AF838919

CONSTITUTIONAL REASONING IN LATIN AMERICA AND THE CARIBBEAN

This book examines the reasoning practice of 15 constitutional courts and supreme courts, including the Caribbean Commonwealth and the Inter-American Court of Human Rights. Enriched by empirical data, with which it strives to contribute to a constructive and well-informed debate, the volume analyses how Latin American courts justify their decisions.

Based on original data and a region-specific methodology, the book provides a systematic analysis utilising more than 600 leading cases. It shows which interpretive methods and concepts are most favoured by Latin American courts, and which courts were the most prolific in their reasoning activities.

The volume traces the features of judicial dialogue on a regional and sub-regional level and enables the evaluation and comparison of each country's reasoning culture in different epochs. The collection includes several graphs to visualise the changes and tendencies of the reasoning practices throughout time in the region, based on information gathered from the dataset.

To better understand the current functioning and the future tendencies of courts in Latin America and the Caribbean, the volume illuminates how constitutional and supreme courts have actually been making their decisions in the selected landmark cases, which could also contribute to future successful litigation strategies for both national constitutional courts and the Inter-American Court for Human Rights.

This project was made possible due to the collaboration and funding provided by the Rule of Law Programme for Latin America of the Konrad Adenauer Foundation and the Law School of the University of San Francisco de Quito.

Volume 3 in the Constitutionalism in Latin America and the Caribbean series

Constitutionalism in Latin America and the Caribbean

Series editors:

Richard Albert
Carlos Bernal
Catarina Santos Botelho

The Constitutionalism in Latin America and the Caribbean series publishes outstanding scholarship on the law and politics of the many varieties of constitutionalism in Latin America and the Caribbean. From single-jurisdiction and cross-national studies to inquiries into the relationship between constitutional and international law in multilevel legal orders in the region, the series welcomes submissions that identify, contextualise, illuminate, and theorise the origins, challenges, foundations, and future of constitutional law and politics in these understudied – but fascinating and important – parts of the world. Scholarship published in this series covers the range of methodologies in law and politics, including but not limited to comparative, doctrinal, empirical, historical, and theoretical perspectives. The series editors invite preliminary inquiries as well as full proposals for monographs and edited volumes in what aims to be the leading forum for the publication of exceptional public law scholarship on Latin America and the Caribbean.

Recent titles in this series:

Constitutional Erosion in Brazil: Progresses and Failures of a Constitutional Project
by Emilio Peduso Neder Meyer

Puerto Rico's Constitutional Paradox: Colonial Subordination, Democratic Tension and Promise of Progressive Transformation
by Jorge M Farinacci-Fernós

Constitutional Reasoning in Latin America and the Caribbean
edited by Johanna Fröhlich

Constitutional Reasoning in Latin America and the Caribbean

Edited by
Johanna Fröhlich

•HART•
OXFORD • LONDON • NEW YORK • NEW DELHI • SYDNEY

HART PUBLISHING

Bloomsbury Publishing Plc

Kemp House, Chawley Park, Cumnor Hill, Oxford, OX2 9PH, UK

1385 Broadway, New York, NY 10018, USA

29 Earlsfort Terrace, Dublin 2, Ireland

HART PUBLISHING, the Hart/Stag logo, BLOOMSBURY and the Diana logo are trademarks of Bloomsbury Publishing Plc

First published in Great Britain 2024

Copyright © The editor and contributors severally 2024

The editor and contributors have asserted their right under the Copyright, Designs and Patents Act 1988 to be identified as Authors of this work.

All rights reserved. No part of this publication may be reproduced or transmitted in any form or by any means, electronic or mechanical, including photocopying, recording, or any information storage or retrieval system, without prior permission in writing from the publishers.

While every care has been taken to ensure the accuracy of this work, no responsibility for loss or damage occasioned to any person acting or refraining from action as a result of any statement in it can be accepted by the authors, editors or publishers.

All UK Government legislation and other public sector information used in the work is Crown Copyright ©. All House of Lords and House of Commons information used in the work is Parliamentary Copyright ©. This information is reused under the terms of the Open Government Licence v3.0 (http://www.nationalarchives.gov.uk/doc/open-government-licence/version/3) except where otherwise stated.

All Eur-lex material used in the work is © European Union, http://eur-lex.europa.eu/, 1998–2024.

A catalogue record for this book is available from the British Library.

A catalogue record for this book is available from the Library of Congress.

Library of Congress Control Number: 2024937570

ISBN: HB: 978-1-50996-017-0
ePDF: 978-1-50996-019-4
ePub: 978-1-50996-018-7

Typeset by Compuscript Ltd, Shannon

To find out more about our authors and books visit www.hartpublishing.co.uk. Here you will find extracts, author information, details of forthcoming events and the option to sign up for our newsletters.

To my Ecuadorean students

SERIES EDITORS' FOREWORD

This first-of-its-kind volume on *Constitutional Reasoning in Latin America and the Caribbean* offers readers an invaluable resource for understanding how supreme, constitutional, and supranational courts perform their role as interpreter and arbiter of constitutional meaning. Focusing on 15 jurisdictions, this book shines a much-needed light on what has thus far been a woefully understudied region of the world. Drawing upon 600 landmark decisions, this rich comparative analysis puts forward an unparalleled study of judicial dialogue on a regional and sub-regional level. Moreover, the book masterfully navigates the omnipresent gulf between the written constitution and the real constitution as applied and enforced in each constitutional jurisdiction. The field of constitutional studies is both stronger and more interesting thanks to this outstanding book.

Richard Albert
Carlos Bernal Pulido
Catarina Santos Botelho
Austin/Dayton/Porto, March 2024

FOREWORD

In writing his monumental *The Concept of Law*, HLA Hart began by noting the 'persistent questions' that law raised. What is law for; what makes it distinct from other forms of social ordering; how is it effective; how does it function as something different from just a raw exercise of power? Hart identified some of the keys to answering these questions in the rule-based nature of law, in the development of institutionally-embodied systems secondary rules, and in adopting a perspective that analyses law from the internal view of those who are direct participants in the social practice of law.

Those questions and insights are certainly central to constitutional law as well, but constitutionalism also has its more specific 'persistent questions', which are linked to Hart's but also arise from the particular aims and functions of constitutions. What are constitutions for? How do they maintain the necessary balance between legitimating and empowering state institutions for the common good and restraining the powers of the state to preserve liberty and pluralism and self-government? How does constitutional law provide the stability and certainty that is needed for order and social peace, while still having the flexibility and responsiveness that allows it to adapt to the changing needs and realities of the political society? Is a constitution principally a programme of action, a strategic plan to be revised periodically according to the shifting ideological currents of the time? Or is it a more general framework of rules and institutions within which social priorities can be deliberated and decided in evolving ways by a fluctuating diversity of political actors over time?

All of these persistent questions of law and constitutionalism form the clear common substratum of the collected studies in this volume and animate the book's overall ambitions. And within the terrain they demarcate all of them are linked by a common thread. Their resolution pulls constitutional systems toward one or the other of two modes, each in perennial tension with the other: the classical and the romantic understandings of law and of constitutionalism. That contrast can apply to constitutions as a whole. Classical models tend more toward economy of language and concepts, minimalism, the restraint and separation of powers, and an emphasis on form over substantive outcomes. They are more willing to bracket the immediate substantive justice at stake in a social controversy, in order to advance the structural and longer-term goods immanent in a commitment to form. Romantic models, instead, tend more toward a maximalism of political and economic goals, the expression of transformative social visions, and the legitimation of powers to achieve those aspirations. Formalism and its more diffuse systemic goods must give way to the more urgent demands of substantive justice in the case at hand. As Mary Ann Glendon acutely observed three decades ago, the distinction between a classical and romantic ethos is particularly apt for describing the self-image and the work of judges, and especially those involved in constitutional adjudication. This brings us, finally, to the *fil rouge* of this volume. As so well detailed here, the deep and ineradicable tension between classical and romantic judges and adjudication is on full display in the application of reason-giving methods of interpretation in the Latin American and Caribbean constitutional tribunals.

It is tempting simply to see the overall trend in the region as a decisive and unqualified shift toward the romantic and anti-formalist, at times to the point of utopianism, at the expense of classicism and formalism. But even if that certainly comes through as the dominant trend of the last 20+ years, the carefully researched and nuanced studies of the diverse national systems paint a richer and more complex picture as well. As if stepping back from a close-up view of a pointillist painting, taking the whole into the scope of our vision allows us to see that there is more to the image. Because they are rooted in the persistent questions like those that Hart had identified, the tensions and contrasts between romantic and classical modes of constitutional law and constitutional adjudication are deeply intertwined, and in fact always coexistent and symbiotic to some meaningful degree in every functioning system of constitutional law.

How those tensions are best managed, and what balance is drawn between them, is not fixed and static, nor does it admit of only a single, abstract, correct answer. Rather, it evolves and is fluid over time, and in any given moment it has much to do with historical contingencies. We can see clearly in these chapters the presence and features of discernable common lines of thought and practice, institutionally embodied and temporally extended, weaving together (loosely) the Latin American region. It is to be welcomed that the editor and authors here have both recognised and received the ongoing presence of that tradition and also engaged it critically. Hart generated his insights into law in the mid-twentieth century, with which these remarks began, through his reception and critical dialectic with the intellectual traditions of English positivism he had inherited. Just so, identifying, working within, and critically examining the traditions of Latin American constitutionalism yields new insights into its present contours as well as the direction it may, and ought to, take in the future. The Latin American story of constitutionalism has never been reducible to a foil of its North American or Continental European counterparts, and since colonial times the region has represented a dynamic synthesis of borrowing, rejecting, and innovating that has generated its own distinctive heritage. The natural law tradition has consistently formed part of that heritage and can be seen as resurgent in new and surprising ways in the present romantic turn.

The constitutional contingencies that shape the balance of classicism and romanticism in adjudication also include moments of rupture that puncture the continuity of constitutional traditions. Among the 'constitutional moments' – to borrow Bruce Ackerman's concept – that have left behind the most enduring effects on Latin American constitutional systems, we consistently see in this book the constitutional traumas of dictatorship, democratic breakdown, gross and systematic violations of human rights, and widespread social exclusion. So much so that contemplating this broad horizon on Latin America helps us to perceive the extent to which so many other constitutional systems have a physiognomy stamped indelibly with the reactions to their own constitutional traumas, whether the original sin of slavery in the United States or the experience of war and genocide in Western Europe and the burden of totalitarian dictatorship in the post-communist world.

Where does this study take us, then, in discerning the possible future(s) of constitutional law and adjudication in Latin America and the Caribbean? Undoubtedly, we are in a time of continued ferment and uncertainty. In the two years before the appearance of this volume, no country in the region has seen as intense and sustained a debate over fundamental constitutional questions and models than Chile, with two successive constitutional conventions producing two wildly different texts and substantive visions of its constitutional future, only to have both decisively rejected by the Chilean people in popular referenda. It seems that the 'unavoidable crisis of authority' that Johanna Fröhlich speaks of in her contributions here is always more apparent. Perhaps this is indicative of a deeper and inchoate desire to swing the pendulum back toward less romantic constitutional adventures and toward a more constrained and formal constitutional climate. But it is too early to tell, and the Chilean context only provides one very particular example. Will the long and steady swing of the pendulum toward romanticism in recent decades continue? Or will there be a return toward more classical forms? In the context of democratic backsliding, populism, and their threat to institutionality and the normative authority of law, the question of which would most effectively buttress the stability of the rule of law is an ever more urgent central question.

In its combination of multiple methods of attentive observation and analysis, an appreciation for the nuance of both commonalities and differences within the region, and its theoretical sophistication, the present volume is a significant contribution to our capacity for understanding that predicament, and for discerning the best way forward. It can provide us with guideposts not only for constitutional reasoning and adjudication in Latin America and the Caribbean, but by casting its light on the persistent questions embedded in law and constitutionalism more generally it can illuminate our understanding of and judgement about the parallel challenges facing the rest of the world as well, from the newest constitutional systems to the most venerable.

Paolo G Carozza
University of Notre Dame
January 2024

SPECIAL NOTE FROM THE DIRECTOR OF THE RULE OF LAW PROGRAM FOR LATIN AMERICA OF THE KONRAD ADENAUER FOUNDATION

Constitutional law is one of the legal branches that has most impacted our current democracies and has acted to support the guarantee of the rule of law. Constitutional interpretation has served to delineate the legal course of ordinary legislation and has allowed – in specific instances – the expansion of the recognition of certain rights based on an evolutionary interpretation of the magna carta derived from a thorough and responsible reading of international and inter-American standards on human rights.

Therefore, the interpretative work of constitutional judges is more than essential for: (a) guaranteeing individual rights 'making them the center of discussion'; (b) the institutional strengthening of public agencies or offices that draft laws and are responsible for their compliance; and (c) guiding a constitutional reading that promotes equality and non-discrimination in all their dimensions. Thus, the rule of law should be regarded as an essential foundation that judges should account for in their reasoning when resolving cases that come before them.

As such, 'constitutional reasoning' acquires an important relevance in terms of the reasons or motives behind a judgment. There are many factors that can influence this reasoning such as the context, the norm or norms to be interpreted, the case's circumstances that must be analysed in a respectful and conscientious way, and the knowledge about certain specialised aspects. These aspects are reinforced by the use of other sources of law such as doctrine, custom, and jurisprudence, and also by the use of key concepts such as democracy, non-discrimination and equality of law, and historicity in some cases, such as the indigenous issue, just to mention an example.

Based on this extremely important relationship between the rule of law and its elements that support constitutional reasoning, we are very happy to present this work entitled *Constitutional Reasoning in Latin America*. Professor Johanna Fröhlich initiated and academically coordinated the project, which was supported by Dr Marie-Christine Fuchs, as Program Director, and Miguel Barboza, current Project Coordinator of the Program.

This work, in a brilliant and timely way, explains what is behind constitutional reasoning in various countries of Latin America and the Caribbean Commonwealth. To make this possible, the authors identified landmark judgments from their countries, to which a questionnaire of 50 questions was applied to identify central and common aspects of constitutional reasoning. Added to these country chapters are several that are more generic, covering the Rule of Law; the Inter-American Court of Human Rights; the Constitutional Tradition in Latin America; and the dialogue between the Inter-American Court of Human Rights and the European Court of Human Rights.

There is no doubt that this work will foster and advance discussions on constitutional reasoning in Latin America and will also serve as the basis of the important role played by inter-American justice in this field, such as in the Inter-American Court of Human Rights and its European counterpart, the European Court of Human Rights. In this sense, I sincerely hope that these discussions will not conclude here, but that this work will continue to generate ideas at the level of the constitutional courts and high courts of the region, as well as in the different ordinary courts, which, in the end, recognise important references in the constitutional judgments that can be utilised when making their own decisions.

I would like to acknowledge and congratulate the authors of this work on their substantial efforts to complete an academic endeavour of almost three years in the making. I know that the planning of this project, the construction of its methodology and building the CORE Dataset have required a tremendous amount of work from the beginning – work that did not cease despite the exceptional circumstances that we encountered due to the pandemic – an aspect that makes this effort even more laudable.

At the KAS, we work to promote the principles of the rule of law in the different countries of Latin America, this through our different areas of activity, such as business and human rights, legal pluralism, women's rights, criminal law and constitutional law. These are legal matters that undoubtedly find an important space for discussion at the level of the high courts and constitutional courts of Latin America, which will unquestionably be more than enriched when analysing and studying this work.

We therefore welcome this text and hope that it will be of the utmost interest to academia, civil society, States and the general public.

Hartmut Rank
Director of the Rule of Law Program for Latin America
Konrad Adenauer Foundation

KONRAD ADENAUER STIFTUNG
ESTADO DE DERECHO · LATINOAMÉRICA

EDITOR'S PREFACE

I lived in Latin America, with all its beauty and turmoil, for just under a decade. A lot of this time was spent on this work that I am finishing as I now return to my home country.

The work on this volume started almost immediately after arriving in Ecuador in 2016, when I decided to apply the CONREASON methodology to measuring the reasoning practice of the Constitutional Court of Ecuador. The curiosity ignited by this first study took me to the Max Planck Institute for International Public Law and Comparative Law in Heidelberg, Germany, where I was granted a fellowship to study the literature on constitutional reasoning in Latin America. The diverse and spontaneous environment, and conversations especially, but not exclusively, with Mariela Morales Antoniazzi, Jimena Soley, and Rainer Grote, were essential for the advancement of this project.

Once the project was officially created, it enjoyed the financial and institutional support of the University of San Francisco de Quito, Ecuador, for which I remain grateful to Farith Simon, Dean of the Law School.

In both research groups I set up at USFQ, first dedicated to the analysis of the Ecuadorean Constitutional Court (CORREG), and then to constitutional and supreme courts of the whole region (CORE Latam, see at www.corelatam.com), I was fortunate to count on the unwavering and wholehearted support of students from the USFQ Law School. I could rely on them during several stages and many different aspects of this research, including long after I had left Ecuador. I would like to express my gratitude to Amalia Fernández-Salvador and Adriana Rodas Merino, my two excellent research assistants, and Sebastián Abad Jara, Katherine Velástegui-Arias, Sol González, Emily Samanta Moya Guerra, María Paula Marroquín, María Emilia Vintimilla, Sebastián Correa, Johanna Guerra Uscocovich, Sebastián Arrieta, Valeria Elizabeth Rosales, Luis Miguel Chiriboga, Melissa Coba, Martín Cordovez, Bernarda Haro, Diana Guevara and Alejandra Ati, all members of the research project. I am also grateful to several professors of the USFQ Law School, such as Marco Morales and Francisco Albuja, for their help during the initial stage of the project, to Juan Pablo Aguilar for sharing with me his ideas on the nature of law in Ecuador, to Daniela Salazar for commenting on the preliminary results of the project and on the Ecuadorean chapter, and to Karla Andrade Quevedo, Andrés Martínez-Moscoso, Hernán Pérez Loose, David Cordero and Ramiro Ávila Santamaría, for participating in academic events that I dedicated to sharing the outcome of the project. I would like to express my gratitude to the external experts of the project, András Jakab, Paolo G Carozza, Julio Ríos-Figueroa, Mátyás Bencze and Gisela Ferrari, who helped with their valuable insights, advice and comments.

I have taken the project and its results in distinct stages to various meetings and conferences. In 2019, thanks to the generous support of the Faculty of Law of the

Pontifical Catholic University of Chile, the project had its first meeting dedicated to the methodology of the research. I invited Mátyás Bencze to speak about the challenges of measuring the quality of judicial reasoning in June 2019. Andrea Castagnola visited USFQ to talk about her work on manipulating courts in new democracies in October 2019. Because of the pandemic, the second annual meeting of the research group was organised online, in June 2020. It was closely followed by a Work-in-Progress Workshop organised at the Columbia Law School in the United States, where I received valuable comments from a group of excellent scholars, coordinated by Jamal Greene and Madhav Khosla. Our research project was granted a separate panel at the Global Summit of Constitutional Law in January 2021 and at the ICON-S Mundo Conference in July 2021. Our preliminary results were also shared at the 'Thursday Seminars' of the Philosophy of Law and International Private Law Department of the University of Alicante in 2021. Furthermore, I had the opportunity to present our results at the XXVII Meeting of Constitutional Courts, Supreme Courts and Constitutional Chambers of Latin America, held in Santiago in September 2022. These instances were important for sharing our dilemmas and preliminary results and exchanging ideas about their meaning. I am immensely grateful to Mila Versteeg, David Landau, Julio Ríos-Figueroa, Yaniv Roznai, Katalin Capannini-Kelemen, Tania Groppi, Manuel Atienza and many others for their on-point insights.

Marie-Cristine Fuchs, as former director of the Programme of Rule of Law for Latin America at the Konrad Adenauer Foundation (KAS) decided to support the project in 2019, which made most of these interactions possible. I am more than thankful for her endorsement that went beyond a plain donation and has borne important academic fruits. I am further grateful to Hartmut Rank, current director of the Programme of Rule of Law for Latin America for his continuing support in key moments and to Miguel Barboza for his reassuring presence, support and patience.

I am indebted to Sebastián Umpierrez de Reguero, who has provided the expertise to manage the dataset from all jurisdictions, and whose unconditional help accompanied me until the very end of the work. I am similarly grateful to Julienne Grant, who selflessly took care of not only the English translation of several chapters, but also the English proofread and formatting of various others. Both Sebastián and Julienne accepted last minute requests with kindness and patience, for which I am especially grateful.

András Jakab is not only an expert on this project, but a mentor, who was key to embarking on this project on the first place. His permanent and unconditional presence and patient and careful guidance have been essential over the past years.

I am very grateful to Hart Publishing, and especially to Kate Whetter, whose compassion and patience sustained this project despite all difficulties.

Last, but not least, I am very grateful to my husband, Pier, who has relentlessly consoled and encouraged me during these last eight years, and took care of our small children, Jacinta and Elías, to help me to finish this work.

Johanna Fröhlich
Santiago de Chile, 2024 January

TABLE OF CONTENTS

LIST OF CONTRIBUTORS

Miguel Ángel Barboza Lopez, Project Coordinator, Programme of Rule of Law for Latin America, Konrad Adenauer Foundation, Colombia.

Rafael Bellem de Lima, Assistant Professor, Insper, Brazil.

Juan Berríos Ortigoza, Universidad Católica Andrés Bello and Universidad del Zulia, Venezuela.

Andrea Castagnola, Adjunct Professor, Department of Political Science and International Relations, Law School, University of Torcuato Di Tella, Argentina.

Alejandro Chechtman, Professor of Law, Law School, University of Torcuato Di Tella, Argentina.

Magdalena Inés Correa Henao, Research Professor, Universidad Externado, Colombia.

María Alejandra Espino Layza, Lecturer, Pontifical Catholic University of Peru.

Johanna Fröhlich, Assistant Professor, Faculty of Law, Pontifical Catholic University of Chile, Chile.

Marie-Christine Fuchs, Universität des Saarlandes, Germany.

Maria Paula Garat Delgado, Professor of Law, Pontifical Catholic University of Uruguay.

María José García Ascolani, Professor of Law, Universidad Católica Nuestra Señora De la Asunción, Paraguay.

Ivar A Hartmann, Associate Professor of Law, Insper, Brazil.

Pablo González Domínguez. Staff Attorney, Inter-American Court of Human Rights; Lecturer, Universidad Panamericana, Mexico.

Tania Groppi, Full Professor of Public Law, University of Siena, Italy.

Juan Camilo Herrera, Cofundador de Greystone Consulting Group Latinoamérica y Jurídica Herrera Sattler & Ossa, Colombia.

Juan Pablo Irrazabal, Doctoral Candidate, University of Bonn, Germany.

Ariana Macaya Lizano, Professor of Law, University of Costa Rica.

Anna Maria Lecis, Associate Professor of Public Law, Sciences Po Bordeaux, France.

Rosa Natalí Llique Ramírez, Lecturer, Pontifical Catholic University of Peru.

Carlos Meléndez Guerrero, Researcher, Center for Studies of Social Conflict and Cohesion. Associate Professor, Universidad Diego Portales, Chile.

Sergio Muro, Guest Professor, University of Torcuato Di Tella, Argentina.

Roberto Niembro Ortega, Mexican Supreme Court of Justice, Mexico.

Derek O'Brien, Reader in Law, Oxford Brookes University, UK.

Alfredo Ortega Franco. Lecturer, Universidad Rafael Landívar, Guatemala.

Pier Paolo Pigozzi, Associate Professor of Comparative Constitutional Law, Ludovika – University of Public Service, Hungary.

Jorge Ernesto Roa Roa, Research Professor, Universidad Externado, Colombia.

Abraham Siles Vallejos, Professor of Law, Pontifical Catholic University of Peru.

Irene Spigno, General Director, Academia Interamericana de Derechos Humanos, Mexico.

Sebastián Umpierrez de Reguero, Research Associate, European University Institute, Italy.

Francisco Javier Urbina, Associate professor, Law school, University of Notre Dame, US.

Raúl Sánchez Urribarrí, Associate Dean and Senior Lecturer, School of Humanities and Social Sciences, La Trobe University, Australia.

Carlos Arturo Villagrán Sandoval, Emile Noël Postdoctoral Fellow, Jean Monnet Center for International and Regional Economic Law and Justice, New York University, US.

Cristián Villalonga Torrijo, Assistant Professor, Pontifical Catholic University of Chile.

Sergio Verdugo, Professor of Law, IE University Law School, Spain.

Anna Luisa Walter de Santana, Professor of Law, Pontifical Catholic University of Paraná, Brazil.

Diego Werneck Arguelhes, Associate Professor, Insper, Brazil.

NOTE ON THE ONLINE MATERIALS

The CORE Latam Dataset, consisting of the 15 Excel Tables from all jurisdictions as well as the aggregate data, is available on the Harvard Dataverse at: Fröhlich, Johanna; Sebastián, Umpierrez de Reguero, 2024, 'CORE Latam Dataset', https://doi.org/10.7910/DVN/WT00YP, Harvard Dataverse, V1. The dataset is accompanied by the Codebook, the Questionnaire and the list of selected landmark judgments from each jurisdiction.

Additionally, in collaboration with the Konrad Adenauer Foundation's Rule of Law for Latin America Programme, all lists of selected landmark judgments are also available through a repository on the webpage of the IUSLAT project, where the selected cases of the project are accompanied by standardised summaries in Spanish. See, www.iuslat.com.

PART I

Foundations and Methodology

1

Introduction – Conceptualising and Measuring Constitutional Reasoning in Latin America and the Caribbean Commonwealth

JOHANNA FRÖHLICH, SEBASTIÁN UMPIERREZ DE REGUERO AND CARLOS MELÉNDEZ GUERRERO

Latin America is claiming a leading position in global constitutional trendsetting, as its rich constitutional traditions continue to inspire new experiments and novel constitutional theories amid the region's search for human rights, social justice and structural change. Recent constitutional theories[1] have entrusted ordinary judges, especially constitutional court judges, with considerable responsibility to eliminate both structural deficiencies and the violence that prevails in so many Latin American societies. After a long history of judicial interbranch crises and numerous attacks on judges and judicial institutions, some scholars[2] posit that there has been an 'ideological shift' concerning the role of judges in the region. This shift is said to have brought not only the dominance of human rights in modern constitutionalism but also a self-empowered image of judges, which has been adapted to the task of approximating the gap between a deficient social, political and institutional environment and law's aim to transform society. A robust empirical component, however, has been lacking to test constitutional courts' activities and their outcomes under the 'post-war paradigm'.[3] To better understand judicial decision-making through reasoning, as well as the current trends and future perspectives of constitutional review in the region, it is essential to seek verifiable answers about how courts are actually functioning in Latin America and the Caribbean. Has the transformative paradigm shift really occurred in the region's constitutional courts, and if so, what do we know about it? What does the alleged constitutional turn mean regarding

[1] R Uprimny, 'The Recent Transformation of Constitutional Law in Latin America: Trends and Challenges' (2011) 89 *Texas Law Review* 1587.

[2] G Helmke and J Rios-Figueroa (eds), *Courts in Latin America* (Cambridge University Press, 2011) 2.

[3] LE Weinrib, 'The Postwar Paradigm and the American exceptionalism' in S Choudhry (ed), *The Migration of Constitutional Ideas* (Cambridge University Press, 2007) 84–112.

those courts' reasoning strategies? What are the interpretive methods and key concepts that can most powerfully appeal to a proper justification of landmark decisions made by the region's constitutional and supreme courts?

The objective of this research, therefore, is to provide an empirically comprehensive understanding of the reasoning practices of constitutional and supreme courts in Latin America and the Caribbean Commonwealth, based on a mixed (quantitative and qualitative) research method of analysing 40 preselected landmark cases from each jurisdiction included in this volume. The selected caselaw from the 15[4] jurisdictions in Latin America and the Caribbean allowed us to systematically analyse the interpretive methods and concepts that have been most frequently invoked. By including two special jurisdictions, the common law Caribbean region and the Inter-American Court of Human Rights (IACtHR) in the project, we expected to create a set of samples that could effectively reflect on the plural and diverse constitutional traditions of this part of the world. The robust dataset also enabled us to establish patterns, trends and a detailed understanding of the most relevant divisions among the region's courts. Besides identifying similarities and differences among countries and subregions, the subsequent analysis helped us test prevalent theories and hypotheses about constitutional adjudication while identifying those arguments that have the potential to successfully influence the outcome of constitutional cases in Latin America and the Commonwealth Caribbean.

I. The Context and Issue of Constitutional Reasoning in Latin America and the Caribbean

Countries in Latin America and the Caribbean enacted more than 200 constitutions before the latest wave of constitutionalism,[5] a history that has firmly established the area's renown for constitutional imagination and legal experimentation.[6] This abundant constitutional history is, however, in sharp contrast to the deficiency of institutional, social and legal settings that most of the region's countries and constitutions face. The proliferation of constitutions in this context might demonstrate on the one hand that political elites have always been willing to expend considerable resources on constitutional law as a means of imagining, constructing and attempting to control the state. On the other hand, the accrual of new constitutions points to the complex nexus between law and society on a more profound level in Latin America and the Caribbean. The role of courts and their attempt to offer justifications that simultaneously define themselves through the act of judicial reasoning is therefore central to the understanding of how constitutions work in practice in the region.

[4] The jurisdictions are the following: Inter-American Court of Human Rights, Argentina, Bolivia, Caribbean Commonwealth, Chile, Colombia, Costa Rica, Brazil, Ecuador, Guatemala, Mexico, Paraguay, Peru, Uruguay and Venezuela.

[5] R Gargarella, *Latin American Constitutionalism, 1810–2010: The Engine Room of the Constitution* (Oxford University Press, 2013); JL Cordeiro, 'Constitutions Around the World: A View from Latin America' (2008) *IDE Discussion Paper* no 164.

[6] C Hübner Mendes, R Gargarella, and S Gaudi (eds), *The Oxford Handbook of Constitutional Law in Latin America* (Oxford University Press, 2022) xvi–xxiv.

Latin American courts and their communities[7] have dramatically changed over the past several decades. Whereas some of the constitutional courts sampled for this study were effectively created in the 2000s, judges in those courts currently have different backgrounds.[8] According to earlier studies, judges' pre-constitutional court experiences are decisive in terms of the type of approach those judges take and the interpretive methods they use while on the bench.[9] Academic profiles are more common not only because more judges have come directly from universities than before but also because those who graduated in the 1970s or 1980s from North American law schools were influenced by the Warren Court and its activist stance.[10] Constitutional and legal scholarship has undergone a sea change in the last 25 years, driven by new constitutional theories like transformative constitutionalism and neo-constitutionalism. During this period, the legal academy has produced more constitutional law treatises and launched more journals have been founded on this topic, and more law deans have had constitutional law backgrounds than in previous decades.[11] Treatises that this generation has authored[12] have attracted attention in English-speaking academic circles and have greatly emphasised the doctrine of human rights and its protection through the constitutional control of legislation.[13] Besides signalling a great Dworkinian influence in the region, these academic works have contributed to a conceptual and linguistic metamorphosis in the constitutional law discipline.

The rise of constitutional scholarship in the region[14] has occurred concurrently with a 'conceptual revolution'[15] that transpired in the late 1980s amid an approaching change in viewing the constitution as a 'higher law constitutionalism'.[16] This approach has been increasingly popular in Latin America and the Commonwealth Caribbean and has offered a powerful innovative narrative to enable courts and judges to strengthen and safeguard human rights and eradicate structural inequality as part of an ample transformative mission. It has been argued that courts and judges have not only started to enjoy greater formal institutional protection from political interventions but also a larger capacity to influence policy, which has put them in a unique and unprecedented

[7] A-M Slaughter, 'The Global Community of Courts' (2003) 44 *Harvard International Law Journal* 191.

[8] S Basabe-Serrano, 'The Judges' Academic Background as Determinant of the Quality of Judicial Decisions in Latin American Supreme Courts' (2019) 40 *Justice System Journal.*

[9] By using the Colombian Constitutional Court as a case study, David Landau showed that before 1991 more judges had been working in the ordinary courts and therefore more often represented the traditionalist-positivist approach, while after 1991 more judges came from academia who had more exposure to neo-constitutional ideas, which made them interpret the constitution more broadly. See, D Landau, 'The Two Discourses in Colombian Constitutional Jurisprudence: A New Approach to Modeling Judicial Behavior in Latin America' (2005) 37 *The George Washington International Law Review* 709–11.

[10] J Couso, 'The Seduction of Judicially Triggered Social Transformation: The Impact of the "Warren Court" in Latin America' in H Sheiber (ed), *The Global Impact of the Warren Court* (Lexington Books, 2007) 237–63.

[11] J Couso, 'The Transformation of Constitutional Discourse and the Judicialization of Politics in Latin America' in J Couso, A Huneeus, and R. Siedel (eds), *Cultures of Legality* (Cambridge University Press, 2010) 147–48.; R Pérez Perdomo, 'Legal Education in the Late Twentieth Century Latin America' in LM Friedman, R Pérez-Perdomo and MA Gómez (eds), *Law in Many Societies. A Reader* (Stanford University Press, 2011) 56.

[12] For instance, Yale graduate Carlos Nino on *Fundamentos de Derecho Constitucional. Analisis filosofico, jurıdico y politologico de la practica constituciona* (The Foundation of Constitutional Law: A Philosophical, Legal, and Politological Analysis of Constitutional Practice), published in 1992.

[13] Couso (n 10) 152–54.

[14] ibid 146.

[15] ibid 152.

[16] A Stone Sweet, *Governing with Judges: Constitutional Politics in Europe* (Oxford University Press, 2000).

position.[17] Furthermore, the legal and constitutional aspects as well as the courts' role have become more influential in political decision-making, which has triggered rearrangements not only in law but also in the political arena, which has experienced an intense process of judicialisation.[18] Beginning in the 1980s, new constitutional theories emerged in Latin America and the Caribbean that originated in Europe, such as neo-constitutionalism in Italy, which evolved into something specifically Latin American. Transformative constitutionalism, Andean neo-constitutionalism or different combinations of these theories sprouted from an academic initiative to influence new constitutions and the design and practice of constitutional control. Several chapters in this work reference these constitutional theories using different names since during the last several decades more positions have emerged regarding both their denominations and actual content. To reflect on the complexity and richness of this debate, this volume dedicates a separate chapter to the constitutional traditions of Latin America and the Caribbean, which describes and critically examines the region's constitutional theories.[19]

Besides the change of formal institutional rules and competences[20] and the novel academic theories, the deeper legal culture must also be considered. Alongside the creative, progressive narrative, there is another aspect that concerns law's authority and the constitution in Latin America. The deficiencies of normativity in the region nonetheless have roots in the colonial legacy; that heritage is still present and oftentimes actively reproduced in different forms in the legal culture.[21] As constitutions are the purest reflection of a society's idea and image of law, judicial reasoning, specifically constitutional reasoning, is a realm where we can best analyse law's authority and limits as well as those values that uphold the legal system's edifice. If law's authority is deficient, then the meaning of law will necessarily share this quality. Thus, it is relevant to question how authority is approached in Latin America and the Caribbean and how that authority affects constitutional reasoning.

Our dataset reveals a new aspect of the problem with legal authority that centres around a false dichotomy concerning law's authority (submission versus revolt), which directly affects the interpretative practices of the region's courts as will be demonstrated in this work's conclusion. The decadence of authority in Latin America primarily has historical and social explanations,[22] as it has been affecting the region's constitutions

[17] J Ríos-Figueroa, 'Institutions for Constitutional Justice in Latin America' in Helmke and Ríos-Figueroa (n 2) 27–54.

[18] N Tate and T Vallinder, *The Global Expansion of Judicial Power* (New York University Press, 1995); D Kapiszewski and MM Taylor, 'Doing Courts Justice? Studying Judicial Politics in Latin America' (2008) 6 *Perspectives on Politics* 741–67; J Couso, A Huneeus and R Sieder (eds), *Cultures of Legality. Judicialization and Political Activism in Latin America* (Cambridge University Press, 2010) 3.; D Kapiszewski and K Newman, 'Judicialization of Politics' in Hübner et al (n 6) 430–43.

[19] See Pigozzi (ch 2).

[20] G Helmke and S Levitsky (eds), *Informal Institutions and Democracy: Lessons from Latin America* (Johns Hopkins University Press, 2006).

[21] 'A belief in law's potential to assist in the creation of a more just order, co-exists with "the (un)rule of law," or lawless violence and a weak presence of the state, including state justice (Mendez, O'Donnell, and Pinherio 1999).' in Couso et al (n 18) 5.

[22] The problems related to law's authority in the region were influenced by an interview conducted with Chilean sociologist Pedro Morandé, on 19 December 2023. See also, P Morandé, *Cultura y Modernización en América Latina* (Instituto de Estudios de la Sociedad, 2017).

since the very beginning of these countries' democratic histories. Constitutional reasoning is like a litmus paper of a society's relationship to legal authority. Various academic works have analysed different aspects of this relationship,[23] but they have lacked an empirical component that assesses the process of constitutional meaning-making – that is, when the normative text becomes a hard reality. We have built a dataset to test existing theories about law and constitutional reasoning in Latin America and the Caribbean and now better understand the features and tendencies of judicial reasoning practices. Our dataset shows that in Latin America and the Commonwealth Caribbean, judges' attitudes towards the normative text have a crucial effect on their justificatory practices, which has contributed to a relevant division in the interpretive landscape in the region, one that lies between a submissive, formalist approach and one that is subversive and anti-formalist. While the detailed picture of this division and the bits and pieces of past and current tendencies are examined in the last chapter,[24] in the following pages, we explain the main features of the methodology used to create a more informed starting point for the subsequent chapters of this volume.

II. The Empirical Pillar of Measuring Constitutional Reasoning in Latin America and the Caribbean

A. Conceptualising Constitutional Reasoning in Latin America and the Caribbean

The study of constitutional reasoning is relatively new in scholarly work. The question regarding the comparability of different constitutional reasoning practices has been put forward before by Jakab and colleagues,[25] asking if '[constitutional reasoning] means the same in the United States as in Taiwan? In Germany as in the United Kingdom?' Even though the response is no, the term 'constitutional reasoning' can travel through different cases by using comparable concepts and indicators to capture the essence of decision-making among the analysed jurisdictions. The CONREASON Project[26] designed such a methodology, which we borrowed and adapted to the Latin American and Caribbean regional circumstances, as explained in the following sections.[27]

Earlier contributions have satisfactorily defined the ontological and secondary attributes of constitutional reasoning and the different interpretive methods. Implicitly,

[23] For extensive citations to literature, see M García-Villegas, 'Disobeying the Law: The Culture of Non-Compliance with Rules in Latin America' (2011) 29 *Wisconsin International Law Journal* 263.; J Esquirol, *Ruling the Law: Legitimacy and Failure in Latin American Legal Systems* (Cambridge University Press, 2020).

[24] See Fröhlich (ch 20).

[25] A Jakab, A Dyevre and G Itzkovich, *Comparative Constitutional Reasoning* (Cambridge University Press, 2017) 10.

[26] ibid.

[27] An important aspect was to ensure the comparability of our results, not only with the CONREASON project but also with other applications of the same mixed research methodology, such as the project concentrating on the Northern European countries (currently in progress, led by Katalin Kelemen at the Örebro University, Sweden, see www.oru.se/nordic-conreason/) and the Turkish Supreme Court. See S von Steinsdorff, E Göztepe, M Abad Andrade and F Petersen (eds), *The Constitutional Court of Turkey. Between Legal and Political Reasoning* (Nomos, 2022).

research on comparative constitutionalism has worked with a minimalist structure,[28] which in theory can adjust to a larger number of cases.[29] Accordingly, existing literature has formulated definitions from the perspective of comparative constitutional law, in which the indisputable role of judges and constitutional courts is self-evident for the study of the concept, but to the detriment of contextual factors. Ontological attributes of constitutional reasoning are thus rooted in its etymology: that is, what we mean by 'constitutional' and by 'reasoning', although, both terms require some clarification in the Latin American and Caribbean context.

With a legal-rational appraisal, accentuated by methodological individualism and the assumption of bounded rationality, reasoning emerges from the individual justifications, which in turn induces a certain course of action. This course of action, which can be exemplified by the decision of a non-elected judge or a (group of) legislators, resolves disputes or collective action dilemmas.[30] On occasion, reasons are the equivalent of motivations and mental processes that prompt the agent to decide one course of action or another; other times, they are meant to provide explanations related to the factual circumstances of concrete situations.[31] In the framework of this research, reasoning equates to the agent's justificatory attempt to provide reasons for why – in this case, to choose a certain constitutional meaning.[32] Thus, whereas reasoning concerns those justifications that make judges choose certain types of methods over others to define what the constitution means, it also involves a cognitive construction and the agent's inherent incentives, which suggest an action as a form of last cause.[33] Indeed, several philosophers have approached the concept of reasoning as propositions that induce action or the concept of argument as a 'publicly expressed tool of persuasion',[34] along with the emotional effects generated by the use of arguments that fail to fit the standard for the definition of an argument. In turn, through deliberation and choice a reason for action guides a determined agent to do something (or contrarily, to refrain from acting) because of the good-making characteristics of the identified and selected option in front of them. Simply put, constitutional reasoning is a special case of legal reasoning, differentiated by the objective that the agent[35] has in mind, as its principal goal is to maintain and enforce the constitution's authority and scope of its protection.

[28] T Groppi and MC Panthoreau, *The Use of Foreign Precedents by Constitutional Judges* (Hart Publishing, 2013); A Jakab, 'Judicial Reasoning in Constitutional Courts: A European Perspective' (2013) 14 *German Law Journal* 1215; Jakab (n 25); J Goldsworthy (ed), *Interpreting Constitutions. A Comparative Study* (Oxford University Press, 2006).

[29] G Sartori, 'Concept misformation in comparative politics' (1970) 64 *American Political Science Review* 4, 1033–53.

[30] N Frohlich and JA Oppenheimer, *Modern political economy* (Prentice-Hall, 1978).; DN Walton, 'What is Reasoning? What is an Argument?' (1990) 87 *The Journal of Philosophy* 399–419.

[31] See generally J Fröhlich, 'Law as Reason for Action' in M Sellers and S Kirste (eds), *Encyclopedia of the Philosophy of Law and Social Philosophy* (Springer, 2019).

[32] V Rodriguez-Blanco, *Law and Authority under the Guise of Good* (Hart Publishing, 2014); G Webber, 'Asking why in the study of human affairs' (2015) 60 *The American Journal of Jurisprudence* 1.

[33] J Elster, 'Belief, Bias, and Ideology' in M Hollis and S Lukes (eds), Rationality and Relativism (MIT Press, 1982); Jakab et al (n 25); J Lenman, 'Reasons for Action: Justification vs. Explanation' in *The Standford Encyclopedia of Philosophy* (2013) at plato.stanford.edu/archives/win2011/entries/reasons-just-vs-expl/.

[34] T Govier, 'Critical Thinking as Argument Analysis' (1989) 3 *Argumentation* 117.

[35] BJ Diggs, 'A Technical Ought' (1960) 69 *Mind* 301–17; L Alexander and E Sherwin, *Demystifying Legal Reasoning* (Cambridge University Press, 2008); SJ Brison and W Sinnott-Armstrong, *Contemporary Perspectives on Constitutional Interpretation* (Westview, 1993).

In the Latin American and the Caribbean context, as we will see more extensively in the conclusion of this edited volume, rhetorical arguments are quite common, which makes it especially difficult at times to differentiate between a simple proposition and one that links a reason to the elected option through a certain logical connection.

Our reference to 'constitutional' reasoning is directed to the formal framework of law – that is, a de jure, codified or written constitution, denominated by legal scholars as a large-c constitution. Large-c constitutions describe their own status as higher, fundamental or as a supreme law(s) that operates as the standard of validity and constitutionality in the legal system. A constitution in this sense also explicitly denotes a state's structure, powers and basic procedural rules. On the other hand, constitutions that are de facto, unwritten, or uncodified or consist of an informal (set of) law(s), are recognised as small-c constitutions, which are studied within the field of political science rather than constitutional law.[36] Thus, they are detached from the ontological attribute of constitutional reasoning. In fact, research areas regarding small-c constitutions comprise the causes and consequences of political regimes (eg, democracies versus autocracies), government (eg, parliamentary versus presidential) or electoral systems (eg, proportional representation versus plurality-majority rules).[37] So, for purposes of the present research, 'constitutional reasoning' concerns the courts' practice to justify the election of certain interpretive methods and concepts to give meaning to the constitution's normative text. This is why reasoning without links to the large-c constitution or reasoning that provided justifications for interpreting ordinary laws instead of the constitution was not considered for inclusion in our database.

The present project concerned judgments that were adopted within the constitutional review competence[38] of constitutional courts, supreme courts, or constitutional chambers of supreme courts. Therefore, judgments of ordinary courts and lower courts were not included in our case selection. Furthermore, following the CONREASON Project methodology, each jurisdiction selected 40 landmark judgments from the jurisprudence of the court that has constitutional review competence; therefore, our case selection mostly reflects the features of hard and complex constitutional law cases and cannot be considered representative of a given jurisdiction's entire jurisprudence.

As the region's constitutions have introduced courts with a combination of various models of constitutional control,[39] the design of the institution that exercises constitutional control varies greatly among the selected jurisdictions. For example,

[36] DS Law, 'Constitutions' in P Cane and HM Kritzer (eds), *The Oxford Handbook of Empirical Legal Research* (Oxford University Press, 2010).

[37] JA Cheibub, *Presidentialism, parliamentarism, and democracy* (Cambridge University Press, 2007); A Lijphart, *Patterns of democracy: Government forms and performance in thirty-six countries* (Yale University Press, 1999); T Persson and G Tabellini, *The economic effects of constitutions* (MIT Press, 2005); MS Shugart and JM Carey, *Presidents and assemblies: Constitutional design and electoral dynamics* (Cambridge University Press, 1992).

[38] However, the principal type of case we included was constitutional review, as courts that have that competence can also have other competences, such as *amparo* or different types of remedies and individual complaints (*tutelas*), which concern enforcing the constitution and remedying constitutional violations. Therefore, these types of cases could also be among those selected.

[39] P Navia and J Ríos-Figueroa, 'The Constitutional Adjudication Mosaic of Latin America' (2015) *Comparative Political Studies*.

we find specific courts[40] dedicated to exercising the competence of constitutional review in Ecuador (the Ecuadorean Constitutional Court), Colombia (the Colombian Constitutional Court), Guatemala (the Guatemalan Constitutional Court), Chile (the Chilean Constitutional Tribunal), Bolivia (the Bolivian Plurinational Constitutional Tribunal) and Peru (the Constitutional Court of Peru). Most Andean countries' courts are found on this list, as well as the region's youngest courts, as many of these countries adopted new constitutions at the end of the 1990s and the beginning of the 2000s. Those countries that have the oldest constitutions in the region, such as Mexico (1917), Argentina (1853) and Uruguay (1976), allocate the competence of constitutional control to the highest ordinary court, specifically the Mexican Supreme Court of Justice, the Argentine Supreme Court and the Supreme Court of Uruguay, respectively. In addition, we find the same model in Paraguay (Paraguayan Supreme Court) and in Brazil (Federal Supreme Court of Brazil). In Venezuela and Costa Rica, conversely, there are separate chambers within those nations' supreme courts, which are dedicated to the exercise of this competence (the Constitutional Chamber of the Supreme Court of Justice in both countries). Finally, the Commonwealth Caribbean subregion is an exception methodologically, as two courts represent this jurisdiction, the Judicial Committee of the Privy Council (JCPC) and the Caribbean Court of Justice (CCJ), which was created in 2006.

B. Methodological Variations of the CORE Research Design

The goal of creating an index is to explain a phenomenon, set of events or circumstances by describing most, if not all, of its aspects. While typologies organise and classify information following a well-defined theoretical framework, indices reduce indicators, which are a subset of items, to facilitate obtaining an aggregate understanding of a given phenomenon, in this case, constitutional reasoning. Building an index[41] increases the likelihood of comparing its constitutive components within and across cases, thus allowing the display of different facets of constitutional reasoning over time and across jurisdictions – one of the CORE Latam dataset's main purposes. A mixed methodology[42] such as that of the present initiative, bridges qualitative and quantitative research and combines the advantages of both approaches. It requires and takes advantage of a familiarity with cases and enhances the empirical data with a deeper knowledge of each jurisdiction's context and the history. Through the combination of doctrinal expertise and a cross-national time-series original dataset, our index is capable of pinpointing cross-case patterns and explaining complex causal conditions on a regional level or in individual countries or subregions. Yet, the sample was non-randomised and the data was extracted using the researchers' expertise while at the

[40] Helmke and Ríos-Figueroa (n 2) 7.

[41] GL Munck and J Verkuilen, 'Conceptualizing and measuring democracy: Evaluating alternative indices' (2002) 35 *Comparative political studies* 5–34.

[42] CC Ragin, *The Comparative Method. Moving Beyond Qualitative and Quantitative Strategies* (University of California Press, 1987); B Rihoux and CC Ragin (eds), *Configurational Comparative Methods: Qualitative Comparative Analysis (QCA) and Related Techniques* (Sage, 2008).

same time maintaining a strict internal validation for external members capable of corroborating a systematic data treatment (see the next subsection). Indeed, the main limitation of our dataset is a smaller scope for identifying regional trends and patterns thus precluding a global comparison. In a similar vein, not all landmark cases in each jurisdiction correspond to standardised years; therefore, the data is unbalanced, having, for instance, outliers that date back to the early 1900s (ie, in Argentina).

As noted above, this project relied on the main features of the CONREASON project,[43] although the original list of indicators was modified and completed following regional specificities. At the very beginning of the project, in 2017, a preliminary case study was conducted on the Ecuadorean Constitutional Court by using the original CONREASON methodology. The analysis of 40 landmark cases, which were pronounced between 2009 and 2016, was an experiment to determine how the original methodology worked in a different context. This dataset was later completed by a second selection of 40 cases from the jurisprudence of the new composition of the Ecuadorean Constitutional Court, to capture meaningful within-country variations that mirrored the drastic ideological split between two distinct governments.[44] Once the project was set up, there was a group of five courts (Costa Rica, Argentina, Mexico, Colombia, and the IACtHR) that each sent three sentences to complete a pilot project regarding which indicators should be added and how the existing indicators should be modified to reflect the Latin American and Caribbean context. As a result of these preliminary studies, we added 13 more indicators, such as the top-down or bottom-up involvement (concerning who or what body initiated the case); length of the judgment; pro homine principle; government system by power structure (concerning the principle of federalism); post-material values; family; transition; economic, social, cultural and environmental rights; activism; and finally an indicator on the overall weight of the arguments.

In the case of several indicators, we created subcategories for a possible affirmative option. For instance, if a sentence contained an international law argument, we asked whether it was a binding international norm from the Inter-American System, outside the regional human rights system or international soft law. Such calibration was introduced in eight indicators, offering an opportunity to produce more sophisticated results about certain characteristics.

i. Sample, Data Sources and Internal Validation

Fifteen jurisdictions of Latin America and the Caribbean comprise the sample of the CORE Latam Dataset. The jurisdiction covers most of South America, Central America, Mexico and a significant part of the Caribbean (ie, Antigua and Barbuda, Barbados,

[43] See Jakab et al, 'CONREASON – The Comparative Constitutional Reasoning Project. Methodological Dilemmas and Project Design' (2015) 9 *MTA JTI Law Working Papers* at jog.tk.hu/mtalwp/conreason-the-comparative-constitutional-reasoning-project-methodological-dilemmas-and-project-design.

[44] J Wolff, 'Ecuador after Correa: the struggle over the "citizens' revolution"' (2018) 38 *Revista de Ciencia Política*, 281–302; AS Castellanos Santamaría, R Dandoy and S Umpierrez de Reguero, 'Between a Rock and a Hard Place: Ecuador during the COVID-19 Pandemic' (2021) 41 *Revista de Ciencia Política* 321–51.This explains why we have two times 40 (=80) selected cases from Ecuador, which is referred to as 'the first and the second Ecuadorean court' or simply as 'Ecuador 1 and Ecuador 2', respectively, in the subsequent chapters.

Belize, Bermuda, Guyana, Jamaica, Saint Lucia, Saint Vincent and the Grenadines, The Bahamas and Trinidad and Tobago), adhering to a meaningful cross-country variation. Despite being a non-probabilistic sample, delving into 40 landmark cases (the unit of observation), 15 jurisdictions can be illustrative of certain features of constitutional reasoning in Latin America and the Caribbean and can point to current and emerging tendencies on a regional level.

The CORE Latam dataset essentially relies on primary sources. It compares unbalanced temporal iterations of 15 jurisdictions from Latin America and the Caribbean: Mexico, Costa Rica, Guatemala, Colombia, Venezuela, Ecuador, Brazil, Bolivia, Peru, Chile, Argentina, Uruguay, Paraguay, the Commonwealth Caribbean and the region's human rights tribunal, the IACtHR. For most of the countries, performing an empirical analysis of the constitutional or supreme court's jurisprudence is unprecedented and therefore has the potential to add a novel perspective and introduce a new range of research questions related to these jurisdictions. Furthermore, the inclusion of the regional human rights court created an original opportunity to have a fresh look at the IACtHR's practice and even compare it to that of the European Court of Human Rights (ECtHR) and the European Court of Justice (ECJ) by using the data of the CONREASON Project.

The temporal distribution of the selected landmark cases,[45] as shown in Graph 1, indicates that most of the identified landmark cases were from the last two decades, while there are numerically fewer from the preceding decades. This phenomenon might be explained by the fact that several of the currently functioning constitutional and supreme courts were created in constitutions adopted after the 2000s.

Graph 1 Temporal distribution of the selected judgments from all jurisdictions

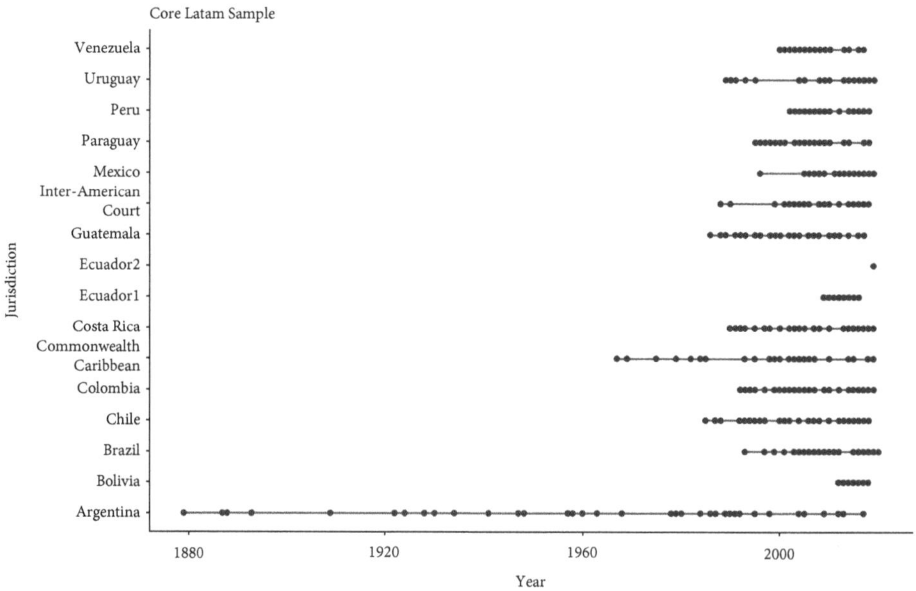

[45] The period for case selection closed in December 2019. By this date, all judgments from all 15 jurisdictions had to be selected. Therefore, all cases after this date could only be mentioned as part of the doctrinal analysis and could not be included in the dataset.

The procedure to collect and synthesise the information was standardised for all jurisdictions and the coding implied internal validation processes. First, experts in each jurisdiction selected a set of 40 landmark cases.[46] This process was evaluated by constitutional law scholars and experts external to the CORE Latam project, but who had expertise in the respective jurisdictions. Once authors from each jurisdiction had the definitive list of 40 landmark cases, they coded all selected judgments by using the set of indicators provided by the CORE Latam Codebook.[47] The CORE Latam dataset relied on categorical coding for most items. The number of pages and the year of each landmark judgment comprised the only set of scale variables. Hence, most responses were coded as '1' or 'YES', otherwise '0' or 'NO', when the condition was not satisfied. Undoubtedly, this coding logic provides uniformity and reduces potential biases related to the expert's constitutional interpretation. In sum, the total number of dataset observations was 640, which means that the authors of this work analysed altogether more than 43,000 pages of judicial landmark decisions.

As somewhat underscored above, Latin America is a geographical region and a complex historical, cultural, political and linguistic concept,[48] which was chosen as the focus of this project precisely because of its intricate constitutional culture, which sets the scene for constitutional reasoning. However, not all countries of South and Central America and the Caribbean were included (for instance, those countries without constitutional review, such as Cuba,[49] were excluded), but we are confident that the present sample adequately reflects the diversity of constitutional traditions in Latin America and the Caribbean Commonwealth. Furthermore, while Brazil was already included in the CONREASON project, it was important to cover this influential jurisdiction again in the present initiative, which is why Brazil is represented in this volume with a new set of selected landmark judgments.

The Caribbean region was expressly added to the project to emphasise its importance as a separate region and recognise its constitutional culture. The comparability aspect of the Caribbean Commonwealth countries may arise since the rest of the analysed jurisdictions primarily belong to the civil law tradition that reigns in Latin America. Besides the fact that common law countries were already represented in the CONREASON dataset, it was pivotal (and also a great opportunity) to highlight Latin America's constitutional diversity by including the Caribbean Commonwealth's experience. The Caribbean region, especially its constitutional systems and constitutional review jurisprudence, is quite under-researched, and while there have been recent academic contributions to fill this void,[50] a chapter dedicated to the analysis of the Caribbean Commonwealth's constitutional jurisprudence can contribute to a better understanding of the region's constitutional culture.

[46] See the dilemmas and reasons behind this methodology, Jakab et al (n 43).

[47] See in the Appendix at the end of this volume.

[48] A von Bogdandy, E Ferrer Mac-Gregor, M Morales Antoniazzi, F Piovesan and X Soley, *Transformative Constitutionalism in Latin America. The Emergence of a New Ius Comune* (Oxford University Press, 2017) 30; M Tenorio-Trillo, *Latin America. An Allure and Power of an Idea* (The University of Chicago Press, 2017) 76.

[49] JC Gaunche, 'Cuba' in Hübner et al (n 6) 170.

[50] R Albert, D O'Brien and S Wheatle, *The Oxford Handbook of Caribbean Constitutions* (Oxford University Press, 2020).

ii. A Note on the 'Overall Weight of the Arguments' Indicator

There is one indicator that differs from the rest of the new indicators in our dataset. Coding the 'overall weight of the arguments' implied the need for more academic judgement than the already challenging identification of different arguments in the selected opinions. The attempt to measure the overall weight of the argument was a reaction to the ample use of rhetorical[51] reasoning, a common feature of various constitutional landmark decisions from the region. Interpretive methods and concepts are frequently invoked rhetorically, which means that they are only mentioned and not actually used to reach the conclusion of the case at hand. There can be several explanations for arguments that are mentioned but not used, as they could have a decorative or ornamental mission as well as a pedagogical aim, and they are sometimes applied to distract the reader and leave the constitutional problem unresolved or ambiguous. Independent from the motivations behind the use of rhetorical arguments, the new indicator focuses on identifying this rhetorical factor and displaying its features across cases and jurisdictions.

As earlier academic attempts were developed to measure the quality of judicial decisions in different conceptual and empirical frameworks,[52] the indicator measuring the rhetorical use of arguments had to be designed from the ground up. The idea was to determine the degree of weight of those interpretive methods and concepts that were already identified from the coding and which appeared in the selected judgment's conclusion.[53] The logical relationship between the previously invoked arguments and the conclusion, together with the level of authority, is referred to as the overall weight of the arguments. The weight can vary according to the type of relationship that the reasoning establishes between the arguments and the conclusion. The Codebook established three kinds of relations: (1) arguments could be categorised as conclusive (or ratio decidendi) arguments if they directly supported the conclusion; (2) arguments could be categorised as supportive (or obiter dictum) if they were inconclusive but were invoked as an additional support for the conclusion; and (3) arguments could be identified as rhetorical arguments if they did not add any weight to support the conclusion.

Once the weight of each previously identified argument was categorised following the above scale, our authors counted all arguments to check if those that carry any weight in relation to the conclusion are in the majority; or, conversely, if there were more unweighted arguments; or, if there were an equal number of arguments with or without argumentative weight. The results of this experiment can be found in this book's conclusions (chapter twenty).

III. The Doctrinal Pillar of Constitutional Reasoning

The empirical dataset alone cannot be properly understood and analysed without extensive knowledge of the relevant political, social and academic backgrounds of

[51] M Bencze and GY Ng, *How to Measure the Quality of Judicial Reasoning* (Springer, 2018).

[52] S Basabe-Serrano, 'The Quality of Judicial Decisions in Supreme Courts: A Conceptual Definition and Index Applied to Eleven Countries in Latin America' (2016) 37 *Justice System Journal* 331–47; Bencze and Ng (n 51).

[53] By the conclusion of the judgment, we mean the Case Disposition under Q4 of the Codebook.

each selected jurisdiction. The idea of the doctrinal pillar, following the CONREASON project, is rooted in providing the appropriate context necessary for a complete analysis of constitutional reasoning in the specific jurisdiction. One of the main goals was to guarantee comparability among the studied jurisdictions, either in this volume or in other (previous and forthcoming) works that use this same methodology. Besides comparability, it was also essential to ensure that the same information was available about every court's jurisprudence in a homogenously structured and coherent way. This was especially important for jurisdictions where the constitutional or supreme court's jurisprudence was rather underrepresented in the body of international research on this topic.

Within the framework of the empirical pillar, authors of each country report had to complete an Excel table regarding the codification of the selected landmark judgments. The cornerstone of the doctrinal pillar was a Questionnaire[54] that author(s) of each country chapter had to follow while describing the political, social and academic contexts of their respective jurisdictions. Besides the necessary adjustments, this Questionnaire was also completed to adequately capture the unique features of the Latin American and Caribbean region. Along with describing the legal and cultural contexts that surround constitutional reasoning, all authors of the country reports were asked to consider specific questions about the court and its litigation, the selection process and profiles of judges, and the legal scholarship and specific approaches to constitutional reasoning in the given academic discourse. This contextualisation served as a condition for moving beyond simply reporting the results of the empirical analysis, making sense of them and offering competing explanations of the possible reasons behind the quantitative picture.

The image drawn by the 15 country reports and the additional chapters offers a fascinating and complex depiction of the constitutional reason-giving practices in Latin America and the Caribbean, which can point to various details, cases, connections and explanations about each studied jurisdiction's jurisprudence and cross-regional connections.

IV. A Jigsaw Falling into Place – Towards the Solution of an Argumentative Puzzle

Following Ackerman's classic thesis written almost 30 years ago, courts that were born in a 'new beginning' scenario will possibly reward a redemptive style of constitutional adjudication.[55] Latin America and the Caribbean have had a rather continuous narrative of new beginnings, based on several regime changes, instances of coups d'état and authoritarian regimes and recoveries from dictatorships followed by transitional periods under new democratic constitutions. The new beginnings rhetoric has almost

[54] The updated and edited version of the Questionnaire for purposes of this volume can be found in the Appendix. Its structure was borrowed and modified per Jakab et al (n 24). See more about the methodology in Jakab et al (n 43).

[55] B Ackerman, 'The Rise of World Constitutionalism' 83 *Virginia Law Review* (1997).

always accompanied these changes, followed by new courts and competences that usually granted more power to constitutional or supreme courts precisely to enable them to lead the newly assigned transformative responsibilities. We can argue, on the one hand, that a redemptive style of adjudication is therefore something that is naturally coded in the region's constitutional changes and is present in most of the courts' jurisprudence analysed here, since at least the 1990s. On the other hand, the desire for a fresh start[56] has a direct link to the emergence of neo-constitutional trends.[57]

However, this seems to be accurate from a bird's eye view, our methodology of measuring concrete features and traits of courts' argumentative practices can help provide a more detailed and complete explanation. To recognise and unearth all possible entanglements of the Latin American and Caribbean constitutional reasoning practices, this volume includes additional chapters to build an informative explanatory framework for the country reports. After this Introduction, the reader will find a chapter dedicated to the 'Constitutional Tradition in Latin America and the Caribbean,' authored by Pier Paolo Pigozzi, which provides an essential insight into the short history and different constitutional theories in the region. Pigozzi's perceptive chapter serves as a companion to the country reports and their authors' efforts to uncover the constitutional theoretical background that surrounds the argumentative practices of their respective courts.

The country reports, incorporating the Questionnaire responses and the results of the empirical analysis, comprise the majority of the volume. However, there are certain patterns, features, and historical phases that the reader can expect to see regarding the courts discussed in each chapter. Specifically, the studied courts first enter a dictatorial or de facto period that either precedes, or for a short period, overlaps the current constitution, followed by a more modest period of the respective court's jurisprudence, and then by a more creative phase, or one characterised by certain irregularities that several courts' practices share, such as ambiguity and rhetorical practice. Simultaneously, each court's jurisprudence displays specific features that collectively amount to a truly diverse and colourful mosaic of constitutional argumentation in the region.

The Costa Rican expression 'put it a salacuartazo!', referring to the review competence of the Fourth Chamber (Sala Cuarta) of the Supreme Court of Costa Rica, adequately reflects the impact and magnitude of constitutional review for many Latin American and Caribbean societies. Renewal, however, exists hand in hand with a rather stubborn persistence of certain enduring features that have created various layers in the constitutional reasoning culture. Andrea Castagnola, Alejandro Chehtman and Sergio Muro, authors of the chapter on Argentina, explain how an institutional design heavily influenced by the US Constitution, with strong continental European features, plays out in the current regional context of constitutional reasoning. The prevalence of the classical interpretive methods and unanimous decisions, together with the emergence of human rights cases, the use of multiple arguments and a growing emphasis on international law, make the Argentine case study an illuminating example of the

[56] KL Scheppele, 'Aspirational and Aversive Constitutionalism: The Case for Studying Cross-Constitutional Influence through Negative Models'(2003) 1 *International Journal of Constitutional Law* 296.

[57] T Győrfy, *Against the New Constitutionalism* (Edward Elgar, 2016).

coexistence of previous classical practices and new creative methods. Similarly, the evolution of the Constitutional Court of Chile represents another example of the coexistence of a more formal and restrictive judicial argumentative style and a recently emerging cosmopolitan profile. As Cristián Villalonga Torrijo and Francisco Urbina explain in the chapter on Chile, this creative turn paradoxically coincided with the decline of the Chilean Constitutional Court's legitimacy due to certain pathologies that weakened its institutional reason-giving function, such as complex and unwieldy opinions and the court's inability to maintain a robust system of settled precedents. Chile is not the only case where the struggle to abandon a formalistic judicial practice has resulted in shortcomings in the court's jurisprudence.

Roberto Niembro Ortega and Irene Spigno eloquently present the Mexican Supreme Court of Justice as it manoeuvres through an argumentative transition concerning not only its argumentative style and practice but also its audience. Similar processes of argumentative transition are underway in other courts' jurisprudence too, such as in Peru, Colombia and Guatemala. As Abraham Siles Vallejos, Rosa Natalí Llique Ramírez and María Alejandra Espino Layza show, during and not long after the period of a captive court, the Peruvian Constitutional Court's jurisprudence was mostly viewed as an institutional part of formalistic and legalistic traditions, which changed in 2000 when the court was 'liberated' under the new democratic leadership. The regime change triggered an innovative argumentative approach in a framework in which the court began to reject the literal interpretation of the constitution, preferring a systematic reading together with the harmonisation of its provisions with regional and international legal sources and a reliance on legal doctrine. Not all courts have advanced at the same pace in this transition. Our dataset suggests that the Supreme Court of Paraguay is a tribunal that is still at a relatively early stage of the abovementioned creative turn. María José Garcia and Juan Pablo Irrazabal, authors of the Paraguay chapter, describe a court that has strong North American and European doctrinal influences but is still struggling to develop a firm analytical capacity to reason and conceptualise and still lacks openness to the content of foreign cases and doctrine.

Besides those mentioned earlier, many other country reports confirm a strong correlation between political regime change and interpretive practices. Carlos Arturo Villagrán, in his chapter on the Constitutional Court of Guatemala, offers a sophisticated account of the evolution of a cosmopolitan court in that Central American country. The Guatemalan court is unique not only in its path to becoming a prominent political player in Guatemalan politics but also in its use of constitutional reasoning to maintain its political power. For instance, its reductionist approach to foreign sources, precedents and other interpretive sources has allowed the Guatemalan court to remain vague, underdetermined and able to consciously leave rules of interpretation undefined to maintain its influence in changing political circumstances. While the Chilean Constitutional Court was unable to establish a clear regime of settled precedents, and it weakened its position as a political actor by overturning prominent judgments without any clear discipline, the Guatemalan court seems to have used similar reductive techniques without the backlashes reported in the Chilean case.

The Bolivian case study adds further bits and pieces to the understanding of deficient argumentative practices. Sergio Verdugo, author of the chapter on the Bolivian

Constitutional Court, demonstrates that multiple self-attributed roles of the same court can contribute to its argumentative style, such as its role in implementing the transformative goals of the ruling political movement, establishing a post-liberal and plurinational political system and emphasising social and indigenous rights along with its role to protect the core institutional arrangements of the democratic system. Unnecessarily long judgments, selective arguments, and inconsistent methodologies used and cited in a decontextualised manner, are all features of the Bolivian court that are generally not uncommon, especially in the Andean region. The Ecuadorean Constitutional Court, as shown by Johanna Fröhlich in the corresponding chapter, is another example of the dearth of elaborated tests and the quest to include indigenous principles and indigenous ways to understand legal norms. In this chapter, the author uses and compares two separate datasets to contrast the court's argumentative practices applied during Ecuador's regime changes, which reflect a complete overhaul of that court's membership. The two samples allowed us to track those interpretive techniques that pertained to the deeper constitutional culture, and those that depended more on reigning ideological influences.

The augmentation of competences and greater judicial autonomy and creativity consequently caused additional difficulties for the study, such as identifying a single voice in the courts' rulings as the Chilean and Mexican examples demonstrate. Undoubtedly, the primary example of a truly hyperbolic court is found in Brazil. Diego Werneck Arguelhes, Rafael Bellem de Lima and Ivar A Hartmann, authors of the chapter on the Supreme Federal Tribunal of Brazil, expertly illustrate the court's transition from a formalist tribunal to one that uses an inexhaustible number of interpretive methods and concepts within the jurisdictional framework that the court itself has gradually broadened 'to a point where it has become virtually impossible to know what it cannot do'.[58] Lengthy and multiple individual rulings, dozens of references to previous decisions without contextualisation and the weak argumentative force of written constitutional provisions have led to problems with the authoritative nature of that court's judgments.

An additional challenge that seemingly contributes to the overall picture of constitutional reasoning in the region is the courts' capacity and willingness to address structural, interbranch cases along with cases concerning human rights.[59] The Colombian Constitutional Court, for instance, is well-known as a transformative, activist, human rights defender, but these features are absent in much of its jurisprudence and the selected landmark judgments. Magdalena Correa Inés Henao and Jorge Ernesto Roa Roa, authors of the Colombian chapter, paint a picture of a sophisticated court that has two contrasting features. Specifically, the court is a strong guarantor of fundamental rights, although more deferential and restrictive when it comes to the legislator's and executive's competences, especially those of a financial, tax and budgetary nature; those that relate to the distribution of powers in the territorial sphere; those that involve economic policies or public international treaties; and finally, those

[58] See Werneck Arguelhes, Bellem de Lima, and Hartmann (ch 5).

[59] See the comparison of horizontal and vertical control exercised by courts in Latin America in Helmke and Ríos-Figueroa (n 2) 9–10.

that related to the state of emergency decreed during the COVID-19 pandemic. The Colombian case, however, is quite different than Costa Rica's experience. In the chapter focusing on the latter, Ariana Macaya Lizano unfolds the powerful history and main features of a court that, besides serving as a tool to improve democracy, the rule of law and fundamental rights and liberties, has also managed to strike a new balance in the context of governmental power. Furthermore, although its jurisprudence has been sharply criticised for its activism and broad interpretation of its own competences, the Fourth Chamber of the Costa Rican Supreme Court's short and concise style and moderate reasoning practice sharply contrast with the otherwise similar path its Brazilian and Colombian counterpart has chosen.

Some courts in the region have evidently not joined the transformative paradigm in their constitutional jurisprudence. María Paula Garat Delgado and Anna Luisa Walter de Santana depict the Supreme Court of Uruguay as a modest and deferential court that guide a coherent and relatively foreseeable jurisprudence, placing greater emphasis on the procedural aspects of standing and legitimisation than the substantive aspects of a case. By contrast, the Constitutional Chamber of the Venezuelan Supreme Court has been actively participating in the development of *Chavismo* as a political regime – that is, the progressive dismantlement of democracy and the eventual surge and consolidation of authoritarian rule. Raúl Sánchez Urribarri and Juan Berríos share the intriguing evolution of the Constitutional Chamber through the lenses of the different stages of regime changes up to the current hegemonic authoritarian regime. The Venezuelan case offers important lessons not only 'to those who place too much faith on the judiciary as a bulwark of democratic rule' as the authors argue but also to those who claim that certain interpretive methods can ensure a just and correct outcome. The Constitutional Chamber regularly relies on the constitution's authoritative text, which makes it a clear outlier in the region. However, in a highly politicised context, the use of any interpretive method becomes dubious, as it is motivated more by the interests of governance and political survival than by the provision of a proper justification for the decision at hand.

The volume includes two special jurisdictions, neither of which is a country. It is perhaps unsurprising that these jurisdictions' reason-giving practices also stand out. One of these jurisdictions is the Caribbean Commonwealth region, which encompasses various smaller countries, while the other is the regional human rights tribunal, the Inter-American Court of Human Rights (IACtHR). To accurately cover the Caribbean region, the author of this chapter, Derek O'Brien, chose to include two courts: the Judicial Committee of the Privy Council (JCPC), which assumed jurisdiction over the British Empire's new territories at the beginning of the eighteenth century and was retained as the final appellate court in the new constitutions after independence, and the Caribbean Court of Justice (CCJ), which was created recently, in 2006. O'Brien offers a fascinating account of these courts' jurisprudence and their relation to each other and other courts in the region, highlighting the radical departure of the CCJ from the JCPC's jurisprudence. While the JCPC seems to utilise a moderate style of constitutional reasoning – mostly the classical methods of interpretation – the CCJ turns to creative methods, employs lengthy judgments and concurring opinions and 'disregard[s] the text of the constitution where this is not compatible with the 'underlying sentiments and principles' of the constitution'.[60]

Pablo González Domínguez and Alfredo Ortega Franco describe the IACtHR, taking special care to note the court's complexities that have developed over its 44-year history. The authors show that the IACtHR favours interpretations that maximise the scope of rights and expand the influence of its decisions at the state level through the principles of effectiveness, *pro personae* and evolutive interpretation. The court has established itself as a regional reference point for constitutional adjudication while new realities and challenges have simultaneously prompted the IACtHR to adjust and revise its argumentative practices. The latter has occurred especially when more sophisticated and contested questions are brought to the court, such as the validity of peace agreements or controversies involving economic, social or cultural rights.

In its third and closing section, the book tackles the principal tendencies of constitutional reasoning present or emerging on a regional level. This is the core topic of 'The Notion of the Rule of Law in the Constitutional Reasoning of Latin America and the Caribbean', a chapter authored by Marie-Christine Fuchs, Juan Camilo Herrera and Miguel Barboza. The enormous amount of work for this chapter, which required an analysis of all the selected landmark judgments that contained a reference to the principle of the rule of law, involved a collaboration with colleagues from the Programme of Rule of Law for Latin America of the Konrad Adenauer Foundation. Thanks to their efforts, we have a much clearer picture of what is behind the relatively high number of judicial references to the rule of law, as well as a broader understanding of constitutional reasoning in the region. Furthermore, Tania Groppi and Anna Maria Lecis's chapter, 'The Constitutional Dialogue Between the Inter-American and the European Courts of Human Rights: Toward an Increasing Influence of the Inter-American Jurisprudence?', sheds light on the tendencies of cross-regional judicial dialogue. The authors highlight the newest transjudicial communication trends, according to which the ECtHR and IACtHR are leading a more dynamic dialogue, where the IACtHR has been a more of an extra-systemic receiver than contributor.

Finally, the aggregate data from all jurisdictions, as well as specific measurements and graphs that depict regional trends, are analysed in the chapter entitled 'The Argumentative Turn in the Constitutional Reasoning in Latin America and the Caribbean', which was authored by Johanna Fröhlich, the volume's editor. The author argues here that the database and the doctrinal analysis point to a clear creative turn in the reason-giving practices of the 15 jurisdictions covered in the book. The creative element of reasoning, however, is not the only relevant factor; it is accompanied by a weakened textual component and a strong and complex rhetorical factor, which together are more capable of illuminating the true characteristics and tendencies currently emerging in Latin America and the Caribbean.

In sum, this volume is based on an initiative to better understand constitutional reasoning in Latin America and the Caribbean. To meet this objective, we applied a mixed methodology that included a robust empirical pillar with a detailed and

[60] See O'Brien (ch 6).

homogenous doctrinal component. This combination made it possible to contrast theories with actual judicial practices, offer a firm scientific basis to form more informed opinions on courts' practices and define and analyse current and emerging tendencies. The chapters reflect the strength and effectiveness of our project's methodology and the resulting high-quality dataset, which the authors have utilised to answer several pressing questions regarding the argumentative practices of the profiled courts.

2

Constitutional Tradition in Latin America and the Caribbean

PIER PAOLO PIGOZZI

I. Introduction

A Latin American constitutional tradition would be the metaexplanatory background that would help make sense regarding the constitutional reasoning of constitutional and supreme courts in the region. This is why each chapter starts with an explanation of the key features of each court's political, legal and academic context. The more solid such a tradition is, the clearer the foundations of each decision to change or to follow previous case law. Yet, drastic constitutional changes and refoundational moments are frequent throughout the history of Latin America and pose a considerable obstacle to reading the series of changes as a novel.

This poses a basic problem of intelligibility for constitutional changes and amendments as well as for constitutional reasoning. The lack of a sustained narrative makes it hard to understand continuities, changes and ruptures with the past. There have been important efforts in reconstructing such Latin American and Caribbean traditions of constitutional thought.[1] However, they faced significant critics,[2] and they remain few. This is an area worthy of sustained effort from searching and systematising primary sources, to writing new findings beyond what might be relevant to the burning interests of the moment.

Things have been different during the last half-century. Already by 1974, the foundation of the Ibero-American Institute of Constitutional Law in Buenos Aires attested to collaborative endeavours throughout the region (in this case, between Mexican and

[1] See R Gargarella, *Latin American Constitutionalism, 1810–2010: The Engine Room of the Constitution* (Oxford University Press, 2013), and M Bernd, *Historia constitucional comparada de Iberoamérica. las seis fases desde la revolución de 1810 hasta la transnacionalización del siglo 21* (Ibáñez, 2016).

[2] See eg J Aldeman, 'Review of The legal foundations of inequality: Constitutionalism in the Americas, 1776–1860 by Roberto Gargarella' (2011) 43 *Journal of Latin American Studies* 372; C Andrews, 'Review of The legal foundations of inequality: Constitutionalism in the Americas, 1776–1860 by Roberto Gargarella' (2012) 44 *Estudios de Historia Moderna Contemporánea de Mexico* 198, R Breña, 'Review of The legal foundations of inequality constitutionalism in the Americas, 1776–1860, by Roberto Gargarella' (2012) 19 *Política y gobierno* 384, and JA Aguilar-Rivera, 'Review of The legal foundations of inequality: Constitutionalism in the Americas, 1776–1860 by Roberto Gargarella' (2014) 47 *J. Latin American Studies* 180.

Argentinian jurists) aiming at the creation of a 'comparative constitutional discourse in the service of democratic aims.'[3] This group of scholars sought to promote values of constitutionalism in times of authoritarian regimes. It is noteworthy then that it was about aspirational efforts, and not so much about an interest in a rigorous historical study.

Throughout the last decades, there has been an identifiable background with three common trends in Latin American Constitutionalism becoming the driving ideas behind constitutional changes. The secondary sources cited in this chapter are, for the most part, those that dare to speak of a regional narrative. This chapter did not add up individual country's narratives to come up with a minimal common denominator for the region. In that respect, the ideas and ideals on constitutionalism that remain influential to Latin American constitutional and supreme court's reasoning date from the 1980s, when many Latin American States were transitioning from authoritarian regimes to constitutions that favoured democratic values, rule of law, and human rights.

From the outset, constitutional ideas had a transformative bent. The aim of the transition was not only to return to democracy, but to do it in order to tackle the acute social challenges in terms of poverty, exclusion (affecting acutely indigenous peoples), violence and lack of environmental protection. The constitutional changes in Brazil (1988) and in Colombia (1991) rightly illustrate the rise of the *Nuevo Constitucionalismo Latino Americano* (NCLA).[4] Some claim that the constitutions of Ecuador (2008) and Bolivia (2009) introduced a yet newer trend of a post-liberal or Andean transformative constitutionalism (ATC).[5] In tandem, *ius constitutionale commune* in Latin American Constitutionalism (ICCAL) gained momentum as a scholarly and judicial agenda.

II. Present Trends in the Latin American and Caribbean Constitutional Tradition

After Jon Elster's study in 1995[6] and Cappelletti's *Judicial Review in the Contemporary World* (1971), it is very common to find public law scholars looking for waves of constitutional changes and the main features that set them apart from each other. The study of constitutional changes in Latin America is not an exception. From the 1970s up to the present, human rights and constitutional law scholars[7] have continued to

[3] A von Bogdandy, 'Ius constitutionale Commune en Latino América. Observations on Transformative Constitutionalism' in A von Bogdandy et al (eds), *Transformative Constitutionalism in Latin America. The Emergence of a New Ius Commune* (Oxford University Press, 2018) 29.

[4] In Spanish, *nuevo constitucionalismo latinoamericano*.

[5] See R Gargarella, 'Lo "viejo" del "nuevo" constitucionalismo latinoamericano' *Seminar in Latin America on Constitutional and Political Theory: Inequality*, Brazil (2015) available at law.yale.edu/sites/default/files/documents/pdf/SELA15_Gargarella_CV_Sp.pdf; R Uprimny, 'The Recent Transformation of Constitutional Law in Latin America: Trends and Challenges' (2011) 89 *Texas Law Review* 1587.

[6] See J Elster, 'Forces and Mechanisms in the Constitution-Making Process' (1995) 45 *Duke Law Journal* 364, 368–73.

[7] See eg H Gros Espiell, 'El constitucionalismo latinoamericano y la codificación en el siglo XIX' (2002) 6 *Anuario Iberoamericano de justicia constitucional* 143; J Carpizo, 'Tendencias actuales del constitucionalismo latinoamericano' (2009) 23 *Revista Derecho del Estado* 7; M Carbonell et al (coords), *Tendencias del constitucionalismo en Iberoamérica* (IIJ-UNAM, 2009); D García Belaunde, 'Los vaivenes del constitucionalismo latinoamericano en las últimas décadas' (2014) 89 *Revista de Derecho Político* 391; Uprimny (n 5).

research the recent trends, with the peculiarity in Latin America that such studies have attained a sort of normative force as if the latest constitutional innovation had become a standard to follow by next constitutional interpretation, constitutional changes or amendments. References to New Latin American constitutionalism or *ius commune* seek to exert influence over the constitutions of the region and sometimes over the jurisprudence of the Inter-American Court of Human Rights and national high courts.

The enthusiasm for constitutional and human rights innovation has to do with the urgent need to address problems of poverty, violence, corruption, week institutions and the disregard for the values of rule of law. Any new formula has the appeal of hope. Since the 1970s constitutional innovations have attained a heightened normative effect in academia and in politics.

It was as if, against the mushrooming of dictatorial regimes from the 1940s to the 1970s, the region felt the need of a constitutional model that would be able to resist the overthrowing of democratically elected authorities. Thus, the need for legal and political reform has been phrased in the language of favouring democracy and human rights, whereas opposing reforms has been increasingly related to the defence of the status quo of violence, arbitrariness, and poverty – to put it succinctly.

Elster verified that waves of constitution-making were usually triggered by some sort of exceptional circumstance that exerts influence over several countries and that the response of constitution-making by one of them serves as an inspiration to be followed by the rest.[8] The end of dictatorial regimes throughout Latin America throughout the late 1970s and the 1980s, and the social and financial crisis of the end of the 1990s triggered waves of constitution-making in the region that coincided with the ones in Europe after the fall of dictatorships in Southern Europe in the 1970s and the adoption of new constitutions in Central Europe after the fall of communism in 1989[9] while African countries had already been through a second wave of constitution-making.[10]

The consolidation of democratic regimes throughout the whole region during the 1980s and 1990s gave way to discussing constitutional reforms that featured developments intended to further the instantiation of democratic values and human rights. Nolte and Schilling-Vacaflor recognise 'four reform clusters [that] were undertaken after the late 1980s that can be associated with good governance' in Latin America.[11]

Following Nolte and Schilling-Vacaflor, the first cluster of reforms was aimed at introducing neo-liberal constitutional reforms such as the deregulation of the market and privatisation of state-owned companies. A second cluster targeted the decentralisation of the state. The third cluster dealt with reforms to the judiciary – which included the institutional design of bodies for horizontal accountability (ie *consejos de la judicatura*), the reform of criminal procedures, and sometimes the creation of

[8] See Elster (n 6) 372.

[9] ibid 368–70, listing seven waves of constitution-making.

[10] See eg C Fombad, 'Challenges to Constitutionalism and Constitutional Rights in Africa and the Enabling Role of Political Parties: Lessons and Perspectives from Southern Africa' (2007) 55 *American Journal of Comparative Law* 1, 2, and GT Hessebon, 'The Fourth Constitution-Making Wave of Africa: Constitutions 4.0?' (2014) 28 *Temple International and Comparative Law Journal* 185, 186–89.

[11] See D Nolte and A Schilling-Vacaflor, 'Introduction: the times they are a Changin': Constitutional Transformations in Latin America since 1990s' in D Nolte and A Schilling-Vacaflor (eds), *New Constitutionalism in Latin America. Promises and Practices* (Ashgate, 2012) 15.

specialised constitutional courts or ombudsman offices. A fourth cluster of reforms sought to promote political rights, direct democratic participation, and the constitutionalisation of guidelines for key policy areas.[12] The constitutional changes in Brazil (1988), Colombia (1991), Peru (1993) and Ecuador (1998) provide good examples of these reforms.

The first three clusters of reforms as described by Nolte and Schilling-Vacaflor correspond to the rise of *nuevo constitucionalismo latinoamericano*. Roughly speaking, the fourth cluster will be included and expanded under the title of Andean Transformative Constitutionalism. In parallel to these two clusters runs the *ius constitutionale commune in América Latina* (ICCAL), which makes more explicit the relation between Latin American constitutionalism and the Inter-American system for the protection of human rights.

A. Nuevo Constitucionalismo Latino Americano

Let us bear in mind that the label *nuevo constitucionalismo latinoamericano* – and its derivations such as *nuevo derecho or neoconstitucionalismo latinoamericano* – is also the generic name which many use to refer to all the clusters of constitutional changes within the past 30 years in Latin America, including *Neoconstitucionalismo Andino Transformador* and ICCAL.[13] For the purposes of this work *nuevo constitucionalismo latinoamericano* (and its derivations) refers only to the trend that starts with the 1988 Constitution of Brazil and ends with the 1998 Ecuadorean Constitution.

This is not to deny that the conceptualisation of '*nuevo constitucionalismo latinoamericano*' is a contentious field. The disagreement comes from many different angles ranging from those who see nothing new in Latin American constitutionalism[14] to those who see that Latin America is just following neoconstitutionalism from Europe, to those who believe that Latin American has ruptured with liberal constitutionalism and started its own breed of constitutionalism.[15] In any case, even those authors who remain sceptical with regard to the depth and breadth of the constitutional changes[16] also refer to a 'nuevo constitucionalismo latinoamericano' in order to take part in the debates on constitutional changes in Latin America that were inaugurated by the Brazilian Constitution of 1988 and end with the 1998 Ecuadorean constitution.[17]

[12] ibid.

[13] ibid; and F Curcó Cobos, 'The new Latin American constitutionalism: a critical review in the context of neo-constitutionalism' (2018) 43 *Canadian Journal of Latin American and Caribbean Studies* 212.

[14] See Uprimny (n 5) and Gargarella (n 5).

[15] See L García Jaramillo, 'El "nuevo derecho" en Colombia: ¿entelequia innecesaria o novedad pertinente?' (2008) 29 *Revista de Derecho Universidad del Norte* 289.

[16] For example in Ecuador, see F Corral, 'La seguridad jurídica' *Diario El Comercio*; F Corral, 'La discrecionalidad' *Diario El Comercio*, www.elcomercio.com/opinion/opinion-columnistas-discrecionalidad-ley.html; F Corral, '¿Dictadura judicial?' *Diario El Comercio* www.elcomercio.com/opinion/dictadura-judicial.html. In Colombia, see also J Tamayo Jaramillo, 'El Nuevo Derecho, el escepticismo antelas normas y el uso alternativo' (2006) 36 *Revista Facultad de Derecho y Ciencias Políticas* 361.

[17] The Venezuelan Constitution of 1999 represents the transition from that nuevo constitucionalismo latinoamericano to what here we label as a Neoconstitucionalismo Andino Transformador. On authors that defend the depth of the constitutional transformation, referring to the wave of changes especially from

Nuevo constitucionalismo latinoamericano purports to distance itself from other contemporary trends on neoconstitutionalism. It is *nuevo* because it learned lessons from Europe, and the Latin American strand purports to develop and improve upon the European version. It is *latinoamericano* because it has sought to incorporate new constitutional designs to address problems endemic to Latin America such as violence, weak institutions, poverty, exclusion of indigenous peoples, and the protection of the environment.

Moreover, special emphasis on the distinction from the European variant is key for legal scholars to invite anticolonial theories from social sciences. Latin American neoconstitutitionalists often enter a dialogue with other disciplines in order to borrow theoretical justifications for claims regarding legal pluralism, indigenous rights, and the constitutional protection of the environment. In order to underscore that distance from European neoconstitutionalism, Latin American scholars usually recognise the extent to which they drew from Spanish and Italian literature,[18] but claim to have produced a greater degree of refinement or detail in the implementation and to have brought original contributions to neoconstitutionalism that are visible in the 1991 Colombian Constitution and the jurisprudence of its Constitutional Court (see, for example, chapter eight on Colombia in this book).

The Latin American borrowing from European *neoconstitucionalismo* can be summarised in three main features: the constitutionalisation of the law, strengthened constitutional courts, and a renewed role for legal scholars.[19] The constitutionalisation of the law[20] begins with the assertion that new constitutions are made of directly binding provisions in contrast to what is perceived as a nineteenth century conviction that constitutional provisions were merely political exhortations for legislators, who were responsible for passing binding statutes. Legislatures are criticised for their lack of care for their constituents[21] and for defending instead the interests of the elite. Neoconstitutionalism sought to remedy this problem by having plebiscitary constitutions directly enforceable by courts, which means that in practice the constitution approved via plebiscite would always prevail against any laws or regulations that may oppose the rights or principles enshrined therein.

Another consequence of the constitutionalisation of the law is that constitutions are difficult to amend. The principles of supremacy of the constitution and its direct applicability are corollaries of constitutional rigidity. In the narrative of

the 2009 Constitution of Venezuela, see B de Sousa Santos, 'Refundación del Estado en América Latina: Perspectivas desde una Epistemología del Sur' (2010) *International Institute on Law and Society* 8–10.

[18] Some of the German, Italian and Spanish scholarly works that are most often cited by Latin American constitutional law scholars are K Hesse, 'La fuerza normativa de la constitución' in *Escritos de derecho constitucional* (Centro de Estudios Constitucionales de Madrid, 1983); R Guastini, 'La "constitucionacionalización" del ordenamiento jurídico' in M Carbonell (ed), *Neoconstitucionalismo(s)* (Editorial Trotta, 2003); E García de Enterría, *La Constitución como norma y el Tribunal Constitución* (Civitas, 1991).

[19] For the seminal text on the distinction between nuevo constitucionalismo latinoamericano and European neoconstitucionalismo see R Viciano Pastor and R Martínez Dalmau, 'Fundamentos teóricos y prácticos del nuevo constitucionalismo latinoamericano' (2011) 48 *Gaceta Constitucional* 307. For a similar appraisal by a Brasilian and Portuguese speaker scholar see LR Barroso, 'El neoconstitucionalismo y la constitucionalización del derecho en Brasil (El triunfo tardío del derecho constitucional en Brasil' (2007) 12 *Revista de Derecho de la Universidad de Montevideo* 25, 28–32.

[20] See R Guastini, 'La "costituzionalizzazione" dell'ordinamento italiano' (1998) VI(11) *Ragion Pratica* 185.

[21] See García Jaramillo (n 15) 299.

neoconstitutionalism, this is to ensure that constitutional rights will prevail in every situation, before any authority and above any other political or legal consideration. Neoconstitutionalists would argue that the constitutionalisation of the law affects the understanding of legal positivism by requiring an analysis of material content in order to assess the *formal* validity of a statute. Constitutional rights became the values that occupy the top spot in the hierarchy of legal sources. Due to their direct applicability, Colombian legal scholars dared say that the liberal understanding of rule of law as *estado de derecho* would no longer be the best available paradigm, and should be replaced by the rule of rights (ie *estado de derechos*)[22] because the power of the state would not find its final constraint in a formal understanding of the law, but on the substantive understanding of rights.

The second main takeaway from European neoconstitutionalism is a less formalistic approach to legal interpretation by constitutional courts, which usually have acquired enhanced powers under the new constitutions. Judicial review by constitutional courts includes both the power to adjudicate the constitutionality of legislation, and to decide on judicial remedies for the protection of constitutional rights. This feature of neoconstitutionalism overlaps with *garantismo*. *Garantismo* was popularised in Latin America through the work of Italian publicists such as Norberto Bobbio[23] and Luigi Ferrajoli[24] and it reaches beyond constitutional law to due process of law in criminal cases (ie *garantismo penal*).

In deciding on the constitutionality of statutes or on the adjudication of judicial remedies, constitutional courts are charged with the duty to safeguard the supremacy of the catalogue of constitutional rights, principles and underlaying values. Gustavo Zagrebelski's *Il diritto mite* is often cited among Latin American neoconstitutionalists in order to advocate for 'meek law' (*diritto mite*), that is, a transformation in which the rigid application of the black letter of national legislation yields to a richer understanding of law that gives way to the direct enforcement of human rights and constitutional principles.[25] From a neoconstitutionalist point of view, the former epitomises a formalistic understanding of the law, whereas the latter is presented as the zeal of neoconstitutionalism.

Neoconstitutionalists defend a purportedly novel centrality of constitutional principles instead of legal rules. The centrality of legal rules is a feature of the previous and outdated constitutional model, whereas the centrality of rights and principles is a feature of the neoconstitutional model. For the everyday practice of the law, this means that the application of the law to a particular set of facts through the logical operation

[22] ibid 301.

[23] See N Bobbio, *L'età dei diritti* (Giulio Einaudi Editore, 1989).

[24] See L Ferrajoli, *Diritto e ragione. Teoria del garantismo penale* (Laterza, 1989); L Ferrajoli, 'Le garanzie costituzionali dei diritti fondamentali' (2007) 1 *Teoria Politica* 11. In Spanish, the most influential works of Ferrajoli include *Derechos y garantías. La ley del más débil* (Trotta, 1999); *Los fundamentos de los derechos fundamentales* (Trotta, 2005); *El Garantismo y la Filosofía del Derecho* (Universidad Externado de Colombia, 2001); and *Garantismo. Una discusión sobre derecho y democracia* (Trotta, 2006). Yet, the origin of the term *garantismo* might be traced as far back as Charles Fourier in France. See generally C Fourier, *Le nouveau monde industriel et sociétaire, ou, Invention du procédé d'industrie attrayante et naturelle, distribuée en séries passionnées* (Éditions Flammarion, 1829) available at gallica.bnf.fr/ark:/12148/btv1b86221373.texteImage.

[25] See generally G Zagrebelski, *Il diritto mite. Legge, diritti, giustizia* (Giulio Einaudi Editore, 1992) (translated to Spanish as *El Derecho dúctil*, 1995).

of the syllogism (or *subsunción*) has to give way to interpretative methods (such as the weighing or '*ponderación*' of constitutional rights and principles; balancing, proportionality and reasonability tests; the *effet utile* of rights or '*maximización de los efectos normativos de los derechos fundamentales*'; as well as the German *Drittwirkung* or horizontal effect of rights and *Wesensgehalt* or the reading of a core or essential content of rights).[26]

For Latin American scholars of neoconstitutionalism, perhaps the two most influential works in this regard are Dworkin's *Taking Right Seriously* and Robert Alexy's *A Theory of Constitutional Rights* – plus shorter texts available in Spanish on the balancing test.[27] The transplantation of those two authors to Latin America does not necessarily take the texts at face value as intended by Dworkin and Alexy.[28] On the one hand, Dworkin's interpretive theory of rights is transplanted into public law, where it does not find the constraints of the chain novel approach provided by common law and by a deep-rooted legal culture on judicial precedents. On the other hand, the method of weighing to apply those rights and principles draws importantly from Robert Alexy. Precisely, one may see the adaptation of both theories in Latin America where the gaps in the legal culture in regard to judicial precedents and its application to public law are filled in through the adaptation of Alexy's derivative constitutional rights norms[29] (*normas adscriptas de derecho fundamental*[30]).

The balancing test or weighing epitomises the purported change in constitutional adjudication as a breakthrough from legal positivism and formalism. Through weighing, it becomes possible to rationalise (ie *argumentar*) judicial decisions that might be at odds with the black letter of the statutes in the name of justice through the direct application of constitutional rights.[31] To put it in one sentence, '[t]he judge is no longer regarded as a servant of the law but as an absolute lord of law.'[32] Constitutional judges receive the name of 'virtuous judges' (*juez virtuoso*) or 'judges for the new law' ('*juez del nuevo derecho*')[33] and their duty is not confined to judicial review or the safeguard of rights, but constitutional courts become a co-legislator and have the duty to actively specify the content of open-ended constitutional provisions and rights.[34] The lengthier catalogues of rights advanced by neoconstitutionalism reveal a renewed

[26] See García Jaramillo (n 15) at 302.

[27] Other influential commentators on the main works by Dworkin and Alexy include L Prieto Sanchís, *Sobre principios y normas. Problemas del razonamiento jurídico* (Palestra Editores, 1992); N Bobbio, *Teoria Generale del Diritto* (Giappichelli, 1993).

[28] There is a famous example provided by Diego López Medina in his 'Impure Theory of the Law' regarding the Latin American reading of HLA Hart. Latin American legal scholars take Hart to be a critique of legal formalism. See, D Lopez Medina, *Teoría impura del derecho. La transformación de la cultura jurídica latinoamericana* (Legis, 2004).

[29] R Alexy, *A Theory of Constitutional Rights* (Oxford University Press, 2002) 33–38. The original term in German is *zugeordnete Grundrechtsnormen*. R Alexy, *Theorie der Grundrechte* (Shurkamp, 1994) 57–63.

[30] R Alexy, *Teoría de los Derechos Fundamentales* (Centro de Estudios Políticos y Constitucionales, 1993) 66–73.

[31] García Jaramillo (n 15) 297.

[32] JA García Amado, 'Retórica, Argumentación y Derecho' (1999) 21 *Isegoría* 131.

[33] See R Uprimny, 'Estado social de derecho y decisión judicial correcta: un intento de recapitulación de los grandes modelos de interpretación jurídica' in D Botero Uribe (ed), *Hermenéutica Jurídica: homenaje al maestro Darío Echandía* (Ediciones Rosaristas, 1997).

[34] García Jaramillo (n 15) 303. See also C Gaviria, 'Prólogo' in AF Nanclares (ed), *Los jueces de mármol* (La Pisca Tabaca, 2001).

interest in moral debates and a thicker philosophical foundation for the constitutional texts. Therefore, the *new* judge has to be aware that her enhanced powers require her to be able to engage with pressing questions of moral philosophy and constitutional theory in her time and place.

In the third place, neoconstitutionalism considers that legal academia must fulfill a double function as a *metagarantía del ordenamiento jurídico.*[35] Legal scholars shall contribute to the creation of the new law and oversee the judiciary. The legal academy in Latin America is entrusted to work on the adaptation of foreign theories as well as on supporting the courts with original developments in order to further explain unprecedented constitutional provisions, or to solve contradictions between neoconstitutionalism and previous understandings of the law.

Nuevo constituticionalismo latinoamericano lacks thematic or methodological unity and it is very comfortable with a self-perception of a 'mosaic of trends'.[36] Yet, a quick glance at law reviews and journals reveals that there are recurrent topics. Thus, a methodological and jurisprudential backbone is there, but it seems to be unfledged, instead of absent all together. Some of these recurrent topics are the conceptualisation of rights (especially of social and economic rights), the justiciability of rights, personal autonomy, indigenous rights, multiculturalism, legal pluralism, and topics related to judicial activism.

The self-description of the 'mosaic of trends' allows *nuevo constituticionalismo latinoamericano* to get away with blending the theories of rights of Alexy and Dworkin with the perceived anti-legal formalism in their readings of Hart, the legal realism of Holmes, different versions of Mangabeira Unger's critical theories of social change through law, and a long etcetera.[37] The mosaic of legal theories behind *nuevo constituticionalismo latinoamericano* might not have thematic coherence, yet they share at their core the driving idea that a utopian transformation of society can be achieved – mainly – through the law. Where there is no *fit*, nor a *faithful justification*, the Dworkinian Hercules type of constitutional judge comes to life to level legal restraints through its interpretative might.

Anti-formalism is a defining postulate for the philosophy of *nuevo constituticionalismo latinoamericano*. It is not necessarily a systematic rejection of formalism.[38] Anti-formalism would be better understood as a 'criticism of a jurisprudence and judiciary [as well as legal academia] considered to be out of touch with the world.'[39] *Nuevo constituticionalismo latinoamericano's* aversion to 'formalism' is actually a criticism of the stiffness in the judiciary, legal profession, and legal academy when they all seemed uninterested in modern philosophical debates and lacking robust jurisprudential debates.

It would be more precise to understand 'anti-formalism' as anti-stiffness, anti-superficiality, and anti-simplistic approaches to understanding and applying the law.

[35] Ferrajoli (2006) (n 24) 33 et seq.

[36] See Carbonell (n 18).

[37] García Jaramillo (n 15) 294.

[38] For a review on the concept of legal formalism and its criticism, see generally H-P Haferkamp, 'Legal Formalism and its Critics' in H Pihlajamäki et al (eds), *The Oxford Handbook of European Legal History* (Oxford University Press, 2018).

[39] ibid 929.

It actualises through our claims on the erosion of the principle of legal certainty and the suspicion against textual interpretation as being prima facie oversimplistic. Such critical appraisals give way to a culture of binding precedents by constitutional courts and invite legal academia to elaborate on doctrines and to check the decisions on the courts in the new anti-formalistic paradigm.

With *nuevo constitucionalismo latinoamericano*, the basis for judicial review and judicial remedies (such as writs of *amparo*) is a constitution with a weakened text that is constantly modified through constitutional adjudication. The constitution, that is, its text as modified by the codified jurisprudence, 'irradiates' its binding effects and supremacy to all branches and acts of power.

Hand in hand with the constitutionalisation of the law and the increased importance of judicial precedents, constitutional law reaches out to international human rights law and to indigenous customary law. Therefore, another recurrent need in neoconstitutionalist scholarship in Latin America is to revisit the theory of the sources of the law[40] together with an understanding of legal pluralism.[41] Other topics that are also frequently reviewed as part of the Latin American appraisal of neoconstitutionalism are implicit rights and new rights; the justiciability of social, economic and cultural rights as an expression of the welfare state (*Estado Social de Derecho*); the domestication of international law (especially Inter-American human rights law); the expansion of judicial remedies for the violations of constitutional rights even against judicial decisions by ordinary courts, and the tensions between the text of the constitution and the outcomes of referenda or plebiscites.[42] Often, when these topics are addressed, there is a latent question of whether these traits were developed throughout the second half of the twentieth century in Europe, or if they are innovations of *nuevo constitucionalismo latinoamericano.*[43]

However, political unrest continued throughout the 1990s–2000s, and the promise of social transformation through the constitutionalisation of the legal order was not realised. Decades of *nuevo constitucionalismo latinoamericano* did not deliver.[44] Proponents of ICCAL (see below), asses that state authority and law tend to be weak in Latin America due to 'the structural adjustment programs pushed by the Washington Consensus in the 1980s and 1990s.'[45] For instance, Argentina faced its 'great depression' between 1998 and 2002,[46] while Uruguay and Brazil faced similar financial crises in 2002.[47]

[40] See eg I Núñez-Leiva, 'Constitución, neoconstitucionalismo y lagunas jurídicas (normativas y axiológicas)' (2012) 10 *Estudios constitucionales* 511, 518–20.

[41] See eg J Montaña Pinto, *Teoría utópica de las fuentes del derecho ecuatoriano* (Centro de Estudios y Difusión del Derecho Constitucional de la Corte Constitucional para el Período de Transición, 2012).

[42] See Uprimny (n 5).

[43] See Donald Lutz's description of European trends and Lint Van Cott's description of Latin American traits in Nolte and Schilling-Vacaflor (n 11) 22–23.

[44] See generally Project Latin America 2000 by the Helen Kellogg Institute for International Studies, especially by JE Mendez et al (eds), *The (Un)Rule of Law and the Underprivileged in Latin America* (University of Notre Dame Press, 1999).

[45] Von Bogdandy (n 3) 15.

[46] See eg J Saxton, 'Argentina's Economic Crisis: Causes and Cures' *Joint Economic Committee*. Washington, DC: United States Congress (2003) available at www.jec.senate.gov/public/_cache/files/5fbf2f91-6cdf-4e70-8ff2-620ba901fc4c/argentina-s-economic-crisis---06-13-03.pdf.

[47] See 'South America's financial crisis. A region prays it will not slide down Argentina's slope' *The Economist* (27 June 2002) www.economist.com/node/1203798.

In Ecuador, three democratically elected presidents had been overthrown from 1996 to 2004, and by 2000 Ecuador faced what the International Monetary Fund labels the worst economic crisis in Ecuadorean history.[48]

B. Andean Transformative Constitutionalism

The 2008 and 2009 constitutional changes in Ecuador and Bolivia (and to a certain extent, the 2022 Chilean project) declared the demise of the liberal constitutional paradigm of rule of law and welfare state. In its stead, these constitutions marked the beginning of a new 'multicultural constitutional framework' and a 'plurilegal order.' No matter how hard proponents of *nuevo constitutionalismo latinoamericano* had emphasised it was homegrown and new, it was evidently created in the 'Global North' to address 'Western' concerns. Therefore, the deficiencies at the core were ones of pertinence and effectiveness.

As a matter of pertinence, the new constitutional paradigm should have emerged from (and not just consider) the distinctive social, economic, and political backgrounds in Latin America. As a matter of effectiveness, the constitutional paradigm should have been daring to discard old formulae and classical-western constitutional principles if needed to effectively answer to Latin American problems of exclusion, violence, and poverty.

It is not generally accepted that Andean Transformative Constitutionalism is a different trend than *nuevo constitucionalismo latinoamericano*, or even than (European) neoconstitutionalism in general. In this case, the heart of the debate is whether constitutional changes in 2008 and 2009 came so far as to redefine the rule of law and the liberal state and thus to signal the birth of a quite different form of constitutionalism.

In a sort of middle-ground, Detlef Nolte and Almut Schilling-Vacaflor[49] argue that the 'transition from a homogenous state model to the constitutional recognition of multicultural societies and of multi-ethnic or plurinational states' only happened with the constitutions of Ecuador (2008) and Bolivia (2009). For them, these constitutions signal the advent of a 'post-liberal type of democracy'[50] and thus of a new constitutional paradigm.

In contrast to the 'asymmetrical [and still neoliberal] multiculturalism' of the 1991 Colombian Constitution, and even in contrast with the 1999 'socialist constitution' of Venezuela – Nolte and Almut Schilling-Vacaflor observe – the new constitutional paradigm implemented in Ecuador and Bolivia is unique in recognising indigenous peoples and their political, juridical, and economic systems as part of the structure of the State.

[48] See eg LI Jácome H, 'The Late 1990s Financial Crisis in Ecuador: Institutional Weaknesses, Fiscal Rigidities, and Financial Dollarization at Work' *International Monetary Fund Working Paper* (2004) www.imf.org/external/pubs/ft/wp/2004/wp0412.pdf.

[49] See Nolte and Schilling-Vacaflor (n 11) 22–27. See also A Schilling-Vacaflor, 'Bolivia's New Constitution: Towards Participatory Democracy and Political Pluralism' *GIGA Working Papers* No. 141 (2010), www.giga-hamburg.de/en/publication/bolivia's-new-constitution-towards-participatory-democracy-and-political-pluralism.

[50] See D Nolte and A Schilling-Vacaflor, 'Conclusions' in D Nolte and A Schilling-Vacaflor (eds), *New Constitutionalism in Latin America. Promises and Practices* (Ashgate, 2012) 391–97.

Andean Transformative Constitutionalism – as multicultural or multi-ethnic paradigm – is deeper and wider than the recognition of indigenous peoples' social struggles. The new paradigm inaugurated in Ecuador 2008 and Bolivia 2009 purports to be decolonial and experimentalist as a whole and for the benefit of the entire nation, indigenous and non-indigenous alike. Andean Transformative Constitutional draws from local idiosyncrasies to experiment with new constitutional and institutional designs to answer to endemic problems in Latin America – not just those affecting indigenous peoples.

Throughout the years, *nuevo constitutionalismo latinoamericano* became increasingly concerned with showing openness to social sciences and critical studies' findings – which in time informed constitutional adjudication.[51] Still, Andean Transformative Constitutionalism social sciences and critical studies are part of the core theoretical framework. Andean Transformative Constitutionalism shares with *nuevo constitucionalismo latinoamericano* several features and foundations such as *garantismo*,[52] yet the new paradigm adds – or drastically accentuates – *participacionismo*, democratic experimentalism and plurinationalism – as well as indigenous values such as sumac *kawsay* and *suma qamaña* that are central to the understanding of the catalogue of rights and institutional design.

If inquiring on the theoretical underpinnings of *nuevo constitucionalismo latinoamericano*, one must be satisfied with the explanation that it blends a 'mosaic of trends'. It is not only that so much has been written about it for decades, but so many authors have kept the same label when they mean something drastically different. Andean transformative constitutionalism also takes pride in being a 'mosaic of trends' and it is more than willing to sacrifice methodological coherence if that is the price for social transformation. Yet, since it has only been actualised in two constitutions, the pedigree of its ideals and foundations of Andean Transformative Constitutionalism can be traced with more ease.

Narrators of the Ecuadorean constitutional change in 2008 have found at least two distinctive groups of anti-liberal intellectuals and activists involved in the drafting of the document.[53] There was a group of social movements leaders and NGOs staffers whose thinking was very much influenced by *participacionismo* (or *democracia participativa*). A second group of intellectuals consisted mainly of legal scholars belonging to *garantismo* and *neoconstitucionalism* (in its different variants). One must not forget the involvement of Spaniard neo-constitutionalist scholars Roberto Viciano Pastor and Rubén Martínez Dalmau, who were senior advisors to constitutional assemblymen in Venezuela (1999), Ecuador (2008) and Bolivia (2009).[54]

[51] See Fröhlich (ch 20) on the rising numbers of references to non-legal arguments, mainly from sociology.

[52] For example, the conceptualisation of rights, new rights, justiciability of rights, personal autonomy, indigenous rights, multiculturalism, legal pluralism, and topics related to judicial activism, anti-formalism and erosion of the principle of legal certainty.

[53] See P Andrade, 'El reino (de lo) imaginario: Los intelectuales políticos ecuatorianos en la construcción de la Constitución de 2008' (2012) 85 *Ecuador Debate* 35.

[54] The Washington Post reports that '[t]he leader [of this group was] Roberto Viciano Pastor, constitutional law scholar at the University of Valencia, whose technical, and some say ideological, assistance in writing the constitutions is generating new scrutiny across South America.' J Partlow, 'Latin America's Document-Driven Revolutions' *Washington Post* (17 February 2009) (on file with author).

'Democratic experimentalism' and *participacionismo* were offered to the constitutional assembly as a methodological framework. 'Democratic experimentalism' encourages trying new constitutional designs that draw from practices and social customs followed by the marginalised sectors of society. This was further complemented by *participacionismo*, which 'envision[s] the maximum participation of citizens in their self-governance (especially in sectors of society beyond those that are traditionally understood to be political e.g., the household and workplace).'[55] Here lays the distinctive decolonial promise to address the problems of inequality and exclusion in a manner that is effective to the challenges in Latin America.

Moreover, when understanding what is new in Andean Transformative Constitutionalism from previous neo-constitutionalism, it is of paramount importance to grasp the centrality of these concepts from social theory. In that sense, it is Boaventura de Sousa Santos' proposal that is central to the new constitutional paradigm, which sets aside competing ideas on democratic experimentalism by, for example, the critical legal scholars Roberto Mangabeira Unger.[56]

In 1996, Mangabeira Unger had already exposed the limitations that judicial activism would find in bringing about deep social changes in the United States. Whereas many other legal scholars had become advocates of judicial activism as means for social transformation, Roberto Mangabeira Unger saw several limitations in the strategic litigation before high courts, for example, that they were designed to uphold legal arrangements on private property, which in turn are central to preserving social hierarchies that directly benefited judges and their elitist circles.[57]

Instead, Mangabeira Unger advocated for democratic experimentalism to create new institutions and policies that would allow for the pursuit of material progress and individual emancipation from social division and hierarchy.[58] Mangabeira Unger had in mind the same sort of experiment as the participatory budget that had been implemented in some cities of Brazil as an alternative form of municipal government.[59]

Boaventura de Sousa Santos is averse to Unger's experimentalism because it relies on already existing institutional arrangements, which are only open to 'members of the middle-class with the economic and cultural capital'.[60] Thus, the resulting experiments will be again the top-down exclusionary impositions and 'those at the bottom are either incorporated only once the institutional blueprint has been fully laid out or are not incorporated at all.'[61]

[55] JD Hilmer, 'The State of Participatory Democratic Theory' (2010) 32 *New Political Science* 43. See B de Sousa Santos, *De la mano de Alicia: lo social y lo político en la postmodernidad* (Siglo del Hombre & Universidad de los Andes, 1998) 332.

[56] See generally R Mangabeira Unger, *What Should Legal Analysis Become* (Verso, 1996).

[57] ibid 110–19.

[58] ibid 1–6.

[59] WR Nylen, 'Testing the Empowerment Thesis: The Participatory Budget in Belo Horizonte and Betim, Brazil' (2002) 34 *Comparative Politics* 127.

[60] B de Sousa Santos and C Rodríguez Garavito, 'Law, politics, and the subaltern in counter-hegemonic globalization' in B de Sousa Santos and C Rodríguez Garavito (eds), *Law and Globalization from below. Towards a Cosmopolitan Legality* (Cambridge University Press, 2005) 1–9.

[61] ibid.

When Boaventura de Sousa Santos addressed the Constitutional Assemblies in Ecuador[62] and Bolivia[63] he presented a radical form of participatory democracy that he labelled '*demodiversidad*' or '*democracia intercultural*.' Santos describes it as a 'bottom-up' process of experimentalism that draws from 'the myriad of legal rules created and enforced by such disparate social actors',[64] especially those emerging from the practices of '[s]ocial movements involving some of the most marginalised classes in the global South – landless peasants, subsistence farmers, and indigenous peoples.'[65]

Central to this quest for a new constitutional design is Santos' anticolonialism. That is why the constitutional design shall be original and draw from 'subaltern forms of legality'.[66] In Boaventura de Sousa Santos' views, the hard questions posed by urgent social issues have only weak answers in present political theory because they have been developed in the 'global North' and they are inadequate for the problems of the 'global South'.[67] In the absence of any suitable alternative theory, Santos praised the emergence of different 'transformative practices' (*prácticas transformadoras*) within the 'global South'.

'*Demodiversidad*' or '*democracia intercultural*' is the strand of *participacionismo* and a central feature of the new constitutional paradigm. First, it exemplifies the conceptual framework of Andean Transformative Constitutionalism that is neither constitutional liberal theory, nor political liberal theory. Second, it is much more complex than the sort of direct democracy promoted for the adoption of new constitutions as central to Viciano's et al. Third, its starting point is the failure of any form of liberal constitutionalism, and it already poses a criticism to previous forms of democratic experimentalism within the framework of a previous (ie liberal) institutional design. Fourth, it calls for an unbounded *participacionismo*, beyond elected officials, technocrats or scholars (here at odds with Inter-American Courts' conventionality control).

To be clear, the centrality and distinctiveness of *demodiversidad* or *democracia intercultural* to the Andean Transformative Constitutional does not mean it stands as a backbone that gives coherence neither to the actual Constitutions of Ecuador or Bolivia, nor to a new paradigm in abstract. Still the old European *garantismo* and judicial activism by strengthened Constitutional Courts[68] made their way into the Constitutions of

[62] See B de Sousa Santos, *Las paradojas de nuestro tiempo y la plurinacionalidad* (Asamblea Nacional Constituyente del Ecuador, 2007). Available on file with author. (Santos encouraged the exploration of 'subaltern democratic practices', such as those daily communal practices of indigenous communities, as having the same potential for becoming valid legal propositions as the norms of the typical 'Eurocentric' legal system.).

[63] See B de Sousa Santos, *La reinvención del estado y el estado plurinacional* (Centro de Comunicación y Desarrollo Andino-CENDA, 2007) www.boaventuradesousasantos.pt/media/reinvencion%20del%20estado%20y%20estado%20plurinacional_Bolivia.pdf.

[64] de Sousa Santos and Rodríguez Garavito (n 60) 4.

[65] ibid 2.

[66] B de Sousa Santos, 'Epistemologies of the South and the future' (2016) 1 *From the European South* 17, 18–19. See also B de Sousa Santos, *Epistemologies of the South. Justice against Epistemicide* (Routledge, 2014) and B de Sousa Santos, *Toward a New Common Sense: Law, Science and Politics in the Paradigmatic Transition* (Routledge, 1995).

[67] See (n 62) 4.

[68] Neoconstitutionalists' primary concern was to sketch a constitutional design that includes safeguards and remedies that would assure that rights are regularly enforced. The most widespread literature on

Ecuador 2008 and Bolivia 2009,[69] in spite of being openly contradictory to the justification of the sort of experimentalism that drives the new constitutional paradigm.

When we look at the concrete changes in the constitutional provisions, we find that the transformation sought to strike at the very definition of the liberal state. The welfare state and the rule of law (*Estado Social de Derecho*) is set aside and replaced by the rule of legal pluralism and rights (*Estado de derechos*). The state is intercultural and multinational in Ecuador,[70] and plurinational-communitarian and pluralist in Bolivia[71] (and could have been plurinational, intercultural and ecologic in Chile).[72] It recognises the existence of several legal systems with no predetermined preeminence of any of them above the others – just like Santos suggested.[73] For the Ecuadorean justice and legal scholar, Ramiro Ávila Santamaría, this sort of constitutional innovation amounted to the latest expression of 'critical thinking,' to the extent that he proclaims the birth of a new trend within the critical theories in Latin America: 'Andean Constitutionalism.'[74]

In theory, the main features of this Andean trend consist of 'surpassing' the mere proclamation of rights and going even beyond modern trends on – for example – the full justiciability of economic and social rights. Instead, in the model inaugurated by the Ecuadorean Constitution of 2008, the depth of the change reaches the substance of what used to constitute the limitations to the exercise of power, which is not the rule of law anymore, but the rights and the cultural practices of precisely those persons and communities disenfranchised under the rule of law. Now the indigenous conceptions (ie subaltern forms of legality) *sumak kawsay, suma qamaña* (an indigenous notion of living well and in harmony)[75] and *pachama* (living in harmony with the Mother Earth)[76] take central place.

Sumak kawsay and *suma qamaña* et al are (re)foundational principles for a whole new paradigm in constitutional design by replacing the former centrality of concepts of welfare state and the common good. The catalogue of what used to be social and economic rights is no longer grounded in a material conception of welfare for the protection of human dignity, but in the indigenous notion of harmony with past, present, and

neoconstitutionalism in Latin America are the compilation of essays by M Carbonell (ed), *Teoría del neoconstitucionalismo. Ensayos escogidos* (Trotta-UNAM, 2007); M Carbonell and L García Jaramillo, *El canon neoconstitucional* (Trotta, 2010); and Carbonell (n 18).

[69] J Montaña Pinto, *Teoría utópica de las fuentes del derecho ecuatoriano* (Centro de Estudios y Difusión del Derecho Constitucional de la Corte Constitucional para el Período de Transición, 2012) 76 (Montaña refers to what in this chapter has been labelled as *participacionismo* with the term 'revolutionary socialists').

[70] Constitución de la República del Ecuador, Registro Oficial 449, 20 de octubre de 2008, at Art.1. Unofficial version in English available at www.constituteproject.org/constitution/Ecuador_2015.pdf.

[71] The Constitution of Bolivia, Art 1.

[72] Proyecto de Constitución Política de la República de Chile, Art 1, 4 de julio de 2022. www.constituteproject.org/constitution/Chile_2022D.

[73] R Ávila Santamaría, 'El constitucionalismo ecuatoriano: breve caracterización de la Constitución de 2008' in M Carbonell et al (coords), *Tendencias del constitucionalismo en Iberoamérica* (IIJ-UNAM, 2009) 953, 970–71, available at biblio.juridicas. unam.mx/libros/6/2701/34.pdf.

[74] R Ávila Santamaría, *Neoconstitucionalismo transformador, el estado y el derecho en la constitución de 2008* (Rosa Luxemburg Stiftung, 2011) 16–17.

[75] See generally the Preamble of the Ecuadorean Constitution ("Hereby decide to build A new form of public coexistence, in diversity and in harmony with nature, to achieve the good way of living, the sumak kawsay"). See also Arts 14, 250, 275 and 387.

[76] See the Preamble of the Bolivian Constitution.

future generations, as well as with Mother Nature. It is not a minor detail that constitutions have 444 and 411 Articles each. The lengthy catalogue of rights governed by *sumak kawsay and suma qamaña* purport to bring the constitutional principles to bear in every aspect of personal, family and social life; and that is what is known as the 'omnipresence of the constitution.'[77]

The Constitutional Court of Ecuador received unprecedented power to oversee the implementation of seven judicial remedies (*garantías judiciales*) for the protection of constitutional rights.[78] Besides the traditional judicial review of statutes and regulations, the new Ecuadorean Constitutional Court has the power to actively fill in gaps and voids of the legal system in order to make constitutional rights immediately applicable if the legislative system has not issued enough regulations. The Court can also declare the unconstitutionality of public policies issued by local governments or by the national executive, and it serves as the final authoritative interpreter of the Ecuadorean Constitution, which used to be in the hands of the legislative branch.[79]

There are also constitutional provisions that remained intact from previous constitutions. One of the important challenges of the new constitutional model is to articulate a new constitutional theory that is capable of both guiding the implementation of the constitutional innovations and explaining how the remnants of liberal constitutionalism will coexist with the new constitutional model.

The purported change of paradigms brought about by the Ecuadorean Constitution of 2008 is that it manifestly seeks to brush aside general principles of constitutional law[80] and international human rights that used to serve as the foundations of constitutions in Latin America.[81] Although the new constitutional model still borrows from the language of those general principles and maxims, they are restated to attain a different meaning according to the guiding ideals and professed goals of the new constitutional paradigm.

C. Ius Constitutionale Commune en América Latina (ICCAL)

Whereas the relationship between the new Latin American and Andean transformative constitutionalism can be appraised as an evolutive stage, the nexus between both with the ICCAL may be represented as an alternative or complement. After the adoption of the 1991 Colombian Constitution with its decisive openness towards international

[77] Montaña Pinto (n 69) 45–46.

[78] See Arts 86–94 of the Ecuadorean Constitution.

[79] See Art 436 of the Ecuadorean Constitution,.

[80] For example, the constitution of Ecuador has left behind the foundational notion of rule of law (*estado de derecho*) and replaced it with the rule of rights and justice (*estado de derechos y justicia*). See Art 449 of the Ecuadorean Constitution. See also R Ávila Santamaría, 'Ecuador Estado constitucional de derechos y justicia' in R Ávila Santamaría (ed), *La Constitución del 2008 en el contexto andino. Análisis desde la doctrina y el derecho comparado* (Ministerio de Justicia y Derechos Humanos del Ecuador, 2008) 31 et seq; LF Ávila Linzán, 'El acceso a la justicia y la emancipación social de las personas excluidas' in R Ávila Santamaría (ed), *Neoconstitucionalismo y Sociedad* (Ministerio de Justicia y Derechos Humanos del Ecuador, 2008) 180–84; R Llasag Fernández, *Plurinacionalidad: una propuesta constitucional emancipadora*, in the same volume at 324 and 329.

[81] See Arts 12 et seq of the Ecuadorean Constitution.

human rights law, together with an increase in the activity of the Inter-American Court of Human Rights (IACtHR), the studies on Latin American neoconstitutionalism and the Inter-American Human Rights System began to overlap.

While neoconstitutionalists addressed different forms of internationalisation of the constitutional order, an accompanying trend emerged on the constitutionalisation of Inter-American human rights law. ICCAL is an offspring of the intersection of these two areas of the law. Armin von Bogdandy is the German scholar who, together with others, conceptualised the academic and judicial project of ICCAL almost 20 years ago. It is certain that there are nuanced and diverging opinions among ICCAL proponents, but it is also clear that there is a main set of goals and means that they have in common. This sets ICCAL apart from Latin American *neoconstitucionalismo(s)*. Neoconstitutionalists do not like to identify their core tenets, and this is why so much literature has been devoted to the debate on whether a proposal amounts to new neoconstitutionalism or not. This is an important difference when compared to ICCAL, that allows for a clearer analysis and criticism, as opposed to neoconstitutionalism that is more of a moving target.

According to von Bogdandy, *ius constitutionale commune* in Latin America (ICCAL) is an academic and judicial project of transformative constitutionalism. It is transformative because it aims at impacting the acute social challenges faced by Latin America[82] in terms of social exclusion and inequality, high levels of violence, and the presence of relatively weak state institutions that include problems of corruption.[83]

Its academic and judicial nature are concerned with ICCAL's approach to public law, which is 'an argument based on methodological orientation to principles over rules and a high valuation of comparative law for the protection of human rights.'[84]

Such an approach to public law does not have its origin in Latin America (although it is complementary to the reigning anti-formalism). Instead, the 'argument based on methodological orientation to principles over rules …' is what German jurists had been studying from the late 1990s under the title of *Gemeineuropäisches Verfassungsrecht*, that is, the emergence of a European Constitutional Law.[85] Yet, if something of the same nature existed beyond the boundaries of Europe, German academia could claim that its reading of a *Gemeineuropäisches Verfassungsrecht* is not just the most accurate description of public law for Europe, but the beginning of a new paradigm of Global Law. In this sense ICCAL is also an agenda, and to that effect, an academic and judicial agenda for a global (transformative) constitutionalism coined in Germany.

[82] A von Bogdandy Armin et al, 'Ius Constitutionale Commune en America Latina: A Regional Approach to Transformative Constitutionalism' in A von Bogdandy et al (eds), *Transformative Constitutionalism in Latin America. The Emergence of a New Ius Commune* (Oxford University Press, 2018).

[83] A von Bogdandy et al (coords), *Ius Constitutionale Commune en América Latina. Textos básicos para su comprensión* (IIJ-UNAM, 2017).

[84] A von Bogdandy, 'Ius Constitutionale Commune en América Latina: Observations on Transformative Constitutionalism' (2015) *American Journal of International Law Unbound* 109, 110.

[85] In this train of thought, some of the foundational ideas of ICCAL can be traced back to Peter Haberle. In 1999 Haberle coined the term '*ius commune americanum*' that foresaw something similar to the *Gemeineuropäisches Verfassungsrecht* (European Constitutional Law). The reason was that Haberle was able to see in Latin America the basis of an openness by constitutions towards the Inter-American human rights system. P Häberle, 'México y los Contornos de un Derecho Constitucional Común Americano: Un Ius Commune Americanum' in P Häberle and M Kotzur (eds), *De la Soberanía al Derecho Constitucional Común: Palabras Clave Para un Diálogo Europeo-Latinoamericano* (IIJ-UNAM, 2001).

Nuevo constitucionalismo latinomaericano and – especially – Andean Transformative Constitutionalism have sought to get along with decolonial theories and their new approaches to law. One can also trace in ICCAL an interest in the 'emancipatory potential of constitutional law.'[86] Yet, the radical proposals of subaltern legal practices that would be at ease under Andean Transformative Constitutionalism will be at odds with the German authorship over a new paradigm on Global Law. ICCAL accords value to the 'European legacy' over Latin America's 'common legal discourse'[87] and promotes the realisation of the central promises of liberal constitutions and western ideals of rule of law, international human rights law and democracy. Andean Transformative Constitutionalism is wary of European legal constructs as colonial forms of oppression.

Returning to von Bogdandy's conceptualisation of ICCAL, the project states three goals (human rights, democracy and rule of law), which are achievable by means of judicial dialogue, inclusion and legal pluralism. Against this triad of ends and means, ICCAL identifies three challenges to be found in the in the social status quo of Latin America: exclusion and inequality, violence and weak state institutions.

ICCAL builds upon *nuevo constitucionalismo latinoamericano's* lengthier catalogues of rights, the strengthened competences of constitutional courts, and judicial guarantees. ICCAL is also enthusiastic about antiformalism. Yet, ICCAL 'builds, far more than neoconstitutionalism, on the Inter-American system of human rights, whose influence in the region the authors of the 1990s could not foresee.'[88] Also, ICCAL draws important lessons from comparative public law or, in its own words from 'the transnational interaction of domestic public law in various countries both horizontally and with international institutions.'[89]

ICCAL gives a central role to human rights, and in doing so ICCAL embraces the proposition that the law is the adequate tool for social transformation. Armin von Bogdandy explains that human rights are the transformative content of constitutions, and he observes that human rights strategic litigation is already the main tool of choice by social actors immersed in transformative efforts throughout Latin America and the Caribbean. In turn, the judicial decisions regarding human rights strategic litigation 'provide legal energy' to the aspirations of advocacy groups.[90]

Moreover, Latin America and the Caribbean have a unique experience in the practice of human rights. In the Inter-American System, the international protection of human rights has been deployed against gross forms of violence,[91] to tackle problems of exclusion,[92] and to acknowledge a collective dimension in the protection of human dignity – as evidenced in the jurisprudence on indigenous peoples.[93] This case-law – in

[86] Which von Bogdandy describes as an 'idealistic and optimistic' outlook that all proponents of ICCAL share See von Bogdandy (n 3) 32.

[87] ibid 30.

[88] von Bogdandy (n 82) 20.

[89] ibid.

[90] von Bogdandy (n 3) 33.

[91] ibid.

[92] See PG Carozza, 'La perspectiva histórica del aporte latinoamericano al concepto de los derechos económicos, sociales y culturales' in A Ely Yamin (ed), *Derechos Económicos, Sociales y Culturales en América Latina: Del Inventivo a la Herramienta* (APRODEH – Centro Internacional de Investigaciones para el Desarrollo, 2006) 52–53.

[93] *Mayagna (Sumo) Awas Tingni Community v Nicaragua*, Merits, Reparations and Costs. Judgment, Inter-Am. Ct. H.R. (ser. C) No. 66 (1 February 2000); *Moiwana Community v Suriname*, Preliminary Objections, Merits,

the view of ICCAL– is an invitation to push harder for 'concreteness and incrementalism in approaching human rights.'[94]

Besides the protection of human rights, ICCAL pursues the strengthening of democracy and rule of law.[95] This translates into building up *institucionalidad*, which entails strengthening the normative power of law as well as securing the independence of courts and public offices. ICCAL's diagnosis of the political and legal culture in the region takes note of the great dissatisfaction with the performance of the political branches of power. This impression leads ICCAL to bet heavily on the transformative potential of courts.

ICCAL does not ignore the limitations of the judiciary throughout Latin America and the Caribbean. In varying degrees, ICCAL acknowledges that the culture of legal argumentation is formalistic courts throughout the region creates an important backlog of cases, and is sometimes virtually inaccessible for large portions of marginalised population.[96] Moreover, even for average-to-well-functioning courts, the threat of authoritarian executives to pack up or dismantle courts looms large within the region.

Whereas the theoretical foundations of Andean Transformative Constitutionalism turned its back on the strained capacity of courts to bring about social change, ICCAL doubles down on the judiciary as the main agent for social transformation. First, because, constitutional reforms have already focused on strengthening or creating judicial procedures as the preferred means for the protection of human rights. Second, because of the perception of positive outcomes in the dialogue among the IACtHR and its national counterparts.

If human rights are prominent among the goals, judicial dialogue takes central stage among the key concepts or means for the realisation of ICCAL's goals – precisely because of ICCAL's faith in transformative potential human rights judgments. Inclusiveness and legal pluralism are required features that the judicial dialogue shall observe. In ICCAL's words, it is about a 'progressist judicial dialogue centred in the jurisprudence of the Inter-American Court of Human Rights with a particular inclination that provides an expansively evolving interpretation of the protection of human dignity.'[97]

The judicial doctrines that enable the type of judgments and judicial dialogue that ICCAL compliments are of two – albeit complementary – kinds: those that uphold the internationalisation of constitutional law, and those that constitutionalise international human rights law. The list includes conventionality control and the idea of a human rights *corpus iuris, cláusula abierta, bloque de constitucionalidad*, among others.

Reparations and Costs. Judgment, Inter-Am. Ct. H.R. (ser. C) No. 124 (15 June 2005); *Yakye Axa Indigenous Community v Paraguay*, Merits, Reparations and Costs. Judgment, Inter-Am. Ct. H.R. (ser. C) No. 125 (June 17, 2005); *Sawhoyamaxa Indigenous Community v Paraguay*, Merits, Reparations and Costs. Judgment, Inter-Am. Ct. H.R. (ser. C) No. 146 (29 March 2006); *Saramaka People. v Suriname*. Preliminary Objections, Merits, Reparations and Costs, Judgment, Inter-Am. Ct. H.R. (ser. C) No. 172 (28 November 2007); and *Xákmok Kásek Indigenous Community v Paraguay*, Merits, Reparations and Costs. Judgment, Inter-Am. Ct. H.R. (ser. C) No. of 214 (24 August 2010).

[94] See von Bogdandy (n 3) 35.

[95] ibid 35–38.

[96] von Bogdandy (n 82) 10–11.

[97] A Rodiles, 'The Great Promise of Comparative Public Law for Latin America Toward Ius Commune Americanum?' in A Roberts et al (eds), *Comparative International Law* (Oxford University Press, 2018) 509.

ICCAL sees in the doctrine of conventionality control[98] the 'legal centerpiece'[99] for judicial dialogue. In brief, this doctrine infers from Articles 1.1 and 2 of the American Convention on Human Rights (ACHR) together with Articles 26 and 27 of the Vienna Convention on the Law of the Treaties (VCLT) that there is an international obligation for national judges (and arguably, state officials)[100] to review domestic laws against the jurisprudence of the IACtHR, and to refrain from enforcing any national law that might be at odds with the ACHR and the IACtHR's case law. To put it briefly, through this doctrine, the IACtHR has accorded *erga omnes* binding character to its jurisprudence.[101]

The doctrine of conventionality control is often coupled with the notion of an Inter-American *corpus iuris* on international human rights law. The doctrine of the *corpus iuris* is the IACtHR's understanding that the ACHR cannot be read in isolation from other international human rights treaties.[102] The IACtHR referred explicitly to such *corpus iuris* in its 1999 Advisory Opinion No. 16 when it concluded that there was a human right implicit in the right of consular officers under Article 36 of the Vienna Convention on Consular Relations to be notified of the arrest of nationals of their sending State. The IACtHR understood that Article 36 of the Vienna Convention expands the right to a fair trial as enshrined in Article 8 of the ACHR.

Since that opinion, the IACtHR has steadily applied this rationale, for example, it went on to assert that through the single sentence in Article 19 of the ACHR, the entire Convention on the Rights of the Child was applicable under its jurisdiction – with no further consideration on the status of ratification by American States to the external treaty.[103] In later cases,[104] the IACtHR reiterated that international instruments

[98] For a comprehensive review on the origin of the conventionality control and its different forms, see P González Domínguez, *The Doctrine of Conventionality Control. Between Uniformity and Legal Pluralism in the Inter-American Human Rights System* (Intersentia, 2018).

[99] ibid 46.

[100] See *Garcia and Montiel Flores v Mexico*, Preliminary Objections, Merits, Reparations and Costs Judgment, Inter-Am. Ct. H.R. (ser. C) No. 220, ¶ 225, 226 and 233 (26 November 2010); and *Gelman v Uruguay*. Preliminary Objections, Merits, Reparations and Costs Judgment, Inter-Am. Ct. H.R. (ser. C) No. 221, ¶ 193, 239 (24 February 2011).

[101] For critical appraisals to this doctrine see AE Dulitzky, 'An Inter-American Constitutional Court? The Invention of conventionality control by the Inter-American Court of Human Rights' (2015) 50 *Texas International Law Journal* 45, 57; J Contesse, 'The final word? Constitutional dialogue and the Inter-American Court of Human Rights' (2017) 15 *International Journal of Constitutional Law*, 414; PG Carozza and P González Domínguez, 'The final word? Constitutional dialogue and the Inter-American Court of Human Rights: A reply to Jorge Contesse' (2017) 15 *International Journal of Constitutional Law* 436.

[102] See The right to information on consular assistance in the framework of the guarantees of the due process of law, Advisory Opinion OC-16/99, Inter-Am. Ct. H.R. (ser. A) No. 16, ¶ 115 (1 October 1999). ICCAL refers to a list of the instruments making up the Inter-American *corpus iuris* available at www.corteidh.or.cr/instrumentos.cfm.

[103] *Fornerón and daughter v Argentina*, Merits, Reparations, and Costs, Judgment, Inter-Am. Ct. H.R. (ser. C) No. 242, ¶ 137 (27 April, 2012). The Court had held the same opinion on the rights of the child since November 1999, see *Villagrán Morales et al. v Guatemala*, Merits, Judgment, Inter-Am. Ct. H.R. (ser. C) No.63, ¶ 194 (19 November 1999).

[104] See, eg, Juridical Condition and Rights of the Undocumented Migrants. Advisory Opinion OC-18/03, Inter-Am. Ct. H.R. (ser. A) No. 18, ¶ 120 (17 September 2003). *Yakye Axa Indigenous Community v Paraguay*, Merits, Reparations, and Costs, Judgment, Inter-Am. Ct. H.R. (ser. C) No. 125, ¶ 127-128, (17 June, 2005); *Kichwa Indigenous People of Sarayaku v Ecuador*. Merits, Reparations, and Costs, Judgment, Inter-Am. Ct. H.R. (ser. C) No. 245, ¶ 164, (27 June, 2012). *Kuna Indigenous People of Madungandí and the Emberá Indigenous People of Bayano and their members v Panama*. Preliminary Objections, Merits, Reparations

pertaining to the United Nations system may also fall under the IACtHR`s jurisdiction via Article 29.b of the ACHR.[105]

At the receiving end, the mandate of application of the Inter-American *corpus iuris* through the doctrine of conventionality control has been welcomed in a variety of fashions by the constitutions and high courts of several Latin American states.[106] ICCAL highlights the judicial doctrine of the block of constitutionality[107] and the constitutional provisions on *cláusula abierta*.[108] *Cláusula abierta* has been understood by some national courts as creating an *erga omnes* legally binding effect on the case law of the IACtHR.[109] Furthermore, the opinions of national courts and their interpretative endeavours in building constitutional blocks are the voice with which they enter into dialogue with the IACtHR.

Together they constitute the pillars of what Mariela Morales – following Klaus Vogel – labels as 'open statehood'[110] and contribute to further softening the dividing line between national and international law in favour of the type of global law that ICCAL advocates for. The latest constitutional reforms of the region show a tendency towards including provisions that reaffirm the openness of the constitutional order to international law human rights law, and to even accord them with the highest hierarchy among legal sources.[111]

and Costs, Judgment, Inter-Am. Ct. H.R. (ser. C) No. 284, ¶118 and 142, (14 October 2014); *Community Garifuna Triunfo de la Cruz & its Members v Honduras*, Preliminary Objections, Merits, Reparations and Costs, Judgment, Inter-Am. Ct. H.R. (ser. C) No. 305, ¶ 103 (8 October 2015).

[105] For a critical appraisal of *corpus iuris*, see AE Dulitzky and K Carpintero, 'Mecanismos formales e informales para el reconocimiento de nuevos derechos y la disfuncionalidad del sistema interamericano de derechos humanos' (2017) 20 *Iuris Dictio* 19, 27–28.

[106] On the receptive end, the most cited example may be the Mexican Supreme Court in *Expediente Varios 912/10*. More recently, also the Ecuadorian Constitutional Court (in Cases 10-18-CN/19 and 11-18-CN/19) has implemented an advisory opinion (OC-24/17) of the IACtHR as if it was directly binding and it had conventionality control over the text of the Constitution. On the aloof end, the Argentinian Supreme Court has declined to fulfil a decision of the IACtHR to revoke a 2001 decision that led to the *Fontevecchia and D'Amico* case before the IACtHR. The Supreme court reasoned that the Inter-American Court lacked the authority to order the revocation of a domestic judgment, as doing so exceeded its powers under the American Convention. See J Contesse, 'Resisting the Inter-American Human Rights System' (2019) 44 *The Yale Journal of International Law* 180.

[107] For a study on the block of constitutionality within the framework of ICCAL, see ME Góngora Mera, 'The Block of Constitutionality as the Doctrinal Pivot of a Ius Commune' in A von Bogdandy et al (eds), *Constitutionalism in Latin America. The Emergence of a New Ius Commune* (Oxford University Press, 2018). Generally see L Favoreu, 'El bloque de constituticionalidad' (1990) *Revista del Centro de Estudios Constitucionales*, 46–47. Available at www.cepc.es/rap/Publicaciones/Revistas/15/RCEC_05_043.pdf.

[108] Provisions on *cláusula abierta* recognise the incompleteness of positivised catalogues of rights and asserts that nothing should preclude the recognition of other rights inherent in human nature. See eg Constitución Política de Colombia [C.P.C.] 1991. Article 94. 'See also Constitution of Uruguay, article 72; Constitution of Bolivia, article 13; Constitution of Paraguay, article 45; Constitution of Venezuela, article 22; Constitution of Honduras, article 63; Constitution of Peru, article 3; Constitution of Argentina, article 33; Constitution of Brazil, article 5,2; Constitution of Panama, article 17; Constitution of Ecuador, article 11,7; Constitution of Dominican Republic, article 74; Constitution of Costa Rica, article 74; Constitution of Nicaragua, article 46'. See, C León Bastos and VA Wong Meraz, 'Cláusulas de apertura al derecho internacional de los derechos humanos: constituciones iberoamericanas' (2015) 18 *Foro* 93.

[109] See eg Ecuadorian Constitutional Court, 12 de junio de 2019, Caso 10-18-CN/19.

[110] M Morales Antoniazzi and P Saavedra Alessandri, 'Inter-Americanization. Its Legal Bases and Political Impact' in A von Bogdandy et al (eds), *Constitutionalism in Latin America The Emergence of a New Ius Commune* (Oxford University Press, 2018) 235–54.

[111] See eg Art 1(1) of the Mexican Constitution; Art 11.3. of the Ecuadorean Constitution; Art 13.4. of the Bolivian Constitution.

The application of these doctrines and their accompanying corollaries are justified ultimately in terms of a *pro homine* interpretation of rights. The interpretation *pro homine* epitomises both ICCAL's critical stance towards the perceived formalistic and unsophisticated legal culture in the region, and the creative type of legal interpretation that chooses to focus on principles as the preferred legal sources for the project of social transformation through the law. This principle 'basically states that the most favourable interpretation to the "human person" is to be preferred, enabling the judge to construe the widest expression of the (human) right at hand.'[112] Within Latin American and Caribbean constitutions and judicial opinions, this principle is also referred to as the principle of favourability,[113] and it embodies the anti-formalism that is common to all 'new law in Latin America.'[114]

The very social problems that ICCAL seeks to tackle are its main obstacles. Social exclusion and inequality and high levels of violence undermine the legal culture in Latin America and the Caribbean and make institutions prone to corruption. Yet, the problem is not in the quality of the laws. There may be 'admirable legal frameworks' in force, but they 'are not abided by or they are applied in a selective fashion'[115] in a way that discriminates against those who live at the margins of society.

Discrimination is aggravated by the immense gap in the distribution of wealth and bad economic performance of Latin American and Caribbean countries. The inability of democratically elected governments to address poverty undermines the trust of people in democracy and opens the path for populism. The proponents of ICCAL perceive populist and plebiscitarian regimes as grave threats to Latin American democracies because populist leaders are often willing to 'sacrifice' civil and political freedoms under the justification of prioritising social and economic rights. Instead, the lack of accountability often leads to corruption, and corruption further undermines the authority of law and the legitimacy of democratic institutions.

Proponents of ICCAL are aware of the internal contradiction of their 'transformative agenda through legal process' in a region where law and democratic state institutions are weak. Yet, their emphasis on the law (as principles and rights) and on the judiciary signals a commitment 'to find the actual channels that are available to address the needs of the most vulnerable groups',[116] while trying not to overstep into the democratic legislative process in this quest. Notwithstanding the problems referred to as lack of *institucionalidad*, weak normative power of the law, lack of access to courts, and low credibility of courts,[117] the judiciary might be in a privileged position to make good use of the constitutional reforms that have strengthened the competence of constitutional courts. What could have been regarded as 'questionable judicial activism, are, under the new paradigm, regarded as appropriate to the judiciary of a

[112] A Rodiles, 'The Great Promise of Comparative Public Law for Latin America Toward Ius Commune Americanum?' in A Roberts et al (eds), *Comparative International Law* (Oxford University Press, 2018) 515.

[113] See eg the Constituional Court of Colombia, 28 de mayo de 1997, Sentencia C-251; C.C.C 15 de marzo de 2006, Sentencia C-187 and C.C.C 12 de febrero de 2004 Sentencia T-116.

[114] See J Esquirol, 'The Turn to Legal Interpretation in Latin America' (2011) 26 *American University International Law Journal*, 1031.

[115] ibid.

[116] ibid 12.

[117] von Bogdandy (n 3) 37.

constitutional democracy which incrementally seeks to make its new constitutional project a reality.'[118]

Furthermore, Von Bogdandy foresees the 'tremendous challenge' of fitting the principles of indigenous law into modern constitutionalism and he leaves it as a pending question. Also, he recognises the tension between having at one end of the dialogue the IACtHR constantly expanding its competences, and at the other end the highest courts of each country trying to reassert their powers and competences while leaving room for indigenous peoples' jurisdiction. For Von Bogdandy, the key concept of pluralism means acknowledging that '[d]ivergences and differences are unavoidable in such a loosely structured, dynamic, and politically delicate relationship',[119] so ICCAL seeks solutions that all sides can support, which does not mean looking for 'harmony' (in the sense of uniformity) across the region.[120]

III. Conclusions

Rights and courts figure prominently in these trends of Latin American constitutionalism. Only in the Andean Transformative Constitutionalism's blueprint did rights and courts take a secondary role to subaltern legal practices. However, as the Ecuadorean and Bolivian constitutions showed, *garantismo* enlarged the attributions of constitutional adjudicators and strengthened the catalogue of rights. In the absence of significant instances of *demodiversidad* or other actualisations of subaltern legal practices, courts and rights now reign within Latin American constitutionalism.

Or so the conventional narrative says. This applies neatly to Bolivia, Brazil, Colombia, Ecuador, Mexico, Peru and Venezuela, but what about the list of countries that do not have important reforms or changes between the 1950s and now? The idea would be that this narrative, and one – or several – of the trends herein described, apply also to the rest of the countries precisely through constitutional interpretation. Is that the story each country-chapter is going to tell?

All three trends would presuppose that 'the virtuous judge' now occupies central stage. Whereas the old and formalistic judge (and lawyer) in Latin America was unfamiliar with modern philosophy and jurisprudence, the new Latin American judge should be well aquatinted with philosophy, jurisprudence, social theory and with the international *corpus iuris* of human rights. What, then, are the philosophical and jurisprudential stances of Latin American high court 'virtuous judges'? How have they sorted out the opposition between highly specific indigenous practices when at odds with a global corpus iuris on human rights?

These trends in Latin American constitutionalism speak of the supremacy of rights. Nevertheless, not all three seem to speak of the same rights, nor to find the same foundations for what they back up as a catalogue of rights. Is there in the case-law an identifiable strand of ideas on the contours of human dignity for Latin Americans?

[118] ibid.
[119] von Bogdandy (n 3) 47.
[120] ibid.

How compatible are the anthropocentric international human rights project and the interpretation of rights in light of subaltern legal and moral practices?

The new judge has at hand several doctrines and principles to assert the supremacy of its judgments and to free its interpretation from the (backwardness of the) blackletter of rules. Does the new judge understand its attributions to go as far as to try experimentalism and *demodiversidad* themselves via constitutional interpretation? Who are the judges that dress in herculean robes? Are they elite or middle class lawyers? Do they speak faithfully for 'those at the bottom'? Or do judges make sure people are 'incorporated only once the institutional blueprint has been fully laid out or are not incorporated at all'?

PART II

The Mosaic of Constitutional Reasoning in Latin America and the Caribbean

3

The Supreme Court of Argentina

ANDREA CASTAGNOLA, ALEJANDRO CHEHTMAN AND SERGIO MURO

I. Introduction

This chapter seeks to identify and account for some of the main traits of the constitutional reasoning of the Argentine Supreme Court.[1] Argentina constitutes an interesting case study insofar as it presents a legal system which combines the institutional design heavily influenced by the American Constitution, with strong Continental European influences on its substantive law and doctrine. It is also characterised by a convoluted history of democratisation, military coups, political instability, and gross human rights violations, which have evidently transpired to the Court and its work. Furthermore, the Supreme Court has played a significant role in the political life of the country, insofar as the Court transplanted early on the doctrine of judicial review on the Argentine judiciary.[2] Examining the main features of the style, materials, and strategies of its judicial reasoning will shed light not only on Argentina's legal culture, main political, economic, and social challenges, but also on the behaviour of justices in conditions of instability.

Perhaps most significantly, this chapter explores constitutional reasoning across almost 150 years and under both conditions of stability and prosperity and of severe institutional fragility and deep economic and political crises. We have selected our 40 cases taking into consideration the different Supreme Courts that have operated in Argentina. As it is often stated, Argentina is somewhat an outlier in Latin America. During the late nineteenth century and early twentieth century it was famously among the most prosperous countries in the world, with a higher GNP per capita than Austria, Japan, and even Spain. At the peak of its deep economic and political crisis in 2001, the GNP per capita had reached a level similar to that of other countries in the region, such as Brazil, Colombia and Peru. Between these two periods Argentina suffered five coups, electoral fraud, the proscription of the majoritarian party for 18 years, a period of state

[1] In this chapter we follow as closely as possible the main sections and subsections identified by the editors. However, due to the particularities of the Argentine case, we combined some subsections to present the analysis in a more consistent and cohesive way.

[2] See *Sojo, Eduardo c/Cámara de Diputados de la Nación*, Fallos 32:120 (1867).

terrorism, and cyclical economic crises. The Argentine Supreme Court was immersed in and was a relevant part of this process. This context can provide some insights to better understand different traits in the constitutional reasoning of courts.

The chapter proceeds as follows. Section II(A) presents the context in which the Argentine Supreme Court operates, including its main institutional and legal features. Section II(B), in turn, addresses the institutional instability at the Argentine Supreme Court. Section II(C) presents an overview of the prevailing legal culture in Argentina. Centrally, Section III identifies and critically examines the different type of constitutional arguments employed by the Court. Section IV situates the court in the broader regional context. Section V briefly concludes.

II. Legal, Political, Institutional and Academic Context

A. The Context of Constitutional Reasoning and Constitutional Litigation

In order to understand the particularities of constitutional reasoning in the Argentine Supreme Court we need to briefly consider the political, institutional, and legal context in which the Court operates. This section provides a brief introduction to Argentina's legal system and the institutional role the Supreme Court plays in it. It includes the regulation of access to the Court, its internal organisation, its relationship with other branches of government over the course of Argentina's constitutional history, and the legal culture in which it is immersed. Each of these elements will inform the quantitative analysis which is the substantive contribution of this study.

After a few failed attempts,[3] Argentina became constitutionally organised in 1853–60.[4] The resulting Constitution, which although the object of several reforms has survived with significantly minor changes, provides a bill of negative and positive rights – the latter added through reforms in the twentieth century – and creates a system of checks and balances based on a tripartite national government and a federal structure.[5] The federal model was partly geared – in the origins of the republic – to amalgamate the different provincial centres without concentrating power in an authoritarian figure. As in other parts of the region, the prevailing constitutional arrangement is the result of an alliance between conservative and liberal groups, often at the expense of other more radical sectors.[6] National authorities comprise an executive, a bicameral congress, and

[3] See Dirección Nacional del Sistema Argentino de Información Jurídica (ed), *Constituciones Argentinas. Compilación histórica y análisis doctrinario* (Ministerio de Justicia y Derechos Humanos, 2015) www.saij.gob.ar/docs-f/ediciones/libros/Constituciones_argentinas.pdf. A similar failed attempt also existed in the United States with the Articles of Confederation and Perpetual Union (1778).

[4] See FN Barrancos and Vedia, *La Corte Suprema de Justicia en la Historia Constitucional Argentina* (Academia Nacional de Ciencias Morales y Políticas, 2000) 202.

[5] See MJ Garcia-Mansilla, 'Separation of powers crisis: the case of Argentina' (2004) 32 *Georgia Journal of International and Comparative Law* 307.

[6] See R Gargarella, *La sala de máquinas de la Constitución: dos siglos de constitucionalismo en América Latina (1810–2010)* (Katz, 2015).

the judiciary. The latter is exercised by the Supreme Court -instituted in 1863 – and other inferior tribunals established by Congress.[7]

The Supreme Court's role centrally involves being the final interpreter of the Constitution – rather than making law – and performing judicial review of the legislation and other acts emanated from the legislative and executive branches.[8] Nevertheless the Court has expanded its role often interpreting substantive law and revising decisions of lower courts through a mechanism the same court sanctioned concerning possible 'arbitrary' decisions.[9] Its balancing role has been vividly present since the court's inception, as President Mitre called it – in 1863 – a moderating power, to be especially useful when political passions lead other branches of government to reach beyond the constitutional limit of their powers.[10]

The Court intervenes both through its original jurisdiction (that is, first instance court in very specific matters) and as the appellate court of last resort.[11] Its original jurisdiction is used for cases related to foreign ambassadors, ministers or consuls, or cases between provinces or a province and a foreign state.[12] The appellate jurisdiction,[13] in turn, includes cases decided by courts of federal, national (ie, local courts of the city of Buenos Aires),[14] federal/national (ie, criminal cases from federal or national standing that reach the Federal Criminal Cassation Court), or provincial jurisdiction.

The standard appellate jurisdiction is known as Extraordinary Appeal '*Recurso Extraordinario Federal*' and it has three different sources. First, when a case questions the validity of a treaty, federal law or action undertaken under federal authority and the local court holds against the validity of the treaty, law, or the federal authority. A second alternative arises when the validity of a provincial law, decree or act has been questioned as unconstitutional or contrary to a treaty or federal law, and the provincial court decides in favour of the validity of the provincial measure. Finally, the Supreme Court may intervene when a party invokes a constitutional clause, treaty, law, or grant of federal authority and the provincial court decides against the norm or privilege invoked.[15] Under exceptional circumstances, an appeal may be granted on the grounds that the decision of the lower court was arbitrary '*Recurso Extrarodinario por sentencia arbitraria*' (hereinafter '*Arbitrariedad*').[16]

[7] See Art 91 of the 1853 Argentine Constitution (current Art 108).

[8] See at www.csjn.gov.ar/institucional.

[9] See the seminal G Carrió, *Recurso extraordinario por sentencia arbitraria: en la jurisprudencia de la Corte Suprema* (Abeledo Perrot, 1967).

[10] See President's Mitre circular to the governors sent on 16 January, 1863 and cited by Barrancos and Vedia (n 4) 202.

[11] When the Argentine Parliament established the Supreme Court appellate jurisdiction, it followed closely the US Judiciary Act of 1789.

[12] Art 117, Constitution of Argentina. Art 1, Act 48 (*Organización y Competencia de los Tribunales Nacionales*).

[13] In most of these cases, the Supreme Court possesses appellate jurisdiction, save for those cases concerning foreign ambassadors, ministers and consuls, and in those cases in which a province shall be a party, where the Court has original and exclusive jurisdiction. Art 117, Constitution of Argentina., 2018). See, accordingly, Art 1 of Law No 48.

[14] Art 4, Law No 48.

[15] Art 14, Law No 48. There is a separate kind of mandatory appellate jurisdiction known as ordinary appeals, which are reserved for cases in which the state is a party, and the amount of the claim exceeds a certain figure. This latter form of appellate jurisdiction is subjected to different rules. It is not addressed in this study.

[16] See, eg Supreme Court decisions in *Sanatorio Otamendy Miroli Ltda. c/ Recúpero, Alfredo*, Fallos 302:1191 (1980), and *Menendez, Carlos N. c/ Giovannoni, Nélida Fallos* 300:535 (1978).

The Court has a large and complex professional bureaucracy, which has grown and diversified over the years. At the time of writing, it is composed by seven judicial departments organised around areas of the law,[17] an Office of Original Cases, and one of Environmental cases, each headed by an official with a rank equivalent to a judge in any federal appeals court in the country. Each justice at the Court is assisted by personnel in an office '*Vocalía*' with a significant number of legal clerks of different internal ranks and levels of seniority. The Court also has a large bureaucracy that covers both administrative, technical and legal matters, including a Direction in charge of communications and protocol, an economic analysis of law unit, a Direction of Case-Law, and other Units including Institutional Development, Administration, and an Office for Women, an Office of information concerning minors, and an office in support of domestic violence cases.[18] Until the creation of the Council of the Magistracy '*Consejo de la Magistratura*' through the 1994 Constitutional Reform, the Court was also the administrative head of the federal judiciary.

When an appeal reaches the Supreme Court, it is distributed to the Judicial Department specialised in the specific area of the appeal.[19] The relevant Judicial Department conducts a preliminary assessment and may keep the file for internal drafting before circulating it among the justices. In other cases, it distributes it across the justices, often starting with one with particular specialisation in an area (before going to the others).[20] In addition, files will typically be sent to the office of the Attorney General '*Procurador General de la Nación*' for a non-binding opinion.[21]

When cases are distributed to the Justices '*vocalías*', an initial majority draft is written in the office of the first Justice in the circulation. If a Justice down the line proposes a different solution, that second opinion is added to the circulating file. Eventually, the latter opinion may become the majority opinion. Each Justice will usually make a decision on the petition after reviewing the appeal file by issuing (or joining in) a reasoned or boilerplate opinion, or by reference to a previous case decision or the non-binding opinion of the Attorney General.[22] Referencing in this context means that a decision or vote will merely invoke a previous decision or opinion as the grounds for the present ruling, without explaining how or why it applies to the particular circumstances. Justices' opinions may come in the form of a majority vote, a separate concurring vote (classified by the Supreme Court as '*por su voto*'), a dissenting vote (partial or total) (classified by Supreme Court as either '*en disidencia*' or '*en disidencia parcial*') or even a no vote.[23] Formally, the decisions are taken on Tuesdays when Justices officially get

[17] See S Muro et al, 'Testing Representational Advantage in the Argentine Supreme Court' (2018) 6 *Journal of Law and Courts* 1–23.

[18] See at www.csjn.gov.ar/institucional/organigrama.

[19] A description of the thematic area of specialisation of each Judicial Department is provided in ibid.

[20] Tax law appeals are always analysed by the relevant Judicial Department (Secretaría Judicial N° 7). Interview A-3.

[21] The *Procurador General* is often equated to the figure of the Attorney General in the US. It formally sits outside the structure of the executive and judicial power and is charged with the protection of the general interests of society and the defence of the constitution (see Art 120, Constitution of Argentina). The *Procurador General* is nominated by the president and is confirmed by two thirds of the members of the Senate.

[22] It should be noted that there is no rule mandating a minimal amount for circulation of each file or that each Justice should receive the file through the circulation process.

[23] Not voting on a case is a fairly widespread practice in Argentine collegial courts, commonly attributed to the large docket sizes those courts handle.

together to sign the opinions they have made on the different cases. Such meetings may also serve to discuss other cases in the pipeline.[24] Formal hearings are extremely rare.[25]

The fact that the Supreme Court has jurisdiction over a case does not guarantee that the Court will arrive at a decision on the merits. In effect, the Court has had to adopt different strategies to deal with the ever-growing number of appeals it receives each year. For instance, the Court sometimes rejects appeals on the grounds that they were insufficiently grounded '*rechazo por falta de fundamentación autónoma*', because there is no proper constitutional issue '*sin cuestión federal*', or because the constitutional issue was raised extemporaneously. In 1990, Congress reformed the Code of Civil and Commercial Procedure, giving the Supreme Court discretion to dispose of appeals based on a lack of substantive importance.[26] This type of decision is referred to as Article 280, which provides the legal basis for these types of dismissals. Since then, the Supreme Court has routinely made use of the discretionary power to reject appeals on the grounds that the matters raised by the appellant are either insignificant or inconsequential. In 2007 the Court introduced substantial formal requirements to all appeals and routinely rejects appeals for failing to comply with them.[27]

Nevertheless, in order for the Supreme Court to reject an appeal it must deliver a decision,[28] typically of the boilerplate type (a short, formulaic decision that is repeated with almost no variations). Rulings on an appeal's admissibility and, eventually, on the substance of the case are included in the same decision. As a result, some admitted appeals carry Article 280 dissents and some rejected appeals have dissents admitting the appeal and analysing the merits. Decisions are reached through a simple majority. Yet, the Argentine legal system does not have an explicit rule mandating Justices to vote in a particular case. Given the history of institutional instability it is not surprising that at some point during the second part of the twentieth century, CSJN justices started considering it acceptable and, in fact, unproblematic to simply abstain from voting. Abstentions are currently common not only on decisions to dismiss appeals but also on appeals decided on the merits.[29]

B. Judges and Institutional Instability in the Supreme Court

The Argentine Constitution does not establish the number of Justices that integrate the Court but, as in the US System, this is decided by Congress. Supreme Court Justices (locally known as '*Ministros*') are appointed by the president with the confirmation of a two-thirds majority of the Senate (before 1994, this required a simple majority). The original text of the National Constitution of 1853 (Article 19) established a fixed

[24] When discussing cases, Justices may question officers leading the relevant specialised Judicial Departments on the details of the case. Informal meetings where Justices (or their clerks) discuss cases are somewhat frequent.

[25] On this, see MA Benedetti and MJ Sáenz, *Las audiencias públicas de la Corte Suprema. Apertura y límites de la participación ciudadana en la justicia* (Siglo XXI Editorial, 2016).

[26] Arts 280 and 285, *Código de Procedimiento Civil y Comercial de la Nación, Ley 23.774.*

[27] On the appeal document's formal requirement, see Muro et al (n 17).

[28] Notably, this type of decision has the same majority requirements as a decision on the merits.

[29] Muro et al (n 17). It is also noteworthy that lower courts justices do not have this prerogative under Argentine federal law.

number of nine sitting Justices for the Supreme Court, but the reform of 1860 eliminated that Article and since then there has been no specific regulation. Therefore, it is up to Congress to decide the actual number of sitting Justices in the Court. Even though the Court had been traditionally composed by five Justices, there were some periods in time in which that number fluctuated.[30] During Frondizi's government (1960) the Congress issued a bill to increase the number of Justices to seven[31] and six years later the de facto Onganía regime took them back to five.[32] During the first Menem presidency (1990), the court was packed by increasing its number from five to nine Justices. This led to the creation of the so-called 'automatic majority' – a reference to the commonality of decisions in favour of Menem's government by a group of Justices.[33] In 2006, and after a political crisis in the Court that created many vacancies, a bill was passed to reduce to five the number of Justices in the court.[34] Until 1990 the Attorney General was considered to be 'part' of the Court, at least for purposes of protocol and image.

One striking historical fact about the Supreme Court is that, despite Justices being appointed for life, since 1947 presidents have had a significant power to manipulate the composition of the high court.[35] Before 1947 Justices remained in office for 10.6 years on average, while afterwards the average tenure was reduced to 5.7 years; many scholars consider that year as a critical juncture in executive-court relations. The accession of Perón to the presidency in 1946 and the ensuing purges of the court by military and civilian administrations reinforced the pattern of the instability of Justices in office associated with an unstable political context. This pattern of judicial instability associated with the political context of the country exceeds the Argentine case since it is also present in other Latin American countries.[36] Moreover, if one concentrates only on the last democratic period (1983–2009), the average tenure for a Justice has been 6.5 years, not that different from the average for the entire period 1947–2009 which is 5.7 years. This high rate of instability of Justices, even after the return of democracy, indicates that both civilian and military executives have manipulated the Court.[37]

Preliminary descriptive analysis of judicial turnover in the country reveals that on several occasions more than half of the sitting Justices have simultaneously departed from the bench in a given year, mainly as a result of changes in the type of regime (from democracy to military and vice versa). The Court has been abruptly reshuffled[38] on seven different occasions, starting in 1947 with Perón and ending in 1983 with the return of democracy. Three of those reshuffles happened as the result of a military

[30] Art 6, Act 27.
[31] Art 21, Act 15.271.
[32] Art 1, Act 16.985.
[33] G Helmke, *Courts under Constraints. Judges, Generals, and Presidents in Argentina* (Cambridge University Press, 2005).
[34] Art 32, Act 26.183.
[35] A Castagnola, *Manipulating courts in new democracies. Forcing judges off the bench in Argentina* (Routledge, 2018).
[36] A Pérez Liñán and A Castagnola, 'Judicial Instability and Endogenous Constitutional Change: Lessons from Latin America' (2016) 46(2) *British Journal of Political Science* 395.
[37] A similar pattern of political manipulation of the courts takes place in the provincial Supreme Courts, since the alternations between military and democratic regimes have also affected the composition of the local courts, producing reshuffles in most provinces, see A Castagnola, '*I Want It All, and I Want It Now*: The Political Manipulation of Argentina's Provincial High Courts' (2012) 4(2) *Journal of Politics in Latin America* 39–62.
[38] This happens when more than half of the sitting justices depart from the bench in a given year.

coup (1955, 1966, and 1976), while the other four occurred as the result of the return of democracy to the country (1947 and 1973 under the Perón administration, 1958 under Frondizi, and 1983 under Alfonsín). Evidently, the ultimate goal of these abrupt reshuffles has likely been to remove unfriendly justices from the bench. From the total 86 Justices that served the Court between 1900 and 2014, 37 per cent of them departed due to natural causes and 63 per cent due to political causes. Departures in the Argentine Supreme Court are not a rare event as happens in established democracies but rather the consequences of changes in the political realignment of the forces in government. The manipulation of high courts in the country has ended up producing a self-reinforcing process that still takes place, in other words it ended up producing a long-lasting political manipulation of the judiciary.

C. Legal Culture and Constitutional Reasoning in Argentina

In order to conduct our study concerning the dominant forms of reasoning in the Court, we must say a few words on the prevailing legal culture in the country. Admittedly, legal systems are seldom if ever reducible to a single source of inspiration.[39] Argentina is not the exception. In its case, natural law theories[40] and legal positivism[41] together with the Madisonian influence have contributed to create the singular texture of the legal system. The codification movement started after the enactment of the constitution – borrowing specially from the French legal tradition – and highlights the eclectic foundations of Argentine Law where the political organisation followed Anglo-Saxon models and the civil laws were anchored in continental Europe's traditions.[42] The impact of the latter and of legal positivism on the legal system were especially felt. They led to a strong practical inclination towards abstraction, whereby Argentine lawyers and judges are often skilful in handling statutes and deducing solutions from general propositions.[43] The same inclination towards abstraction has led to a somewhat loose sourcing of judicial precedents, often insufficiently grounded in legal propositions.[44] This general attitude of receiving foreign legal institutions has also influenced the great importance often attributed to foreign scholarly work.

The many sources that have inspired the development of the Argentine legal system have also influenced the theories of interpretation used by tribunals.[45] In the case of

[39] For instance, Madison wasn't merely influenced by Scottish thinkers, but also by the French enlightenment. See CA Sheehan, 'Madison and the French Enlightenment: The Authority of Public Opinion' (2002) 59 *The William and Mary Quarterly* 925.

[40] See V Tau Anzoátegui, *Las ideas jurídicas en la Argentina (siglos XIX – XX)* (Editorial Perrot, 1977).

[41] See NG Wenzel, 'Matching Constitutional Culture and Parchment: Post-Colonial Constitutional Adoption in Mexico and Argentina' (2010) *Historia Constitucional* 11.

[42] See Tau Anzoátegui (n 40) 83; J Reinaldo Vanossi, 'Breves Reflexiones Sobre Forma y Estilo en la Interpretación Judicial de la Constitución Histórica' (Comunicación en sesión privada de la Academia Nacional de Ciencias Morales y Políticas, 2003) at www.ancmyp.org.ar/user/FILES/Forma_y_estilo-Vanossi-2003.pdf.

[43] See H Spector, 'Constitutional Transplants and the Mutation Effect' (2008) 83 *Chicago-Kent Law Review* 129. cf GR Carrió, *Recurso de Amparo y Técnica Judicial* (Abeledo-Perrot, 1987) 174.

[44] ibid.

[45] Interpretation is a complex issue that has been studied extensively in Argentina. See eg CS Nino, *Fundamentos de derecho constitucional. Análisis filosófico, jurídico y politológico de la práctica constitucional* (Astrea, 1992).

the Supreme Court, it has employed many different interpretative criteria throughout its history to provide meaning to the legal texts under review.[46] These criteria include identifying the literal, popular, specialised, realist, systematic, dynamic, teleological, external, constructive or intentional meaning of the text to be interpreted. In addition, other Supreme Court decisions have sought to use the legislator's will, fairness or what an ideal legislator would have had in mind to arrive at a solution.[47] The variety of interpreting methods has led to a degree of unpredictability, with some authors highlighting the lack of a concerted effort to find a solution to this problem.[48] It has been further reinforced by a strong adherence to the principle of *iura novit curia* (the justices know the law) throughout the legal system. It is also accompanied by a very weak understanding of the doctrine of precedent, even in the Argentine Supreme Court.

The seeming multitude of judicial answers which may arise from different interpretation methods increases concerns related to the constitutional limits of judicial decision-making.[49] Indeed, the plurality of potential legal answers to a given question brings about an element of judicial discretion.[50] And it is this discretion that gives rise to the criticism of judicial activism, that is 'judges inject[ing] their substantive preferences and decid[ing] questions that ought to be left to political determination.'[51] There have been many decisions by the Supreme Court that could be labelled as instances of activism[52] – eg the judicial recognition of the '*acción de amparo*', creating new constitutionally recognised rights or incorporating the per saltum appeal,[53] nevertheless many authors consider that restraint – in the form of judicial acquiescence to the executive – has been the court's norm.[54] This view has received some empirical support as Helmke and Sanders find that most Argentine judges are motivated by

[46] N Sagüés, *Interpretación constitucional y alquimia interpretativa. (El arsenal argumentativo de los tribunales supremos)* (Lexis Nexis, 2004).

[47] ibid.

[48] See R Gargarella, 'De la alquimia interpretativa al maltrato constitucional. La interpretación del derecho en manos de la Corte Suprema Argentina' in R Gargarella (coord), *Teoría y Crítica del Derecho Constitucional* (Abeledo Perrot, 2008).

[49] See F Easterbrook, 'Do Liberals and Conservatives Differ in Judicial Activism' (2000) 73 *University of Colorado Law Review* 1401; FM Racimo, 'El Activismo Judicial. Sus Orígenes y su Recepción en la Doctrina Nacional' (2015) 2 *Revista Jurídica de la Universidad de San Andres* 89.

[50] See Gargarella (n 48).

[51] See JS Schacter, 'Putting the Politics of "Judicial Activism" in Historical Perspective' (2017) *The Supreme Court Review* 209.

[52] The definition of judicial activism is subject to some debate. See C Rayburn Yung, 'Flexing Judicial Muscle: An Empirical Study of Judicial Activism in the Federal Courts' (2011) 105 *Northwestern University Law Review* 1. ('From those perspectives and definitions, the following elements emerge as signs of judicial activism: overruling actions by other federal branches or state governments, failing to follow textual meaning, departing from history or tradition, issuing maximalist and not minimalist holdings, using broad remedial powers, basing decisions upon partisan preferences, failing to follow an originalist view of the Constitution, issuing an opinion inconsistent with prior precedent, exercising power beyond a court's jurisdiction, creating new rights or theories, altering prior doctrines or interpretations, establishing substantive policy, and failing to use an accepted interpretative methodology.').

[53] See Racimo (n 49); PA Maraniello, 'El Activismo Judicial, una Herramienta de Protección Constitucional' (2012) 5(32) *Tla-Melaua. Revista de Ciencias Sociales* 46.

[54] See AB Bianchi, 'Una meditación acerca de la función institucional de la Corte Suprema' (1994) 1997-B *La Ley* 994; Barrancos and Vedia (n 4). An early example of the restraint shown by the court can be seen in the decision in the case *Cullen v Llerena*, Fallos 53:420 (1893) where the Supreme Court accepted the notion of non-justiciability of political matters.

career survival[55] – something which, as previously discussed, may be traced to the history of judges' removal.

III. Arguments in Constitutional Reasoning – Descriptive Statistics

This section presents the descriptive statistics on constitutional reasoning at the Argentine Supreme Court. Our dataset contains a total of 40 Supreme Court cases, the first one decided in 1879 and the last one in 2017.[56] We aim to capture the fundamental traits, as well as the variances of judicial reasoning at the Argentine Supreme Court. Due to this long period of time and the significant changes in the political stability of the country and its effects on the judiciary, we shall divide the analysis into three periods.

A. Main Features: Structure, Framing, Type of Argument, and Length

The first period encompasses the first decades of the Supreme Court until 1929, the year before the first military coup took place in the country. This period can be conceived as the foundational years of the court, basically a court free from political manipulation. The second period encompasses all the oscillations between military and democratic regimes that the country experienced between 1930 to 1983. Within this timeframe there were six military coups (1930, 1943, 1955, 1962, 1966 and 1976) and the Supreme Court was constantly purged after every regime change. Even though this second period can become an interlude within the historical analysis of the Supreme Court rulings, it also sheds light on how the justices were able (or not) to guarantee the rule of law and the respect for individual rights. Finally, the third period runs from 1984 until present day and it represents the return of democracy in the country. Based on this periodisation 20 per cent of the cases fall within the foundational years, 32 per cent within the years of political instability, and 48 per cent after the return of democracy. Throughout this whole period of time there was substantial agreement within the Court (on average 78 per cent of the decisions were unanimous). This is hardly surprising given the pervasive instability in the Court and the recurrent purges it suffered. The average length of the judgment of 41 pages, ranging from 2 to 259 pages, indicates a Court prone to extensive treatment of the legal issues, but also relying on an extensive and very sophisticated judicial bureaucracy. In half of the docket of cases analysed the court made a ruling considering a particular legal provision to be unconstitutional. 88 per cent of the cases were bottom up initiated.[57]

[55] See G Helmke and MS Sanders, 'Modelling Motivations: A Method for Inferring Judicial Goals from Behavior' (2006) 68(4) *The Journal of Politics* 867.

[56] See Fröhlich, Umpierrez De Reguero and Meléndez (ch 1).

[57] The Argentine legal system, as most civil law countries, is deeply influenced by the principle of *jura novit curia*. Nevertheless, given that the Argentine Supreme Court does not provide access to the appeals, it is not possible to determine the extent to which it relies upon, or takes into consideration, the arguments expounded by the parties in a case, or by other legal materials such as *amici curiae*. The empirical research on public

The appeals reaching the Argentine Supreme Court are based on cases based on a myriad of substantive legal topics. Graph 1 below shows the incidence of different types of constitutional cases in our sample, divided into fundamental rights, state organisation, or procedural cases (in addition to a catch all category of 'other'). Throughout the years, the cases in our sample referred to fundamental rights issues in at least 50 per cent of the events in each of the studied periods of time. The peak incidence of fundamental rights cases arises unsurprisingly during the 1930–1983 period – perhaps the darkest of the Argentine Republic – where violations of basic human rights became unfortunately common. In this period, fundamental rights cases included milestone judicial decisions recognising a constitutional writ going beyond the *habeas corpus* protection against illegal detentions.[58] In Siri, for instance, the Court used *habeas corpus* to protect the right to freedom of expression when facing the administrative closure of a local newspaper. It explicitly stated that Constitutional rights 'exist and protect individuals by their sole inclusion in the Constitution' and that 'judges must apply them in their full scope, without altering or debilitating them with vague interpretations or ambiguities concerning the express meaning of their text.'[59]

State organisation cases, by contrast, were less frequent occurrences – that is, if we were to omit the single occurrence of the 'other' category.[60] The incidence of the State Organisation category was 0 per cent among the landmark cases in our sample during the 1930–1983 period. This is perhaps unsurprising given the dictatorial nature of several of the regimes in power during this period and the fact that each new government basically appointed most of the members of the Court.

Graph 1 Common topics among the selected rulings (Q5)

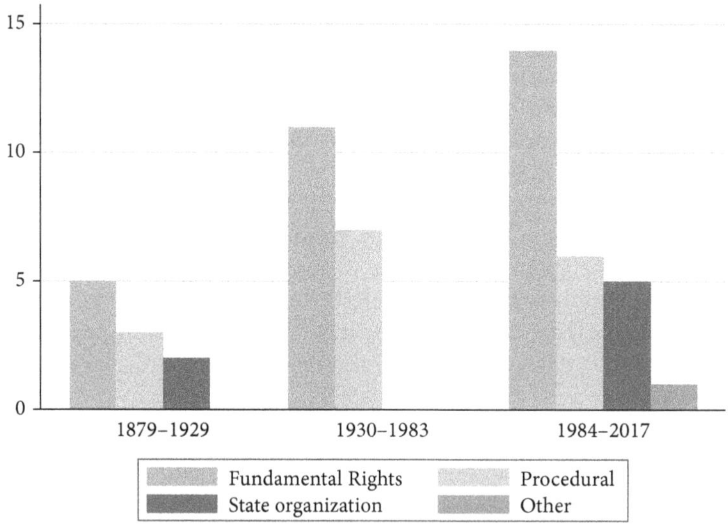

hearings, however, suggests that the Court has been quite reluctant to rely on arguments made by the parties in them. See Benedetti and Sáenz (n 25).

[58] Decisions of the Supreme Court: in *Siri, Angel S. s/ acción de amparo*, Fallos 239:459 (1957); *KOT, Samuel S.R.L. s/ Acción de amparo. Acto de particulares* (5-958), Fallos 241:291 (1958).

[59] Siri, ibid 463.

[60] Others refer in some cases to emergency powers (*Peralta, Luis Arcenio y otro c/ Estado Nacional (Mrio. de Economía – BCRA.) s/ amparo*, Fallos 313:1513 (1990)).

A key element of this study is to help identify the types of arguments frequently used by the Argentine Supreme Court while deciding landmark cases. At a formal level, legal arguments are constructed following a logical form. This part uses the categories developed in Jakab to determine the different logical form a legal argument can adopt.[61] Under this analysis there are three prototypical structures of legal arguments: (i) conclusive arguments, inclusive of a chain of arguments in a linear sequence; (ii) parallel arguments, each independently supporting the same conclusion; and (iii) cumulative arguments, where each individual argument is inconclusive but all of them together become conclusive.

Different argument structures have been prominent in landmark cases throughout the Argentine Supreme Court's history, as it is shown in Graph 2 below. While during the initial period all the studied structures were utilised with similar prominence, during the 1930–1983 period one-line conclusive arguments seem to have reigned supreme, as they appear in over 60 per cent of the cases in our sample. Later, parallel arguments clearly overtook the other remaining categories which jointly represent less than 40 per cent of the cases in our sample. While our data is insufficient to identify the reasons behind this change, it is possible to ponder whether the different institutional setting played a role in it. Specifically, during the latter period, the court was not serving merely at the whim of the new political or military leader in power (as was the case during the 1930–1983 period), at least not for the longest part of the period.[62] By contrast, it was largely a period in which judges from very different political parties coincided in the Court and, most importantly, a period of regained republican normalcy. As such, it could be speculated that the court placed additional value in making sure that the decisions made were robust in the eyes of not only different political actors but also the civil society (and the legal community) at large, particularly after the steep legitimacy crisis of the Court in 2001. A preference for this technical approach may have been used as a way of increasing the court's own reputation and social capital. In other words, if a decision made by the court could be supported by several different independent, yet individually conclusive arguments, the chances of a broader agreement with the achieved outcome tends to increase.

Other factors could have also played a role in explaining this shift towards favouring parallel conclusive arguments. For instance, the higher incidence of dissents in landmark decisions during this period (95 per cent during the 1983–2017 period, relative to 69 per cent during the 1930 to 1982 period) may have influenced the design of majority opinions. Dissents, especially reasoned ones, are known to alter the behaviour of the majority leading it to create longer opinions where a dissent is present.[63] Parallel conclusive arguments can be a way to make a majority opinion more robust in the face of a dissenting minority. Yet other factors, such as the development of technology – facilitating the identification of sources and arguments and

[61] See A Jakab, 'Judicial Reasoning in Constitutional Courts: A European Perspective' (2018) 14(8) *German Law Journal* 1215.

[62] A problematic period here was Menem's automatic majority. See Section II(B) above.

[63] See L Epstein et al, 'Why (and When) Judges Dissent: A Theoretical and Empirical Analysis' (2011) 3 *Journal of Legal Analysis* 101–37; S Muro et al 'Exploring Dissent in the Supreme Court of Argentina' (2020) 63 *International Review of Law and Economics* 105909.

Graph 2 The structure of the arguments among the selected rulings (Q9)

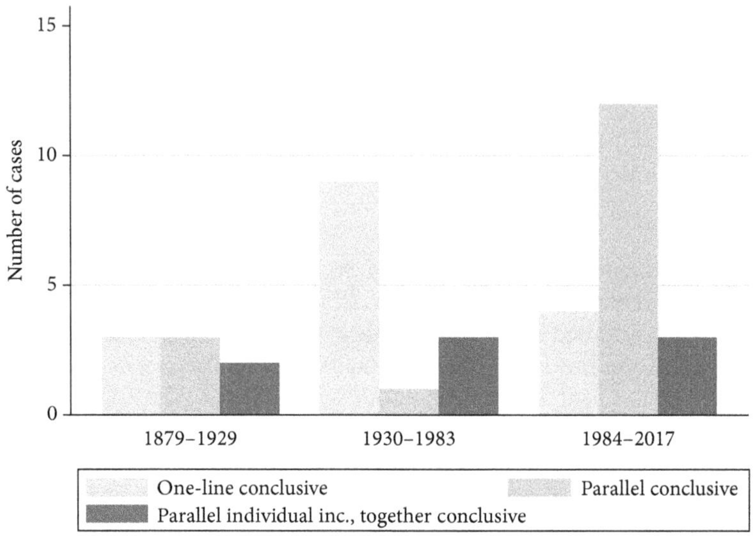

their restatement – may have also played a role in fostering a preference for parallel arguments. Ultimately, this is a positive aspect to highlight since parallel arguments reinforce the main features of democratic governments and deliberative aspects of the court.

Graph 3 shows that the Argentine Supreme Court is essentially a formalist court, significantly attached to the text of the Constitution. Indeed, the Court has significantly maintained a textual approach, which has even intensified in more recent times (see also Section III on the frequency with which the Court refers to the ordinary meaning of words). To illustrate, the Court in Sojo (1887) famously adopted the doctrine of constitutional review from the US Court without citing any provision of the Argentine constitutional text (only broad references of the similarities with the US Constitution and specific legal opinions of the US Supreme Court). In the Leandro N Alem case (1924), in turn, the Court considered it appropriate to 'logically deduce from this constitutional text that the central objective of the state of emergency "*estado de sitio*" was the defence of the Constitution and the national authorities that it creates'.[64] More recently, in Verbitsky (2005), the Court examined the situation in the prisons of the Province of Buenos Aires by centrally referring to the explicit terms of Article 18 of the Constitution, and its reference to prisons being 'healthy and clean, for the security and not for the punishment of the prisoners confined therein'.[65]

[64] See *Alem, Leandro N. y Candioti, Mariano N. (causa CCCLIII)*, Fallos 54:432 (1893) 455.

[65] See *Recurso de hecho deducido por el centro de Estudios Legales y Sociales en la causa Verbitsky, Horacio s/ habeas corpus*, Fallos 328:1102 (2005).

Graph 3 Constitutional discussions within the selected judgments (Q10 & Q11)

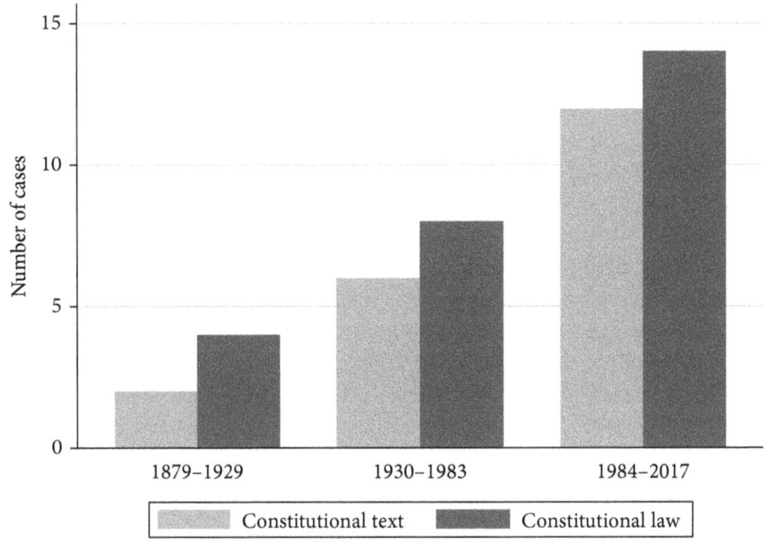

B. Argumentative Style and Key Concepts

There are two ways in which the argumentative style can be assessed, both of which are captured in Graph 4. The first one is absolute, as a feature of the relative weight of different materials at the basis of the Supreme Court's reasoning. During the first period examined, the Argentine Supreme Court had a marked preference for arguments based on foreign law (88 per cent), as well as on the purpose or aim of the provision in question (teleological textual, 75 per cent), and on scholarly work (62.5 per cent). This is probably unsurprising in a new Court trying to find its voice and authority within a new legal system. It is also compatible with the Creole elite in Argentina and Latin America looking to Europe and the US as sources of 'civilisation'. In the mid-period, characterised by institutional and political instability inside and outside the Court, the preferred argumentative strategy of the Court was relying on precedent (77 per cent), followed by an attempt to harmonise different Articles or provisions in the Argentine Constitution (domestic harmonising, 69.23 per cent), and scholarly work (61.5 per cent). The third period involved the return and consolidation of democracy, a greater sophistication of the legal profession and the expansion of the Court's areas of interest through the doctrine of '*arbitrariedad*'. This period, in turn, is perhaps most clearly characterised by the far larger array of relevant materials the Court utilised to ground its decisions, including scholarly work (95 per cent) and precedent (89 per cent), but also teleological textual arguments (84 per cent), harmonisation within the Argentine Constitution (79 per cent), and harmonisation with international legal instruments (69 per cent). The Court also used arguments considering the drafter's purpose or intention (teleological historical arguments, 69 per cent), foreign law (68 per cent), and even extensive use of non-legal (ie, explicitly moral, religious, economic, scientific, or sociological) and other arguments (58 per cent, respectively).

The second relevant analysis concerns the variances within each of the categories along with the history of the Court. Some changes are to be expected. Precedent evidently played a much smaller role during the first period of the operation of the Court than during the other two (37.5 per cent against 77 and 89 per cent, respectively). Scholarly work has always been influential although it has become the prevailing source of argumentation in line with changes in legal training that operated at a global level (going from 62.5 per cent up to 95 per cent in the third period). The influence of international law, by contrast, has grown significantly during the third period after slightly decreasing in the second one (25 per cent, 18 per cent and 69 per cent, respectively). This is most likely the result of the growing importance of international legal rules in domestic spheres, which in the case of Argentina even ended in a Constitutional reform incorporating human rights treaties within the Constitution.[66] Perhaps the most eloquent variation in the data is the evolution of pro persona arguments, which went from 25 per cent during the first period to 0 during the period of military coups and institutional instability, to 37 per cent since the return of democracy. Professionalisation of the legal profession may also explain the general increase and diversity of argumentative style in judgments, leading to a more sophisticated and rich legal practice.

Graph 4 Interpretive methods among the selected judgments

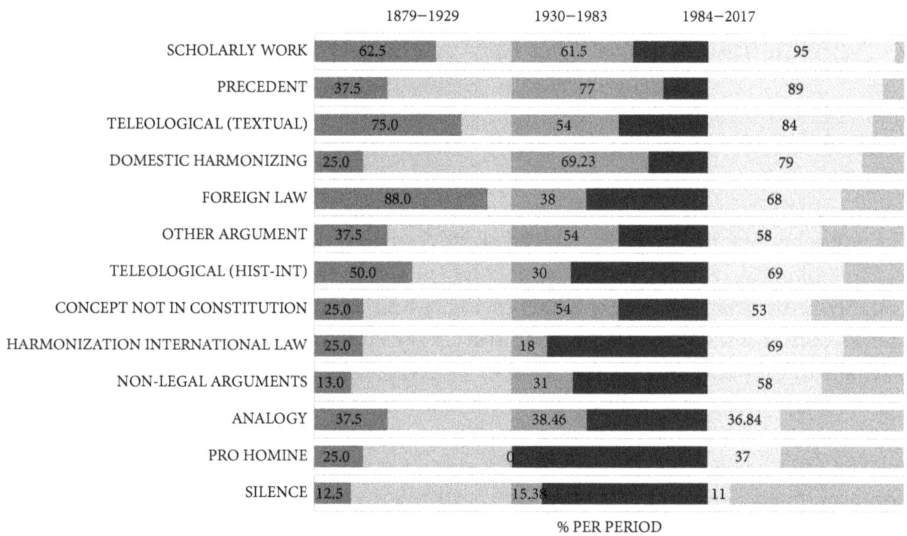

Graph 5, in turn, shows some of the key concepts used by the Court in its rulings. Again, we may consider the presence of these central concepts both in terms of their relative appearance in the overall case-law of the Court, as well as in terms of its variance across our three relevant periods. From the first perspective, the Court has referred most

[66] See respectively, PH Verdier and M Versteeg, 'International Law in National Legal Systems: an Empirical Investigation' (2015) 109 *American Journal of International Law* 516; A Chehtman, 'Constitutions and International Law' in C Hubner Mendes et al (eds), *The Oxford Handbook of Constitutional Law in Latin America* (Oxford University Press, 2022), for information on Argentina and Latin America more broadly.

often to the 'rule of law', 'justice', 'state', and 'human dignity'. This seems paradoxical in a country which has suffered political violence, reiterated Coups d'État, and ultimately the perpetration of heinous human rights violations against part of its population. By contrast, the least mentioned concepts are 'secularism', 'judicial independence', 'transition', 'family' and, perhaps most notably, 'freedom of expression'.

The variance in the references to each of these terms is of particular interest. For instance, 'democracy' was not mentioned during the founding period, it appeared in 15 per cent of the decisions during the turbulent years which included fraud, political violence, Coups, and the proscription of one of the majoritarian parties and went up to 53 per cent since the return of democratic rule in 1983. The 'right to privacy' had a similar evolution from 0 per cent mentions in the first period, to 15 per cent in the second, and finally to 42 per cent. 'Secularism', although not very popular overall, became a more significant constitutional issue after 1983 (going from zero mentions in the first two periods to 16 per cent in the third). We also note a steady growth in the use of concepts such as 'human dignity', 'constitutional rights', but also a greater overall reference to these concepts.

The concept of 'state' played an important role during the founding period (referenced twice as much as the second most cited concept), significantly decreasing its importance both vis-à-vis the previous period and vis-à-vis the other concepts. It became largely relevant again in the third period. By contrast, the concept of 'nation' has maintained a consistently low presence overall. Curiously, we see more references to 'economic, social, cultural, and environmental rights' during the period of authoritarian and/or turbulent rules than even after the return of democracy and the constitutionalisation of human rights instruments in 1994. Similarly, 'rule of law' was mentioned in almost half of the cases in the middle period even though the period was inaugurated by a coup, and suffered continuous breaks to the constitutional order, and many affronts to democratic rule.

Graph 5 Key concepts among the selected judgments

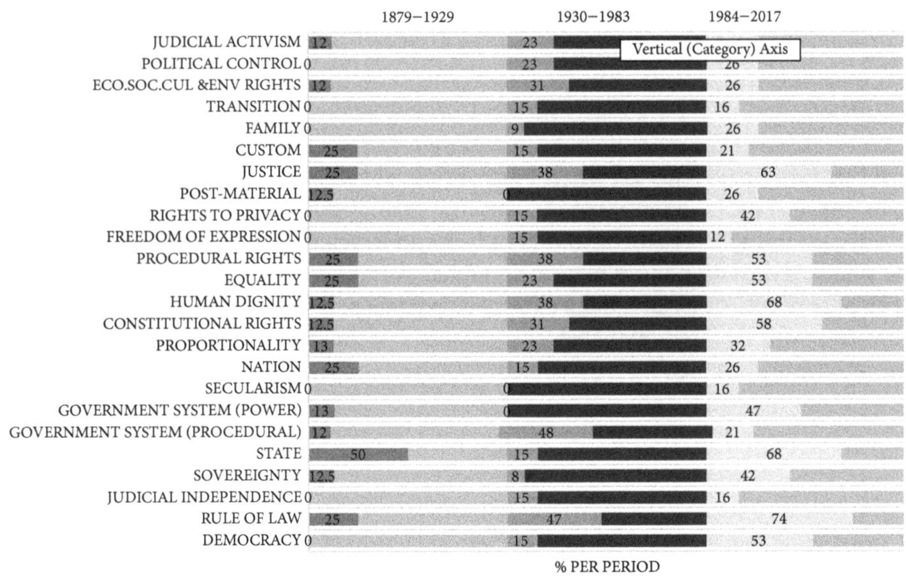

IV. Comparative Perspective

Common trends can be observed when analysing the way in which the Argentine Supreme Court and its peer institutions in the region apply their reasoning. At its core, the cases analysed in this chapter focus mostly on fundamental rights (75 per cent), a figure that is similar to that of the cases analysed for peer countries (Brazil, Colombia, Mexico) and slightly higher to that of the regional average (68.5 per cent). Moreover, the structure of the arguments made by the Argentine Supreme Court are at par with those of other High Courts. Specifically, four-fifths of all arguments delivered by the Argentine Supreme Court were either one-line or parallel conclusive arguments, similar to the regional average (79 per cent). Nevertheless, it is unclear whether other courts in the region have also started to more frequently opt for parallel conclusive arguments.

When it comes to the types of arguments favoured by the Argentine Supreme Court and the concepts it tends to root those arguments in, several peculiarities make the court stand out. *Ordinary meaning of words* (ie grammatical-literal interpretation of the provisions of the constitution) and *textual teleological* (ie the purpose or aim of a provision based on the text) arguments are used at a much higher rate than the regional average (in each case the usage is almost one standard deviation higher than the regional mean). A similar pattern can be observed by the high rate of reference to scholarly work. The results are typically sophisticated legal opinions, that are nonetheless tightly anchored to the legal text. That is not to say that the High Court is starkly different in the types of arguments it uses to those of its peers. In fact, for both the Argentine Supreme Court and the regional average, precedent-based arguments sit among the top types of arguments used (75 per cent and 80 per cent, respectively).

As per the concepts the Argentine Supreme Court tends to root its arguments in, two distinctive characteristics appear to emerge. On the one hand, the court uses the concepts of sovereignty (ie state authority), state form (ie republic) and procedural structure (ie presidential system) much more frequently than its peers, on average.[67] In a way, the Argentine Supreme Court seems to frequently find a way to connect to the organisation of the state as a means to reach its conclusions. On the other hand, closely connected concepts such as human dignity, justice, basic procedural rights and core constitutional rights are cited much more frequently by the court than they are by its regional peers, on average. As with the case of state organisation, concepts that describe an individual's worth to themselves and in relation to others are used at least one standard deviation more than the regional average. The high prevalence of the two types of concepts described before (ie state organisation and an individual's worth) is consistent with an often textualist interpretation of the constitution, as they mirror its two structural elements.[68]

[67] In the case of state form, it is the court that makes the most use of this concept (applied in 47% of cases).

[68] The Argentine constitution is organised in two parts: a bill of rights section, and an authorities of the nation section.

V. Conclusion – Evaluation, Pathology and Criticism

This chapter seeks to capture the main traits of the legal reasoning at the Argentine Supreme Court. We decided to examine this both in absolute terms, as well as historically, following a standard periodisation of Argentina's constitutional history. A number of important findings may be highlighted. On the one hand, some of the variations can be attributed to global trends, such as the professionalisation of the legal profession (as captured by an increased recourse to doctrine and more sophisticated argumentative styles) and the growing salience of international law in domestic settings. On the other hand, several variations can be traced to Argentina's main political history. For instance, cases dealing with the organisation of the State were more frequent during the democratic years than during the most turbulent years of the country. During periods with military governments the key issues became procedural and concerning rights rather than regarding the organisation of the state. By contrast, the structure of judicial reasoning became more inclusive and complex during democratic periods vis-à-vis the years of military governments in which one-line conclusive arguments reigned. Finally, there are traits that arguably characterise the Argentine Supreme Court across time. For instance, the prevalence of unanimous decisions (particularly during turbulent times) eloquently shows a reaction of judges against instability and external threats. Similarly, the use of multiple argumentative styles and tools for reasoning reveals a collective effort of the justices in promoting more cohesive and legitimate decisions. Finally, the Court has largely focused on decisions on fundamental rights over other issues, most notably political organisation.

4

The Jurisprudence of the Bolivian Constitutional Court

SERGIO VERDUGO

I. Legal, Political, Institutional, and Academic Context

A. Legal and Political Culture as Context for the Constitutional Reasoning

Evo Morales was elected in 2005 with a platform that sought to challenge the ruling elite, taking advantage of the dissatisfaction with the existing political parties and offering an alternative platform that promised to reset the Bolivian constitutional system. Morales won the election with an overwhelming majority and immediately promoted the establishment of a constituent assembly. The assembly initiated its functions in 2006, and the MAS constitutional designers (*Movimiento al Socialismo*, Morales' supporting political coalition) promoted a plebiscitary and majoritarian approach that was initially resisted by the right-wing political opponents of the MAS.[1] In the end, and after a confusing and complicated process, and a failed and illegal attempt to call for a referendum,[2] the Morales regime was forced to negotiate with the opposition and succeeded to plebiscite the constitutional text.[3]

Although constitutional designers moderated the text, in the end the Constitution's final version still reflected the critical goals of the MAS program. Elsewhere, I have claimed that the resulting text included a sort of political insurance to prevent the MAS regime from becoming hegemonic and Morales from extending its rule outside the regular elected channels.[4] Joshua Braver has referred to this process as an example of what he calls an extraordinary adaptation constituent power procedure.[5] The final

[1] M Mendoza-Botelho, 'Revisiting Bolivia's Constituent Assembly: Lessons on the Quality of Democracy' (2016) 29 *Asian Journal of Latin American Studies* 19, 40.

[2] See F Lehoucq, 'Bolivia's Constitutional Breakdown' (2008) 19 *Journal of Democracy* 110.

[3] See F Uggla, 'Bolivia: Un Año de Vivir Peligrosamente' (2009) 29 *Revista de Ciencia Política* 247. Also, A Mokvist Uggla, 'Bolivia: Un Año de Consolidación' (2010) 30 *Revista de Ciencia Política* 191.

[4] S Verdugo, 'The Fall of the Constitution's Political Insurance. How the Morales Regime Broke the Insurance of the 2009 Bolivian Constitution' (2019) 17 *International Journal of Constitutional Law*.

[5] J Braver, 'Constituent Power as Extraordinary Adaptation', papers.ssrn.com/sol3/papers.cfm?abstract_id=3571507.

referendum confirmed the Constitution with 64.2 per cent of the votes, and the MAS controlled an overwhelming majority of both chambers of the legislative assembly.[6]

That 2009 Bolivian Constitution is generally understood as establishing a post-liberal and plurinational political system, emphasising social and indigenous rights, and recognising transformative commitments in areas such as the administration of land, natural resources, the economy, and political institutions.[7] Some scholars think that the neobolivarian project is not liberal,[8] even post-liberal.[9] The Constitution was conceived as an aspirational and forward-looking document that is rich in social rights and that seeks a radical approach to democracy.[10]

All of these considerations are relevant for understanding the expectations on constitutional reasoning that were placed on the *Tribunal Constitucional Plurinacional* (hereinafter, the TCP). Even though the TCP's official and formal aim – as declared explicitly in the Constitution – is to assure constitutional supremacy, exercise judicial review powers, and 'safeguard the respect and enforcement of rights and constitutional guarantees,'[11] those declarations are, of course, insufficient to understand the TCP's constitutional function. To understand its function, we need to look at the primary constitutional purposes of the MAS regime and the controversial constitutional enactment process, which partly explains the MAS's concessions to the opposition.[12] To simplify, I assume that the TCP's function is twofold.

The first function of the TCP was to help implement the MAS constitutional project, including its plurinational, post-liberal, and decolonising aims, all of which inspired the members of the constituent assembly. This first goal required the TCP to be an activist[13] or a protagonist of the plurinational state[14] and increase its power compared to the

[6] See A Alpert, M Centellas and M M Singer, 'The 2009 Presidential and Legislative Elections in Bolivia' (2010) 29 *Electoral Studies* 757.

[7] See eg J Wolff, 'New Constitutions and the Transformation of Democracy in Bolivia and Ecuador' in D Nolte and A Schilling-Vacaflor (eds), *New Constitutionalism in Latin America. Promises and Practices* (Routledge, 2012); A Schilling-Vacaflor, 'Bolivia's New Constitution: Towards Participatory Democracy and Political Pluralism' (2011) 90 *European Review of Latin American and Caribbean Studies* 3; H Tórtora Aravena, 'El Carácter Descolonizador Como Rasgo Material Del Nuevo Constitucionalismo Latinoamericano' in J Gajardo and Francisco Zúñiga (eds), *Constitucionalismo y Procesos Constituyentes. Una Revisión Crítica al Nuevo Constitucionalismo Latinoamericano*, vol 2 (Thomson Reuters, 2019). See a nuanced approach in M Benente, 'El Estado y los derechos humanos en la Nueva Constitución Política del Estado Plurinacional de Bolivia' (2017) *XLX Boletín Mexicano de Derecho Comparado* 49.

[8] Z Elkins, 'Constitutional Revolution in the Andes?' in R Dixon and T Ginsburg (eds), *Comparative Constitutional Law in Latin America* (Edward Elgar, 2017) 109.

[9] Wolff (n 7).

[10] See Schilling-Vacaflor (n 7). As the neoboliviarian constitutional projects tend to organise the state in a detailed way, and are rich in principles and goals, it should come to no surprise to find a particularly long text. Indeed, as Elkins has reported, the Bolivian Constitution has around 40,000 words, while the mean word count is of 13,270 words. Elkins (n 8) 114.

[11] See Art 196.1 of the Bolivian Constitution.

[12] See D Landau, 'Constitution-Making Gone Wrong' (2013) 64 *Alabama Law Review* 924; GI Deheza, 'Bolivia: ¿Es Posible La Construcción de Un Nuevo Estado? La Asamblea Constituyente y Las Autonomías Departamentales' (2008) 28 *Revista de Ciencia Política* 61; Uggla, 'Bolivia: Un Año de Vivir Peligrosamente' (n 3); Lehoucq (n 2).

[13] B Clavero, 'Tribunal Constitucional En Estado Plurinacional: El Reto Constituyente de Bolivia' (2012) 94 *Revista Española de Derecho Constitucional* 29, 31.

[14] ME Attard Bellido, 'Un Mate de Coca y Unas Breves Reflexiones Dialógicas Entre La Diosa Themis y Mama Ocllo. ¿Es El Tribunal Constitucional Plurinacional Un Modelo Polifónico de Justicia Constitucional?' (2019) XXV *Anuario de Derecho Constitucional Latinoamericano* 409, 413. Also, ME Negrón Pino, 'Diálogo Intercultural Para Una Efectiva Coordinación y Cooperación Entre Sistemas Jurídicos' (2012) 13, 102.

traditional constitutional judges in Bolivia.[15] I call this first function the *enabling* function. The second role that the TCP was supposed to perform was to preserve the institutional arrangements that aim to keep the competitiveness of the democratic system even against Bolivia's post-liberal values. This is the TCP's *insurance* function.

Of course, a book chapter on constitutional reasoning cannot fully evaluate whether a court like the TCP succeeded in achieving its roles. However, a focus on constitutional reasoning helps identify the way the TCP perceived its own function, the types of arguments it used to justify its outcomes, and how those arguments were supportive – or not – of its twofold role.

I focus on the TCP's activity between 2012 and 2018 – which coincides with the Evo Morales administration – and claim that in the politically salient and landmark cases examined in my sample of 40 selected rulings, the TCP used arguments that favoured the incumbent regime when the political stakes were high. The chapter also shows that the TCP incorporated post-material values consistent with Bolivia's constitutional project. Nevertheless, if the sample of rulings examined in this chapter is an indication of the TCP's regular activity, then it seems that the TCP's judicial style has yet to build a jurisprudence based on consistent tests that can release predictable doctrinal interpretations.

B. The Court and Constitutional Litigation

The TCP has several enumerated powers,[16] including abstract review powers to evaluate legislation, organic laws, and administrative regulations. The president, a group of legislators, or the superior regional authorities could challenge these norms and bring the cases to the TCP. The TCP also resolved conflicts of jurisdiction among diverse branches of government and solved appeals against judicial decisions that had decided a range of legal actions to protect fundamental rights. The TCP could also be consulted about the constitutionality of legislative bills, and it reviews international treaties before the state ratifies them. It had the power to solve procedural claims presented during the legislative procedure of constitutional amendments, among others.

The TCP decisions were released by either the Court's plenary or one of the three two-judge chambers,[17] The fundamental rights cases were typically decided by a particular chamber, while the plenary usually decided abstract challenges and conflicts of jurisdiction.[18] Among the 40 rulings examined in this chapter, 17 were enacted by the plenary. This is a disproportionate distribution compared to the normal docket because the two-judge chambers receive a large majority of the cases.[19] However, this study's disproportionate chamber-plenary distribution makes sense because abstract challenges are typically more politically salient and tend to be over-represented in qualitative studies like this one.

[15] See eg P Talavera, 'La Privilegiada (Pero Crucial) Posición del Juez en el Estado Constitucional. Una Mirada Sobre Bolivia' (2012) 13 *Revista Boliviana de Derecho* 22.

[16] See Art 202 of the Bolivian Constitution, and Art 12 of the Ley 027 2010.

[17] Art 26 of the Ley 027 2010.

[18] See Arts 28–32 of the Ley 027 2010.

[19] See eg in the first semester of 2017, the three chambers solved 1,430 cases out of 1,522. TCP, *Rendición Pública de Cuentas – Informe Parcial I 2017 (Primer Semestre)*: tcpbolivia.bo/tcp/sites/default/files/pdf/rendicion/RPC_PARCIAL_AGOSTO_2017.pdf.

Most of the TCP's docket comprised decisions solving appeals against other courts' rulings that have resolved an action protecting fundamental rights.[20] In 2015, for example, 88.14 per cent per cent of the new cases were *acciones de amparo* or *acciones de libertad*. In 2016's second semester, the TCP released 2,109 decisions solving fundamental rights claims, out of a total of 2,234 rulings.[21]

As I stated earlier, this chapter only focuses on 40 judicial decisions enacted by the TCP between 2012 and 2018. This period coincides with the Evo Morales regime, and I ignored the decisions passed by the transitory tribunal that worked before 2012.[22] Even though the TCP frequently cites judicial decisions enacted before 2012,[23] I excluded the rulings enacted before that year because the TCP followed different organisational rules and its judges were appointed in different ways.[24] In other words, even though both the transitory tribunal and the TCP were supposed to enforce the 2009 Constitution, they were different judicial bodies. For the same reasons, I also excluded the decisions enacted by the Constitutional Court that operated before the 2009 Constitution was implemented.[25]

C. The Judges

Since its independence, Bolivia has had 17 constitutions,[26] but Bolivian constitution-makers only implemented the first Constitutional Court in 1998.[27] Before the 2009 Constitution was enacted, the Evo Morales regime had managed to dismantle the Constitutional Court that operated between 2006 and 2007 with a combination of impeachment threats, judicial resignations, and the MAS capacity to paralyse new appointments procedures.[28] The 2009 Constitution established the current Court: the TCP, which started to operate in 2012.[29]

[20] TCP, *Informe de Gestión 2015*: tcpbolivia.bo/tcp/sites/default/files/pdf/rendicion/INFORME_FINAL_2015.pdf.

[21] TCP (2016): *Rendición Pública de Cuentas – Informa Parcial II 2016 (Segundo Semestre)*, tcpbolivia.bo/tcp/sites/default/files/images/pdf/RendicionDeCuentas/Rendicion_TCP_II_2016_FINAL.pdf.

[22] The TCP started to review the cases that were brought after 31 December 2011. The transition was regulated by Ley 212 2011. See BW Arias López, 'Estado de Transición Constitucional y Nuevas Líneas Jurisprudenciales Del Tribunal Constitucional Boliviano' (2011) 12 *Revista Boliviana de Derecho* 44.

[23] See TCP SCP 1954/2014, 426/2015-3.

[24] While the transitory tribunal was mainly composed of interim judges appointed by President Evo Morales, judges of the TCP were popularly elected. See Decreto Supremo 432 2010.

[25] Although it makes sense not to consider the judicial decisions enacted by the Court that was in place before the Morales Constitution replaced it with a new institution – as it operated under a different Constitution and the judicial body had a different institutional design – some of the decisions of that Court have been cited by the later TCP when looking for precedents to justify its doctrines. Examples of important judicial decisions of that time are the rulings that elaborated the constitutional block doctrine, which incorporates rights of international human rights law to the set of rights that the court can enforce. See STC 95/2001. The constitutional block doctrine was later incorporated in the 2009 constitutional text.

[26] See G Negretto, 'Replacing and Amending Constitutions: The Logic of Constitutional Change in Latin America' (2012) 46 *Law & Society Review* 749, 752; Elkins (n 8).

[27] See the Ley 1836 1998.

[28] See A Castagnola and A Pérez-Liñán, 'Bolivia. The Rise (and Fall) of Judicial Review' in G Helmke and J Ríos-Figueroa (eds), *Courts in Latin America* (Cambridge University Press, 2011) 299–302; Lehoucq (n 2) 119–20. Also, See G Helmke and JK Staton, 'The Puzzling Judicial Politics of Latin America: A Theory of Litigation, Judicial Decisions, and Interbranch Conflict' in G Helmke and J Ríos-Figueroa (eds), *Courts in Latin America* (Cambridge University Press, 2011) 308.

[29] Besides the 2009 Constitution and its amendments, relevant statutory legislation should also be considered. See the following pieces of legislation: Ley 027 2010, Ley 212 2011, and the Ley 254 2012.

The TCP was composed of seven elected judges and seven substitute judges. However, a 2017 amendment increased the number to nine.[30] The electoral process required that two-thirds should approve judicial candidates of the legislative assembly. Specific quotas were needed, among other rules.[31] The MAS had the necessary votes to control the judicial nominations. Judges served for six non-renewable years, and the Electoral Organ controlled the electoral information given to the voters.

An issue that has become important among scholars studying the TCP is whether its judges are truly independent. The design of the judges' careers may seem to impair their true independence, mainly because of their nomination procedure and their exceptionally brief tenure. One possible indicator – but not a definitive one – is whether the TCP can rule against the incumbent regime. The TCP has ruled, at least partially, against challenged statutes, decrees, or lower court decisions in 24 out of 34 cases – six cases cannot be categorised like this.

Despite these numbers showing that the TCP can confront incumbent authorities, some scholars have still questioned the independence of the TCP.[32] They have reported how the regime opponents distrusted the TCP as a partial and unreliable institution,[33] criticised the judicial electoral process,[34] denounced that the elections merely confirm the partisan nominations made by the assembly,[35] complained against a possible impeachment against constitutional judges,[36] and even questioned the economic vulnerability of judges that cannot run for re-election after a brief judicial term.[37] As I show later in this chapter, the decisions associated with the *insurance* function of the TCP suggest that the TCP played a role in allowing MAS regime to become hegemonic during the Evo Morales administration. This partly confirms the scholars' scepticism.

D. Legal Scholarship and Constitutional Reasoning

It is helpful to distinguish between scholars working within the Bolivian constitutional system and comparative or global scholars with an *outsiders*' perspective. The latter group of authors typically group the 2009 Bolivian Constitution with the 'neobolivarian'

[30] Ley N° 960.

[31] See Arts. 197–199 of the Bolivian Constitution, and Ó Antonio Millán Terán, 'El Sistema Electoral Para La Elección de Los Magistrados Del Tribunal Constitucional Plurinacional' (2015) 35 *Ciencia y Cultura* 107.

[32] See eg MA Baldivieso Jinés, 'La Independencia En La Administración de Justicia. Elección de Autoridades Judiciales En Bolivia' (2012) *Anuario de Derecho Constitucional Latinoamericano* 349, 352–53; E Cícero Landívar Mosiño, 'Indigenismo y Constitución En Bolivia (Un Enfoque Desde 1990 a La Fecha)' (2015) 19 *Revista Boliviana de Derecho* 470, 504; Millán Terán (n 31) 123–26.

[33] GI Deheza, 'Bolivia 2011: Gobernando Con El Conflicto' (2012) 32 *Revista de Ciencia Política* 31, 38; A Driscoll and MJ Nelson, 'The 2011 Judicial Elections in Bolivia' (2012) 31 *Electoral Studies* 628, 630.

[34] Driscoll and Nelson (n 33); A Driscoll and MJ Nelson, 'Judicial Selection and the Democratization of Justice: Lessons from the Bolivian Judicial Elections' (2015) 3 *Journal of Law and Courts* 115; A Driscoll, 'Bolivia's "Democracy in Transition": More Questions than Answers in 2016' (2017) 37 *Revista de Ciencia Política* 255.

[35] R Baldivieso Guzmán, 'Breve Examen de Algunos Temas Constitucionales' (2012) 14 *Revista Boliviana de Derecho* 10, 18–19.

[36] W Durán Ribera, 'La Constitución Vigente y Sus Leyes de Desarrollo. ¿Guardan Compatibilidad Con La Idea Estado de Derecho?' (2011) 11 *Revista Boliviana de Derecho* 6, 17.

[37] FB Escobar Pacheco and AM Russo, 'Elección Popular de Jueces En Bolivia: Aportes Del Derecho Constitucional Comparado al Debate' (2019) *XXV Anuario de Derecho Constitucional Latinoamericano* 657, 676–77.

trend that started with the 1999 Venezuelan Constitution, and also include the 2008 Ecuadorian Constitution.[38] The neobolivarian movement developed a left-wing socialist constitutional idea that mixed indigenous and post-colonial elements[39] with a personalised perspective on political representation and institutional legitimacy.[40] This made sense for the MAS regime. After all, Morales was a crucial indigenous leader, and Bolivia possesses a high number of indigenous peoples.[41] The Constitution also emphasised the MAS transformative project, giving an enhanced role to the executive branch and relaxing the checks and balances principle. However, contrary to other transformative constitutional projects such as those of Colombia (1991) and South Africa (1996), the Bolivian transformative project did not require establishing a strong and independent court able to challenge the regime. For this reason, one may think, as Jorge Roa does, that the Bolivian Constitution was not a truly transformative project.[42] If judicial independence is a necessary condition for transformative constitutionalism, then Roa is correct. Nevertheless, most scholars will probably agree that the Bolivian constitutional project had transformative goals[43] and even recognise that the TCP helped advance those aims.[44]

Most of the comparative literature studying the TCP focused on either the insurance or the enabling function, but not on both. Scholars looking at the enabling function generally agree that the TCP has achieved its purposes. For example, they have claimed that the TCP has recognised indigenous and social rights, reaffirmed the plurinational nature of the new state and the decolonisation process, and enforced InterAmerican human rights law, among other associated tasks.[45] On the other side of the spectrum, scholars focusing on the insurance function generally examine the cases regarding Evo Morales' re-election to argue that the TCP has failed to protect core democratic principles.[46] My findings appear to show that there are arguments to confirm both types of scholarship: while the reason-giving activity of the TCP supports the values and principles of the transformative constitution, it also helped to justify the removal of term limits in favour of a political coalition that attempted to become hegemonic.

From an internal scholarly perspective, the evaluation and description of the TCP tend to be legalistic and sometimes formalistic. Scholars are interested, for example, in

[38] See P King, 'Neo-Bolivarian Constitutional Design' in DJ Galligan and M Versteeg (eds), *Social and Political Foundations of Constitutions* (Cambridge University Press, 2013); Elkins (n 8).

[39] See the Constitution's preamble.

[40] JM Díaz de Valdés and S Verdugo, 'The ALBA Constitutional Project and Political Representation' (2019) 17 *International Journal of Constitutional Law* 479.

[41] Comisión Económica para América Latina y el Caribe (CEPAL), *Los Pueblos Indígenas En América Latina. Avances En El Último Decenio y Retos Pendientes Para La Garantía de Sus Derechos* (Naciones Unidas, 2014).

[42] See J Roa, 'El Rol Del Juez Constitucional En El Constitucionalismo Transformador Latinoamericano' [2020] MPIL *Research Paper* No. 2020-11.

[43] See A von Bogdandy et al (eds), *Transformative Constitutionalism in Latin America: The Emergence of a New Ius Commune* (Oxford University Press, 2017); A von Bogdandy, 'Ius Constitutionale Commune En América Latina: Observations on Transformative Constitutionalism' (2015) 109 *AJIL Unbound* 109.

[44] See eg Attard Bellido (n 14).

[45] See eg ibid 413–14.

[46] See eg J Cortez Salinas, 'El Tribunal Constitucional Plurinacional de Bolivia. Cómo Se Distribuye El Poder Institucional' (2014) 139 *Boletín Mexicano de Derecho Comparado* 287; LA Nocera, 'Contradicciones constitucionales: el Tribunal Constitucional Plurinacional boliviano y la reelección de morales. ¿Una práctica de abusivismo?' (2019) 23 *Anuario Iberoamericano de Justicia Constitucional* 491.

claiming that the TCP decisions are final and that appeals are not allowed.[47] Despite some concerns about the fact that the TCP's statute also empowers the legislative assembly to interpret the Constitution, most scholars tend to agree that the Constitution requires the TCP's interpretation to be final.[48] Those scholars are also interested in the interpretation tools that the TCP is supposed to follow. According to the Constitution, the TCP should preferably use the will of the constitution-makers according to the documents, acts and resolutions of the constituent assembly, and the literal meaning of the constitutional text.[49] The TCP's statute adds that judges should use a systematic, contextual, and teleological approach to the Constitution[50] and that the rights included in international treaties should be enforced when their norms are more 'favourable'.[51] State actions are presumed compatible with the Constitution until the TCP declares its unconstitutionality.[52]

However, the Constitution does not detail a more precise methodology, and the way those tools of interpretation should be used seems to remain vague. It appears, as one scholar has tried to show, that the interpreter should use both the originalist and textualist tools simultaneously and that those tools do not exclude using other criteria.[53] Moreover, some scholars note that the conflictive nature of Bolivia's constitution-making process – including the unavailability of many documents, the lack of genuine debates and a true legal consensus – raises practical difficulties for the originalist method,[54] and early cases show that the TCP does not typically explain the methodology it uses.[55]

The vagueness of the tools of interpretation adds another complication: the TCP is also supposed to interpret constitutional and legal texts that include several open-textured principles. For example, the Constitution establishes a list of moral principles taken from indigenous cultures, such as the principle of preventing people from becoming lazy (*Ama Qhilla*) and the harmonious life-principle (*ñandereko*),[56] it provides an extensive list of principles such as dignity, equilibrium, a peaceful state, redistribution, and social justice,[57] and it recognises constitutional hierarchy to international human rights treaties.[58] Statutory legislation also adds some principles. For example, the statutory legislation regulating the TCP establishes 13 principles such as social harmony and peace culture.[59]

[47] Art 203 of the Bolivian Constitution. See TCP SCP 1954/2014. See E Peña Venegas, 'Aspectos de Interpretación Constitucional Ante La Nueva Constitución Política Del Estado Plurinacional de Bolivia' (2015) 19 *Revista Boliviana de Derecho* 428, 436; MA Baldivieso Jinés, 'Interpretación Constitucional En Bolivia (¿Suicidio Del TCP? Estudio de Caso)' (2017) 23 *Revista Boliviana de Derecho* 16, 29–30.

[48] See a discussion in AE Vargas Lima, 'Reflexiones Críticas Sobre La Nueva Ley Del Tribunal Constitucional Plurinacional En Bolivia' (2011) 9 *Estudios Constitucionales* 639, 661–66. Also, H Andaluz Vegacenteno, 'Constitución, Derechos y Jurisprudencia' (2013) 15 *Revista Boliviana de Derecho* 10, 35.

[49] Art 196.II of the Bolivian Constitution.

[50] Art 6.II, Ley 027 2010.

[51] Art. 2.II, Ley 254 2012.

[52] Art. 5, Ley 027 2010.

[53] Andaluz Vegacenteno (n 48) 39–40.

[54] Vargas Lima, 'Reflexiones Críticas Sobre La Nueva Ley Del Tribunal Constitucional Plurinacional En Bolivia' (n 48) 668. Also, Andaluz Vegacenteno (n 48) 29. On the conflictive nature of the Bolivian constitution-making process, see J de la Fuente Jeria, 'El Difícil Parto de Otra Democracia: La Asamblea Constituyente de Bolivia' (2010) 45 *Latin American Research Review* 5.

[55] Andaluz Vegacenteno (n 48) 29.

[56] See Art 8.I of the Bolivian Constitution.

[57] See Arts 1, 8.II, 9 and 10 of the Bolivian Constitution.

[58] Art 410.II of the Bolivian Constitution.

[59] Art 3, Ley 027 2010, and Art 4, Ley 254 2012.

If we consider that Bolivian judges are elected, that the Bolivian Constitution is rich in open-textured principles and ambiguous in its rules of interpretation, it is reasonable to assume that the Court can become a consequential actor, particularly in its enabling role. The later sections show examples that seem to confirm that the justifications given by the TCP fit with this assumption.

II. Arguments in Constitutional Reasoning

This section discusses examples of reasons that the TCP has given to justify decisions in specific cases, considering the 40 selected judicial decisions. As I am not interested in identifying the average or median rulings but landmark and politically salient decisions, I did not select the judicial decisions randomly. Instead, I used a guided selection procedure to include diverse themes and consider the decisions' importance. Even though this procedure does not allow for generalisation, examining 40 decisions that meet these features is helpful because they illustrate the kinds of arguments that the TCP develops when engaging with those cases. I considered the rulings highlighted by the TCP on its website as 'relevant rulings,'[60] which generally emphasise decisions that are doctrinally relevant by, for example, consolidating or explaining a specific legal doctrine in matters such as the due process in criminal cases and privacy rights. I also added judicial decisions that legal scholars have cited in the *Revista Boliviana de Derecho* and other judicial decisions that have been important for political reasons – ie, decisions engaging with term limits.

The sample includes 27 rulings that engage with fundamental rights, 19 rulings that solve state structure issues, and 18 decisions partly based on due process arguments. Governmental agencies initiated 15 cases. Even though the selected cases are not representative of the TCP's general docket, all the chosen decisions are significant for legal or political reasons. Many can be understood as landmark cases. As landmark cases typically involve innovative arguments and larger justifications, we should not expect those rulings to be good examples of the ordinary practice of the TCP.

A. The Structure of Constitutional Arguments

The TCP has elaborated a practice of providing abstract arguments that are not connected to the legal issue at stake to justify concrete rulings. This is connected to the way the TCP uses the idea of a precedent – see below – but it is not the only example. Another example relates to the right to legal security. The TCP started explaining Article 1 of the Constitution, the meaning of the decolonisation project, the need to transcend the liberal state, and the importance of neo-constitutionalism.[61] Confirming this practice of including many values and principles, sometimes unrelated to the case, the data extracted from the 40 selected decisions show that, among those 40 cases, 17 have parallel conclusive arguments and 18 rulings use a parallel, individually inconclusive argument. The TCP does not really use one-line arguments, and the use of obiter dictum is widespread.

[60] See tcpbolivia.bo/tcp/. The 'relevant rulings' showed by the website can vary.
[61] TCP SCP 1787/2013. See also TCP DCP 8/2014.

B. Types of Arguments in Constitutional Reasoning

i. Analogies

I only found one case in which the TCP arguably used an argument structured in the form of an analogy. However, the TCP used the idea of an analogy not as a ratio decidendi, but to explain how precedent should work.[62] According to the TCP, to be used as a precedent, a previous decision should have similar facts to the new case, which involves the use of an analogical argument for the TCP. I will come back to the use of precedents later.

ii. Debating the Applicability of the Constitution

The TCP rarely discusses whether the Constitution is applicable to the case or not, as it usually assumes that it is. I did not find cases invoking a doctrine such as the political question doctrine. However, it is possible that the TCP discusses whether a specific mechanism included in the Constitution is applicable to the case in point. I found two cases. In one of them, for example, the TCP argued that the amparo legal action was not able, in that case, to protect the right to legal security.[63]

In contrast, the TCP has expanded the applicability of the Constitution to cases where the legal action was formulated in a non-constitutional formal manner. According to the TCP, The Bolivian Constitution recognises the principle of direct applicability of the fundamental rights, which requires that formal requirements should not be invoked to prevent their protection and that specific remedies should be understood in a flexible way.[64] For example, the TCP has declared that it is 'obliged to protect all the rights, even dispensing from the hateful formalism'.[65] It has also stated that the principle of direct application requires rights to have 'full effectiveness beyond [...] extreme formalities that may prevent their full validity'.[66] In another decision, the TCP has also stated that judicial and administrative procedures should not only be constituted by simple formal norms but that it should secure 'full rights' efficacy', including material justice, due process, and fundamental rights.[67]

Sometimes the TCP identifies and is aware of a formal or procedural irregularity that, legally, should make the TCP reject a claim. However, it relaxes the formal and procedural requirements when it generally identifies that a minority or underprivileged group has been harmed. In one case, the TCP argued that errors in presenting the legal actions should not prevent the judges from exercising jurisdiction.[68] With similar arguments, the TCP has also expanded the scope of the '*acción de amparo*' to a takings case so that a possible rights infringement can be evaluated by a judge when a specialised jurisdiction

[62] TCP SCP 846/2012.
[63] TCP SCP 1787/2013.
[64] Andaluz Vegacenteno (n 48) 14–15.
[65] TCP SCP 1864/2013. Also, See TCP SCP 1357/2013, SCP 828/2014.
[66] TCP SCP 790/2012. Also, See TCP SCP 691/2017-S3.
[67] TCP SCP 140/2012.
[68] TCP SCP 258/2012. See also of a case in which the TCP relaxes the requirements of a legal remedy, though it is not part of the 40 selected decisions, in TCP SCP 1478/2012.

does not yet exist.[69] Another example considers a case where the TCP decided that the 'reconduction' of a legal action that was presented wrongly, is possible to benefit exclusively those who have impaired difficulties, minorities, indigenous peoples, people from African descent, the elderly and pregnant women.[70] Sometimes this type of decision is justified with a decolonial argument based on the need to abandon the formalism typically associated with classic colonial constitutionalism to advance material principles.[71]

iii. Ordinary Meaning of the Words of the Constitution

The TCP sometimes uses the literal text as an argument, connected to the ordinary meaning of the words. Although this seems to be a common practice – and a constitutionally required tool of interpretation – the TCP has rarely acknowledged this practice explicitly. I counted only three cases where the TCP openly invokes a provision's literal meaning. An example includes a case in which the TCP expressly appealed to an article's 'literal sense'.[72] The TCP has also declared that a literal interpretation of an infra-constitutional rule may violate the Constitution and that the constitutional interpretative tools should be preferred, such as the *pro homine* principle.[73]

iv. Harmonising Arguments

The TCP frequently uses harmonising arguments (I counted 21 cases), as it is part of one of the preferred ways to make sense of how legal norms should be compatibilised with the Constitution. It also uses harmonising arguments to make sense of domestic and international law: 18 rulings cite international instruments, 19 decisions refer to other sources of international law, and 14 rulings quote soft law norms. Only 14 cases omit any reference to international law.

Inter-American human rights law seems particularly important, though it is not the only quoted international source. The TCP tends to invoke the block of constitutionality, a legal doctrine that considers international human rights and constitutional rights part of the same canon. I'll come back to that doctrine later.

Sometimes the use of international human rights law is used in an arguably deceiving or decorative way. An important example is a decision regarding the removal of term limits. In that case, the TCP argued that term limits infringe the political rights recognised in Article 23 of the American Convention on Human Rights. It also claimed constitutional term limits involved a sort of discrimination, violating Article 24 of the Convention. The TCP cited some decontextualised decisions from the Inter-American Court of Human Rights in supporting these arguments.[74] However, none of the cases related to the issue, but the TCP used them to argue that American Convention required the TCP to enforce those Articles against national norms. The TCP arguments were

[69] TCP SCP 693/2012.
[70] TCP SCP 617/2016-S2.
[71] See TCP SCP 487/2014.
[72] TCP SCP 2143/2012.
[73] TCP SCP 874/2014.
[74] TCP SCP 84/2017, at 15–57.

wrong.[75] The Inter-American Court had never reviewed term limits (in fact, it later claimed that there was no human right to be re-elected[76]) as the Venice Commission had previously stated.[77]

v. Precedents

There is an argument to be made saying that the Bolivian Constitution requires the TCP to respect its previous precedents because of the equal protection and legal security clauses.[78] The TCP recognised this idea in a landmark case conceptualising a doctrine regarding the use of precedents in 2012,[79] The TCP added that Article 203, referring to the obligatory nature of the TCP's judicial decisions, included a stare decisis legal effect. The TCP added that its jurisprudence is a direct source of law, that precedents are crucial for the legal system's coherence, and that changing the precedents is possible. It also differentiated between dicta and genuine precedents.

Looking at the 40 decisions of the sample, one can find that the TCP frequently and almost always cites previous decisions to justify a ruling – 39 out of 40 cases cite previous decisions. Also, it is normal for the TCP to reproduce paragraphs that were included in those previous decisions literally. However, it is uncommon to see the TCP referring to the specific legal issue that was solved in the cited previous case. The previous rulings are typically presented in a decontextualised way, and they generally consist of literal reproductions of abstract forms to understand specific principles or constitutional norms. Many cases are not genuinely related to the substantive law applicable to the case but secondary themes. For example, they reproduce paragraphs reflecting on the use of the TCP's powers or general doctrines that are irrelevant to the controversy. These rulings are part of an obiter dictum argument. Thus, it is unclear whether the promise included in the doctrine of the 2012 decision can be sustained.

The TCP may generally cite previous rulings to show additional – but unnecessary – justifications for its outcomes. Still, it is also possible that a genuine commitment to legal consistency exists. That commitment may be reflected in the fact that the TCP publishes what it understands as '*sentencias relevantes*' on its website, a list of selected rulings the TCP highlights to the legal community.

However, even though a practice of referring to previous decisions seems to exist, the methodology is somehow arbitrary or unexplained – how the cited cases were selected? – it is unclear whether the cases the TCP citations are engaging with the same legal issues at stake – they are usually presented in a decontextualised way – and, therefore, it is unlikely for the TCP to use techniques such as *distinguishing*.

[75] D Landau and R Dixon, 'Abusive Judicial Review: Courts Against Democracy' (2020) 53 *UC Davis Law Review* 1362–63; S E Roca Serrano, 'La Injerencia del Órgano Ejecutivo sobre el Tribunal Constitucional: El Caso Boliviano' (2020) 37 *Academia Colombiana de Jurisprudencia* 235.

[76] *Interamerican Court of Human Rights* OC-28/21, 7 June 2021.

[77] See Venice Commission's criticisms against the decision in European Commission for Democracy Through Law (Venice Commission), *Report on Term – Limits* (Part I, pp 16–17) CDL – AD (2018). Another example shows that the TCP also tends to invoke international law in a vague and unclear way, without referring to a particular instrument and using phrases such as 'from the comprehension of the different national and international instruments …'. TCP SCP 874/2014.

[78] See eg Andaluz Vegacenteno (n 48) 37.

[79] TCP SCP 846/2012. Also, see Attard Bellido (n 14) 415; Andaluz Vegacenteno (n 48) 33.

vi. Doctrinal Analysis of Legal Concepts or Principles

The TCP sometimes analyses legal concepts of principles in a lengthy way. I show two connected examples: the constitutional block doctrine and the idea of legal pluralism.

The Bolivian version of the block of constitutionality involves abandoning the universalistic approach to human rights and recognising a pluralistic and inter-cultural perspective that seeks to secure the population's wellbeing.[80] The doctrine includes the protection of international human rights law,[81] which arguably possesses a supra-constitutional legal value,[82] and the existence of a pluralistic judicial review system composed of several judicial systems, such as the indigenous jurisdiction – all of which are subject to the TCP's jurisdiction.[83] The TCP remains the apex court. The 2009 Constitution recognises these features explicitly, and they became operative before the new TCP was actually implemented in 2012. However, the origin of the block of constitutionality doctrine in Bolivia can be connected to previous judicial decisions that considered rulings from the Inter-American Court of Human Rights,[84] and the rulings of the previous Constitutional Court operating before the enactment of the 2009 Constitution.[85]

The TCP has also conceptualised the kind of legal pluralism that the plurinational State requires. For the TCP, legal pluralism should enable an inter-cultural dialogue supported by the fact that there is no unique source of law and the need to constantly seek a new meaning for the rights involved in the specific cases.[86]

The TCP has repeatedly reaffirmed the integration of international human rights treaties within the constitutional canon,[87] and restated its mission in protecting fundamental rights, typically with a strong language – though many of the phrases included in those decisions are dicta. For example, it has recognised the constitutional rights' 'principle of direct and effective application' to avoid the need for 'legislative recognition or extreme formalisms' that could prevent the rights' application.[88] It has also stated that the new State's model is justified by rights included in the constitutional block, which 'breaks with the neoliberal State' and 'redirects the country towards a social model where the search for the well-being predominates'.[89] Moreover, the TCP

[80] Attard Bellido (n 14) 417.

[81] The TCP's landmark decision interpreting the 2009 Constitution in this way is earlier than the period this chapter examines. See TCP SCP 110/2010-R.

[82] Compare Durán Ribera (n 36) 10; Andaluz Vegacenteno (n 48) 16.

[83] See eg TCP SCP 300/2012, SCP 1227/2012, SCP 2143/2012, DCP 6/2013 and SCP 778/2014. Also, Negrón Pino (n 14).

[84] See Arias López (n 22) 110–11; Andaluz Vegacenteno (n 48) 15–17; AE Vargas Lima, 'La Evolución Histórica Del Control de Constitucionalidad En Bolivia y Su Proyección Hacia Un Modelo Plural' (2018) 13 *Precedente* 81, 105–107.

[85] AE Vargas Lima, 'Los Principios Ético-Morales de La Sociedad Plural y El Bloque de Constitucionalidad. Configuración y Desarrollo En La Jurisprudencia Constitucional Boliviana' (2016) 14 *Estudios Constitucionales* 15, 46–47.

[86] TCP SCP 790/2012.

[87] See eg TCP SCP 972/2014, SCP 783/2015 and SCP 6/2016. Sometimes the reference to international law is vague and lacks a particular reference to a specific international instrument. See eg TCP SCP 874/2014, 37/2018-S4.

[88] TCP SCP 0790/2012.

[89] TCP SCP 1864/2013.

has also declared itself part of the 'neo-constitutionalist' tradition.[90] These types of statements are supposed to be obligatory for the TCP.[91]

vii. Arguments from Silence

The TCP rarely uses arguments from silence. I only found two cases. One of them, referring to whether a local government can use the due process clause to uphold an expropriation, identified a regulatory gap and claimed that it left the parties without access to justice. The TCP concluded that there must be a procedure.[92]

viii. Objective Teleological Arguments

Appealing to the purpose of the text of the Constitution is a standard practice of the TCP. The data shows that the TCP invoked the purpose of the norms in 36 cases. However, many of those arguments refer to reasons unrelated to the court's conclusions.

ix. Subjective Teleological Arguments

Teleological arguments of this kind are constitutionally required. According to Article 196.II of the Bolivian Constitution, the TCP is supposed to seek the will of the constituent power in the 'documents, acts and resolutions, and also on the literal meaning of the text'.[93] The TCP has invoked the intention of the constitution-makers in 14 out of the 40 cases. However, the way the TCP refers to these types of historical arguments varies. Sometimes the TCP is not precise and avoids referring to a specific document, act, or resolution.

An example is related to how the TCP has ruled in favour of the MAS interests when the cases involved high stakes, as these cases provide an opportunity to check the purpose of the constitution-makers. In 2013, the Legislative Assembly enacted a statute – the *Ley de Aplicación Normativa* – allowing Evo Morales and his vice-president to run for re-election, despite a provision that explicitly forbade this option – ie, the *Disposición Transitoria Primera*. In reviewing the statute, which aimed at 'interpreting' the Constitution, the TCP's plenary declared that the sovereign constituent power had established a new state and, therefore, the term limits were rebooted.[94] Thus, the TCP upheld the statute's constitutionality and, despite protests from the opposition, Morales and his vice-president could run for re-election. They won the re-election. In its decision, the TCP conceptualised the constituent power doctrine, defended its sovereign nature, and argued that the new Constitution had established a new state. The TCP also argued that the legislative assembly had derivative constituent power and that it could therefore detail the constitutional norms.[95] None of those arguments helped explain

[90] See eg TCP SCP 1787/2013 and SCP 2180/2012.

[91] CA Goitia Caballero, 'El Derecho a Una Acción Directa de Inconstitucionalidad' (2015) 35 *Ciencia y Cultura* 85, 99.

[92] TCP SCP 693/2012.

[93] TCP SCP 0084/2017, Arts 58–59.

[94] TCP DCP 3/2013. Also, Cortez Salinas (n 46).

[95] The TCP only questioned a specific non-related rule regarding the assembly's power to approve the budget law. TCP DCP 3/2013.

why legislators could enact a statute contradicting and modifying the literal meaning of a constitutional clause,[96] as they only focused on secondary considerations.[97]

Another argument came when the TCP declared the unconstitutionality of term limits. The TCP cited a report enacted by one of the constituent assembly's committees to claim that the constituent power's original will was to allow consecutive re-elections.[98] The TCP did not consider that constitutional designers added the term limits later in the constitution-making process as part of the negotiations with Morales' opponents. Instead, it assumed that a small number of constitution-makers could represent the original constituent power. The TCP's originalist methodology was opaque and selective. So far, it seems that the TCP lacks a predicable originalist methodology.

x. Non-Legal Arguments

The Bolivian Constitution includes many principles and norms that have a moral, sociological, or economic component. However, technically those elements are 'legal' as they explicitly form part of the Constitution, which may justify a claim saying that, after all, when the TCP refers to them, it is acting using an inclusive positivist rationale. In other words, the TCP does not need to invoke non-legal ideas to justify the protection of many social, economic, and moral principles. 31 rulings include principles and norms that have explicit legal recognition, though many (19, to be exact) could connect to social and economic rights, for example.

xi. References to Scholarly Works

The TCP sometimes refers to the work of scholars. In my sample, it did so in 17 out of the 40 rulings. Those decisions tend to be the lengthier and more politically salient ones. For example, in one of the decisions that helped to consolidate Morales' rule, the TCP cited some scholars, such as the Spanish scholar, Ignacio de Otto,[99] to defend the constituent power doctrine and interpret the 2009 Constitution using the lenses of that doctrine. Another example shows that the TCP cited Robert Alexy and Luis Prieto Sanchíz to explain how fundamental rights can be treated as principles.[100]

xii. References to Foreign (National) Law

The TCP has invoked foreign law from other Latin American jurisdictions nine times and non-Latin American jurisdictions eight times. For example, in a case regarding the application of retroactive laws in criminal cases, the TCP cited the Colombian Constitutional Court to reflect on the nature of judicial decisions that are supposed to

[96] An observer claims that this decision helped to 'mutate' the Constitution. See AE Vargas Lima, 'La Reelección Presidencial En La Jurisprudencia Del Tribunal Constitucional Plurinacional de Bolivia' (2015) 19 *Revista Boliviana de Derecho* 446, 462–65.

[97] Baldivieso Jinés (n 47) 38–39.

[98] TCP SCP 0084/2017, 59–60.

[99] TCP DCP 3/2013.

[100] TCP SCP 1787/2013.

be final.[101] However, sometimes the references to foreign law appear disconnected to the conclusions of the case. An example considers a case involving a conflict between two indigenous communities, in which the TCP cited the Constitution of Ecuador to suggest that Latin America is generally following the idea of the '*Estado Constitucional de Derecho*'.[102] Another example refers to a case about the consultation with the indigenous peoples. The TCP offers some descriptions of the idea of centralised judicial review, mentioning the courts of Germany, Spain, Colombia, and Peru as examples.[103]

xiii. Pro Homine *Principle*

The TCP has used the *pro homine* principle in 13 cases. A deceiving example is the case of the removal of the term limits, in which the TCP invoked that principle to give more weight to the political rights recognised in the American Convention on Human Rights.[104]

C. The Overall Weight of the Arguments

Even though the Bolivian Constitution includes interpretation rules, I don't think that the TCP has built, at least considering the cases I have reviewed, a precise way to weigh the different kinds of arguments it uses. Sure, the block of constitutionality, the will of the constitution-maker, and indigenous ideas such as the wellbeing of the people seem to be central in some instances, but it would be a mistake, at least considering the 40 decisions analysed, to build from those cases to generalise a precise method that can assess how those ideas prevail over others. On the contrary, the vague way the TCP uses the idea of the precedent and how the TCP structures its arguments – see section II(B) v – makes this type of exercise challenging. Half of the decisions of the TCP seem to include an equal proportion between ratio decidendi, obiter dictum arguments, and merely decorative or arguably deceptive arguments, and 13 cases mainly presented decorative arguments. Of course, separating what is a mere decorative argument working as obiter dictum and what is the actual reasoning supporting specific outcomes is not an exercise that can be achieved merely by examining the reasons given by the TCP. However, many arguments that are disconnected from the conclusions seem to suggest that this proportion is plausible.

D. Judicial Candour and Judicial Rhetoric

The rulings of the TCP typically fit the following structure: first, the TCP presents the type of procedure and the names of the parties. It then narrates the process, summarising the facts presented by the legal action, the petitioners' legal claims, and explaining

101 TCP SCP 770/2012.
102 TCP SCP 778/2014.
103 TCP SCP 2143/2012.
104 TCP SCP 84/2017, 15–57.

the previous procedural steps. It also outlines the defenders' arguments and, if applicable, the decisions made by the lower judges. After that information is presented, the TCP presents some conclusions on what it considers relevant to start its reasoning. Then, the TCP explains the legal grounds. This is usually the longest part of the ruling, which also includes a summary or reproduction of the legal and constitutional provisions that regulate the procedure. It consists of an explanation of the norms and a reference to previous decisions on them. The rulings then dedicate some paragraphs to explaining how the norms apply to the case. In the end, the TCP enumerates its conclusions. The dissenting opinions are not included in this document, but in separate documents. When the TCP examines an abstract review of a piece of legislation, the structure changes accordingly.

E. Length, Dissenting and Concurring Opinions

The TCP's decisions vary in length. The 40 rulings extension varies from seven to 177 pages, and the average is 31.75. These numbers do not consider a judicial style common in the TCP's jurisprudence: many paragraphs – sometimes pages – literally reproducing parts of previous judicial decisions.[105]

Regarding the existence of dissenting opinions, though the civil law tradition generally prohibits dissenting opinions or promotes anonymous and unanimous decisions,[106] Bolivia, like other Latin American constitutional courts,[107] allows and publishes separate judicial votes. Nevertheless, in Bolivia, dissenting opinions are typically not included in the same document that contains the majority decision but in different documents. One may expect judicial opinions to become more frequent when politically salient cases or landmark rulings exist. Among the cases examined, nine out of 31 have dissenting votes. Most of the dissenting opinions (seven out of nine) were released in cases solved by the TCP's plenary. It is rare – though possible – that a small chamber will enact a decision including a dissenting opinion, perhaps because it may be easier to achieve consensus in a two-judge chamber.

The existence of dissenting opinions could be an indicator associated with assessing the judges' independence. From one perspective, publishing judicial dissents may allow internal fragmentation to become public, and judges will be able to speak to different audiences. From another perspective, judges with short judicial tenures, such as the judges of the Bolivian TCP, may find that the possibility of publishing judicial dissenting opinions can make them accountable to whoever has the power to influence the judges' post-court career. If there are possible consequences, they may prefer to release anonymous or unanimous decisions. A high number of dissenting opinions may indicate

[105] See eg TCP SCP 783/2015-S1, SCP 60/2016, SCP 575/2016-S3, SCP 93/2017.

[106] See eg P Pasquino, 'E Pluribus Unum – Disclosed and Undisclosed Vote in Constitutional/Supreme Courts' in J Elster (ed), *Secrecy and Publicity in Votes and Debates* (Cambridge University Press, 2015).

[107] See eg D Werneck Arguelhes and L Molhano Ribeiro, 'The Court, It Is I? Individual Judicial Powers in the Brazilian Supreme Court and Their Implications for Constitutional Theory' (2018) 7 *Global Constitutionalism* 236; S Basabe-Serrano, 'Determinants of Judicial Dissent in Contexts of Extreme Institutional Instability: The Case of Ecuador's Constitutional Court' (2014) 6 *Journal of Politics in Latin America* 83; LB Tiede, 'The Political Determinants of Judicial Dissent. Evidence from the Chilean Constitutional Tribunal' (2016) *European Political Science Review* 377.

independence because it will show that judges do not fear backlash when showing their genuine preferences. Even though it may seem that the rate of dissenting opinions in Bolivia may be low, considering that judges do not last very long in their positions, it is complicated with this information to argue what exactly are the reasons that explain their particular positions, as a counterfactual case is missing due to the unique nature of the Bolivian Court.

F. Framing of Constitutional Issues

27 cases examined refer to fundamental rights, and 19 relate to separation of powers or state organisation issues. Six cases cannot be classified. 18 cases relate to procedural issues, including due process of law aspects.

G. Key Concepts

The TCP has elaborated on many key concepts. It has invoked the idea of the rule of law 23 times, the concept of legal security 15 times, democracy 10 times, the nation 19 times, human dignity 22 times, justice 21 times, custom nine times, proportionality nine times, equality 28 times and basic procedural rights 23 times, and economic and social rights 19 times.[108] Post-material values are present in 28 rulings, and they often connect to indigenous principles.

This is not surprising. Indeed, some scholars believe that the Bolivian Constitution's main goal was to decolonise the country, recognise the wellbeing ('*Buen Vivir*') principle – a principle that comes from the indigenous cosmovision – and empower indigenous peoples by providing for a series of collective rights.[109] The wellbeing principle is connected to the establishment of the plurinational State and the idea of equality across peoples and generations and the recognition of the natural world – ie, the *Pachamama* – and the protection of the environment. The principle appears in the Constitution's preamble, as part of the state principle and the recognition of constitutional rights, and the TCP has used it in its jurisprudence.

An example is a case involving a controversy between two indigenous communities. In this case, the TCP declared that the paradigm of the wellbeing should guide an inter-cultural interpretation of individual and collective rights, that in inter-cultural contexts the wellbeing is part of the essential core of those rights, that the paradigm requires that the TCP solves the issue at stake considering a pluralistic method including procedures such as ordering anthropological and cultural studies or the development of dialogue within the indigenous communities.[110]

[108] Other types of arguments seem less popular in the jurisprudence of the TCP. The system of government (6), secularism (0), freedom of speech (3), right to privacy (4), family (5) and activism (1), are rarely, if ever, mentioned in the sample of cases that I reviewed.

[109] See eg H Tórtora Aravena, 'El "Buen Vivir" y Los Derechos Culturales de Naturaleza Colectiva En El Nuevo Constitucionalismo Latinoamericano Descolonizador' (2021) 28 *Revista de Derecho* (Coquimbo). Also, See Landívar Mosiño (n 32).

[110] TCP SCP 778/2014.

The TCP has repeatedly recognised the indigenous nations and peoples, along with constitutional pluralism,[111] and it has also frequently invoked indigenous principles in its rulings as direct legal mandates.[112] An example consists of a case where the TCP asked whether the principle of *Ama Qhilla* – which means, do not be lazy – applies to judges, declaring that judicial delay infringes this principle after providing an explanation of the meaning of *Ama Qhilla*.[113] In another case, involving state rights to own good acquired due to illicit activities such as drug trafficking, the TCP used the *Ama Qhilla* along with other indigenous principles like *Ama Lulla* – which means do not lie – and *Ama Suwa* – which means, do not steal, to solve the case.[114]

A critical case typically referred to in the literature is the TIPNIS case, involving the indigenous peoples' rights to be consulted when policy projects may affect their interests under the ILO Convention 169.[115] The Morales regime violated the indigenous peoples' right to be previously consulted when a measure may affect them when ordering the construction of a road crossing an indigenous territory and national park (TIPNIS). The indigenous peoples of that area protested, and the police force repressed them.[116] The authorities enacted a statute to guarantee that the road won't be built. Still, another group of indigenous peoples – which had the support of the Morales administration – initiated demonstrations against that statute.[117] The conflict within indigenous groups allowed the government to amend the mistake and begin a consultation process so that the road could be built. The government enacted a law regulating the consultation procedure, and a group of indigenous peoples asked the TCP to declare the unconstitutionality of that law. The TCP proclaimed that the law was constitutional but only if the regulation was understood as requiring that the procedure be organised in agreement with the indigenous peoples,[118] thus, challenging the government.

Other cases that I cannot fully develop here show that the TCP has generally taken seriously the evaluation of the procedures for consulting indigenous peoples or upholding indigenous rights.[119]

III. Comparative Perspective

The TCP is probably unique in the region because it is the only court that is popularly elected. It is also one of the newest courts in Latin America, established only in 2012. Compared to other courts of the region that possess a transformative aim, such as the Colombian and Ecuadorian courts, the Bolivian TCP is probably more

[111] See eg TCP DCP 6/2013. See also TCP DCP 8/2014, SCP 60/2016, SCP 93/2017.

[112] See Vargas Lima, 'Los Principios Ético-Morales de La Sociedad Plural y El Bloque de Constitucionalidad. Configuración y Desarrollo En La Jurisprudencia Constitucional Boliviana' (n 85).

[113] TCP SCP 551/2014.

[114] DCP 2/2013. See also TCP SCP 2056/2012, SCP 1422/2012, SCP 951/2012.

[115] See C Núñez González, 'Trabajo y Pueblos Originarios En Bolivia: La Integración Constitucional Del Convenio 169 de La OIT' (2017) 24 *Revista Boliviana de Derecho* 296.

[116] Landívar Mosiño (n 32) 483.

[117] ibid 484.

[118] TCP SCP 300/2012.

[119] See eg TCP SCP 1250/2012.DCP 1/2016, SCP 426/2015-3, DCP 8/2014, SCP 1787/2013, SCP 300/2012, SCP 6/2016, SCP 60/2016.

indigenous-centred. It also shares the Neobolivarian political project that has been present in countries like Venezuela and Ecuador, even though its structure and functioning differ significantly from the Venezuelan Supreme Court. Probably the court that resembles the TCP more is the Constitutional Court of Ecuador. Both courts are relatively new; both follow a centralised model of judicial review; both use teleological and precedential arguments, though selectively and lacking a clear methodology; both frequently use arguments based on due process and the rule of law, and both use post-material values. Also, the TCP is far from the courts of Chile and Guatemala, which seem to be more conservative. For example, the Chilean Court can appeal to constitutional values connected to the Christian tradition.

The TCP is also part of some shared trends in the region, for example, by invoking the idea of the block of constitutionality, which is popular in the region, and it continuously appeals to international law, even though it can sometimes use arguments taken from that trend in a legally dubious way.

IV. Evaluation, Pathology, and Criticism

The 2009 Bolivian Constitution established the TCP, replacing the previous Constitutional Court. Former president Evo Morales and the MAS promoted the constitution-making process as part of their transformative plan to decolonise Bolivia, reboot the political institutions, and protect social and indigenous rights. As I stated in the introduction, the TCP was supposed to play a double role in Bolivia's constitutional project: First, an *enabling role* aimed at helping to implement the MAS transformative project, which included the preservation and promotion of its indigenous, post-liberal, plurinational, and decolonising aims. Second, an *insurance* role aimed at protecting the core institutional arrangements of the democratic system. This chapter has focused on the TCP's activity between 2012 and 2018 and used 40 selected judicial decisions to assess how those TCP rulings have helped justify or support its double role.

After reviewing these decisions, it is easy to conclude that the TCP's constitutional reasoning helps justify the TCP's *enabling* functions. Of course, this does not mean that the TCP has succeeded in performing this function – an academic project focusing on constitutional reasoning cannot make that judgement. However, the findings suggest that the TCP seems to be loyal to its first role, at least in its reason-giving activity. Examples include decisions using post-material values, invoking the block of constitutionalism and legal pluralism, international law, and others. Nevertheless, this chapter has also identified some problems with the reason-giving activity of the TCP, particularly in the way the TCP uses the precedents and frequently presents lengthy rulings that include too many obiter dictum arguments that sometimes seem to be deceiving arguments.

The TCP's reasoning style sometimes involves rulings that are unnecessarily long, with selective arguments that lack consistent or predictable methodologies, sources cited in decontextualised ways, jumping from abstract considerations about general principles to specific solutions without explaining the connecting links, and, even though they are familiar with ideas such as dignity and proportionality, they have not yet elaborated sophisticated tests that can be used consistently, according to the facts of each case. Sure, these types of criticisms are possibly valid in other constitutional courts. What probably makes the TCP unique – or, at least, remarkable for comparativists – is the way the TCP has been able to use legal frameworks that seek to include the indigenous principles and indigenous ways to understand norms, regardless of whether the justifications used have normative or consistency flaws.

Regarding the TCP's second role – the *insurance* function – I had argued that the TCP generally favoured the incumbent regime when the political stakes were high, confirming what other scholars and I have claimed elsewhere.[120] The problem is not only related to the outcome of these types of cases. The problem is that the TCP has built unconvincing and legally dubious doctrines that arguably seem to deceive the reader with legal reasons that are highly implausible, including, following Dixon and Landau's criticism, an 'abusive' use of the constituent power theory,[121] and a wrong approach to the connection between political rights and international human rights law.

[120] See Verdugo (n 4); Landau and Dixon (n 75).

[121] See R Dixon and D Landau, *Abusive Constitutional Borrowing: Legal Globalization and the Subversion of Liberal Democracy* (Oxford University Press, 2021).

5

The Jurisprudence of the Supreme Federal Tribunal of Brazil

DIEGO WERNECK ARGUELHES, IVAR A HARTMANN AND RAFAEL BELLEM DE LIMA

I. Legal, Political, Institutional, and Academic Context

A. Legal and Political Culture as Context for Constitutional Reasoning

Brazil transitioned to democracy in 1985, with the election of the first civilian president since the military coup of 1964 established a dictatorship. In 1987, an elected National Constitutional Assembly (NCA) convened to draft a new constitution, in a delicate political climate in which the outgoing regime still exerted significant influence. The 1988 constitution, the country's eighth, is long and detailed, with hundreds of articles and more than 100 specific provisions establishing rights. It has clear transformative ambitions, with several positive rights and many clauses requiring or even directly establishing specific social policies. The constitution empowered courts, and specifically the Supreme Court (Supremo Tribunal Federal, STF). It greatly expanded access to the STF's constitutional review jurisdiction, allowing a host of public authorities, political actors, and civil society organisations to file direct, abstract review lawsuits.

In the 1990s, social expectations and the legal profession were often at odds with the STF regarding the implications of this new constitution. Though entrusted with powerful mechanisms to redeem constitutional ambitions, the Court displayed a more restrained view of the break with the authoritarian past. When the NCA convened in 1987, nine of the 11 STF judges had been appointed by the military regime. Unsurprisingly, in the first few years after the transition, the court looked at the new constitution through old lenses. Brazilian legal and judicial culture was then generally considered 'formalist', but the STF's stance toward the new constitution was characterised less by fidelity towards the text and more by a traditional, constrained approach to the judicial role, often in tension with the constitutional text itself.[1]

[1] D Werneck Arguelhes and M Mota Prado, 'Resistance by Interpretation?: Supreme Court Justices as Counter-Reformers to Constitutional Changes in Brazil in the 90s' in R Albert et al (eds), *Constitutional Change and Transformation in Latin America* (Hart Publishing, 2019).

The new constitution created the *Mandado de Injução* to give courts the power to intervene in legislative omissions – specifically when a fundamental right's additional, enabling legislation is never enacted by congress or the president. In its *MI-QO 107* (1989)[2] ruling, however, the STF decided it could only issue a formal declaration of omission, without taking any further measures. Invoking separation of powers and deviating from an explicit choice of the constitutional assembly, the STF refused to set provisional rules, or so much as a deadline for Congress.[3]

Until the early 2000s, the court was generally careful in not blocking the government's main agenda. Presidents used (and expanded) their broad legislative powers granted in the constitution to promote their goals within Congress, and the court's jurisprudence helped shape a regime in which political dynamics often trumped constitutional law in defining presidential influence in the legislative process. While the STF did enforce some limits on presidential law-making and veto some policies and reforms on the margins, judges typically steered away from the daily workings of coalition presidentialism.[4]

Nonetheless, the 1990s court played a relevant role in some cases involving executive power and interbranch relationships. President Collor filed several lawsuits during his impeachment trial, dragging it on for several months in 1992. The court then intervened in congressional proceedings to protect due process. Still, it ultimately confirmed the Senate's decision to see the trial through and convict Collor despite his resignation during the proceedings. Moreover, in 1993, the Court first decided that a constitutional amendment could be struck down as unconstitutional for violating 'eternity clauses' – a landmark affirmation of judicial power in Brazilian constitutional law.[5] The decision ultimately did not prevent the government from charging ahead by simply using a different legal measure.

Fundamental rights cases were scarce at the STF in the 1990s. The court decided important issues of criminal law and procedures, as well as rights related to tax law and civil service careers. Beyond that, rights cases were rare. The court focused mostly on the separation of powers, procedural guarantees, federation issues, and the scope of its own review powers. STF judges generally did not speak in the vocabulary of fundamental rights and vulnerable minorities, even when dealing with issues that could be framed in those ways.[6] In 2000, for example, when asked to answer whether the constitutional clause that textually granted maternity leave to pregnant women could also be interpreted to include adoptive mothers, the Second Panel issued a short, unanimous decision, in which only the reporter presented a (five-page) written opinion.[7] The court decided that in choosing the word 'pregnant' the constitution explicitly linked this right to a biological condition not encompassing adoption.

[2] STF MI-QO 107 Reporter M Alves, 1989.

[3] This position would change in the *MI 670 decision* (Reporter M Correa, 2007).

[4] See eg DM Brinks, 'Faithful Servants of the Regime: The Brazilian Constitutional Court's role under the 1988 Constitution' in G Helmke and J Rios-Figueroa (eds), *Courts in Latin America* (Cambridge University Press, 2011).

[5] STF ADI 939 Reporter S Sanches, 1993.

[6] D Werneck Arguelhes, 'Ellwanger e as transformações do Supremo Tribunal Federal: um novo começo?' (2022) 13(3) *Revista Direito e Práxis*.

[7] STF RE 197807 Reporter O Gallotti, 2000.

Eventually, the STF changed – for various reasons and along multiple dimensions. The last pre-democratisation judges retired in 2003, which also marked the first major alternation of power in the presidency since democratisation. In his first term (2003–2006), President Lula appointed six new STF judges, four in his first two years in office.

In the last two decades, constitutional judicial review has become routine in Brazil. The *Ação Direta de Inconstitucionalidade* (Direct Action of Unconstitutionality or ADI) is the main kind of abstract review procedure. Between 2010 and 2019, in more than 37 per cent of them, the STF agreed at least partially with the constitutional challenge.[8] Furthermore, the drastic power to strike down constitutional amendments, based on the constitution's 'eternity clauses', has become part and parcel of the STF's business. Between 1988 and 2020, it annulled or suspended at least partially more than 40 per cent of the 37 constitutional amendments challenged in abstract review.[9] While the court has not struck down the core of a major reform so far, amendments have been regularly shaped by rulings and the shadow of the STF's power.

Moreover, the STF today openly creates rules in cases of legislative omissions. In 2019, it held that, when the Constitution defines 'racism' as a crime, this should include homophobia and transphobia. Article 5, XLI of the Constitution states that 'the law shall punish any discrimination which may attempt against fundamental rights and liberties'. Congress had enacted statutes criminalising discrimination based on several factors (such as gender or social class) but did not mention homophobia.[10]

Since 1988, the STF's power has undergone several reforms, but always towards expansion. No legislative proposals to change appointment mechanisms or restrict court powers and competencies have been enacted. In the 1990s, Brazil's system of diffuse judicial review devoid of binding precedents enabled the opposition to challenge and delay, before lower courts, key parts of the government's regulatory agenda – such as the major privatisation efforts in the first Cardoso administration (1995–1998).[11] National political players took an interest in centralising judicial power at the STF.[12]

Since the 2000s, the STF has established a central, albeit ambiguous position in national politics. On the one hand, it has consistently interpreted its powers in very expansive terms, as well as successfully resisting (in the public sphere and in the legislative arena) all would-be attempts to tone down its powers and prerogatives. It also developed internal practices whereby individual Justices wield considerable individual power, with almost no effective accountability mechanisms.

On the other hand, however, the impressive powers the court has developed and spread around its individual components are used rather selectively. Since 1988, the

[8] A Barbosa Paz and I Fitipaldi, 'Uma análise do padrão de julgamento do Supremo Tribunal Federal (STF) sobre ações diretas de inconstitucionalidade entre 2010 e 2019' (2021) 18 *Revista Direito GV* (data includes federal laws, state laws, and other types of statutes). In 23 cases in our sample of 40 high-profile decisions, the court decided at least partially against the constitutionality of the challenged statute, decision, or measure.

[9] F Luci de Oliveira and D Werneck Arguelhes, 'O Supremo Tribunal Federal e a Mudança Constitucional' (2021) 36 *Revista Brasileira de Ciências Sociais* (Rev Bras Ci Soc).

[10] STF MI 4733 Reporter E Fachin, 2019.

[11] MM Taylor, *Judging policy: courts and policy reform in democratic Brazil* (Stanford University Press, 2008).

[12] See R Bastos Arantes, 'Jurisdição Política Constitucional' in MT Sadek (ed), *Reforma do Judiciário* (Centro Edelstein de Pesquisas Sociais, 2010).

STF has avoided direct confrontation with governing coalitions, rarely striking down statutes central to the government's agenda.[13] Clashes with Congress have always been much more frequent than direct confrontation with the President; when the two political branches converge, the STF has tended not to interfere.

B. The Court and Constitutional Litigation

The STF is a multi-purpose court, playing many roles beyond constitutional review.[14] First, it is a court of last resort, at the summit of a judicial system in which all judges exercise concrete constitutional review. Appeals in such cases are a traditional STF competence, hailing back to the 1891 constitution. In this role, the STF decided whether a national association of musicians had to obey due process before expelling its members (2005);[15] whether the right to education entailed the state's obligation to provide free childcare (2005);[16] and whether it was constitutional for a statute to require a journalism degree for someone to be employed as a journalist (2009).[17]

Second, as a constitutional court, the STF has the sole power to decide abstract review challenges based on the federal Constitution. Here, the two most important procedures are the aforementioned ADI and the *Arguição de Descumprimento de Preceito Fundamental* (Allegation of Non-Compliance with a Fundamental Precept or ADPF). Apart from relevant technical differences, they both allow a specific, limited set of state and social entities listed in the constitution to challenge a federal or state action (or omission) in abstract terms, independently from application in a specific case. All state governors and legislative assemblies, all political parties with at least one seat in Congress, the National Bar Association, and civil society organisations that fulfil certain criteria can file ADIs and ADPFs. These accessible procedures make it extremely likely that any controversial political issue will find its way to the Court.[18]

For example, several parties used ADIs to challenge an electoral 'performance clause' preventing small parties from obtaining access to public resources during elections (*ADI 1351* and *1354*, decided in 2006);[19] the Attorney-General filed an ADI to ask the court to decide whether authorising stem cell research violated the right to life and human dignity (*ADI 3510*, decided in 2008);[20] the national association of health workers asked the STF to declare that the termination of a pregnancy with a brainless foetus cannot be prosecuted as abortion, as this would violate the woman's human dignity

[13] See eg L Da Ros, 'Poder de decreto e accountability horizontal: dinâmica institucional dos três poderes e medidas provisórias no Brasil pós-1988' (2008) 16 *Revista de Sociologia e Política* (Rev de Sociol e Polit) 143–60. The Bolsonaro government (2019–2022) seems to be an exception. V Elias de Oliveira and L Mori Madeira, 'Judicialização da política no enfrentamento à covid-19: um novo padrão decisório do STF?' (2021) 35 *Revista Brasileira de Ciencias Sociais.*

[14] J Falcão et al, *I Relatório Supremo em Números: O Múltiplo Supremo* (Fundação Getulio Vargas, 2011); O Vilhena Vieira, 'Supremocracia' (2008) 4 *Revista Direito GV* 441–64.

[15] STF RE 201819 Reporter E Gracie, 2005.

[16] STF RE 436996 Reporter C de Mello, 2005.

[17] STF RE 511961 Reporter G Mendes, 2009.

[18] In our sample, in more than 30 cases the lawsuits were not brought by government institutions.

[19] STF ADI 1351 and 1354 Reporter M Aurélio and M Corrêa, 2006.

[20] STF ADI 3510 Reporter A Britto, 2008.

(*ADPF 54*, decided in 2012);[21] and, in an ADI filed by the National Bar Association (*ADI 4650*, decided in 2015),[22] the STF struck down as unconstitutional a statute allowing private companies to make unlimited contributions to electoral campaigns.

Third, the STF has original jurisdiction over injunctions involving acts by the houses of Congress, the President, and other superior courts. This includes *habeas corpus* petitions against such authorities. The STF ruled on injunctions filed by President Collor against his 1992 Senate conviction, as well as by individual members of Congress disputing the rule that a legislator should lose their mandate after switching parties during the term (the party fidelity cases, in 2007 and 2008);[23] and the 2003 *Ellwanger habeas corpus*, filed by a publisher of antisemitic propaganda against a ruling by the Superior Court of Justice (STJ) that had confirmed his conviction for the crime of racism.[24]

Fourth, the STF is also a powerful criminal court. It has sole, original, and final jurisdiction over criminal investigations and trials of all congress members and ministers of state – over 600 public authorities. Here, the STF acts as a trial court, authorising and supervising investigative measures (including provisional detention and temporary suspension from public office), hearing witnesses, analysing documents and other evidence, deciding factual questions, as well as issuing a verdict. These competencies have been a key ingredient in the STF's rise to power in the last decade, since the *Mensalão* (*AP 470*) judgment in 2013[25] when the court decided a criminal lawsuit involving 40 defendants. Since then, the Court's pull over criminal lawsuits against political actors has uplifted the judges as much as (if not more than) their constitutional review powers.

Brazil has a diffuse, US-like model of constitutional review operating in the same legal system as a 'kelsenian' concentrated, abstract *erga omnes* mechanism.[26] Judicial review exercised in concrete cases, however, only binds the parties (with a couple of potential exceptions we will discuss below). Because Brazil lacks a formal system of stare decisis, the STF often decided thousands of appeals in 'repeat' cases discussing identical legal issues and often involving the same defendant, such as public companies, large banks, or the federal government itself.

This system underwent major changes. Congress enacted statutes to consolidate and expand abstract review tools in the 1990s, and Constitutional Amendment 45 of 2004, known as the 'Judicial Reform Amendment', created two mechanisms that centralised power in the STF: the *Súmula Vinculante* (SV) and the *Repercussão Geral* (RG). The two mechanisms were proposed as solutions for the STF's long-standing problem of an ever-expanding number of incoming cases (with a record of over 110,000 new cases in 2005).

The SV is a binding statement comprising the court's interpretation of a given statutory or constitutional provision, which must be approved by two-thirds of its judges. It allows the court to formalise, as a general binding rule, the understanding it adopted in a specific ruling. Lower courts and the public administration must abide by the SVs,

[21] STF ADPF 54 Reporter M Aurélio, 2012.
[22] STF ADI 4650 Reporter L Fux, 2015.
[23] STF MS 26.602; 26.603 and 26.604 Reporters E Grau, C de Mello and C Lucia, 2007.
[24] STF HC 82424 Reporter M Alves, 2003.
[25] STF AP 470 Reporter J Barbosa 2007. See MM Taylor, 'The Troubling Strength of Brazilian Institutions in the Face of Scandal' (2019) 15 *Taiwan Journal of Democracy* (TJD) 91–111.
[26] R Bastos Arantes, *Judiciário e política no Brasil* (Educ, Idesp, 1997).

thus preventing waves of thousands of repetitive appeals from reaching the STF. Since 2006, the court has created 58 SVs.

The RG allows the court to decline to hear an appeal, by a vote of two-thirds of its members, if the topic lacks 'general repercussion'. In practice, RG has developed not just as a filter for incoming cases – a docket control device – but also as a mechanism for the STF to shape lower court decisions. RG allows the STF to set a case apart as a 'paradigm' so that lower courts have to apply the same decision in all past (temporarily suspended, awaiting the 'paradigm' decision) and future similar cases. In Brazilian procedural law, this is not technically the same as a 'binding precedent' or a decision with *erga omnes* effects; however, a lower court decision diverging from an RG decision on a 'paradigm case' can be more easily challenged before the STF.

The STF is composed of 11 judges (officially called *Ministros* and *Ministras*). Decisions are made in the plenary court, when all the ten Associate Justices and the Chief Justice (CJ) sit together, or in one of the two five-judge panels. The CJ is excluded from the routine allocation of cases and does not sit on the panels during their two-year tenure. Since 2007, the court's plenary (11 judges) and two panels (with five judges each) have coexisted with a body named the 'Virtual Plenary' (*Plenário Virtual*, PV) – an asynchronous voting platform to which judges upload their opinions within a certain time frame.[27]

In the two panels or in the plenary court, all STF deliberations have been public for more than a century. Since 2002, plenary court deliberations are broadcast live on the official court channel *TV Justiça* – and, since 2006, are streamed via the court's official YouTube channel. Print and televised media, as well as social networks in Brazil, are full of images, clips, and memes of individual STF judges. From a comparative perspective, the STF's level of official transparency and its pioneering engagement with public communication are remarkable.[28] The court has been an active player in shaping its own public image. It has its own TikTok and Instagram accounts and is very active on social media.[29] Because deliberations are public, judges lack institutionalised, formal fora to privately discuss cases. There is anecdotal evidence that at least some judges meet informally and exchange views before official deliberations, especially in high-profile cases. Still, the occurrence of such meetings and interactions is denied by other current and former judges, some of which have criticised such practices.[30] In deciding, judges are not expected or required to interact beyond public deliberations.

While plenary court decisions in *TV Justiça* attract most of the public attention, decision-making procedures and powers in the STF are heavily decentralised. The court is characterised by strong individual powers of agenda-setting and decision-making.[31]

[27] In recent years, each of the two panels have also adopted 'virtual' platform versions of their decision-making procedures.

[28] MC Ingram, 'Uncommon Transparency: The Supreme Court, Media Relations, and Public Opinion in Brazil' in R Davis and D Taras (eds), *Justices and journalists: the global perspective* (Cambridge University Press, 2017).

[29] See M Lanos and C Tibi Weber, 'High Courts and social media in Latin America'(2021) *German Institute for Global and Area Studies* (GIGA).

[30] See eg the interviews of C Velloso, R Mayer, C Peluzo, M Aurélio, N Jobim and R Barroso in the Supreme Court Oral History project (F Fontainha et al, *Historia Oral do Supremo Tribunal Federal*, vols 1, 4, 5, 7, 9, 11).

[31] See D Werneck Arguelhes and L Molhano Ribeiro, '"The Court, It Is I?" Individual Judicial Powers in the Brazilian Supreme Court and Their Implications for Constitutional Theory' (2018) 7 *Global Constitutionalism* 236–62.

In particular, the trajectory of each case until a collective decision depends greatly on the case reporter, a judge who is randomly assigned to every new case that enters the docket. The reporter alone decides whether to conduct public hearings with experts or civil society organisations. The reporter can autonomously issue emergency injunctions in some conditions and dismiss an appeal or petition that is manifestly void of legal grounds or goes against the STF's settled case law. The entire life span of most cases begins and ends with the reporters' individual rulings.

Most importantly, reporters have the sole power to decide when (and if) a lawsuit is ready to be decided by the (plenary or panels). More recently, they also gained the power to decide whether a case will be discussed synchronously or asynchronously (in the PV). This means that reporters have absolute, negative agenda-setting powers over their cases.[32] Still, once a case is cleared for judgment, the CJ or panel head has the exclusive power to decide which cleared cases they will include in the schedule of judgments. All such decisions – the reporter's, the CJ's and the panel head's – are considered discretionary, and judges need not provide reasons for such choices.[33]

Court sessions include oral arguments by lawyers, followed by opinion delivery and debates by the judges. The STF is a *seriatim* court. There is no 'opinion of the court', only individual opinions.[34] We consider a 'majority decision' the set of all individual opinions issued by the largest number of justices who agree on a given outcome. Strictly speaking, all opinions are either concurrences (if they agree with the prevailing outcome) or dissents (if they voted for a defeated outcome). In coding cases, we have considered a certain variable to be present in the court's final decision whenever we found it (substantively, not just in passing) in either: (i) the decision reporter's opinion, or (ii) any of the concurrences by other judges in the winning coalition.

The deliberative quality of STF opinions and debates has been the target of sustained criticism. In many high-profile cases, judges – anticipating the public attention the decision will draw – will simply read aloud their opinions in session, without engaging their colleagues or considering how other opinions relate to their own positions.[35] While in some cases the court considers which arguments and outcomes have the support of a majority, in the typical STF decision (even a unanimous one) finding the shared ratio decidendi is a daunting task.[36]

Although they can state their opinion as succinctly as 'I follow the reporter', in high-profile cases each Justice typically brings to session their own fully developed written opinion. As each opinion reveals information about the likely outcome, the behaviour

[32] ibid.

[33] For a comprehensive account of agenda-setting mechanisms in the STF, see LF Gomes Esteves, 'A construção da pauta do Supremo Tribunal Federal: quem, o quê, e como' (2022) *PhD thesis University of São Paulo*.

[34] C Hübner Mendes, 'O Projeto de uma Corte Deliberativa' in A Vojvodic et al (eds), *Jurisdição Constitucional no Brasil* (Malherios Editores, 2012) 53.

[35] V Afonso da Silva, 'Deciding Without Deliberating' (2013) 11 *International Journal of Constitutional Law* 557; C Hübner Mendes, 'The Supreme Federal Court in Brazil' (2017) *Comparative Constitutional Reasoning* 115; A Jakab et al (eds), *Comparative Constitutional Reasoning* (Cambridge University Press, 2017) (calling the STF a 'soloist court').

[36] A Vojvodic et al, 'Escrevendo um romance, primeiro capítulo: precedentes e processo decisório no STF' (2009) 5 *Revista Direito GV* 21.

of subsequent voting judges might be affected by strategic considerations, such as avoiding unnecessary defeats to display collegiality.[37]

Statutes entitle lawyers to meet judges in person, in their chambers, to discuss the case. Meeting the case reporter is an opportunity to persuade them to issue an injunction, or to clear (or not) a case for judgment. This practice has been criticised for lacking transparency and potentially favouring high-profile lawyers, parties, and public authorities in litigation.[38]

Appeals represent most of the court's vast workload. In recent years, even after the effects of the Judicial Reform Amendment were felt, the court still received more than 60,000 new cases per year. Since 1988, though, more than 95 per cent of the STF's cases have been disposed of by individual decisions. Between 1988 and 2019 only 1 per cent of all procedures included at least one specific decision by either the plenary or one of the panels in synchronous decisions.[39]

Before the pandemic, the PV had limited relevance. In March 2020, the PV's scope was expanded to include all cases and procedures, with potentially far-reaching implications. In the PV, there is no interaction between judges, and voting is asynchronous; once the reporter submits their vote, other judges as a rule have a deadline of six days to submit theirs, in no predetermined order. There are no debates or actual deliberations.[40]

Both in virtual and synchronous decision-making procedures, each judge can request for a judgment to be suspended so that they can further study the facts and arguments presented by their colleagues – a *pedido de vista*, a formal request to examine the case files. Judges often hold *vistas* for months and even years, way past the legal deadlines.[41] Because there is no formal mechanism to control or sanction such behaviour, judges often use *vistas* to delay or even prevent a decision on a case for a variety of motives. The PV has replicated this decentralised agenda-setting dynamic.[42]

C. The Judges

The STF is composed of 'eleven Justices, chosen from among citizens over 35 and under 65 years of age, of notable juridical learning and spotless reputations' (Article 101 of the Constitution). Judges are nominated by the President and confirmed by an absolute majority of the Senate in a secret vote, after public hearings (called *sabatinas*) conducted

[37] See eg F de Mendonça Lopes, 'Dissent aversion and sequential voting in the Brazilian Supreme Court' (2019) 16 *Journal of Empirical Legal Studies* 933.

[38] J Cesario Alvim Gomes, 'Cancelas Invisíveis: Embargos auriculares, legitimidade ativa e a permeabilidade social seletiva do Supremo Tribunal Federal' (2020) 6 *Revista Estudos Institucionais* 55.

[39] T Pereira et al, *VIII Relatório Supremo em Números: Quem decide no Supremo? Tipos de decisão colegiada no tribunal (1988–2018)* (FGV Direito Rio, 2020). The rest of the decisions were made individually, in 'virtual' (asynchronous) platforms or as part of lists of dozens of identical, supposedly 'easy' cases that reporters bring to session to dispose of summarily.

[40] The post-2020 high profile cases we selected were decided synchronously. Our sample does not include PV cases.

[41] D Werneck Arguelhes and I Alberto Hartmann, 'Timing Control without Docket Control: How Individual Justices Shape the Brazilian Supreme Court's Agenda' (2017) 5 *Journal of Law and Courts* 105.

[42] In December 2022, the Court reformed its internal rules of procedure to establish that, after 90 days, cases under *vista* will be automatically cleared for deliberation. It is expected that this new mechanism will limit individual agenda-setting powers in the Court.

in that house's commission of judicial affairs. The public hearing before the Senate vote is a relatively recent practice, having been adopted in the 1980s. Once confirmed, judges remain in office until the mandatory retirement age of 75.[43]

While the Senate has not rejected an appointee in a century, this veto power is not irrelevant.[44] The president probes and negotiates with legislators beforehand; names that run a high risk of rejection do not make it to an actual formal appointment by the President; the President typically makes the necessary informal efforts – lobbying and bargaining in Congress – to ensure a favourable outcome for their appointee.[45]

The court has only ever had three female judges since its establishment in 1890 – Ellen Gracie (2000–2010), Carmen Lúcia (2006–), and Rosa Weber (2011–2023). In the STF, the Chief Justice is the senior judge who has not yet been CJ, serving a tenure of just two years. Judges Gracie, Lúcia and Weber were CJs in 2006–2008, 2016–2018, and 2022–2023 respectively. The first (and so far only) African-Brazilian judge, Joaquim Barbosa, was appointed in 2003 and served on the court until 2014 (being CJ between 2013 and 2014).

Since 1988, most STF judges have been recruited from the ranks of a set of elite public legal professions, which wield considerable power and prestige in Brazil – the judiciary, the *ministério público* (independent prosecutors), and the public attorneys who serve as counsel and litigators for the federal government (*Advocacia-Geral da União*) or states (*Procuradorias do Estado*). With one exception, all judges on the current court previously held positions in one of the institutions mentioned above.[46] With very few exceptions, STF judges are almost always professional insiders, part and parcel of the legal community's elite.[47] They are highly familiarised with and strongly connected to the different corporations and institutions in the Brazilian justice system. However, while often politically connected, STF judges are seldom politicians. At the time of writing, the only current Justice who held elected office is Flavio Dino, who was a state governor, a federal deputy and a senator. Before Dino, the last two judges who held elected offices in their careers retired in the mid-2000s.

Each judge works with dozens of clerks and other staff. Since the 1990s, the balance between career (civil servants) and non-career (freely appointed by the judge) legal clerks seems to have changed. They have more often been recruited amongst recent law school graduates, often with professional ambitions beyond civil service. In the late 2000s, the court created the possibility of appointing 'auxiliary judges' chosen from the lower courts, which can perform roles such as supervising procedures in criminal investigations.

[43] The 1988 constitution originally established the mandatory retirement age at 70, but, in 2015, a constitutional amendment extended it to 75. This was immediately applicable to current judges, in a clear congressional manoeuvre to prevent President Rousseff from making more appointments.

[44] See M Llanos and L Barreiro Lemos, 'Presidential Preferences? The Supreme Federal Tribunal Nominations in Democratic Brazil' (2013) 55 *Latin American Politics and Society* 77.

[45] F Recondo, 'As indicações para o Supremo Tribunal Federal: ontem, hoje e amanhã' in MT Sadek et al (ed), *O Judiciário do Nosso Tempo* (Globo Livros, 2021).

[46] The exception being Justice Cristiano Zanin (appointed in 2022), who had exclusively been a practising lawyer before his appointment.

[47] See R Mafei Rabelo Queiroz et al, 'De las aulas universitarias a la toga: la trayectoria académica de los ministros del Supremo Tribunal Federal brasileño (1988–2013)' (2016) 8 *Precedentes* 97; R Bastos Arantes and R Martins, 'O antes influencia o depois? Trajetórias, nomeações e votos dos ministros do STF' (2020) 44 *Encontro Anual ANPOCS*; F de Castro Fontainha et al, 'Os três poderes da elite jurídica: a trajetória político-partidária dos ministros do STF (1988–2013)' (2018) 49 *Revista de Ciências Sociais* 93.

Since the 2000s, STF judges are typically law professors as well, and many of them take former or current students to the court as their clerks. Of the current court, six of the 11 judges already had positions in traditional law schools in public universities before their appointment. But this should be put into the specific context of Brazilian legal academia, which is far from insulated from legal practice and often instrumentalised by the legal profession. Very few law professors – even when they formally have full-time appointments in public universities – have academia as their main professional activity, and no legal scholar who was not also a practising lawyer, a judge, a prosecutor, or a public attorney has been appointed to the STF since 1988. The court has strong connections with an academic establishment that is largely dominated by lawyers and the same elite legal professions from which STF judges are recruited.

D. Legal Scholarship and Constitutional Reasoning

Ideas inside the STF greatly changed since the 1990s, matching transformations in constitutional discourse. As in other Latin American countries, 'neoconstitutionalist' ideas became increasingly popular in the 1990s.[48] In Brazil, this involved two major changes. First, an expanded conception of methods of constitutional interpretation and adjudication (including specific approaches to apply constitutional principles, such as proportionality analysis, and an emphasis on purposive interpretation in lieu of text-centred approaches). Second, an expansive view of the judicial role, with separation of powers taking a back seat to 'effectiveness' in enforcing constitutional rights and guarantees.

Shaped by these two features, the academic discourse would push the STF in a very different direction from the 1990s, making the court more flexible – sometimes unbound – in its approach to constitutional reasoning and more activist in its relationship with the other branches. Charges of activism are common but carry little weight in the legal community, which is generally deferential towards the court and supportive of judicial intervention in politics. Criticism in the media and in the specialised press is a recent, but rapidly increasing phenomenon. Moreover, politicians themselves are constantly asking the court to intervene in the political decision-making process, often in a highly visible fashion.

In the mainstream view in Brazil, legal interpretation is an eclectic enterprise which requires a combination of strategies. No single method or approach to interpretation is considered prima facie more adequate or sound. Judicial decisions and legal treatises often remark on the lack of priority between different methods. In practice, actual forays into legislative intent – for example, using records of congressional debates – are rarely found in judicial opinions in Brazil.

Citation practices centre heavily on scholarly ('doctrinal') authorities. STF judges are connected to the academic mainstream, and often cite both classic works and treatises

[48] J Couso, 'The transformation of constitutional discourse and the judicialization of politics in Latin America' in J Couso et al (eds), *Cultures of legality: Judicialization and political activism in Latin America* (Cambridge University Press, 2010) 141, 149; JL Esquirol, 'The Turn to Legal Interpretation in Latin America' (2010) 26 *American University International Law Review* 1031.

and recent monographs (sometimes even unpublished dissertations) on novel issues. The STF *circa* democratisation was more conservative in its citation practices, but the current court seems eager to cite the latest rounds of scholarship.

II. Arguments in Constitutional Reasoning

A. The Structure of Constitutional Arguments

As we mentioned in section I(B), the STF decides in a *seriatim* way. Considering this institutional setting, the most frequent structure of reasoning was the 'legs of a chair' (23 out of 40 cases). Judges include in their individual opinions several arguments that are (concurrently) presented as sufficient for a decision. This might be due precisely to the *seriatim* structure of the decision-making process; since judges present their individual opinions, they often approach the case from very different perspectives. As we considered all the opinions converging on the majority-supported outcome when coding for this question, this might have led to more cases of 'parallel' reasoning (because different judges present different arguments to justify the same outcome).

Of the 17 cases with different structures, 11 cases displayed a single argument or a chain of reasoning in which arguments derive or follow from one another (a surprisingly high number, perhaps, considering the voting structure we discussed above), and six cases displayed a more 'dialogic' reasoning structure (in which several independent considerations, which are in themselves insufficient, are added up to support a given outcome by their combined strength). In any event, we recommend caution when reading this data against in the context of *seriatim* voting procedures.

B. Types of Constitutional Arguments

Arguments from precedents and scholarship appear in every single one of the 40 cases (100 per cent), while domestic harmonising arguments appear in all but one of the cases (97.5 per cent). Teleological-purposive arguments were present in 35 of the 40 cases (87.5 per cent), while subjective-historical arguments appeared in 32 cases (80 per cent). In 29 cases, we found 'other types' of arguments, which we could not easily fit into the existing categories.

As we discussed in section I(C) above, citing scholarship to justify arguments is a traditional practice in the Brazilian legal professions, and the STF judges are often law professors as well. We should emphasise, however, that those references do not necessarily mean the judge is substantively engaging with the arguments presented in the cited sources. More often than not, making an argument from scholarship in the STF means citing scholars as authorities for the adoption of a certain interpretation of legal materials or a certain version of a legal concept. In this sense, for example, the fact that a certain author presents a certain interpretation of a constitutional clause counts as an argument for the adoption of such understanding as the correct one, even if the citing judge does not elaborate on why this understanding is the correct one.

Citations to foreign authors, in particular, are a common and traditional practice in Brazilian legal academia, displaying different waves of influence over time. Until the 1990s, opinions often relied on Portuguese authors on constitutional law, Italian scholarship on procedural law (and on constitutional review procedures), as well as German criminal law, French administrative law, and US scholarship and cases on specific issues (such as the separation of powers or federative arrangements). Since then, however, German and US authors have gained increased prevalence in Brazilian legal discourse and in the STF.

Perhaps the best two examples are the legal theorists Robert Alexy and Ronald Dworkin. They have become almost synonymous with reasoning with constitutional principles itself and are often cited by judges and lawyers all around the country. Critics have pointed out that judicial uses of such authors, however, are often decontextualised, non-rigorous, and ultimately superfluous – attempts more to show erudition or attunement to the neo-constitutionalist *zeitgeist* than actual engagement with specific ideas.[49] By citing Dworkin or Alexy, judges are perhaps signalling to their audiences that they are aware of supposedly 'modern' ideas on constitutional interpretation, the application of constitutional principles, and the judicial role – even when they do not substantively engage with what those authors are saying, or discussing how they are relevant for the case outcome.

The pervasiveness of precedent-based arguments is perhaps unexpected in a legal system in which there is no formal doctrine of stare decisis, and in which judicial decisions are formally not seen as a source of law. However, this finding deserves careful interpretation. We have included in our analysis cases in which judges point to the existence of previous decisions as an argument for the adoption of a certain interpretation or outcome in the present case. This very minimalistic understanding of an 'argument from precedent' is compatible with very different conceptions of precedent-based reasoning (sometimes in the same decision).

Indeed, scholars have criticised the STF precisely for the lack of consistency in its use of precedent-based arguments – sometimes citing decisions to illustrate a point the judge substantively agrees with, sometimes using it to indicate that the court must obey its past decisions whatever their specific content, and at other times mentioning previous cases without articulating why exactly that past decision is specifically relevant now.[50] Previous cases are often mentioned for mostly rhetorical purposes.

Domestic harmonising arguments – *interpretação sistemática* – appear in all but one of the cases. This might be an expression of the widespread belief in the centrality of the idea of the constitution as a 'unity' of meaning, which would require judges to interpret separate provisions to reconcile them with one another, thus granting maximum effectiveness to the constitution as a whole.[51] The usefulness of this idea as something

[49] See eg R Bellem de Lima, 'Proporcionalidade no Supremo: uma ideia fora de lugar' (2021) 6 *REI* 184; C Michelon, 'Princípios e Coerência na argumentação jurídica' C Barbieri and R Macedo (eds), *Direito e interpretação: racionalidades e instituições* (Saraiva, 2011).

[50] See F Leal, 'Força autoritativa, influência persuasiva ou qualquer coisa: o que é um precedente para o Supremo Tribunal Federal?' (2020) 7 *Revista de Investigações Constitucionais* 206.

[51] See eg LR Barroso and AP de Barcellos, 'O começo da história: a nova interpretação constitucional e o papel dos princípios no direito brasileiro' (2003) 232 *Revista De Direito Administrativo* 141.

specific to constitutional interpretation is questionable.[52] Still, 'constitutional unity' is widespread in Brazilian legal discourse, which might explain the pervasiveness of harmonising arguments.

Teleological arguments are very frequent. Contrary to our initial expectations, subjective-historical arguments were also frequent – the fourth most frequent type of argument, appearing in 80 per cent of the cases. We should consider, however, that such historical arguments are usually discussions of contexts of enactment, not structured analyses of legislative debates. Moreover, consistently with scholarly images of judicial adjudication in Brazil, the court more often mentions the 'objective' purpose of the statute or provision (87.5 per cent) more often than the 'subjective' intent of legislators.

In contrast, the incidence of arguments from the ordinary meaning of words (45 per cent of the cases, 18 out of 40) is relatively low. Of the traditional elements typically considered in legal interpretation, the textual meaning seems to be the least favoured by STF judges. This might be another indicator of the court's recent drive towards expanding its powers, as it becomes increasingly unbound by textual constraints.[53]

Non-legal arguments appear in 75 per cent of the cases. Sociological arguments appear in 25 cases, economic arguments appear in 21 cases, and scientific/medical arguments appear in 15 cases. Consistent with findings in previous studies, then, the STF is fertile ground for judges and parties engaging with non-legal arguments.[54] Moreover, our sample suggests this trend might be accelerating in recent decades. One reason for this might be the increasing popularity, in the court, of convening public hearings (*audiências públicas*) with scientists or other experts. The first such public hearing took place in 2008, within the *Stem Cell Research Case* (*ADI 3510*),[55] which is included in our sample, and this practice has become more frequent since then. Scholars have criticised the court for cherry-picking elements from expert briefs and for not establishing clear criteria on which kinds of cases would recommend calling for a public hearing in the first place.[56]

High-profile STF rulings have begun to include international law references and Interamerican Court of Human Rights decisions more often since the 2000s, although such references only took place in roughly one-third of the cases (13 of the 40 rulings). Citations to foreign jurisdictions, however, are pervasive. In our data, 36 majority opinions (90 per cent) include references to foreign law, and references to legal materials from Latin American countries appear in 19 cases. However, while in 17 of such cases the Court is referring only to non-Latin American jurisdictions (typically Western European countries and the US), in just one case the court refers only to legal materials

[52] V Afonso da Silva, 'Interpretação Constitucional e Sincretismo Metodológico' (2005) *Interpretação Constitucional.*

[53] F Leal, 'A Constituição diz o que eu digo que ela diz': formalismo inconsistente e textualismo oscilante no Direito Constitucional Brasileiro' (2019) 12 *Revista Brasileira De Direitos Fundamentais & Justiça* 99.

[54] Mendes (n 35), D Kapiszewski, 'Tactical Balancing: High Court Decision Making on Politically Crucial Cases' (2011) 45 *Law & Society Review* 471.

[55] STF ADI 3510 Reporter A Britto, 2008.

[56] F Leal et al, 'Uma década de audiências públicas no Supremo Tribunal Federal (2007–2017)' (2018) 5 *Revista de Investigações Constitucionais* 331.

from Latin America. References to Latin American legal materials almost always appear in conjunction with references to other regions. Citation practices in the Court, not unlike what happens in the rest of the legal community, are still highly influenced by traditional jurisdictions in the 'global north' countries. Specifically, decisions from the US and Germany are frequently used to illustrate or contextualise arguments favoured by individual judges. Still, citations to Latin American jurisdictions are on the rise in the last two decades.

Arguments from constitutional silence (16) and analogy (14) are not uncommon. *Pro homine* or *pro persona* principles (eight) and discussions on the applicability of constitutional law (seven) are rarer, and there was only one instance in which the court discussed what counts as constitutional text.

C. The Overall Weight of Arguments

The STF has been recurrently criticised for employing arguments for purposes unconnected to what is necessary to dispose of the case. Judges might mention things in their decisions to appear knowledgeable or connected to certain professional audiences, or sensitive to certain moral or political issues. The court has also been criticised for employing principles and norms that are considered 'important' even when they have no bearing on specific outcomes in the case at hand. Human dignity is a case in point. Since the Brazilian Constitution explicitly guarantees many fundamental rights which are most likely directly and specifically related to the case at hand, using a principle as broad and comprehensive as human dignity is often unnecessary from a legal reasoning point of view, and is often done for purely rhetorical purposes.

The data provides some support for such criticisms. In our sample, in only five cases we considered that most arguments had a primarily rhetorical, deceptive, or decorative role, and in 12 cases we found a practically equal balance between rhetorical/decorative/deceptive and substantive arguments. In 23 cases (57.5 per cent) we believe that most of the arguments mentioned in the majority opinion could be considered at least as obiter dicta. Still, even if they are not purely rhetorical, obiter dicta arguments are still unnecessary to justify the outcome defended by the majority opinion – a situation we find often in the cases in our sample. Moreover, non-rhetorical arguments can still be (and often are) underdeveloped in their application to the specific case, as well as lacking in logical rigour or transparency of their assumptions. In this sense, testing the scholarly criticisms of STF's rhetorical use of arguments would require further analysis.

D. Judicial Candour and Judicial Rhetoric

The STF is a highly individualistic court – also in the style of writing and reasoning. Some judges develop highly personal voices and styles, which become immediately recognisable by observers familiar with the court's output. Moreover, due to the fact that deliberations have always been public (even before *TV Justiça*), every opinion (or comment during debates) issued by the judges is, in principle, simultaneously directed both at internal (the other judges in session) and external audiences.[57] External audiences can include public authorities in other branches of government; other courts; the legal profession and scholarly community; the general public and the media, among other possibilities.

The relative weight of different audiences might have changed over time. Decisions in the 1990s used a more restrained language and tone, and rhetoric was arguably targeted toward legal audiences. In contrast, in the context of the court's increased public exposure since the 2000s, more recent opinions tend to include 'soundbites' – short, catchy statements with the potential to grab immediate attention in the press and social media. *ADI 4815*[58] (on unauthorised biographies and the right to privacy) is a good example. Judge Carmen Lúcia uttered the informal expression '*Cala a boca já morreu*' (literally, 'shut up' is dead' – in that context, a reference to censorship practices of the military dictatorship being long gone). That expression, with no clear legal content, made headlines the following day and is still associated with that ruling in public debates.

Also, perhaps due to the greater role of external audiences, STF plenary decisions can sometimes be very conflictive, with heated debates between the judges, as they explicitly remark on a colleague's mistake or use strong language to criticise one another.

E. Length of Opinions, Dissenting and Concurring

As we explained, because of the *seriatim* voting procedure, all opinions that follow the judge whose opinion ultimately prevails on the outcome are formally concurring opinions. From a substantive perspective, however, it is possible that some opinions simply follow or completely mirror the winning judge's reasoning – or simply state 'I follow the reporter' or 'I follow the diverging opinion of judge X'. Therefore, although formally all opinions are concurrences, it is in principle possible to verify whether they are in practice 'substantively joining' another judge's reasoning or 'substantively concurring' – agreeing with the outcome but presenting a different rationale.

Analysing the substance of STF opinions in this way, however, is a complex task. In high-profile cases, opinions are full of potential *dicta*. Moreover, opinion length has grown considerably since the 1990s, and scholars have investigated whether the broadcasting of live deliberations on *TV Justiça* can explain this transformation.[59] The average length of the *acórdãos* in our sample is 260 pages. Discounting an average of ten pages with the report of the case facts, and assuming each judge presented an opinion – which often occurs in high profile cases – we have an average of 22 pages per opinion. Such estimates, however, can be misguiding. First, cases in which all 11 judges vote are uncommon. Typically, at least one member of the court will be either absent or will have

[57] C Hübner Mendes, *Constitutional Courts and Deliberative Democracy* (Oxford University Press, 2013); V Afonso da Silva, 'O STF e o controle de constitucionalidade: deliberação, diálogo e razão pública' (2009) 250 *Revista De Direito Administrativo* 197.

[58] STF ADI 4815 Reporter C Lúcia, 2015.

[59] I Alberto Hartmann et al, 'A influência da TV Justiça no Processo Decisório do STF' (2017) 4 *Revista de Estudos Empíricos em Direito* 38; F Lopes, 'Television and judicial behavior: Lessons from the Brazilian Supreme Court' (2018) 9 *Economic Analysis of Law Review* 41.

recused himself or herself.[60] Second, the average includes extreme variation, as a typical reporter's opinion will usually be much longer than the rest.

90 per cent of the cases included at least one dissent (defined as opinions proposing an outcome that is different from the one that obtained a majority of votes).[61] For the same reasons we explained above, data on formal unanimity allows for limited conclusions on the nature and extent of divergence within the court. A unanimous STF decision simply means that all judges agree on the 'outcome', defined as accepting, partially accepting, or rejecting an appeal or a constitutional challenge; or issuing an injunction or not. This tells us very little about whether judges converged in more substantial ways, including if they share the same ratio decidendi – or even if they framed the underlying legal problem in the same terms.[62]

In many non-unanimous cases, we have a single dissenting opinion – typically Judge Marco Aurélio, who in this tenure on the court (1990–2021) crafted a public judicial persona of a 'great dissenter'. Consider, for example, the *Inquérito 4781*, nicknamed '*the Fake News Investigation*'. In 2019, the court started proceedings to investigate coordinated online disinformation and threats to the court and the judges. A political party filed *ADPF 572*, asking the court to decide whether the investigation powers it was employing were compatible with constitutional provisions on due process of law and separation of powers. The court answered in the affirmative.[63] In one of the most controversial and politically salient rulings of the last decade, Marco Aurélio was the sole dissenter – a frequent situation during his long career in the court, shaping the rate of unanimity of the STF's decision and posing challenges for the interpretation of this kind of data.[64]

F. Framing of Constitutional Issues

The STF's decisions are characterised by an eclectic combination of different approaches to constitutional interpretation, but also to the framing of issues. Few decisions are framed as being exclusively about one kind of issue or another – rather, the judges often add different layers of framing to the same case. However, as we already discussed, there have been significant changes since the 1990s in how the court uses certain perspectives to frame issues. Fundamental rights talk, a widespread feature in the court's vocabulary today, was largely absent in the 1990s. While we have coded all the cases of the 1990s in our sample as involving fundamental rights, this is our classification of the underlying issues involved – not necessarily reflective of how the court articulated the questions in

60 E Rosevear et al, 'Disagreement on the Brazilian supreme court: an exploratory analysis' (2015) *SSRN Electronic Journal*, available at ssrn.com/abstract=2629329.

61 Existing empirical studies note that that most constitutional review cases in the STF are decided unanimously. See eg J Mariano Silva, 'Mapeando o Supremo: as posições dos ministros do STF na jurisdição constitucional (2012–2017)' (2018) 37 *Novos Estudos Cebrap* 35.

62 Vojvodic et al (n 36).

63 STF ADPF 572 Reporter E Fachin, 2020.

64 See eg F Luci de Oliveira, 'Supremo relator: processo decisório e mudanças na composição do STF nos governos FHC e Lula' (2012) 27 *Rev Bras Ci Soc* 89. S W Desposato et al, 'Power, Composition, and Decision Making: The Behavioral Consequences of Institutional Reform on Brazil's Supremo Tribunal Federal' (2015) 31 *Journal of Law, Economics, & Organization* 534.

those cases. Moreover, criminal law and criminal procedures are almost always framed as being different from the rest, requiring the application of specific methods and decision-making approaches. The STF consistently treats criminal issues as belonging to a specific realm of legal reasoning.

G. Key Concepts

The most frequent concepts in the decisions analysed in our sample are rule of law (32 cases), democracy (28 cases), proportionality (27 cases), the essential core of rights (27 cases), human dignity (25 cases) and equality (25 cases).

Although human dignity is frequently mentioned in relevant decisions of the court, it does not necessarily play a relevant justificatory role, for reasons we discussed in previous sections. Of the 25 decisions evoking it, in only two we consider that the court's reasoning was indeed building on human dignity to justify a specific result. Consider, for example, the court's decision on transgender persons' right to change their first name in public records.[65] Overruling a Superior Court of Justice (STJ) decision requiring sex reassignment surgery as a condition for changing one's name, the STF discussed the rights to equality and to privacy, private life, honour, image, and health of transgender persons. However, one of the most compelling reasons for the STF's decision was the acknowledgement that the obligation to live under a name that does not match their identity would violate the dignity of transgender individuals. This is a case in which dignity was central to the outcome.

Similarly, the principle of human dignity played an important role in the *ADPF 54*, in which the court guaranteed the right to terminate pregnancies of anencephalic foetuses.[66] At the time, abortion was only legal in cases of rape or the pregnant woman's life being at risk, and arguments about individual freedom and bodily autonomy were not deemed decisive. The majority argued that forcing a woman to carry to term pregnancies in cases of anencephaly would violate her human dignity.

In the remaining 23 cases, however, we did not consider human dignity decisive or necessary for the outcome. It mainly reinforces the importance of other more specific rights – such as the prohibition of discrimination on ethnic and religious grounds (*HC 82424*),[67] land ownership by *quilombola* communities (*ADI 3239*)[68] or freedom to work as a journalist without a degree in journalism (*RE 511961*).[69]

Proportionality was present in almost three quarters of our sample (27 cases), but this does not say much about how the STF scrutinises laws or public measures that restrict fundamental rights. Just as it happens with the court's citations to scholarship in general, references to proportionality analysis might show only that judges wanted to signal awareness of current academic debates. Proportionality had its heyday in the court in the 2000s when it seemed to be everywhere in STF opinions. This rise was

[65] STF ADI 4275 Reporter M Aurélio, 2018. STF RE 670.422 Reporter D Toffoli, 2014.
[66] STF ADPF 54 Reporter M Aurélio, 2012.
[67] STF HC 82424 Reporter M Alves, 2003.
[68] STF ADI 3239 Reporter C Peluso, 2018.
[69] STF RE 511961 Reporter G Mendes, 2009.

increasingly followed by (justified) scholarly criticisms on the judges' lack of rigour or consistency in applying proportionality tests.[70]

The first major decision in our sample involving proportionality, from 2001, illustrates these problems. That case involved a government decree-law rationing electricity during a major power shortage. Opinions mention proportionality and some of them explain its structure but do not take any of its three tests seriously to assess government claims on the restrictive measures. Judges concluded that the government measure was either proportional or disproportional, depending on their views, without actually explaining why it was so. Rather than working as a framework that channels the reasoning for grounds that can justify maintaining or revising a government measure, the idea of proportionality was generally used by STF judges simply to endorse their positions on the case.

In our sample, this 'confirmatory' use of proportionality can be noted in the opinions of judges Marco Aurelio and Gilmar Mendes in the *Ellwanger* case (*HC 82.424*).[71] Although they disagreed on the merits of the constitutional question at stake, both appealed to proportionality in a very similar way. In a few pages, they described in detail and in the abstract each of the three stages of the test (suitability, necessity, and proportionality in a narrow sense), but then proceeded to abruptly conclude that punishing the publication of an anti-Semitic book as racism was evidently suitable, necessary, and proportional in a narrow sense (judge Gilmar Mendes), or that it was evidently unnecessary and not proportional in a narrow sense (judge Marco Aurélio).

It is possible, however, that the scholarly criticisms of the misuse of proportionality in the last two decades have also been taken to heart. Our reading of the cases suggests that it is becoming less frequently used – and, when it is evoked, it seems more likely to be articulated with the facts and arguments of the case.

Equality (25 cases) appears more often than freedom of expression (13) or privacy (8); social and economic rights appear in 21 cases, and 'justice' appears in 19 cases. At least in how they write opinions, the judges seem more focused on substantive, material equality than on individual prerogatives and freedoms. For a court tasked with redeeming a transformative constitution, this is expected.[72] However, as discussed above, judges might be signalling their attunement to certain (bold) ideas on the court's role and power even in cases in which the actual outcome they are prepared to defend is very modest.[73]

Around one-third of the cases include references to regime transition, suggesting that the court has been somewhat sensitive to the potential differences between the political contexts in which statutes and constitutional norms were enacted. 'Family' and 'secularism' appear in roughly 25 per cent of the cases, which suggests that, as the STF produced many decisions in our sample, it had to balance potentially competing considerations involving traditional *mores* and the separation of religion and state.

[70] VA da Silva, 'O proporcional e o razoável' (2002) 798 *Revista dos Tribunais* (RT) 23.

[71] See n 23.

[72] O Vilhena Vieira, 'Ambitious constitutions: prominent courts' in R Dixon and Tom Ginsburg (eds), *Comparative Constitutional Law in Latin America* (Edward Elgar, 2017) 253.

[73] For discussion of this mismatch in the STF's 'transformative' role, see D Werneck Arguelhes, 'Transformative Constitutionalism: a view from Brazil' in P Dann et al (eds), *The Global South and Comparative Constitutional Law* (Oxford University Press, 2020) 165.

Within the 'rule of law' category, 19 cases discuss legal certainty (*segurança jurídica*). In judicial review cases, the STF often discusses the temporal effects of its decisions – in particular, if it will consider the laws it strikes down null and void *ab initio* (*ex tunc* effect), or whether it will consider them void starting from the official ruling date (*ex nunc* effect). While the former is the default in Brazilian law, a 1999 statute empower a two-third majority of the court to opt for *ex nunc* effects – or even to set a future date after which the statute becomes unconstitutional.[74] However, even in the 1990s, the STF already discussed the 'modulation' of decision effects, and the data shows the court has been consistently sensitive to the impact of its decisions on legal structures and legitimate social expectations arising from even an unconstitutional statute.

Issues related to the structure of government, national sovereignty, or federalism appear rarely. In contrast, mechanisms of political control (16 cases) and judicial activism (17 cases) appear often. This might suggest that, while STF judges rarely considered the nuts and bolts of government structures, they very often discussed the limits of government action. However, while the court often raises the necessity of effective accountability and control mechanisms for the other branches of government, but it rarely did so when discussing its own powers. Indeed, while the idea of judicial activism appears in more than one-third of the cases, the conclusion judges ultimately reached is that the STF was not trespassing its institutional limits. There is perhaps a mirrored relationship between accountability and judicial activism in the court's decisions: because there must be control mechanisms for government action, judges must be empowered to make certain decisions. Only rarely do majority opinions in the STF assert that the court could not do something in principle.

References to post-material values (17) and basic procedural rights (16) are not uncommon. Custom (11) and State form (nine) appear less often, references to sovereignty (6) and the idea of nation (two) are rare. In only three cases the government system is explicitly discussed in more abstract terms (although the court often interprets and applies specific rules regarding presidential powers and interbranch relationships).

In many cases (75 per cent) the judges cite ideas and concepts that are not expressly mentioned in the constitutional text. This often takes the form of the formulation of a 'legal principle' that is both implicit in the text (often as a specific version of a more general ideal) and, to the judges, very important from a substantive point of view. This is the case, among other examples, of the 'principle of equal opportunity between political parties' that appears in some opinions in cases on electoral laws in our sample.

III. Comparative Perspective

As already mentioned, the selected STF rulings are on average 260 pages long. Many exceed 400 pages. The STF today produces lengthy opinions, unlike any other Latin American court, and the size of opinions and the number of citations to precedents are on the rise.[75] Naturally, the tendencies and average lengths differ between our selection

[74] Federal Law No 9.868, 1999 (BR).

[75] F Leal et al, *IX Relatório Supremo em Números: a justificação de decisões no Supremo: extensão das decisões e aplicação de precedentes* (FGV Direito Rio, 2020).

of high-profile cases and the court's docket. The vast majority of STF decisions are brief appeal denials, only a couple of dozen pages long, without any mention of precedent or legal scholarship. Even among such typical cases, however, the increase in length has been noticeable.

In salient cases, judges cover every possible angle, regardless of their actual pertinence to the core issue. Opinions read as if judges felt no need to identify and leave out irrelevant arguments. This context must be accounted for when reading the data on arguments from scholarship and arguments from foreign law jurisdictions – something the STF arguably does more than other courts in this project. Such citations to foreign law are not borne by an appreciation of how comparative law might help decide certain issues. Rather, as it is the case with so many reasoning patterns in the STF, judges cite foreign law to add yet another dimension or perspective to what can seem like a potentially endless line of reasoning. Foreign lawyers reading STF opinions should further keep in mind that, in this overburdened court that decides cases in a *seriatim* voting procedure, judges have little institutional incentives not to include something – be it citations to foreign laws, scholarship, precedents, non-legal arguments – in their opinions.

IV. Evaluation, Pathology and Criticism

Even after many reforms, the number of incoming cases and decisions issued remains enormous. While judges decry the workload, this phenomenon has persisted even after the court was equipped with different tools to summarily dismiss new appeals and disincentivise oncoming ones. There is always a pool of thousands of open cases from which judges can discretionarily choose. In practice, complete decision-making autonomy combined with an endless supply of new cases (and a considerable number of cases that have been in the court's docket for years) has provided the court with immense power to choose what to decide and when to decide it. The fact that all 40 cases in our sample were decided in the Plenary makes them part of the privileged one per cent of cases that were not decided individually, asynchronously, and/or as part of a list of dozens of identical lawsuits.[76]

The lack of a clear ratio decidendi in most STF collegiate rulings, sometimes because of subpar deliberation conditions, has been criticised for decades. But problems of truncated reasoning also affect individual rulings (which represent most of the court's output). One such problem, connecting reasoning deficits in collegiate and individual rulings with the increase in opinion length, is argumentative 'saturation'.[77] Judges pile up one argument after another making it almost impossible to detect a unifying string of reasoning or to identify which arguments are decisive and which are accessory.[78] The problem is not that they never engage with one another's argument – they often do in many cases in our sample. Rather, the problem is the lack of institutional incentives not to present as many of your arguments as you can, in your opinion, in your own voice,

[76] Pereira et al (n 39).

[77] F Leal, 'Less is More?: Against Argumentative Saturation in Legal Decision-Making' in M Nogueira de Brito et al (eds), *The Role of Legal Argumentation and Human Dignity in Constitutional Courts* (Nomos, 2019).

[78] See Leal et al (n 75).

citing your own preferred scholarship, foreign law, and precedents. Moreover, the court decides so many relevant cases in a given month (and packs so much information in each opinion) that even trained professionals have a hard time identifying each opinion's ration decidendi and following up on its implications.

Precedent citation, in this context, has all but lost meaning. References to previous decisions are lined in decisions, sometimes by the dozen, without contextualisation or explanation about the facts and ratio deciding in each prior case being cited, leading to two problems. On the one hand, the volume of precedents mentioned in a given paragraph becomes itself the guiding force of the argument – it becomes a matter of quantity, not legal reasoning. On the other hand, the same STF ruling ends up cited in diverse contexts to support competing positions, indicating a low appreciation for the role of precedents in the development of future rulings. Individual decision-making and opinion-writing add another layer of problems, as some judges begin to develop their own preferred decisions, which they cite in their individual rulings and opinions. It seems unlikely that the court will ever agree not just on what it means to use a 'precedent', but also on which of the STF's decisions express the court's position on a given issue.

Scholarship is selectively cited in salient cases, endowing judges with an aura of knowledgeability about subjects ranging from forestry (*ADC 42*)[79] to race-based affirmative action in higher education in many different legal systems (*ADPF 186*).[80] Every single decision in our sample includes references to academic publications, but these often amount to very short arguments from authority.

The use of non-legal arguments is frequent and problematic. Although they might feel comfortable making and discussing varied non-legal claims, STF judges rarely provide evidence or justification in a more structured fashion. Even when they attempt to do so, the evidence included in the opinions tends to be selective and anecdotal. The STF has so far not attempted to develop a clear, articulate set of standards to deal with scientific evidence or empirical arguments. Even so, the judges are generally undaunted by arguments beyond their legal training and expertise.

The STF has a strained relationship with legal texts. The wording of constitutional clauses is always mentioned, but never decisively. Even clear rules are easily trumped by vague constructions of (sometimes implicit) legal principles.[81] Provisions on the court's powers are almost always reinterpreted expansively. Increasingly so in the last decade, the court gradually broadened its own competence to a point where it has become virtually impossible to know what it cannot do. The STF court has armed itself with enough such interpretations that it can in theory reach any decision about anything, even when it decides not to take use such powers in a particular case.

[79] STF ADC 42 Reporter L Fux, 2018.
[80] STF ADPF 186 Reporter R Lewandowski, 2012.
[81] F Leal, 'A Constituição diz o que eu digo que ela diz': formalismo inconsistente e textualismo oscilante no Direito Constitucional Brasileiro (2018) 12 *Direitos Fundamentais & Justiça* 99.

6

The Jurisprudence of the Commonwealth Caribbean

DEREK O'BRIEN

I. Legal, Political, Institutional and Academic Context

A. Legal and Political Culture as Context for the Constitutional Reasoning

The independent[1] countries of the Commonwealth Caribbean comprise a group of islands and archipelagos – Antigua and Barbuda, the Bahamas, Barbados, Belize, Dominica, Grenada, Jamaica, St Kitts and Nevis, St Lucia, St Vincent and the Grenadines, and Trinidad and Tobago – which form a wide arc between Florida to the north and Venezuela to the south. To this group must be added the mainland countries of Belize in Central America and Guyana in South America. Though occupying a wide geographic region and separated, in some instances, by vast expanses of sea, what links these countries, and what distinguishes them from their neighbours in the Caribbean region and in Central and South America, is their shared experience of colonial rule under the British Empire. Not only are their legal systems based predominantly on the English common law, but upon attaining independence – at different times in a period spanning the 1960s through to the 1980s – each country adopted a Constitution (the 'Independence Constitution') which incorporated the so-called 'Westminster model' of government; albeit within a context in which the Constitution is the supreme law and in which certain fundamental rights and freedoms are guaranteed by the constitution.[2]

Until relatively recently, the Judicial Committee of the Privy Council (JCPC) served as the final appellate court tasked with dealing with constitutional matters for the entire

[1] The label 'independent' is used to distinguish them from the United Kingdom's Overseas Territories in the region, which have markedly different constitutional systems and are not, therefore, considered in this chapter.

[2] Except for the Bill of Rights Chapter in the Constitution of Trinidad and Tobago, which was based on the Canadian Bill of Rights, the Bills of Rights contained in the Constitutions of the other countries in the region were based on the European Convention of Human Rights.

Commonwealth Caribbean. However, in 2006, a new final appellate court was established by governments in the region, the Caribbean Court of Justice (CCJ), with the ambition that, eventually, this would replace the JCPC as the final appellate court for the entire Commonwealth Caribbean. This ambition has not however, been realised, for reasons which I allude to below.

i. The Judicial Committee of the Privy Council and the Caribbean Court of Justice

With the growth of the British Empire in the early eighteenth century, the JCPC assumed a jurisdiction as the final court of appeal from Britain's colonies around the world. However, upon independence, or soon thereafter, the majority of these former colonies abolished the right of appeal to the JCPC and established their own final appellate court. In defiance of this trend, upon independence Commonwealth Caribbean countries not only enshrined, but deeply entrenched, the JCPC as the final appellate court in their Independence Constitutions. Though it is true that Guyana abolished the right of appeal to the JCPC four years after independence, it was in this, as in many other respects, somewhat of an outlier within the region.[3] Even now, with the establishment of the CCJ in 2006, only four countries have ratified its appellate jurisdiction – Barbados, Belize, Dominica and Guyana – which means that the JCPC remains the final appellate court for the majority of Commonwealth Caribbean countries. Though a detailed discussion of reasons for this are beyond the scope of this chapter, it would be fair to say that whilst the CCJ's appellate jurisdiction is supported by a number of governments in the region this has not translated into popular support for the CCJ. As a result, it has not proved possible to satisfy the referendum requirements needed to affect the constitutional amendment necessary to replace the JCPC with the CCJ.[4]

Though they sit on separate courts, the judges of the JCPC and CCJ share much in common from a legal perspective. Both are steeped in the English common law. Indeed, some of the judges of the CCJ have undertaken at least part of their legal education in the UK. They are also both familiar with a constitutional system based on the Westminster model of government;[5] with all that this implies in terms of foundational principles such as representative democracy, the rule of law and the separation of powers. Despite this shared legal and political culture, an analysis of their jurisprudence reveals a striking difference in their approaches to constitutional interpretation and the respective roles of legislators and judges in effecting constitutional change. This is discussed in more detail below, but at the risk of oversimplification, the judges of the JCPC adopt, on the whole, a much more deferential approach to

[3] As well as abolishing the right of appeal to the JCPC in 1970, Guyana replaced the Queen as head of state with a ceremonial President, and in 1980 abandoned the Westminster model of government, opting instead to become a 'co-operative socialist republic'.

[4] As demonstrated by the referendums on replacing the JCPC with the CCJ in Grenada in 2016 and again in Grenada and Antigua and Barbuda in 2018. On each occasion, the replacement of the JCPC with the CCJ was supported by the incumbent government but rejected by the voters.

[5] With the exception of Guyana, which is based on a hybrid presidential/parliamentary system.

constitutional review of decisions of local legislatures and executives than their CCJ counterparts. This may be due in part to their discomfiture in exercising jurisdiction, extra-territorially, over countries which they may never have visited and about which they are candid enough to admit they know very little.[6] They are also much more concerned with respecting the text of the constitutions they are being asked to review, a mode of interpretation which reflects the traditional English approach to statutory interpretation.[7] By contrast, the judges of the CCJ, being indigenous to the region,[8] and much more aware of the failure of local legislatures to hold their executives to account, tend to be much less deferential in matters of constitutional review. They are also much less concerned with being faithful to the text of the Constitutions they are reviewing, which they regard as lacking, in some respects, democratic legitimacy, being non-autochthonous products of the Imperial Parliament in Westminster.[9]

This contrast in approach to constitutional reasoning is at its most profound in cases which involve the effect of saving laws clauses upon the fundamental rights and freedoms guaranteed by the constitution. Such savings laws clauses, which are a central feature of Commonwealth Caribbean constitutions, preserve existing laws, rendering them immune from constitutional challenge on the grounds of inconsistency with the Bill of Rights included in each constitution. There are two kinds of saving laws clauses. The first kind of savings clause, which I will call a *partial* savings clause, preserves all forms of punishment that were lawful prior to independence.[10] The second kind of savings clause, which I will call a *general* savings clause, is even more extensive, affording immunity from constitutional challenge to all laws that were in force at the time of independence. The constitutions of some countries only contain partial saving laws clauses,[11] while the remainder contain both partial and general saving laws clauses.

The presence of these savings clauses has posed formidable interpretive challenges for both the JCPC and CCJ when confronted with colonial laws or forms of punishment, in particular, the death penalty, that are not only inconsistent with the freedoms guaranteed by the region's Bills of Rights but are also repugnant to contemporary human rights norms. It should, therefore, come as no surprise that, of the 32 landmark judgments that were heard by the JCPC, almost half (14) were concerned with the operation of the death penalty in the region. At a very practical level an additional reason for the preponderance of death penalty cases is the work of the Death Penalty Project (DPP), a group of lawyers based in London, dedicated to seeking the removal of the death penalty through constitutional litigation. The fact that these lawyers worked on a pro bono basis was significant because legal aid is rarely, if ever, available in the Commonwealth Caribbean to complainants wishing to bring appeals from their local court of appeal to the JCPC.

[6] See comments of Lord Hoffmann available at www.jamaicaobserver.com/news/privy-council-judge-supports-ccj/.

[7] See F Bennion, *Bennion on Statutory Interpretation*, 5th ed (Lexis Nexis, 2008) 469.

[8] With only two exceptions to date: Justice Hayton and Justice Wit.

[9] With the exception of Belize, the independence Constitutions of all the other countries in the region came into force as a result of an Act of the UK Parliament. See further T Robinson, 'Our Inherent Constitution' in D Berry and T Robinson (eds), *Transitions in Caribbean Law* (Ian Randle Publishers, Caribbean Law Publishing Company, 2013).

[10] See Constitution of Jamaica, s 17(2).

[11] Antigua and Barbuda, Belize (but now expired), Dominica, Grenada, St Kitts, St Lucia and St Vincent.

Following the DPP's success, in 1994, in the case of *Pratt and Morgan A-G Jamaica*,[12] in which the JCPC declared that executions more than five years after the imposition of the death sentence were presumptively unconstitutional, there followed a flood of cases in the early 2000s in which the DPP sought to persuade the JCPC to impose further limitations on the operation of the death penalty. The high water mark was a series of cases at the beginning of the 2000s in which the DPP successfully argued: first, that death row prisoners could not be executed while their petitions to international human rights bodies were pending; and, second, that in those countries whose constitutions included partial savings clauses, laws prescribing a mandatory death penalty for murder were unconstitutional, though the same did not apply to countries whose constitutions also included a general savings clause.

As a result, by the time that the CCJ opened its doors for business in 2006 most of the constitutional issues surrounding the death penalty had been exhaustively argued and it is notable that, of the eight landmark judgments that were heard by the CCJ, only two were concerned with death penalty issues.

B. The Courts and Constitutional Litigation

None of the Commonwealth Caribbean constitutions expressly provide for a power of constitutional review of legislation, but it was held by the Court of Appeal of Trinidad and Tobago in *Collymore and Abraham v A-G*[13] that such a power may be derived by way of necessary implication from the text of these constitutions. Though the Court of Appeal of Trinidad and Tobago is not a final appellate court, its judgment in *Collymore* has never been overruled by the JCPC, and may, therefore, be regarded as authoritative on the question of the origins of the power of constitutional review in relation to Trinidad and Tobago. Moreover, while the Court of Appeal Trinidad and Tobago is a national and not a regional court, its judgment in *Collymore* is generally regarded as seminal for the other constitutions in the region which share a similar constitutional structure to Trinidad and Tobago. Indeed, it has even been described by some commentators as the Commonwealth Caribbean's equivalent of *Marbury v Madison*.[14]

In reaching its conclusion about the Courts' powers of constitutional review, the Court of Appeal in *Collymore*, relied on a network of provisions in Trinidad's independence Constitution. Firstly, pursuant to section 36, Parliament's power to make laws was expressly 'subject to the provision of this Constitution'. Secondly, section 2 provided that no law shall abrogate, abridge or infringe or authorise the abrogation, abridgement or infringement of any of the rights and freedoms guaranteed by the Constitution.[15] Thirdly, pursuant to section 6, if any person alleged that their fundamental rights as guaranteed by the Constitution were being, or were likely to be, violated they could apply to the High Court for redress. On the basis of these provisions Chief Justice Wooding was moved to declare that:

[12] [1994] 2 AC 1 (PC).

[13] *Collymore and Abraham v A-G* (1968) 12 WIR 5 CA (Trinidad and Tobago).

[14] 5 US 137 (1803).

[15] Subject to the provisions of ss 3, 4 and 5.

> I am accordingly in no doubt that our Supreme Court has been constituted, and is, *the guardian of the Constitution*, so it is not only within its competence but also its right and duty to make binding declarations, if and whenever warranted, that an enactment passed by Parliament is *ultra vires* and therefore void and of no effect because it abrogates, abridges or infringes (…) one or more of the rights and freedoms recognized and declared by [Chapter 1].[16]

Notwithstanding its importance for the region as a whole, the reach of the Court of Appeal's judgment in *Collymore* is limited by the fact that in *Collymore* the Court was concerned with its power to review legislation which contravened the fundamental rights guaranteed by the Constitution, rather than legislation which contravened other constitutional provisions. *Collymore* does not, therefore, provide the juridical basis for reviewing legislation which is alleged to infringe the other provisions of the constitution, ie the non-Bill of Rights provisions. So far as these are concerned, there are two possible sources for the power of constitutional review.

The first source is to be found in a number of Commonwealth Caribbean Constitutions – Antigua, Dominica, Grenada, Guyana, St Kitts, and St Vincent – which contain a right to apply to the High Court for redress in respect of violations of the non-Bills of Rights provisions of the Constitution.[17] By analogy with the judgment in *Collymore*, in which the Court of Appeal attached considerable weight to the enforcement provision in section 6 of the Trinidadian Constitution in respect of violations of the fundamental rights guaranteed by the Constitution, it is arguable that the enforcement provision in respect of non-Bill of Rights violations in these other constitutions, combined with a supreme law clause, similarly empowers courts in these countries to review the constitutionality of legislation that violates the non-Bill of Rights provisions of the Constitution.

The second potential source of the power of constitutional review is relevant to those constitutions, such as the Jamaican Constitution, that do not contain an express enforcement provision for the non-Bill of rights provisions of the constitution. In the case of these constitutions, it is arguable that a power of constitutional review is necessarily implied by the inclusion of a supremacy clause which provides that laws that are inconsistent with the Constitution shall be void.[18] This is essentially the approach that the JCPC adopted in *Hinds v The Queen*,[19] in which the JCPC, adopting a line of reasoning based on the related principles of the rule of law and the separation of powers, struck down certain provisions of Jamaica's Gun Court Act, which purported to confer on the Full Court Division of the Gun Court, which was composed of persons qualified and appointed as resident magistrates, a jurisdiction which under the provisions of Chapter VII of the Constitution could only be exercised by a person qualified and appointed as a judge of the Supreme Court. *Hinds* is of particular significance because it was the first piece of legislation enacted by a post-independence parliament in the Commonwealth Caribbean to be struck down by the JCPC.

[16] At 9A-8.
[17] See eg Constitution of Antigua, s 119.
[18] See eg Constitution of Jamaica, s 2.
[19] *Hinds v The Queen* [1977] AC 175.

More recently, the courts' power to review the constitutionality of legislation has even been extended, by statute, in some countries, to permit the Attorney General on behalf of the Cabinet to refer to the Court of Appeal questions concerning, inter alia, the interpretation of the Constitution and the constitutionality or interpretation of any legislation enacted by parliament.[20] Thus, in *Attorney General's Reference (Constitutional Questions), Re*[21] the Court of Appeal of St Lucia was asked to answer a series of questions regarding the Eastern Caribbean Supreme Court (Rates of Pension) Judges (Act) and the constitutional entitlement to a pension of a judge who has retired from office before the constitutionally mandated retirement age.

Though constitutional review has traditionally been available only in proceedings brought by a claimant against the state, and all of the 40 landmark cases selected for this empirical research involve proceedings brought by claimants against the state, the reach of constitutional review has been extended in Jamaica by section 13(5) of the Jamaican Charter of Fundamental Rights and Freedoms (2011) to permit claimants to bring proceedings for constitutional review against 'natural or juristic persons if, and to the extent that, it is applicable, taking account of the nature of the right and the nature of any duty imposed by the right'. Applying this provision, in *Brendan Courtney Bain v The University of the West Indies*,[22] the Supreme Court of Jamaica treated the University of the West Indies as a juristic person in upholding a claim against the University for violating the Charter rights of the claimant.

C. The Judges

The judges who sit on the JCPC are, in the main, the 12 Justices of the UK's Supreme Court, who divide their time about equally between the JCPC and the Supreme Court. The procedure for appointment of these Justices is governed by the Constitutional Reform Act 2005 (CRA 2005). Suitable candidates for the position of Justice of the Supreme Court are recommended by a selection commission, chaired by the President of the Supreme Court, and convened by the Lord Chancellor. The other members of the selection commission are a senior judge, other than a Justice of the Supreme Court, and a member of each of the Judicial Appointments Commissions (JACs) of England and Wales, Scotland, and Northern Ireland, nominated by the Chairman of the relevant JAC. At least one of these members must be a lay person. Once the selection commission has made its decision it must submit a report to the Lord Chancellor which must state who has been selected. In certain closely defined circumstances, the Lord Chancellor can invite a reconsideration or can reject a candidate. If the Lord Chancellor is content with the selection commission's recommendation, the candidate's name is forwarded to the Prime Minister who, in turn, sends the recommendation to the Queen who makes the formal appointment. Justices of the Supreme Court can only be removed on a petition to both Houses of Parliament.

[20] See eg Antigua, The Attorney General's Reference (Constitutional Questions) Act 2009. See also St Lucia, The Attorney General's Reference (Constitutional Questions) Act 2005.

[21] *Attorney General's Reference (Constitutional Questions), Re* LC 2010 CA 8 (unreported).

[22] *Brendan Courtney Bain v The University of the West Indies* JMFC FULL 3.

On occasion, judges from outside the UK will sit. When this occurs, it will usually be a senior judge from the country from which the appeal emanates. Quite apart from the local knowledge that the judge can bring, having a judge from the country from which the appeal emanates helps to reinforce the point that the JCPC is sitting as the highest appellate court of the country in question and is applying the law of that country.

The JCPC does not sit *en banc*. Usually, appeals are heard by panels of five Justices. However, in cases of the highest constitutional importance – for example, where the JCPC is considering overruling one of its own decisions – the appeal will be heard by a panel of nine Justices.[23]

The procedure for the appointment of Justices of the CCJ was greatly informed by the widespread concern that had been voiced by opponents of the CCJ about the role of politicians in the judicial appointments process. In order to address this concern, it was accepted by the Heads of Government that it was crucial to insulate, as far as possible, the appointment of Justices to the CCJ from political interference. Accordingly, responsibility for the selection and appointment of the Justices of the CCJ, with the exception of the President, is vested in the Regional Judicial Services and Legal Commission (RJSLC).[24] This is a very unusual arrangement for an international court, where the normal procedure is for judges to be appointed by governmental nomination and/or election, but it is a system with which the Heads of Government were familiar from their experience of the appointment of judges to their own national courts. If political interference was to be avoided, however, the independence of the RJLSC was also crucial. Therefore, it was agreed by the Heads of Government that membership of the RJLSC should not be dominated by either politicians or lawyers but would include other sections of the wider community. As a result, the RJLSC is composed of 11 members, including: the President of the CCJ as Chair; two lawyers; two lay people; two academics; two representatives of the regional Bar; and two chairs of the Public Service Commissions and Judicial and Legal Service Commissions of the member states (appointed by rotation in alphabetical order).[25]

In order to be eligible for appointment as Justice of the CCJ, a candidate must satisfy one or other of the following requirements. Either they must, for a period of not less than five years, have been a judge of a higher court in the territory of a Contracting State (ie a state that has ratified the Agreement Establishing the CCJ) or another Commonwealth country or a state exercising civil law jurisprudence common to that of the Contracting States and distinguished themselves in that office. Or they must, for a period of not less than 15 years, have been either a legal academic or a practising lawyer in a Member State of CARICOM or in another Commonwealth country or a state exercising civil law jurisprudence common to that of the Contracting States and distinguished themselves in the legal profession. To date, most of those who have been appointed as Justices have been experienced judges from the appellate courts of Contracting States, though there have been two Justices, who were former Professors of Law: Justice David Hayton and Justice Winston Anderson.

[23] See eg *A-G Barbados v Boyce and Joseph* [2006] CCJ 1 (AJ).
[24] Agreement Establishing the Caribbean Court of Justice (Agreement), Art V.
[25] Agreement, Art I.

With the exception of the President, appointments of the CCJ's Justices by the RJLSC are made by a majority vote of all members.[26] Once appointed, a judge may sit until he reaches the age of 72.[27]

A judge may only be removed from office for inability to perform the functions of his office, whether arising from illness or any other cause, or for misbehaviour;[28] and only then after a majority vote of all members of the RJLSC, having first been referred to a tribunal, consisting of a chairman and not less than two other members selected by the RJLSC from among persons who have held a senior judicial appointment.[29]

Separate provision has been made with regard to the President who is appointed by a qualified majority vote of three quarters of the Heads of Government.[30] This would appear to offer more scope for interference by the Heads of Government, but this is limited by the requirement that the Heads of Government must appoint as President someone recommended by the RJLSC.[31] The President holds office for a non-renewable term of seven years or until he reaches the age of 72, whichever is earlier.[32] The President may be removed from office by a qualified majority vote of three quarters of the Heads of Government.[33] However, as with his appointment, the President's removal is subject to the recommendation of the RJLSC, which itself must act on the advice of a tribunal which can only be appointed if at least three of the Heads of Government represent to the others that the question of the President's removal ought to be investigated.[34] In such a case the members of the tribunal are selected by the Heads of Government.[35]

As we will see in Section II below, the insulation of the Justices of both the JCPC and CCJ from political interference ensures that the judges are free to adopt whatever line of constitutional reasoning and argumentation they deem to be appropriate in any given case without fear that this will result in their removal from office or a prejudicial alteration to their terms and conditions of service.

D. Legal Scholarship and Constitutional Reasoning

With some notable exceptions, the jurisprudence of the JCPC has not attracted a great deal of interest from constitutional scholars outside the Commonwealth Caribbean; though it has attracted considerable criticism from constitutional scholars from within the region, as discussed below.[36] In turn, as we will see in Section II(B), the judges of the JCPC, rarely, if at all, engage with the work of constitutional scholars, whether

[26] Agreement, Art IV, para 7.
[27] Agreement, Art IX, paras 1 and 3.
[28] Agreement, Art IX, para 4.
[29] Agreement, Art IX, para 6(a).
[30] Agreement, Art IV, para 6.
[31] ibid.
[32] Agreement, Art IX, para 2.
[33] Agreement, Art IX, para 6(b).
[34] ibid.
[35] ibid.
[36] See especially T Robinson, A Bulkan and A Saunders, *Fundamentals of Caribbean Constitutional Law* (Sweet and Maxwell, 2015).

within or without the region, in their judgments; though they do frequently refer to the judgments of other constitutional courts and international human rights bodies. This failure to engage with constitutional scholarship may be partly the result of the paucity of constitutional scholarship within the UK on Caribbean Commonwealth constitutional matters and a lack of familiarity with the work of Commonwealth Caribbean constitutional scholars. It may also be due to the sharp divide amongst senior UK judges between practising lawyers who go on to become senior judges and legal academics who rarely go on to become senior judges.[37]

Their lack of engagement with constitutional scholarship has also meant that, until relatively recently, the judges of the JCPC were not in the habit of articulating their reflections on matters of constitutional interpretation.[38] However, in the last two decades, with the emergence of a transnational judicial conversation about constitutional rights,[39] they have been much readier to expound their own approach to constitutional interpretation and to refer to the development of constitutional interpretation in other common law jurisdictions.

Broadly speaking, it is possible to identify three main approaches that have been adopted by the JCPC – the 'ordinary meaning', the 'structural', and the 'purposive' – always remembering that this taxonomy is subject to two caveats. The first is that the JCPC's interpretive approach is flexible and is inevitably influenced by the subject matter of the case and the nature of the constitutional provision in issue. The second is that the JCPC tends to sit in panels of five judges rather than *en banc* so that, as we will see, differently constituted panels sometimes favour different interpretive approaches to the same issue. As we will also see, even within the same panel the majority and dissenting judges often divide sharply over the correct interpretive approach.

i. *The Ordinary Meaning Approach*

The ordinary meaning approach to constitutional interpretation is based on the presumption that the meaning of the constitution is derived from the text of the constitution itself as it would be understood by the reasonable reader.[40] This is not to say that the intentions of the framers are irrelevant, but rather that the best way of discovering those intentions is by reference to the words that they used. This version of the textual approach is closely related to the traditional English approach to statutory interpretation, as defined in the leading English text on the subject:

> An enactment has the legal meaning taken to be intended by the legislator. In other words the legal meaning corresponds to the legislative intention … [T]he function of the court is to find out and declare that intention [which] is the paramount, indeed only ultimate, criterion.[41]

[37] The three notable exceptions are: Lady Hale, a former President of the UK Supreme Court, who had previously been a Law Professor at the University of Manchester; Lord Sumption, who was, briefly, a Fellow at Magdalene College, Oxford; and, most recently, Lord Burrows, formerly, Norton Rose Professor of Commercial Law at St Hughes College, Oxford.

[38] P Hogg, 'Canada from Privy Council to Supreme Court' in J Goldsworthy (ed), *Interpreting Constitutions* (Oxford University Press, 2007) 84.

[39] See C McCrudden, 'Common Law of Human Rights?: Transnational Judicial Conversations on Constitutional Rights' (2000) 20 *Oxford Journal of Legal Studies* 499.

[40] A Barak, *Purposive Interpretation in Law* (Princeton University Press, 2005) 269.

[41] Bennion (n 7) 469.

This resembles but is, emphatically, not identical to the *originalist* approach popular in the US, which requires the interpreter to use historical methods to determine the meaning of the constitution by reference to its public meaning as at the time of its ratification.[42] Though the JCPC has sometimes had regard to the history of the drafting of Caribbean independence constitutions,[43] it has never regarded this as decisive, preferring always to base its conclusions on the meaning of the constitution as understood by the reasonable reader.

ii. The Structural Approach

As expounded by the JCPC, the structuralist approach looks to the broad principles which are said to underpin the text of the constitution, such as the separation of powers, representative government, equality and the rule of law, to interpret specific provisions where the constitution is vague or ambiguous, or to fill a lacuna.[44] The high water mark of this approach is the Board's decision in the case of *Hinds* to strike down Jamaica's Gun Court Act on the basis that it violated a number of implied principles on the Jamaican Constitution, in particular the rule of law and the separation of powers.

iii. The Purposive Approach

This approach can be traced to Lord Wilberforce's judgment in *Minister of Home Affairs (Bermuda) v Fisher*.[45] Tasked with the question of deciding whether the term 'child' in section 11 of the Constitution of Bermuda, which guaranteed freedom of movement, included an 'illegitimate child', Lord Wilberforce observed that the starting point in answering this question was to recognise that a constitution is a *sui generis* instrument, 'calling for principles of interpretation of its own'. This did not mean there were no rules of law which should apply to the interpretation of a constitution. 'Respect must be paid to the language which has been used and to the traditions and usages which have given meaning to that language'.[46] However, the broad and ample style in which the constitutional guarantees of rights and freedoms were drafted, influenced as they were by the European Convention on Human Rights, and 'laying down principles of width and generality', called for:

> a *generous* interpretation avoiding what has been called 'the austerity of tabulated legalism', suitable to give individuals the full measure of the fundamental rights and freedoms referred to (emphasis added).[47]

This approach has had a profound influence on the JCPC's approach to constitutional interpretation over the ensuing decades and has been deployed on a number

[42] See A Scalia, 'Originalism: The Lesser Evil' (1989) 57 *University of Cincinnati Law Review* 849.
[43] See eg *Newbold and Others v Commissioner of Police* [2014] UKPC 12, para 24.
[44] J Goldsworthy, 'Australia: Devotion to Legalism' in J Goldsworthy (ed), *Interpreting Constitutions* (Oxford University Press, 2007) 129.
[45] *Minister of Home Affairs (Bermuda) v Fisher* [1980] AC 319.
[46] ibid 329 E–F.
[47] ibid 328 G–H.

of occasions by the JCPC to impose restrictions on the operation of the death penalty in the region, though it has not ultimately been enough to overcome the barriers erected by the saving clauses, which immunise the death penalty itself from being declared unconstitutional.

In contrast to the JCPC, the CCJ has been greatly influenced by the work of Caribbean constitutional scholars, who are consistently cited by the CCJ in its judgments. Their willingness to engage with constitutional scholarship may have something to do with the fact that many of the CCJ's Justices were taught by these same constitutional scholars when undertaking their law degree at the University of the West Indies.[48] Additionally, the current President of the CCJ, Justice Adrian Saunders is, himself, one of the co-authors of the leading text on Caribbean constitutional law.[49] In this monograph, the authors who, in addition to Justice Saunders, include two of the region's leading constitutional scholars, Tracy Robinson and Arif Bulkan, provide a forceful critique of the JCPC's approach to constitutional interpretation. They advocate as an alternative what I have elsewhere called the 'holistic approach',[50] which conceives of the constitution as more than the sum of its written provisions. In effect, this means treating the constitution 'not as a set of discrete written provisions which derive their formal authority from their legal enactment, but as a normative structure which is based on certain foundational principles that are the deepest source of its authority'.[51]

At first glance, there would appear to be considerable overlap between the holistic and the structural and purposive approaches as they have been applied by the JCPC, but there are important differences. The holistic approach lies much further along the spectrum of judicial creativity in terms of the interpretive licence it affords to judges. Unlike the purposive approach, which requires judges 'to pay respect to the language which has been used and to the traditions and usages which have given meaning to that language', the holistic approach directs judges to eschew the usual and ordinary meaning of the words used if that meaning is too technical or overly legalistic or has the effect of 'undermining the broad intent of the constitution'.[52] Even a provision, the meaning of which appears to be plain on the face of it, 'may have to be reconciled with other provisions or core principles of the constitution that, on a broader review, it is in tension with'.[53] This requires judges to adopt not the plain or natural meaning, but rather the meaning which is most compatible with the 'underlying sentiments and principles' of the constitution.[54] These unwritten foundational principles are to be treated as supreme and binding on all state actors 'even in the absence of and, in

[48] See in particular, S McIntosh, *Caribbean Constitutional Reform: Rethinking the West Indian Polity* (Caribbean Law Publishing Company, 2002).

[49] See Robinson et al (n 36).

[50] D O'Brien, 'The Interpretation of Commonwealth Caribbean Constitutions: Does Text Matter?' in R Albert, D O'Brien and S Wheatle (eds), *The Oxford Handbook of Caribbean Constitutions* (Oxford University Press, 2020).

[51] J Goldsworthy, 'Constitutional Interpretation' in J Goldsworthy (ed), *Interpreting Constitutions* (Oxford University Press, 2007) 2.

[52] Robinson et al (n 36) 147.

[53] ibid 158.

[54] ibid.

extraordinary cases, in spite of, an explicit constitutional provision'.[55] What is needed, it is argued, is a mode of interpretation that honours fundamental rights and freedoms 'without being entirely undone by textual restrictions within the constitution'.[56] As we will see in Section II(B) this is reflected in the willingness of the CCJ Justices to ignore the ordinary meaning approach in favour of a more purposive/holistic approach in cases involving fundamental rights.

II. Arguments in Constitutional Reasoning

Before examining the structure and type of constitutional arguments most common to Commonwealth Caribbean judges it should be noted that of the 40 landmark judgments that formed the basis of the empirical study, 32 were judgments delivered by the JCPC and the remaining eight were judgments of the CCJ.

A. The Structure of Constitutional Arguments

In the majority of judgments (26), the arguments were one-line conclusive. This probably reflects the parsimonious approach of the common law towards adjudication, only deciding what is necessary for the resolution of the case.

There was only one example of an, arguably, parallel, individually inconclusive, but together conclusive argument. This was the judgment of the CCJ in *McEwan et al v A-G Guyana*.[57] This case was a radical departure from the approach to constitutional interpretation previously taken by the JCPC and marked a watershed in the implementation of the region's Bills of Rights. It is understandable, therefore, that the CCJ wished to avail itself of as many arguments as possible, especially as no single argument was individually conclusive of the issue at hand.

B. Types of Arguments

i. *Analogies*

On the understanding that an analogy involves applying a norm to a situation, which does not actually fall under its scope, there were only four examples of argument by analogy. A good example of this type of argument can be found in the case of *Campbell-Rodrigues v AG Jamaica*. In this case, which concerned the right to property under section 18(1) of the Jamaican Constitution, the JCPC drew an analogy between the assumption by the Minister of Finance of the temporary management of certain companies whose affairs were under investigation and the creation of a toll road by public authorities.

[55] Robinson (n 9) 250.
[56] ibid 249.
[57] *McEwan et al v A-G Guyana* [2018] CCJ 30 (AJ).

ii. Establishing the Text of the Constitution and the Applicability of the Constitution

Generally speaking, neither the text of the Constitution, nor the applicability of constitutional law, was a live issue in any of the leading cases. However, there were a number of cases – *Boyce and Joseph*[58] and *Nervais v The Queen*,[59] for example, in which the JCPC and the CCJ, respectively, had to decide whether a modifications clause contained in the legislation under which the Constitution was enacted was of an equivalent legal status to the Constitution and would thus mitigate the immunising effect of a saving clause to be found in the Barbados Constitution. In another case, *Mitchell v DPP*, the JCPC had to have regard to whether a decree enacted during the Grenada Revolution had constitutional force, even though it was not enacted in accordance with the procedure prescribed by the Constitution.

iii. Harmonising Arguments

Domestic harmonising arguments in the sense of interpreting one constitutional provision in the light of another, or using two constitutional provisions together to establish the constitutional standard, were relatively common: 14 out of 32 judgments of the JCPC and six out of the eight judgments of the CCJ. The preponderance of these types of arguments in the leading cases before the CCJ, arguably, reflects its holistic approach to constitutional interpretation.

International harmonising arguments in the sense of using international law in order to interpret the Constitution were also relatively common: 16 of the leading cases made reference to international human rights law, which correlates very closely to the number of cases involving constitutional challenges to the death penalty. In these cases, the appellants referred to the state party's obligation under international human rights law; the majority of countries in the region being signatories to one or both of the Inter American Convention on Human Rights (ACHR) and the Universal Declaration of Human Rights (UNDHR). Though all of the Commonwealth Caribbean countries have dualist legal systems there is a strong presumption that domestic law can and should be read consistently with international law and that domestic decision-makers can (some judges would say 'should' in the case of fundamental rights) take these international obligations into account when reaching their decision.[60] In the case of Guyana, Article 39(2) of the Constitution expressly mandates the courts 'to pay due regard to international law' when interpreting any of the fundamental rights provisions contained in the Constitution.

iv. Precedents

Unsurprisingly, in countries with legal systems that are based on the common law doctrine of stare decisis almost all of the listed leading cases make reference to the JCPC's precedents. As the volume of its case law has begun to grow, so too the CCJ has

[58] *A-G Barbados v Boyce and Joseph* [2006] CCJ 1 (AJ).
[59] *Nervais v The Queen* [2018] CCJ 19 (AJ).
[60] Lord Mance, *International Law in the UK Supreme Court*, 13 February 2017, at www.supremecourt.uk/docs/speech-170213.pdf.

increasingly begun to refer to its own precedents. There are, however, two noteworthy points about the use of precedents amongst the list of leading cases.

The first is the willingness of the JCPC to ignore the doctrine of stare decisis and overrule its own earlier judgments in two cases: *Pratt and Morgan* and *Boyce and Joseph*. This is highly unusual, since the customary way for a court to avoid an inconvenient precedent is to *distinguish* the unhelpful precedent. The willingness of the JCPC to overrule its own precedents reflects the extraordinary challenges that the saving clauses included in the region's constitutions present for judges when faced with existing laws that are immunised from constitutional review, but which are clearly repugnant to international human rights norms.

The second noteworthy point is the approach of the CCJ towards the JCPC's precedents. In *A-G Barbados v Boyce and Joseph*, the CCJ explained how it would go about developing its jurisprudence:

> [W]e shall naturally consider very *carefully and respectfully* opinions of final courts of other Commonwealth countries and particularly, judgments of the [JCPC] which determine the law for those Caribbean states that accept the [JCPC] as their final appellate court (emphasis added).

In *Nervais*, the CCJ added that the development of its jurisprudence would require '*evolution* and change in relation to the approach of decisions of the [JCPC]'.[61]

v. Arguments from Silence

Though it was not a dominant argument amongst the leading cases, there were at least six instances in which the court invoked the absence of words in the constitution under review or the common law in reaching its conclusion. For example, in *Collymore*, the JCPC referred to the absence of the right to strike under the English common law when interpreting the right to freedom of assembly under the Constitution of Trinidad and Tobago. In *De Freitas v Permanent Secretary of Ministry and Agriculture*,[62] the JCPC referred to the absence of a suitable exemption when striking down a statutory provision prohibiting civil servants from expressing opinions on matters of national political controversy. In *A-G Guyana and Richardson*,[63] the CCJ referred to the absence of any express constitutional limitation on parliament's power to impose a two-term limit on Presidents. Finally, in *Ram v AG Guyana*,[64] the CCJ referred to the absence of any express distinction in the Constitution between a member of parliament's participation and vote on a motion of no confidence and on any other motion.

vi. Teleological (Textual) Arguments, Historical-intentional and Ordinary Meaning

As alluded to above, it is only relatively recently that the judges of JCPC have begun to expound the theoretical underpinning of their approach to constitutional interpretation.

[61] See *Nervais* (n 59), para 7.
[62] *De Freitas v Permanent Secretary of Ministry and Agriculture* [1999] AC 69.
[63] *A-G Guyana and Richardson* [2018] CCJ 17 (AJ).
[64] *Ram v AG Guyana* [2019] CCJ 14 (AJ).

None could be said to be *originalists* in the sense that that term is used to describe the approach of a number of Justices of the US Supreme Court, most famously Justice Scalia. The judges of the JCPC have, however, from time to time had regard to the purpose of a constitutional provision when interpreting its meaning. A good example is the JCPC's judgment in *Watson v The Queen*,[65] in which the court sought to rationalise the existence of the savings clauses in the Constitution of Jamaica as a means of securing the orderly transition from colonial rule to independence.

From time to time the judges of the JCPC also invoke the intentions of those who drafted the Constitution when interpreting its provisions (10 out of the 32 listed leading cases). It is important to note, however, that this is not by reference to the historical record of the drafters' intention, but rather to the judges' own hypothetical assumptions about what the drafters must have intended. So, for example, in *Hinds*, Lord Diplock referred to the presumed intentions of the drafters with regard to the implied principle of the separation of powers in the Jamaican Constitution. Again, in *Sharma v A-G Trinidad*,[66] Lord Bingham referred to the presumed intentions of the drafters when finding in the Trinidad Constitution an implied right for members of parliament to be paid for their services. If anything, the judges of the CCJ appear to be even more ready to invoke the presumed intentions of the drafters to support their conclusions. Thus, in six out of the eight leading cases before the CCJ, the judges referred to the drafters' intentions. This possibly reflects the CCJ's Justices' greater sense of ownership of the region's Constitutions and their correspondingly greater insight into the intentions of the drafters.

In line with the traditional approach to statutory interpretation, the judges of the JCPC frequently refer to the ordinary meaning of the words of the Constitution (14 out of 32 cases) and the ordinary meaning of the words of the Constitution is also referred to in no less than three of the eight listed leading cases before the CCJ. However, the judges of both courts have shown themselves prepared to ignore the ordinary meaning approach where they believe that a purposive or a holistic approach is better suited to the protection of fundamental rights.

vii. Non-Legal Arguments

There were no examples of cases amongst the 40 landmark judgments in which such arguments informed the judges' reasoning, though there are occasional references by the JCPC to the economic position of these, largely, small developing states. Also, in the death penalty cases there were passing references to the anguish suffered by death row prisoners and the inhumanity of prolonged delays in the carrying out of the death penalty, but the constitutional challenge was ultimately based on a legal rather than a moral argument: for example, by reference to the constitutional guarantee of 'the protection of the law', 'due process,' or the prohibition against 'cruel and unusual punishment'.

[65] *Watson v The Queen* [2004] UKPC 34.
[66] *Sharma v A-G Trinidad* [2007] UKPC 41.

viii. References to Scholarly Work

As noted above, in Section I(D), references to scholarly work by the JCPC were relatively rare. Out of the 32 leading cases before the JCPC only five contained references to scholarly works. Of these five, only one was a reference to a work by a Commonwealth Caribbean scholar, Margaret Demerieux. References to scholarly work were far more frequent in the leading cases before the CCJ: five out of the eight leading judgments referred to scholarly work. Additionally, CCJ judges were more likely to refer to the scholarly work of leading Commonwealth Caribbean scholars, such as Francis Alexis,[67] Simeon McIntosh,[68] Tracy Robinson and Arif Bulkan.[69] This suggests a much greater willingness on the part of CCJ Justices to engage with the commentary of Commonwealth Caribbean scholars when reaching their decisions.

ix. References to Foreign (National) Law

There was a relatively strong presence of references to foreign (national) law: 14 out of the 32 leading cases before the JCPC. The presence of so many references to foreign law reflects the growth in a transnational judicial conversation about fundamental rights that began to emerge in the 1990s. References to foreign law was especially marked in the death penalty cases, with JCPC judges citing judgments of the constitutional courts of other English-speaking countries, such as the US and Indian Supreme Courts and the Constitutional Court of South Africa. These were chosen for the support they offered to the JCPC's conclusions about the incompatibility of various aspects of the operation of the death penalty in the Commonwealth Caribbean with the constitutional prohibition against cruel and unusual punishment or inhuman treatment.

The reference to foreign law is even more marked in the case of the CCJ: seven out of eight of the leading cases include references to foreign law. This may reflect the CCJ's status as a relatively new court, seeking to establish its own corpus of distinctively Caribbean jurisprudence, but supporting this novel jurisprudence by pointing out its consistency with the jurisprudence of other well-respected constitutional courts. For these purposes, I have not treated references by the CCJ to judgments of the JCPC as references to foreign law.

x. Pro Homine *or* Pro Persona *Arguments*

For the purposes of this analysis the *pro homine* principle has been treated as the equivalent of the 'purposive' approach discussed above. Though it was originally outlined by Lord Wilberforce in 1979, in the case of *Minister of Home Affairs (Bermuda)*, the purposive approach really began to impact on the JCPC's jurisprudence following its landmark judgment in *Pratt and Morgan*, 15 years later. Following *Pratt and Morgan*, the purposive approach has been invoked by the JCPC in no less than 12 of its leading

[67] *Changing Caribbean Constitutions* (Antilles Publications, 1983).
[68] See McIntosh (n 48).
[69] T Robinson and A Bulkan, 'Constitutional Comparisons by a Supranational Court in Flux: The Privy Council and Caribbean Bills of Rights' (2017) 80 *Modern Law Review* 380.

cases. This means that in total it has been invoked by the JCPC in a total of 15 out of its 32 leading cases. The frequency of references to the purposive approach is even more notable in the case of the CCJ, being invoked by the CCJ in six out of the eight leading cases before the CCJ, though in the case of the CCJ it may be more accurate to label this approach holistic.

C. The Overall Weight of the Arguments

As one would expect in a common law system based on the doctrine of *stare decisis* (binding precedent), the majority of arguments mentioned in the landmark judgments formed part of the ratio decidendi. Neither the Justices of the JCPC nor the Justices of the CCJ used rhetorical or decorative arguments. However, as noted above, in cases involving fundamental rights there was a clear preference for the purposive over the ordinary meaning approach to constitutional interpretation.

D. Judicial Candour and Judicial Rhetoric

In a common law system, the judges' immediate audience, when handing down their judgments are the parties to the proceedings and their lawyers. Through their reasoning the judges must justify their decision, in the first instance, to the parties to the proceedings. However, because the common law system is based on binding precedent, the judges must also, through their reasoning, offer guidance to future litigants on whether a constitutional challenge based on analogous facts is, or is not, likely to succeed.

As an extra-territorial court, composed almost exclusively of judges with no connection to the Commonwealth Caribbean, the judges of the JCPC are also acutely aware of the need in their reasoning to be sensitive to local sensibilities, particularly in relation to issues like the death penalty, which continues to enjoy popular support in the Commonwealth Caribbean, a region with some of the highest homicide rates in the world. This means that the judges must be careful to ensure that their *legal* reasoning is capable of justifying the decision that they have reached and that they cannot be accused of usurping the functions of local legislatures or executives.

It also means that the judges tend scrupulously to avoid legally irrelevant political and/or emotional language in the text of their judgments. Where such language appears in the judgments it tends to be directed toward their fellow judges, most particularly in relation.to those judgments where the judges have disagreed about whether an ordinary meaning or purposive approach is more appropriate.[70]

E. Length, Dissenting and Concurring Opinions

Though it is not possible to be precise about the average length of the JCPC's judgments because the judgments are delivered in a number of different formats, there is

[70] See especially the judgment of Lord Hoffmann in *Boyce and Joseph* (n 23).

a noticeable increase in the length of JCPC judgments delivered in the 1990s when compared with earlier judgments. This coincides with the JCPC's judgments becoming available on the internet and counsel for the parties citing an increasing number of precedents in support of their arguments. Another factor contributing to the increase in the length of JCPC judgments from the 1990 onwards is the complexity of the constitutional challenges presented to the JCPC and the increase in the number of its own precedents as a result of the rise in the number of appeals in the 1990s and 2000s.

Because they are all delivered in the same format it is possible to be precise about the length of the average CCJ judgment, which is 63 pages, though it should be noted that this figure is skewed by one case, *AG Barbados v Boyce and Joseph*, which is 179 pages in length. A major contributor to the length of the CCJ's judgment is the number of minority opinions. Amongst the JCPC's 32 leading cases, there were only ten which included minority opinions, and these were found most frequently (nine out of the ten) in death penalty cases where the Justices of the JCPC were, often deeply, divided about the correct approach to take to the interpretation of the constitutional provision in issue. By contrast, seven out of the eight judgments of the CCJ included minority opinions. In the main, these were concurring opinions, either in full or in part, with only three dissenting opinions (see further below).

Though dissenting judgments are usually taken for granted as an integral feature of the common law,[71] up until 1966 the principle of 'Unity in Judgment', which was unique to the JCPC, precluded the publication of dissenting judgments. Indeed, even following the change of rule in 1966, only two opinions are permitted: a collective majority opinion and a dissent. Even then, it would be expected that 'a shared legal culture, widely accepted reasoning criteria, and the momentum of an established body of cases, refined by the high level of resources which are mobilized'[72] at the level of a final appellate court, would most often tend to consensus. The fact that there were dissenting opinions in ten of the 32 landmark judgments handed down by the JCPC comes, therefore, as something of a surprise, but may be explained by the fact that nine of these cases were concerned with the operation of the death penalty and reflected a profound disagreement between the judges about the limits of judicial law-making power in relation to efforts to restrict the operation of the death penalty. As John Alder has observed:

> In the case of final appellate courts, it is a reasonable hypothesis that many of the disagreements that give rise to dissents will concern incommensurables since one of the functions of the highest tribunal is to consider cases where, although the law may be tolerably clear on a technical level, issues of justice or policy arise.[73]

By contrast, both dissenting and concurring opinions are permitted by the CCJ and it is notable that seven of the eight landmark judgments handed down by the CCJ contain one or both dissenting and concurring opinions. In two out of these seven judgments there were two concurring opinions. In another two, there were three concurring opinions. And in one remarkable judgment there were no less than five concurring opinions.[74]

[71] J Alder, 'Dissents in Courts of Last Resort: Tragic Choices' (2000) *OJLS*.
[72] ibid 226.
[73] ibid.
[74] *Joseph and Boyce* (n 23).

The multiplicity of concurring opinions accounts for the greater length of the judgments of the CCJ when compared to the JCPC average and may be attributable to the desire of the Justices of the CCJ not only to present a unified front, but also to raise their jurisprudential profile, in a bid to market their jurisdiction to those countries which continue to send their appeals to the JCPC in London. Of the three cases which included dissenting opinions, only two of these were full-blown dissents; the other being a partial dissent in which the dissenting Justices agreed with the majority that the appeal should be allowed but disagreed with their reasoning.

F. Framing Constitutional Issues

For the reasons outlined above, almost half of the cases decided by the JCPC involved fundamental rights issues, particularly those surrounding the operation of the death penalty. However, as a result of the efforts of the DPP most of these legal issues had been resolved by the JCPC by the time of the inauguration of the CCJ. This may help to explain why the eight leading cases before the CCJ were much more varied in terms of content than those of the JCPC. Almost half of the leading cases before the CCJ emanate from Guyana. Only one of these is a Bill of Rights case, with the remainder being concerned with issues that are of a more institutional character: such as presidential term limits, the appointment of the Chair of the Electoral Commission, and the validity of a vote of no-confidence in the Government. This reflects the recent political turbulence in Guyana, following the prorogation of parliament in 2016 and the subsequent refusal in 2018 of the incumbent President to resign following a vote of no-confidence.

G. Key Concepts

The most popular arguments used by the JCPC and the CCJ in the 40 leading cases were: 'basic procedural rights' (16 cases), 'the rule of law' (11 cases), 'proportionality' (10 cases) and 'sovereignty' (8 cases). The second most popular set of arguments were: 'freedom of expression' (3 cases), 'equality' (2 cases), and 'custom' (4 cases). The frequency of these arguments, in the context of the Commonwealth Caribbean, requires some explanation. The reason why arguments about basic procedural rights featured so prominently was the existence of the mandatory death penalty for murder (six out of the 11 cases invoking basic procedural rights). The argument in these cases was that the condemned man was being denied his basic procedural rights because there was no opportunity for a judge to take account of mitigating circumstances when imposing the sentence for murder. Arguments about the rule of law also featured prominently in mandatory death penalty cases (four out of the eight cases invoking the rule of law). Here the focus was on the separation of powers between the judiciary and the executive, and the latter's role in deciding whether to exercise the prerogative of mercy. 'Sovereignty' was most often invoked in the context of the relationship between parliament and the judges. This argument was at its most intense in cases where the judges of the JCPC were divided over whether to use the modifications clause (see above) to read down laws prescribing a mandatory death penalty for murder, or whether it should be for local legislatures to remove saving laws clauses which prevent the courts from striking down such laws. 'Proportionality' has been a familiar argument in the JCPC's jurisprudence, following the test laid down by the JCPC in *De Freitas v Permanent Secretary of Ministry of Agriculture*[75] and is often invoked by the judges in discussions about the potential disproportionality of the mandatory death penalty.

Though 'freedom of expression' was invoked by way of argument in three cases, in at least two of these the constitutional right to freedom of expression was directly in issue (*De Freitas* and *Panday v Gordon*).[76] In the third case, (*Mc Ewan et al*) a case involving a group of men who had been prosecuted for cross-dressing for an allegedly improper purpose, freedom of expression was invoked by way of argument even though violation of their constitutional right to freedom of expression was not directly relied upon by the appellants. Of the three cases in which 'equality' was invoked as an argument, one (*Suratt v AG Trinidad*)[77] was concerned with the establishment of the Equal Opportunities Commission; one was concerned with indigenous land rights (*Maya Leaders Alliance*);[78] and the third was concerned with the right to equality of the group of men referred to above who had been prosecuted for cross-dressing (*McEwan et al*).

'Custom' in this context is a reference to the common law and has been invoked in a judicial debate about the relationship between rights that existed under the common law prior to independence and the rights guaranteed by the independence Constitutions. This debate first arose as a result of Lord Devlin's insistence in *DPP v Nasralla*[79] in 1967 that the rights contained in the region's independence constitutions were merely declaratory of the rights that already existed under the common law prior to independence.

III. Comparative Perspective

The JCPC is one of the oldest courts in the region, being of a similar vintage to the Mexican Supreme Court, whilst the CCJ is one of the youngest, being only a year older than the Ecuadorian Constitutional Court. Like many constitutional courts in Latin America the jurisdiction of the JCPC and CCJ is enshrined in the constitutions of the countries which subscribe to their appellate jurisdiction.

In other respects, however, both the CCJ and JCPC are *sui generis* courts. Unlike Latin American constitutional courts, they function within a common law system. Consequently, when their judges wish to engage with comparative constitutional law, they most often look to the judgments of other common law constitutional courts rather than the constitutional courts of Latin America. Unlike the constitutional courts of Latin America, they are also both regional courts: the CCJ because it was established to serve as the final appellate court for all of the independent English-speaking countries

[75] *De Freitas v Permanent Secretary of Ministry of Agriculture* [1999] 1 AC 69.
[76] *Panday v Gordon* [2005] UKPC 36.
[77] *Suratt v AG Trinidad* [2008] UKPC 38.
[78] [2015] CCJ 15.
[79] *DPP v Nasralla* [1967] 2 AC 238.

in the region; and the JCPC because its judgments are binding on the courts of all the other countries that subscribe to its appellate jurisdiction. Moreover, the judges of both courts are appointed by independent bodies which are not susceptible to political influence and may only be removed from office in the most exceptional circumstances. This means that in both cases the judges have no reason to fear or favour the government of any country subscribing to their appellate jurisdiction. This may help to explain why, in contrast to many constitutional courts in Latin America (see, for example, Mexico), the judges of both courts are less deferential when reviewing the constitutionality of actions of the executive and those of the legislature.

Functioning within a common law system based on the doctrine of *stare decisis*, both courts are predictably more heavily influenced by precedential reasoning than their Latin American counterparts, though, as we noted above, the JCPC has been surprisingly willing to overrule its own earlier judgments, whilst the CCJ has made it clear that it will respect but will not regard itself as bound by judgments of the JCPC. Moreover, the CCJ, like the constitutional courts of Mexico, Colombia and Costa Rica, and unlike the JCPC, is much less influenced by the text of the constitution.

Finally, it is worth noting that as in Latin America, the landmark judgments of the JCPC tend to be dominated by human rights issues, for the reasons considered above.

IV. Conclusion – Evaluation, Pathology and Criticism

Analysis of the landmark cases selected for this empirical research reveals a number of important insights into the modes of constitutional reasoning by JCPC and CCJ judges.

First, it demonstrates that the majority of appeals that reached the JCPC were concerned with human rights issues, in particular, the operation of the death penalty. Though some of the appeals to the CCJ were also concerned with human rights issues, there were far more cases concerning what might be categorised as 'institutional' matters, concerning, for example, presidential term limits. So long as the CCJ is restricted to hearing appeals from less than a handful of countries, it is difficult to say whether this is a reflection of the nature of politics in the countries from which the CCJ hears appeals or is indicative of a broader trend in terms of constitutional adjudication.

Second, it reveals that judges of the JCPC and CCJ frequently deploy both domestic and international harmonising arguments, with particular emphasis on the ACHR and UNDHR and that the judges of both courts frequently invoke foreign law, in particular the judgments of other well-known and well-respected English-speaking constitutional courts.

Third, it reveals a surprising attitude towards precedent and the doctrine of stare decisis on the part of the JCPC in terms of its willingness to overrule its own earlier judgments as well as a willingness of the CCJ to depart radically from the jurisprudence of the JCPC, which might have been expected at the very least to be treated as being of persuasive authority.

The willingness of the CCJ to depart radically from the jurisprudence of the JCPC is also reflected in a difference in approach to constitutional reasoning which is revealed by our analysis of the selected landmark case. It is notable, for example, how much more ready CCJ judges are to reference scholarly works. It is also notable that the length of CCJ judgments dwarf those of the JCPC, lengthy concurring judgments being much more common in the case of the CCJ's jurisprudence. Most notable of all, however, is the willingness of the CCJ to go far beyond the JCPC's purposive approach to constitutional reasoning and to disregard the text of the constitution where this is not compatible with 'the underlying sentiments and principles' of the constitution.

7

The Jurisprudence of the Chilean Constitutional Court

CRISTIÁN VILLALONGA TORRIJO AND FRANCISCO JAVIER URBINA*

I. Introduction

The Chilean Constitutional Tribunal (hereinafter, CHCT) was designed as a veto player to protect a set of constitutional values from political majorities. Unlike the previous constitutional court – which functioned as an umpire in conflicts of competences between branches of government from 1971 until the 1973 coup – the CHCT was introduced in the 1980s Constitution as one of several enforcement mechanisms to secure more substantive policy goals and principles established in that Constitution, such as strong protection of property and economic freedom. The literature on politics has referred to the CHCT's design to illustrate a kind of authoritarian bent in Chilean constitutional development.[1] Despite this, the CHCT has developed as a consequential judicial forum, particularly in the last 15 years or so.[2] Somewhat paradoxically, its increase in relevance in the past years coincides with the decay of its legitimacy. This work explains the evolution of the CHCT's reasoning and how the deterioration of its reason-giving function is associated with its loss of legitimacy.

As part of the Constitutional Reasoning in Latin America Project (CORE Latam), our study examines the CHCT's 40 most relevant decisions in the period between its re-establishment in 1981 and 2019, filling a major gap in the literature on the CHCT. The bulk of the scholarship on the CHCT is doctrinal, 'black-letter' analysis.[3] Empirical

* I am grateful for the support of the Kellogg Institute for International Studies at the University of Notre Dame, where I was a Visiting Fellow during the Spring term of 2022, and to the Faculty of Law of the Pontificia Universidad Católica de Chile, to which I was affiliated while I was writing this chapter.

[1] T Ginsburg, *¿Fruto de la parra envenenada? Algunas observaciones comparadas sobre la constitución chilena* (Estudios Públicos, 2014) 14; C Fuentes, *El Pacto. Poder, constitución y prácticas políticas en Chile (1990–2010)* (Universidad Diego Portales, 2012) 31–34; R Barros, *Constitutionalism and Dictatorship. Pinochet, the Junta, and the 1980 Constitution* (Cambridge University Press, 2002) 236–40.

[2] J Couso and L Hilbink, 'From Quietism to Incipient Activism. The Institutional and Ideological Roots of Rights Adjudication in Chile' in G Helmke and J Rios-Figueroa (eds), *Courts in Latin America* (Cambridge University Press, 2011) 117–21.

[3] See eg P Zapata, *Justicia constitucional. Teoría y práctica en el Derecho chileno y comparado* (Editorial Jurídica de Chile, 2008); H Nogueira, *El Tribunal Constitucional Chileno y perspectiva comparativa con tribunales constitucionales latinoamericanos* (Tirant Lo Blanch, 2019).

studies of the CHCT's rulings focus on justices' votes, attempting to expound general patterns of judicial behaviour.[4] Few studies have undertaken empirical systematic analyses of the content of the Tribunal's verdicts, usually focusing on specific areas.[5] Although all this literature is crucial in furthering understanding of the CHCT, it has not addressed its reason-giving function as an object of empirical analysis.

We offer three hypotheses to interpret the evolution of the CHCT's reasoning. First, the Tribunal has been prone to repeal legislation only from 2006 onwards. As other commentators, we notice that the CHCT's behaviour changed after the 2005 constitutional amendments, which inaugurated a new political cycle in the country and, among other things, empowered the CHCT and modified the process for appointing its judges.[6] Second, and more important, we show that this change in the CHCT's behaviour overlaps with a transformation in its style of reasoning, adding to the usual formalist interpretative methods a new repertoire of arguments. These new arguments are associated with what has been called 'neo-constitutionalism' – an influential academic trend proposing an expansive understanding of fundamental rights, an anti-formalist method of interpretation and adjudication in fundamental rights cases, and a robust role for judges.[7] Third, we argue that the expansion of the CHCT's repertoire is associated with some pathologies that weaken its reason-giving institutional function, such as the existence of complex and unwieldy opinions and the inability to keep a robust system of settled precedents. Exploring an issue rarely tackled by law and politics scholarship, we finally suggest that the CHCT's jurisprudential pathologies and other internal dynamics have contributed to diminishing its standing.[8]

II. Legal, Political, and Academic Context

A. The CHCT's Institutional Design

The current Chilean constitution was adopted in 1980, during the Augusto Pinochet dictatorship. Even though the Constitution provided for the permanence of the dictatorship for eight more years in its transitory provisions, its main text contemplated several institutions familiar to constitutional democracies. It provided for an independent judiciary, a (mostly) elected congress, an elected president, and a constitutional court. Whether this design was sufficiently democratic – considering that several of

[4] See eg R Carroll and L Tiede, 'Judicial Behavior on the Chilean Constitutional Tribunal' (2011) 8(4) *Journal of Empirical Legal Studies* 873–74; D Pardow and S Verdugo, 'El Tribunal Constitucional chileno y la reforma de 2005. Un enroque entre jueces de carrera y académicos' (2015) XXVIII *Revista de Derecho* (Valdivia) 123–44.

[5] See eg A Álvez and B Vicente, 'Estudio legal empírico sobre el uso del Derecho Comparado por parte del Tribunal Constitucional de Chile' (2018) XXXI(2) *Revista de Derecho* (Valdivia) 155–74.

[6] Pardow Lorenzo and Verdugo Ramírez (n 4).

[7] For the judicial role in new constitutionalism, see C Villalonga Torrijo, 'Analizando el modelo de juez racional. Reflexiones sobre la teoría de la jurisdicción en el neoconstitucionalismo' (2019) 46 *Revista Chilena de Derecho* 765.

[8] K Whittington, and G Vanberg, 'Constitutional Courts in Comparative Perspective: A Theoretical Assessment' (2015) 18 *Annual Review of Political Science* 167.

its provisions constrained political majorities – has been the subject of much of Chile's constitutional debate.[9] The Constitution was amended on dozens of occasions, the most important of which were the reforms of 1989 and 2005. Both entailed a broad agreement of political forces on a comprehensive set of reforms, altering the original structure of interbranch relations to make the constitution more democratic.[10]

The CHCT predates the Constitution of 1980. The 1970s amendment to the Constitution of 1925 established a constitutional court attempting to resolve the recurrent conflicts between the executive and congress.[11] The drafters of the Constitution of 1980 conceived a more ambitious role for the CHCT, one of guardian of the Constitution, ensuring respect for the norms and principles of the Constitution.[12] The 1980s CHCT was composed of three judges of the Supreme Court chosen by that same court, two judges selected by the Council for National Security,[13] one judge chosen by the president, and one nominated by the Senate. The judiciary's influence in the CHCT was secured, given that the Supreme Court had the largest share of appointments of any single organ and that the members nominated by the President and the Senate had to have served in the Supreme Court as non-career pro tempore judges for at least three consecutive years.[14] Judicial justices joined the CHCT imbued of the distinctive institutional culture of the Chilean judiciary, one that strongly emphasised its apolitical nature.[15]

From 1971, Chile had a bifurcated system of constitutional review that vested this function in two bodies. On the one hand, the Supreme Court had the power of declaring a legal provision unconstitutional as applied in a specific case, with effect only for that case (*inaplicabilidad*). On the other hand, the CHCT was granted the power of constitutional review of bills, constitutional reform projects, and provisions in treaties under discussion in Congress, all with general application.[16] The original design of the 1980 Constitution preserved this division, but granted to the CHCT additional powers. It could review the constitutionality of all 'constitutional organic laws' and of laws interpreting the Constitution. It could decide on the constitutionality of any part of a bill, proposal of constitutional reform, or treatise, under discussion in Congress. The CHCT also held powers of review of presidential decrees and could decide on conflicts of competence, as well as on the constitutionality of political movements and of individual persons' responsibilities according to Article 8 of the Constitution (which forbade

[9] Fuentes (n 1) 31–32; F Atria, *La constitución tramposa* (Lom, 2013).

[10] E Pfeffer, *Reformas Constitucionales 2005. Antecedentes, Debates, Informes* (Editorial Jurídica de Chile, 2005); F Zúñiga (ed), *Reforma Constitucional* (LexisNexis, 2005).

[11] E Silva Cimma, *El Tribunal Constitucional de Chile (1971–1973)*, 2nd edn (Cuadernos del Tribunal Constitucional, 2008) 24–25.

[12] See eg J Guzmán, 'La definición constitucional' (1980) 15 *Revista Realidad* 17, especially at 36–37; L Ríos Álvarez, 'El nuevo tribunal constitucional chileno' (2007) 1 *Anuario Iberoamericano de Justicia Constitucional* 243, 250.

[13] Because the Council was composed in its majority by members of the armed forces, it was seen as one of the 'authoritarian enclaves' of the Constitution. Among other reforms, the 2005 constitutional amendment stripped the Council of its legal powers to turn it into an advisory body.

[14] Art 81, Politic Constitution of the Republic of Chile 1980, (original text).

[15] L Hilbink, *Judges beyond Politics in Democracy and Dictatorship: Lessons from Chile* (Cambridge University Press, 2007).

[16] JI Martínez, 'Recurso de inaplicabilidad, Tribunal Constitucional y juez ordinario en la reforma constitucional' in H Nogueira (ed), *La Constitución Reformada de 2005* (Librotecnia, 2005) 460.

the propagation of doctrines that attacked family, promoted violence, totalitarianism or class struggle).[17]

B. The Judges

The 2005 constitutional amendment – the product of a broad political agreement – altered the original structure of interbranch relations substantively and reinforced the democratic legitimacy of the political regime. This reform introduced important changes in the composition of the CHCT and gave it new powers.[18] The composition changed from seven to ten judges, three of which were to be chosen by the Supreme Court, three by the president, and four by Congress. The reform eliminated the requirement that judges appointed by the President and Congress had to have served in the Supreme Court, and established an incompatibility between serving in the CHCT and belonging to the judiciary. The judiciary thus lost much of its influence over the CHCT.

C. Constitutional Litigation before the CHCT

The CHCT's jurisdiction includes different legal powers, which do not represent an equal share of its docket in the period under study. For instance, there are decisions where the Tribunal uses its power to undertake mandatory abstract review of interpretive and organic constitutional legislation and international treaties dealing with matters of organic constitutional law (a power granted in Art 93 N°1 of the current Chilean Constitution; *n*: 681); others where the CHCT exercises powers of non-compulsory abstract judicial review of provisions in legislative bills during their discussion in Congress (Art 93 N°3, *n*: 88); others regard presidential executive decrees (Art 93 N°16, *n*: 34), etc. There are also specific actions to declare the unconstitutionality of political parties and movements (Art 93 N°10, *n*: 4); and to resolve conflicts of competences between administrative authorities and ordinary courts (Art 93 N°12, *n*: 66), among other subjects.

There is also the *inaplicabilidad*, namely, the judicial review of legal dispositions as applied in specific judicial proceedings (Art 93 N°6, *n*: 6,250), Crucially, the 2005 constitutional reform moved the *inaplicabilidad* from the Supreme Court to the CHCT and granted the CHCT a new power to declare unconstitutional a law once it had been already declared 'inapplicable' at least once. There was broad agreement in favour of moving *inaplicabilidad* from the Supreme Court to the CHCT, as it was widely acknowledged that this prerogative had been idle in the Supreme Court's hands.[19] In moving *inaplicabilidad* to the CHCT, its scope was amplified: since then, it became possible to present it in cases before specialised (and not only ordinary) courts and for the *a quo* court to initiate the process of *inaplicabilidad*.[20] The CHCT became empowered and this

[17] Art 2 (original text), Politic Constitution of the Republic of Chile 1980.

[18] Some authors spoke of a 'new Constitutional Tribunal'. See eg N Massmann, 'La inadmisibilidad del recurso de inaplicabilidad: a tres años de la reforma' (2009) 15 *Ius et Praxis* 263, 264.

[19] Martínez (n 16) 457–58.

[20] ibid 457–62.

was reflected quickly in its docket. Between 1981 and 2005, the Tribunal never decided more than 36 cases a year. Since 2006, the CHCT's caseload continuously grew, spurred by the increase in petitions of concrete review.

The total number of the CHCT's rulings contain several asymmetries. Figures 1 and 2 show that while abstract review remained stable over time, the quantity of petitions for concrete review (*inaplicabilidad*) grew, particularly since 2016. Some of the rulings address acute inter-branch conflicts, like the judicial review of presidential executive decrees, and others are not directly associated with open political struggle, like most decisions of *inaplicabilidad*. The tribunal decisions are unevenly distributed in time since about 93.6 per cent of them were adopted in cases of concrete judicial review after the 2005 constitutional amendment.

Figure 1 Ex-ante abstract reviews

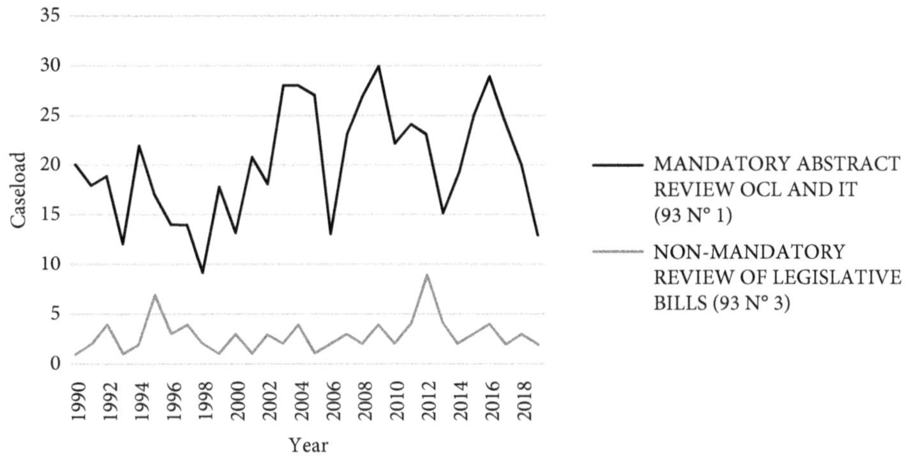

Note: *OCL*: Organic Constitutional Legislation. *IT*: International Treatias. Elaboration of the authors.

Figure 2 Ex-post concrete judicial reviews

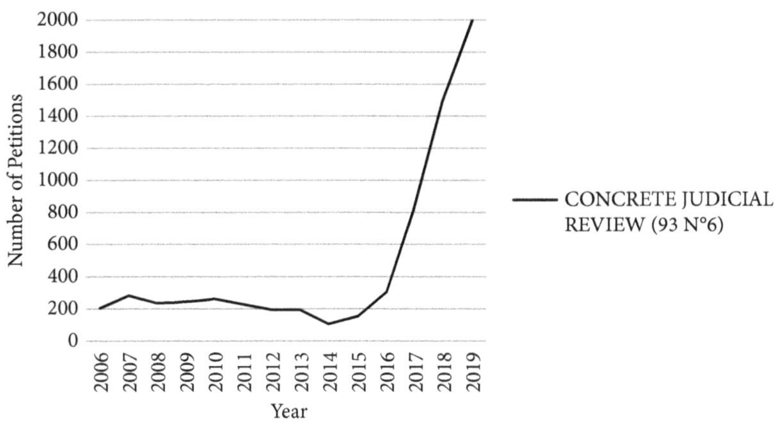

D. Legal Scholarship and Constitutional Reasoning

The academic context in which the CHCT has deployed its activity has experienced a profound transformation in the last 30 years. And to a great extent, the CHCT has been a protagonist of such a gradual change. Like other Latin American countries during the mid-twentieth century, the Chilean legal culture promoted judicial restraint and the enforcement of formal legal standards. In the Chilean case, political constraints and the theoretical influence of textual positivism from Continental Europe also shaped a professional ideology of judicial apoliticism. In so doing, courts understood their role to be restricted to law finding and avoiding law-making, exhibiting a clear deferential behaviour.[21]

The legal culture of the region in general, and in Chile in particular, has undergone a deep shift, however. Over the last 30 years, neo-constitutional thought has become the mainstream in legal academia, even beyond constitutional law. Importing scholarship from Germany, Spain, and Italy, local legal scholars have reformulated a more ambitious role for courts in enforcing an expansive view of fundamental rights. Debates on judicial discretion, the application of human rights standards, and the proportionality test made inroads into the Chilean legal academy, replacing text positivism.[22] This academic shift coincided with a more robust constitutional jurisdiction and more sophisticated litigation. This chapter illustrates such a transformation at the level of the CHCT's reasoning.

III. Arguments in Constitutional Reasoning

Following the CORE LATAM's methodology, we looked for 40 leading judgments of the CHCT according to political relevance and jurisprudential influence.[23] Naturally, this sample mirrors only a tiny part of the CHCT's decisions in the period covered in our study (between the CHCT's re-establishment in 1981 and 2019). Since the selected rulings extend for almost 40 years, a longitudinal analysis can provide a representation of how the Tribunal's reasoning has evolved. Table 1 shows different distributions of the indicators.

[21] Hilbink (n 15); C Villalonga Torrijo, 'Dwindling Professional Authority: Legal Elites and the Division of Governmental Labor in Chile, 1932–70' (2021) 46 *Law & Social Inquiry* 226–51.

[22] J Couso, 'The Transformation of Constitutional Discourse and the Judicialization of Politics in Latin America' in J Couso, A Huneeus and R Sieder (eds), *Cultures of Legality. Judicialization and Political Activism in Latin America* (Cambridge University Press, 2010) 141–60. Villalonga Torrijo (n 7) 765.

[23] We presented a shortlist of the decisions we deemed the 40 most relevant of the Tribunal's rulings to a group of five constitutional law scholars who have conducted extensive research on the Tribunal (Marisol Peña, Carlos Carmona, Patricio Zapata, Arturo Fermandois, and Sergio Verdugo). None of them proposed to exclude more than one of the rulings we listed. In this work we exceptionally refer to other CHCT's rulings for illustrative purposes.

Table 1 The longitudinal multi-layered analysis. Jurisprudential continuity (underlying formalist legal culture)

	85	87	88	92	93	94	95	96	97	00	01	02	04		06	07	08	10	12	13	14	15	16	17	18
Ord. Meaning	1	2	1	2	1	1	1	1	1	1	1	1	1		1	1	2	2	2	1	1	3	1	1	
Dom. Harmon.	1	2		1		1		1	1	1	1	1	1		1		2	3	2	1	1	4	1	2	
Tele Historical	1	1	1				1		1		1	2					1	3	1			2	1	1	
Tele. Textual	1	2	1	1					1	1	1	2				1	2	1					1	2	
Analogy				1				1		1	1	1			1	1		3			1	2	2	2	1
New Principle		1	1	1	1				1	1		1				1	2	2	1		1	3	1	2	1
Rule of Law	1	2	1	1	1	1	1		1	1	1				1	1	1	2			1	4	1	1	1

Table 2a Jurisprudential Change (the transformation towards new-constitutionalism)

	85	87	88	92	93	94	95	96	97	00	01	02	04		06	07	08	10	12	13	14	15	16	17	18
Precedents			1	2		1	1	1	1	1	1		1		1	2	3	3	2	1	1	4	2	2	1
Non-Legal			1				1									1	1	1		1		3	2	2	1
Scholarly Work			1		1		1		1		1	1			1		2	2	2		1	3	2	2	1
Foreign Law							1			1		1			1	1	2	2	2		1	3	2	2	1
Core of Rights		1		1					1				1			1	2	2			1	3	2	1	

Table 2b Jurisprudential Change (the transformation towards new-constitutionalism)

Proportionality		1									1						2	2	2	1		1	2	1	1
Human Dignity		1															1	2				1	2	2	
Justice																1	1	1	2	1		1	1	1	1
Int. Law																	1	2	1		1	3	1	2	

Table 3 Political Behaviour and External Demand

	85	87	88	92	93	94	95	96	97	00	01	02	04		06	07	08	10	12	13	14	15	16	17	18
Parallel Struct.							1						1			1	1	1				3	2	2	1
Repealing	1	2	1	3			1					1	1			1	3	2	1			3	2	2	1
Equality		1	1	1			1			1							3	2	2	1		3	2	1	1
Democracy		2	1	1												1	1			1		2		2	
Eco., soc. rights											1							1			1	2	1		

Table 2a shows indicators that tend to be evenly distributed over time, such as the ordinary meaning of words and harmonisation with domestic law. These are formalist methods of constitutional interpretation, characteristic of a formalist legal culture. Table 2b illustrates a different set of arguments that complements the formalist approach, which we associate with the trend that is referred to as 'neo-constitutionalism'. These arguments include some not employed before 2006 (eg, international law) or some employed much more frequently after 2006 (eg, scholarly work). Finally, Table 3 collects arguments that show important changes in their use after 2006, which, we suggest, respond to certain patterns related to political behaviour, judicial rhetoric, and external demands to the CHCT.

A. Judicial Behaviour, Judicial Candour, and Judicial Rhetoric

Our analysis of the CHCT's rulings shows important changes both in its political behaviour (eg, deference/no-deference) and in the judicial rhetoric of its leading judgments.[24] To interpret the variations illustrated above, mostly in Table 3, we divide our analysis into three cycles: (i) a brief period towards the end of the authoritarian government (1985–1992), (ii) the years of the democratic consolidation and centripetal politics (1993–2005), and (iii) a new political cycle of gradual political polarisation (2006–2019).

The first cycle took place from the mid-1980s until the first years of democracy (1992). During that phase, the CHCT decided cases concerning the electoral system in four out of seven landmark rulings, reflecting the centrality of the Tribunal as an arbitrator in the matters of uttermost concern of politics during the transition to democracy. At the same time, it was open to selectively reverse legislation in a sort of strategic fashion, granting the petitions in five out of seven leading judgments. These rulings were consequential. They paved the way for channelling political conflict into a democratic competition and consolidated the constitution's economic and legal preferences in the long run.

Indeed, during the convulsed political years of the mid-1980s, the military junta passed four organic constitutional statutes that dealt with electoral regulation according to the new 'protected' democracy enshrined in the Constitution of 1980. Since these statutes did not provide for equitable rules regarding crucial aspects of the plebiscite of 1988 (the plebiscite on the regime's continuity), the opposition looked at them as a sort of façade for controlling the electoral process. Through high-stakes decisions in cases of abstract review of these statutes, the CHCT instilled equitable standards to those laws, contributing decisively to the consolidation of the process of democratisation.[25] In a well-known decision called *Tribunal Calificador de Elecciones* (TC 33/1985), the CHCT reviewed the time of entering into force of the electoral courts that would oversee the

[24] Similarly, P Ahumada, 'El Tribunal Constitucional en Chile: tres ensayos de justicia constitucional' in C Huneeus and O Avendaño (eds), *El sistema político chileno, 1990–2017. Instituciones, actores y desempeño democrático* (LOM, 2018) 396–406.

[25] Barros (n 1); S Verdugo, 'The Civil Law Tradition, the Pinochet Constitution, and Judge Eugenio Valenzuela' in R Abeyratne and I Porat, *Towering Judges. A Comparative Study of Constitutional Judges* (Cambridge University Press, 2021) 290–307.

1988 plebiscite, whose functioning had been postponed for after the plebiscite. The CHCT ruled that the permanent principles of the Constitution required an impartial court to watch over any election, including the 1988 plebiscite. In its *Partidos Políticos* decision (TC 43/1987), the CHCT declared unconstitutional several statutory provisions that indirectly limited the establishment of opposition parties, and in *Votaciones Populares y Escrutinios* (TC 53/1988), it asserted that the Constitution mandated providing equitable opportunities for independent citizens and political parties in electoral propaganda.[26]

These landmark decisions reflect a form of strategic behaviour. Initially, the CHCT confined itself to repealing legislation that compromised the fairness of an electoral process increasingly supported by the population.[27] But when justices perceived greater political threats, they deferred to the regime. For instance, the CHCT declared the socialist leader Clodomiro Almeyda responsible for disseminating Marxist-Leninist doctrines in a ruling issued months after a murder attempt against Pinochet, applying the prohibitions on totalitarian ideas established in the controversial Article 8 of the Constitution (TC 46 /1987).

At the beginning of the first democratic administration, the CHCT also safeguarded policy goals that were at the core of the Constitution. In *Publicidad Caminera* (TC 146/1992), the CHCT reversed the statutory ban on advertising in the highways, affirming that such a prohibition unduly restricted economic freedom and private property by failing to regulate highway advertisement by statute rather than by decree. And in *Gobiernos Regionales* (TC 155/1992), the Tribunal reasserted the limits between administrative regulations, ordinary statutes, and organic constitutional statutes, which were instrumental in securing the core of the legislative scaffolding built by the 1980 Constitution.

A second cycle of the CHCT's behaviour developed between 1993 and 2005. We record only three decisions repealing legislation out of 11 leading judgments in this phase, suggesting that the CHCT turned deferential in its most politically and legally visible rulings.[28] Such a behavioural pattern coincides with a period of centripetal politics in which the two larger coalitions of the country reached compromises around economic policy, democracy and the rule of law.[29]

This behaviour found doctrinal expression in the judicial doctrine of reasoned deference, which asserted that the CHCT must respect lawmakers' sphere of autonomy on the grounds that the acts of the legislature enjoy a robust presumption of constitutionality. In 2000, for instance, a group of congressmen challenged the ratification of the Convention of the International Labour Organization on Indigenous and Tribal Peoples, alleging that some of its norms contradicted property rights and equality before the law. The CHCT, however, dismissed the challenge, asserting that all the norms passed by the political branches enjoyed a strong presumption of

[26] See also TC 141/1992 and TC 38/1986.

[27] S Verdugo, 'How can judges challenge dictators and get away with it?' (2021) 59 *Columbia Journal of Transnational Law* 555.

[28] Beyond that political compromise, the court was open to repeal legislation. See TC 220/1995; TC 346/2002, and TC 423/2004.

[29] A San Francisco, 'Chile y el fin de la historia' (2002) 1 *Bicentenario. Revista de Historia de Chile y América* 5.

constitutionality and that the Tribunal only could overturn them when it reached a firm conviction that they contravened the Constitution (TC 309/2000). This doctrine appeared in several of the CHCT's decisions, and it was broadly employed by litigators and political actors.[30]

Finally, we can identify a third cycle initiated after the 2005 constitutional amendment reinforced the CHCT's powers and modified its rules of appointments. In a period of increased political fragmentation, the CHCT faced social demands for greater democracy, legal equality, and economic justice. A brief review of our landmark rulings provides several illustrations. For instance, the Tribunal tackled more ambitious attempts at statutory regulation of economic activity. In 2010, the CHCT reviewed the price determination of private health insurances, banning the unilateral increase of premiums according to the clients' sex and age (TC 1710/2010). And in 2015, it upheld a statute forbidding the reception of public funds by charter schools that selected their students (TC 2787/2015). Furthermore, the CHCT began to decide cases related to social issues. For example, the Tribunal banned the morning-after contraception pill in 2008, allowed the decriminalisation of abortion in specific circumstances in 2017, and decided cases on same-sex marriage in 2010 and 2019.[31]

During these years, the Tribunal grew more prone to repeal legislation than in the previous period, granting petitions in 15 out of 22 judgments in our sample (as opposed to 8 of 19 in the previous period). So, while the CHCT employed the doctrine of reasoned deference to defer to law-making before 2006, by that date it was moving in the opposite direction, reasserting its role as the guardian of the constitution in landmark cases. The CHCT defied governments, risking high political costs, in its new consequential role. In 2008, for instance, the CHCT reversed two administrative decrees authorising a loan to fund the public transportation system of Santiago at its deepest crisis, asserting that this matter should be regulated by statute.[32]

Why did the CHCT became less deferential and employed a less formalistic repertoire of arguments after 2006? Some literature suggests that the constitutional amendments of 2005 allowed the incorporation of judges from politics and academia, who envisioned a more ambitious role for constitutional adjudication.[33] This is true, though the CHCT's new behaviour may have also stemmed from other variables on the demand side. In the last ten years or so, repeat players employed a larger set of arguments in litigation as part of a deep transformation in legal culture, resorting extensively to constitutional petitions to challenge legislation. Furthermore, the increasing level of fragmentation in partisan politics has contributed to more contentious law-making. Although this did not create a higher demand for abstract review, it may have produced other indirect effects on the CHCT, like the absence of a reference framework for the CHCT from the political fora and an internal division in the CHCT's own composition.

[30] Zapata (n 3).
[31] TC1881/2010 and TC7774/2019.
[32] Couso and Hilbink (n 2) 110.
[33] Pardow and Verdugo (n 4); JL Cea, 'Imagen del juez y de la justicia constitucional en América Latina' in JL Cea, *Escritos de Justicia Constitucional* (Cuadernos del Tribunal Constitucional, 2007) 170–92.

B. Framing of Constitutional Issues

The CHCT framed most of its decisions as fundamental rights issues (n = 33), usually combining such a frame with procedural considerations or reasonings associated with the structure of the government and its branches (n = 22). Within those parameters, there are some tendencies. Before 2006, the CHCT often frames its rulings uniquely as a matter of constitutional structure, or another framing other than fundamental rights (with the exception of basic procedural rights, n=5). Few landmark decision of the period are about fundamental rights (other than basic procedural rights), excluding other constitutional issues. By contrast, after 2006, all the rulings of the CHCT include fundamental rights as one of their arguments (n = 22), and ten of them were framed only as a matter of fundamental rights. There is no correlation between the framing employed by the Tribunal and the legal power under which it delivered its rulings.

C. Transformation of the Tribunal's Repertoire: The Overall Weight and Type of Arguments

The data suggests that the 2005 amendment represents the main watershed in the CHCT's reasoning. Before the reform, the Tribunal employed mostly the traditional formalist legal repertoire that dominated the legal culture of the country. In this vein, the CHCT resorted to arguments centred on the ordinary meaning of words, on the coherence of the interpreted constitutional passage with the rest of the Constitution, on the constitution-makers' purpose as manifested in historical records, and analogy. It is not surprising that these four main arguments were already sanctioned for statutory interpretation by the Chilean Civil Code (1855) and that, previously, the Supreme Court had employed them for constitutional interpretation. The CHCT regularly resorted to key legal concepts within the same legal culture, such as principles associated with procedural readings of due process and formal rule of law-values such as legal certainty.[34]

In this more formalist period, the CHCT relied on a specific style of judicial reasoning characterised by relatively brief decisions written in a plain style that eschewed parallel and rhetorical argumentation. Even when their language is technical, they are not hard to understand for lawyers. The structure of their ruling starts by describing the arguments of the parties and their standing in the petition. Then, the Tribunal defines the constitutional controversy. It then explains the meaning of the invoked constitutional provisions and how the interpreted text matches other passages within the constitutional framework. If these arguments are not enough to reach a decision, the CHCT relies on the constitution-making process records, particularly on the opinion of the members of the commission that elaborated the complete draft of the 1980 Constitution.

[34] This is so even when they may have thought that constitutional interpreters had more interpretive tools at their disposal. See eg E Valenzuela Somarriva, *Criterios de Hermenéutica Constitucional aplicados por el Tribunal Constitucional* (Cuadernos del Tribunal Constitucional, 2003).

The predominance of this formalistic type of reasoning had an impact on the Tribunal's outcomes, tending towards deferential behaviour. When the CHCT exceptionally repealed legislation, justices tended to resort more to teleological analysis on the objective purpose of the text. This argument was present in five out of the eight cases of our sample where the CHCT repealed legislation before 2005. Perhaps, the judgment on electoral tribunals mentioned above is the best illustration of this (TC 33/1985).

As mentioned before, after 2005 the CHCT made use of a new set of arguments associated with neo-constitutional thought. Accordingly, the CHCT embraced purposivism and principled adjudication, and replaced its emphasis on reasoned deference by reasserting its role as the guardian of the Constitution.[35] Here we need to distinguish two kinds of arguments that gained prominence in the period. First, arguments rarely present in its jurisprudence before 2005, the application of which became more common after 2005, such as the use of precedent, non-legal arguments, scholarly work, appeal to foreign law, and the proportionality test. Second, new arguments, like human dignity, reflections on substantive justice, and international law, which were not present at all in our sample before 2005.

i. Non-legal Arguments

The CHCT employed extensively non-legal arguments after 2005, resorting to this type of argument in 12 out of 22 cases of our sample. Its engagement with non-legal arguments is intuitive, cherry-picking from scholarly literature, without considering competitive hypotheses. The best example of this is the judgment upholding the statutory ban for charter schools, in which the CHCT used economic and sociological studies concerning the correlation between educational quality and equity in OCDE countries (TC 2787/2015). Occasionally the CHCT has relied on medical science, as in the cases on the morning-after pill and abortion (TC 740/2007 and TC 3729/2017).

ii. Scholarly Work and Foreign Law

The CHCT has increasingly employed scholarly work and foreign law to provide additional support for its decisions.[36] In the 18 leading judgments before 2005, we found rulings with some references to Chilean, Argentinian, or Spanish writers of constitutional doctrine ($n = 8$), and some generic mentions to foreign law that were indirectly taken from scholarly literature ($n = 3$). In the 22 decisions issued after 2005, the CHCT cited to academic sources with more recurrence ($n = 16$). It also broadened its scholarly citations in decisions about rights, adding references to authors linked to neo-constitutionalism thought, such as Luigi Ferrajoli and Robert Alexy. Likewise, the CHCT extensively cited foreign law, mainly legislation from Spain and other Latin American countries

[35] See TC 2935/2015, consideration No. 15.

[36] This data is coincidental with the finding of Álves and Vicente (n 5) 172, who conclude that comparative law was relevant in the outcomes of only 263 out of 1,212 rulings in which the CHCT used this argument between 2006–2012.

(*n* = 16), resorting exceptionally to judicial decisions from common law jurisdictions and the European Union. Sometimes, such considerations do no substantial work in the reasoning of the decision, as is the case in the judgment on lawyers' obligation to provide free legal aid, which employed rhetorically historiographical scholarship (TC 755/2007).

iii. The Proportionality Test and Core of Rights

Another development is the increasing use of the idea of proportionality and balancing, including the use of the three or four-part 'proportionality test'.[37] Chilean scholars debate whether the CHCT really applies the proportionality test,[38] but it is clear that the CHCT refers to 'proportionality' to describe analytically distinct demands. In some cases, it uses explicitly the structured proportionality test known in several other jurisdictions broadly consisting of requirements of legitimate aim, adequacy, necessity, and proportionality (eg, TC 2922/2015). In others it alludes more vaguely to requirements such as that limitations of rights be 'measured and reasonable' (eg, TC 2487/13).[39] While there is very little allusion to proportionality in our sample before 2005 (n=2), the use of the concept becomes common after 2005 (n=12). Because proportionality entails a less formalistic methodology to rights adjudication, this confirms the move away from the prior traditional formalist approaches. Something similar occurs with regard to the idea of the core of a right. While the 1980 Constitution already establishes a guarantee that statutes limiting fundamental rights 'cannot affect rights in their essence' (Article 19 number 26 of the Chilean Constitution), we see a greater incidence of this idea in the sample starting in 2005 (n=4 before 2005, n=12 after 2005).

iv. Substantive Justice

We find an even greater contrast regarding the use of 'substantive justice'. While before 2005 this argument does not appear in our sample, after 2005 it is featured in roughly half of the cases to support a decision (n=10 out of 22 cases). Arguments of justice appear sometimes straightforwardly, pointing to a deficiency in terms of substantive justice, for example, arguing that something would be 'unfair' or not 'equanimous' (TC 2487/2013). This link to equality or unfairness is reflected as well in the fact that of the 10 decisions in the sample alluding to this argument, eight also use 'equality' as an argument (out of 15 that use equality in the post-2005 period). The CHCT has also referred, in relation to interests for outstanding tax payments, to measures that are 'disproportionate, unjust, and abusive' (1951(1952)/2011).

[37] On the different formulations of the test, see FJ Urbina, *A Critique of Proportionality and Balancing*, (Cambridge University Press, 2017) 4–9.

[38] I Covarrubias, '¿Emplea el Tribunal Constitucional el Test de Proporcionalidad?: 128 sentencias del Tribunal Constitucional en la perspectiva de la jurisprudencia constitucional alemana, de la Cámara de los Lores y del Tribunal Europeo de Derechos Humanos' (2014) 12 *Estudios constitucionales* 163.

[39] On the different requirements under the rubric of 'proportionality', see E Lim and FJ Urbina, 'Understanding Proportionality in the Illegality Defense' (2020) 136 *Law Quarterly Review* 575, 580–84.

v. International Law

Before 2005, the CHCT did not properly resort to international law in its reasoning, even in cases that directly dealt with international law issues, which were resolved by application of domestic norms (ie, TC 309/2000, and TC 346/2002). This absence mimicked the reluctance of the ordinary judiciary to use international law. After 2005, however, the CHCT gradually started to engage with Inter-American Human Rights Law. Between 2006 and 2010, the CHCT cited to decisions of the Inter-American Court of Human Rights in only six out of almost 1,000 rulings, including some cases on imprisonment of employers due to social security debts (eg, TC 519/2006) and on the right to identity in family determination (TC 1340/2009).[40] As Figure 3 shows, the CHCT has progressively cited more frequently to Inter-American Human Rights Law, asserting, for example, that the Interamerican Court is the authentic interpreter of the American Convention on Human Rights (eg TC 2493/2013).

Figure 3 The CHCT's Engagement with International Law

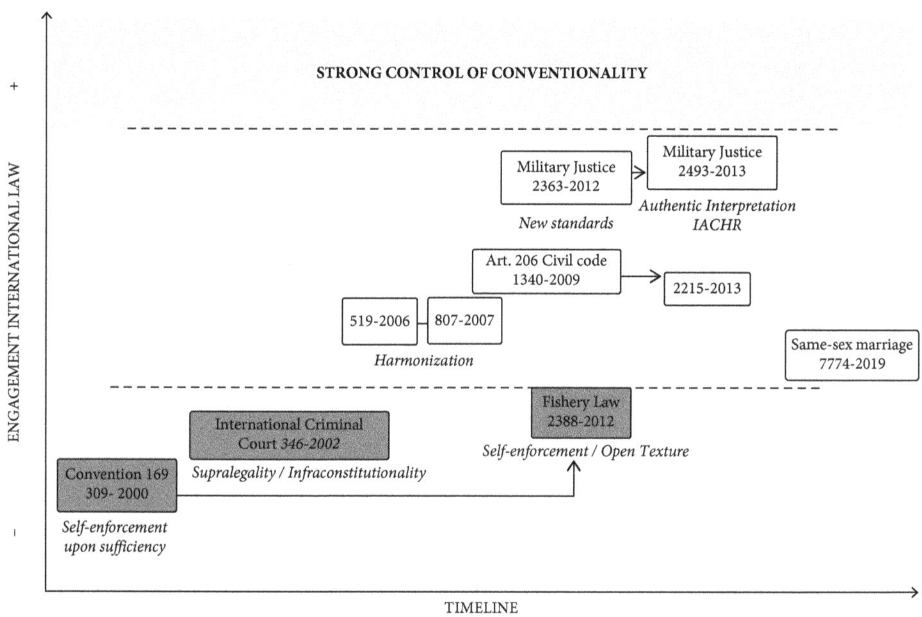

D. Key Concepts

The CHCT faced more demands for legal equality and economic justice after 2005. Accordingly, it has resorted to equality in 15 out of 22 rulings of the period. It has also engaged with socio-economic rights that were almost absent in the pre-2005 cases.

[40] L Galdámez, 'El valor asignado por la jurisprudencia del Tribunal Constitucional a la jurisprudencia de la Corte Interamericana de Derechos Humanos' (2014) 12(1) *Estudios constitucionales* 330.

And it has appealed again to the argument of democracy, which had been missing from the CHCT's repertoire since the late 1980s. In a judgment on the private health insurances' premiums, for instance, the CHCT states that the right to social security entails the elements of solidarity, universality, sufficiency, and uniformity (TC 1710/2010). In a similar vein, the CHCT has upheld statutory quotas for each sex in primary elections, stating that they operate as a mechanism of social inclusion within the democratic process (TC 2777/2015).

E. Length, Dissenting and Concurring Opinions

Since 2005, the reasoning of the CHCT has developed some pathologies. These pathologies are more than the unintended consequences of principled and purposive adjudication and are probably associated also with the justices' greater political fragmentation and the efforts to face the increasing social pressure on the Tribunal.

In the first place, the CHCT's reasoning has turned increasingly complex, and many times confusing. Although our sample is discrete, careful observation can provide some clues on this phenomenon. While the CHCT used to write short decisions in a syllogistic style before 2005, it has produced longer decisions after 2005. As Table 2 shows, the average judgments' length in our sample went from 43 pages before 2005 to 125 pages in the period starting after that year (subsample 2006-2019 A). If we exclude decisions on concrete review (*inaplicabilidad*) introduced in the 2005 amendment, to homologate our comparison (subsample 2006–2019 B), the average length reaches 182 pages. As Table 4 shows, the page length is not only related to the cases' number of issues that required a judicial pronouncement.

Table 4 Opinions Attributes

	1985–2005 (*n* 18)				**2006–2019 A (*n* 22)**				**2006–2019 B (*n* 12)**			
	Mean	SD	Min.	Max.	Mean	SD	Min.	Max.	Mean	SD	Min.	Max.
Length (per pages)	43	23.1	23	93	125	90.7	36	329	182	87.8	45	329
Substantive issues (per ruling)	3	2.6	1	11	2.7	3.2	1	11	3.9	2.62	1	11

Table 5 Argumentative Structure

	1985–2005 (*n* = 18)	**2006–2019 A (*n* = 22)**	**2006–2019 B (*n* = 12)**
MAJORITY			
one line conclusive argument	88.8	77	83
parallel lines conclusively individually	11.2	41	50

(continued)

Table 5 ***(Continued)***

	1985–2005 (n = 18)	2006–2019 A (n = 22)	2006–2019 B (n = 12)
parallel lines conclusively jointly	0	13.6	16.6
CONCURRING SEPARATE VOTES (Majority)	0	9	16.6
one line conclusive argument	5.5	4.5	8.3
parallel lines conclusively individually	0	4.5	8.3
parallel lines conclusively jointly	0	0	0
DISSENTING OPINIONS	72	50	50
one line conclusive argument	66.6	45.5	41.6
parallel lines conclusively individually	5.5	4.5	16.6
parallel lines conclusively jointly	0	0	0
DISSENTING SEPARATE VOTES	0	40.9	50
one line conclusive argument	0	36.3	50
parallel lines conclusively individually	0	0	0
parallel lines conclusively jointly	0	4.5	8.3

However, confusing reasoning as a jurisprudential pathology is not primarily about the decisions' length or the fact that the CHCT displays a broader argumentative repertoire. The main deficiency of the new rulings is the emergence of separate votes and different types of parallel lines of reasoning. Justices have gradually introduced separate votes both in the concurring majority and in the dissenting opinions. This practice began by adding different arguments to clarify any aspect needed to reach a verdict, evolving into separate opinions coalescing on the same outcome but differing from one another on the reasoning. In Table 5, we can observe that decisions began to include separate votes after 2005, particularly within subsample 2006–2019 B (excluding concrete review). They have emerged mainly in the dissidences in high-profile cases of abstract review, as 50 per cent of the cases in that subsample have separate dissenting votes. Perhaps, the sentence on statutory reform of collective labour bargaining (TC 3016/2016) is the best example of a great variety of outcomes and opinions. In this, the Chief Justice tie-breaking vote decided three out of four issues, and two separate opinions joined the majority regarding two matters. There were dissident opinions in the four issues, complemented by two partial dissents and a separate vote that joined one of the latter. It is not surprising that some of those sentences include a roadmap explanation to navigate such a labyrinth.

Table 6 Judgment on collective labour bargaining TC 3016/2016

Issues	Majority A	Majority B	Dissidency A	Dissidency B	Dissidency C
1	repealing		upholding		
2	repealing partially		upholding	partial dissidency	1 separate vote
3	upholding	1 separate vote	repealing	partial dissidency	
4	upholding	1 separate vote	repealing		

The CHCT has also begun to complement one-line opinions of syllogistic style, adding parallel arguments conclusive at the individual level and parallel, individually inconclusive, but jointly conclusive assertions. It is common to reach a verdict repealing legislation on the grounds of its unconstitutionality applying several fundamental rights, each of which could serve individually to challenge the legislation in question.

For example, regarding the first issue in the case on collective labour bargaining explained in Table 6, the Tribunal applied freedom of association, freedom of unionisation, the right to bargain, and legal equality, each of whom could serve to repeal the relevant provisions in the statutory reform. Table 5 indicates that the use of different types of parallel argumentation increased in its recurrence after 2005, even though they still are less common than one-line reasoning. Evidence also indicates that parallel argumentation only seems to be more relevant in majority votes.

These tendencies achieve their more pathological form in cases where the CHCT is quite simply unable to provide a single majority reasoning. Perhaps the clearest illustration of this are the many decisions relating to the law on 'arms control'. The CHCT has declared 'inapplicable' in countless cases a statutory provision establishing mandatory prison sentences for crimes committed with certain arms. In many such decisions (eg TC 4802/2018), the CHCT introduces its reasoning warning that while all judges in favour of declaring 'inapplicable' the relevant provision do so because of the same 'constitutional infractions', 'there exists among them differences as to the direction of the line of argument used', recording that there are two main different approaches. That the CHCT was unable to provide a unified opinion in a low-stakes decision that they must reproduce hundreds of times, speaks volumes of the difficulties of the CHCT in reaching consensus in the final part of the period under study. Furthermore, despite the fact that the decision is reproduced verbatim in other cases, the CHCT may also change the disposition of the case if, for example, there is one justice less in the Tribunal (eg TC 4685/18).

The CHCT sometimes does not even try to provide a unified argument. This occurred in a recent case where the CHCT declared 'inapplicable' a criminal provision applied for breach of restrictions on movement imposed regarding the COVID-19 pandemic. There, the CHCT quite simply stated that it would reproduce the reasoning of the different judges, since there was no agreement on the arguments for the decision (TC 8950/2020).

Regarding complex and confusing argumentation, we found several phenomena after 2005: lengthier judgments, greater conceptual diversity, a broader repertoire of arguments, and as we have analysed in this section, the introduction of separate votes and parallel reasoning. Although neither of these is atypical at the comparative level, they entail a considerable change, overshadowing the previous constitutional practice and the usual traits of the Chilean legal culture. The concentration of all these changes in high-profile rulings in a brief period, however, gave more visibility to them, triggering lawyers' complaints about the unintelligibility of the Tribunal's opinions.

F. The Use of Precedents

A second jurisprudential pathology is associated with contradictory decisions or precedents. Although the Chilean legal system has never developed a case-law culture, higher courts have traditionally referred to past cases to add weight to their reasoning. We can observe that the CHCT began to cite its own decisions increasingly after 2005. On average, within our sample, decisions issued before 2005 cited the Tribunal's precedents 1.72 times, while they did so 10.5 times in the sample after that year. Simultaneously, we found that the CHCT has been reluctant to cite Supreme Court decisions throughout all the period analysed.

Although the CHCT has increasingly referred to prior decisions,[41] it is not always clear what this entails, and occasionally, citations refer to aspects that are not directly linked to the core argument of the cited ruling. Exceptionally, we also find some manipulative use of precedents. For example, the CHCT upheld the legislation authorising abortion in specific circumstances, alleging that legal personality began at birth (TC 3729/2017, para 23). Among other reasons, the CHCT asserted there was no settled precedent in this matter. The Tribunal assumed that a prior verdict on organ transplantation had indicated that life began at birth (TC 220/1995), while on another decision on the provision of the morning-after pill, the CHCT had ruled that the unborn's life began at conception (TC 740/2007). In doing so, however, the majority omitted mentioning that the first decision concerned a case where the beginning of human life was not at issue.

Although we have not conducted a systematic analysis on the precedents' stability, we observe that recently the CHCT has overturned precedents in other high-profile cases. In 2015 the CHCT declared constitutional legislation banning schools with lucrative purposes, disregarding a previous decision that asserted that the Constitution contained no limitation for the educational institutions' legal personhood other than those linked with its exclusive educational end (TC 2787/2015, TC 1363/2009). In another striking example, the CHCT handed down two contradictory decisions on

[41] JF García, '¿Precedente horizontal de facto en el Tribunal Constitucional?' (2018) Special Issue, *Revista de Derecho Público* 247.

statutory authorisations to withdraw social security savings to mitigate the economic consequences of the COVID-19 pandemic.[42] In December 2020, the CHCT decided a petition in favour of the executive, asserting that only the executive branch could introduce a bill on social security reform. However, in a controversial ruling of April 2021, it denied the executive's standing to file an analogous petition concerning a similar piece of legislation, claiming that its decisions 'can change in successive cases, within the framework of legitimate hermeneutical activity'.[43]

IV. Comparative Perspective

The CHCT's reasoning presents some features closely associated with its place in the democratisation of Chile and changes in the legal culture of civil law countries. Within that framework, the correlation between formalist reasoning/deferential behaviour and non-formalist reasoning/nondeference seems the most significant matter of comparative inquiry that the Chilean case offers. At the beginning of the period under analysis, the CHCT mirrored textual positivism as most Latin American and Continental European nations. This style of reasoning employed a plain style, which centred on the ordinary meaning of words, domestic harmonisation, and the constitution-makers' intentions. That reasoning was instrumental in maintaining a focus on law-finding and deferential behaviour. When the CHCT exceptionally challenged the other branches of government, it did so by resorting to teleological analysis on the objective purpose of the text. As we have extensively explained throughout this chapter, the CHCT resorted to a new argumentative repertoire after 2005, showing less deference in landmark cases (cases in our sample). The association between less formalist reasoning and nondeference seems to be also present in other jurisdictions (eg Colombia). However, only a more systematic comparative examination could conclude it is not an idiosyncratic feature in constitutional reasoning in Chile.

V. Evaluation, Pathologies and Criticism

The CHCT played a critical role in Chilean politics, facilitating the return to democracy and contributing to the consolidation of the rule of law during the last decades. After the 2005 constitutional reforms modified its composition and strengthened its functions, the CHCT attempted to be more responsive and occasionally took significant political risks in repealing legislation. As we have analysed throughout this chapter, in this period the justices' opinions also adopted a new style of reasoning by adding to the CHCT's original repertoire of reasons related to textual positivism a broader repertoire closer to so-called 'neo constitutional' thought. Thus, the CHCT attempted to increase the legitimacy of its decisions by using additional sources (eg, international law, foreign

[42] TC 9797/2020 and TC 10774/2021.
[43] TC 10774/2021, Consideration 36.

law) and gained more interpretive leeway in adjudication by means of arguments like the proportionality test and allusions to substantive justice.

Despite its growing influence, the quick transformation in the Tribunal's practices and the gradual political fragmentation of Chilean politics have contributed to the erosion of the CHCT's authority within the political process. Here we have not attempted to provide a comprehensive account of the causes leading to the loss of legitimacy of the CHCT. We only focus on one, often neglected, part of the story: the weakening of its reason-giving function. To fully understand the loss of legitimacy of the CHCT one would have to consider a broader context.

An important part of that context, which we cannot develop here, is that the CHCT's greater influence aroused the political parties' interest in exerting more direct control in it. After 2006, the executive and the legislative branches nominated well-respected legal and political actors to the CHCT's bench (eg former minister and senator José Antonio Viera-Gallo, undersecretary Jorge Correa Sutil, and former senator Hernán Vodanovic). However, gradually, the appointment process deteriorated, together with the prestige of some members of the Tribunal. For instance, in 2009 and in 2013, the incumbent executives appointed close legal advisors to the CHCT – justices Carmona and Brahm – who later were accused of sexual and of work harassment respectively. In 2015 Congress chose justices Letelier and Pozo, who, in turn, were active militants in parties of the right and the left respectively. They lacked the needed expertise and there was no public debate on their appointment, which was known only the same day of the vote. Quickly accusations of plagiarism (Pozo) and of illicit campaign funding (Letelier) were raised regarding these candidates. These appointments had a negative impact in the relations of justices in the CHCT, producing a sense of political partisanship inside the Tribunal which transcended to the media.[44]

It is only natural that partisan nominations and quarrels between judges would affect the legitimacy of the Tribunal. Yet we believe there is an important additional cause of the loss of legitimacy of the CHCT: the innovations in the CHCT's argumentation have not been free of troubles. Besides lengthier sentences and a broader repertoire, the Tribunal introduced separate votes and parallel reasoning, particularly in high-profile cases. Although these traits are not uncommon in other jurisdictions, they have made it increasingly difficult to understand the reasoning of the Tribunal. At the same time, the CHCT has been unable to establish a methodologically clear regime of settled precedents, overturning prominent judgments without clear discipline.

All things considered, the abovementioned difficulties have undermined the very core of the CHCT's constitutional role, which entails the work of impartial judges applying pre-existing constitutional criteria through sound legal reasoning. While political appointments and internal conflict make it harder to perceive the CHCT as impartial, a defective system of precedents and the disordered complexity in the reasoning of some decisions has diminished the authority of the CHCT's judgments. These difficulties emerged at a time when the CHCT became more consequential and needed greater legitimacy, after more than a decade of deferential behaviour (1992–2005).

[44] J Contesse, 'The Downfall of a Constitutional Court' *Verfassungsblog on Matters Constitutional* (28 April 2020) www.verfassungsblog.de/the-downfall-of-a-constitutional-court/.

8

The Jurisprudence of the Constitutional Court of Colombia

MAGDALENA CORREA INÉS HENAO AND JORGE ERNESTO ROA ROA

I. Legal, Political, Institutional and Academic Context

A. Legal and Political Culture as Context for the Constitutional Reasoning

Since the beginning of its independent history, the Colombian State has followed a legalistic tradition. All political, social and economic processes and conflicts are resolved through the law. In the nineteenth century, eight constitutions were approved. This tradition has determined the predominantly formal value of the law as the supreme legal norm. In this context, the Constitution has specifically been understood to be a norm of a political nature.

The judicial function has been decisive in the history of Colombian institutions. Despite its formalism and adherence to the letter of the law rather than to the objective of pursued justice, the judiciary has been the branch of public power that has most closely complied with the principles of the rule of law. However, this does not signify that there is an overall positive assessment of the functioning of the administration of justice[1] or that this constitutional function is exercised without any interference or problems with corruption.[2] In comparative terms within Latin America, Colombian judges and courts are recognised as being relatively independent.[3]

The great revolution in Colombian legal thought commenced in 1991. Since then, different methods of reasoning have survived and competed, but distinct forms of judicial reasoning have also been harmonised. On the one hand, with the traditional rule of

[1] R Uprimny, C Rodríguez Garavito and M García Villegas, 'Las cifras de la justicia' in M García Villegas, C Rodríguez Garavito and R Uprimny, *¿Justicia para todos? Sistema judicial, derechos sociales y democracia en Colombia* (Grupo Editorial Norma, 2006).

[2] D Rico Chavarro, 'La rama Judicial del poder público en Colombia: "Independencia versus intervencionismo"' (2011) 3 *Criterio jurídico garantista* 12–31.

[3] M García Villegas and MA Ceballos Bedoya (eds), 'Estudio preliminar. Derecho, justicia y sociedad en Colombia' in *Democracia, justicia y sociedad: Diez años de investigación en Dejusticia* (Dejusticia, 2016) 26–27.

law and its particularities, it was understood that the judge's function was to subsume the resolution of the specific case under what is established in the law. On the other hand, the more complex decisions based on constitutional interpretation[4] are premised on the normative structure of constitutional rules that are built from notions of broad, varied and debatable contents.

For their part, the ordinary and contentious-administrative courts have sustained over the years a relative tension with the jurisprudence of the Constitutional Court of Colombia (CCC). Although this tension is generally not continuous, it is certainly clear that these courts do not always follow the CCC's pronouncements. This situation has been dubbed a 'train wreck', which occurs with the application of the action of legal protection (*tutela*) against judicial decisions. Indeed, the CCC has often revised decisions of the Supreme Court of Justice and the Council of State, which has resulted in the revocation of those judgments in which the claimants had been denied the protection of their rights.

B. The Court and Constitutional Litigation

According to Article 241 of the Constitution, the Court is responsible for 'the safeguarding of the integrity and supremacy of the Constitution'. This responsibility is executed through three types of activity: (i) deciding on petitions of unconstitutionality or exercising the automatic review of the constitutionality of laws and decrees with the force of law, including reformative acts of the Constitution, referenda or a Constituent Assembly to amend the Constitution; referenda on laws and popular consultations and plebiscites with a national scope; bills opposed by the Government; proposed statutory bills; and international treaties and their approving laws; (ii) revising, in accordance with the law, judicial decisions related to the *tutela* action of constitutional rights; and (iii) resolving jurisdictional conflicts. This chapter only addresses the first two types.[5]

i. Function of Constitutional Review

The CCC's exercise of constitutional review has two variations. The first is the product of the exercise of the unconstitutionality action, and the second is automatic or exercised at the request of the national Government. Both variations are decided in the CCC's Plenary Chamber, although their processing is carried out by the office of one of the judges who sits on the panel.

Public action can be exercised by any natural person who has Colombian citizenship.[6] However, this does not preclude foreigners and legal entities, under both

[4] R Gargarella, 'La dificultosa tarea de la interpretación constitucional' in *Teoría y Crítica del Derecho Constitucional* (Abeledo Perrot, 2008) 123–47.

[5] Constitutional review judgments are identified with the letter 'C', and *tutela* judgments are usually identified with the letter 'T'. When their nomenclature begins with the acronym 'SU' (unification judgments), they correspond to *tutela* reviews that the Plenary Chamber has adopted. See R Uprimny, 'Should Courts enforce social rights? The Experience of the Colombian Constitutional Court' (11 October 2006) *Dejusticia* 4–5, at www.dejusticia.org/wp-content/uploads/2017/04/fi_name_recurso_67.pdf.

[6] JE Roa Roa, *La acción pública de constitucionalidad a debate* (Universidad Externado de Colombia, 2015).

private and public law, from going before the CCC to file lawsuits against legal norms they consider to be contrary to the Constitution. These claims must be channelled through a natural person with citizenship because this is the only party who has standing (*legitimación*) to initiate the case.[7]

The Court also reviews a certain number of bills or laws, acts and legislative decrees whose constitutionality must be assessed, without the need for a lawsuit. The case arrives at the Court either because the Constitution directly mandates an automatic review petition or at the Government's request (Government objections prior to the approval of laws). These reviews must be initiated prior to the approval of the normative text (statutory laws call for mechanisms of citizen participation) or after it (legislative decrees or acts reforming the Constitution).

In the procedures of the two variations of constitutional review, there are no actual procedural parties because the process is objective, or it challenges legal norms. The participation of the *Procurador General de la Nación*, or whoever acts on his or her behalf, is mandatory. In addition, during the relevant procedural phases, both the President and the Congress of the Republic may submit written briefs expressing their views on the matter. Likewise, the magistrate who hears the case may invite public entities, private organisations and experts on related topics, or anyone who participated in the norm's drafting, to submit briefs that communicate their views on the case.[8]

It has been understood that not only any citizen but also any person or organisation, *motu proprio* and within the procedure, may also submit a brief regarding the review under discussion. In this way, it is becoming increasingly common to identify in the proceedings different types of contributions that the Court recognises as interventions, *amicus curiae* or opinions (*conceptos*).[9]

In addition, in abstract review proceedings – and also in the *tutela* reviews resolved in the Plenary Chamber – any magistrate may request that public hearings be held, which the Court will decree, 'considering the background of the act subject to constitutional judgment and the importance and complexity of the issues' to be resolved.[10]

Although the action of unconstitutionality is public, the lawsuit must meet minimum requirements.[11] Indeed, it is necessary to identify the challenged rules and the constitutional norms that have allegedly been infringed. Additionally, it is essential to precisely draft a complaint of infringement (*concepto de violación*) that contains a clear (understandable), certain (or that relies on an existing and unambiguous legal proposition), specific (where the description of how the challenged norm violates the Constitution is presented in an objective and verifiable form), pertinent (or that the accusations are of a constitutional nature) and sufficient (in argumentative and probative elements of judgment that produce the least doubt about the alleged unconstitutionality).[12]

[7] Judgment C-163/2021.

[8] Roa Roa (n 6).

[9] Judgment C-294/2019.

[10] JE Roa Roa, *Control de constitucionalidad deliberativo. El ciudadano ante la justicia constitucional, la acción pública de inconstitucionalidad y la legitimidad democrática del control judicial del legislador* (Universidad Externado de Colombia, 2019) 213–393.

[11] Judgment C-1052/01.

[12] Roa Roa (n 10) 213–393.

According to CCC statistics, between 1992 and September 2021, the Court received 14,407 actions of unconstitutionality,[13] which resulted in a total of 4,426 decisions[14] on those actions. This signifies that the CCC only admits or is aware of approximately 30 per cent of all unconstitutionality claims. And based on the approximate number of those that the Court accepts, only 33 per cent of the decisions reach the merits of the case – that is, they resolve the constitutional issues that citizens have raised.

When the CCC carries out a comprehensive review, the Court must address the norm at issue within the totality of the Constitution's precepts. Decisions on the merits have the effect of constitutional *res judicata*, and they are binding and have *erga omnes* effect on the rule's operative part. The section of the rule that describes its purpose is only an auxiliary criterion for judicial use and for the application of legal rules in general.

The issued judgments have been of various types, and they respond to what has been called the 'modulation of the decision's effects' ('*modulación de los efectos de la sentencia*').[15] With regard to their content, the judgments contain declarations of clear, simple or conditioned constitutionality or unconstitutionality, whether these are interpretive, integrated or substituted. And regarding temporal effects, the decisions of unconstitutionality are retroactive, deferred or immediately effective.[16]

On this last aspect, the general rule is that the declaration of a norm's unconstitutionality or unenforceability means that it is excluded from the legal order, and it therefore cannot be applied once the CCC's ruling has been published. The decision is not properly an annulment because such a measure usually takes effect in the future unless the Court determines otherwise.[17]

Finally, the function of constitutional review is not exclusive to the Constitutional Court. The Constitution establishes what the jurisprudence itself calls a 'diffuse functional' ('*difuso funcional*') model.[18] On the one hand, the Constitutional Court and the Council of State are the organs responsible for the abstract review of constitutionality, the latter having residual jurisdiction; 'on the other hand, all judges and corporations (…) must decide on *tutela* actions or resolve actions and remedies provided for to guarantee constitutional rights or when making use of the exception of unconstitutionality in the specific cases submitted for their consideration'.[19]

ii. Function of the Review of the Tutela

As Rodrigo Uprimny has described, the *tutela* action, 'enacted by the 1991 Constitution (art. 86) and regulated by Decree 2591/91, (…) is the judicial action by which any person can request a speedy decision (within 10 days) by a judge to protect his or her fundamental rights'.[20] It is an informal action, which does not require legal technicalities

[13] Statistics of the Constitutional Court, Constitutional Court of Colombia, at www.corteconstitucional.gov.co/lacorte/estadisticas.php.
[14] ibid.
[15] Roa Roa (n 6).
[16] ibid.
[17] ibid.
[18] C-1154 of 2008.
[19] C-1154 of 2008 and C-415/2012. Italics added.
[20] See Uprimny (n 5) 5.

or a lawyer, and which all individuals can request without distinction of nationality, sex, age or ethnicity.

Unlike in the constitutional review procedure, in the *tutela*, there are procedural parties that can be either natural or legal persons. On the one hand, the standing of petitioner(s) as plaintiff(s) of a *tutela* in an active case is established by being nothing more than the subject(s) of a fundamental right that is considered violated or threatened, although the Ombudsman (*Defensor del Pueblo*) is also empowered to exercise a *tutela* 'on behalf of any person who requests it or who is in a situation of helplessness and defencelessness'.[21] On the other hand, the *tutela* is directed against the authorities or individuals (under certain circumstances) who cause or are responsible for the indicated violation or threat.

Under specific rules of apportionment and competence, all domestic judges, other than those of the CCC, are responsible for handling *tutelas*. The process has two stages although the appeal is not mandatory. The CCC's role becomes decisive because 'all cases end up in the docket of the CCC, which can discretionally review, by a sort of *certiorari*',[22] although all the decided and binding *tutelas* reach the CCC and enter the Court's selection process.[23] The latter can be requested by the parties who acted as plaintiffs or defendants during the initial proceedings. When a *tutela* is not included in the selection, the parties may insist,[24] which is also an option 'of the Ombudsman, the *Procurador General de la Nación*, the National Agency for Legal Defence of the State or a Magistrate of the Constitutional Court'.[25]

Once the *tutela* decision to be reviewed has been selected, in the procedure, like in abstract reviews, the judge who examines it can admit evidence. In that context, the judge can request opinions or interventions from persons or entities with expertise, which allows the reviewing chamber to have better materials to examine when deciding the case.

The review's purpose may be to revoke or modify the lower court's decision, unify constitutional jurisprudence or clarify the general scope of constitutional norms.[26] According to the CCC's statistics, it is estimated that of the total number of *tutela* decisions that reach the Court,[27] it selects only about 0.23 per cent.[28]

The decision is usually made by a review chamber comprised of three judges.[29] The CCC itself has recognised two different types of orders or remedies that it confirms or establishes in the *tutela* review process to address situations involving the infringement of fundamental rights. Namely, these are 'simple orders and complex orders, depending on

[21] Art 46, Decree 2591/1991.

[22] See Uprimny (n 5) 5.

[23] This process is carried out by a selection chamber composed of two magistrates who decide on a monthly basis the *tutelas* that will be reviewed.

[24] This takes the form of a letter of 'insistence' ('*insistencia*') in which the parties reiterate the selection request.

[25] Art 55, Agreement 02/2015. Constitutional Court. Italics added.

[26] Art 35, inc. 1° of Decree 2591/1991.

[27] 8,295,032 filings.

[28] This percentage is obtained by comparing the universe of *tutela* rulings that were filed with the number of review decisions that the Court issued between 1992 and June 2021 (19,446 T and 447 SU).

[29] However, in some cases identified by the letters SU, it is the Plenary Chamber that decides, adopting unification rulings.

the characteristics of the case and the degree of complexity that the resolution requires, which is determined from such variables as (i) the number of actions or abstentions that are incorporated in the order; (ii) the number of subjects and/or authorities to whom the order is addressed; and (iii) the period required for its execution'.[30]

iii. Institutional Impact, Effectiveness and Transformative Power of the CCC's Decisions

The CCC's decisions have different levels of effectiveness, depending on their content. Apart from those that confirm the constitutionality of norms, which do not propose any alteration of the legal order, those with provisions that are declared unconstitutional (and especially when their constitutionality is conditioned) can be relatively complex to execute, which is dependent on the clarity of the order and not necessarily on the order itself.[31]

However, where the effectiveness of the Court's judgments is most often discussed is in the *tutela* reviews. In general, these judgments are not fulfilled. This is due to the criticism they evoke when imposing the obligated authorities' unforeseen fees or budgetary allocations, or because they imply an inequitable distribution of scarce resources that benefits less-disadvantaged groups compared to others that do not access the *tutela*. Further, if the judgments are truly transformative, when confronted with preponderant political or economic interests, the sentences are not executed.[32]

The prestige and power that the CCC has garnered since its formation has prompted various reactions from the Government, the legislative branch and other authorities and private institutions – specifically, openly reticent when the judgments have altered decisions of economic public policy, and in a biased way when they affect measures of political interest. So far, however, the foregoing has not necessarily meant that the CCC has altered its way of exercising review of the acts of the Government and the legislator.

C. The Judges

The CCC is composed of nine magistrates elected by the Senate of the Republic from shortlists prepared by the President of the Republic, the Supreme Court of Justice and the Council of State. Their eight-year terms are personal in nature, and the judges cannot be re-elected.[33] They can be tried in a special procedure at the request of the Congress of the Republic,[34] and they can only be removed from their positions for 'crimes committed in the exercise of their duties, for indignity, for misconduct or for common crimes'.[35]

[30] SU-092/2021.
[31] C-123/2014.
[32] SU-039/1997.
[33] Art 238, Constitution of Colombia.
[34] Arts 174 and 175, Constitution of Colombia.
[35] Art 329 et seq, Law 5a/1992.

Since its creation in 1991, and its formation the following year, the CCC's institutional stability has been preserved despite several attempts to weaken its power directly or indirectly by reforming some of its constitutional competences.[36]

During the CCC's 30 years of existence, its magistrates have mostly been career judges, trial lawyers and academics. Although regional representation has not been especially limited, ethnic and cultural minorities have not been represented on the bench. As of 2020, only six women have been elected judges of the Court; currently, five of the nine members are female.

The most relevant changes in constitutional jurisprudence can be found less in the variations in the Court's composition and more in the occurrence of social and cultural phenomena, as well as in political changes and offshoots of ordinary constitutional reforms[37] or the peace process.[38]

II. Types of Arguments in Constitutional Reasoning

A. The Structure of Constitutional Arguments

The sample judgments included in this study accurately reflect the argumentative structure of Colombian constitutional jurisprudence. This structure tends to be complex because it is built with either independent-inconclusive arguments together with conclusive arguments, or with parallel-conclusive arguments (35 cases). This prevalence might be explained by the fact that the constitutional judge has a wide range of principled constitutional norms from which to choose.

B. Types of Arguments in Constitutional Reasoning

The CCC's tenor and the characteristics of the selected judgments envision that judicial reasoning is constructed from an unequivocal acceptance of the Constitution's normative value, although the types of arguments the Court uses are quite varied.

i. Constitutional Nature of Norms

Five judgments include discussions about the constitutional nature of norms relevant to the cases. The nature of these cases' constitutional issues, and the scopes of what

[36] JE Roa Roa, 'Activismo judicial, legitimidad democrática de la protección judicial de los derechos e incidente de impacto fiscal' (2017) Año XXIII *Anuario de Derecho Constitucional Latinoamericano* 455–82.

[37] (Constant) use of states of emergency (C-070/2009, C-252/2010), government initiatives on gross legal reforms (C-038/2004, C-030 of 2008, C-175 of 2009), and acts of constitutional reform, such as the call for a constitutional referendum (C-551/2003), and the legislative acts that introduced the possibility of presidential re-election (C-1040/2005, C-141/2010).

[38] Copious jurisprudence was produced related to the CCC's central function, fulfilled during the implementation process of the Peace Agreement through the transitional constitutional norms, whereas the CCC would carry out automatic abstract control, either before or after, of the totality of the norms dictated by the Constituent Assembly, the legislator and the Government: C-699/2016, C-332/2017 and C-274/2017.

they aim to resolve, explain the reasons to include this kind of argument. One case is associated with the constitutional value conferred on the popular referendum.[39] Two decisions seek to determine the contours of the constitutional protection of progressive rights: one involves people in a vegetative state's right to health,[40] and the other is an abstract review case that addresses the rights of peasants (*campesinos*).[41] And two of the five cases are related to the scope of the constitutional competence to review public international treaties along with the substantial number of constitutional rules invoked: one decision declares unconstitutional those supervening norms of the Concordat that had entered into force prior to the 1991 Constitution,[42] and another recognises the constitutionality of the measures provided for in the Rome Statute but without compromising or binding national judges.[43]

ii. Debating the Applicability of Constitutional Law

The analysis of 'the constitutional enforceability and justiciability' of the Constitution, or whether it can be applied directly to resolve a case, is identified in 16 decisions of which half are among the selected rulings that were issued during the CCC's first 10 years. This is understandable given the importance of establishing the binding power of constitutional mandates from the CCC's jurisprudence. Twelve cases are *tutela* reviews due to the nature and legal basis of constitutional rights, which consist of a fundamental, constitutional and binding international human rights law (IHRL) and a somewhat broad or narrow legislative configuration, found by examining civil[44] and political[45] liberties, the right to equal treatment in equal situations[46] and non-discrimination[47] as well as social rights[48] and even economic freedoms and rights.[49] Four constitutional cases refer to matters in which it is vital to define the obligatory content of constitutional norms, either to review public international treaties,[50] the power of constitutional reform and the Constitution's irreplaceable content[51] or the harmonisation with the American Convention on Human Rights (ACHR).[52]

No decision expressly includes the question of the control of conventionality[53] in the argumentation. However, in an opinion in which freedom of expression is safeguarded under very broad contours of protection, inter-American jurisprudence is a fundamental part of the argumentation.[54] In a judgment that addresses a legal norm, which invokes another constitutional rule that provides fewer guarantees than Article 23 of the

[39] C-699/2016.
[40] T-057/15.
[41] C-644/2012.
[42] C-027/1993.
[43] C-578/2002.
[44] SU-337/99, T-391/2007 and SU166/1999.
[45] SU-047/99.
[46] T-494/1992 and T-590/2017.
[47] T-1090/2005.
[48] T-406/1994, T-881/2002 and T-418/2010.
[49] T-629/2010 and T-543/2017.
[50] C-073/1993 and C-578/2002.
[51] C-332/2017.
[52] C-111/2019.
[53] This is a doctrine that creates an international obligation for State parties to the Pact of San José to interpret any national norm in accordance with the ACHR and, in general, with the Inter-American *corpus iuris*.
[54] T-391/2007.

ACHR (specifically, for the removal of popularly elected authorities), the Court resolved whether there is a disparity between these norms and explained the value it attaches to the inter-American jurisprudence on the matter.[55]

iii. Analogies

There are only four decisions in the sample that allude to analogy. This result is partly explained by the sample itself and partly by the CCC's proclivity to employ methods of constitutional interpretation. Analogy only had a useful impact in one decision, where it served to explain the reasons why it could not be applied to the definition of the Court's procedural powers when it exercises the constitutional review of constitutional reforms.[56]

iv. Ordinary Meaning of the Words of the Constitution

In nine judgments, there were references to the ordinary meanings of the Constitution's words/phrases/articles: of these, seven involved abstract review and two were *tutela* reviews. In the first group, the majority adopted it as one of its basic arguments, rejecting it as the exclusive method of interpretation to establish the meaning of concepts used in the constitutional review rules (issued by the legislator[57] and by the national government during states of emergency[58]) or review parameters (involving constitutional reforms[59] or laws calling for an approval of a constitutional referendum[60]).

The Constitution's words were presented as the argument *par excellence* in the dissenting opinions to the *tutela* decision adopted by the Plenary Chamber regarding same-sex marriage. Notwithstanding the Constitution's provisions on the composition of the family by marriage, the majority recognised that the fundamental right to enter into a marriage contract also applies to same-sex couples.[61]

v. Domestic Harmonising Arguments

The type of interpretation that has prevailed most often in Colombian constitutional jurisprudence is that of the systemic or integrative understanding of the Constitution: 38 decisions expressly recognise this as a type of argumentation. This is explained by the reception of the principle of constitutional unity that serves both to interpret specific constitutional norms as part of a complex and coherent system and to expand the scope of the rights and institutional guarantees provided therein.

vi. International Harmonising Arguments

A rather remarkable element of the CCC's judicial reasoning is the Court's common use of international law requirements to interpret the Constitution and to decide the

[55] C-111/2019.
[56] C-699/2016.
[57] C-590/05 and C-591/05.
[58] C-070/2009 and C-252/2010.
[59] C-332/2016.
[60] C-141/2010 and C-699/2016.
[61] SU-214/2016.

cases. A good number of the decisions (28 judgments) incorporate them, in most cases combining references to norms of the Inter-American Human Rights System (IAHRS) and other norms of hard and soft international law.

Regarding the use of binding, conventional and universal IHRL, although the Constitution establishes a difference between the 'constitutionality block' *stricto sensu* or *lato sensu*,[62] it also establishes that both substantially comprise international instruments of hard law. However, the CCC has not been particularly rigorous in interpreting and applying one[63] or the other.[64]

vii. Precedents

The sample aptly reflects the most important change that has occurred in Colombian law since the issuance of the Charter in 1991 – that is, the value that the CCC has placed, from the beginning, on constitutional precedent within the system of sources of law as a fundamental argument in which the Constitution is interpreted and in which the case's issues are addressed. Apart from the first selected judgment from 1992, the others all contain references to a precedent-based argument.

The strength of precedent is largely a conception of the Court itself, since in the Constitution, jurisprudence is an auxiliary criterion of judicial proceedings (Art 230, Const.). Precedent-binding force has been recognised based on the principles of legal equality and certainty (Arts 13 and 29, Const.) in relation to the right of access to justice (Art 229, Const.). However, horizontal and vertical precedents for ordinary and contentious-administrative justice are not insurmountable. Judges, in the exercise of their functional independence, may stray from those as long as the reasons for doing so are justified.[65] On the contrary, the constitutional precedent is mandatory since it is based on the effects of constitutional *res judicata* provided for in the Constitution for the substantive decisions that the CCC adopts (Art 243, Const.).[66] Changes or alterations can only be made by the Court and by satisfying argumentative requirements that the current jurisprudence would be erroneous or inadequate due to (i) a '*subsequent social change*';[67] (ii) 'being contrary to the values, objectives, principles and rights on which the legal system is based';[68] and (iii) 'a change in the positive legal system'.[69]

viii. Doctrinal Analysis of Legal Concepts or Principles

Similarly, the CCC quite frequently includes principles in its reasoning that are not expressly specified in the constitutional text – that is, in 25 cases out of 40 in the sample.

[62] ME Góngora-Mera, 'The Block of Constitutionality as the Doctrinal Pivot of a Ius Commune' in A von Bogdandy, E Ferrer Mac-Gregor, M Morales Antoniazzi, F Piovesan and X Soley (eds), *Transformative constitutionalism in Latin America. The emergence of a New Ius commune* (Oxford University Press, 2017) 248.
[63] C-070/2009.
[64] T-417/2010, C-182/16 and T-590/2017; C-644/12, C-674/2017 and C-T-236/17.
[65] C-621/2015.
[66] C Bernal Pulido, 'El Precedente en Colombia' (2008) 21 *Revista Derecho del Estado* 81–94.
[67] C-836 of 2001.
[68] C-228 of 2002.
[69] C-111/2019.

They serve mainly to recognise unnamed fundamental rights[70] and to interpret rights and principles of a political nature,[71] procedural guarantees,[72] and Government, administrative[73] and judicial[74] competences and functions.

ix. Arguments from Silence

The Court relied on *argumentum ex silentio* in five judgments as part of the reasoning for its decisions, drawing on an omission or lack of express reference to a right or principle in the Constitution or a law,[75] and explaining that constitutional or legal silence does not necessarily prohibit or exclude certain interpretations.[76]

x. Teleological/Purposive Arguments

Teleological arguments are instead a constant: 20 judgments refer to the purpose of the text and 16 to the intention of the Constitution-maker.[77] Recourse to these arguments can be understood as a sign of the CCC's interest in legitimising its interpretations of the Constitution rather than presenting its own views on the function that each of the constitutional provisions has in the constitutional order, which is already clear from the Charter's text or from the Constituent Assembly's preparatory work.

xi. Non-Legal Arguments

Also noteworthy is the high number of decisions (26 out of 40) in which non-legal arguments are utilised, operating either to measure the problem that the case poses or to resolve it. Arguments of a sociological (16 cases), economic (13 cases), scientific (8 cases) and moral or religious nature (7 cases) are used alone or combined.[78] This practice reflects a constant in the CCC's reasoning, which assumes that constitutional law is a legal discipline but whose contents, guarantees, effectiveness, development and noncompliance are not only understood from its normative sources but also from the interaction of these with other areas of knowledge.

xii. References to Scholarly Works

Another factor that demonstrates the CCC's interpretative openness in fulfilling its function as the Constitution's interpreter is the Court's recurrent references to scholarly works (29 cases). The most common references are to IHRL experts, both Latin

[70] SU-166/99, T-025/04, C-355/06, C-644/12 and T-057/15.
[71] C-141/10.
[72] C-1052/01, C-141/10 and C-674/17.
[73] C-578/02, C-332/17 and T-617/2010.
[74] C-578/02, C-332/17 and T-617/2010.
[75] C-371/00, SU-383/03 and T-057/2015.
[76] SU-214/16 and C-699/2016.
[77] C-027/93.
[78] 13 use only one type of non-legal argument, and 13 combine different ones.

American and those from the global North and South. Citations to foreign constitutional law scholars are also observed, with preference shown for European and North American authors. Although this practice is not the judgment's definitive or exclusive argument, references to doctrine (especially foreign) is an auxiliary criterion that the CCC uses to elucidate the constitutional State's range of principles, rights and institutions that are relevant to the cases. Additionally, in some cases, doctrine is cited to understand the properties or characteristics of the institutions that regulate the norms under review.

xiii. References to Foreign (National) Law

Although they lack any binding force, references to the experiences of foreign legal institutions also occupy a prominent place in the CCC's argumentation. This practice is presented as a kind of pragmatic use of comparative law for the interpretation of domestic law (substantive) or as an interpretive technique in and of itself (procedural).[79] In other words, the Court does not follow the guidelines of the comparative law discipline since it focuses on analysing the normative texts issued in other States. The weight given these sources is apparent in the understanding of the subject matter under analysis, especially in judgments that address difficult issues or are of great constitutional significance.[80]

xiv. Pro Homine/Pro Persona *Principles*

The *pro persona* principle is unquestionably a major premise within the CCC's reasoning for constructing the interpretation that best guarantees fundamental rights and the definition of the purposes that justify functions, institutions and competences. Thus, it is surprising that express reference to the principle is only reported in three decisions,[81] although it is the implicit basis for many others in which the objective or subjective infringement of constitutional rights is raised.

xv. Other Methods

Finally, 27 rulings use other types of arguments or methods. For cases related to the regulation or limitation of fundamental rights, the argument types that stand out are weighing, the reasonableness and proportionality test, the equality test with its different levels of depth (depending on the compromised right's scope or its holders' affectation) and the regressivity test. When 'organic' problems or the development of constitutional competences must be resolved, the assessment of the jurisdictional forums, the

[79] A Baraggia, 'Challenges in Comparative Constitutional Law Studies: Between Globalization and Constitutional Tradition' (2017) *Special Issue – Comparative Law, Law and Method* 7.

[80] Abortion (C-355/2006); freedom of expression (T-391/2007); same-sex marriage (SU-214/2016); the 'right to try' in health (T057/2015) and the right to nondiscrimination in taxation based on gender (C-117/2018); the ruling that declared the second presidential re-election unconstitutional (C-141/2010) and the first decision that examined the special legislative procedure (C-699/2016).

[81] C-221/1994, T-881/02 and C-182/2016.

legislative immunity and the *in dubio pro legislatore* are notable, along with cases where the Court judges acts of constitutional reform, the syllogism that is part of the constitutional substitution test.

The Court uses all these methods, without any rule's permission or prohibition. Their inclusion in constitutional judicial reasoning derives from the CCC's own interpretation of their constitutional functions.

C. The Overall Weight of the Arguments

The complete review of the arguments noted in the sample shows an imprint in the CCC's reasoning that can be traced from the beginning of the Court's existence. The CCC is a court that hears demands for justice, which are presented by way of action of unconstitutionality or *tutela* – including the most difficult cases, conjointly with various types of arguments used interchangeably, with the Court seeking to demonstrate the rationality of its case analyses and the accuracy and legality of its decisions.

Not all the arguments satisfy the same function since some are part of the obiter dictum and serve as context to understand the case's subject matter, and others are useful for identifying and resolving the constitutional issue of the case. With regard to the latter, there is a clear preference for methods of constitutional interpretation that include legal arguments or the Constitution as a norm along with its system of sources, with binding and enforceable principles, guarantees and purposes. In cases where a power allocation is reviewed, the argumentation is constructed from constitutional unity and the comparable value of all constitutional assets. In those where fundamental rights are compromised, the argumentation is less weighted because in general it is crafted to justify either the least possible restriction or the most desirable comprehensive protection. The argument accounts for reality, scientific knowledge, data and information to describe how the case's legal issue materialises and to foster the idea of the Constitution as a living norm.

This is confirmed because 30 of the 40 analysed judicial opinions are structured with the ratio decidendi and obiter dictum arguments, these being the longest. With the passage of time, it can be observed in the judgments that the ratio decidendi is becoming more technical and improving in clarity and defining the reasons, contents and effects of the ruling. Of the remaining 10 cases, seven are practically equal in terms of 'the proportion between the ratio decidendi and obiter dictum arguments (…) and the decorative, rhetorical or deceptive arguments'.[82] And in just three, the judicial opinion's majority uses mostly rhetorical or deceptive arguments. In both groups, the results could be explained in terms of the complexity of the issues to be resolved, by involving or stressing principles, rights or constitutional functions that compromise or confront deep-rooted political,[83] social, cultural and institutional conceptions.[84]

[82] See the CORE Latam Codebook Question 50 on the 'Overall Weight of the Argument' in the Appendices of this volume.

[83] C-221/1994, C-578/2002, C-141/2010, C-252/10, C-123/2014, SU-214/16 and T-590/2017.

[84] SU-383/03, C-591/05 and C-699/16.

D. Judicial Candour and Judicial Rhetoric

In general, the CCC's decisions are extensive, as it is shown in Table 1.

Table 1 The average extension of the CCC's decisions for the duration of its existence

TIME PERIOD	Avg. No. of Pages
1992–2019	163.5
1992–2000	90.1
2001–2009	183.091
2010–2016	202.272
2017–2019	175.88

Undoubtedly, such lengthiness accounts for the weight of obiter dicta and the breadth of arguments it usually garners. Over time, this has been compounded by the detailed presentations of the increasingly numerous interventions during the procedure, which also evaluate and assist when describing the legal problem and resolving it while developing specific opinions on the matter. But constitutional jurisprudence has been assuming the role of serving as the source from which not only constitutional law is explained but also substantive and procedural principles of public and private law that relate to the case's constitutional issue. In this sense, the target audience of the judgment's reasoning is not only the parties or stakeholders in the process but also the general public.

However, since the Court generally uses technical language, it could be assumed that it is primarily intended for judges, courts and the legal community, including academics and law students. Besides, in terms of clarity, the judgments' length and language make them extravagant and difficult to understand and make it challenging to disseminate constitutional doctrine and the subrules it contains.

E. Length, Dissenting and Concurring Opinions

The page lengths of the judgments in the sample, which can be seen in the table above as averages per time period, reflect their enlargement over time, with a slight decrease in recent years. The importance or representative nature of the selected decisions can be added to the reasons above. All in all, this is a common feature of the CCC's jurisprudence, and in this sense, the cases that the Court hears are not always particularly complex. Thus, it is the Court's own unique reasoning that best explains the 'long' sentences.

The recurrent formulation of dissenting and concurring opinions – which can be seen in 28 of the 40 judgments in the sample – according to the legislation, can be raised by Court members who disagree with either the decision or with the majority's arguments. In any event, their value, in addition to making the judgments even longer, reflects pluralistic positions that feed the debate and that encourage the evolution of precedent or the improvement of argumentation.

F. Framing of Constitutional Issues

The sample includes 18 *tutela* review judgments and 22 constitutionality rulings. However, even with this variance, the results on the general topics to which the judgments refer (see Figure 1) can be considered indicative of the ways in which the law is interpreted and how the CCC practices its constitutional judicial function, with variations barely apparent during the last short period subject to the selection.

Figure 1 General topics in the selected rulings of the CCC for the duration of its existence

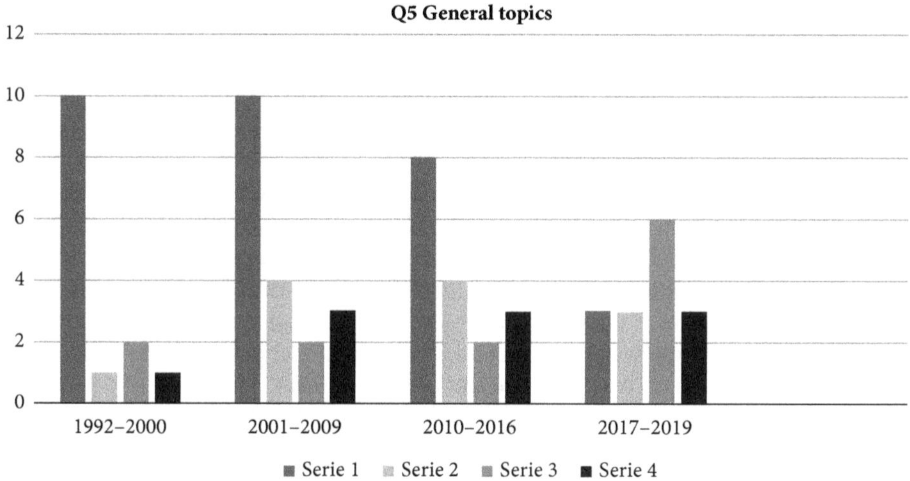

Note: Series 1 refers to Fundamental rights, Series 2 refers to Organisation of the State, Series 3 refers to Due process, and Series 4 to other materials.

Apart from *tutela* review judgments, it is natural that fundamental rights and due process are recurring topics in the Court's jurisprudence. It is a distinction of the CCC's reasoning to place special value on the substantive aspects of cases, even in seemingly formal matters. Therefore, in decisions also involving State organs, public functions and powers, or processes and procedures, the constitutional judge values the exactness of the norms, the fulfilment of procedural requirements and the worthiness of the constitutional functions attributed to the State's powers and authorities. However, the judge also appeals to the principles on which these created organs and powers are based.[85]

As for the results of the 22 constitutional judgments, 12 were upheld and 10 dismissed. The balance between them is a product of the relevance of the chosen cases. This is not entirely representative of the jurisprudence of objective review, where approximately only one-third of the decisions fully or (most often) partially accept the claims of unconstitutionality. In this type of review, the constitutional judge is usually deferential to the legislator, applying both self-restraint and the principle of the preservation of the law.

[85] This has been observed, for example, in the decisions on legislative decrees declaring states of emergency (C-070/2009 and C-252/2010) and in the interpretation of the competence to review reformatory acts of the Constitution (C-141/2010).

The case of *tutela* review judgments is distinct. All 18 in the sample were upheld – that is, they protected the claimed fundamental rights (and others), issued orders and set remedies. This reflects the CCC's *tutela* jurisprudence, since in most cases, the *certiorari* is exercised precisely to reinforce fundamental rights.

G. Key Concepts

The sample offers a very revealing panorama of the importance that the best liberal tradition of Colombian constitutionalism still harbours – in principles, rights and in the deeply rooted structure of the State's system of government and institutional design. This system developed concurrently with an openness to guarantee, pluralism and deliberation in interpretation and constitutional adjudication and with the recognition of the State's reinforced social dimension (broad in terms of guarantees), which the Constitution of 1991 introduced.[86]

The liberal tradition itself is represented in 26 judgments, which accounts for different manifestations of the rule of law that the Constitution includes (Arts 1, 6, 29, 95, 113, 121 and 209, Const.), such as constitutional supremacy, legality and legal certainty. The same number of judgments consider the democratic form of government, which also reflects its status as a core principle of the Colombian Constitution, both in its procedural and substantive aspects (preamble, Arts 1, 2, 3 and 40, Const.; and another 23 constitutional norms of a substantive and organic nature).

Judicial independence, whose importance to the Colombian State extends far beyond what is provided for in the Constitution (Art 228, Const.) and in transitional constitutional norms that introduced the Special Jurisdiction for Peace (*Jurisdicción Especial para la Paz*) (eg, Arts 7, para. and 12 of Legislative Act 1/2017), is considered in seven judgments, where it is especially relevant either as external,[87] internal,[88] organic[89] or functional[90] independence.

The concept of sovereignty is addressed in eight judgments, with its double constitutional meaning (Arts 3 and 9, Const.) of popular and representative sovereignty and external sovereignty in the context of international relations.

As far as principles are concerned, no fewer than 29 judgments refer to equality before the law (Art 13, Const.) and political equality (Arts 40 and 258, Const.).[91] And there are five decisions that address secularism, one of the most firmly established advances of the 1991 Constitution.[92] On civil and political fundamental rights, 16 decisions consider basic procedural rights, while freedom of expression is the subject of three in which serious legal positions are established in defence of the least possible restriction of that freedom and its link to the right to information as part of the fundamental

[86] L Villar Borda, 'Estado de derecho, Estado social de derecho' (2007) 20 *Revista Derecho del Estado* 74–96.
[87] C-027/1993, C-578/2002 and SU-214/16.
[88] C-590/05 and T-590/2017.
[89] C-674/17.
[90] T-590/17 and C-591/2005.
[91] T-1090/2005, T-629/2010 and C-182/2016.
[92] J Aguirre and CA Peralta, 'La Constitución Política de 1991 y la diversidad religiosa: un análisis de la discusión doctrinal sobre la laicidad del Estado colombiano' (2021)(50) *Revista Derecho del Estado* 135–64.

core of consumer rights.[93] And the five decisions that address the right to privacy do so in connection with private autonomy and the general principle of freedom.[94]

With regard to the State's institutional design and structure, five judgments highlight the republican form of government. This form, in place since the nation's initial establishment as an independent State, is an irreplaceable element of the Constitution, which is part of its identity[95] and which explains the 'impermanence of power' of the democratically elected authorities, along with 'periodic, competitive and free elections'.[96]

Regarding the government system by procedural structure, it is striking that only seven decisions include it in their key concepts. Apart from the cases that address government powers in states of emergency[97] or administrative powers in emergency situations[98] and presidential decisions,[99] only two materially consider hyper-presidentialism,[100] which is so much a part of the constitutional historical imprint that it has not been surmounted by the Charter of 1991 and its development. In other words, hyper-presidentialism has not been raised before the CCC as problematic, nor does the Court attribute greater meaning[101] to the 'checks and balances' system, which is unbalanced towards the Executive, and which proves to be something assumed or taken for granted and accepted, being what Roberto Gargarella[102] deems 'the identity mark of constitutionalism' of the region.[103]

Something similar could be inferred in terms of the State government's structure and system. Although Colombia's nineteenth-century history was immersed to a large extent in bloody civil wars fought between centralist and federalist elites,[104] the centennial Constitution of 1886 established the State's unitary form, which was maintained in the 1991 Constitution although tempered by the principles of pluralism (Arts 1, 7 and 8, Const.), decentralisation and territorial autonomy (Arts 1, 246 and 288, Const.). In the CCC's most significant jurisprudence, the difficulties posed by the propensity for the centralisation of national power have not been litigated and are absent. This explains why only two judgments address territorial autonomy and the principle of subsidiarity,[105] while five consider the concept of nationhood and within it the question of plurality.

For the same reason, and notwithstanding its broad constitutional provision, only four judgments in the sample pertain to the mechanisms of political control. Despite being the fundamental political component of the system of 'checks and balances',[106]

[93] C-578/2002; T-391/2007 and T-543/2017.

[94] C-221/94, SU-337/99, C-355/06, T-391/07 and T-629/10. See JC Upegui Mejía, *Transparencia estatal y datos personales: el problema de la publicidad de la información personal en poder del Estado: estudio comparado México-Colombia* (Bogotá, Universidad Externado de Colombia, 2020).

[95] C-699/2016 and C-674/17.

[96] C-141/2010.

[97] C-070/2009 and C-252/10.

[98] C-318/95.

[99] C-578/02 and C-699/16.

[100] C-141/10 and C-332/17.

[101] SU-383/03, T-236/17, C-644/12, C-117/18 and C-123/14.

[102] R Gargarella, 'Sobre el "Nuevo constitucionalismo latinoamericano"/The "new Latin American constitutionalism"' (2018) 27 *Revista Uruguaya de Ciencia Política* 109–29.

[103] C-599/16 and C-332/17.

[104] C Sixirei Paredes, 'Federalismo y centralismo en los orígenes de la Colombia contemporánea' (2014) 33 *História* (São Paulo) 330–45.

[105] T-617/2010 and C-123/2014.

[106] C-252/10 and C-699/16.

the cases reveal that there are no mechanisms that make it enforceable,[107] and although there are fiscal-administrative and disciplinary actions available to pursue inefficient or corrupt actions,[108] their results are quite meagre.

The express constitutional reference to human dignity as one of the foundations of the social rule of law (Art. 1, Const.) anticipates that this is a concept that the CCC recurrently uses and recognises as the sustenance of all rights.[109] In fact, 26 judgments appeal to human dignity, among which one stands out that laid the foundations of its structure, comprised of aspects of freedom, material equality and non-discrimination.[110]

Without being provided for in the Constitution, 17 cases of those selected (eight of constitutionality and nine of *tutela* review) resort to proportionality as a formula for controlling arbitrariness in the use of emergency powers; within the regressivity test[111] for norms that reduce the scope of social and economic rights; within the equality judgment when considering norms or situations of fact; and for resolving collisions between rights and other legal assets. The study's sample provides a good idea of what proportionality has represented in the CCC's jurisprudence – as an immanent method of adjudication derived from the openness with which the CCC has understood the Constitution from the beginning – along with the sources and interpretive methods that were transplanted, first subtly,[112] then with the mixed structure built from the use of the proportionality judgment in Europe and North America, according to the subject matter and nature of the measure judged.[113]

In the same vein, although it was only added to the Constitution in 2011, the core of constitutional rights is employed in 14 judgments, generally with an argumentative value more rhetorical than normative. The qualitative analysis of the decisions highlights the introduction of pluralistic thinking, noted in the concept of family, which is considered in seven decisions and under different constitutional connotations. The same is found in the concept of justice, which is addressed in 11 judgments appearing in the form of corrective justice, which guides the exercise of the parliamentary function and especially the judicial function, others as distributive justice as a defining element of the social rule of law, which manifests itself in the protection of freedoms and equalities, between maximum and minimum. In addition, 10 cases include references to post-material values, which have in common their appearance when referring to the recognition of the fundamental rights of minorities, communities and individuals that warrant special protection.

As a hallmark of this dynamic conception of the Rule of Law that the sample reveals, seven cases address the concept of transition. Four reference the 'process of remodelling social and cultural institutions', which brought about the Constitution of 1991 and the

[107] SU-047/99.

[108] T-418/10 and C-111/19.

[109] B Carvajal, *La dignidad humana como norma de derecho fundamental* (Universidad Externado de Colombia, 2020).

[110] T-881/2002.

[111] M Correa and MA Osorio, 'Socio-Economic Rights in the Colombian Constitutional Jurisprudence: Proportionality Analysis and the Prohibition of Regressive Measures' in L Clérico, X Pou and E Restrepo (eds), *Proportionality and Transformation: Theory and Practice from Latin America* (Cambridge University Press, 2022 [forthcoming]).

[112] C-318/95.

[113] C-709/2002, C-1041/2007, C-417/2009 and T-466/2019.

social, legal and culture transformations, and in three cases, the transition is understood as a transformational process from a domestic conflict to a state of peace. And although only one decision resorts to the notion of constitutional custom, its use had a large impact on the judgment.[114]

Finally, in the key concepts of the sample, the incorporation of social constitutionalism is apparent in the 12 judgments that address issues related to the enforceability of economic, social, cultural and environmental rights. These decisions expose how the very concept of fundamental rights has been understood from the notion of the social rule of law's perspective, where what is inherent in the human person is not only associated with civil and political individual freedoms and rights but also with the satisfaction of basic needs,[115] while the areas of free personality development are also safeguarded by access to public services.[116] With the guarantee of the rights to life, physical integrity and the personal security of the victims of the conflict, it is also essential to provide policies, goods and services that meet at least essential requirements,[117] while the guarantee of the right to prior consultation and collective property has been carried out to protect both indigenous and black communities,[118] as well as the collective assets of the environment and cultural diversity that their territories preserve. And the presidential powers in states of emergency, and the legislative powers needed to develop or distribute competences between the nation and local powers, have been centred around the most suitable satisfaction of social and economic rights.[119]

Among all the aforementioned decisions, 18 refer to judicial activism, used as an argument to support the dissenting and concurring opinions to salvage or clarify judicial votes[120] or to justify the orders that the Court uses to remedy deficits in the protection of required areas of fundamental rights.[121]

III. Comparative Perspective

One of the fundamental findings in comparative public law is the existence of courts accorded high levels of prestige. These are courts that are prominent in comparative constitutional jurisprudence because of their judgments' content, methodology, operation or their decisions' impact. In Latin America, the Constitutional Court of Colombia has distinguished itself globally for three reasons: its transformative character (content and impact of its rulings), its public hearings (methodology) and the opening of constitutional review to citizens (operation).

Unlike other courts that occupy this position due to their location (eg, the Supreme Court of the United States) or their intrinsic power (eg, the Court of Justice of the

[114] T-629/10.

[115] T-406/92 and T-881/2002.

[116] C-221/94 C-355/06, T-629/2010 and C-644/2012.

[117] T-025/2004.

[118] SU-383/03 and T-236/17.

[119] C-252/2010, C-644/12 and C-123/14.

[120] C-141/10, C-644/12, SU214/16, C-332/17 and C-674/17.

[121] T-406/92, C-027/93, C-221/94, C-239/97, SU047/99, SU-337/99, T-025/04, C-355/06, T-391/07, T-418/10, T-617/10 and C-123/14.

European Union), the CCC offers analysis and commentary that are useful to resolve common problems through a global comparative conversation. This role has had a positive internal effect associated with civil society's progressively higher level of awareness of the Court's design, integration and decisions. From the normative system's domestic structure, the Constitutional Court promotes a long, slow and difficult process towards the progressive constitutionalisation of the legal system and a culture of constitutional deliberation. And from the social perspective, the CCC has triggered an empowerment of people or groups for whom the doors of the ordinary judiciary were closed and for whom traditional actions did not permit the channelling of a jurisdictional claim for the protection of their rights.

For the Court, these circumstances involve a constant, fluid and loyal dialogue with the standards of other courts (domestic and international), an open look at comparative law and the awareness of being a local judicial actor immersed in a global dialogue. A fundamental challenge that the Court faces is the preservation of its independence in an environment in which its greater legal and social power makes it attractive to public and private actors' interference. And, of course, judges must understand that their actions occur in contexts marked by deep inequality, exclusion, and poverty in which the Constitution's public values are aspirational. This means that, through dialogue between powers and with citizens, the Court must seek institutional and social allies to promote real transformations that bring people's reality closer to constitutional promises.

Likewise, this position is not synonymous with infallibility. The Court should not assume that any decision or grounds based on its prestige must be accepted. As such, it is important to note that this qualification does not imply unanimity or the absence of disagreements among the judges about their rulings. On the contrary, since decisions are more relevant, they elicit a high degree of internal debate. Even disagreements that seem unimportant internally are widespread and have a far-reaching external impact. In addition, the Court must work deliberatively and transparently to invite society's highest level of scrutiny. So, it is not a question of endorsement but rather an obligation of deliberation, diligence, care, and above all, the maintenance of the material conditions of independence and methodology that have led the Court to its current position.

IV. Evaluation, Pathology and Criticism

The sample does not fully reflect the CCC's judicial reasoning, but as a whole, it serves as a good representation of the Constitutional Court's best-known profile: strong, a guarantor and a seasoned activist, which in exercising its functions, responds positively to the transformative mandate of the 1991 Constitution. However, this assessment hardly represents a large part of its jurisprudence.

Indeed, in the objective review of constitutionality, there have been significant developments in the CCC's jurisprudence on organic or institutional components, in which an equal guarantor position is observed as long as fundamental rights are clearly not compromised, albeit conservative in the interpretation of others and therefore highly deferential to the legislator and the Executive. Among them, it is worth highlighting the very weak constitutional review of matters of a financial, tax and budgetary nature, of the distribution of powers in the territorial sphere and of economic policies,[122] public international treaties[123] and of the state of emergency measures decreed during the COVID-19 pandemic.[124]

For its part, in the function of *tutela* review, the Court has been much more transformative, although the activism attributed to it is more symbolic than material.[125] This does not suggest, however, that the CCC's recognition in the international arena, at least in the global South, is not without support. It has been a strong constitutional court, not only because of the indisputable shortcomings of representation and the political will to develop the Colombian Constitution's normative mandates identified as aspirational,[126] but also for historical reasons (the tradition of judicial review in Colombian constitutionalism), normative reasons (the competences the Constitution grants to the CCC) and conceptual reasons (the constitutional norm and the function of interpreter and guarantor).

Finally, the Constitutional Court does not only have a broad agenda; the progressivism of its decisions has approached the character of a transformative court.[127] However, the transformative character of the judiciary is exhibited, if not daily, then with each of its opinions and with the sustained maintenance of a jurisprudence that is transformative. On the contrary, the transformative potential of constitutional justice is not, as often believed, a type of capital that accumulates and can be squandered. Citizens demand, on a daily basis, the protection of constitutional promises. And that is the duty of the Constitutional Court.

[122] D Landau, 'Instituciones políticas y función judicial en Derecho Constitucional comparado' (2011) 13 *Revista de Economía Institucional* 13–83.

[123] M Inés Correa Henao, 'El control de constitucionalidad de los acuerdos de inversión en Colombia. Análisis desde la cláusula de expropiación indirecta' in A von Bogdandy, P Salazar, M Morales Antoniazzi and FC Ebert (coords), *El constitucionalismo transformador en América Latina y el derecho económico internacional. De la tensión al diálogo* (UNAM, MPI, DFP, 2018) 511–45.

[124] R Gargarella and JE Roa Roa, 'Diálogo democrático y emergencia en América Latina (Democratic Dialogue and Emergency in Latin America)' Max Planck Institute for Comparative Public Law and International Law Research Paper, no 2020-21, June 2020 at papers.ssrn.com/sol3/papers.cfm?abstract_id=3623812.

[125] JE Roa Roa, 'El rol del juez constitucional en el constitucionalismo transformador latinoamericano (The Role of Constitutional Courts in Latin American Transformative Constitutionalism)' Max Planck Institute for Comparative Public Law and International Law Research Paper, no 2020-11, May 2020, at papers.ssrn.com/sol3/papers.cfm?abstract_id=3571507.

[126] M García Villegas, 'Constitucionalismo aspiracional' (2013) 15 *Revista Iberoamericana de Filosofía, Política y Humanidades* 77–97.

[127] JE Roa Roa, 'La ciudadanía dentro de la sala de máquinas del constitucionalismo transformador latinoamericano' (2021) 49 *Revista Derecho del Estado* 35–58.

9

The Jurisprudence of the Fourth Chamber of the Supreme Court of Costa Rica

ARIANA MACAYA LIZANO

The Constitutional Chamber of the Supreme Court of Justice was created by means of a Constitutional amendment in 1989. The jurisprudence of the Constitutional Chamber has been characterised, since its inception, by a certain judicial activism, which is reflected in the methods of interpretation used. In this study, 40 relevant judgments were chosen, covering the more of 30 years of activity of the Chamber. Through the study of this sample, we can underline three main characteristics: the tendency to self-reference, with the constant use of its own precedents as a way of reaffirming its legitimacy; the recourse to International Law, in particular to International Law of Human Rights, as a way to update a constitutional text more than 70 years old, and, finally, a complexification of the structure of the decisions, which reflects the difficulty of finding consensus among a Chamber that has become a vector of the judicialisation of politics in Costa Rica.

I. Legal, Political, Institutional and Academic Context

A. Legal and Political Culture as the Context for Constitutional Reasoning

i. The 1949 Constitution and Constitutional Review before 1989

The current Constitution in Costa Rica was drafted in 1949. After the Civil War of 1948, one of the first actions of the Founding Board of the Second Republic was to convene a Constituent Assembly and entrust the drafting of the new Constitution to a Committee of Jurists. This Committee drafted a progressive project for the time, however, the newly elected Constituent Assembly decided to discard this project and to base this discussion on the previously valid Constitution, the Constitution of 1871. Therefore, the current Constitution largely assumed the 1871 text and its main amendments, in particular the chapter on social guarantees introduced in 1943. Since its entry into force, the Constitution has been subject to 62 amendments, one of the most important being the creation of the Constitutional Chamber in 1989.

Prior to 1989, the constitutional control system was extremely complex. Indeed, the original wording of Article 10 of the 1949 Constitution determined that it was up to the Supreme Court of Justice 'to declare the unconstitutionality of the provisions of the Legislative Branch and of the decrees of the Executive Branch'. Writs of habeas corpus, by virtue of Law No. 35 of 1932, were also heard by the Supreme Court, while writs of amparo, in application of Law No. 1161 of 1950, were heard by criminal judges. Another obstacle to the development of constitutional control was that a majority of 2/3 was needed to be able to declare a norm unconstitutional. This system was increasingly decried as being illogical, cumbersome, and, consequently, not sufficiently effective.[1]

ii. The Constitutional Amendment of 1989: The Creation of the Constitutional Chamber as a Legal Revolution

In May 1989, Articles 10 and 48 of the Constitution were amended to create a specialised Chamber in the Supreme Court in charge not only of a concentrated constitutional review, but also of the protection of human rights through habeas corpus and the writ of amparo. This reform was completed with the approval of the Constitutional Jurisdiction Act in October of the same year. These amendments provided the new judicial body with the power to re-establish the long-forgotten supremacy of the Constitution.[2] It has also had an impact in the distribution of powers between the different branches of the government, allowing a close control of all normative acts, as a guarantee of the rule of law.

iii. The Constitutional Chamber as a Political Figure: Between Activism and Self-Restrain

Since its inception, the work of the Chamber has meant an alteration to the balance of powers designed by the constituent of 1949, and the constitutional review that it exercises goes beyond its written competences, which has empowered it to the point of turning it into one of the fundamental political actors on the Costa Rican political scene.[3] This is reinforced by a broad interpretation of its own powers that has led the Chamber to fill potential power gaps that have occurred in other branches. Hence, it is possible to witness in Costa Rica a process that has become widespread in several countries of the continent: the judicialisation of politics.

To this phenomenon must be added, especially in the first years of the Constitutional Chamber, a tendency towards judicial activism by its judges. The argumentation methods used by the Chamber in the cases chosen for this report reflect a certain tendency

[1] R Baker, 'Constitutional Adjudication in Costa Rica' (1986) *University of Miami International Law Review* 246.

[2] O Rodríguez, 'The Costa Rican Constitutional Jurisdiction' (2011) *Duquesne Law Review* 253.

[3] A Brenes and E Martínez, 'Cortes Supremas y Candidaturas Presidenciales en Centroamérica' (2012) 158 *Revista de Estudios Políticos* 178.

towards activism, especially in its expansive conception of its own competence and in the use of more constructivist interpretation techniques, such as the theory of the Living Constitution.[4] The recourse to structural rulings to try to solve endemic problems of the national reality[5] is another indication of this activism of the Constitutional Chamber.

However, faced with the risk that the power of the Chamber will lead the system to a government of judges, a marked tendency towards self-restraint can be noted in recent years. Indeed, although the judicialisation of politics is not in itself a good or bad phenomenon, it can lead to the politicisation of justice. Since the beginning of the twenty-first century, an increase in criticism of the work of the Judiciary in general, and the denunciation of a certain politicisation of the Constitutional Chamber can be verified, especially when it deals with controversial cases, such as the presidential re-election or the approval of free trade agreements. According to the public think tank *Estado de la Nación*, citizen assessment of the Supreme Court of Justice has deteriorated over time. Between 2004 and 2018, trust in the institution went from 61.9 to 52.9 points on a scale of 0 to 100.[6] Regarding the Constitutional Chamber itself, according to opinion studies published by the Centre for Research and Political Studies (CIEP) of the University of Costa Rica, in 2012, the Constitutional Chamber was rated according to its performance with a 6.9/10 grade, while for 2020 the rating dropped to 5.8/10.[7]

Three phenomena can illustrate the trend towards a mutation in the judicialisation of politics and a certain self-containment starting in the 2000s. First, a decrease in the number of actions of unconstitutionality filed against acts of the Legislative Assembly can be verified: from an average of 144.5 per year in the 2005–2015 period, to 113 in the 2016–2018 triennium.[8] There is also a tendency on the part of certain groups to direct their strategic litigation not to the Constitutional Chamber, but to supranational instances, such as the Inter-American Court of Human Rights. It is considered that litigation before the jurisdiction of this International Court, whose judgments and even its advisory opinions are considered binding by the Constitutional Chamber,[9] is a more effective avenue for achieving social change. The foregoing is demonstrated in the

[4] Constitutional Chamber of the Supreme Court (Costa Rica), Resolution No. 678-1991, 27 March 1991.

[5] Following Miranda, structural rulings or injunctions can be defined as rulings 'that seek to concretize the reorganization of a social institution and repair, through said organizational reform, the damage that public agencies themselves have produced by violating certain constitutional rights' (H Miranda, 'Las sentencias estructurales en la actuación de la Sala Constitucional de Costa Rica' (2018), *Revista IUS Doctrina*). This kind of injunction can be found in the resolutions of the Inter-American and European Courts of Human Rights, and in the jurisprudence of the Constitutional Court of Colombia. In Costa Rica, the use of this kind of injunction is recent, and one example can be found in Constitutional Chamber of the Supreme Court (Costa Rica), Resolution No. 5560-2019, 29 March 2019. This resolution is one of the 40 landmark cases selected for this report and addresses the structural problem of patient's waiting lists before the Social Security System.

[6] Programa Estado de la Nación, 'El Poder Judicial como actor del sistema Político', *Tercer Informe Estado de la Justicia* (CONARE, 2020) 192.

[7] CIEP, *Informe de resultados del estudio de opinión sociopolítica*, Noviembre 2020 (ciep.ucr.ac.cr/informe-del-estudio-de-opinion-sociopolitica-noviembre-2020/) and *Encuesta de opinión octubre-noviembre 2012*, (ciep.ucr.ac.cr/wp-content/uploads/2021/04/Informe-de-resultados-del-Estudio-de-Opinio%CC%81n-Sociopoli%CC%81tica-octubre-2012.pdf).

[8] Programa Estado de la Nación, 'El Poder Judicial como actor del sistema Político' 199.

[9] The Constitutional Chamber has established that 'if the Inter-American Court of Human Rights is the natural body to interpret the American Convention on Human Rights (Pact of San José, Costa Rica), the binding effect its decision when interpreting the convention and prosecuting national laws in light of this

case of In Vitro Fertilisation[10] and in the case of same-sex marriage,[11] where the Inter-American Court pronounced, respectively, in its contentious and advisory powers, resolutions which led to changes in the Court's own jurisprudence and, more generally, in Costa Rican society.

At the same time, the number of rejections of unconstitutionality actions increased significantly in the same period. Of the total actions filed between 2005 and 2015, 83.3 per cent were not admitted for study by the constitutional court, and between 2016 and 2018 that value rose to 91.7 per cent.[12] This high volume of rejection demonstrates a certain self-restraint on the part of the Court.

Finally, the Chamber itself in its jurisprudence has begun to mention the principle of self-restraint as a determining factor in the delimitation of its jurisdiction.[13]

B. The Court and Constitutional Litigation

According to Articles 10 and 48 of the Constitution and 2 of the Constitutional Jurisdiction Act, the Constitutional Chamber has three main competences: the guarantee of rights

regulation, either in a contentious case or in a mere consultation, will have – in principle – the same value of the interpreted rule' Constitutional Chamber of the Supreme Court (Costa Rica), Resolution No. 2313-1995, 9 May 1995.

[10] In 2000, the Constitutional Chamber ruled that the IVF technique was unconstitutional, considering that it could affect the right to life. (Constitutional Chamber of the Supreme Court (Costa Rica), Resolution No. 2306-2000, 15 March 2000). The practical result of this resolution was the effective ban of this technique in Costa Rica. A group of persons affected by this ban decided to present a claim before the Interamerican System. In 2012, the Interamerican Court of Human Rights ruled Costa Rica responsible for the violation of the right to private and family life and the right to personal integrity in relation to personal autonomy, sexual health, the right to enjoy the benefits of scientific progress and technology and the principle of non-discrimination for the ban of the IVF technique (Corte IDH, *Caso Artavia Murillo y otros Vs. Costa Rica.* Excepciones Preliminares, Fondo, Reparaciones y Costas. Sentencia de 28 de noviembre de 2012, Serie C No. 257). Compliance with the sentence was particularly complicated in this case, since the political forces in the Legislative Assembly could not reach a consensus to regulate IVF through legislation. Finally, to comply with what was ordered by the Court, the Executive Branch decided to regulate the technique by means of an Executive Decree. However, the Constitutional Chamber, in its decision 1692-2016 declared this decree unconstitutional, considering it contrary to the principle of reserve of law (Constitutional Chamber of the Supreme Court (Costa Rica), Resolution No. 1692-2016, 3 February 2016). This decision of the internal jurisdiction motivated an unprecedented action by the Inter-American Court: by means of a supervision resolution, it considered that the decree declared unconstitutional by the Constitutional Chamber should be kept in force to comply with what was ordered by the Court (Corte IDH, *Caso Artavia Murillo y otros Vs. Costa Rica.* Supervisión de cumplimiento de Sentencia. Resolución de 26 de enero de 2016).

[11] One of the main points of the campaign of President Solis in 2014 was marriage equality, but once in power, the President faced a deadlock in the Legislative Assembly, where a majority of conservative legislators was against any form of same-sex unions. The government decided to request and advisory opinion on the matter to the Inter-American Court. The result was the Advisory Opinion Oc-24/17 of 24 November 2017, about Gender identity, and equality and non-discrimination of same sex couples. Considering the jurisprudence of the Chamber recognising binding force to Advisory Opinions of the Inter-American Court, the Constitutional Chamber incorporated this opinion in his ruling of 2018, considering the ban of same-sex marriage unconstitutional (Constitutional Chamber of the Supreme Court (Costa Rica), Resolution No. 12782-2018, 8 August 2018).

[12] Programa Estado de la Nación, 'El Poder Judicial como actor del sistema Político' 199.

[13] See Constitutional Chamber of the Supreme Court (Costa Rica), Resolution No. 5347-1998, 24 July 1998. This resolution is one of the 40 landmark cases selected for this report. For an analysis of this jurisprudence cf. A Fallas and T Gómez, *¿Es suficiente la autocontención del juez constitucional para garantizar el principio de seguridad jurídica?: un análisis a la jurisprudencia de la Sala Constitucional* (Tesis para obtener el grado de Licenciatura en Derecho, Universidad de Costa Rica, 2018) 88.

and freedoms through the writ of amparo and the habeas corpus; constitutional review a priori and a posteriori and to solve conflicts of competence between the Supreme Power of the State.

The Constitutional Chamber is, by far, the busiest jurisdiction of the Supreme Court with an average caseload of 20,000 cases and a production of more than 18,000 decisions each year. The competence exercised most often is the guarantee of rights and freedoms through the writ of amparo. Indeed, since the inception of the Court, the writ of amparo was designed as a flexible, broad, and informal remedy. It has no formal requisites, and it can even be presented on a napkin or by email by any person or group. Indeed, one of the main aims of the 1989 constitutional amendment was to bring citizens closer to the Constitution.

This determination to provide citizens with a more open constitutional justice system is also reflected in the constitutional review procedures. Even if the unconstitutionality action is a more formal remedy and requires an issue pending resolution before the courts in which the unconstitutionality of the norm is invoked, the Constitutional Jurisdiction Act allows a sort of *actio popularis* (direct and abstract standing) for the defence of diffused interests or matters that concern the community (section 2, Article 75). Section 3 also allows the public Comptroller, the Attorney General and the Ombudsman to present unconstitutionality actions without the need of a pending resolution. Hence, the Constitutional Chamber can be described more of a bottom-up jurisdiction, most of the matters initiated by citizens, as reflected by the landmark cases selected for this report where more than 82 per cent of the cases were initiated by citizens. This openness has nevertheless resulted in an increasing caseload for the Constitutional Chamber that impacts on the distribution of the time spent by the Magistrates deciding such cases.

The Constitutional Chamber has developed an expansive interpretation of its own powers. From a literal interpretation of the Constitution and the Constitutional Jurisdiction Act, it follows that the powers of the Chamber are limited, in the case of actions of unconstitutionality filed against Articles of the Constitution, and that the Chamber is only competent to review the constitutionality of norms emanating from the derivative constituent, and only with respect to the procedure for its approval.[14] Indeed, if it is considered that there is no hierarchy between constitutional norms, it is difficult to establish a control of the constitutionality of the Constitution itself. However, the Constitutional Jurisdiction Act also grants the Chamber, the competence to exercise control of 'the conformity of the internal legal system with International

[14] This interpretation was the position of the majority in the Resolution No. 7818-2000, nevertheless two Magistrates dissented and considered that the 'the Constitutional Chamber does have full jurisdiction to know of the unconstitutionality and order the consequent annulment or, where appropriate, the non-application or, of course, the interpretation and consistent application of the constitutional norms themselves – reformed or even the original ones – when these must give way before others, or before principles or values of the Law of the Constitution – in its full extension and intensity, which includes, privilegedly, the Law of Human Rights, both internal and international – and are, therefore, likely to incur, themselves, in the vice of unconstitutionality' (Constitutional Chamber of the Supreme Court (Costa Rica), Resolution No. 7818-2000, 5 September 2000. This resolution is one of the 40 landmark cases selected for this report). Two years later, the position of the dissenting judges was admitted by the majority of a newly appointed chamber and the Constitutional Chamber (Constitutional Chamber of the Supreme Court (Costa Rica), Resolution No. 2771-2003, 4 April 2003. This resolution is one of the 40 landmark cases selected for this report).

Law' (Article 2, subparagraph b). Likewise, the Chamber has recognised the supra-constitutional nature of those international human rights instruments that grant broader protection than the Constitution itself.[15] In this way, from the union of these two considerations, the Chamber has then interpreted, although not unanimously, its competence to conduct a conventionality control on the provisions of the Constitution itself.

C. The Judges

i. Appointment

The Constitutional Chamber is a part of the Supreme Court of Justice; therefore, its justices receive the title of 'Magistrates' and must comply with the requirements established by the Constitution in a general way for any Magistrate of the Judicial Branch. In accordance with Articles 157 and 158 of the Constitution, Magistrates are elected by the Legislative Assembly for a period of eight years, with the possibility of indefinite re-elections. Since a constitutional amendment approved in 2003, for their appointment they need the votes of two-thirds of the totality of the members of the Legislative Assembly. In the performance of their functions, they must act with efficiency and could be considered re-elected for equal periods, unless the contrary is agreed in a vote of no less than the two-thirds part of the totality of the members of the Legislative Assembly. Alternate or substitute Magistrates are appointed by the Legislative Assembly from a list of nominees presented by the Supreme Court of Justice for a four-year period. To be a Magistrate, according to Article 159 of the Constitution, a person must be Costa Rican by birth of Naturalisation, at least 35 years old and to possess a law degree.

In practice, for the appointment of a Magistrate, a procedure has been established through which a public contest is held in which applicants for the office of magistrate submit their names, these are evaluated by a Commission of the Legislative Assembly which verifies the requirements and a score is assigned to them, with this score a shortlist is made that is presented to the Legislative Plenary for the respective election vote.[16] Nevertheless, the Assembly can vote for a candidate outside of the shortlist. This can open a gate for politisation, promoting a vote for political reasons over actual qualifications. Furthermore, the appointment of Magistrates by the Legislative Assembly, a political body, can be interpreted as a threat for the independence of the judges.[17]

Another unique feature of the election of Magistrates is aimed at their re-election, in the sense that they are practically considered re-elected for equal periods, except

[15] The Constitutional Chamber has indeed considered that 'The international human rights instruments in force in the Republic in accordance with the reform of art. 48 of the Constitution, are integrated in the legal system at the highest level, ie, at the constitutional level, as they complement it in what favours the person' Constitutional Chamber of the Supreme Court (Costa Rica), Resolution No. 5759-1993, 10 November 2003.

[16] See A Burgos Mata, 'El Nombramiento de los Magistrados Suplentes de la Sala III de la Corte Suprema de Justicia en Costa Rica' (2019) *Revista Iudex* 185.

[17] The Special Rapporteur on the independence of judges and lawyers of the UN, also denounced in his report before the Human Right Councils in 2018 the risk of politicising judicial appointments (Human Rights Council, Report of the Special Rapporteur on the independence of judges and lawyers, May 2nd, 2018, A/HRC/3838, §51).

that a vote of no less than two-thirds of the totality of the members of the Legislative Assembly otherwise agreed (reverse vote). This characteristic note has been widely criticised because it results in successive re-elections until retirement, but it is also praised by another sector of opinion given that it offers stability to the person in office and there is a distancing or separation from the properly political actors.[18]

ii. Composition

The Constitutional Chamber is composed of seven Judges and 12 alternates (Article 4 of the Constitutional Jurisdiction Act). It has been criticised for its lack of diversity: since its creation, none of the full-time Magistrates has been chosen from a minority group. Only three women have been appointed as full-time Magistrates since 1989, hence gender equality has never been achieved in the full-time composition of the Chamber. Nevertheless, since the last appointment of alternates magistrates in December of 2021 parity was finally achieved: six of the 12 alternates are women.

Magistrates of the Constitutional Chamber come from different legal backgrounds: Academia, the Judiciary Branch, and, in a lesser proportion, from a political career or private practice. In its current conformation (December 2021), six of the seven Magistrates have a PhD.

D. Legal Scholarship and Constitutional Reasoning

The creation of the Constitutional Chamber meant a true turning point in the development of the doctrine and teaching of Constitutional Law in Costa Rica. Indeed, although in the 1970s, under the impulse of professors trained in Europe such as Eduardo Ortiz Ortiz, Rodolfo Piza Escalante (who would later become a Magistrate of the Constitutional Chamber), Rubén Hernández Valle or Hugo Muñoz, constitutional justice appeared in the Syllabus of the two courses taught at the Faculty of Law,[19] the creation of the Chamber and the subsequent development of its abundant jurisprudence, implied a profound change in the teaching not only of Constitutional Law, but of Law in general. The diversity of topics covered by the decisions of the Chamber, as well as its effect on the institutional and social development of the country, made the jurisprudence of the Chamber a subject of compulsory study in almost all branches of Law.

The abundant jurisprudence of the Court has given rise to the development of an important doctrinal production destined for its comment and criticism, by not only constitutionalists but also academics from all branches of the Law. The commentary on the Chamber's jurisprudence is a common theme in the doctrine articles of national

[18] See B Arias Ramírez, 'Comisiones y Nombramientos en la Asamblea Legislativa Costarricense' *Ponencia presentada como investigación base para el Informe Estado de la Nación en Desarrollo humano Sostenible*, 2009 (hdl.handle.net/20.500.12337/1098).

[19] R Hernández Valle, 'Reseña histórica sobre la creación de la Sala Constitucional' (2019) *Revista de la Sala Constitucional* (revistasalacons.poder-judicial.go.cr/images/Catalogo/Articulo/PDF/Reseña%20histórica%20sobre%20la%20creación%20de%20la%20Sala%20Constitucional.pdf).

legal reviews and the Constitutional Chamber itself created its own doctrine review in 2019. Also, due to the social impact of its powers, the decisions of the Chamber are often the subject of media coverage in the country's main newspapers and editorials in the Opinion sections.

II. Arguments in Constitutional Reasoning

A. The Structure of Constitutional Arguments

The Constitutional Chamber does not follow a single model in the structure of its arguments. From the study of the 40 cases, it can be noted that the majority (29 cases) contain parallel arguments, and only in 11 cases could a single line of arguments that reach a conclusion be observed. Indeed, the plaintiffs, when presenting the actions of unconstitutionality, as well as the writs of amparo or habeas corpus, present numerous arguments, to which the Chamber responds exhaustively. Likewise, in unconstitutionality actions, the Chamber must give a hearing to the Attorney General's Office, who usually presents extensive briefs with new arguments to be considered by the Chamber. Finally, following the principle of *iura novit curia*, the Chamber may also incorporate arguments or considerations that were not alleged by the plaintiffs.

B. Types of Arguments Used in Constitutional Reasoning

i. Ordinary Meaning of the Words of the Constitution

The Constitutional Chamber used textualist arguments only in five of the resolutions studied. In general, the literal or grammatical interpretation is conducted by the Chamber referring to the definition in the Dictionary of the Royal Academy of the Spanish Language.[20] However, on some occasions it can include general definitions of what it is going to understand by a word or expression, without making an express reference to the source of its definition.

ii. Harmonising Arguments

Article 2 of the Constitutional Jurisdiction Act establishes that the Chamber has the competence to control not only the constitutionality of the norms, but also the 'conformity of the internal legal system with International or Communitarian Law'. Likewise, Article 48 of the Constitution specifies that the amparo writ and habeas corpus guarantee the rights enshrined in the Constitution as well as those 'of a fundamental nature established in international instruments on human rights'. In this way, since its creation, the Constitutional Chamber has conducted a control of conventionality, so arguments of harmonisation with international regulations are a usual resource in its resolutions.

[20] Constitutional Chamber of the Supreme Court (Costa Rica), Resolution No. 18643-2014, 12 September 2014.

Thus, of the 40 landmark cases studied, 28 of them contain an argument of harmonisation with international regulations, in most cases, with respect to Treaties on Human Rights.

It is important to remember, as was done above, that the Chamber has broadly interpreted its jurisdiction in matters of conventionality control. First, the Chamber has considered the possibility of controlling the conventionality of constitutional norms, for this, its jurisprudence has developed the concept of 'supra constitutionality' of those international instruments in the field of human rights if they confer greater freedoms or a greater scope of protection.[21] Likewise, in addition to this line of jurisprudence, the Chamber has considered that the normative block through which it exercises this control of conventionality is made up not only of formally approved Human Rights Treaties, but also other instruments such as the Universal and American Declarations of Rights,[22] to which the Chamber has given full legal force. Indeed, among the 40 landmark cases studied, 13 refer to the Universal Declaration and nine to the American Declaration.[23] Usually, the Chamber does not differentiate between International Treaties and other soft law instruments.[24]

Among the block of conventionality that the Chamber uses to conduct its control, references to norms of the Inter-American System are the most frequent. Indeed, of the 40 resolutions analysed, 25 refer to some instrument of the Inter-American System, in particular the American Convention on Human Rights and its Protocol on Economic, Social and Cultural Rights (Protocol of San Salvador). The Chamber also makes frequent reference to the jurisprudence of the Inter-American Court, considering that both the American Convention on Human Rights, as well as the rulings of the Inter-American Court of Human Rights, are not only applicable as they are part of the Law of the Constitution, but to the extent that they provide greater coverage or protection of human rights, they prevail over the Fundamental Norm.[25] However, the Chamber has also refused to apply *mutatis mutandi* precedents of the Inter-American Court, if the facts of the case examined clearly differs from those analysed by the Inter-American Court.[26] On the other hand, the Chamber has come to consider that 'the Advisory Opinions of the Inter-American Court of Human Rights have full value in this country and that, in the case of Human Rights, their decisions bind the Costa Rican State'.[27]

[21] See G Armijo, 'La tutela supraconstitucional de los derechos humanos en Costa Rica' (2003) *Ius et Praxis* 39, 62.

[22] 'In this aspect, it is necessary to rescue the specific reference that the Constitution, in its current version, makes of "international instruments", meaning that not only conventions, treaties or agreements, formally signed and approved according to the constitutional procedure itself […], but any other instrument that has the nature of the protection of Human Rights, even if it has not undergone this process, is valid and applicable in the country' Constitutional Chamber of the Supreme Court (Costa Rica), Resolution No. 9685-2000, 1 November 2000.

[23] Due to this recognition of full normative force, references to these instruments were considered as references to binding international instruments and not as soft law.

[24] Constitutional Chamber of the Supreme Court (Costa Rica), Resolution No. 3656-2003, 7 May 2003.

[25] Constitutional Chamber of the Supreme Court (Costa Rica), Resolution No. 9685-2000, 1 November 2000.

[26] See V Orozco, 'El valor normativo de los Instrumentos Internacionales en materia de Derechos Humanos en el Sistema de Justicia Constitucional Costarricense: el caso particular de la jurisprudencia de la Corte Interamericana' (2014) *Revista Judicial* 11, 32.

[27] Constitutional Chamber of the Supreme Court (Costa Rica)), Resolution No. 1682-2007, 9 February 2007.

The Court has also made references to the jurisprudence of the European Court of Human Rights.[28]

iii. Precedents

Costa Rica is part of the countries with a Civil Law tradition, thus, unlike Common Law countries, the jurisprudence of the higher courts does not directly bind the lower ones, nor does it expressly create rules of law.[29] There is an exception to this rule, since Article 13 of the Constitutional Jurisdiction Law establishes that the precedents of the Constitutional Chamber are binding *erga omnes*, except for itself.

Although the Chamber is not bound by its own precedents, its main argumentation strategy is the use of its own jurisprudence. In this way, of the 40 landmark cases studied, 36 make references to previous pronouncements of the Chamber. The remaining four cases correspond to rulings from the Chamber's first five years, when it was still developing its own jurisprudence.

This argumentative strategy reflects the will of the Chamber to give itself legitimacy, emphasising that, despite being able to change its position, its rulings are based on legal arguments that go beyond the possible political cleavages of its conformation or the circumstances of the case. Likewise, the use of precedents also allows to strengthen the interpretations that the Chamber can build of the constitutional norms, in its role as authentic interpreter of the Constitution.

iv. Doctrinal Analysis of Legal Concepts or Principles

The Constitution of Costa Rica is more than 70 years old. Although it has been amended on multiple occasions, the Constitutional Chamber, thanks to its jurisprudence, has contributed to updating the constitutional text by refining general principles or new rights through interpretation. That is why it is not surprising to find that the Chamber mentions a principle or a right that is not explicitly enshrined in the constitutional text in half of the resolutions studied.

The Chamber itself has given a definition of these principles, indicating that 'The recognized constitutional doctrine defines as constitutional principles the fundamental ideas about the legal organisation of a community, emanating from the social conscience, which fulfil fundamental and at the same time interpretative functions with respect to the of the legal system'.[30] These principles and rights are not simply created by the Chamber, in general, they respond to a systematic or evolutive interpretation of the text of the Constitution itself.[31] The Chamber has also deduced from a systematic

[28] For example, in Constitutional Chamber of the Supreme Court (Costa Rica), Resolution No. 12782-2018, 8 August 2018, the Chamber referenced several resolutions to illustrate the pilot judgment procedure used by this Court. In several individual opinions, the Magistrates also referenced extensively the *Schalk & Kold v Austria* case, among others.

[29] V Orozco, 'La Jurisprudencia como fuente del Derecho: el caso de Costa Rica' (2017) *Revista Judicial* 225.

[30] Constitutional Chamber of the Supreme Court (Costa Rica), Resolution No. 2771-2003, 4 April 2003.

[31] Constitutional Chamber of the Supreme Court (Costa Rica), Resolution No. 980-91, 24 May 1991.

interpretation of the Constitution the democratic principle, the principle of interdiction of arbitrariness, of the subjection of public powers to the Constitution, and of equality of individuals before justice,[32] as well as the principle of gender parity,[33] among others.

The Chamber has devoted entire resolutions explaining the emergence of a principle or a right not explicitly enshrined in the Constitution. Such is the case of the ruling on due process of law,[34] or the consecration of peace, first as a constitutional value,[35] to later consider it as a fundamental right implicitly contained in the Constitution but fully enforceable in the writ of amparo.[36]

v. Teleological/Purposive Arguments

The main manifestation of this kind of interpretation is the recourse to the genetic or historical method of interpretation, used in 13 of the 40 landmark cases studied. In most of the cases studied, the Chamber, when resorting to the historical method, expressly mentions the opinions voiced by the representants recorded in the minutes of the 1949 Constituent Assembly, however, in four cases, it simply makes a reference to the 'will of the constituent' or that 'is clear from the minutes' without explicitly citing any of the representants.[37]

It is important to remember that the Constituent Assembly used the 1871 Constitution as the basis for its discussion, which it largely reproduced. However, the Constitutional Chamber does not refer to the preparatory work of this Constitution and only takes as a parameter the opinions issued in 1949. This limits the recourse to historical interpretation, since many Articles of the current Constitution, were not subject to detailed discussion in 1949. However, it is important to highlight that the Chamber has used the discussion of the draft Constitution of the Governing Board that was finally rejected as a tool in its historical interpretation.[38] Likewise, it also mentions, in individual votes, not only the specific discussions on an Article, but also the more general discussions that took place in the Constituent Assembly, to define the concept of 'Social and democratic Rule of Law.'[39]

[32] Constitutional Chamber of the Supreme Court (Costa Rica), Resolution No. 2771-2003, 4 April 2003.

[33] Constitutional Chamber of the Supreme Court (Costa Rica), Resolution No. 13885-2015, 4 September 2015.

[34] Constitutional Chamber of the Supreme Court (Costa Rica), Resolution No. 1739-92, 1 July 1992.

[35] Constitutional Chamber of the Supreme Court (Costa Rica), Resolution No. 9992-2004, 8 September 2004.

[36] Constitutional Chamber of the Supreme Court (Costa Rica), Resolution No. 9122-2013, 5 July 2013.

[37] Constitutional Chamber of the Supreme Court (Costa Rica), Resolution No. 3220-2000, 18 April 2000; Constitutional Chamber of the Supreme Court (Costa Rica), Resolution No. 2323-2010, 2 February 2010: Constitutional Chamber of the Supreme Court (Costa Rica), Resolution No. 6247-2013, 9 May 2013, and Constitutional Chamber of the Supreme Court (Costa Rica), Resolution No. 13885-2015, 4 September 2015.

[38] In both resolutions about presidential re-election (Constitutional Chamber of the Supreme Court (Costa Rica), Resolution No. 7818-2000, 5 September 2000, and Constitutional Chamber of the Supreme Court (Costa Rica), Resolution No. 2771-2003, 4 April 2003).

[39] Constitutional Chamber of the Supreme Court (Costa Rica), Resolution No. 9469-2007, 3 July 2007, Separate opinion of Magistrates Armijo and Cruz.

vi. Non-Legal Arguments

Among the cases studied, the Chamber used extra-legal arguments on 14 occasions, either to justify its majority decision or in the argumentation of individual opinions by the Magistrates.

The Chamber has the power to request reports on different topics, especially when the constitutional matter involves taking technical aspects into consideration. For example, in a case where the Chamber declared Internet access as a fundamental right, to define what 'functional access' means and to understand the fair use policy, the Chamber requested the technical criteria of the School of Sciences of Computing and Informatics of the University of Costa Rica.[40]

The recourse to sociological arguments can also be a tool to verify a change in circumstances that would justify the recourse to an evolutive interpretation. This argumentative technique was used in the vote on same-sex marriage, to demonstrate the evolution of the notion of family.[41] Economic arguments can also be considered to contextualise the resolution. Thus, in the ruling on the 2018 tax reform, the Chamber extensively cited reports on the difficult financial and fiscal situation of the country, to put the decision to endorse this tax plan in context.[42] Likewise, the economic effects can be considered when measuring the effects of a declaration of unconstitutionality. For example, in the decision on female quotas in public employment, Justices Castillo and Rueda in a separate opinion proposed considering the possible 'dislocations to the social and economic order' that could be caused by a declaration of unconstitutionality without dimensioning.[43]

The Chamber does not make frequent use of religious or ethical arguments. Among the cases studied, we only found one example of a religious argument, and it was advanced to distinguish the institution of religious marriage from civil marriage when analysing the unconstitutionality of the prohibition of same-sex marriage.[44] Regarding ethical criteria, it is worth underlining the reference to the Kantian imperative of not treating human beings as a means, used by the Chamber when considering the IVF technique as contrary to the right to life.[45]

vii. References to Scholarly Works[46]

The Constitutional Chamber makes a modest use of the arguments of doctrine. Indeed, of the 40 resolutions studied, only 11 make any mention of doctrine. Likewise, it should be noted that in seven of these 11 cases, the judgment does not make a particular mention of a doctrinal citation or an author, but merely makes a general remark of

[40] Constitutional Chamber of the Supreme Court (Costa Rica), Resolution No. 11212-2017, 14 July 2017.

[41] Constitutional Chamber of the Supreme Court (Costa Rica), Resolution No. 12782-2018, 8 August 2018.

[42] Constitutional Chamber of the Supreme Court (Costa Rica), Resolution No. 19511-2018, 23 November 2018.

[43] Constitutional Chamber of the Supreme Court (Costa Rica), Resolution No. 13885-2015, 4 September 2015. Separate Reasons of Magistrates Castillo and Rueda.

[44] Constitutional Chamber of the Supreme Court (Costa Rica), Resolution No. 12782-2018, 8 August 2018.

[45] Constitutional Chamber of the Supreme Court (Costa Rica), Resolution No. 2306-2000, 15 March 2000.

[46] In this category, only references to legal doctrine were considered. References to doctrine in other disciplines were addressed in the category of non-legal arguments.

analysis carried out by 'some authors',[47] to 'comparative doctrine and jurisprudence',[48] or simply of 'the relevant doctrine'.[49]

Among the four rulings that make a specific mention of an author, it should be noted that in one of them the quote is found in an individual vote, and it is a quote from the author of the vote itself.[50] On two other occasions, national authors are referenced: Eduardo Ortiz Ortiz[51] and Rubén Hernández Valle.[52] In the latter case, the citation of doctrine is a comment on the jurisprudence of the Chamber, which reaffirms the trend towards self-reference developed by the Court. There is only one mention of a foreign author: a reference to Argentine professor Nestor Pedro Sagüés in the ruling on same-sex marriage.[53] It is interesting to note that, although the author is mentioned, there is no citation of a particular article or book.

viii. References to Foreign (National) Law

Of the 40 cases studied, only ten make some mention of foreign legislation (eight cases do so in the majority vote, while two cases mention foreign legislation in individual votes). In some cases, the Chamber does not make a precise reference to a law or act, but only refers to expressions such as 'precedents in comparative law'[54] or establishes in a general way how an institution or practice is regulated in other countries,[55] without precisely mentioning the standards on the matter. In other cases, it refers to historical legislation that has served as a model, such as the English Magna Carta of 1215[56] or the Spanish Water Law of 1879.[57]

In general, the Chamber, when using comparative law, prefers the reference to the jurisprudence of other Constitutional Courts or Supreme Courts, to the mention of specific national regulations. In this way, the so-called 'dialogue between judges' is deepened, which not only takes place vertically (with respect to Supranational Courts, as seen in the section on harmonisation), but also a horizontal dialogue between Supreme Courts or Constitutional Courts. Particularly noteworthy are the citations to judgments of the Supreme Court of the United States, the Spanish Constitutional Court, the German Federal Constitutional Court, the Italian Constitutional Court, the French Constitutional Council, and the Colombian Constitutional Court.[58]

[47] Constitutional Chamber of the Supreme Court (Costa Rica), Resolution No. 980-91, 24 May 1991.
[48] Constitutional Chamber of the Supreme Court (Costa Rica), Resolution No. 1739-92, 1 July 1992.
[49] Constitutional Chamber of the Supreme Court (Costa Rica), Resolution No. 1313-93, 26 March 1993.
[50] Constitutional Chamber of the Supreme Court (Costa Rica), Resolution No. 18643-2014, 12 September 2014, Individual vote of Magistrate Jinesta.
[51] Constitutional Chamber of the Supreme Court (Costa Rica), Resolution No. 10540-2013, 7 August 2013.
[52] Constitutional Chamber of the Supreme Court (Costa Rica), Resolution No. 6247-2013, 9 May 2013.
[53] Constitutional Chamber of the Supreme Court (Costa Rica), Resolution No. 12782-2018, 8 August 2018.
[54] Constitutional Chamber of the Supreme Court (Costa Rica), Resolution No. 6247-2013, 9 May 2013.
[55] Constitutional Chamber of the Supreme Court (costa Rica), Resolution No. 7818-2000, 5 September 2000, and Constitutional Chamber of the Supreme Court (Costa Rica), Resolution No. 10540-2013, 7 August 2013.
[56] Constitutional Chamber of the Supreme Court (Costa Rica), Resolution No. 1739-92, 1 July 1992.
[57] Constitutional Chamber of the Supreme Court (Costa Rica), Resolution No. 6922-2010, 16 April 2010.
[58] See H Miranda, 'La utilización de jurisprudencia constitucional extranjera por la Sala Constitucional' (2017) *Revista Judicial* 257, 284.

ix. Pro Homine *or* Pro Persona *Principle*

Although it is not explicitly mentioned (in fact, of the 40 landmark cases, only four make an explicit mention of the principle), the *pro homine* or *pro persona* principle is present across the board in the jurisprudence of the Constitutional Chamber, especially in cases where it harmonises with international legislation on human rights. In effect, it should be remembered that according to constitutional jurisprudence, human rights instruments that offer greater protection to the person have a rank equal to and even higher than the Constitution, in application of the principle.

x. Other Methods

In addition to the argumentation techniques described above, the Chamber also resorts on some occasions to analogies to complement an analysis (four occurrences among the landmark cases). Likewise, another method that it usually favours is the realisation of a historical study of the norms that regulate a precise subject, either to justify an evolutive interpretation or to show the permanence of an institute in the legal history of the country. For example, to analyse the constitutionality of the Law of the Historical-Architectural Heritage of Costa Rica, the Chamber began its analysis by conducting a historical study of the regulation of property rights in the constitutional history of Costa Rica, since our first Constitution of 1821, to conclude that 'with regard to the constitutional regulation of property, only limitations 'of social interest' dictated for reasons of public necessity are admissible'.[59]

C. The Overall Weight of the Arguments

In more than half of the 40 cases studied, most of the arguments presented represent the ratio decidendi of the case, explicitly showing the relationship of the argument with the object of the case. However, in these cases a frequent recourse to obiter dicta can be observed. Indeed, the Chamber often deals with issues related to the main topic of the case and presents legal arguments and conclusions even though they are not part of the questions raised by the petitioners.

In some resolutions, despite raising a specific problem, the Chamber can take the opportunity to make more general considerations and clarify general principles that will be applied in other resolutions. Such is the case of resolution 1739-92, where a judge specifically consulted on whether due process had been respected in a criminal proceeding, and the Chamber used this consultation to make a general development on the different principles that make up due process of law.[60]

On some occasions, the Chamber complements its resolution with numerous arguments that may seem more rhetorical or even decorative. Indeed, in one decision, the Court even quoted the French writer Victor Hugo. This recourse to rhetorical arguments, however, may respond to a pedagogical will, to frame the main arguments in a

[59] Constitutional Chamber of the Supreme Court (Costa Rica), Resolution No. 3656-2003, 7 May 2003.
[60] Constitutional Chamber of the Supreme Court (Costa Rica), Resolution No. 1739-92, 1 July 1992.

deeper and more detailed explanation of the general theme. We can find this formula in the decision of the Chamber on historical heritage.[61]

In the same way, the Chamber can present superabundant arguments on the same topic, to the point that they become decorative or rhetorical. The reference to dozens of international treaties or soft law instruments, without really explaining their content or their specific relationship with the object of the procedure, in the decision on the principles of environmental law can be an example of this technique.[62]

D. Judicial Candour and Judicial Rhetoric

When qualifying the style, rhetoric and judicial candour of the resolutions of the Chamber, two factors must be taken into account: first, the increasing caseload of the Chamber, which implies that it cannot dedicate much time to drafting of resolutions, and the system according to which each matter is assigned to an 'instructing' magistrate (*magistrado o magistrada instructor*), who is in charge of drafting the resolution and who, consequently, can imprint his personal style on it. The resolutions of the Chamber use technical legal language, with arguments arranged around large chapters numbered in capital letters and later with subsections in Roman numerals.

During the first years of the Chamber, its resolutions were generally short and clear, however, the constant recourse to precedent as an argument has not only lengthened the resolutions but can also make them difficult to read. Starting in the 2000s, a tendency to reproduce long paragraphs of previous resolutions can be observed.

Another element that affects the drafting style of the Chamber's resolutions is the increasingly frequent recourse to minority opinions. Traditionally, minority votes (whether dissenting or concurring) are presented as an annex. However, the magistrates of the Constitutional Chamber not only draft concurring or dissenting opinions, but also resort to the drafting individually or together with other magistrates of notes or additional reasons, which are presented not at the end of the resolution in annex, but in the body of the resolution, in the chapter that refers to the subject of this note. In this way, on some occasions the majority arguments are intertwined with those of the minority, which makes the understanding of the vote more complex.

The argumentative structure used by the Chamber can also respond to a pedagogical will, and certain resolutions have a style that makes them resemble an article of doctrine or even a lecture giving in a Law School.[63]

E. Length, Dissenting and Concurring Opinions

The decisions of the Constitutional Chamber are particularly extended. The length of the selected landmark cases ranges from a low of three pages, to a high of 129 pages,

[61] Constitutional Chamber of the Supreme Court (Costa Rica), Resolution No. 3656-2003, 7 May 2003.
[62] Constitutional Chamber of the Supreme Court (Costa Rica), Resolution No. 6322-2003, 3 July 2003.
[63] Constitutional Chamber of the Supreme Court (Costa Rica), Resolution No. 1313-93, 26 March 1993.

with an average of 22.7 pages.[64] In general, the decisions concerning constitutionality affairs (unconstitutionality actions and constitutional consultations) are longer,[65] with an average of 24.3 pages. A detailed description of the procedures, the transcription of the arguments presented by the parties and the tendency to reproduce extensive excerpts of its own precedents, contribute to the length of the decision.

Decisions at the Constitutional Chamber are taken by simple majority. The Chamber is always composed of seven Magistrates, either full-time or alternates, for which a majority of four votes is required to reach a decision. The Costa Rican legislation allows any member of a Tribunal or Court to draft a dissenting opinion if he does not agree with the opinion of the majority (Article 154 of Civil Procedure Code). In practice, judges do not only draft dissenting opinions, but also concurring opinions and even notes are added by the Magistrates to provide supplementary arguments or clarifications.[66] The use of minority vote (dissenting or concurring) is frequent in the Constitutional Chamber. Thus, 25 out of the 40 selected cases have at least one minority vote. It can also be observed that as the Chamber has evolved, its ability to reach consensus has been decreasing, in this way while in 2005 more than 80 per cent of the decisions reached in the resolution of unconstitutionality actions (excluding the ones that were dismissed by an admissibility ruling) were unanimous, in 2015 this proportion dropped to 48 per cent.[67] Likewise, it can be observed that the personal position of the Magistrates can affect its argumentation, and that the composition of the Chamber can have an impact on its jurisprudence, as demonstrated in the case of presidential re-election.

In recent years, the inclusion of several minority opinions in the decisions also influenced the length of the decisions. Of the 40 selected cases, 25 have at least one minority opinion. In the period ranging from 2013 to 2019 (14 landmark decisions) all but one decision has minority opinions. Furthermore, a single decision can be the object of several minority opinions. The decision concerning the parliamentary consultation of the Central American Free Trade Agreement (CAFTA),[68] with nine minority opinions (two notes, six partially dissenting opinions and one concurring opinion), is a revealing example of the dangers of this trend.[69] Nevertheless, this abundance of arguments contributed to a very opaque decision, difficult to read and understand, undermining the legitimacy of the rationale of the main decision of the Constitutional Chamber.

[64] Since the migration to a new database (https://nexuspj.poder-judicial.go.cr), the decisions of the Constitutional Chamber are no longer publicly available in Word format. They can only be downloaded in PDF or plain text format, with no margins or any formatting. This setting hinders the possibility of comparison with other countries. For example, the resolution 12782-2018 in the actual format is 86 pages long, but transformed into a word file, with normal margins, times new roman, 12-point font is 287 pages long.

[65] Nevertheless, in the 40 landmark cases, the lengthiest decision was a writ of amparo (resolution 6922-2010), but this case is very atypical. Excluding this decision, in the 40 landmark cases, the average length of a writ of amparo is of 12.3 pages and of a decision concerning the constitutionality of a norm (including unconstitutionality actions, Parliamentary and Judiciary consultations), is practically the double, 24.3 pages.

[66] For statistical purposes, these 'notes' are considered and counted as minority concurring opinions.

[67] Data from the Programa Estado de la Nación, 'El control constitucional: patrones de votación, *Segundo Informe Estado de la Justicia* (San José, CONARE, 2017) 196.

[68] Constitutional Chamber of the Supreme Court (Costa Rica), Resolution No. 9469-2007, 3 July 2007.

[69] It can seem contradictory that a Court composed by 7 Magistrates can draft 9 minority opinions in the same decision, nevertheless, the same Magistrate can write different minority opinions to distinct aspects of the decision. In this case, two groups of Legislators presented two parliamentary consultations of the procedure

The overuse of minority opinions can even replace and erase the need for the construction of a single rationale for a majority decision of the Chamber. Therefore, it is possible to find decisions when a majority is reached for a particular result (the constitutionality/unconstitutionality of the norm or the effects of the declared unconstitutionality), but it was impossible to reach a consensus on the reasoning behind the result. Hence, instead of a single core argumentation written by the majority, the decision only presents independent notes or minority opinions drafted by the different judges who composed the majority. This was the case of decision 12782-2018 about marriage equality. The Court reached a majority deciding that the norm object of constitutional review (Article 14 subsection 6 of the Family Code that forbids a marriage between two persons of the same sex) was unconstitutional but did not reached consensus on the consequences of this declaration of unconstitutionality.

F. Framing Constitutional Issues

In general, all the decisions of the Constitutional Chamber contain formal and substantive arguments, in the sense that the Chamber rules on the procedural requirements of the action or writ presented as well as on its merits in the same decision. Indeed, even in amparo and habeas corpus writs, which have few formal requirements, the Chamber rules on the matter.

Focusing on the merits of the case, we can see that in 31 of the 40 landmark cases, the main issue is fundamental rights. This underlines the fact that the Chamber was created and has been consecrated as an instance to protect fundamental rights, rather than a technical instance to safeguard constitutional supremacy in abstract. It can also be attributed to the fact that the competences of the Chamber were endowed, not only by the coverage of rights directly applicable from the Constitution, but also by incorporating international human rights standards via the conventionality control.

G. Key Concepts

The most recurrent concept among the 40 landmark cases is that of the 'Rule of Law', present in 26 of the 40 cases, either expressly or through its derived principles of legality (17 cases) or legal certainty (ten cases). In many judgments, the concept of

of approval of the CAFTA agreement, both consultations were joined by the Constitutional Chamber under the same file. The Chamber, composed of the Judges Luis Fernando Solano (presiding), Luis Paulino Mora, Ana Virginia Calzada, Adrián Vargas, Gilbert Armijo, Ernesto Jinesta and Fernando Cruz, ruled on 4 issues: first, by a vote of 5 to 2, on the admissibility of the two consultations (Judge Calzada dissented on the admission of the second consultation, Judge Mora dissented the admission of both consultations); second, by a vote of 5 to 2, on the constitutionality of the International agreement (Judges Armijo and Cruz dissented and presented a joined dissenting opinion, judge Armijo also presented a solo dissenting opinion, judges Mora and Jinesta presented a joined concurring opinion, three notes were added: one by Judge Vargas, one conjointly by judges Mora and Armijo, and a third by judge Armijo alone); third, on the inadmissibility of the consultation about the legislative procedure, by a vote of 5 to 2 (Judges Armijo and Cruz dissented and presented a joined dissenting opinion), and, finally, they declared unanimously the inadmissibility of a supplementary request of a group of legislators.

'Rule of Law' is used as a matrix principle or as an ideal that, without being expressly contained in constitutional norms, serves as the source for deducing new principles and rights or as the basis for the actions of any public authority.[70] For its part, the principle of legality was the basis for the development of the right to due process.

The Chamber has defined the principle of legal certainty as 'the sum of certainty, legality and proportionality'.[71] Likewise, this principle is often used to justify the dimensioning of a declaration of unconstitutionality, in order not to affect the rights acquired in good faith or situations already consolidated.

Another of the key concepts that appears in numerous landmark cases are economic, social, and cultural rights and post-material values, especially in those resolutions that have to do with environmental law. Indeed, although the Constitution has had an Article since 1994 that enshrines the right to a healthy environment, it is above all the jurisprudence of the Constitutional Chamber that has been responsible for developing a whole series of derived rights and guarantees, nurturing the development of the environmental law with elements such as the obligation to carry out environmental impact studies, or the principle of progressivity in environmental matters.

In the same way, the principle of proportionality appears in numerous resolutions (on 12 of the landmark cases). Indeed, the proportionality test is one of the tools frequently used by the Chamber to examine possible clashes between fundamental rights, resorting to the weighting mechanism and thus establishing that any limitation to a right must not only respond to a public interest, but also which must be proportional.

III. Evaluation, Pathology and Criticism

Judge Rodolfo Piza E, part of the first composition of the Constitutional Chamber, used to paraphrase the famous phrase of Justice Charles Evans Hughes, according to which 'the Constitution is what the judges say it is', considering that 'the Constitution says what the Constitutional Chamber says that it says'.[72] There is no doubt that the creation of the Constitutional Chamber has played a fundamental role both in the protection of fundamental rights and the appropriation by citizens of the Constitution, as well as in the restructuring of the balance of powers, and the development of Constitutional Law. The development of the Constitutional Jurisdiction clearly became an instrument to improve democracy, the rule of law, and fundamental rights and liberties.[73] But this success has also been accompanied by profound criticism of the Chamber's broad interpretation of its own powers, as well as its role in the judicialisation of politics and the activism of some of its members.

The success of the Constitutional Chamber can be measured in quantitative terms. For the year 2021, the Chamber received 26,031 actions and recurses (all competences confused) and issued a total of 28,704 resolutions. But, beyond these numbers, the

[70] Constitutional Chamber of the Supreme Court (Costa Rica), Resolution No. 980-91, 24 May 1991.

[71] Constitutional Chamber of the Supreme Court (Costa Rica), Resolution No. 2771-2003, 4 April 2003.

[72] Quoted by O Rodríguez, 'Seeking Governance without Undermining the Constitutional Jurisdiction in Costa Rica' (2013) *Duquesne Law Review* 432.

[73] O Rodríguez, 'The Costa Rican Constitutional Jurisdiction,' (2011) *Duquesne Law Review* 256.

impact of the Chamber's work on people's daily lives can be illustrated by two examples. First, the expression 'to put a salacuartazo', referring to the 'Sala Cuarta – Fourth Chamber', the journalistic name that has been given to the Constitutional Chamber as it is the fourth Chamber of the Supreme Court, is part of the Costa Rican vocabulary, being viewed as the solution to any problem, from the closure of a municipal park to the lack of access to a medicine in the Social Security system. Second, the Chamber itself, on its 30th anniversary, undertook a video project that shows the impact of the Constitutional Chamber's resolutions on people, under the title 'the Chamber changed my life'.[74]

The Chamber has also contributed to a new balance of powers, placing limits on the work of the legislator[75] and guaranteeing not only constitutional supremacy, but also the superiority of any instrument that guarantees human rights, through development from its first years of a control of conventionality, even before the Inter-American Court developed it as an obligation of every State. For some commentators, the inception and development of the Constitutional Chamber 'meant a change in government. It meant passing from a moderate presidential system to a co-governing body of the political branches of government and the Constitutional Chamber'.[76] The foregoing has been accompanied by a development of Constitutional Law and, more generally, of Human Rights Law, as doctrinal and academic disciplines in the country, deeply focused on the commentary of the Chamber's jurisprudence.

However, after more than 30 years of existence, the work of the Chamber is not exempt from criticism. First, the Chamber is a victim of its own success. The number of cases heard by the Chamber has continued to increase, and the financial and human resources allocated to the Chamber cannot keep up with the volume of work. Some describe the Chamber as a true 'resolution factory'. These structural problems have given rise to certain objectionable practices. For example, the Constitutional Jurisdiction Law imposes deadlines for the resolution of certain writs or actions (habeas corpus, parliamentary consultations). However, due to the material impossibility of dealing with the case backlog, the Chamber on many occasions only publishes the resolutive part of the judgment, leaving the actual wording of the resolution and eventual minority opinions pending. This is therefore communicated to the press and the public, who know the general decision, but not the reasons for it. It may be months before the full resolution is known. Likewise, the public reaction to the vote could even influence the wording of the full resolution. On the other hand, the number of matters known by the Chamber prevents due follow-up on their compliance, which implies a questioning regarding the effectiveness of the Chamber's resolutions in matters of habeas corpus and amparo writs, particularly when it comes to amparos against private law persons.

[74] See salaconstitucional.poder-judicial.go.cr/index.php/la-sala-cambio-mi-vida.

[75] As O Rodríguez summarises '[t]hrough the 1989 amendments to the Constitution, the legislators implicitly limited their own power in favour of a juridical system based on binding analysis of procedural matters (not on substantive matters) that would place constitutional principles and values ahead of future legislation'. See Rodríguez (n 72) 440.

[76] HA Muñoz, 'Sistema Presidencial Moderado Parlamento Racional y sin el Cogobierno de la Sala Constitucional' (2008) *Revista Parlamentaria* 264.

The Chamber itself has internally implemented modifications to its working methods to deal with the growing number of cases backlogged. Likewise, several bills have been proposed to modify the Constitution and the Constitutional Jurisdiction Act. Some projects have raised the need to create sections within the Chamber, so that matters can be voted by a smaller number of magistrates. The possibility of eliminating the parliamentary consultation has also been raised. The doctrine has also raised the need for reforms, proposing a radical change in the very nature of the Chamber, turning it into a Tribunal, independent to the Supreme Court, also creating subordinate courts that would hear amparo and habeas corpus writs.

According to Article 13 of the Constitutional Jurisdiction Act, the Constitutional Chamber is not bound by its own precedents. This can amplify the dangers of politisation because a change in the composition of the Chamber can imply a change in its jurisprudence, therefore a politically motivated change in its composition can also affect the stance of the Court. This threat was denounced in the early 2000 when the Constitutional Chamber was asked, twice, to review a constitutional amendment of 1969 prohibiting the presidential re-election in a widely politised context.[77] In its first resolution, the Chamber concluded on the constitutionality of the reform, considering only procedural arguments.[78] Nevertheless, a new action challenging the constitutionality of the same amendment was presented two years later. In the meantime, two new Magistrates were appointed to the Constitutional Chamber.[79] This newly conformed Chamber delivered, in 2003, a new resolution, considering the amendment of 1969 unconstitutional, opening the path to former Presidents to seek re-election. The Chamber held as central argument that re-election can be considered as a political fundamental right and that a partial amendment of the Constitution cannot limit a fundamental right, as the derived constitutional power can only expand but not diminish this kind of rights.[80]

Therefore, the main critic to the Chamber focuses on its role in the judicialisation of politics and the alleged activism that it has developed. Some authors consider that the Chamber overreaches the interpretation of the Constitution.[81] The leading role of the Chamber in controversial issues such as presidential re-election, in vitro fertilisation, or the approval of free trade agreements, has led some authors to consider

[77] At that time, a former President of the Republic, was seeking the possibility of being a candidate for a new term, but, since 1969, the re-election of a former President was prohibited in Costa Rica. Not having the political force in the Legislative Assembly to promote a new constitutional amendment allowing re-election, his legal team challenged the 1969 Amendment of the Constitution before the Constitutional Chamber.

[78] Constitutional Chamber of the Supreme Court (Costa Rica), Resolution No. 2000-7818, 5 September 2000.

[79] As Brenes and Martínez point out, the newly appointed Magistrates, had judicial and academic careers and had not previously held political office. Nevertheless, the most relevant media in the country published articles denouncing more or less explicitly how the new magistrates could have been appointed at the request of the former President who was seeking re-election, who knew their stance on the matter, to influence the conformation of a Chamber favourable to his position and political interest. See Brenes and Martínez (n 3). The same explanation can be found in O Vargas Rojas, 'Sistema de elección de magistrados(as): talón de Aquiles de la justicia costarricense' (2009) *Revista de Ciencias Jurídicas* 106.

[80] Constitutional Chamber of the Supreme Court (Costa Rica), Resolution No. 2771-2003, 14 April 2003. This resolution is one of the 40 landmark cases selected for this report.

[81] See A Solís, La Constitución es lo que los jueces dicen. El problema de la interpretación constitucional (Investigaciones Jurídicas, 2009).

that the Chamber not only makes legal decisions, but has become a power political, leading Costa Rica to become a true government of judges. The foregoing can be problematic if it is combined with an apparent popular discredit that the Chamber has received since the twenty-first century. However, in its 30s, the Chamber has also shown signs of wanting to move towards greater self-control to deal with these criticisms.

10

The Jurisprudence of the Ecuadorean Constitutional Court

JOHANNA FRÖHLICH*

I. Legal, Political, Institutional and Academic Context

A. Legal and Political Culture as a Context for Constitutional Reasoning

Prior to the end of World War II, Ecuador adopted 15 different constitutions, all of them marking sharply divisive political epochs in which the oppositions' shifting triumphs and demises found constitutional recognition. New constitutions usually emerged in times of crisis,[1] although socioeconomic crises and regime collapses have been common throughout Ecuador's history.

The rhetoric of crisis usually helped frame the discourse on new constitutions, as their purpose was to signal a symbolic regime change rather than to alter the law of the land. However, while the driving force behind new constitutions was not to reform the rules of human and social conduct,[2] but to recognise the prevailing political power

* I owe special gratitude to all members of the CORREG research group, and its continuation, the CORE Latam research group at University of San Francisco de Quito USFQ, for their hard work since 2016. I am extremely grateful to USFQ Faculty of Law for the research grants supporting the completion of this chapter; to Pier Paolo Pigozzi, Tania Groppi, Daniela Salazar, Juan Pablo Aguilar, Hugo Echeverría, András Jakab, Rainer Grote, Ximena Soley, Mauricio Guim and Danny Cevallos for their valuable comments and suggestions; to Pamela Aguirre for providing useful information about the procedures of the Ecuadorian Constitutional Court; to the participants of the 2 February 2017 workshop and the 24 November 2017 workshop hosted by the USFQ Faculty of Law, for their critical remarks; to the Max Planck Institute for International Public Law and Comparative Law for providing a rich and impulsive environment and for supporting this research project; to the participants of the Younger Scholars Forum in 2018, especially to the members of the Section on Populism, for their useful comments; and to all participants of the 'Thursday Seminars' at the Philosophy of Law and International Private Law Department of the University of Alicante in 2021. Finally, I am grateful to Julienne Grant for the English proofreading.

[1] See J Elster, 'Forces and Mechanisms in the Constitution-Making Process' (1995) 45 *Duke Law Journal* 364.

[2] See R Borja Cevallos, 'Breves apuntes sobre el desarrollo constitucional del Ecuador, 1830–1980' in L Mora Ortega, E Ayala Mora, and F Ávila Paredes, *Política y Sociedad* (Corporación Editora Nacional, 1980) 88–89.

and its programme, the result was a legally impotent vision of the constitution with far-reaching effects on its function and social perception. One of these effects was that Ecuador's constitutions have typically had truly little impact on quality of life and legal institutions. Each new constitution, by marking a salient contrast with its predecessor, paradoxically induced the adoption of yet another constitution every time a political crisis ensued. The inefficacy of the constitution,[3] the society's indifference to it, and the vicious cycle of 'failed law'[4] created a conducive environment for charistmatic strongmen and populists, along with their abusive practices.

Ecuadorian scholars have explained the often-insuperable gap between law and reality from various perspectives, ranging from the heritage of the hacienda system,[5] the country's geographic extremities[6] and the disproportionate concentration of executive power,[7] to the high level of poverty and the constant constitutional reforms depicted as an 'epidemy'.[8] The general historical and social context in Ecuador can serve as a remarkably rich and deep source of explanation that deserves great scholarly attention, as it permits the observation of the delicate interplay between several contradictory elements in the country's social and political fabric. As revealed in the following sections, the Ecuadorean model of constitutional review and constitutional reasoning is, in large part, a product of these powerful contradictions.

i. The New Constitution of 2008 and the Andean Transformative Constitutionalism

Inspired by transformative constitutionalist trends, the new Constitution of 2008[9] (hereinafter 'the Constitution') is the twentieth[10] since Ecuador fought for its independence in 1830 and is the most progressive in its history. In line with the global and regional trends of transformative constitutionalism,[11] the Constitution attempts to overcome the structural problems of society, such as poverty, inequality, and violence, through the progressive exercise of constitutional review with a focus on human rights.

[3] M García Villages, 'Disobeying the Law: The Culture of Non-Compliance with Rules in Latin America' (2012) 29 *Wisconsin International Law Journal* 263.

[4] J Esquirol, 'The Failed Law of Latin America' (2008) 56 *American Journal of Jurisprudence* 75.

[5] O Hurtado Larrea, 'El proceso político contemporáneo' in Mora Ortega et al (n 2) 36–37.

[6] J Salvador Lara, 'Historia del Ecuador y caudillismo' in Mora Ortega et al (n 2) 125.

[7] A von Bogdandy et al, 'Ius Constitutionale Commune en América Latina: A Regional Approach to Transformative Constitutionalism' in A von Bogdandy et al (eds), *Transformative Constitutionalism in Latin America* (Oxford University Press, 2017) 14.

[8] G Barragán Romero, 'El constitucionalismo en el Ecuador, 1830–1980' in Mora Ortega et al (n 2) 118 (author's translation).

[9] Official Registry No. 449 (22 October 2008). For the English translation, I used the database of the Constitute Project, www.constituteproject.org/constitution/Ecuador_2015?lang=en.

[10] See E Ayala Mora, *Evolución constitucional del Ecuador. Rasgos históricos* (Quito Universidad Andina Simón Bolívar) 139. This figure could be higher if we count the Quito State Charter of 1812 or the Constitution of Great Colombia of 1821.

[11] As neoconstitutionalism, because of its European origins, is related more to liberal constitutionalism, while the Ecuadorean model aspires to create something distinctly Andean in its origins, it seems more appropriate to use the term 'transformative'. For more details on these trends, see Pigozzi (ch 2) in this volume.

Despite public disapproval and institutional dysfunctions[12] plaguing the judicial branch, the Constitution has been influenced by theories that have failed to recognise the perils of the broad abyss existing between social reality and legal rules. In the scheme of aspirational constitutionalism,[13] the lack of enforceability is not necessarily a sign of law's weak authority, but a consequence of the creative jurisprudence of courts that have attempted to reinforce social progress. Similarly, the inefficacy of rights is viewed as 'a culmination of a struggle to change the status quo'.[14] Therefore, the Constitution's authority is understood in the context of 'the "drama" of inequality'[15] where legal rules serve the dominant political elite and where those rules have historically been corrupted by injustice and abuse of power, including in contemporary times. This approach implies a very particular vision of law's normativity and its relation to legal hierarchy, where all types of sources of law, including international law, could and should be utilised directly to rectify inequalities – without reliance on principles of the formal rule of law, such as legal hierarchy or foreseeability.

The new Constitution has been influenced by the Andean version of transformative constitutionalism, which departs from several of neoconstitutionalism's important tenets, such as normativity, democracy, and the rule of law. Andean transformative constitutionalism heavily emphasises social, economic and cultural rights rather than political and civil rights; it gives more weight to participatory democracy (in Ecuador, popular referendums and social controls is a separate branch of power) than to representative democracy; it recognises collective subjects as political actors (eg indigenous people's rights of participation); it creates special legal and institutional means to vindicate the rights of indigenous people (see, plurinational state); and finally, it increases state intervention in the economy to counter neoliberalism and the free market system.[16]

The Constitution was adopted under the presidency of Rafael Correa[17] in a constitution-making procedure accompanied by considerable political turmoil.[18] The constitution-making procedure started with a presidential decree in 2007 that called for a plebiscite on the formation of a national Constituent Assembly. In February of the same year, voters approved the call for a plebiscite primarily due to President Correa's threats to otherwise dissolve Ecuador's National Assembly. The National

[12] G Helmke and J Ríos-Figueroa (eds), *Courts in Latin America* (Cambridge University Press, 2011) 1–2, 4.

[13] See MC Dorf, 'The Aspirational Constitutionalism' (2009) 77 *George Washington Law Review* 1633.

[14] ibid.

[15] R Gargarella, *Latin American Constitutionalism, 1810–2010: The Engine Room of the Constitution* (Oxford University Press, 2013) 196.

[16] von Bogdandy et al (n 7) 18.

[17] See CM Conaghan, 'Ecuador: Correa's Plebiscitary Presidency' (2008) 19 *Journal of Democracy* 46, 47–48.

[18] See N Massüger and Y Welp, 'Legality and Legitimacy: Constituent Power in Venezuela (1999), Bolivia (2006–2009) and Ecuador (2007–2008)' in F Méndez and J Wheatley, *Constitution-Making and Popular Participation* (Ashgate, 2013); D Landau, 'Abusive Constitutionalism' (2013) 47 *UC Davis Law Review* 189, 207. See P Andrade A, *El reino (de lo) imaginario: Los intelectuales políticos ecuatorianos en la construcción de la Constitución de 2008* (2012)85 *Ecuador Debate* 38–40, 45; R Ávila Santamaría, 'El constitucionalismo ecuatoriano. Breve caracterización de la Constitución de 2008' in M Carbonell et al (coord), *Tendencias del constitucionalismo en Iberoamérica* (UNAM, 2009) 960.

Assembly approved the draft of the new constitution in July 2008, and by September, the document had been ratified in a national referendum.[19]

The Constitution is highly specific with 444 articles, followed by 30 Transitory Provisions and another 30 articles of the Transition System; in total, the document spans approximately 215 pages. As for flexibility, the Constitution introduced three different amendatory procedures with progressively entrenching rules for matters with increasing levels of impact. The Ecuadorean Constitutional Court (hereinafter ECC), which was created by the Constitution, became a central political actor with the power to choose the suitable amendatory procedures and approve the proposed amendments.[20]

In line with Andean transformative constitutionalism, the Constitution introduced a distinct catalogue of rights and guarantees (*garantismo*). The novelty of the new catalogue is not only that it is extensive and detailed; it also has a unique Andean character, and the lack of a hierarchy among the different rights accords well with the catalogue's cosmological approach.[21]

As the traditional classification of rights was set aside, the catalogue applies the indigenous concept of the 'good way of living' (*Buen vivir* or *Sumak Kawsay* in Quechua) and 'Mother Earth' (*Pacha Mama*) to garner a new and distinct understanding of wellbeing. The Constitution promotes the enforcement of rights, not only by specifying that rights can be exercised and enforced individually and collectively (Art 11.1), but also by explicitly acknowledging the collective rights of Ecuador's different communities, nations, and peoples (Arts 56–60). Indeed, the Constitution draws upon the country's diverse social and cultural background (*plurinacionalidad*), which is why concepts such as nation are notably absent from most of the ECC's landmark decisions. Finally, the Constitution grants significant authority to the citizenry to direct democracy, creating a new branch of power called the 'Transparency and Social Control Function'. However, some scholars were initially critical of the sweeping competences of this new institution, arguing that its rules and procedures were unclear and their application uncertain.[22] Hence, ten years after the institution's creation, it was the transitional Council for Public Participation and Social Control that triggered the reprise of the ECC (see Section II(A) in this chapter).

Furthermore, the Constitution of 2008 in its Article 427 lays down the basic rules for constitutional interpretation. According to this Article, the textual meaning of the Constitution shall be the principal method of constitutional interpretation. Secondary methods, in case of doubt, are those that are the most favourable to the full and effective enforcement of rights and that best respect the will of the constituent in accordance with the general principles of constitutional interpretation.

[19] See A Grijalva, 'Courts and Political Parties: The Politics of Constitutional Review in Ecuador' 151–52 (unpublished PhD dissertation, University of Pittsburgh) d-scholarship.pitt.edu/7334/.

[20] J Fröhlich, 'More flexibility in favour of constitutional stability? – What breaking amendment rules in Ecuador can teach us' (2021) 19 *International Journal of Constitutional* 974.

[21] A Grijalva Jiménez, *Constitucionalismo en Ecuador*, in Pensamiento Jurídico Contemporáneo no. 5 (Corte Constitucional para el Período de Transición, 2012) 28.

[22] ibid 33.

B. The Court and Constitutional Litigation

The history of the ECC can be divided into two distinct periods: (1) its first ten years operating during the Correa presidencies with Correa-appointed judges; and (2) its second period, which commenced in early 2019 with a complete turnover of its judicial composition. In this chapter, the opportunity exists to analyse the ECC's reasoning using a separate dataset for each historical period of the Court.[23] However, the comparability of the two datasets has limitations; for the first ECC, there is data available from an eight-year period (between 2008 and 2016),[24] while for the actual ECC, there is data only about its first year (2019), until the closure of the dataset. With a careful and self-reflective approach, however, these datasets can shed light on the reshaping of complex political environments, which serve as the context for the executive's and the different ideological groups' continuous struggle for domination over the ECC and its consequential impact on constitutional reasoning.

i. The Two Main Periods of the ECC

The political battle for power has oftentimes led to the manhandling of judges[25] and left the ECC with procedural and formal deficiencies. The first period (2008–2018) of the ECC started with irregularities. Due to an ambiguity about the regime of transition, members of the predecessor of the ECC who were appointed already by then President Correa adopted a resolution[26] to self-appoint themselves immediately as judges of the ECC competent to enforce the new rights and guarantees. The 'ECC of the Transitional Period' lasted until 2012, contributing to half of the selected landmark cases from the jurisprudence of the first ECC.

However, the ECC's members cannot be impeached, nor can they be removed from office 'by those who appoint them' (Art 431). In 2018, the ECC's judges were again replaced after Lenin Moreno, who had served as Correa's vice president, ascended to the presidency and began the process of reinstitutionalisation.[27] After a popular referendum that empowered the transitional Council for Public Participation and Social Control to evaluate the overall performance of the first ECC, the council removed all nine judges on the grounds of irregularities in their selection, their failure to protect rights and guarantees and their misuse of public funds.[28] After a 60-day constitutional vacancy, new judges were appointed to the ECC at the end of 2018.

[23] For purposes of this chapter, the ECC of the first period is referred to as 'the first' or 'the previous', while the ECC from the second period is called 'the actual' or 'the current' ECC.

[24] The reason for not having data from the years 2017 and 2018 is that the project was born and set up in those years after the discoveries of the study on Ecuador.

[25] See A Grijalva, Courts and Political Parties. The Politics of Constitutional Review in Ecuador (VDM Verlag Dr Müller, 2010); A Grijalva, 'Constitucionalidad, Institucionalidad y Derecho en el Ecuador' (2007) 71 *Ecuador Debate* 31; A Isaac, 'Los problemas de consolidación democrática en Ecuador' in F Burbano de Lara (comp), *Antología: democracia, gobernabilidad y cultura política* (FLACSO, 2003).

[26] Resolution of the Court, No. 451, 22 October 2008.

[27] See J Fröhlich and PP Pigozzi, 'Ecuador' in R Albert et al (eds), *2018 Global Review of Constitutional Law* (I·CONnect-Clough Center, 2019) 88–89.

[28] Resolution No. PLE-CPCCS-T-O-089-23-08-2018 (23 August 2018), paras 558, 653–60.

ii. The Competences of the ECC

According to Article 429 of the Constitution, the ECC is 'the supreme body for controlling, constitutionally interpreting and administering justice'. Ecuador has a 'hybrid'[29] or 'eclectic'[30] constitutional review model, which is an accrual of several different designs. The ECC has the final word on constitutionality, and at the same time, every ordinary judge is explicitly called upon to exercise constitutional control, which is in line with the principle of the Constitution's direct applicability as set forth in Articles 11.3 and 426.

It is a widely held view that the ECC has broad and cumulative competences to put the Constitution's ideology into practice. While its predecessor's decisions were not expressly enforceable, the decisions of the ECC are binding, and the Court can also issue 'binding jurisprudence' in selected cases originating in ordinary courts.[31]

The ECC's competences are codified in different constitutional provisions and in various statutes. Academic sources[32] usually divide these competences into the following four categories: a posteriori review powers (unconstitutional action; action of unconstitutional omission; judicial consultation; a posteriori review of declarations of state emergencies; and noncompliant actions), a priori review powers (control of international treaties; preventive control of laws; preventive control of constitutional reforms; preventive control of calls for popular referendum; and control of dissolution of the National Assembly), constitutional and jurisdictional guarantees (direct protection of jurisdictional guarantees, such as the writ of amparo and selected cases originating in ordinary courts), conflicts of competences and other political competences. This current design promotes accessibility by eradicating the requirements for a concrete violation of rights, instead introducing *actio popularis* for cases of abstract constitutional review.

One of the criticisms of the first ECC was that it purposefully refrained from deciding politically sensitive cases. Indeed, the first ECC decided only a small number of cases[33] as its average caseload per year was around 370. Consequently, the current ECC has had to handle a large backlog of cases, which has been languishing for years.[34] The competence exercised most often is by far the writ of amparo (*acción extraordinaria de protección*), which is an exclusive competence to review the constitutionality of judicial decisions or acts of state authorities. Every ECC decision is publicly available, and the ECC regularly holds public hearings, just like ordinary courts.

[29] P Navia and J Ríos-Figueroa, 'The Constitutional Adjudication Mosaic of Latin America' (2005) 38 *Comparative Political Studies* 189.

[30] J Castro-Montero and G van Dijck, 'Judicial Politics in Unconsolidated Democracies: An Empirical Analysis of the Ecuadorian Constitutional Court (2008–2016)' (2017) 38 *Justice System Journal* 380, 385.

[31] See Art 236.6. portal.corteconstitucional.gob.ec:8494/Grafos.aspx?opcion=relatoria&provincia=&anio=0, see under 'PJO'.

[32] A Ruiz Guzmán, P Aguirre Castro, and D Ávila Benavidez, '*Desarrollo Jurisprudencial de la Primera Corte Constitucional (Noviembre 2012–Noviembre 2015)*' in Jurisprudencia constitucional no 7 (Corte Constitucional del Ecuador, 2016); R Oyarte, *Derecho Constitucional: Ecuatoriano y Comparado,* 2nd edn (Quito, Corporación de Estudios y Publicaciones, 2016); N Jervis Secaira, 'El Common law en las competencias de la Corte Constitucional Ecuatoriana' (2010) (unpublished paper, Universidad de las Américas).

[33] The first ECC decided only around 3,500 cases before 2018.

[34] The actual ECC inherited 10,500 ongoing cases from the previous court and decided almost 600 cases during its first year. portal.corteconstitucional.gob.ec:8494/Grafos.aspx?opcion=relatoria&provincia=&anio=0.

Another disparity between the first and current ECC is their contrasting approaches to petitions received from citizens, civil organisations, and state authorities. The previous ECC often took a deferential approach towards the executive and favoured petitions with a top-down involvement originating from state organs.[35] Among the selected cases of the first ECC were 13 petitions with top-down involvement, seven out of which were decided in favour of the state's interests regarding political participation, the collective rights of indigenous communities or refugee rights. However, this approach seems to have changed with the current ECC, which has consciously departed from the previous line of jurisprudence – not only taking on a more critical stand towards the executive, but explicitly rejecting the doctrine that supports the idea of the state as a rights holder.[36] The selected judgments of the current ECC show that the number of cases with top-down involvement was almost the same as its predecessor (10), but there were only four cases where the Court decided in favour of state interests.

While the Constitution includes several innovations, the success of its extensive rights catalogue has been put into doubt. The Constitution lists 99 different rights, making it the constitution with the highest number of rights in a global comparison.[37] However, its enforcement has failed to live up to expectations, especially during the Constitution's first decade in force. Irregularities in enforcement can be found particularly in the realms of economic, social, cultural and environmental rights,[38] as exemplified in a case involving the 2009 Mining Act.[39] In this decision, the first ECC argued that, although indigenous communities have the right to participate in questions related to their ancestral land, the lack of consultation in question was not unconstitutional because 'the enactment of the Mining Act happened in an exceptional context' of transition, which justified the absence of enforceable regulations on how to exercise that right. Another example for the Court's strategic voting is the River Vilcabamba opinion,[40] where it took seven years for the first ECC to sanction a road construction project that had already been completed without sufficient proof of possible environmental harm.[41] Regarding the performance of the actual ECC, it is still too early to form a well-founded opinion.

C. The Judges

The Constitution specifies that the ECC shall be composed of nine judges with non-renewable terms of nine years.[42] The Constitution also prescribes a rule for rotation,

[35] This was confirmed by other empirical studies that claimed that ECC judges, between 2008 and 2016, 'strategically vote[d] in favour of the government depending on the political salience of the cases'. Castro-Montero and van Dijck (n 30) 381.

[36] Decision of the ECC, No. 282-13-JP/19.

[37] Data derived from the Comparative Constitutions Project, at comparativeconstitutionsproject.org/ccp-rankings/.

[38] See C Rodriguez-Garavito, 'Beyond the Courtroom: The Impact of Judicial Activism on Socioeconomic Rights in Latin America' (2011) 89 *Texas Law Review* 1669.

[39] Decision of the ECC, No. 001-10-SIN-CC.

[40] Decision No. 11121-2011-0010, Provincial Court of Loja, Ecuador.

[41] Decision of the ECC, No. 012-18-SIS-CC.

[42] Art 433 Constitution of Ecuador.

according to which one-third of the ECC's members shall be re-elected every three years. De facto independence is more problematic as interruptions in the judges' constitutional mandate and job security demonstrate.[43] In 2007, President Correa packed the CT and replaced its judges with his political allies.[44] Then, six out of the nine ECC judges were replaced again by cronies from President Correa's close political circles during the Transitional Period until 2012.[45] The judges of the first ECC were mainly coming from the executive branch, and they were generally perceived as lacking professional skills and favouring the interests of the executive.[46] This bias, as it later turned out, led to serious corruption charges lodged against the members of the Court.[47] Six out of the nine judges were women.

The new composition of the second ECC reflects the intent to provoke a paradigm shift in constitutional adjudication in Ecuador. In line with this aspiration, the profiles of the new judges contrast with those of the previous ECC's members. All the current judges earned PhDs from European or North American universities, as well as master's degrees from Ecuador, the United States or Europe. All the new judges were previously academics or practiced law independently, and currently one has prior judicial experience. Some of the current EEC judges actively shaped the debates during the constitution-making procedure in 2008.[48] Five out of the nine judges are women.

D. Legal Scholarship and Constitutional Reasoning

The position of the legal academy and its treatment of the ECC is controversial. On the one hand, when the previous ECC voted strategically because of pressure from the executive, such as in cases involving the collective rights of indigenous people, the academic community criticised the ECC. On the other hand, in politically neutral cases, or when the political climate changed, the judges of the first ECC tried to appease activists, civil society and the academic community by deciding in favour of their interests. An example of the former is the ECC's opinion that granted freedom of choice for personal identity and gender,[49] and for the latter, its decision on the constitutionality of the amendment to eliminate presidential term limits.[50] The general audience of the first

[43] S Basabe-Serrano, 'Judges without Robes and Judicial Voting in Contexts of Institutional Instability: The Case of Ecuador's Constitutional Court, 1999–2007' (2012) 44 *Journal of Latin American Studies* 127.

[44] Castro-Montero and van Dijck (n 30) 384.

[45] See 'El oficialismo se filtra en Corte Constitucional, el más poderoso ente en Ecuador' *El Universo* (11 November 2012), at www.eluniverso.com/2012/11/11/1/1355/oficialismo-filtra-mas-poderoso-ente-pais.html.

[46] S Basabe, 'Corte Constitucional = inoperancia + corrupción + pusilanimidad, Cuatro Pelagatos' (7 August 2018).

[47] Recently, all the judges of the first ECC were formally charged with corruption. See at periodismodeinvestigacion.com/2018/08/08/los-secretos-financieros-de-los-jueces-constitucionales/.

[48] R Ávila Santamaría, *El neoconstitucionalismo transformador: El estado y el derecho en la Constitución de 2008* (Quito, Abya-Yala, Universidad Andina Simón Bolívar, 2011); R Ávila Santamaría, A Grijalva Jiménez and R Martínez Dalmau (eds), *Desafíos constitucionales. La Constitución Ecuatoriana de 2008 en perspectiva* (Ministerio de Justicia y Derechos Humanos, 2008), www.corteidh.or.cr/tablas/25562.pdf.

[49] Decision of the ECC, No. 133-17-SEP-CC.

[50] Decision of the ECC, No. 018-18-SIN-CC. The first ECC published its decision four years after the amendment, just before its judges were removed.

ECC was mainly the political elite and the executive, and in some cases, the various civil society groups. This seems to have changed with the actual ECC, which is still functioning in an atmosphere of institutional instability and job insecurity, but nevertheless has chosen to take a critical stance towards the executive branch.

Legal scholarship in Ecuador seems to share some characteristics with the broader Latin American attitudes towards legal education and academia in general. The approach to legal theories and legal literature is mostly influenced by European and North American scholars, while local voices with original ideas are still relatively scarce.[51] This asymmetry seems to be especially true for the Ecuadorean legal academy, which is widely known for its body of literature that has been characterised as a '[commentary] of cited foreign authority'.[52] In Ecuador, one group of scholars represents the classic commentary genre, which is critical of the transformative constitutional trends, and therefore is critical to the current ECC.[53] On the other hand, especially in the last decade or so, a new type of academic legal community has emerged, mostly influenced by progressive and critical theories. Many members of this new community are admirers and advocates of Andean transformative constitutionalism, seeking ways to reconstruct Ecuador's legal system following the principles of equality and non-discrimination. According to the general criticism, 'legal scholarship has not played a fundamental role in the development of constitutional law in Ecuador',[54] and it is seen rather as a means of political advocacy.

II. Types of Arguments in Constitutional Reasoning

A. The Structure of Constitutional Arguments

There has been an interesting longitudinal change in the structure of the ECC's arguments across the Court's two periods. While the majority of the first ECC's opinions relied on one-line argumentation (24 out of 40 cases), and only one-quarter of its cases applied a parallel conclusive structure (12 out of 40 cases), the current ECC employed parallel reasoning at least twice as frequently as its predecessor (26 out of 40 cases), and it only used one-line argumentation 11 times out of 40. Although in Ecuador it is common to base an action on several different grounds, this shift in reasoning strategy can be explained by the ECC's transitory character and its intent to convey a fully responsive and comprehensive opinion to its audience. The dialogic structure of

[51] C Rodríguez-Garavito, 'Remapping law and society in Latin America. Visions and topics for a new legal cartography' in C Rodríguez-Garavito (ed), *Law and Society in Latin America: A New Map, Law, Development and Globalization* (Routledge, 2015).

[52] ibid 3.

[53] L Fernando Torres, 'El Activismo Judicial en la era Neoconstitucional' 13 *Iuris Dictio* (2013); S Zaidán, *Neoconstitucionalismo: Teoría y práctica en el Ecuador* (Quito, Cevallos, 2012).; M Atienza, 'Ni positivismo jurídico ni neoconstitucionalismo: una defensa del constitucionalismo postpositivista', en *Filosofía del derecho y transformación social* (Trotta, 2017).

[54] D Salazar, 'The Constitutional History of Ecuador: Twenty Constitutions and Counting' in C Hübner Mendes et al (eds), *The Oxford Handbook of Constitutional Law in Latin America* (Oxford University Press, 2022).

argumentation appeared in only four of the first ECC's cases and in three of the current ECC's selected jurisprudence.

B. Types of Arguments in Constitutional Reasoning

Having two datasets available on the constitutional reasoning practices of the Ecuadorean Constitutional Court provides a means to compare two distinct tribunals. The contrast is marked, not only by an abrupt halt and a period of discontinuity, but by how the ECC used different argumentative strategies in different periods. Almost all of the Court's statistical results have decreased quantitatively with the actual ECC, with just a few exceptions. This would be a surprise if there was a direct correlation between the number of arguments and the quality of the Court's reasoning, but in the Ecuadorean case such correlation cannot be confirmed. The previous ECC took advantage of citing several distinct sources and employing distinct types of arguments in its decisions; but for the most part, these decisions did not possess an argumentative character per se, and they failed to add any discernible level of persuasiveness or credibility to the Court's opinions. The actual ECC seems to have chosen a different strategy in this regard.

i. Analogies

There was only one opinion out of the 40 in the dataset of the first ECC where an analogy was employed. In that case, Decision No. 309-16-SEP-CC, the first ECC made an analogy between people with disabilities and pregnant women to support the proposition that, in both situations, the ECC must apply fundamental guarantees as prescribed in the Constitution.

ii. Debating the Text of the Constitution and the Applicability of the Constitution

The EEC has rarely relied on arguments based on doubts about what counts as the text of the Constitution. The first ECC invoked this type of 'constitutional block' argument in five cases, however the current ECC has only used this type of argument twice.[55] The previous ECC usually drew upon the 'constitutional block' theory together with the concept of the Constitution's supremacy. In Decision No. 031-11-SEP-CC, the first ECC argued that the supremacy of the Constitution and the supremacy of international law can coexist since the Constitution assigns a constitutional rank to binding international treaties.

The current ECC has appealed even more to international law in the framework of Andean transformative constitutionalism as demonstrated in its landmark decision on same-sex marriage. There the Court argued that international human rights instruments

[55] Decision of the ECC, No. 2-19-IC-2019 (competences of the Transitory Council); Decision of the ECC, No. 11-18-CN/19 (same-sex marriage).

are incorporated in Ecuador's Constitution.[56] Furthermore, the current ECC declared that the Transitory Provisions and the competences of the Transitory Council are integral parts of the Constitution and have constitutional rank.[57]

Regarding the indicator on the applicability of constitutional law, the previous ECC never invoked this type of argument, while the current ECC utilised it four times – for example, in an opinion involving the legislator's constitutional discretion to adopt legislation.[58]

iii. Ordinary Meaning of the Words of the Constitution

The use of ordinary meaning, or textual interpretation, has never been an influential method in the ECC, and its use has decreased even more in the current ECC. While the first ECC made textual arguments in almost half of its landmark cases (18 out of 40), the actual ECC used this type of argument only 13 times. Invoking an argument, however, does not always lead directly to a decision, although it can serve as a rhetoric function – a common feature of the first ECC's reasoning practice. The quality and sophistication of the Court's textual arguments have varied widely. For instance, in Decision No. 080-13-SEP-CC, the previous ECC relied on the dictionary of the Royal Spanish Academy of Languages to determine the meaning of 'discrimination'. However, in another case, Decision No. 001-14-PJO-CC, the first ECC attempted to clarify the literal meaning method and applied it in a case on data protection.

Textual arguments are almost always superseded by other types of arguments, such as scholarly opinions or even comparative sources. For instance, in Decision No. 002-09-SAN-CC, the first ECC considered it necessary to draw on the Argentinian experience to justify the expansion of constitutional control over related norms, even though the Constitution expressly provides for this option. Textual arguments in the practice of the first ECC were decisive only in one case, which addressed the freedom of information.[59]

The current ECC seems to take a more transparent approach to its argumentative strategy when it treats textual method as secondary. The current ECC invoked this method a total of 13 times: 11 times in majority opinions and twice in minority opinions. Although there is a clear division between those judges who prefer classic methods with a textual basis, and those who favour creative methods, the data suggests that judges from the second group still mention textual methods, but they place more emphasis on other techniques, such as the application of international law.

iv. Harmonising Arguments

Two types of harmonising arguments were analysed for this study: domestic and international. Both types of harmonising methods appeared in approximately every second

[56] Decision of the ECC, No. 11-18-CN/19, para 10.
[57] Decision of the ECC, No. 2-19-IC/19, paras 26–27.
[58] Decision of the ECC, No. 002-19-DOP-CC.
[59] Decision No. 182-12-SEP-CC.

selected case in the jurisprudence of the previous ECC, while the use of the domestic harmonising method decreased substantially in the selected jurisprudence of the current ECC:

Overall, the first ECC used a domestic harmonising argument in 22 of its selected 40 decisions, while the current ECC utilised it in only eight of its landmark cases.

Beyond simply reading two or more constitutional provisions concurrently, the previous ECC supplemented the principle of constitutional unity, which is usually referred to as a 'systematic' or 'integral' argument (eg, the first ECC's Decisions in Nos. 110-14-SEP-CC and 0001-09-SIC-CC). The first ECC frequently applied arguments invoking inner unity within the Constitution alongside the new theories of Andean constitutionalism. In Decision No. 148-12-SEP-CC, for example, the first ECC found a substantial nexus between personal dignity and the right to decent housing as part of its 'integral interpretation'. But this was part of a broader argument related to 'contemporary theories of constitutionalism' and the rejection of legal formalism, which often resulted in a finding that the lower courts' decisions were unconstitutional. In the opinions of the current ECC, the number of domestic harmonising arguments was less than half the number used in the previous ECC. This decline is likely a reflection of the general downturn in the use of classic methods of argumentation based on the text of the Constitution.

The previous ECC also relied heavily on arguments related to international law, as has the current ECC. In half of the selected cases of the first ECC, binding international law was cited, especially the American Convention on Human Rights (ACHR) and other regional treaties. Further references can be found to several charters and conventions on fundamental and human rights, such as the Universal Declaration of Human Rights (UDHR). As happened with several other arguments and concepts, the first ECC preferred to reference international legal sources in its decisions, but in most instances, it was unclear if these sources carried any weight when the Court made its final decision. As explored in a subsequent section, the first ECC's use of international law is a prime example of rhetoric and deceptive reasoning.

The selected landmark opinions of the current ECC produced similar empirical data, but a crucial difference lies in the weight that the Court assigned to international law. Contrary to its predecessor, the current ECC not only invokes international law; it also assigns decisive levels of importance to it. The indicators show that most of the time (17 times out of 40), the current ECC refers to the various sources that comprise the Inter-American System of Human Rights and assigns considerable weight to binding international law outside the regional system (eight instances) and so-called soft law (eight instances). The actual ECC's use of international law seems to signal a more qualitative than quantitative level of importance of this interpretive method; the heavy, sometimes even disproportionate, reliance on regional human rights law has evolved into a symbol of politically sensitive cases where the current ECC wanted to exhibit its transformative power.

v. Precedents

One of the most frequent interpretive methods that the first ECC utilised was to rely on precedents (28 cases out of 40), and this technique is similarly dominant in the current

Court's landmark opinions (23 cases out of 40). Prior to 2012, there were fewer decisions containing references to precedential opinions, while all the ECC's post-2012 selected cases invoked precedent-based arguments. This can be explained easily by noting the 2012 end date of the first ECC's transitory period; not so long afterwards (in 2015), the Court first mentioned 'settled case law' (*jurisprudencia reiterada*) in connection with procedural issues in a case involving parental rights and children's best interests. The set of the current ECC decisions referenced precedents almost as frequently as the previous ECC. In several cases, however, the current ECC expressly deviated from the case law of its predecessor.

vi. Doctrinal Analysis of Legal Concepts or Principles

The most monumental change that occurred between the previous and current ECC regarding empirical results concerns the interpretive method of employing legal concepts. While the first ECC utilised this method in only 11 cases (out of 40), the current Court used doctrinal analysis of legal concepts for the purpose of constitutional interpretation 24 times.

Among the first ECC's favoured concepts was the doctrine of principles (as in a case on arbitration), the principle of *pro homine* (eg, in a case granting protection to a Cuban refugee), and the concept of 'protected legal good' (*bien jurídico protegido*) invoked in the well-known *Cocha* case involving indigenous justice. Furthermore, the previous ECC used the principle of *in dubio pro legislatore* in the case involving the 2009 Mining Act, as well as in a tax law case concerning airports.

The current ECC, however, gives greater weight to legal concepts in its interpretations. Drawing more from such concepts presupposes strong academic backgrounds which, according to studies on judicial behaviour,[60] has direct implications for the quality of judicial decisions. As we shall see later, the increasing use of concepts and principles that are not textually present in the Constitution is also a sign for judicial self-empowerment, and apparently an important aspect of the judicial argumentative style in the region.

vii. Arguments from Silence

According to the datasets, both the previous and current ECC only utilised this type of argument (*argumentum ex silencio*) two times each.

viii. Objective Teleological Arguments

While the current EEC's most frequently used method of interpretation invokes doctrinal concepts, the previous ECC's most frequently used method was the objective teleological method, which was applied 33 times out of 40.

[60] S Basabe-Serrano, 'The Judges' Academic Background as Determinant of the Quality of Judicial Decisions in Latin American Supreme Courts' (2019) 40 *Justice System Journal*.

In academic literature, extracting and invoking a purpose that is recognisable in the normative text is regarded as both a persuasive and an authentic method of interpretation since it combines creative interpretive elements with the legitimacy of the binding constitutional text.[61] In light of this, the result was a bit surprising, as the main criticism of the first ECC was precisely that it failed to seek creative and responsive solutions to its cases. One possible explanation might be that the Ecuadorian Constitution includes various references to the purposes or objectives of the rules and legal institutions it incorporates; in turn, this can provide ammunition for teleological arguments. It is noteworthy that, in almost two-thirds of those cases (19 out of 33), these arguments were used to support procedural matters – namely, to define and delimit the Court's own proceedings. Focusing on the procedural aspects of constitutional matters in general was one of the strategies the first ECC used to avoid dealing with the substantive aspects of constitutional cases.

In a few cases, however, the first ECC took advantage of the purposive method's potential, mainly in cases on human rights or the rule of law. Furthermore, the previous ECC used a teleological method to argue that the Constitution's text must be interpreted in a way that gives effect to every part of it – that is, to its entirety.[62]

In the selected landmark cases of the actual ECC, this type of teleological argument is important, but less so than it was for its predecessor. The actual ECC invoked the purpose of the Constitution 18 times, primarily in rights cases. Considering the changes in ideology and judicial character that have accompanied the current ECC, this result could be interpreted as simply a reflection of the Ecuadorian Constitution's aspirational character and its stronger stand against the state in rights cases.

ix. Arguments Referring to the Intention of the Constitution-Maker

Drawing on the intent of the National Assembly or the Constitutional Assembly as an interpretive method was rather rare in the selected jurisprudence of both periods of the ECC (three and four times out of 40, respectively), even though this method is explicitly mentioned in Article 427 of the Constitution.

Perusing the three cases of the previous ECC, two are related to indigenous rights, and in both decisions, the intent of the Constitution's drafters was used against the complainants. In the first case of the two, the ECC declared that the law permitting mining activities without consulting the affected indigenous communities was in line with the Constitution.[63] In the other case, the previous ECC decided that the indigenous and ordinary justice systems are distinct and incomparable; therefore, the prohibition of double jeopardy did not apply, and the defendants could be tried by the state as well.[64]

The current ECC refers to this type of argument as the 'spirit of the constitution', as it is utilised to contend that the purpose of certain mechanisms of constitutional

[61] A Jakab, 'What makes a good lawyer?' (2007) 2 *Zeitschrift für öffentliches Recht* 275–87.
[62] Decision of the ECC, No. 0006-09-SIC-CC; Decision of the ECC, No. 002-09-SAN-CC.
[63] Decision of the ECC, No. 001-10-SIN-CC.
[64] Decision of the ECC, No. 113-14-SEP-CC.

amendments is not to make significant changes to the text per se.[65] Furthermore, the Constitution's drafting history was invoked in a case involving the civil registry of same-sex couples to justify the 'evolutive' interpretation of legal institutions.[66]

x. *Non-Legal Arguments*

The use of non-legal arguments was quite common in the selected cases of the first ECC (16 out of 40), and this technique remained important in the group of decisions of the current ECC (11 out of 40). Looking just at the numbers, the ECC's practices during the two periods appear to be similar; but, striking differences emerge when noting references to external sources.

The first ECC made typical political, economic, and sociological arguments, appealed to an 'effective justice administration', or referred to the circumstances of certain vulnerable groups. Among these were the 'negative social perception' of individuals carrying the HIV virus, the 'new environment' to which a child must adapt if his or her habitual residence changes, the health problems of the elderly, the vulnerability of mothers during the period of lactation and the 'history of social exclusion of women'.

In contrast, the current ECC utilised non-legal arguments in nine out of 11 of those flagged cases, the Court relied on sociological arguments, and less on moral, economic, or scientific ones. Furthermore, the weight of sociological arguments increased, for instance, in the case on same-sex marriage, the ECC referred to sociological arguments six times in total throughout the majority decision.

xi. *References to Scholarly Works*

Besides domestic harmonising arguments, another method with decreased use in the actual ECC is that of referencing scholarly works. In the selected jurisprudence of the first ECC, this was the second most common method (28 cases out of 40), but in the current ECC's practice, there were only 13 cases that mentioned academic literature.

Numbers reflecting the use of scholarly works might serve at least two purposes: they could serve as a useful indicator for the academic community and the culture that specifically surrounds the legal academy, and/or they might serve as a measurement of the academic skills of the judges themselves. In terms of the first supposition, the general prestige of the academy is rather low in Ecuador, and its output of scholarly works is not often known or cited outside that orbit. In Germany, which is considered a model of the continental academic culture, the same indicator was 37,[67] while in Colombia, famous for its strong academic culture in the region, this number is 29 (see, chapter eight on Colombia in this volume). Regarding the profiles of the ECC judges, those of the current Court have stronger ties with academia and better academic credentials than the first ECC's judges. So, looking at both aspects together, it is rather surprising

[65] Decision of the ECC, No. 1-18-RC/19, paras 20, 51.

[66] Decision of the ECC, No. 11-18-CN/19, para 153.

[67] A Jakab, A Dyevre and G Itzcovich (eds), *Comparative Constitutional Reasoning* (Cambridge University Press, 2017) 378.

that this number was so high in the jurisprudence of the first ECC and so much lower in the current ECC's selected opinions.

Looking at the scholarly works that were referenced by the first ECC, it is possible to differentiate between three types. The vast majority were Italian authors (and sometimes Spaniards), such as Luigi Ferrajoli, Gustavo Zagrebelsky and Norberto Bobbio, whose ideas were used to support the theories of the Andean version of neoconstitutionalism.[68] References in the second group were made to works authored by the great names of legal and constitutional theory, such as Hans Kelsen, Robert Alexy and Ronald Dworkin. The inclusion of Alexy and Dworkin might be explained by the Court's attempt to eschew the often-blamed formalistic legal culture and support the new and more creative roles of judges in the region.[69] The third group consists of regional Latin American legal literature, including those Ecuadorian authors, constitutional scholars and theorists. References made to the latter group's work primarily supported the idea of an Ecuadorian version of Andean transformative constitutionalism related to, for instance, the 'rule of rights and justice' (the Ecuadorian understanding of the rule of law), the system of constitutional guarantees and the participative nature of state powers.

The current ECC used only half as many references to scholarly works as its predecessor, and the numbers of scholarly references were reduced to one or two per decision. Furthermore, the character of the referenced sources also changed. The Italian authors who were so prevalent in the first ECC's decisions are less cited than before; their places have been taken by Argentinian and Spanish authors. In the current ECC's selected decisions, there were no references made to eminent legal theorists, such as Hart, Alexy or Dworkin, and Ecuadorean scholars were referenced only rarely. One possible explanation for this could be that the current ECC employed a less pompous and more pragmatic decision-making style in general.

xii. References to Foreign (National) Law

In 14 cases out of 40, the previous ECC invoked foreign law to interpret the Constitution, while this number dropped to 10 in the jurisprudence of the actual ECC.

Looking at the previous ECC's cases, the jurisprudence of the Colombian Constitutional Court was the most cited foreign source.[70] Cases from Argentinian courts were also popular, as were the decisions of the European Court of Human Rights, the Supreme Court of the United States, and the Federal Constitutional Court of Germany. Justification for using foreign jurisprudence, however, was lacking in the first ECC's opinions, and there was seemingly no attempt made to craft a coherent method for choosing certain sources over others. This is anything but a uniquely Ecuadorian characteristic,[71] but in the instance of the first ECC, cherry-picking and the deceptive

[68] See S Pozzolo, 'Un constitucionalismo ambiguo' (2002) *Revista de la Facultad de Derecho de México* 139; P Comanducci, 'Formas de (neo)constitucionalismo: un análisis meta teórico' in M Carbonell (ed), *Neoconstitucionalismo(s)* (Trotta, 2003) cited by Bogdandy et al (n 7) 15–16.

[69] von Bogdandy et al (n 7) 38.

[70] The Constitutional Court of Colombia was quoted about diverse topics, including once on tax regulation. See Decision No. 003-09-SIN-CC.

[71] T Groppi and M Ponthoreau (eds), *The Use of Foreign Precedents by Constitutional Judges* (Hart Publishing, 2014).

use of comparative sources were both prevalent. For example, in the case invoking the 2009 Mining Act, the first ECC chose a decision of the Colombian Constitutional Court as an example of *ultima ratio*,[72] making the argument that the lack of prior consultation was not unconstitutional,[73] instead of another one that opined that the absence of a prior consultation requirement in legislative acts that directly affect indigenous people is unconstitutional.[74]

Like its predecessor, the current ECC's favourite foreign constitutional court was the Colombian Constitutional Court, which was cited at least a dozen times in the selected cases, while other Latin American constitutional courts were referenced only once or twice. The only courts that the current ECC referenced from outside of Latin America were the European Court of Human Rights, the Supreme Court of the United States, and the German Federal Constitutional Court.

xiii. Pro Homine *or* Pro Persona *Principle*

With the dataset of the current ECC, the objective was to measure the dominance of an emerging principle in Latin American constitutional adjudication. According to the *pro homine* principle, formal legal rules and hierarchy should be superseded by a more substantial and open type of legal hierarchy that favours the augmentation of rights and guarantees to expand equality and human rights.[75] The current ECC applied this principle in five of the selected landmark decisions, specifically in cases related to defendants' rights in criminal proceedings and the rights of same-sex couples.

xiv. Other Methods

Regarding the first ECC's practice, arguments classified as 'other' did not fit into another category. There were six cases in which the previous ECC used 'other' argument types, which were mainly relevant to the new Ecuadorian paradigm of constitutionalism. These arguments were usually made to emphasise that law's validity is dependent on the rights and guarantees it envisages – for instance, by claiming that judges' roles have been transformed and are now unrestrained by legal formalism;[76] through the rejection of formal hierarchies among human rights ('legal Darwinism'); or through incorporating all state powers in the Constitution instead of exclusively promoting legal validity.[77]

The current ECC has employed a similar line of argumentation within the framework category of 'other' methods, against formalism and in favour of an 'evolutive'

[72] Decision C-065/97 of the Constitutional Court of Colombia.

[73] Decision of the ECC, No. 001-10-SIN-CC.

[74] Decision C-030/08 of the Constitutional Court of Colombia. See MF Saulino and LJ Torres Asencio, 'The protection of the environment' in JF González-Bertomeu and R Gargarella (ed), *The Latin American Casebook: Courts, Constitutions, and Rights* (Routledge, 2016) 177–81.

[75] See eg Y Negishi, 'The *Pro Homine* Principle's Role in Regulating the Relationship Between Conventionality Control and Constitutionality Control' (2017) 28 *European Journal of International Law* 457; A Peters, 'Supremacy Lost. International Law Meets Domestic Constitutional Law' (2009) 3 *Vienna Online Journal of International Constitutional Law* 170.

[76] Decision of the ECC, No. 302-15-SEP-CC.

[77] Decision of the ECC, No. 002-09-SAN-CC.

interpretation, especially in its opinions on same-sex marriage. Additionally, classic types of logical arguments fit in this category as well, such as *argumentum a contrario* and *argumentum ad absurdum*.

C. The Overall Weight of the Arguments

No evidence exists in any of the ECC's decisions of attempts to build a coherent doctrine about the justification or prioritisation of methods and arguments. Both judicial panels of the ECC were silent about the relative weight of the arguments they used; however, it was the first ECC that seemingly invoked arguments in a rather deceptive way by mentioning, but not applying arguments that resulted in vagueness surrounding the propositions and overall conclusions of the decisions. Although decorative and rhetorical arguments are part of the tool kits of all constitutional courts, their quantity and nature[78] are worth analysing in more depth.

The indicator of overall weight shows that the first ECC was ambiguous relative to the arguments that led to final decisions about constitutionality. Ten times out of 35 (the rest of the cases were not relevant), the first ECC simply recalled the facts of the case, noted the mistakes of the lower courts, and stated that the rules were incompliant – rather than providing justifiable reasons. In another nine cases, the first ECC relied on arguments about the procedural aspects of the case without addressing the substantive issues.[79] In the rest of the cases, the methodologies that led most frequently to the Court's conclusions were precedent-based arguments (six times), while it used non-legal arguments in five cases. Teleological, scholarly, and international harmonising arguments served as conclusive arguments in three decisions.

The current ECC employed more coherent arguments, which revealed their levels of importance. In most of the selected cases (37 times out of 40), the current ECC made a clear, textually perceivable connection between its arguments and the conclusions it reached. Still, in several cases, the Court seemed to continue the pattern of its predecessor, using ordinary legal (instead of constitutional) arguments to support conclusions on constitutionality. It occurred only in three cases, that the number of arguments with clear weight and the ones that were only decorative or deceptive were around the same.

D. Judicial Candour and Judicial Rhetoric

The format and structure of the decisions followed the same design in both periods of the ECC. First, the Court provided a summary of the petitions and arguments of state

[78] IM Copi and C Cohen, *Introducción a la Lógica*, 2nd edn (Limusa, 2013) 7; M Bencze and GY Ng (eds), *How to Measure the Quality of Judicial Reasoning* (Springer, 2019) 91–96, 97.

[79] For instance, in an environmental law case about business activity in a mangrove on indigenous territory. Decision of the ECC, No. 065-15-SEP-CC.

authorities and other third parties, which was followed by the legal-constitutional questions arising from the facts. The first ECC usually dedicated many pages to procedural issues, using language that was diffuse and pedantic, and that lacked clear or logical connections among the propositions. Another common feature of the ECC in both of its configurations was the lack of discussing counterarguments in the judgments; only in dissenting opinions were there some inferences to the critical points of the majority decisions.

In terms of a target audience, the previous ECC's was primarily politicians, and in certain cases that were not too politically sensitive, the first ECC crafted its decisions for a narrow group of scholars and activists. The transformation of the profiles of the ECC judges, however, triggered a change in the Court's target audience, which now consists of activist groups, civil society, and to a certain degree, the academic community. What this means in terms of judicial candour and rhetoric is reflected in the attempt of the ECC's progressive majority to speak plainly and in a succinct manner for pedagogical reasons and to also establish a cordial relationship with the complainants.

E. Length, Dissenting and Concurring Opinions

The switch in the ECC's target audience, as well as in the profiles of the judges, also led to a change in the style and length of the Court's decisions. The length of the selected landmark cases of the first ECC ranged from a low of five pages, to a high of 117 pages (separate opinions included), with an average of 31 pages. The three longest decisions (78, 116 and 117 pages) were all cases where the first ECC rejected complaints involving overly sensitive issues, such as indigenous justice and income tax rates. These lengthy decisions could be due to the inclusion of separate opinions and the overall high pressure to justify the dismissal of cases. In contrast, the average length of the current ECC's selected decisions was only 16.5 pages. The shortest decision from that group was four pages long (involving the double taxation treaty between Ecuador and Japan), and the two longest decisions (50 and 87 pages) were those addressing the constitutionality of civil marriages between same-sex couples.

The practice of releasing separate opinions was remarkably similar in both Court's historical periods. During the period of the first ECC, there were four dissenting opinions and three concurring among the 40 landmark decisions, while the current ECC produced three dissenting and one concurring opinion during its first year. The small number of dissenting opinions could be explained in several ways. First, following the internal rules of procedure, ECC judges can vote against a decision only if they file a dissent or a concurrence. Additional obstacles to submitting these types of opinions are short deadlines and the now former requirement to reproduce the complete structure of the full sentence as if it were a majority decision. The current ECC abolished the latter requirement, so now dissenting judges need only concentrate on those aspects that are about the actual disagreement; however, the conditions for dissenting votes and the ungenerous three-day long deadline to issue a separate opinion presents challenges that still seem rather insurmountable.

Furthermore, voting against the majority opinion or expressing discordant reasons publicly might encourage the use of procedural loopholes. One such loophole is that, since there is no formal obligation in the ECC's rules for judges to vote, they can simply refrain from being present for a voting session or leave the session before the vote is called. Second, the exchange and open confrontation of different views involving a mutual respect of disagreement is uncommon in academic discourse in Ecuador. Difference of opinion, even in academia, is seen as a personally or politically motivated attack rather than an opportunity for mutual growth. To avoid an appearance of weakness or division, the current ECC judges try to exhibit an image of unanimity even if there are deep ideologic fractures among them.

F. Framing Constitutional Issues

The prevalent topic among the selected cases of the first ECC was procedural rights (in 21 cases). In the remaining 19 opinions, the main general topic was fundamental rights, which indicates that the first ECC did not hear any cases on interbranch issues – that is, those cases that deal with the structural relationships among the different state powers. The current ECC, however, had a more balanced docket in terms of the general subject matter of its landmark cases. Fifteen were dedicated to rights matters, 10 to interbranch controversies, 18 to procedural rights issues, and in some cases, rights matters were combined with structural controversies. However, the number of cases involving procedural rights was still relatively high, and the current ECC has seemingly taken a stronger position on issues related to clashes of state powers.

G. Key Concepts

In the instance of the first ECC, basic procedural rights and equality were the key concepts of its constitutional reasoning practice. The former appeared in 17 cases, while the concept of equality was prevalent in 10. Freedom of expression and privacy rights appeared once; controversies involving democratic principles were addressed twice; proportionality was an issue in three cases; and human dignity and the concept of nation were at issue four times each. Other concepts, like sovereignty, state and government form, secularism and federalism were practically invisible in the previous ECC's jurisprudence. In contrast, the first year of the actual ECC revealed a quite different landscape in terms of its treatment of key concepts. Although references to the rule of law dropped by half (from 14 to seven, out of 40), its treatment of the concepts of democracy and proportionality increased substantially (from two to 11, and from three to 10, respectively). Basic procedural rights were apparently still the leading general topic among the current ECC's cases (18 out of 40), although it is no longer the leading concept used in argumentation (in six cases). Furthermore, the Court's reliance on new concepts (in nine cases) appears to be on the rise, as is the use of various post-material values (in eight cases), such as references to indigenous terms, peace, ancient knowledge, and biodiversity.

III. Comparative Perspective

However, the two periods of the ECC share distinct features in some important respects, the ECC in general seems to follow the regional trend of using less classical, text-based methods and more creative methods. In comparison with other countries from the region, in both periods the argumentative diversity and conceptual diversity of the ECC is low, which is especially true about the second ECC for the reasons mentioned above. In this aspect, ie, regarding how many different methods of interpretation and concepts a court employs in its decisions, the ECC looks more like Paraguay and Guatemala, the Caribbean Commonwealth or Uruguay then its regional counterparts.

However, when we look at the type of methods and concepts the ECC refers to, the similarity with other courts in the Andean region becomes clear. The first ECC seemed to exhibit characteristics that are like those of the Bolivian Plurinational Constitutional Court, where teleological and precedential arguments are highly influential, and the applications of international law and non-legal arguments are likewise dominant. In terms of key concepts, the Bolivian court also frequently relies on rule of law and procedural rights arguments in decorative or deceptive ways. On the other hand, the current ECC seems to share the argumentative preferences of the Mexican, Colombian and Costa Rican constitutional courts, particularly because they all exhibit a waning interest in using textual arguments, and because they share a proliferating interest in weaving contemporary legal concepts and international law sources into the national constitutional jurisprudence.

IV. Evaluation, Pathology and Criticism

The fact that we have two datasets about the two periods of the ECC, allows us to differentiate between features of the ECC's reasoning that run deeply within the Ecuadorean constitutional culture and were displayed by the ECC in both analysed periods, and those that seem to be less static and might be the result of the judges' educational backgrounds, ideologies, or independence. Starting with the characteristics that are not engraved in the genetic code of Ecuadorean constitutional traditions, the attitude towards governmental power is relevant. Serious doubts about the independence of the first ECC affected its caseload and efficiency, as well as constitutional doctrines and everyday legal practice. The current ECC tries to differentiate itself from its predecessor's jurisprudence (*see*, for example, a specific opinion involving the state's fundamental rights). The constitutional jurisprudence of the current ECC reflects higher levels of professional and academic standards than those of the first ECC – through more coherent and straightforward language and its hospitable tone with petitioners.

Furthermore, the new ECC takes a more vehement posture on the protection of rights, which consequently implicates or results in more activist decision-making, a greater influence of international law and legal concepts, and – perhaps as a result – a sharper divide between the classic approach and the evolutive or creative approach of constitutional reasoning. Activism was only expressly mentioned in the decisions on same-sex marriage, but just like several other issues, it is implicitly present in almost all ideologically sensitive cases, such as those involving economic rights. These, and similarly sensitive issues, are intertwined with a new cosmopolitan feature in the reasoning of the current ECC, which is most visible in the dominance of international law over national law, and the expanded use of legal concepts and non-legal arguments.

Those features that seem to be more independent from the composition of the ECC are related to the general constitutional culture. Principally, we can find the overall aversion to using arguments grounded in the text of the Constitution. Although the Ecuadorian Constitution includes rules on constitutional interpretation including a reference to the textual approach, there is no evidence that the judiciary has applied it coherently or developed an alternative theory relative for constitutional adjudication. The ECC from both periods – for quite different reasons – refrained from formulating arguments based explicitly on the constitutional text and instead chose methods of interpretation on an ad hoc basis, without applying pre-existing standards. As a result of the tensions that this longstanding pattern triggered, the gap between the classic and creative legal approaches has become larger.

In the Ecuadorian legal culture, high aspirations are often bonded together with the rejection of legal formalism and distrust in the rule of law. Failures of the legal and political system are blamed on 'law' and the bitter experience of simply recalling its text against substantial justice claims throughout Ecuador's history. The current ECC has continued to lean towards adopting transformative Andean constitutionalism, and it is seemingly filling the empty space left behind by a constitution doomed for disharmony with the norms of international law.

The ECC, with its accompanying constitutional powers, has become one of the most precious fruits of Ecuador's new constitutional system. It embodies several legitimate pledges to provide a more effective and just package of rights and guarantees, trying remedy a centuries-long pattern of abuses of power and violations of human rights. However, these aspirations can only be achieved with a prudent and coherent reliance on the constitution's authority and an appeal for a judicial dialogue where national courts are not only followers of foreign decisions and tendencies but are active and equal peers in a relationship based on mutual respect for the constitutional system each country represents.

11

The Jurisprudence of the Constitutional Court of Guatemala

CARLOS ARTURO VILLAGRÁN SANDOVAL*

The legal reasoning of the *Corte de Constitucionalidad de Guatemala* (Guatemalan Constitutional Court, GCC) has evolved over its lifespan, as the Court adapts its methods of reasoning to different political contexts. This chapter demonstrates how the court has changed its method of reasoning over three very distinctive periods of time. Despite the changes, however, the analysis also shows that some traits of constitutional reasoning are constant. Chief amongst them is the Court's preference for indeterminacy and vagueness, which has helped the GCC to become a prominent player in Guatemalan politics, but which also justifies the need to read between the lines of the GCC's abstract approach to constitutional reasoning.

I. Legal, Political, Institutional and Academic Context

A. Legal and Political Culture as Context for the Constitutional Reasoning

The current Constitution of Guatemala was made in 1985, following almost 40 years of devastating civil war (1960 to 1996) that involved gross human rights violations and genocide. Reflecting the desire to mark a clear break with the past and the social injustices that fuelled the conflict, the Constitution gave prominence to human rights with a strong inclination to social justice.[1] It created a series of complex procedures and new institutions, including a Human Rights Ombudsman and the GCC itself, to

* I give thanks to Anna Dziedzic, Juan Pablo Gramajo and Edgar Ortiz for their peer review, providing me with invaluable comments and editing assistance in the development of this chapter.

[1] E Ulate, *Del Patrimonio Constitucional Centroamericano al Derecho Constitucional Centroamericano: Estudios de Derecho Comparado* (ISOLMA S.A., 2015) 26.

effectively limit public power.[2] In this, the 1986 Constitution sought to promote a new image of Guatemala to the world[3] and to the region.

This Constitution was the first in the region to explicitly recognise international human rights instruments as a superior source of law over domestic law, including the Constitution itself.[4] The meaning and effect of this provision has been heavily debated by various benches of the GCCs, as will be discussed later in the chapter. Even though the new Constitution introduced a new discourse of human rights, much of the state apparatus and institutions stayed the same.[5] As such, under this Constitution, Guatemala still has a tendency to hyper-presidentialism, in which Presidents have a strong oversight and overriding role in governance, including in the creation, development and implementation of norms.[6] Therefore, Guatemala is categorised as a hybrid regime of governance.[7] In this hybrid regime, Congress is portrayed as a weak player. Congress is usually dominated by the executive or private interests. This is due to Guatemala's weak representation schemes, enabled by the electoral laws. In addition, Guatemalan laws allow private actors to participate in many public decision-making arrangements.[8] Private interests (such as strong economic chambers), consequently have a direct voice in the formulation of labour, monetary and tax policies.[9]

Although the Constitution includes various open-ended clauses recognising a plurality of human rights sources – particularly international human rights instruments – it still reflects conservative values.[10] There are provisions that recognise the place of the family and marriage, as traditionally conceived, at the centre of Guatemalan society. The Constitution also states that life begins at conception.[11]

During the 1990s, along with the rest of Latin America, Guatemala entered a period of liberalisation and privatisation.[12] Yet, the newly adopted development model did not bring relief to the rising inequality and discrimination.[13] Guatemala has the

[2] Art 274, Constitution of Guatemala.

[3] B Loveman, *The Constitution of Tyranny. Regimes of Exception in Spanish America* (University of Pittsburgh Press, 1993) 91–136.

[4] Art 46, Constitution of Guatemala.

[5] R Gargarella, *Latin-American Constitutionalism 1810–2010: The Engine Room of the Constitution* (Oxford University Press, 2013).

[6] MC Mirow, *Latin American Constitutions: The Constitution of Cádiz and Its Legacy in Spanish America* (Cambridge University Press, 2015) 230–37.

[7] T Karl, 'The Hybrid Regimes of Central America' (1995) 6 *Journal of Democracy* 72.

[8] R Brett and A Delgado, 'The Role of Constitution-Building Processes in Democratization: Case Study Guatemala' (2005) *International Institute for Democracy and Electoral Assistance. Democracy-Building & Conflict Management* 11.

[9] SM Puig and D Sánchez-Ancochea, 'Central America's Triple Transition and the Persistent Power of the Elite' in SM Puig and D Sánchez-Ancochea (eds), *Handbook of Central American Governance* (Routledge, 2014) 5.

[10] Art 44, Constitution of Guatemala.

[11] Arts 1, 3 and 47, Constitution of Guatemala.

[12] A Schneider, 'The Great Transformation in Central America. Transnational Accumulation and the Evolution of Capital' in D Sánchez-Ancochea and SM Puig (eds), *Handbook of Central American Governance* (Routledge, 2014) 29.

[13] R Sieder (eds), *Cultures of Legality. Judicialization and Political Activism in Latin America* (Cambridge University Press, 2010) 165.

highest poverty and malnutrition rates in the Latin American region,[14] particularly among its indigenous peoples.[15] Therefore, and as noted by the UN Human Rights High Commissioner, Guatemala still exhibits the same conditions of inequality and discrimination that led the country to enter into civil conflict in 1956.[16]

i. The Foundational Period of the GCC's History (1986–1995)

Following the creation of a new Constitution and a new constitutional court in 1986, the GCC faced a situation where it needed to assume a role in Guatemala's transition from military authoritarianism to democracy. This first court was composed of reputed scholars and legal professionals. The legitimacy of the GCC derived from the fact that its judges were considered the finest legal professionals. Consequently, little emphasis was placed on the reasoning of the court in this period, since legitimacy was linked to the prestige of the judges.

The GCC firmly established its role as a prominent player in Guatemalan politics through a case in which it determined the legality of Guatemala's 1993 self-coup.[17] In this case, the GCC acted for the first, and only, time *propio motu*, or without petition by an individual or state actor.[18] In a comparatively short judgment of four pages, the GCC reiterated the supremacy of the Constitution and the role of the Court to defend it.[19] With the support of the public and the army, this judgment was made effective and the president, who led the self-coup and attempted to abolish congress and the courts, fled the country.[20] This judgment consolidated the GCC as a new political player. As explained by Edgar Ortiz, it represented an indicative moment of the transition from military power to civilian rule.[21]

During this period, the GCC also resolved matters relating to the judicial review of laws that were made prior to the promulgation of the new Constitution,[22] the intervention of the executive to the Red Cross in Guatemala[23] and the recognition of

[14] United Nations Development Programme, Human Development Report, Table 3: Inequality-Adjusted Human Development Index hdr.undp.org/en/composite/IHDI.

[15] MR Morales, *Breve Historia Intercultural de Guatemala* (Editorial Cultura, 2014) 111–13.

[16] Comisión Interamericana de Derechos Humanos, Observaciones Preliminares de la Visita in loco de la CIDH en Guatemala, 4 August 2017, at www.oas.org/es/cidh/prensa/comunicados/2017/114a.asp. United Nations Human Rights, Office of the High Commissioner, Statement by UN High Commissioner for Human Rights Zeid Ra'ad Al Hussein at the end of his mission to Guatemala, 19 November 2017, at www.ohchr.org/en/statements/2017/11/statement-un-high-commissioner-human-rights-zeid-raad-al-hussein-end-his-0?LangID=E&NewsID=22415.

[17] E Ortiz, 'Corte de Constitucionalidad: ¿árbitro de última instancia del juego político?' La ruptura con el legalismo in CA Villagrán Sandoval (ed), *Constitucionalismo Guatemalteco frente a lo Global: Estudios de una nueva generación de voces* (Cara Parens, 2020) 48.

[18] R Rohrmoser, 'De cómo viví el Serranazo' (2018) XV *Opus Magna Constitucional.*

[19] Corte de Constitucionalidad, *Coup d'Etat Case*, Inconstitucionalidad General, Expediente 225-93, 25 May 1993.

[20] E Martínez, 'Central American (High) Courts' in D Sánchez-Ancochea and SM Puig (eds), *Handbook of Central American Governance* (Routledge, 2014) 173.

[21] Ortiz (n 17) 48.

[22] Corte de Constitucionalidad, *Correction of Constitutional Jurisdiction Procedures Case*, Inconstitucionalidad de Leyes, Reglamentos y Disposiciones de Carácter General, Expediente 12-86, 17 September 1986.

[23] Corte de Constitucionalidad, *Legality of intervention on Red Cross case*, Amparo en única Instancia, Expediente 93-89, 28 July 1989.

independence of Belize.[24] As will be explained in the next section, it laid down the type of functional and reductionist reasoning in the use of foreign sources, such as international human rights and transnational principles, that would influence later generations of the Court.[25]

Another important case decided in this period related to a former *coup d'etat* President, Efrain Rios Mont. Rios Mont was a general who came into power via a coup. (He was tried in 2011 for genocide committed in the Guatemalan civil war, but his conviction was overturned on procedural grounds in 2013.[26]) In 1990, Rios Mont launched a new bid for election to the Presidency, disregarding the constitutional prohibition on anyone who came to power via a rebellion or constitutional disruption from later standing for election.[27] The GCC reviewed the legality of the constitutional prohibition contained in the new constitution and denied Rios Mont in his bid to run for president, upholding the constitutional prohibition.[28]

This case, and others decided during this time, show that during this foundational period the GCC looked to establish a new understanding of constitutionalism and reinforce its role in upholding it. In this period, the court asserted its powers by setting limits on public power, particularly on the executive and congress, and detailing the function of the constitution.[29]

ii. The Legalist Period (1995–2011)

After the 1993 self-coup attempt, the Guatemalan Constitution was reformed to settle more defined limits on the powers of the Executive, Congress and the judiciary.[30] During this period, Guatemala was transiting through a new economic reform. This reform was embedded in the neoliberal model, which implemented strong privatisation and liberalisation policies and laws.[31] This reform period coincided with the election of a new GCC, which showed much deference to this new neoliberal agenda and was reflective of a new conservative pushback in Guatemala. This conservative pushback was a reaction to the signing of the 1994 peace accords. These reforms were ultimately rejected by the population at a referendum in 1999 due to lack of support of the president, strong public opposition from economic groups and an overly complicated question being put to the population, being still mostly illiterate.[32] The GCC's new conservative approach was first seen in the *ILO 169 Opinion*. In this case, although

[24] Corte de Constitucionalidad, *Belice Recognition Case*, Inconstitucionalidad General, Expediente 290-91 y 292-91, 3 November 1992.

[25] CA Villagrán and AE Garcia, 'De métodos, proporcionalidad y las reformas a la Ley de ONG' (2020) 7 *Pensamiento Jurídico* 20–22. See also Corte de Constitucionalidad, Expediente 96-86, dictamen, resolución de 25 de noviembre de 1986.

[26] CA Villagran Sandoval and S Larios, 'Guatemala' in R Albert et al (eds), *Global Review of Constitutional Law* (I•CONnect and the Clough Center, 2018) 128.

[27] Art 186(a), Constitution of Guatemala.

[28] Corte de Constitucionalidad, *Rios Mont I Case*, Apelación de Sentencia de Amparo, Expediente 280-90, 19 October 1990.

[29] Art 268, Constitution of Guatemala.

[30] EJ Dabrov, *Informe Final: Reformas Constitucionales de 1993 y cambios en el diseño institucional del Estado Guatemalteco* (Universidad de San Carlos de Guatemala, 8 January 2016).

[31] Schneider (n 12) 29.

[32] Sieder (n 13) 165.

the court recognised the human rights character of the 169 ILO Convention, it nevertheless pronounced that it cannot be used as a standard for the review of domestic statutes and laws. In other words, it made it non-justiciable in Guatemala.

In this second period, the GCC can be described as legalist and deferential, in that it took a positivist and formalist approach to constitutional cases and attempted to separate law from politics and morals.[33] In this period, the selection of judges became politicised. As a result, the legitimacy of the GCC derived from the prestige of its members was compromised for the sake of implementation of the government's agendas.[34]

During this period the court would often dismiss cases on procedural grounds. An example is the *Hague Ratification Case*.[35] In this case, the court made clear its idea of legalism by stating that 'interpreting norms' – including the Constitution – must be done 'in accordance to their text'. In this case, the Court rejected the accession of Guatemala to the *Hague Convention* on the grounds that Guatemala cannot 'adhere' – *adherir* – to international instruments.[36] As the Court interpreted, the Constitution of Guatemala does not explicitly mention the word 'adhere' as a faculty of the President to ratify international treaties.[37]

This period coincided with a wider conservative backlash introduction of a liberalisation and privatisation movement in Guatemala. The GCC can be observed also pushing this liberalisation agenda. An example of this is the *Honduras Border Closure Case*.[38] In this case the GCC resolved in favour of major economic chambers who preferred to keep the border open for economic purposes during the 2009 coup against Zelaya in Honduras, disregarding Central American treaties and calls from international organisations to close the border.

During this time, the GCC also limited the application of international law. In various opinions, the GCC held that, although international human rights instruments had a superior status to domestic laws, this did not mean that these instruments were to be interpreted as standards for revising the constitutionality of laws and statutes.[39] A prime example where this trait is observed is when the court refused to recognise the self-executing character of the Inter American Court of Human Rights' (IACtHR) judgments.[40] The GCC, using a legalist approach, explained that to give effect to judgments of IACtHR, particularly those which sought as reparation the reopening of criminal cases against military commanders accused of gross violations of human rights,

[33] J Shklar, *Legalism* (Harvard University Press, 1964) 1–10.

[34] See Ortiz (n 17) 49–52.

[35] Corte de Constitucionalidad, *Case The Hague Convention Ratificacion*, Inconstitucionalidad General Total, Expedientes Acumulados 1555-02 y 1808-02, 13 August 2003.

[36] ibid.

[37] ibid.

[38] Corte de Constitucionalidad, *Honduras Border Closure Case*, Amparo en Única Instancia, Expedientes Acumulados 2420-2009 y 2474-2009, 26 November 2010.

[39] CA Villagrán, 'Una reflexión sobre el «dualismo dentro del dualismo» en la interacción del derecho internacional con el doméstico en Guatemala' in JI Acosta López et al (eds), *De Anacronismo y Vaticinios. Diagnóstico sobre las relaciones entre el derecho internacional y el derecho interno en Latinoamérica* (Universidad del Externado de Colombia, 2017).

[40] CA Villagrán and FF Carvalho 'A Human Rights' Tale of Competing Narratives' (2017) 8 *Direito & Praxis: Perspectivas Críticas do Sistema Interamericano de Direitos Humanos*, 1603.

would violate universal rights such as the prohibition of double jeopardy.[41] This court went even further to declare international instruments, such as the Treaty Constituting the Central America Parliament, unconstitutional in order to release from immunity a former vice-president accused of corruption.[42]

During this period, the GCC reviewed again the constitutional prohibition that prevented Rios Mont from standing for election.[43] However, on this occasion, the Court ruled that the Constitution was not retroactive and therefore could not limit the right for election in relation to acts that happened before the 1986 Constitution was in place. This allowed Rios Mont to run for the presidency. Interestingly, years later this same court reviewed this judgment in a first 'annulment procedure'.[44] It found that, although it could not annul a previous judgment, because it is not in law, it could declare it that it had no effect on precedent.

At the end of this period, and due to mounting international pressure and the influence of human rights groups, the GCC started to introduce human rights discourse into its judgments. At this time, the GCC recognised concepts as *jus cogens*[45] and described the *pro homine* character of the constitution.[46] This coincided with a new wave of judgments against Guatemala by the IACHR, concerning violations of human rights by the state and military during the conflict years.[47] This paved the way for the third, cosmopolitan phase.

iii. The Cosmopolitan Period (2011–present)

The final period of the GCC is the cosmopolitan phase. This period coincides with the election of a new court in 2011 under a left-wing presidency and congress. During this period, a new human rights discourse emerged in Guatemala, partially in response to the series of judgments by the IACHR against the country.

This third period of the GCC is marked by the move from legalist to cosmopolitan approaches to constitutional reasoning. The Court's approach changed from a positivist and formalist mindset to a progressive and anti-formalist mindset. This is observed clearly in the *Judicial Appointments case*. In this case the court clearly sidelines formalistic standing issues raised against the applicants in the case, reversing previous case law.[48]

[41] Corte de Constitucionalidad, Limitation self-execution IACtHR judgments, Amparo en Única Instancia, Expediente 548-2010, 25 August 2010 and Corte de Constitucionalidad, Limitation self-execution IACrHR judgments II, Amparo en Única Instancia, Expediente 386-2011, 13 April 2011.

[42] Corte de Constitucionalidad, *PARLACEN case*, Expedientes Acumulados 12-2004 y 213-2004, 20 July 2004.

[43] Corte de Constitucionalidad, *Rios Mont II Case*, Expediente 1089-2003, Apelación de Sentencia de Amparo, 14 July 2003.

[44] Corte de Constitucionalidad, *Rios Mont Judgment Annulment Case*, Expediente 2395-2006, Solicitud de Anulación, 10 October 2006.

[45] Corte de Constitucionalidad, *Jus cogens recognition case*, Expediente 30-2000, Amparo en única Instancia, 30 October 2000.

[46] Corte de Constitucionalidad, *Pro Homine recognition Case*, Inconstitucionalidad General, Expediente 890-2001, 9 December 2002.

[47] See cases at the Interamerican Court against Guatemala, Myrna Mack, Molina Theissen, Rio Negro and other cases.

[48] Corte de Constitucionalidad, *Judicial Appointments case*, Amparo en Única Instancia, Expedientes Acumulados 4639-2014, 4645-2014, 4646-2014 y 4647-2014, 19 November 2014, 79–80.

The judges of this period were also elected under very politicised scenarios. Perhaps because of this, the GCC, as will be shown in the next section, has resorted to drafting more complex judgments. This has included the use of foreign and international sources as a means to legitimise its decisions and decision-making process. From this moment onwards, and seen through the case law, human rights became the language by which disputes were settled and foreign citation the means of supporting the Court's decisions.

This epoch of the GCC was inaugurated by the recognition of both the Constitutional Block (*bloque de constitucionalidad*)[49] and the Conventionality Control (*control de convencionalidad*).[50] Since then, the Court has decided matters relating to social and economic rights (first seen in the *HIV medication case*[51]), the abolition of the death penalty[52] and the promotion of education in indigenous languages.[53] In addition, the GCC has allowed third parties, not directly affected by government action, to bring suits against it.[54]

However, in politically sensitive cases, such as deciding whether Rios Mont's daughter, Zury Rios, was prohibited from being a candidate for presidential election, this GCC resolved issues in an originalist and formalist fashion.[55] It upheld the prohibition, deciding that, from a historical perspective, the prohibition is an exception to the right to stand for election enshrined in the American Convention on Human Rights.

The recognition of the constitutional block was a significant step in the development of Guatemalan law.[56] It opened Guatemalan laws and state action, or inaction, to review under international law, particularly international human rights treaties. In addition, during this period the Court transplanted principles developed in other jurisprudence, such as proportionality, into Guatemala.[57] Yet, it still maintained a conservative approach in politically sensitive cases, such as the *Genocide Recognition Failure Case*.[58] In this case the GCC did not want to sacrifice its political position and decided to annul the genocide conviction of Rios Mont on procedural grounds.

[49] Corte de Constitucionalidad, *Constitutional Block recognition*, Inconstitucionalidad General Parcial por Omisión, Expediente 1822-2011, 17 July 2012.

[50] Corte de Constitucionalidad, *Recognition Conventionality Control*, Expediente 2151-2011, Apelación de Sentencia de Amparo, 23 August 2011.

[51] Corte de Constitucionalidad, *HIV –Economic and Social Rights- Case*, Apelación de Sentencia de Amparo, Expediente 2846-2012, 18 September 2012.

[52] Corte de Constitucionalidad, *Death Penalty Abolishment Case*, Inconstitucionalidad General, Expediente 5986-2016, 24 October 2017.

[53] Corte de Constitucionalidad, *Education in Native Language Case*, Apelación de Sentencia de Amparo, Expedientes Acumulados 4783-2013, 4812-2013, 4813-2013, 6 June 2016.

[54] See eg Corte de Constitucionalidad, *CICIG Visa case*, Apelación de Sentencia de Amparo, Expediente 5443-2018, 21 December 2018.

[55] Corte de Constitucionalidad, *Zury Rios case*, Expediente 1584-2019, Apelación de Sentencia de Amparo, 13 May 2019.

[56] C Villagrán, 'Una reflexión crítica de la reserva guatemalteca al artículo 27 de la Convención de Viena de 1969 ante un Nuevo Paradigma de Constitucionalismo Global' (2017) 13 *Opus Magna Constitucional* 297.

[57] Corte de Constitucionalidad, *Recognition of Proportionality of Laws case*, Inconstitucionalidad General Parcial, Expediente 2729-2011, 14 August 2012.

[58] Corte de Constitucionalidad, *Genocide Recognition Failure Case*, Inconstitucionalidad General Parcial, Expediente 4371-2011, 9 October 2012.

However, this GCC has received plenty of backlash from some conservative groups. Consequently, some of its precedents have been modified to answer to some of the conservative concerns. This is observed in the court's attempt to limit the application of the constitutional block.[59] Other cases in which the GCC upheld conservative positions include the declaration of illegality of surrogacy in Guatemala[60] and the limitations on the recognition of indigenous rights in intellectual property cases.[61]

Last, the GCC has recently resorted to a practice of not deciding cases where the political cost is high.[62] For example, the court did not decide cases on matters related to the government's expulsion of the International Commission Against Corruption in Guatemala (CICIG), the transfer of the Guatemalan embassy in Israel from Tel Aviv to Jerusalem, or the legality of the Third-Country Agreement between Guatemala and the United States.[63]

B. The Court and Constitutional Litigation

The GCC was created by the new Constitution of 1985. It was not the first constitutional court in Guatemala. In 1965, Guatemala established its first GCC, which was also the first of its kind in the region.[64] Unlike the current Court, this first constitutional court was modelled after the French *Counseil Constitutionnel*.[65]

In contrast to the first constitutional court, the current GCC is influenced by the models of constitutional review originating in Austria and the United States.[66] It not only reviews the constitutionality of statutes post-enactment, but also abuse of power, via action or inaction.[67] The GCC has come to recognise as a violation of the Constitution the inaction of state institutions, such as Congress, when it fails to regulate in certain matters. This is observed most recently in cases where the GCC has reviewed Congress' failure to regulate international obligations ratified by the Guatemalan state, such as the ILO 169 Convention, or to change laws when new international instruments have been ratified.[68]

[59] Corte de Constitucionalidad, *Expansion Content of Constitutional Block*, Inconstitucionalidad General, Expediente 3438-2016, 8 November 2016.

[60] Corte de Constitucionalidad, *Prohibition Surogacy by Constitutional Court*, Apelación de Sentencia de Amparo, Expediente 3590-2016, 20 July 2017.

[61] Corte de Constitucionalidad, *Recognition of Indigenous IP case*, Expediente 2906-2017, Apelación Sentencia de Amparo, 21 September 2017.

[62] Human Rights Watch, 'Running Out the Clock. How Guatemala's Courts Could Doom the Fights Against Impunity' (Human Rights Watch, 2017) 11–12.

[63] See CA Villagrán, *Fighting the Good Fight: Litigating Foreign Relations, International Law and Corruption at the Constitutional Level in Guatemala*. IACL-AIDC Blog, 2019, at blog-iacl-aidc.org/2019-posts/2019/2/15/fighting-the-good-fight-litigating-foreign-relationsinternational-law-and-corruption-at-the-constitutional-level-in-guatemala.

[64] A González, La Corte de Constitucionalidad de Guatemala, archivos.juridicas.unam.mx/www/bjv/libros/1/219/3.pdf, p 20.

[65] J García, *Breve historia constitucional de Guatemala* (Editorial Universitaria, 2010).

[66] R Sanchez-Urribarri, 'Between power and submissiveness: constitutional adjudication in Latin America' in R Dixon and T Ginsburg, *Comparative Constitutional Law in Latin America* (Edward Elgar, 2017) 279.

[67] See *Recognition of Constitutional Block Case*, Corte de Constitucionalidad, Expediente 1822-2011, Sentencia 20 May 2020.

[68] Corte de Constitucionalidad, *Recognition Structural Judgments Doctrine case*, Apelación de Sentencia de Amparo, Expedientes Acumulados 90-2017, 91-2017 y 92-2017, 26 May 2017.

According to the statute regulating the jurisdiction of the GCC, *Ley de Amparo, Exhibicion Personal y Constitutionalidad* (GCC Statute),[69] individuals can access the court through three processes: constitutional injunction (amparo) either directly or on appeal from another court,[70] judicial review of laws (*inconstitucionalidad de caracter general*),[71] and judicial review of laws for individual cases (*inconstitucionalidad en caso en concreto*).[72] The GCC also has an advisory jurisdiction. It may deliver opinions on the constitutionality of laws,[73] and it is *obligated* to do so in cases where Congress decides to overrule a presidential veto of a bill.[74]

Each process has a special writ, and each writ needs to fulfil certain requirements.[75] In addition, the statute only allows those directly affected by public action or inaction to bring suits to the court.[76] This excludes class actions and third parties from bringing actions where they are not directly affected. However, there are recent signs the GCC has relaxed this rule, extending access to the court.[77] Last, the GCC has the capacity to present initiatives to reform the Guatemalan Constitution.[78] However, the court has never presented an initiative during its history.[79]

The majority of suits entertained by the court are amparo. The GCC Statute provides that the amparo is instituted for the purpose of protecting persons against the threats of violations of their rights or to restore the rule of the same when the violation has occurred. It proceeds whenever the acts, resolutions, provisions, or laws of an authority should imply a threat, restraint, or violation of the rights which the Constitution and the laws guarantee.[80]

The GCC Statute obliges the GCC to interpret the statute expansively, meaning to interpret it in a manner that enables the full protection of human rights, the efficient working of the constitutional procedures and the defence of the constitutional order.[81] This makes it very difficult for the GCC to reject a suit brought by an individual. However, during the legalist period the court became very stringent on formalities and restricted access by interpreting formal requirements in a very legalist fashion.[82] In contrast, most of these formalities were waived during the cosmopolitan era, allowing petitioners to claim reparations for violations in a less stringent manner.

The judicial review of laws has been an important tool for the introduction of new doctrines and transnational principles in Guatemalan law. Most recently, judicial review

[69] Decreto 1-86, Ley de Amparo, Exhibición Personal y de Constitucionalidad, 1986.
[70] Art 60, GCC Statute.
[71] Art 133, GCC Statute.
[72] Art 116, GCC Statute.
[73] Art 163 (e), GCC Statute.
[74] Art 163 (h), GCC Statute. However, there are conflicting opinions about the GCC's capacity to act in such manner, see: Corte de Constitucionalidad, Expediente 3003-2010, Opinion Consultiva, 21 December 2010, 2.
[75] Art 21, GCC Statute.
[76] Corte de Constitucionalidad, *Actio Popular in certain circumstances case*, Amparo en Única Instancia, Expediente 461-2014, 7 March 2014.
[77] Corte de Constitucionalidad, *CICIG Visa case*, Apelación de Sentencia de Amparo, Expediente 5443-2018, 21 December 2018.
[78] Art 277, Constitution of Guatemala.
[79] Corte de Constitucionalidad, *Judicial Appointments case*, Expedientes Acumulados 4639-2014, 4645-2014, 4646-2014 y 4647-2014, 19 November 2014, 102–103.
[80] Art 265, Constitution of Guatemala.
[81] Art 2, GCC Statute.
[82] See the selected cases between 1995 and 2011.

of laws has led to the introduction of new remedies, particularly for the inaction of Congress.[83] However, on the topic of remedies, the GCC is limited.[84] Although it has the power to declare a constitutional violation by action or inaction of a state institution or official, the Court does not have a supervisory function. It is left to the individual seeking the remedy to oversee the execution of the judgment.[85] Most recently (and a first) the GCC ordered Congress to inform it why it had not complied with the inclusion of international standards into statute in its *Recognition of Constitutional Block case* of 2011.[86]

C. The Judges

The GCC is composed of five judges.[87] Each judge has their own substitute judge who sits when they have an impediment to review a specific case.[88] One judge is elected by the Executive, another by Congress, a third is elected by the Supreme Court, a fourth is elected by the College of Lawyers and Notaries and the fifth by the *Consejo Superior Universitario de la Universidad de San Carlos* – University Superior Council.[89] The idea behind the election of judges by different entities was to promote balance on the bench and to incorporate academia and liberal experience into the mix.

The judges of the GCC serve for five-year periods.[90] The judges can be re-elected. During the court's lifespan, the court has had seven different benches. To be eligible for appointment as a GCC judge, a person must be of Guatemalan origin, a member of the College of Lawyers (*Colegio de Abogados y Notarios*), of recognised integrity (*honorabilidad*) and have at least 15 years of professional experience after graduation.[91] Yet, as will be shown, despite its complex composition, the GCC does not have a strong culture of dissenting opinions.[92] Rather, dissenting opinions are observed more in relation to certain political cases.

D. Legal Scholarship and Constitutional Reasoning

Guatemala has a civilian tradition of law. Due to its civilian heritage, the judicial approach to problem solving is exegetic.[93] In other words, judges approach cases in

[83] *Recognition Structural Judgments Doctrine case* (n 68) 76–80.
[84] Arts 49 and 51, GCC Statute.
[85] Art 50, GCC Statute.
[86] *Recognition of Constitutional Block Case* (n 67).
[87] Art 269, Constitution of Guatemala.
[88] ibid.
[89] ibid.
[90] Art 269, Constitution of Guatemala.
[91] Art 270, Constitution of Guatemala.
[92] See the Guatemalan results about the number of dissenting and concurring opinions in the empirical dataset.
[93] J Merryman and R Pérez, *The Civil Law Tradition: An Introduction to the Legal Systems of Europe and Latin America* (Stanford University Press, 2009) 80–81.

a heavily doctrinal manner using codes and statutes as their basis of reasoning. This is because statute and codes are an abstract compilation of legal materials meant to be applied in everyday cases.[94] Judges, therefore, are viewed as bureaucrats applying general norms contained in codes and statutes to specific cases. This is also observed in the constitutional cases, where judges take a literal approach to the application of the text of the Constitution to cases. In this process, Guatemalan judges follow a Kelsenian approach to problem solving.[95] The Kelsenian approach is a hierarchical model which places the Constitution at the apex of the Guatemalan legal system and serves as the basis for solivng any dispute.[96]

The study of law in Guatemala is highly conceptual and abstract.[97] It favours exegetic interpretation, in which authors recompile and systematise legal materials, including laws, codes, statutes and judicial decisions.[98] Due to these characteristics, legal scholarship in Guatemala focuses on either defining concepts (eg constitution, process, amparo, etc) or on clarifying procedural and formalist matters (writ requirements, time frames, evidence, etc).[99] This is observed in the reasoning of GCC's case law, where the GCC has resolved a variety of topics by invoking or transplanting foreign concepts.[100] In most of these cases the court merely cites these principles in an abstract way, never actually grounding these in the text of the Constitution. This is particularly observed in the case law on the principle of proportionality, and conflicting interpretations of this principle are revealed in the analysis of its application in many cases.[101]

Analysis of constitutional reasoning is studied within the subject of 'constitutional procedural law' (*derecho procesal constitucional*),[102] rather than, for example, jurisprudence or public law. In this class, there is no focus on jurisprudence or precedent, rather it relates solely to applying the GCC Statute.[103] One example of this type of academic study is the book *The Failed Amparo* (*el Amparo Fallido*).[104] This book, as with much legal scholarship in Guatemala, illustrates the legalist trait of Guatemalan academia by simply mentioning the requirements to correctly submit a writ of amparo.[105] The approach is also reflected in the jurisprudence of the GCC, which has not developed

[94] JA Couso, 'The Transformation of Constitutional Discourse and the Judicialization of Politics in Latin America' in JA Couso, A Huneeus and R Sieder (eds), *Cultures of Legality: Judicialization and Political Activism in Latin America* (Cambridge University Press, 2010) 144.

[95] CM Gutiérrez and J Chacón, *Introducción al Derecho* (Serviprensa, 2016) 33.

[96] H Kelsen, *Teoría General del Estado* (Editorial Nacional, 1948) 160. (Translated by L Legaz Lacambra.).

[97] M Carducci and L P Castillo, 'Comparative Regionalism and Constitutional Imitations in the Integration Process of Central America' (2012) 2 *Eunomia. Rivista semestrale del Corso di Laurea in Scienze Politiche e delle Relazioni Internazionali* 7, 10.

[98] Couso (n 94) 144.

[99] CA Villagrán 'Del funcionalismo al constructivismo en el análisis de jurisprudencia de la Corte de Constitucionalidad' (2019) 4 *Pensamiento Jurídico* 1, 33.

[100] See the Guatemalan results about the general topic of the cases in the empirical dataset.

[101] See Villagrán and Garcia (n 25) 7.

[102] CA Villagrán Sandoval, 'Introducción: La realidad guatemalteca, un constitucionalismo sin método ni metodología' in Villagrán (n 17).

[103] See example as textbook: VM Castillo et al, *Derecho Procesal Constitucional* (Ediciones de Pereira, 2019).

[104] MR Guzmán Hernández, *El Amparo Fallido* (Guatemala, Corte de Constitucionalidad, 2004).

[105] Current bibliography that exhibits this trait, see V Aguilar, *El Amparo: Garantía contra la Arbitrariedad* (Guatemala Serviprensa, 2020).

a theory of stare decisis or the use of precedent. Although the court may cite previous judgments, it tends to do so only to support its argument, rather than analyse the state of the development of the law.[106] This has led to the development of conflicting lines of case law.[107]

Although it still reflects a strong exegetic heritage, scholarship in Guatemala has also seen a certain move from legalism to anti-formalism. However, the new scholarship reflects the same traits as the previous one.[108] Few authors look critically into new developments or the use of transnational principles by the GCC.[109] In addition, very few universities in Guatemala teach comparative constitutional law or methodology. Most courses teach the study of foreign concepts as universally applicable while not actually reviewing the contextual reality of the GCC. As a result, there is little methodological discussion of the court's reasoning.[110]

As will be explained in section IV of this chapter, the method by which the court reasons and uses transnational principles is a reflection of the style of legal reasoning in academia in Guatemala, which is exegetic and reductionist. Reductionism refers to the method by which foreign sources and principles are cited and used without any justification or context.[111]

II. Arguments in Constitutional Reasoning

A. The Structure of Constitutional Arguments

The structure of constitutional argument reflected in the case law has evolved throughout the periods of the GCC. In the foundational GCC, the court tended to link 'one-line conclusive' arguments and 'parallel conclusive' arguments. In other words, chains of one-line arguments would be linked together, following one from another. This may be because this first pioneer GCC was still finding its way in developing a culture of reasoning. This is observed in the first decisions, *Correction of Constitutional Jurisdiction Procedures Case* and *Interpretative Judgments case*, where in each case the GCC made clear the need to interpret doctrine and principles in order to solve disputes. Most of its reasonings could then be used as ratio, since the GCC was laying down the foundations

[106] See the Guatemalan results about the reference to freedom of expression in the selected cases.

[107] The same citation has been used to provide two completely opposite results. About this, there was radical change of interpretation and definition regarding municipal taxes or '*tasa*': see contradiction between: Corte de Constitucionalidad, Inconstitucionalidad Parcial, Expediente 1623-2001, 24 April 2002; Corte de Constitucionalidad, Inconstitucionalidad General Total, Expediente 2751-2004, 26 April 2005; Corte de Constitucionalidad, Inconstitucionalidad General Total, Expediente 794-2007, 6 November 2007; Corte de Constitucionalidad, Inconstitucionalidad General, Expediente 2843-2004, 1 December 2015; Corte de Constitucionalidad, Inconstitucionalidad en Caso Concreto, Expediente 5921-2014, 25 November 2015.

[108] See eg ME Ochoa, 'Neoconstitucionalismo, valores e interpretación constitucional' (2017) XIII *Opus Magna constitucional guatemalteco*, 253.

[109] Villagran and Garcia (n 25) 8–14.

[110] See eg JC Cordón, 'Interpretación de la Constitución y desde la Constitución' (2017) XIII *Opus Magna constitucional guatemalteco* 243–44.

[111] Merryman and Pérez-Perdomo (n 93) 80–81.

of a new normative constitutional system. Yet, the type of reasoning was direct, tailored to the situation at hand without much discussion of the reasoning.[112]

The legalist GCC, due to its formalist character, mostly deployed 'one-line conclusive' arguments. As mentioned, this GCC was mostly concerned in resolving in a formalist fashion, so its arguments were straightforward and sought to avoid difficult issues. Therefore, the GCC provided only the ratio, and did not venture into arguments that did not directly arise from the dispute. A perfect example of this reasoning is the *Exhaustion of ordinary procedures case*,[113] in which the court merely quoted from law the requirements of the amparo in the *CGG Statute* and added a few obiter remarks to say why it was important to exhaust ordinary remedies before initiating an amparo procedure.

Meanwhile, the cosmopolitan GCC has developed a dialogic strategy. Due to its use of foreign sources and transnational principles, the cosmopolitan GCC started to use more obiter. This is observed in the lengthier judgments it has delivered. However, this obiter was more discursive in nature. In other words, it reflected more on the study of abstract principles, rather than solving the case at hand. The GCC also started to use foreign materials as a mechanism to strengthen its legal arguments. However, while the cosmopolitan GCC started to use more obiter, it was not necessarily reflective of the case at hand, but rather was used to justify its approach. An example is the *Recognition of Indigenous IP case*, where the court defines concepts as 'legislative omission',[114] the importance of the relationship between indigenous people and the land, quoting several judgments of the IACHR and international instruments,[115] indigenous territory and custom,[116] indigenous communal land,[117] and Roman law[118] to finally conclude that it has no powers to give protection to indigenous products and Congress must create a law to protect such features of indigenous peoples.[119]

B. Types of Arguments in Constitutional Reasoning

i. *Identification of the Constitution's Text and Discussion of its Applicability*

Regarding the exercise of identification of the Constitution's text (two decisions) and discussion of its applicability (seven), the GCC has paid little attention to the text of the Constitution. This is partly due to the nature of the amparo, which requires little discussion of whether the Constitution is applicable because there is a legal presumption that all cases are justiciable.

[112] See exception, *Belice Recognition Case* (n 24).

[113] Corte de Constitucionalidad, *Exhaustion of ordinary procedures case*, Apelación de Sentencia de Amparo, Expediente 916-9727, May 1998.

[114] Corte de Constitucionalidad, Inconstitucionalidad General Parcial, 8 October 2019, 21–25.

[115] ibid 25–28.

[116] ibid 28–36.

[117] ibid 36–41.

[118] ibid 41.

[119] ibid 47–52.

ii. Analogy and Ordinary Meaning of Words

Common among all three courts is the lack of usage of analogy (one decision). Meanwhile, in the use of ordinary meaning, the legalist GCC engaged heavily in this style of interpretation (nine decisions). As mentioned, under this approach, the GCC left without effect the adhesion to international treaties and effect of international human rights instruments.

iii. Domestic Harmonisation and Harmonisation with International Law

Domestic harmonisation (referred to eight out of 40 decisions) and harmonisation with international law (19 times out of 40 decisions) was used more prevalently in the cosmopolitan GCC. During this last period, the GCC engaged widely with international sources, particularly since the recognition of the constitutional block and conventionality control principles.

iv. Precedents and the Use of Principles or Concepts

All three GCC have relied on principles not mentioned in the Constitution (11 out of 40). However, through the use of these, the legalist GCC did limit the application of the amparo, by establishing procedural limits on the use of amparo and recognising the principle of *in dubio pro legislatoris* (in case of doubt favour the reason of congress). With the introduction of proportionality by the cosmopolitan GCC, this principle has been less invoked by the court.

As mentioned previously, the court in all three periods adopted a functionalist approach to precedent (17 out of 40), in which former cases were cited merely to support a proposition or principle, rather than without analysis of its connection to the case at hand. This type of reasoning may be characterised as utilitarian, since it only uses precedent to present its point of discussion as authoritative. All GCC's have cherry picked precedents for this purpose, even to the extent of citing contradictory judgments.

v. Arguments from Silence and Non-Legal Arguments

Again, common for all three historical GCCs, has been the lack of use of arguments from silence (two out of 40) and non-legal arguments (four out of 40). Due to the nature of Guatemalan legal scholarship being exegetic, magistrates of the court rely on written positive law, rather than using sources that cannot be inferred from it.

vi. Teleological Textual and Historical-Intentional Arguments

As mentioned, the GCC's approach to sources has been in a reductionist fashion. This type of functional reasoning is also displayed in the use of other sources, such as the preparatory text of the Constituent Assembly (again, even using the same reasoning of the assembly to reach two contradictory judgments[120]). This has also led the court to neglect forms of originalist interpretation, disregarding historical (three out of 40) or teleological approaches to determine the meaning of the Constitution (18 out of 40).

vii. Reference to Scholarly Work and to Foreign Law

The GCCs engage with legal scholars (11 out of 40) and foreign law (five out of 40) in a manner that directly benefits the solution provided.[121] However, none of the GCCs discuss the legitimacy of the use of scholarly work of foreign law. This only shows the abuse of the cherry-picking exercise used by all GCCs. Yet, this exercise became more prevalent in the cosmopolitan GCC.

viii. Use of Pro Homine *Principle and Other Methods*

Although the *pro homine* principle was recognised by the legalist GCC, it has seldomly been used since (in five cases). Its uses have not been clear and used to reinforce other arguments, particularly human rights claims. The same can be said for the use of other methods of interpretation (in two cases).

C. The Overall Weight of the Arguments

The foundational GCC sought to lay the foundations of a new legal system in Guatemala. It was concerned with correcting previous procedures and developing a legitimate role for the court. Its judgments were direct and objective and focused on limiting public power. As such, individual rights complaints were not entertained, unless the wording of the Constitution allowed it.[122] It directly resolved the matter at hand without expanding on its reasons, unless it needed to correct certain procedures or concepts along the way.[123] This is exemplified in cases like the *Constitution Overlap 'Sobrevenida' Case*[124] or the *Belice Recognition Case*,[125] where the GCC needed to make clear certain concepts or historical facts. In the first case the GCC sought to explain why it needed to analyse the constitutional validity of statutes that were legal before the entry of the Constitution. Meanwhile, in the second case the GCC was faced with a case of the independence of Belize, with which Guatemala has a historical territorial dispute and

[120] See *Rios Mont II case* (n 43) 49, where it was used to uphold the candidacy, notwithstanding a constitutional prohibition; and *Zury Rios case* (n 55), where the same prohibition was used to not allow her to run for president.

[121] See *Judicial Appointments case* (n 79) 97–98.

[122] Corte de Constitucionalidad, *Capacity to Pay Tax case*, Apelación Sentencia de Amparo, Expediente 167-95, 5 April 1995.

[123] Corte de Constitucionalidad, *Amparo legality case*, Apelación de Sentencia de Amparo Expediente 142-88, 15 June 1988.

[124] Corte de Constitucionalidad, *Constitution Overlap 'Sobrevenida' Case*, Inconstitucionalidad General, Expediente 305-95, 26 September 1996.

[125] Corte de Constitucionalidad, *Belice Recognition Case*, Inconstitucionalidad General, Expediente 290-91 y 292-91, 3 November 1992.

has considered parts of its territory as belonging to Guatemala since the Constitution of 1945.

The legalist GCC was characterised by its positivist and formalistic approach. As such, in many cases the GCC dismissed arguments without giving any direct response to the petitioner. The judgments of this GCC were also direct and short. The GCC would often define the correct procedure and then reject the case at hand on the grounds that it had not met those procedural requirements. This is clearly observed in the *Non-derogability of the Constitution by Constitutional Court Case*,[126] *Exhaustion of ordinary procedures case*[127] and *Limits of Amparo against ordinary judicial judgments case*.[128] In all these cases, the GCC rejected the complaints on formal procedural grounds. In other cases where the court did consider substantive issues, it would analyse the wording of the Constitution in a narrow way. An example is the case of the *CICIG Advisory I*, where the court expressly prohibited an international mission from assuming a role in criminal proceeding or courts.[129]

For its part, the cosmopolitan GCC moved from a 'one-line conclusive' argumentative style towards a 'multiple lines' type of argument. The cosmopolitan GCC usually discusses the potential principles to be applied in the case, using abstract and technical foreign or transnational terms to support its decision making. Consequently, many of its arguments can be auxiliary since they by themselves do not present a concrete line for resolving the case. In the most recent cases during the cosmopolitan GCC, the use of foreign sources become common.[130] However, the use of foreign sources often hides the main line of discussion, if there is one. The citation of foreign sources often disrupts the reading and analysing of ratio decidendi.

Aside from a few judgments of the foundational GCC, the court's reasoning does not usually align with the arguments filed by the petitioner. In complex cases, it does not seem that, historically, the GCC gives much weight to the arguments of the parties. The GCC has focused on solving issues. In this, the Court can be understood as a political arbiter. As such, its type of reasoning has stayed abstract and non-contextualised. Consequently, although it seems that in certain cases the GCC was able to prescribe a rule, this is not always the case and exceptions are always created along the way depending on context.

D. Judicial Candour and Judicial Rhetoric

Since the first GCC, the court's reasoning has been directed at a legal audience. This is an exercise that persists today. The use of abstract principles and rules is more

[126] Corte de Constitucionalidad, *Non-derogability of the Constitution by Constitutional Court Case*, Inconstitucionalidad, Expediente 300-95, 12 March 1996.

[127] Corte de Constitucionalidad, *Exhaustion of ordinary procedures case*, Apelación de Sentencia de Amparo, Expediente 916-97, 27 May 1998.

[128] Corte de Constitucionalidad, *Limits of Amparo against ordinary judicial judgments case*, Apelación de Sentencia de Amparo, Expediente 266-99, 20 May 1999.

[129] Corte de Constitucionalidad, CICIG Advisory I, Opinión Consultiva, Expediente 1250-2004, 5 August 2004.

[130] See *Education in Native Language Case* and Corte de Constitucionalidad, *Death Penalty Abolishment Case*, Inconstitucionalidad General, Expediente 5986-2016, 24 October 2017.

noticeable in the cosmopolitan GCC and shows a lack of didactic reasoning and limits its accessibility for common laypeople. Due to the technicality of the procedures and methods of reasoning, the GCC avoids common language and the use political or emotional sentiment. Some of the vocabulary used by the GCC is so technical and inaccessible, that the GCC has resorted to literally copying pages of precedent when invoking it.[131]

Another consequence of this type of reasoning is that the GCC may invoke any precedent or principle as it sees fit in any particular case.[132] The lack of reasoning by analogy or concrete methodology by which the court assesses cases rarely helps when it comes to predicting outcomes.

E. Length, Dissenting and Concurring Opinions

Judgments in Guatemala have been historically short. The *Self-coup case*, described as the landmark judgment of the Court, was only four pages.[133] The legalist GCC was known for its brevity and did not often include much detail of the facts of the case or the positions presented by the parties. This was a strategy the legalist GCC used to avoid controversial questions about law and politics.

With the cosmopolitan GCC, the length of judgments has increased. However, it is rare to see a judgment go beyond 50 pages. In contrast to the previous GCCs, the cosmopolitan GCC has included more detailed descriptions of the petitioners' pleadings and the arguments laid down in public hearings.

Dissenting and concurring opinions have always been accepted as part of the practice of the GCC, across all three periods.[134] However, there is no strong culture of dissenting or concurring opinions, despite the complex system for the selection of judges of the GCC, which could work to create a court bench that is more likely to disagree than agree. Dissenting and concurring opinions are rare but do appear in particularly hard or controversial cases. This shows that judges provide dissenting opinions in situations of complex political crisis.[135]

F. Framing Constitutional Issues

In framing constitutional issues, each GCC has its own approach. The foundational GCC, under its normative guise, was focused on establishing the limits of public

[131] See Corte de Constitucionalidad, *Judicial Appointments 2 case*, Judgment, Expediente 1169-2020, 6 May 2020.

[132] See the invocation of the estoppel principle in the Expediente 56-2012, Inconstitucionalidad General Parcial, 3 May 2012 (*Estoppel –Actos Propios- case*), changing its precedent on the *PARLACEN case*.

[133] S Larios, 'The Court as a Stronghold for Democracy: The Serrano Elias Case' *IACL-AIDC Blog* (23 July 2020) at blog-iacl-aidc.org/constitutional-landmark-judgments-in-central-and-south-america/2020/7/23/the-court-as-a-stronghold-for-democracy-the-serrano-elias-case.

[134] See *Legality of Congress opinion* Expediente 364-90, Apelación de Sentencia de Amparo, 26 June 1990.

[135] See Corte de Constitucionalidad, Voto Razonado Disidente Magistrada Dina Josefina Ochoa Escribá, Auto de Amparo Provisional, Expediente 2201-2018, 29 May 2018.

powers and public function. This is observed by the court delimiting the functions of the Electoral Tribunal, the capacity of Congress to enact bills or the capacity of the executive to intervene in the activities of private actors.

Meanwhile, the legalist GCC took a positivist and formalist approach to framing constitutional issues. During its time, the GCC was more concerned with defining the characteristics and application of the amparo, the limits of the GCC in reviewing cases and detailing the interaction and limiting the application of international law to domestic law.

On its part, the cosmopolitan GCC has addressed most constitutional issues under a vision of human rights. This was marked by the introduction of the constitutional block, conventional control and the principle of proportionality. Also, the cosmopolitan GCC has expanded the use of social and economic rights, beyond those social economic rights already recognised in the Constitution, such as housing.

With the introduction of human rights concepts the GCC has positioned itself under a counter majoritarian view of protection of human rights. This means it has begun to uphold the rights of minorities, specifically in socio-economic rights litigation. Cases concerning education policies, such as education in indigenous language and the election of magistrates of the Supreme Court and Court of Appeals, have been framed in human rights terms.[136] However, the GCC has continued with some formalist traits of the previous GCC, limiting its own expansive jurisdiction.

G. Key Concepts

The use of key concepts has been uniform and consistent throughout the different periods of the GCC. Since the foundational GCC coined key concepts such as '*principio de legalidad*' (legality), '*estado constitucional de derecho*' (constitutional rule of law), '*supremacia de la constitucion*' (supremacy of the constitution), '*superlegalidad constitucional*' (superlegalilty of the constitution), and '*defensa del orden constitutional*' (defence of the constitutional order), these concepts have become part of the common language of the courts. This last concept is a term taken directly from the Guatemalan Constitution.

The GCC usually mentions these concepts without much explanation, simply citing the cases where these terms have been used as precedent. This exercise is often the only gesture the GCC makes to precedent – that is, citation of previous case law is limited to supporting the statement of key concepts. However, on rare occasions the GCC has ventured out to define these concepts. In the *Recognition of Proportionality case*, the GCC recognised that the concept of '*estado de derecho*' applied in Guatemala is similar to that used in the United States.[137] However, the GCC later went on to incorporate the proportionality test as used by the German Constitutional Court.

[136] See *Judicial Appointments 2 case* (n 131).
[137] *Recognition of Proportionality of Laws case* (n 57) 15.

III. Comparative Perspective

The GCC is not among the older courts of the region (such as the Argentinian or Mexican Supreme Court, or the Chilean Constitutional Tribunal), nor is it the youngest (Ecuador and Bolivia). It is of the same era as the Colombian Constitutional Court, Costa Rica's *Sala Cuarta* (fourth or constitutional chamber) and the Peruvian Constitutional Tribunal. In Central America, the GCC is the only court of its type, that is, an independent free-standing court. Other Central American states have institutionalised their constitutional courts as chambers of their respective supreme courts.

In its reasoning, the GCC shares similar trends to others in the region. After 2005, the GCC, like the Chilean Constitutional Tribunal, began referencing more openly foreign sources, particularly human rights ones.[138] Yet, although Guatemala has one of the highest indigenous populations in the continent, it has not shown any sign of incorporating post-material values, as the Ecuadorian and Bolivian courts have done. In matters relating to abortion and other issues that potentially conflict with traditional Christian values, the GCC is still very much conservative, like the Chilean Constitutional Tribunal.

However, the cosmopolitan GCC has been greatly influenced by other courts in the region, particularly Colombia,[139] as well as those from abroad.[140] Throughout the cosmopolitan stage, the GCC has increased its citation of foreign and international sources.[141] In this, although it is heavily influenced by the Colombian tribunal, its conduct is similar to that of the Ecuadorian Constitutional Court.[142] Thus, it similarly reflects a court in transition that has not adopted a single identity, but rather has changed drastically over its lifespan.

[138] J Fröhlich, 'Traces of Constitutional Reasoning in Latin America and the Caribbean – Regional Cosmopolitanism Without Backlash?' (2020) *Int'l J. Const. L.*, at www.academia.edu/43775166/Traces_of_constitutional_reasoning_in_Latin_America_and_the_Caribbean_Regional_Cosmopolitanism_without_backlash.

[139] See recent examples Expedientes 1267-2019 (Judgment of 4 November 2019), 781-2019 (Judgment of 3 September 2019), 1879-2019 (Judgment of 10 July 2019), 5106-2018 (Judgment of 26 February 2019), 6215-2018 (Judgment of 28 January 2020), 3591-2018 (Judgment of 20 February 2019), 2438-2018 (Judgment of 22 November 2018), 4785-2017 (Judgment of 3 September 2018), 1598-2018 (Judgment of 9 August 2018), 834-2017 (Judgment of 3 May 2018), 5844-2017 (Judgment of 3 May 2018), 259-2017 (Judgment of 26 April 2018).

[140] See eg Germany Expedientes 6094-2017 (Judgment of 3 May 2018), 3076-2016 (Judgment of 21 February 2017), 3978-2019 (Judgment of 30 May 2020), 2729-2011 (Judgment of 14 August 2012), and Spain: 5318-2017 (Judgment of 28 February 2018), 3719-2016 (Judgment of 9 March 2017), 1734-2013 (Judgment of 6 April 2016), 5016-2014 (Judgment of 5 May 2015).

[141] See the Guatemalan results about the general topic of the selected cases and the reference to scholarly work and foreign law that shows a clear difference in the foundational stage, where no citation of foreign sources is observed.

[142] D Carrera and J Fröhlich, 'Constitutional Identity in Transition? The Case on the Human Rights of the State' *IACL-IADC Blog* (9 July 2020) at blog-iacl-aidc.org/constitutional-landmark-judgments-in-central-and-south-america/2020/7/9/constitutional-identity-in-transition-the-case-on-the-human-rights-of-the-state.

IV. Evaluation, Pathology and Criticism

A. Exegetic Approach in Reasoning

The reasoning of the GCC can be characterised as exegetic. Similar to Guatemalan scholarship, the court's reasoning reflects an abstract and conceptual approach to problem solving. As discussed previously, the structure of the GCC's judgments usually starts with a review of the abstracts principles and rules that can be applied. However, this type of reasoning rests on reductionism.

B. Reductionism in Reasoning in the Use of Foreign Sources and Precedents

Reductionism relies on the reduction and decontextualisation of legal concepts and laws.[143] A clear example of this is found in the GCC's approach to comparative law, where it stated that comparison, including the citation of foreign scholars, is to be used to understand 'the law' or principles.[144] As such, comparative law is used in a reductive manner, describing principles or norms, but not taking into account the context in which this principles were invoked or its importing context.

As mentioned before, the GCC has a tendency of reductionism in its legal analysis of cases and reasoning. Reductionism refers to the decontextualisation of the sources used in interpretation, whether these are foreign sources, such as transplants, or local sources such as previous case law. This trait of the GCC becomes problematic because it does not account for features of local or current context.[145]

This type of reasoning has had three consequences. The first is the consolidation of a model of resolving cases through ontological and conceptual models of law, which actually does not take into account local context.[146] Second, it means that the Court has not developed rules or guidance on how to assess comparative jurisdictions and the workability of transplanted foreign principles.[147] And last, this type of reasoning curtails any domestic innovations or case law presented by lower courts.[148]

C. Indefinite Rules for Resolving Cases

Evidence from this study shows that the GCC has been able to pick and choose principles, sources and norms for deciding specific cases. It also shows its readiness to dismiss

[143] M Siems, *Comparative Law* (Cambridge University Press, 2014) 26; G Frankenberg, *Comparative Law as Critique* (Edward Elgar, 2016) 53.

[144] Expediente 2020-2014, sentencia de 7 de agosto de 2014.

[145] P Legrand, 'Are Civilians Educable?' (1998) 18 *Legal Studies* 216, 222.

[146] M Hoecke and M Warrington, 'Legal Cultures, Legal Paradigms and Legal Doctrine: Towards a New Model for Comparative Law' (1998) 47 *International and Comparative Law Quarterly* 495, 497, 532.

[147] This has been called by Cass Sunstein as the 'minimalist basis', see C Sunstein, *One Case at a Time* (Harvard University Press, 1999) xi.

[148] L Pinto, 'Utilización Del Derecho Constitucional Comparado En La Interpretación Constitucional: Nuevos Retos a La Teoría Constitucional' (2007) 5 *Estudios Constitucionales* 251, 270.

the same without any explanation. The lack of use of analogy, cherry picking and the functional approach in order to preserve what it calls *'estado constitucional de derecho'* (constitutional rule of law), shows the careful balance that the GCC seeks to make between law and politics.

A hypothesis of why the GCC has taken this approach to constitutional reasoning, currently and historically, is that the Court sees the value of undefined rules of interpretation. Leaving things open for interpretation leaves the door open for the court to have some leverage in deciding what cases it should resolve and those it should not, based on the political scenario of the time.[149]

Although the GCC has become more open towards foreign sources and international human rights discourse, at heart it still sees itself as a political arbiter. Undefined rules of interpretation are the price it pays to maintain itself as a strong counter-majoritarian actor and to limit other state powers. The court is still reluctant to resolve on matters where there could be strong political or social backlash and carefully measures the cases which it thinks are most suitable to resolve.

V. Conclusion

The GCC has gone through continuous, but also very marked, periods of transformation. Yet, throughout these transformations, certain hallmarks of the court persist. The GCC continues to view itself, and is viewed by the public in turn, as a strong political actor. With this mindset, the court has obtained a strong status in Guatemalan politics. However, this status also exposes the court to backlash and co-option by political actors.

In 2021 a new GCC with legalist traits was established. As such, there has been a return to the formalist traits that defined the second historical period of the court. The tradition of abstract and high-level argumentation allows these strong shifts in styles of constitutional reasoning, while the value of uncertainty allows the court to maintain itself as a hegemonic actor within the legal and political regime in Guatemala.

[149] See H Asgeirsson, *The Nature and Value of Vagueness in the Law* (Hart Publishing, 2020).

12

The Jurisprudence of the Inter-American Court of Human Rights*

PABLO GONZÁLEZ DOMÍNGUEZ AND ALFREDO ORTEGA FRANCO

I. Legal, Political, Institutional and Academic Context

A. Legal and Political Culture as Context for Constitutional Reasoning

i. The Inter-American Court of Human Rights as Part of the Inter-American Human Rights System

The creation of the Inter-American Court of Human Rights (hereinafter 'Inter-American Court', 'Court', 'Tribunal' or 'IACtHR') is part of the multilateral commitments assumed by several States to consolidate a regional system of human rights protection in the Americas (the Inter-American Human Rights System).[1] The Chapultepec Conference of 1945 might be regarded as the first step to consolidate said system. In this Conference, the Republics of the Americas agreed upon committing to the principles of international law regarding the safeguard of essential rights and to the creation of an international system to protect those rights.[2] The Conference was followed by the Ninth International Conference of American States, where the Charter of the Organization of American States (hereinafter, 'OAS Charter') and the American Declaration on the Rights and Duties of Man (hereinafter, 'American Declaration') were adopted in 1948.

The OAS Charter recognised a series of principles that included the proclamation of individual fundamental rights without distinction. Furthermore, it established that

* This chapter represents the opinion of the authors, and it is the result of academic research. Therefore, it is not necessarily representative of the official position or opinions of the Inter-American Court or any of its members. We would like to thank Alexei Julio, Johanna Fröhlich, Ximena Soley and Christian González for their detailed comments and suggestions for the text, and Angélica Suárez Torres and Javier Urizar for their research assistance.

[1] See S García Ramirez, 'The Relationship between Inter-American Jurisdiction and States (National Systems): Some Pertinent Questions' (2015) 1 *Notre Dame Journal of International and Comparative Law* 119.

[2] See Inter-American Conference on Problems of War and Peace, held in Mexico City between 21 February–8 March 1945, Resolution XL.

social justice and social security are the basis for a lasting peace.[3] The OAS Charter also created a political, juridical and social forum for the fulfilment of the purposes and principles adopted by the States. In 1959, the States Party to the Charter created the Inter-American Commission of Human Rights (hereinafter 'Inter-American Commission' or 'Commission').[4] In 1970, the Commission became a principal body of the OAS.[5] The American Declaration is particularly relevant in this regard, since it was the first instrument that – although not binding as a treaty – defined a catalogue of international rights and duties in the region that influenced the adoption of treaties in the future.[6] These developments – institutional and normative – constituted a fundamental step in the creation of international institutions and procedures for the protection of human rights and they are still relevant to this day.

The adoption of the American Convention on Human Rights (hereinafter 'American Convention' or 'Convention') in 1969 is part of the abovementioned institutional and normative developments, and constituted a fundamental aspect in the consolidation of the Inter-American System.[7] This was the first treaty adopted in the region containing a catalogue of human rights and liberties that must be respected and ensured by the States and that also established an obligation to give domestic effects to those rights and freedoms.[8] The Convention was – and has been ever since – a regional instrument that entailed international human rights obligations. Breaches to the Convention give rise to the international responsibility of the State and the duty to repair.[9] The definition of a set of means of protection and procedural basis for the supervision of the compliance with the Convention is also one of the main features of that Treaty.[10] This supervision is guaranteed mainly through the creation of the Inter-American Court and the establishment of a system of individual petitions that allowed the Commission to submit cases of human rights violations committed by State Parties to the Court.[11]

The Court was officially established on 3 September 1979 in San Jose, Costa Rica, after the American Convention entered into force and the States appointed the first judges. Since then, the Court has carried out its jurisdiction without interruption as an autonomous international judicial institution.[12] The main objective of the Court is to oversee all cases concerning the interpretation and application of the American Convention and other treaties of similar nature, provided it has jurisdiction to that end.[13] Along with the Inter-American Commission, the Court constitutes one of the two

[3] See Art 3 and Principles of the Charter of the Organization of American States (Bogota, 1948).

[4] See Fifth Meeting of Consultation of Ministers of Foreign Affairs, held in Santiago, Chile, 12–18 August 1959.

[5] The Protocol of Buenos Aires to the OAS Charter was adopted in 1967 and entered into force in 1970.

[6] See T Burgenthal, 'La relación conceptual y normativa entre la Declaración Americana y la Convención Americana sobre Derechos Humanos' (1989) *Revista del IIDH* 112.

[7] See generally C Medina, *The American Convention on Human Rights. Crucial Rights and their Theory and Practice*, 2nd edn (Intersentia, 2016) 1–56.

[8] See Arts 1 and 2 of the American Convention on Human Rights (San Jose, 1969).

[9] See Art 63.1 of the ACHR; see generally *Velasquez Rodriguez v Honduras*. Reparations and Costs, Judgment, Inter-Am. Ct. H.R. (Ser. C) No. 7, (Jul. 21, 1989) paras 24–25.

[10] See Part II of the ACHR.

[11] See Arts 48–51 of the ACHR.

[12] See Art 1 of the Statute of the Inter-American Court of Human Rights (La Paz, 1979).

[13] See Arts 62–64 of the ACHR.

main organs of supervision in the Inter-American Human Rights System.[14] It is one of the three regional human rights courts in existence, together with the European Court of Human Rights (hereinafter, 'European Court') and the African Court of Human and People's Rights. The Court is, therefore, part of the international mechanisms of protection of human rights.[15]

The existence of the Court does not mean that it has jurisdiction over all the 35 Members of the OAS. Article 62.1 of the Convention indicates that, upon or any time after depositing the instrument of ratification or adherence, any State Party can recognise the jurisdiction of the Court as binding. At the time of writing, 20 States have accepted the jurisdiction of the Court: Argentina, Barbados, Bolivia, Brazil, Chile, Colombia, Costa Rica, Dominican Republic, Ecuador, El Salvador, Guatemala, Haiti, Honduras, Mexico, Nicaragua, Panama, Paraguay, Peru, Suriname, and Uruguay.[16] Some States in the region have not signed or ratified the Convention, like the United States of America, Canada or Cuba. Trinidad and Tobago, as well as Venezuela, denounced the Convention in 1998 and 2012, respectively. These circumstances have created different degrees of obligations in the Inter-American System,[17] and reflects the difficulties of maintaining and strengthening an international human rights system in a region with a plurality of legal and political traditions.[18] The ratification of the American Convention by all the members of the OAS, and the continuance of those States that are already Parties, has been a constant political and juridical goal of the Inter-American System.[19]

At a normative level, there has been a progressive adoption of different binding and non-binding legal instruments by the States in the Inter-American System. These instruments have specified to a greater degree the rights and obligations established in the American Convention, and have expanded the jurisdiction of the Court.[20] This normative production has included different areas: economic, social, cultural and environmental rights (ESCER),[21] death penalty,[22] non-discrimination,[23] women's rights,[24]

[14] See D Shelton, 'The Promise of Regional Human Rights Systems' in BH Weston and SP Marks (eds), *The Future of International Human Rights* (Transnational, 1999) 352.

[15] For an approach of the different international systems of human rights protection, see generally T Buergenthal, D Shelton and DP Steward, *International Human Rights in a Nutshell*, 4th edn (West, 2009).

[16] See Signatures and Ratifications of the ACHR.

[17] See E Salmon, *Introducción al Sistema Interamericano de Derechos Humanos* (Fondo Editorial de la Universidad Católica del Perú, 2019) ch I.

[18] See generally P Carozza, 'The Anglo-Latin Divide and the Future of the Inter-American System of Human Rights' (2015) 5 *Notre Dame Journal of International and Comparative Law* 155.

[19] See Inter-American Commision on Human Rights, *Consideraciones sobre la ratificación universal de la Convención Americana y otros tratados internacionales en materia de derechos humanos* (Washington, D.C., 2014) 3.

[20] See generally *Case of González et al. ('Cotton Field') v Mexico.* Preliminary Objections, Merits, Reparations and Costs Judgment, Inter-Am. Ct. H.R. (Ser. C) No. 205, (16 November 2009) paras 31–65.

[21] Additional Protocol to the American Convention on Human Rights in the area of Economic, Social and Cultural Rights 'Protocol of San Salvador' (San Salvador, 17 November 1988).

[22] Protocol to the American Convention on Human Rights to Abolish the Death Penalty (Asuncion, 8 June 1990).

[23] Inter-American Convention Against Racism, Racial Discrimination and Related Forms of Intolerance, (Antigua, 5 June 2013).

[24] Inter-American Convention on The Prevention, Punishment and Eradication of Violence Against Women 'Convention of Belem Do Para' (Belém do Pará, 9 June 1994).

indigenous peoples rights,[25] disability rights,[26] older persons rights,[27] justice administration,[28] prohibition of torture,[29] and enforced disappearance,[30] asylum, refugees and displaced persons rights,[31] democracy,[32] and terrorism.[33] There have also been regulatory developments in both the Statute and the Rules of Procedure of the Inter-American Court of Human Rights, such as the granting of *locus standi* to the representatives of the victims.[34]

ii. Relevant Social and Political Actors

The Court is an autonomous regional court. Yet, it is not isolated from the actors and events that occur in the international arena, especially in relationship with the OAS and the States Parties to the Convention. From an institutional standpoint, the OAS and the States are the main formal actors with which the Court deals on crucial questions. This is obvious due to the fact that the legal instruments that define the jurisdiction of the Court emerge from the agreements of States that take place in the context of the OAS. The Court also depends on States in matters as important as the appointment of the judges,[35] the approval of its budget,[36] the consideration of the Annual Report,[37] the appropriate substantiation of the cases, and the compliance with its judgments.[38] Furthermore, the Inter-American Commission – which is a principal body of the OAS – and the States are the only actors that may present cases before the Court.[39] This power has allowed the Commission to highly influence the Court's judicial agenda, by defining the factual basis of the cases and most of the legal questions to be answered.

Notwithstanding the centrality of States and the OAS in the institutional design of the Inter-American System, the legal and political culture of the Court is influenced by other actors that have less or no formal institutional linkages. They include civil society (especially NGO's that represent the victims before the Inter-American System), academia, public defenders, ombudspersons, the media, other regional courts (especially the European Court) and specialised institutions of human rights (for instance, the UN Human Rights Council), the high courts of the States, specific branches of government, among others. These actors might be influential in the resolution of cases

[25] American Declaration on the Rights of Indigenous Peoples (Santo Domingo, 15 June 2016).

[26] Inter-American Convention on The Elimination of All Forms of Discrimination Against Persons with Disabilities (Guatemala City, 9 June 1999).

[27] Inter-American Convention on Protecting the Human Rights of Older Persons' (Washington, D.C., 15 June, 2015).

[28] Inter-American Convention Against Corruption (Caracas, 29 March 1996).

[29] Inter-American Convention to Prevent and Punish Torture (Cartagena de Indias, 9 December 1985).

[30] Inter-American Convention on the Forced Disappearance of Persons (Belém do Pará, 9 June 1994).

[31] Convention on Diplomatic Asylum (Caracas, 28 March 1954).

[32] Inter-American Democratic Charter (Lima, 11 September 2001).

[33] Convention to Prevent and Punish the Acts of Terrorism Taking the Forms of Crimes Against Persons and Related Extortion that are of International Significance (Washington, D.C., 2 February 1971).

[34] See Art 25 of the Rules of Procedure of the Inter-American Court of Human Rights (San Jose, 2009).

[35] See Art 53 of the ACHR.

[36] See Art 26 of the Statute of the IACtHR.

[37] See Art 65 of the ACHR.

[38] See Art 68 of the ACHR.

[39] Arts 48–50 and 61 of the ACHR.

through direct actions (like formulating arguments before the Court as representatives in a case, or by presenting *amicus curiae*) or indirect actions (like producing relevant information that is later used to establish the context of a case or interpreting human rights instruments that are used by the Court to interpret a norm of the Convention).[40]

Furthermore, the legal and political culture in the Inter-American System must be understood in relation with the larger spectrum of economic, social, political, and ideological forces that shape the human rights discourse and action in the region. For instance, the history of human rights in Latin America has been characterised by the constant occurrence of gross human rights violations, serious deficits in democracy and the rule of law, and the weak political support that States have historically provide to the Inter-American System.[41] This reality is reflected in the fact that the majority of the Court's decisions have dealt with violations to some of the most basic human rights (life, personal integrity, and personal liberty), and violations to the right to a fair trial and judicial protection.[42] So it is not surprising that the Court has taken an approach prone to expand the protection of rights in the cases subject to its jurisdiction, an attitude that has been shared – and driven – by the Inter-American Commission.[43] With the same logic, the Court has created procedural mechanisms to increase the effectiveness of its decisions, such as the judgment compliance supervision, and the doctrine of conventionality control.[44]

B. The Court and Constitutional Litigation

The powers and jurisdiction of the Inter-American Court are typically classified and distributed as the following: advisory, contentious (individual, inter-state, and the supervision of compliance of its judgments), and precautionary.[45] The following paragraphs will refer only to the contentious jurisdiction, since it is there where litigation mainly occurs before the Court.

[40] See S García Ramírez, 'Foreword. The Inter-American Human Rights Jurisdiction: A Long Journey' in L Burgorgue-Larsen and A Úbeda de Torres, *The Inter-American Court on Human Rights. Case Law and Commentary* (Oxford University Press, 2011) XXI.

[41] See generally D Shelton, 'The Promise of Regional Human Rights Systems' in DL Shelton and PG Carozza (eds), *Regional protection of human rights* (Oxford University Press, 2013) 368.

[42] See generally L Bellocchio and A Santiago (cord), *Historia de la Corte Interamericana de Derechos Humanos (1978-2018)* (La Ley Reuters, 2018) 69-505.

[43] See generally Y Negishi, Conventionality Control of Domestic Law. Constitutionalized International Adjudication and Internationalized Constitutional Adjudication (Nomos, 2022) 17.

[44] On the mechanism for the monitoring compliance with judgments, see generally P Saavedra Alessandri et al, 'Reparación y supervisión de sentencias' in J García Roca et al (coord), *¿Hacia una globalización de los derechos?. El impacto de las sentencias del Tribunal Europeo y de la Corte Interamericana* 228–45 and 254–60 (Thompson Reuters Arazandi, 2017); on the doctrine of conventionality control, see generally P González Domínguez, *The Doctrine of Conventionality Control. Between Uniformity and Legal Pluralism in the Inter-American Human Rights System* (Intersentia, 2018) 1–3.

[45] For a detailed analysis of the competences and procedures before the Court, see generally JM Pasqualucci, *The Practice and Procedure of the Inter-American Court of Human Rights*, 2nd edn (Cambridge University Press, 2013) Part I and II.

The main competence of the Court is the capacity to exert jurisdiction over States Parties in cases concerning the alleged violation of the American Convention, provided it has jurisdiction *ratione materiae*,[46] *ratione personae*,[47] *ratione temporis*,[48] and *ratione loci*. The Commission and the States Parties to the Convention have the exclusive right to bring cases to the Court, which means that there is no direct access. However, victims and their representatives have *locus standi* since reforms to the rules of procedure in 1996 and in 2000.[49] The contentious jurisdiction of the Court requires that the claimant party exhaust the local remedies and the procedure before the Inter-American Commission. The Court cannot discretionally select the cases that will be analysed. Contentious proceedings are regulated in Articles 34 to 69 of the Rules of Procedure.

On average, the Court decides a case approximately two years after it is submitted by the Commission. It is worth mentioning, however, that if counted from the moment a petition is filed before the Commission, and the final decision of the Court, the total time could be between 8 and 10 years, if not more.[50] After a case is ruled upon, a procedure to monitor compliance with the judgment begins.[51] During that procedure, the Court evaluates the information submitted by the parties in order to conclude if the orders of the Court in a judgment have been fully complied with and the case can be closed. Until 2020 there were 237 cases in the supervision of compliance stage, and 40 that have been fully complied with.[52] This relatively small percentage of full compliance with judgments (16 per cent) must be appreciated in context. The Court often provides for a broad array of reparatory measures that might present challenges for States to comply with.[53]

The Court's workload is contingent on the number of cases that are submitted to its jurisdiction. For example, in 2020, the Commission submitted 23 cases to the Court. That year, the Court issued 23 judgments.[54] However, as shown in Figure 1, there has been a steady increase in the Court's output.[55]

[46] See Art 63.1 of the ACHR, and *Case of González et al. ('Cotton Field') v Mexico*, para 37.

[47] See *Case of Granier et al. (Radio Caracas Television) v Venezuela*, Preliminary Objections, Merits, Reparations and Costs Judgment, Inter-Am. Ct. H.R. (Ser. C) No. 293, (22 June 2015) paras 222–27.

[48] See *Case of Radilla Pacheco v Mexico*, Preliminary Objections, Merits, Reparations and Costs Judgment, Inter-Am. Ct. H.R. (Ser. C) No. 209, (23 November 2009) para 23.

[49] See Art 25 of the Rules of Procedure, see generally A Cancado Trindade, *El acceso directo a los individuos a los tribunales internacionales* (Universidad de Deusto, 2001) 49–60.

[50] *cf* AE Dulitzky, 'Muy poco, muy tarde: la morosidad procesal de la Comisión Interamericana de Derechos Humanos' (2015) *JA* 35.

[51] The Court has considered said procedure as part of its contentious jurisdiction. See *Case of Baena Ricardo et al. (270 workers) v Panama*. Monitoring Compliance with Judgment. Order of the Inter-American Court of Human Rights of 6 June 2003.

[52] For a list of cases at the stage of monitoring compliance with judgments, see Inter-American Court of Human Rights, *Annual Report* (2021) 56.

[53] X Soley, 'The Transformative Dimension of Inter-American Jurisprudence' in A Von Bogdandy et al (eds), *Transformative Constitutionalism in Latin America. The Emergence of a New Ius Commune* (Oxford University Press, 2017) 347–48.

[54] See IACtHR, *Annual Report* (2021).

[55] The Court's output includes decisions regarding contentious cases, provisional measures, supervision of compliance, and advisory opinions. This uptick can be attributed to the reforms to the rules of procedure in 1996, 2000, and the Court's opinion in 2003 that asserted its powers to oversee the compliance of judgments.

Figure 1 The Court's output of decisions concerning merits, provisional measures, and supervision of compliance

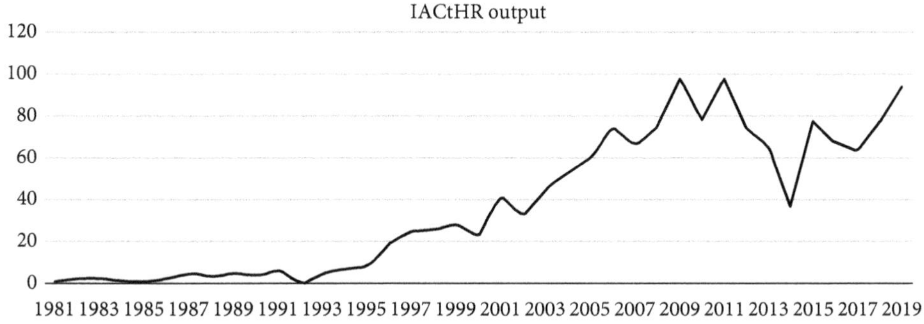

C. The Judges

The Court's bench consists of seven judges, who are elected by secret ballot by an absolute majority votes of the States party to the American Convention during the General Assembly of the OAS. They are appointed for a period of six years that may be reviewed once, from a panel of candidates proposed by the States Party to the American Convention. Article 52.1 of the Convention establishes that judges must be: (a) nationals of the member states of the OAS; (b) elected in an individual capacity, (c) from among the jurists of the highest moral authority; (d) of recognised competence on the field of human rights; and (e) who possess the qualifications required for the exercise of the highest judicial functions in conformity with the law of the state of which they are nationals or the state that proposes them as candidates.[56] States also have the possibility to appoint an ad hoc judge when there is no judge of their nationality in the Court and there is a contentious case originating in an inter-state communication (not in an individual petition).[57] The Court elects its own President and Vice president every two years, and there is no limit for re-election for these positions.[58]

Regarding the background of the judges in the Court's history, we compiled a dataset that shows that, before their seating, 53 per cent of Inter-American judges had some form of formal academic employment, 38 per cent had judicial experience, and 35 per cent had some background as politicians or diplomats.[59] These percentages, however, have changed over time. For example, during the Court's first two decades of existence, there was a strong presence of diplomats and politicians: at least 50 per cent of the judges had some background, training, or experience as such. At the turn of the

[56] See Arts 53–55 of the ACHR.

[57] See Art 55 of the ACHR, and Art 55 of the American Convention on Human Rights. Advisory Opinion OC-20, Inter-Am. Ct. H.R. (Ser. A) No. 20 (Sep. 29, 2009) Operative Paragraph 1.

[58] See Art 12 of the Statute of the IACtHR, Art 12.

[59] These percentages do not amount to 100% as there have been judges, like Sonia Picado, or Eugenio Zaffaroni, that have had concurrent training or experience as academics, judges, and diplomats.

century, the scale tilted towards judges with backgrounds as scholars. In the last decade, the Court has shifted towards members with a background as former constitutional judges. These trends in the conformation of the Court, as we can see in Figure 2, might help to explain the different approaches that the Court has had over time regarding the interpretation of the rights protected by the American Convention and the scope of its powers and attributions.[60]

Figure 2 The Court's composition previous training and background

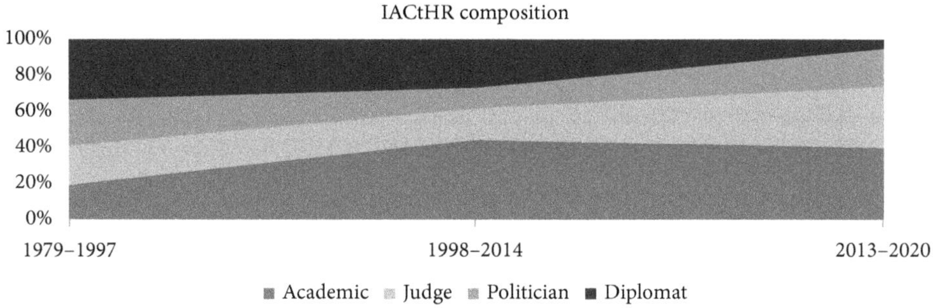

Unlike other international tribunals, there is no public selection process or any previous scrutiny of the nominees. As a result, the nomination and selection process has been deemed by some as lacking transparency, clarity, and accountability.[61] Furthermore, criticisms may be levied due to the lack of gender, ethnic, racial, cultural, national, and ideological representation throughout the Court's history. During most of the Court's existence, States have not enabled any public or independent scrutiny of nominees, nor specified the reasons for nominating a candidate. Voting during the OAS General Assembly is secret, as determined by the American Convention. Therefore, States have had no incentive to disclose the reasons to vote in favour of – or against – any specific nominee. However, there have been efforts from civil society organisations and academia to change this absence of scrutiny. For instance, since 2015 several organisations have convened a politically independent group – meaning not assembled by States – of experts to evaluate candidates for the Court.[62] Moreover, there are initiatives to push for states to ensure gender parity and to address the root causes of gender sub representation.[63]

It is worth mentioning that the Court does not sit permanently in San Jose, Costa Rica. For this reason, the Court celebrates 'regular' and 'special' sessions for the exercise

[60] For instance, 26 of the 40 landmark cases selected for the purposes of this chapter occurred during the period where there was a greater presence of scholars in the Court. This does not necessarily mean that scholars produce better judgments but suggests that they might take decisions that generate greater impact in the Court's jurisprudence.

[61] See O Ruiz-Chiriboga, 'The Independence of the Inter-American Judge' (2012) 1 *The Law and Practice of International Courts and Tribunals* 111–35.

[62] See CEJIL. Press Release: *Independent experts launch report evaluating candidates for the Inter-American Court of Human Rights*, 31 May 2018.

[63] See GQUAL Declaration, presented in September 2015 at the UN.

of its functions.[64] Most sessions are held in Costa Rica. Some sessions are held in other State Parties to the Convention, in an effort to bridge the gap between the Court and the Latin-American legal communities, governments, civil society, and of course, victims of human rights violations. In practice, judges meet several times a year for periods of two or three weeks to decide on cases, have working sessions with the permanent staff, and if necessary, review the most relevant administrative questions. In 2021 the Court celebrated seven sessions.[65] When the Court is not in session, the judges continue to carry out their functions remotely. This work structure highlights the function of Court's Secretariat as an important institutional player in charge of conducting the day-to-day affairs of the Court.[66] The Secretariat, comprised of a multi-national staff, has historically had an important role in the drafting of judgments, and consequently in the criteria and reasoning laid out in the final decisions of the Court.[67]

D. Legal Scholarship and Constitutional Reasoning

It might be challenging to find scholarship that is overtly critical of the Court's work, especially in Latin America. Scholars and practitioners have extensively studied and commented on the Court's decisions thorough its history, generally, in positive terms. Scholarly work tends to acknowledge how the Court has contributed to the protection of human rights in the region.[68] The former might stem from the work of the Court during its first decades of existence, when most cases addressed gross human rights violations and sometimes responded to contexts of authoritarian regimes. Arguably, there was a consensus on the need and benefits from the Court taking a proactive approach towards the cases expanding the scope of protection of the Convention and establishing ample reparations.[69] Yet, during the last two decades the Court has progressively tackled more contemporary legal conundrums (questions about economic, social and cultural rights, the rights of LGBTQ+ persons, democratic governance, and transitional justice, to name a few), which has also led to the increase of critical analysis in academic circles.[70] The criticism has come from those that consider the Court as being too aggressive, or too passive, in its approach to human rights adjudication.[71]

[64] See Arts 11 and 12 of the Rules of Procedure of the IACtHR.

[65] See IACtHR, *Annual Report* (2021) 24.

[66] See Art 10 of the Rules of Procedure.

[67] See J Calderon, 'Dinámicas, procedimientos y elaboración de sentencias', in C Astudillo and S García Ramírez, *Corte Interamericana de Derechos Humanos. Organización, funcionamiento y trascendencia* (Tirant Lo Blanch, 2021) 698–702.

[68] See generally Revista del Instituto Interamericano de Derechos Humanos, published since 1985.

[69] See generally E Ferrer Mac-Gregor, 'Las siete líneas jurisprudenciales de la Corte Interamericana de Derechos Humanos aplicable a la justicia penal' (2014) 59 *Revista del Instituto Interamericano de Derechos Humanos* 29.

[70] See J Contesse, 'Resisting the Inter-American Human Rights System' (2019) 44 *Yale Journal of International Law* and A Paul, 'Decision-Making Process of the Inter-American Court: An Analysis Prompted by the "In Vitro Fertilization" Case' (2014) 21 *ILSA Journal of International & Comparative Law*.

[71] See generally J Acosta, 'Corte Interamericana y política criminal: ¿Quién tiene la última palabra?' (9 February 2022) *IberICONnect*, and D Cerqueira, 'The justiciability of economic, social and cultural rights under the American Convention. On the need to fill in the reasoning gaps of the Lagos del Campo Vs. Peru judgment' (29 May 2018) *DPLF Blog*.

The Court does not cite scholars in the contents of its decisions. We found references to scholarly work in only two out of the 40 selected decisions. Notwithstanding, the Court has constant contact with academic circles in Latin America and beyond. The communication between the Court and academia – although difficult to measure – influences both the decisions of the Court and the work of scholars. The Court's decisions have historically had an impact in legal scholarship regarding human rights in the Americas. Conversely, some ideas and theories developed by scholars are reflected in the Court's jurisprudence. An interesting example of this phenomenon is the recent position of the Court regarding the enforceability of Article 26 of the American Convention. Although many factors were involved in the Court's position, it is reasonable to sustain that the Court was inspired by the writing of some scholars.[72] By the same token, the Court's jurisprudence has made economic, social and cultural rights the subject of increased academic interest within the human rights community in the region.[73]

II. Arguments in Constitutional Reasoning

A. The Structure of Constitutional Arguments

The judgments of the Court usually contain different types of arguments in a single document. However, most legal questions addressed by the Court are decided on a relatively linear manner, based on the direct application of the Convention or a rule or principle (a standard) defined in previous cases. In this manner, the reasoning is usually made by deploying one conclusive argument, or a chain of arguments following from one another. For instance, in the case of *Radilla Pacheco v Mexico* the Court concluded, in a direct fashion, that a case that involved a crime committed by a member of the armed forces could not be judged by a military court. Therefore, the State was in violation of the Convention. This decision was based on a previously – and well settled – standard that established that military courts cannot decide on cases that involved crimes committed by a member of the armed forces and where the victim is a civilian. By the same token, the Court, pursuant to Article 2 of the American Convention, required Mexico to modify its Military Criminal Code to make it compatible with the abovementioned standard.[74]

The Court formulates cumulative-parallel arguments in decisions that require more complex legal analysis. These types of arguments allow the Court to use cumulative arguments based on several rules, principles and sources to support a legal interpretation or conclusion that serves as a new standard. These arguments, however, would suffice on their own, but there is more than one argument pointing in a similar direction.

[72] See T Melish, 'La protección de los derechos económicos, sociales y culturales en el Sistema Interamericano de Derechos Humanos' (2003) *CDES-Yale Law School* 379–92, and V Abramovich and J Rossi, 'La tutela de los derechos económicos, sociales y culturales en el artículo 26 de la Convención Americana sobre Derechos Humanos' (2007) 9 *Revista Estudios Socio-Jurídicos. Universidad del Rosario* 34–53.

[73] See generally E Ferrer Mac-Gregor et al, *Inclusión, Ius Commune y justiciabilidad de los DESCA en la jurisprudencia interamericana: el caso Lagos del campo y los nuevos desafíos* (Instituto de Estudios Constitucionales del Estado de Querétaro, 2018).

[74] See *Case of Radilla Pacheco v Mexico*, paras 274 and 342.

For example, in the case of *Cuscul Pivaral et al v Guatemala*, the Court referred to a series of interpretative methods to define the scope of protection of Article 26 of the American Convention. The Court referred to several interpretative methods to arrive to its conclusion, asserting the independent validity of each one of them. The obiter dicta deployed arguments referring, inter alia, to the ordinary meaning of the terms of the treaty, a systemic approach, the *pro personae* principle, and to the object and purpose of the American Convention. These arguments allowed the Court to assert the direct enforceability of economic, social, cultural, and environmental rights based on Article 26 of the American Convention, including the right to health.[75]

Furthermore, the Court uses dialogic arguments by referring to considerations that are not conclusive by themselves but that taken altogether lead to a certain conclusion. For instance, this type of reasoning is used in decisions where the Court constructs its own conclusions by considering the arguments and practices of other domestic or international institutions that have interpreted certain right. In the case of *Artavia Murillo v Costa Rica* the Court discussed relevant treaties, case law, and decisions by other human rights protection systems such as the Universal Human Rights System, the jurisprudence of the European Court of Human Rights, and the African Human Rights Protection System to define the scope of the protection to the right to life as protected by Article 4.1 of the Convention. Moreover, the Court reviewed interpretations made by constitutional courts at the regional level. Although the reference to comparative law was not conclusive in the Court's reasoning, it reinforced its decision regarding the scope of protection of the right to life.[76]

B. Types of Arguments in Constitutional Reasoning

i. *General Principles of Interpretation*

The general theory of interpretation of the Inter-American Court is based on Articles 31 and 32 of the Vienna Convention on the Law of Treaties, and Article 29 of the American Convention.[77] In the Court's narrative, the Convention is interpreted through the simultaneous and joint application of the criteria of good faith and the ordinary meaning to be given to the terms of the treaty in their context and in the light of its object and purpose. Supplementary means of interpretation are also used for the interpretation of the Convention,[78] but the Court gives secondary interpretative status to the intention of the Parties to the treaty. The Court favours a teleological and evolutive interpretation that reflect the objective values that the Inter-American System seeks to support.[79]

[75] See *Cuscul Pivaral et al v Guatemala*. Preliminary Objections, Merits, Reparations and Costs Judgment, Inter-Am. Ct. H.R. (Ser. C) No. 359, (23 August 2018), paras 75–93.

[76] See *Artavia Murillo et al v Costa Rica*. Preliminary Objections, Merits, Reparations and Costs Judgment, Inter-Am. Ct. H.R. (Ser. C) No. 257, (28 November 2012), paras 224–244 and 254–256.

[77] See The Environment and Human Rights (State obligations in relation to the environment in the context of the protection and guarantee of the rights to life and to personal integrity – interpretation and scope of Articles 4(1) and 5(1) of the American Convention on Human Rights). Advisory Opinion OC-23, Inter-Am. Ct. H.R. (Ser. A) No. 23 (15 November 2017) paras 40–45.

[78] Arts 31 and 32 of the Vienna Convention on the Law of Treaties (Vienna, 23 May 1969).

[79] See *Case of González et al. ('Cotton Field') v Mexico*, para 33.

The methods of interpretation followed by the Court are akin to the idea of systemic interpretation of the American Convention, which is based on Articles 31.3 of the Vienna Convention and Article 29 of the American Convention. These provisions allow defining the content of the rights protected by the Convention in relationship with other norms and principles of international human rights law,[80] and to interpret treaties in a manner that attain its 'appropriate effect' (*efecto útil or effet utile*).[81]

The following paragraphs refer to the main types of arguments that the Court has used in its reasoning, which are theoretically grounded in its general theory of interpretation. The analysis is based on the categories defined by the CORE Project Guide, and on our database of 40 landmark decisions chosen for this project.

ii. Ordinary Meaning of the Words

The Court discussed the ordinary meaning of words in 20 decisions and has referred to historical arguments in 18 decisions. This is not surprising considering that the point of departure for the analysis of cases are the provisions of the American Convention or of any other treaty upon which the Court has jurisdiction. References to the text of the treaty are therefore present in all the decisions, and in some of them are directly discussed by the Court. Notwithstanding these numbers, arguments dealing with the ordinary meaning of the words and the intention of the parties reflected in the *travaux préparatoires* are usually not decisive. They tend to be overruled by other arguments based on comparative sources, legal concepts and principles, or precedents. For example, in the case of *Castañeda Gutman v Mexico*, the Court rejected the argument of the representatives of the victim regarding the adequate interpretation of the word 'only' in Article 23.2 of the Convention asserting that 'it is not possible to disregard paragraph 1 of this Article and interpret paragraph 2 in isolation, nor is it possible to disregard the other provisions of the Convention or the basic principles that inspire it to interpret Article 23 as a whole'.[82]

iii. Harmonising Arguments and Reference to Foreign (National) Law[83]

To establish the scope of the rights recognised by the American Convention, the Court usually relies on the broader system of norms and principles that are part of the *Corpus Juris* of international human rights law, including soft law. The origin of the universalist interpretative approach of the Inter-American Court can be traced back to the *Advisory Opinion OC-1/82*. In that decision, the Court reasoned that there is a common core of human rights based on the attributes of human personality, and from this follows a tendency to integrate the regional and universal systems for the protection of

[80] See The Right to Information on Consular Assistance in the Framework of the Guarantees of the due Process of Law. Advisory Opinion OC-16, Inter-Am. Ct. H.R. (Ser. A) No. 16 (1 October 1999) para 114.

[81] See *Case of Velásquez Rodríguez v Honduras*. Preliminary Objections, para 30.

[82] *Castañeda Gutman v Mexico*. Preliminary Objections, Merits, Reparations and Costs Judgment, Inter-Am. Ct. H.R. (Ser. C) No. 184, (6 August 2008), para 153.

[83] For the purposes of this project, we deemed it necessary to adapt these indicators to match the specific functions of the Inter-American Court of Human Rights.

human rights.[84] In terms of the categories studied in this project, it is possible to say that the Court relies extensively on harmonising arguments with international law, and has recently incorporated references to foreign (national) law as part of its reasoning.

Harmonising arguments with international law are present in instances where the Court seeks to find coherence with the rest of the international legal system, by relying on the case law of other international human rights protection systems or other international courts. To identify trends in this regard, we used the Q15 indicator (Harmonising with international law requirements). As shown in Figure 3, the Court overwhelmingly employs other treaties of the Inter-American System alongside the American Convention. The Court also frequently employs or cites other binding and non-binding sources such as treaties, precedents, opinions, and reports, particularly from the European Court of Human Rights and the UN System.[85] In some instances, these references seem to be highly influential for the reasoning of the Court in asserting the content of rights. Only two cases in our sample do not have any reference to other sources of international law beyond the Inter-American System, and only in two more is there no reference to other sources but the American Convention.[86]

Figure 3 Results for indicator Q15 harmonizing with international law requirements

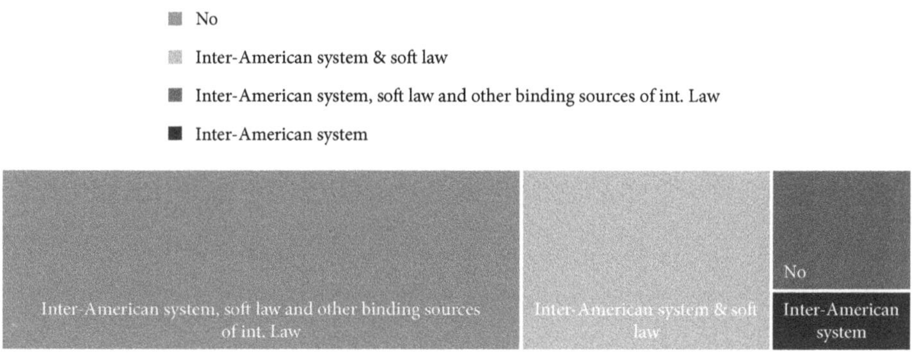

The Court has also referred to foreign (national) law as an argument in and of itself. 14 of the cases had some reference to decisions of Latin American courts, and half of those included citations to constitutional courts beyond State members of the OAS. In this regard, there are important scholarly works that have systematically explored

[84] See generally Other treaties subject to the consultative jurisdiction of the Court (Art 64 American Convention on Human Rights). Advisory Opinion OC-1/82 of 24 September 1982, paras 41–43; for an analysis and discussion on the controversies surrounding the use of external sources to interpret the Convention, see M de Pauw, 'The Inter-American Court of Human Rights and the Interpretative Method of External Referencing' in Yves Haeck et al (eds), *The Inter-American Court of Human Rights: Theory and Practice, Present and Future* (Intersentia, 2015) 3–24.

[85] See *Hacienda Brasil Verde Workers v Brazil*. Preliminary Objections, Merits, Reparations and Costs Judgment, Inter-Am. Ct. H.R. (Ser. C) No. 318, (20 October 2016) paras 259–68.

[86] See *Case of Barrios Altos v Peru*. Merits, Inter-Am. Ct. H.R. (Ser. C) No. 75, (14 March 2001), and Exceptions to the Exhaustion of Domestic Remedies (Arts 46(1), 46(2)(a) and 46(2)(b) American Convention on Human Rights). Advisory Opinion OC-11, Inter-Am. Ct. H.R. (Ser. A) No. 11 (10 August 1990).

this 'judicial dialogue' between the Inter-American Court and domestic courts.[87] It is an established fact that national high courts in the Latin American space are constitutionalising international law, as has been empirically demonstrated through concrete datasets.[88] By the same token, our sample suggests that the Court itself started 'listening' to national courts relatively recently, in 2008. Yet, the Court has not developed a consistent methodology to discuss the opinion of domestic courts and there is no clarity on the normative value that these references have for the reasoning of the Court.

iv. Precedents

Precedents seem to be the most relevant method of interpretation followed by the Court, both from a quantitative and qualitative perspective. From our sample, 38 selected decisions were decided by precedent-based arguments. As mentioned before, when deciding cases, the Court refers to the general principles and rules established previously in its judgments (a standard), and then applies them to the concrete case at hand. The exceptions to this approach are cases where the Court has not previously decided on a similar question. But even then, the Court will usually refer to its previous decisions before addressing new legal questions. Consequently, it is common for the Court to gradually increase the scope of protection of human rights by formulating additions to the principles previously established in other cases – which then serve as the basis for analysing future decisions. Here it is important to highlight that new standard use to emerge as the result of interpretations of the treaty that are 'abstract' – this is not necessarily contingent on the facts of a concrete case, but on the content of the right that is being interpreted. For this reason, it is rare that the Court restrains from the application of precedents by distinguishing the facts of different cases, as it is a practice in common law traditions.

v. Teleological Arguments and the Pro Personae *Principle*

For the Court, the object and purpose of the treaty is the 'protection of the fundamental rights of the human beings'.[89] This notion reinforces the view that the interpretation of the American Convention must be guided by the values protected by the Inter-American System rather than the intention of the Parties. From our sample, the Court referred to arguments on the object and purpose of the text in 22 judgments. However, these references seem to be used more as a complementary argument that reinforces other explicitly decisive arguments. Usually, the Court does not discuss the specific

[87] See A Von Bogdandy, et al (eds), *Ius constitutionale commune en América Latina: Textos básicos para su comprensión* (Instituto de Estudios Constitucionales de Estado de Querétaro, 2017).

[88] See E Gonzalez-Ocantos, 'Communicative Entrepreneurs: The Case of the Inter-American Court of Human Rights' Dialogue with National Judges' (2018) 62 *International Studies Quarterly* 737–50.

[89] See generally The Environment and Human Rights (State obligations in relation to the environment in the context of the protection and guarantee of the rights to life and to personal integrity – interpretation and scope of Articles 4(1) and 5(1) of the American Convention on Human Rights), Advisory Opinion OC-23, Inter-Am. Ct. H.R. (Ser. A) No. 23 (15 November 2017), para 41.

object and purpose of a provision, but the overall objective of the treaty. For instance, in the *Advisory Opinion 24*, the Court interpreted the meaning of the term 'family' in the American Convention. The Court decided the question of gay marriage mainly – although not exclusively – in an interpretation of Article 17 based on sociological and systemic arguments and considerations (paragraphs 174 to 186), but reinforced its conclusion referring to the object and purpose of the treaty (paragraph 187).[90]

With a similar logic, the Court has considered the *pro personae* principle as a guiding element to interpret the Convention from 'the best perspective for the protection of the individual'.[91] This principle requires the content and scope of rights to be interpreted broadly, and restrictions narrowly.[92] The use of this principle of interpretation tends to maximise the content of rights, and limit the possibility of restrictions.[93] The *pro personae* principle may be a cross-cutting notion within the Inter-American system. However, we found that this principle was explicitly referred to in less than half of the selected cases (17 cases). And even when it is mentioned, its purpose is not clear in the Court's reasoning. This could be deemed as a counter intuitive. Yet, we contend that the principle serves as some sort of meta legal principle that inspires the interpretation of the Convention, rather than a substantive argument that impacts the outcome of the decision.

Furthermore, it is possible to argue that a *pro personae* interpretation reinforces the view that human rights treaties are living instruments, and that their interpretation must evolve with the times to become a more effective instrument for the protection of human dignity.[94] The Court has indicated in several instances that the evolutive interpretation is based on the general rules of interpretation established in the Vienna Convention and Article 29 of the American Convention.[95] Evolutive interpretation also relies on systemic and sociological arguments since they are necessary to show how the content of a right has 'evolved'. In this sense, in the case of *'Street Children' (Villagran Morales et. al.) v Guatemala*, the Court stated that international human rights law advances substantially by the evolutive interpretation of international protection instruments.[96]

vi. Other Types of Arguments

As mentioned before, the Court rarely refers to scholarly work in its decisions. From our sample, references to scholarly work were only made in two cases and they were not explicitly discussed in the text of the decisions. The Court used analogies in 14 cases. Regarding the use of arguments of silence, our data showed that they were referred to in

[90] See *Case of Furlan and family v Argentina*, Inter-Am. Ct. H.R. (Ser. C) No. 246, (31 August 2012), paras 38–39.

[91] See Advisory Opinion OC-23, para 41.

[92] See C Medina, *The American Convention on Human Rights. Crucial Rights and their Theory and Practice* (Intersentia, 2014) 52.

[93] See *Case of Petro Urrego v Colombia*, Inter-Am. Ct. H.R. (Ser. C) No. 406, (8 July 2020), paras 94–95.

[94] See *Case of the 'Street Children' (Villagrán Morales et al.) v Guatemala*. Merits, Inter-Am. Ct. H.R. (Ser. C) No. 77, (26 May 2001), para 193.

[95] See *Case of Atala Riffo and daughters v Chile*, para 83.

[96] See *Case of the 'Street Children' (Villagrán Morales et al.) v Guatemala*, paras 193–194.

11 cases. There are other principles used by the Court that were not codified but that are certainly relevant for the reasoning of the Convention, such as the principle of subsidiarity or complementarity,[97] or the notion that human rights are universal, indivisible, and interdependent.[98] These principles are part of the concepts of international human rights in general, and of the Inter-American System in particular. They also have important relevant normative consequences in the interpretation of treaties. Finally, regarding this point, the Court has referred to arguments based on the principles of dignity, equality, or proportionality, which are also common language in constitutional law.[99]

C. The Overall Weight of the Arguments

From a quantitative and qualitative perspective, the arguments that have the greater weight in the Court's jurisprudence are those based on precedent. This is not a definitive rule, since the Court is not legally obligated to follow its precedents, and there are exceptions and even contradictions in the Court's jurisprudence. Yet, our sample confirmed that in most aspects, the Court tends to decide legal questions in accordance with its previous decisions. In cases that present a novel question, or where there is a change in the Court's criterion, the reasoning of the Court seems to be based – first and foremost – on arguments that reflect the application of principles that increase the protection of human rights. In that sense, one could argue that the principles of effectiveness, *pro personae* and evolutive interpretation are implicitly dominant in the Court's reasoning. These principles help to explain the incrementalistic approach of the Court's interpretations, and its tendency to reject arguments that are too deferential with States or that may result in a narrow understanding of the content of rights.

The cases studied show that other arguments are also important, especially for determining the content of the rights recognised by the Convention. These arguments may explore the ordinary meaning of the words, or the subsequent practice of states, or what other courts and committees have said regarding a similar question. The use of these arguments seems to be focused on giving the provisions of the Convention the most effective – usually expansive – understanding of rights. An example of this can be seen in cases like *Indigenous Community Yakye Axa v Paraguay*, where the Court concluded that the right to 'communal property' was protected by Article 21 of the American Convention (right to private property).[100] This conclusion had much more to do with increasing the protection of human rights of indigenous communities than with exploring the meaning of the term 'private property' or the subsequent practice of States.

[97] See *Case of Las Palmeras v Colombia*. Merits, Inter-Am. Ct. H.R. (Ser. C) No. 90, (6 December 2001), para 33, see generally P Carozza, Subsidiarity as a Structure Principle of International Law (2003) 97 *American Journal of International Law* 79.

[98] See Vienna Declaration and Programme of Action, 25 June 1993, para 5.

[99] See below, section II(G) on 'Key Concepts'.

[100] See *Case of the Yakye Axa Indigenous Community v Paraguay*, Inter-Am. Ct. H.R. (Ser. C) No. 125, (17 June 2005), para 137.

D. Judicial Candour and Judicial Rhetoric

The format and the structure of the reasoning component of judgments – referred to as *consideraciones* – usually consists of two different parts. In the first part, the Court indicates the relevant guiding rules and principles for the decision. As mentioned before, these standards are mainly construed by referring to previous decisions, the American Convention, other human rights treaties, and a variety of sources of international and domestic law, all interpreted through various methods. It is usually in this section where the Court creates new legal standards that then are applied in future cases. In the second part of the reasoning component, the facts of the case are analysed based on the allegations of the parties, the applicable legal standards, and the evidence. Sometimes new legal standards are developed in this section, although it tends to be more focused on solving concrete legal questions. The language used by the Court in this section tends to be objective and logical, with not too much consideration of non-legal arguments or value judgments.

In terms of the target audience, the Court's judgments are formally addressed to the parties to the case and the Commission. This might help to explain why the Court presents long elaborations on the facts of the case, makes extensive references to different sources of law, and establishes detailed – and extensive – reparations. These elements might also aim to strengthen the legal force of its decisions. This aspect is particularly relevant for the effectiveness of judgments in concrete cases, to avoid the occurrence of similar facts in the future, and to ensure justice for the victims. Furthermore, the Court's decisions may play a role in the elaboration of legal doctrines that contribute to the development of IHRL, to evidence human rights violations in the region, and to contribute to produce changes at the State level. From that perspective, other courts and human rights institutions at the international and domestic level, the academic community, and civil society, are a relevant audience for the Court.

E. Length, Dissenting and Concurring Opinions

The selected judgments have an average length of 107 pages. It is not possible to draw correlations between topics and length, as all cases analysed by the Court concern fundamental rights. However, variations in length can be explained due to other much more circumstantial factors. First, during the early years of the Court, each case entailed three separate decisions: admissibility, merits, and reparations. For this reason, most opinions below 70 pages in our sample are decisions that concern solely the merits of a particular case. Second, in cases such as *Barrios Altos*, the State recognised its international responsibility. Therefore, the Court did not review the evidence and there was no discussion on the facts of the case. Third, we also contend that length will be contingent on factors that relate to the specific circumstances of the case, such as the number of victims[101] or the complexity of evidentiary issues.[102]

[101] See *Case of the Massacres of El Mozote and surrounding areas v El Salvador*, Inter-Am. Ct. H.R. (Ser. C) No. 252, (25 October 2012), para 1.

[102] See *Case of Rodríguez Vera et al. (The Disappeared from the Palace of Justice) v Colombia*, Inter-Am. Ct. H.R. (Ser. C) No. 287, (14 November 2014), para 1.

The practice of judges submitting separate opinions is certainly high, considering that it happened in 32 of the selected decisions. This high presence of opinions seems logical since in landmark cases – such as those in our sample – there is usually more controversy and judges might want to express their views. Furthermore, the requirements for separate opinions established in the Rules of Procedure are simple (they must be reasoned, presented within a time limit established by the President of the Court, and should refer to the case).[103] Yet, it is worth noticing that the sample is not representative of the practice of the Court. By reviewing the historical data, we found the percentage of dissenting and concurring opinions to be much lower in general terms.

F. Framing of Constitutional Issues

The great majority of cases decided by the Inter-American Court involve fundamental rights and due process issues. This should not come as a surprise, since the Court's mandate is precisely to interpret the American Convention and other human rights treaties in the Inter-American System. Additionally, a case can be brought to the Court only after domestic remedies have been exhausted. In other words, most cases that come to the Court do so after domestic remedies were not effective, and there were violations to due process. In fact, basic procedural rights are invoked in 35 cases of our sample (90 per cent), far exceeding the regional average of 35.8 per cent. The Court has not analysed the organisation of the State in any of the cases in our sample. However, when the Court has addressed issues that touch upon government systems, it is mostly to assert that the government structure was an influence in the fulfilment – or lack of fulfilment – of their human rights obligations. The focus on the analysis of fundamental rights issues and due process is a tendency that has been constant in the Court's case law and that reflects its nature as a regional human rights court.

G. Key Concepts

Whilst identifying the Court's key concepts, we found both unsurprising and counterintuitive results. The sample confirmed that the Court relies on notions like dignity (22 cases), equality (22 cases), the *pro personae* principle (17 cases), proportionality (16 cases), or the core of human rights (15 cases). These concepts reflect some basic principles of international human rights law. However, the details in the data also show some unexpected results that are equally telling of the Court's reasoning and ethos. For example, there are no judgments that refer to State form, or very few that address the government system by its power structure or procedural structure, or even mechanisms of political control. This shows that the Court's focus is mainly addressing human rights violations from the standpoint of the claimant party. However, the Court has referred to concepts such as democracy (15 cases), the rule of law (17 cases), judicial independence (7 cases) and post material values (11 cases). By doing so, the Court has touched upon

[103] See Art 65.2 of the Rules of Procedure of the IACtHR.

consequential questions of governance such as the limits of popular referendum,[104] the powers of domestic electoral systems[105] and judicial governance,[106] to name a few.

III. Comparative Perspective

The Court's reasoning has characteristics that are inherent to its role as a regional court of human rights. Naturally, they are distinct to those of constitutional courts. The Court is an international judicial institution whose main purpose concerns the interpretation and application of the provisions of the American Convention or other treaties of similar nature. As such, there are indicators in our dataset where the Court is surely an outlier when compared with constitutional courts. For example, it is expected that an international tribunal harmonise its opinions with international law requirements (Q15). Hence, 95 per cent of the rulings analysed used some form of binding or non-binding instruments of international law. In contrast, 50 per cent is the average for this indicator within the constitutional courts analysed in other chapters.

Notwithstanding, we contend that the Court shares a space of competence and practices with constitutional courts in the region. All constitutional courts must also solve fundamental rights questions and establish the scope and content of rights recognised in their respective jurisdictions. This leads to the use of several concepts and arguments by both types of courts, although the Inter-American Court may use some of these concepts more frequently. In this regard, the Court is one of the leaders among the rest of the tribunals that have been analysed in our dataset in the use of arguments such as proportionality (Q35),[107] human dignity (Q37),[108] or equality (Q38).[109]

It is worth mentioning that the Inter-American Court has more limited powers than constitutional courts in two crucial questions: it does not decide questions on the organisation of power and does not have the power to directly strike down laws or judicial decisions of lower courts. However, as shown in the previous section, this does not mean it has not indirectly addressed these questions. For example, the Court does not perform abstract judicial review of laws, and yet it has ordered domestic legal systems to be changed when a domestic law – applied in a concrete case – is incompatible with the American Convention.[110]

IV. Evaluation, Pathology and Criticism

The Court's reasoning methods and practices have some non-surprising features: they tend to favour interpretations that maximise the scope of rights and that increase the

[104] See *Case Gelman v Uruguay*. Merits and Reparations, Inter-Am. Ct. H.R. (Ser. C) No. 221, (24 February 2011).
[105] See *Case of Yatama v Nicaragua*, Inter-Am. Ct. H.R. (Ser. C) No. 127, (23 June 2005).
[106] See *Case of López Lone et al. v Honduras*, Inter-Am. Ct. H.R. (Ser. C) No. 302, (5 October 2015).
[107] Used in 42.5% of cases; the LAC average is 27.3%.
[108] Used in 52.5% of cases; the LAC average is 29.4%.
[109] Used in 55% of cases; the LAC average is 40%.
[110] See *Case of Radilla Pacheco v Mexico*, para 342.

influence of its decisions at the State level. We contend that this ethos is an operation of the principles of effectiveness, *pro personae* and evolutive interpretation, which work as meta legal principles that inspire the interpretations of the Court, both in substantive and procedural questions. Furthermore, the Court seems to define the content of rights in relationship with the broader system of norms and principles that are part of the *Corpus Juris* of international human rights law. This method allows the Court to accept and incorporate into its cases novel (usually broader) interpretations to define the content of rights. In that regard, the empirical analysis shows that the use of international sources (soft law and the decisions of other international Courts, particularly the European Court of Human Rights) is present in 38 of 40 cases. The ordinary meaning of words and the intention of States is mostly not a defining aspect in the reasoning of the Court, but rather a point of departure for the interpretation of the Convention.

The approach taken by the Court regarding the interpretation and application of the provisions of the American Convention has historically given little space to considerations of the subsidiary position of the Inter-American System, adopting a strict scrutiny on State action and an expansive approach of the scope of rights and reparations. This tendency might be partially explained by the experience of the State's lack of compliance with their human rights obligations, and the serious and blatant human rights violations that have been historically brought to the Inter-American System. Notwithstanding the widespread acceptance that the Court has by and large enjoyed in its first 44 years of existence, some aspects of the Court's methods and practices of interpretation might require adjustment and revision as new realities and challenges exist in the region. These challenges of interpretation might emerge as more sophisticated and contested questions are brought to the Court (such as the validity of peace agreements or controversies of economic, social and cultural rights), and as the States improve their democratic credentials and the Rule of Law at the domestic level.

13

The Jurisprudence of the Supreme Court of Justice of the Nation of Mexico*

ROBERTO NIEMBRO ORTEGA AND IRENE SPIGNO

I. Legal, Political, Institutional and Academic Context

A. Legal and Political Culture as Context for the Constitutional Reasoning

In Mexico, judicial review in a meaningful sense began 25 years ago.[1] Before the constitutional amendment of 1995, which helped reinforce the Mexican Supreme Court as a constitutional court, we cannot think about constitutional reasoning. Once the Supreme Court began to defend the Constitution[2] as an independent institution, it became a binding law, and it is from that moment on that we can talk about constitutional reasoning.[3]

The Mexican Supreme Court was part of the authoritarian regime that ruled during the 70 years of the Institutional Revolutionary Party (PRI, from its initials in Spanish) government. By different mechanisms, such as nominations and dismissals, the President controlled the Court and reduced it to a secondary role.[4] Fortunately,

* The selection of the 40 leading cases is the result of the joint work of the authors. The chapter has been written by Roberto Niembro Ortega (sections I(A), I(B), II(A), II(B), II(C) and IV) and by Irene Spigno (sections I(C), I(D), II(D), II(E), II(F), II(G) and III).

[1] In this part of the chapter, we follow what one of us published before: R Niembro Ortega, 'John Hart Ely in the Mexican Supreme Court' (2021) 19 *International Journal Constitutional Law*.

[2] H Fix-Zamudio, *Estudio de la defensa de la Constitución el ordenamiento mexicano* (Porrúa-Instituto de Investigaciones Jurídicas, UNAM, 2005).

[3] A Jakab, A Dyevre and G Itzcovich, 'Introduction: Comparing Constitutional Reasoning with Quantitative and Qualitive Methods' in A Jakab et al (eds), *Comparative Constitutional Reasoning* (Cambridge University Press, 2017) 12.

[4] See B Magaloni, 'Authoritarianism, Democracy and the Supreme Court: Horizontal Exchange and the Rule of Law in Mexico' in S Mainwaring and Ch Welna (eds), *Democratic Accountability in Latin America* (Oxford University Press, 2003) 287. For Andrea Pozas and Julio Ríos there are three different roles of the justices of the Mexican Supreme Court: from 1917 to 1940 the justices' role was that of adjudicators, from 1941 to 1997 they performed as regime supporters, and from 1998 to 2013 their role consisted on being constitutional interpreters. A Pozas Loyo and J Ríos Figueroa, 'The Transformations of the Role of the Mexican Supreme Court' in A Castagnola and S López Noriega (eds), *Judicial Politics in Mexico: The Supreme Court and the Transition to Democracy* (Routledge, 2016) 10.

the Court has slowly moved towards becoming a stronger and more independent body, through the 1994 reform, the alternation in the presidency of the Republic in the year 2000, and subsequent changes in 2011. In its newly strengthened role, thus, the Court has started to guarantee fundamental rights.

During the authoritarian period, despite the Court's passive role and subordination to the Executive Branch, the Executive Branch needed the Supreme Court to give legal legitimisation to the regime. With the PRI as the single dominant political party, the government was able to enact constitutional reforms that weakened the Court's independence, in particular, the reform of 1928, which allowed the President to propose to the Senate the candidates for Justices, and the reform of 1934, which reduced the lifetime appointment of Justices to a six-year period. In this context, the Supreme Court limited itself largely to the resolution of conflicts of legality and to the maintenance of a cordial relationship with the head of the Executive.[5]

Throughout this period, the Supreme Court resorted to the literal interpretation of the Constitution but it did not have a proper constitutional theory to guide its decisions, which mainly regarded legality issues, and it did not take part in the political processes.[6] Likewise, the counter-majoritarian difficulty of the judicial control of legislation, which was discussed obsessively in the United States,[7] was never a great concern for Mexican political elites or academia.

In a broad sense, the democratic transition in Mexico began in 1977, with the incorporation of elected representatives based on the principle of proportional representation, and ended in 2000, with the alternation in the Republic's presidency.

Once the multi-party system gained strength, and power began to alternate in the Executive Branch – at the local level since 1989 and at the federal level after the presidential election of 2000 – the Judicial Branch started to gain greater relevance as an independent and autonomous political actor.[8] As well, political parties needed a coordination mechanism that would allow them to solve their conflicts.[9] This relevance peaked with the constitutional reforms of 1995 and 2011, which marked a new conception and narrative of the function of constitutional justice in Mexico.

First, the Supreme Court experienced an important change through the constitutional reform of 1995, when its jurisdiction to deal with constitutional procedures of abstract review was established and the cases of conflicts among branches or levels of government were broadened. In 1996, another reform gave the Supreme Court the power to review electoral legislation. In the first 13 years of the 1995-reformed Court, its main areas of concern were conflicts between branches of government and disputes between the Federation, federative entities, and municipalities,[10] and its main function

[5] P Domingo, 'Judicial Independence: The Politics of the Supreme Court in Mexico' (2000) 32 *Journal of Latin American Studies* 705, 706, 710; Magaloni (n 4) 285. See P Mijangos y González, *Historía Mínima de la Suprema Corte de Justicia de México* (El Colegio de México, 2019) 142.

[6] JR Cossío Díaz, *Dogmática constitucional y régimen autoritario* (Fontamara, 2016) 125, 135.

[7] B Friedman, 'The Birth of an Academic Obsession: The History of the Countermajoritarian Difficulty, Part Five' (2002) 112 *Yale Law* Journal.

[8] Domingo (n 5) 728, 731; Magaloni (n 4) 267; A Sánchez, B Magaloni and Eric Magar, 'Legalist versus Interpretativist. The Supreme Court and the Democratic Transition in Mexico' in G Helmke and J Ríos-Figueroa (eds), *Courts in Latin America* (Cambridge University Press, 2011) 215.

[9] Magaloni (n 4) 295.

[10] J Carpizo, 'Reformas Constitucionales al Poder Judicial Federal y a la Jurisdicción Constitucional del 31 de Diciembre de 1994' (1995) 83 *Boletín Mexicana de Dererecho Comparado*.

was to resolve political conflicts[11] which in the past had been solved by the President in his capacity as the party's leader.[12] Hence, during the first phase of the democratic context (1995–2008), the Supreme Court fulfilled the role of being an arbitrator of political conflicts between branches of government[13] – that is, between political elites.[14] These transitions, of course, took place within a democracy understood in a minimalistic way,[15] since the main concern was to ensure a peaceful alternation of power at the federal and local levels. However, over time, constitutional scholars began to critique the Court for being too removed from the citizenry[16] and asked the Court to protect human rights and consider substantive values.[17]

In the second phase of the democratic context (2008),[18] the Supreme Court included human rights on its agenda and adopted a substantial vision of democracy, in which its role as a counter-majoritarian institution is not called into question as long as it guarantees and provides content to fundamental rights. In this 'rights agenda' phase, several methodologies – such as the proportionality test – have been adopted, giving judges a wide margin of action. However, the role of the Supreme Court has been called into question in the new regime inaugurated by the 2018 elections, which urges us to reconsider the role of Mexican judges.

The human rights agenda that started to flourish about 12 years ago gained strength with the constitutional human rights and *Amparo* trial reforms of 2011.[19] Since then, human rights cases have occupied a considerable part of the Supreme Court's docket. The resolution of human rights cases has allowed the Court: (1) to study and apply principles of constitutional interpretation, and (2) to use methodologies to analyse the constitutionality of its restrictions and implement levels of scrutiny.

[11] A Zaldívar Lelo de Larrea, 'La Justicia Constitucional en México. Balance y Retos' in J Vega Gómez and E Corzo Sosa (coords), *Tribunales y justicia constitucional* (UNAM, 2002) 423.

[12] Magaloni (n 4) 293.

[13] Sánchez et al (n 8) 187; A Zaldívar Lelo de Larrea, 'La Suprema Corte en la democracia mexicana' *Revista Nexos*, 1 de septiembre de 2017 at www.nexos.com.mx/?p=33469. For a different opinion see A Castagnola and S López Noriega, 'Are Mexican Justices True arbiters among the political elites? An empirical analysis of the court's rulings from 2000–2011' in A Castagnola and S López Noriega (eds), *Judicial Politics in Mexico. The Supreme Court and the Transition to Democracy* (Routledge, 2016) 87.

[14] B Magaloni, 'Enforcing the Autocratic Political Order and the Role of Courts: The Case of Mexico' in T Ginsburg and T Moustafa (eds), *Rule by Law. The Politics of Courts in Authoritarian Regimes* (Cambridge University Press, 2008) 180; Pozas Loyo and Ríos Figueroa (n 4) 29.

[15] J Schumpeter, *Capitalism, Socialism and Democracy* (Harper & Brothers, 1942).

[16] ibid 272.

[17] AL Magaloni and A Zaldívar, 'El ciudadano olvidado' in R Vázquez (comp), *Corte, Jueces y Política* (Fontamara, 2007) 111–15. For a response see R Lara, R Mejía and F Pou, '¿De verdad deseamos una corte redentora?' in the same book.

[18] I place the beginning of this second phase in 2008 based on the increased number of certioraris granted by the Court in cases related to the interpretation of human rights. See Suprema Corte de Justicia de la Nación, *Los Derechos Humanos en las Solicitudes de Ejercicio de Facultad de Atracción*, Portal de Estadística Judicial at estadisticajudicial.scjn.gob.mx/documents/temasJudiciales/DDHH_en_SEFAS.pdf.

[19] M Carbonell and P Salazar (coords), *La reforma constitucional de derechos humanos. Un nuevo paradigma* (Instituto de Investigaciones Jurídicas-UNAM, 2011); F Pou, 'The Constitution of Mexico' in C Hübner Mendes and R Gargarella (eds), *The Oxford Handbook of Latin American Constitutional Law* (Oxford University Press, 2022) 6. There are two landmark decisions of the Supreme Court related to the human rights reform of 2011: Expediente Varios 912/2010 and Contradicción de Tesis 293/2011. In these cases, the Court established that human rights on international treaties are part of the Constitution. Moreover, the jurisprudence of the Inter American Court of Human Rights is binding for Mexican judges, if it is more progressive than the Mexican.

The Mexican Supreme Court has opted, without further theoretical or jurisdictional discussion, for a theory that legitimises judges to make the final decisions on deeply controversial moral issues.[20] In this regard, Ely's proceduralist theory has had very little influence in Mexico,[21] while other authors such as Ronald Dworkin, Robert Alexy, or the Italian Luigi Ferrajoli have been profusely studied and quoted by the Mexican Supreme Court.

The Supreme Court's adoption of a strong model of judicial review and a substantive conception of democracy, which grounds the legitimacy of constitutional justice in the results that it renders in the protection of human rights, is reflected in the adoption of methodologies such as the proportionality test and, particularly, a maximalist approach of that test.[22] In the Mexican context, the use of this method is part of the gradual departure from formalism[23] and its tools, like judicial syllogisms, to solve cases. Likewise, the strong model is shown in the resolution of landmark cases in which the Court has made an assessment of economic freedoms or fundamental liberties.

In Mexico, as in many other Latin American countries, the primary methodology employed to analyse the constitutionality of limits to fundamental rights is the proportionality test also the Supreme Court uses the reasonableness test.[24] In addition, we have not considered the application of different tests depending on which right is at issue, nor the idea of interests-based balancing[25] in which rights have no automatic preference.

B. The Court and Constitutional Litigation

i. *Jurisdiction*

The Supreme Court's constitutional review powers reside in the resolution of amparo actions, constitutional controversies, and actions of unconstitutionality (abstract review).[26] Sometimes, the Court has called public hearings in some highly controversial cases, for example, when it analysed the liberalisation of abortion in Mexico City or the unconstitutionality of the telecommunications act in 2006.

Only the full Court with a qualified majority decision of eight votes through a general declaration of unconstitutionality in an indirect amparo trial, in actions of unconstitutionality or constitutionality controversies – in the cases set forth in the Article 105,

[20] Cossío Díaz (n 6) 139 ff.

[21] The only quote that we have found of his work in Mexican jurisprudence is a dissenting opinion written by Justice Arturo Zaldívar in the *Acción de Inconstitucionalidad* 63/2017, to argue that the LGBTI community is a social minority. The action was solved by the Full Court on 21 September 2017.

[22] What is distinctive about it is that 'limitations on human rights must be justified by reference to gains on some other interest, principles, or value. The question is whether the gains are enough to compensate for the loss on the side of the right engaged by the measure'. F Urbina, *A Critique of Proportionality and Balancing* (Cambridge University Press, 2017) 18–19.

[23] Pou (n 19) 21.

[24] M Cohen-Eliya and I Porat, 'American Balancing and German Proportionality: The historical origins' (2010) 8 *International Journal of Constitutional Law* 263, 272, 274.

[25] I Porat, 'From Interests-Based Balancing to Rights-Based Balancing: Two Models of Balancing in the Early Days of American Constitutional Balancing' (2007) at papers.ssrn.com/sol3/papers.cfm?abstract_id=1012592.

[26] For a general overview see H Fix Zamudio, *Estudio de la defensa de la Constitución en el ordenamiento mexicano* (Porrúa, 2005).

fraction I, penultimate paragraph of the Constitution[27] – can annul statutes with general effects.

ii. Amparo Action

The amparo is one of the most venerated legal institutions in Mexico. It is a means of constitutional control of norms, acts or omissions that is promoted by individuals who allege the violation of a fundamental right. Any individual has legal standing to promote an amparo action when they allege the violation of a fundamental right and demonstrate a legitimate interest to dispute an act of authority.[28]

The resolutions of the Courts are binding to the authorities and must be promptly obeyed as per article 192 of the Amparo Law.[29] The failure to obey a decision of a federal court has severe consequences for the authorities.[30]

In the amparo, the consequences of the unconstitutionality vary depending on the nature of the contested act or norm. If the contested act is positive (an action), the remedy must restore the full enjoyment of the applicant's violated right. If the contested act is negative (an omission), the remedy will consist in an order for the authority to act in a way that complies with the content of the violated right. Lastly, if the contested act is a law, it will be declared unconstitutional but only regarding the applicant.[31] It should be noted that, normally, the effects of the amparo might only benefit the applicant, but there have been cases in which the court has extended the effects in a way that benefits a whole group of community (for example in the amparo under review 378/2014).[32]

iii. Constitutional Controversy and Action of Unconstitutionality

The constitutional controversy is a means of constitutional control whose purpose is to safeguard the separation of powers between the different branches of the government, the federation, the states, the municipalities, and the autonomous constitutional bodies. It can be filed by: the federal executive power, the federal congress, the local congresses, the governors, the judicial branches of the states and others.

[27] Art 105, fraction I, penultimate paragraph, of the Constitution: 'Provided that the controversies revolve around general provisions of the federative entities, the municipalities, or the territorial demarcations of Mexico City challenged by the Federation; of the municipalities or the territorial demarcations of Mexico City contested by the federative entities, or in the cases referred to in subparagraphs c) and h) above, and the resolution of the Supreme Court of Justice declares them invalid, such resolution will have general effects when approved by a majority of at least eight votes.' Subparagraph c) refers to the controversies between the Executive Power and the Congress of the Union; the Executive Power and either Chamber of Congress or, when applicable, the Permanent Commission. Subparagraph h) refers to the controversies between two powers of a same federative entity regarding the constitutionality of their acts or general provisions.

[28] Art 5, Amparo Law, Regulating Arts 103 and 107 of the Political Constitution of the Mexican United States.

[29] ibid Art 192.

[30] ibid Art 262.

[31] ibid Arts 77 and 78.

[32] Suprema Corte de Justicia de la Nación [SCJN], Amparo en Revisión 378/2014, solved on 15 October 2014, Second Chamber (Mex.), available in Spanish at www2.scjn.gob.mx/ConsultaTematica/PaginasPub/DetallePub.aspx?AsuntoID=166107.

The action of unconstitutionality is an abstract means of constitutional control of general norms. The actions of unconstitutionality can only be filed by 33 per cent of the members of the Chamber of Deputies or the Senate, the Legal Counsel of the Federal Executive Power, the equivalent of 33 per cent of the members of the local legislatures, the national leaderships of the political parties and others.[33]

A declaration of unconstitutionality issued in an action of unconstitutionality has the effect of expelling the contested norm – and all the norms from said law that share the unconstitutionality vice or that derive its validity from said norm – from the legal system.[34] In a constitutional controversy, the remedy set forth by the Court (the declaration of invalidity) shall have general effects if the case falls into the scenarios provided in the law. If it does not fall into any of said cases, the effects will only affect the parties of the trial, but neither the law nor the Constitution establish what kind of remedies the Court might set forth.[35]

iv. Case Load and Litigation

The workload of the Court has constantly grown: during the last 10 years it went from 5,775 cases to 11,723 cases. All cases are published but if there is any sensitive data this information is censored.

During the first half of 2019, the Supreme Court received 11,851 cases (this figure includes cases not related to the review of constitutionality). Of those cases, 94 were actions of unconstitutionality, 5,846 were direct amparos under review, 656 were amparos under review, 259 were controversies of competencies, 365 were thesis contradictions, 293 were constitutional controversies, 505 were requests for the Court to exercise its powers of attraction, 103 were incidents of non-execution of sentences, 63 were appeals for nonconformity, 1,962 were reclamations, and 32 were administrative revisions.[36] Of said cases, 34 per cent of the actions of unconstitutionality, 58 per cent of the constitutional controversies and 64 per cent of the amparos under review were rejected.[37]

C. The Judges

The Mexican Supreme Court of Justice was created by the 1824 Constitution,[38] which provided a composition of 11 Justices (called *ministers*). This number was confirmed by the original version of the current 1917 Constitution and changed through different

[33] Art 105 of the Constitution.

[34] ibid Art 41.

[35] Art 42, Law regulating fractions I and II of constitutional Art 105.

[36] Secretaría General de Acuerdos, *Estadística Mensual, julio 2019*. This information is available (in Spanish) at www.scjn.gob.mx/sites/default/files/pagina/documentos/2019-09/SGAEM0719.pdf.

[37] The information publicly available in the statistics portal of the Supreme Court only covers up until the first half of 2019. Suprema Corte de Justicia de la Nación, *Portal de Estadística Judicial*, estadisticajudicial.scjn.gob.mx/Inicio.aspx.

[38] The reference is to Art 9 of the *Acta Constitutiva de la Federación Mexicana*, issued on 31 January 1824.

reforms during the twentieth century. At the end of 1994, a new reform to the judicial power was consummated, and the Supreme Court returned to its composition of 11 Justices to function in plenary session and two chambers.[39]

The Justices of the Mexican Supreme Court are appointed by the Senate, chosen within a list of three candidates presented by the President of the Republic. They are appointed for a 15-year term,[40] and they cannot serve a second term (unless an interim minister has been appointed and his next term is with the respective appointment).[41] They may be removed only in the case of resignation for 'serious cause',[42] submitted to the executive and approved by the Senate, for unjustified absence for more than one month, permanent physical or mental disability, or death and they must comply with requirements indicated in Article 95, para IV.

Currently,[43] the Court consists of eight men and three women. The current Chief Justice (Arturo Zaldívar Lelo de Larrea) has 25 years of work experience as a lawyer and a strong academic background. The majority of the other Supreme Court Justices (eight out of 10) come from judicial careers, holding previous positions in local and federal courts and tribunals,[44] while only two practised as lawyers;[45] besides, four of them have also an academic profile,[46] and four were engaged in the public service.[47]

D. Legal Scholarship and Constitutional Reasoning

The relationship between legal scholarship and constitutional reasoning has significantly improved since 2011, when the Mexican Constitution was amended to include the Human Rights reform.[48] Before implementing the Human Rights reform, Mexican constitutional doctrine was quite deferential, reverential, and not very critical to the Court case law, as demonstrated by the few good doctrinal works available. However, since 2011, the Mexican constitutional judge has begun to develop advanced jurisprudential criteria that have been placing its judicial doctrine more in line with the constitutional scholarship, especially concerning human rights, thanks also to the presence of academics sitting in the Court.[49] This trend was accompanied by a strengthening

[39] ibid 231 ff.

[40] Art 94, para 12 of the Constitution.

[41] Art 94, para 13 of the Constitution.

[42] It is not specified in the Constitution or in the Organic Law of the Judicial Power of the Federation (*Ley Orgánica del Poder Judicial de la Federación*) which causes enter this assumption. However, Justice Eduardo Medina Mora resigned in 2019 without alleging any justification. According to the press, he resigned for being in the middle of a scandal since he received significant amounts of money incompatible with his salary.

[43] The information recollected in this paper is updated to 31 January 2021.

[44] They are Jorge Mario Pardo Rebolledo, Ana Margarita Ríos Farjat, Norma Lucía Piña Hernández, Javier Laynez Potisek, Luis María Aguilar Morales, Yasmín Esquivel Mossa, José Fernando Franco González Salas and Alberto Pérez Dayán.

[45] The reference is to Ana Margarita Ríos Farjat and Luis María Aguilar Morales.

[46] This is the case of Juan Luis González Alcántara Carrancá, Jorge Mario Pardo Rebolledo, Norma Lucía Piña Hernández and Alberto Pérez Dayán.

[47] They are Alfredo Gutiérrez Ortiz Mena, Javier Laynez Potisek, Yasmín Esquivel Mossa and José Fernando Franco González Salas.

[48] See *ex plurimis* M Carbonell and P Salazar (coords), *La reforma constitucional de derechos humanos: un nuevo paradigma* (Instituto de Investigaciones Jurídicas-UNAM, 2011).

[49] See at the end of the previous section.

of the studies of constitutionalism[50] that has implied not only the study of constitutional texts – that was part of the tradition of legal education in Mexico and somehow still is[51] – but also a more detailed approach to the judgments of the Supreme Court, which has implied from the academy an outstanding analysis of judicial arguments.[52] This process has also been stimulated thanks to the opening of the constitutional jurisprudence to human rights issues and the recognition of the binding nature of those Inter-American Court of Human Rights judgments in which the international responsibility of Mexico for the violation of one or more of the rights recognised in the American Convention on Human Rights is declared (as long as its application is more protective towards human rights, according to Article 1 of the Constitution).[53]

In this sense, the conventionality control required by the Constitution[54] and the binding nature of international decisions has motivated a greater interest from academic and public opinion on the Supreme Court's agenda and, even more, on the constitutional judicial doctrine it develops. Cases such as the long-term preventive prison (known as *arraigo*),[55] the release of Florence Cassez,[56] the legal interruption of pregnancy in Mexico City,[57] the legalisation of same sex marriages,[58] the legalisation of marijuana,[59] and the participation of the army in security tasks,[60] to name just a few, have brought national and international academic attention on the judicial agenda of the Mexican Supreme Court of Justice. This phenomenon was accompanied by a critical and proactive attitude as demonstrated by the large number of academic works developed

[50] The creation of specific centres dedicated to the study of constitutionalism as the Centre for Constitutional Studies of the Mexican Supreme Court of Justice.

[51] On the main features of legal education in Mexico see L Efrén Ríos Vega and I Spigno (eds), *Educación Jurídica y Derechos Humanos. La enseñanza del derecho en el siglo XXI* (Tirant lo Blanch, 2020).

[52] See JR Cossío Díaz and R Lara Chagoyán, '¿Derechos Humanos o jurisprudencia infalible' (2015) *Cuestiones Constitucionales* 32, 81–109.

[53] As established in the Mexican Supreme Court decisions *Varios 912/2011* and *Contradicción de Tesis 293/2011*. See MC Galván Tello, *La Justiciabilidad de los derechos humanos. La Contradicción de tesis 293/2011* (Tirant lo Blanch, 2018).

[54] See E Carpizo, 'Conventionality Control and its Relationship with the Mexican Constitutional System: Towards a Simple Protective Activity of Human Rights' (2013) 46 *Boletín Mexicano de Dererecho Comparado* 939–71.

[55] See *Amparo directo en revisión 1250/2012.*

[56] Florence Cassez is a French citizen accused and sentenced in 2007 to 60 years in prison under the presumption of the commission of the crimes of kidnapping, organised crime, and illegal possession of firearms for the exclusive use of the army and released thanks to the Mexican Supreme Court decision *Amparo en revision 517/2011* for the many irregularities committed during her detention. On this case, see J Mijangos y González, 'El debate de la asistencia consular en la Suprema Corte de Justicia de la Nación. El caso *Florence Cassez*', in LE Ríos Vega and I Spigno (eds), *Mariano Otero, el Diplomático. Dos lecturas del derecho a la asistencia consular* (Tirant lo Blanch, 2017) 165–86.

[57] See *Acción de inconstitucionalidad 146/2007 y su acumulada.*

[58] See *ex plurimis Jurisprudencia 1a./J. 85/2015.*

[59] See *ex plurimis Amparo en Revisión 57/2019.*

[60] See *Acción de Inconstitucionalidad 1/1996.* A set of constitutional reforms approved in 2019 (published in the Official Gazette of the Federation on 26 March 2019) introduced the National Guard, a civil police institution composed of members of the Federal, Military, and Naval Police, responsible for guaranteeing public security. This constitutional reform was integrated by a legislative package that entered into force in May 2019: three new laws (the National Guard Law, the National Law on the Use of Force, and the National Law of the Detention Registry) and a law reforming the General Law of the National Public Security System. See G Hernández, C-A Romero-Arias, 'La Guardia Nacional y la militarización de la seguridad pública en México', (2019) 25 *URVIO Revista Latinoamericana de Estudios de Seguridad* 87–106.

precisely on the analysis of court decisions, conferences, seminars, and different activities on the judicial criteria issued by the Court.

Simultaneously, the dialogue between legal scholarship and constitutional judicial doctrine also emerges in the references the Supreme Court does to scholarly works. Out of the 40 judgments analysed, 19, that is almost 50 per cent, cite doctrinal works. The reference is generally made to 'legal scholarship' or to 'many authors'[61] or throughout the citation of specific parts of scholarly texts,[62] in the main text, or more often in the footnotes.[63]

As far as the perception of the different prestige that constitutional judges have in comparison with constitutional law professors or lawyers is concerned, it should be noted that on the one hand, Supreme Court Justices enjoy a very high prestige that is sometimes related more to their position as public servants rather than to their judicial work or academic ideology, even if in Mexico there are highly prestigious law professors and there have also been some Justices with an extensive prestige both in the Supreme Court and in academia.

II. Arguments in Constitutional Reasoning

To analyse the arguments used by the Mexican Supreme Court in its constitutional reasoning based on 40 relevant cases would seem to many experts to be a futile and misleading exercise since the Court issues more than 7,000 rulings per year. However, we sought to reflect the work of the Court in a broad sense. For that, we chose cases from the 9th and 10th Epochs decided by the Full Court and the two Chambers on competencies and human rights issues. Furthermore, our conclusions match with our broader knowledge of the Court's jurisprudence as constitutional experts.[64]

A. The Structure of Constitutional Arguments

The Court does not speak in a single voice. Among the studied cases, there are 15 rulings with a one-line conclusive argument or a standalone structure, 21 with parallel conclusive arguments in which two or more divergent and self-sufficient considerations

[61] See eg *Amparo Directo Civil 6/2008.*

[62] As in the *Acción de inconstitucionalidad 146/2007 y su acumulada 147/2007*, with reference to a Sergio García Ramírez text on death penalty.

[63] See eg *Amparo Directo en Revisión 2655/2013, Acción de inconstitucionalidad 8/2014, Amparo en Revisión 208/2016, Amparo Directo en Revisión 5490/2016* and *Amparo en Revisión 163/2018.*

[64] We have been working on the Court's jurisprudence in other publications. See R Niembro Ortega, *La argumentación constitucional de la Suprema Corte. A diez años de la reforma derechos humanos* (Instituto de Investigaciones Jurídicas, UNAM, 2021); P Salazar, R Niembro Ortega and C Alonso (coords), *Diez sentencias emblemáticas de la Suprema Corte* (Instituto de Investigaciones Jurídicas UNAM, 2019); R Niembro and AM Alterio, *La Suprema Corte y el matrimonio igualitario en México* (Instituto de Investigaciones Jurídicas UNAM, 2017); LE Ríos Vega and I Spigno (eds), *Estudios de casos líderes nacionales. Vol. V. Los Derechos Humanos en la jurisprudencia de la Suprema Corte de Justicia de la Nación de México* (Tirant lo Blanch, 2020) and LE Ríos Vega and I Spigno (eds), *Estudios de casos líderes nacionales. Vol. XI. Cuestiones actuales de los derechos familiares y de la niñez* (Tirant lo Blanch, 2019).

lead to the same conclusion, and four with parallel inconclusive arguments but together conclusive arguments. This shows a defining feature of the Mexican Supreme Court and a trend that has become even more marked in recent years. The broadcasting of the Plenary sessions on television discourages a collegial court.[65] The consequence has been that in prominent cases the Justices want to have the best argument. So, in some cases, in order to reach a decision, the different arguments presented by the Justices are included in the final ruling because they refuse to give up the argument they put forward in the discussion. This is also reflected by the high number of cases with dissenting or concurring opinions, which we can find in 33 of the 40 cases.

The plurality of arguments has two unfortunate consequences. First, it is sometimes difficult to apply the criteria sustained in the ruling to subsequent cases; however, this also allows the Justices to easily distinguish the 'precedent' from previous decisions and argue that a case is different. Therefore, even though we find 37 cases that cite previous judgments,[66] that does not mean that the Court always follows its precedents in a strict sense. Second, it makes it difficult for citizens to know what the content of the law actually is. They may know what the disposition of the case was, but the plurality of voices of the Court makes it a bit hazy.

B. Types of Arguments in Constitutional Reasoning

i. Identifying the Text and Debating the Applicability of Constitutional Law

The Mexican Supreme Court has no problem in identifying the text of the Constitution. Among the 40 relevant cases there is only one case in which that discussion took place (*Contradicción de Tesis 293/2011*). This case considered the legal rank of the American Convention on Human Rights, and the Court concluded that it has constitutional rank unless the Constitution establishes an exception to it. In contrast, there has been more discussion about the Constitution's applicability. Indeed, we find 16 cases in which the applicability of constitutional law was discussed. Some of these cases refer to the discretion of the legislator. In another one, the Court ruled in 2007 that an act of the Federal Chamber directed towards the Oaxaca Governor was a political question not subject to judicial review (*Controversia Constitucional 140/2006*). Then, in 2014 the Justices argued the applicability of the right to prior consultation for indigenous communities

[65] F Pou, 'Changing the Channel: Broadcasting Deliberations in the Mexican Supreme Court' in R Davis and D Taras (eds), *Justices and Journalists: The Global Perspective* (Cambridge University Press, 2017). About the importance of collegiality see C Hübner, *Constitutional Courts and Deliberative Democracy* (Oxford University Press, 2013).

[66] We refer as precedent to the use of previous judgments or preliminary rulings of the same court. However, in Mexico we can distinguish between persuasive and binding precedents. Since March 2021, in amparo trials it is enough for the Supreme Court to rule once with a qualified majority to establish a binding precedent. On constitutional controversies and abstract review, the ruling needs 8 of the 11 votes of the justices to become a binding precedent. See R Camarena, 'La creación del precedente en la Suprema Corte de Justicia de la Nación' in C Bernal Pulido, R Camarena and A Martínez Verastegui (eds), *El precedente en la Suprema Corte de Justicia de la Nación* (Centro de Estudios Constitucionales SCJN, 2018).

based on Article 2 of the Constitution and Convention 169 of the International Labour Organization (*Controversia Constitucional 32/2012*).

Over time, the Court has expanded its jurisdiction to cover every constitutional conflict, and it does not use the political question doctrine anymore. We must understand this trend within its historical development. Moreover, the 2011 human rights reform brought to the Court the discussion of human rights enshrined in treaties as a part of constitutional law. We cannot find a type of argument that is usually the ratio decidendi. Our conclusion is that the Court has a pragmatic approach and uses the arguments that will make its rulings more convincing.

ii. Analogies and the Ordinary Meaning of the Words of the Constitution

We find six cases that use analogy, mostly including rulings on the topics of fundamental rights and of state organisation and involving, for example, cases regarding the powers of municipalities;[67] the constitutionality of Mexico City's Abortion Law;[68] freedom of speech;[69] and the reparation of moral damage.[70] Also, six cases refer to the ordinary meaning of the text of the Constitution (three of them in the majority decision and one in dissenting or concurring opinions; in two cases such reference is made on both the decision and the opinions).

iii. Harmonising Arguments

Of the 40 leading cases, on one hand, 19 of them expressly refer to domestic harmonising arguments. These include rulings on various topics such as the composition of a state Congress;[71] municipalities powers;[72] the constitutionality of Mexico City's Abortion Law;[73] freedom of speech;[74] human rights recognised in international treaties and the Inter-American Court of Human Rights case law;[75] gender perspective;[76] the constitutionality of long-term preventive prison (*arraigo*);[77] the right of parents to decide the order of their children's surnames;[78] the constitutionality of the Constitution of Mexico City;[79] state advertising, legislative omissions and freedom

[67] *Controversia Constitucional 14/2001*, on the determination if the Organic Law of the municipalities of Hidalgo invades the powers of the municipalities.

[68] *Acción de Inconstitucionalidad 146/2007 y su acumulada.*

[69] *Amparo Directo 28/2010*, in which the Court had to determine whether the expression used by a publishing house to criticise the position of a newspaper was protected by freedom of speech.

[70] *Amparo Directo en Revisión 5490/2016.*

[71] *Acción de Inconstitucionalidad 9/2005.* In this case, the Court had to determine if the changes to the Constitution of the state of Aguascalientes on the composition of the state Congress violated the parameters established in the Federal Constitution on proportional representation, and it also had to analyse the alleged irregularities of the legislative procedure.

[72] *Controversia Constitucional 14/2001.*

[73] *Acción de Inconstitucionalidad 146/2007 y su acumulada.*

[74] *Amparo Directo 28/2010.*

[75] *Contradicción de Tesis 293/2011.*

[76] *Amparo Directo en Revisión 2655/2013* and *Amparo Directo en Revisión 7134/2018.*

[77] *Amparo Directo en Revisión 1250/2012.*

[78] *Amparo en Revisión 208/2016.*

[79] *Acción de Inconstitucionalidad 15/2017.*

of expression;[80] the banning of cockfighting, animal rights and cultural rights;[81] equality, domestic work and social security,[82] and the medicinal use of cannabis,[83] among others.

On the other, three cases refer to international legal instruments from the Inter-American System for the Protection of Human Rights. These pertain to the issues of same-sex marriage, the constitutionality of the analysis of a constitutional reform, and the constitutionality of the Constitution of Mexico City.[84] In addition, three cases refer to other binding sources of international law and one case refers to sources of international soft law. Furthermore, six cases refer to both international legal instruments from the Inter-American System and other binding sources of international law, including cases on the binding force of the Inter-American Court of Human Rights case law, moral damage and compensation, and the right to previous consultation,[85] among three others.[86] Additionally, three cases refer to other binding sources of international law and soft law, including cases on regulations regarding autistic persons and the banning of cockfighting, animal rights and cultural rights.[87] Finally, we find 15 cases that refer to the three types of international law, on issues such the constitutionality of Mexico City's Abortion Law; the rectification of official identification documents for transexual persons;[88] freedom of speech; gender perspective; the human right to the highest level of health;[89] femicide;[90] bullying;[91] state advertising, legislative omissions and freedom of expression, and reparation of moral damage, among others.

In total, there are 31 cases that refer to international law. Of these, only two cases were ruled before 2011.[92] This shows us how important the constitutional reform of 2011 was for the inclusion of international legal instruments in the reasoning of the

[80] *Amparo en Revisión 1359/2015*, in which the Court had to determine whether the omission of the Legislative Branch to issue a law regulating the hiring of state advertising was unconstitutional and affected the freedom of expression.

[81] *Amparo en Revisión 163/2018.*

[82] *Amparo Directo 9/2018.*

[83] *Amparo en Revisión 57/2019.*

[84] *Amparo en Revisión 581/2012, Recurso de Reclamación 9/2016-AI*, and *Acción de Inconstitucionalidad 15/2017*, respectively.

[85] *Contradicción de Tesis 293/2011, Amparo Directo 30/2013* and *Controversia Constitucional 32/2012*, respectively. In the last case, the Court had to determine if the legislative process to reform the Constitution of the state of Michoacán conducted by the state Congress violated the right to previous consultation of the indigenous municipality of Cherán.

[86] *Amparo Directo en Revisión 517/2011* on whether the irregularities of the arrest violated the rights to consular assistance and presumption of innocence of the accused and contrary to due process; *Amparo Directo en Revisión 1250/2012* on the constitutionality of long-term preventive prison (*arraigo*), and *Amparo Directo en Revisión 6564/2015* on whether the claimant was illegally detained or not and if the torture allegedly suffered by the claimant had such an effect on the criminal procedure that it should be reinstated.

[87] *Amparo en Revisión 714/2017* and *Amparo en Revisión 163/2018*, respectively. The other case is the *Acción de Inconstitucionalidad 6/2018*, on the invalidity of general law by scope of constitutional competences.

[88] *Amparo Directo 6/2008.*

[89] *Amparo en Revisión 378/2014.*

[90] *Amparo en Revisión 554/2013.*

[91] *Amparo Directo 35/2014.* In this case, the Court had to determine if the defendant school was responsible for the moral damage suffered by a child as a consequence of the bullying encouraged by one of his teachers and to which the school did not respond appropriately and set the corresponding compensation.

[92] *Acción de Inconstitucionalidad 146/2017 y su acumulada*, on the constitutionality of the Mexico City Abortion Law and *Amparo Directo 6/2008*, on the rectification in birth certificates and other official identification documents in the case of transexual persons.

Court. In our opinion, the Court is part of the second wave of judicial review in which national courts give sharper teeth to international obligations.[93]

iv. Precedents, Doctrinal Analysis of Legal Concepts or Principles and Arguments of Silence

Overall, we find 37 cases that use precedents. In addition, out of the 40 selected cases, 18 of them invoke a concept or a principle that is not expressly specified in the constitutional text, and seven cases consider arguments of silence.

The high number of rulings that use precedents (37) puts into light a Court that, ever since 1995, has been ruling a huge number of cases on constitutional law. However, we must be careful to avoid the assumption that the Court straightforwardly uses precedents to issue a new ruling in the same direction. Occasionally, precedents are used in a judgment precisely to distinguish it from prior decisions. Moreover, the two chambers of the Court consider that they are not bound by the rulings of the other chamber. In fact, each chamber may issue contradictory rulings and the Plenary is in charge to decide which one should prevail. Furthermore, upcoming Justices do not consider themselves bound by the precedents previously issued by the Court. Finally, due to the high number of cases that the Court decides each year (around 7,000), it is hard to follow precedent.[94]

v. Teleological Arguments

Regarding this type of argument, 10 cases explicitly invoke the supposed purpose of the constitutional provision. Moreover, five cases openly refer to the intention of the constitution-maker in the majority decision; in five cases both the majority decision and the concurrent/dissenting opinions refer to the intentions, and in one case such reference is made in the opinions.

vi. Non-legal Arguments, References to Scholarly Work, Foreign Law, and the Pro Persona *Principle*

We also find 15 cases that invoke or consider non-legal arguments such as sociological, economic, moral, or religious reasonings and 19 cases that explicitly invoke scholarly contributions. The relatively high use of non-legal arguments as additional arguments expresses the interest of the Court in strengthening its constitutional argumentation through arguments grounded on externalities to the legal process or the law. There is a frequent reference to sociological arguments present in 11 cases, either alone (six cases) or in combination with economic (one case), moral or religious (one case), or scientific and medical arguments (three cases). Sociological arguments can include

[93] D Lustig and JHH Weiler, 'Judicial Review in the contemporary world-Retrospective and prospective' (2018) 16 *International Journal of Constitutional Law* 327.

[94] DB González Carvallo, 'El autoprecedente en la jurisprudencia de tribunales de cierre: el caso de la Suprema Corte de Justicia de la Nación de México' in C Bernal Pulido, R Camarena and A Martínez Verastegui (eds), *El precedente en la Suprema Corte de Justicia de la Nación* (Centro de Estudios Constitucionales SCJN, 2018).

both strict sociological theories or concepts (as in the *Amparo en Revisión 208/2016* on parents' right to decide the order of their children's surnames, in which there is a reference to the sociological concept of family), or others, including cultural[95] and statistical arguments.[96] Sociological arguments are used with medical ones in highly sensitive cases (as in the *Acción de Inconstitucionalidad 146/2007 y su acumulada*, on the constitutionality of Mexico City's Abortion Law, and the *Amparo Directo 6/2008*, on the rectification of birth certificates and other official identification documents in the case of transexual persons).

Another impression is that the high number of cases that invoke a concept or a principle that is not expressly specified in the constitutional text, non-legal arguments, and scholarly work is due to the jurisprudence of principles that the Justices have adopted. Our conclusion is that most Justices understand that constitutional law is inspired by values.

Furthermore, 13 cases refer to foreign law, most of which pertain to fundamental rights issues such as rectification of official identification documents of transexual persons, freedom of speech, same-sex marriage,[97] gender,[98] marihuana consumption and the right to free development of personality,[99] and medicinal use of cannabis. In detail, eight of the 13 cases that refer to foreign law invoke or consider foreign law both from Latin America and other regions, and five invoke or consider foreign law from other regions. Finally, we also find five cases that explicitly use the *pro persona* principle of interpretation.[100]

C. The Overall Weight of the Arguments

The legal argumentation of the Court has improved over the years. We must consider that the Mexican Supreme Court has been ruling on constitutional cases for only 25 years and on human rights cases for around 12. In this regard, the Court is getting

[95] See *Amparo en Revisión 163/2018.*

[96] See *Amparo Directo 9/2018 (relacionado con el Amparo directo 8/2018)*, a case on equality, domestic work, and social security.

[97] *Amparo en Revisión 581/2012*, in which the Court had to determine if Art 143 of Oaxaca's Civil Code made a discriminatory distinction that excluded same-sex couples from accessing the institution of marriage and the benefits that derive from it.

[98] *Amparo Directo en Revisión 1754/2015*, in which the Court had to determine if the decision to deny the claimant's request for compensatory alimony after her divorce, because she already received a retirement pension, and overlooking her gender and age violated her right to an adequate and decent standard of living.

[99] *Amparo en Revisión 237/2014*, in which the Court had to determine if the set of administrative prohibitions of personal marihuana consumption for recreational purposes in the General Health Law violated the claimants' right to free development of personality.

[100] *Contradicción de Tesis 293/2011*, on the hierarchical situation of human rights recognised in international treaties and the binding force of Inter-American Court of Human Rights case law; *Amparo en Revisión 159/2013*, on equality and non-discrimination; *Amparo en Revisión 554/2013*, the first case of femicide to ever come to the Mexican Supreme Court; *Recurso de Reclamación 9/2016-AI*, on the determination if the Supreme Court can analyse the constitutionality of a constitutional reform, and *Amparo Directo en Revisión 6565/2014*, in which the Court had to determine whether the claimant had been illegally detained and if the torture allegedly suffered by the claimant had such an effect on the criminal procedure so that it should be reinstated.

used to applying different methodologies and usually considers the arguments it mentions and connects them to the conclusion in the case.

The degree of rhetoric is relatively low, almost absent. The Court's tendency is towards using the majority of the arguments mentioned in the judicial opinion as ratio decidendi or obiter dictum arguments (39 out of 40) and seldom does the Court make use of decorative rhetorical or deceptive use of arguments. However, there is no general doctrine that establishes the weight of the methods or arguments that the Court uses. Neither is there a pattern regarding the conclusive arguments. As we have already mentioned, the Court uses pragmatically the argument that is more convincing for most of the justices.

D. Judicial Candour and Judicial Rhetoric

Over time, the role played by the Supreme Court within the Mexican institutional framework has changed, and so its judicial rhetoric is evolving towards a plural decision-making process in which quite often it is possible to acknowledge Justices' value judgments thanks to the high use of concurring and dissenting opinions. Each case discussed and decided by the Court results from a high-intensity debate: out of the 40 leading cases selected for this work, 33 have concurring or dissenting opinions (and in few other cases, some of the judges share their intention to write a separate opinion).

The Court's judgments openly display the underlying values, and the Mexican Supreme Court assumes an open attitude both with parties of the case and with scholars. The language is technical, perfectly understandable for lawyers, and not so easily accessible to non-lawyers. The Court usually uses a concrete, scholarly professional language.

However, the author of the judgment plays a crucial role in the choice of the language and arguments used, and it is possible to identify remarkable differences between the different judges, depending on their personal and professional background, and in relation to their empathy. Generally, there is little political and or emotive language in their reasoning.

E. Length, Dissenting and Concurring Opinions

Decisions issued by the Mexican Supreme Court of Justice are quite long. The average number of pages among the 40 selected leading cases is 150 (there even is a considerable difference between the longest one, which in its full version including concurring and dissenting opinion counts 1,313 pages, and the shortest one, which counts only 33 pages). This high number of pages is mainly related to a quite long reconstruction of the previous phases of the proceeding and the arguments developed by the parties, and it also depends on each judge's writing technique. However, the proper constitutional interpretation is relatively short. Furthermore, each judgment's length is related to the (political or constitutional) relevance of the issue at stake.

Also, there is usually a long descriptive part of normative and jurisprudential issues throughout the copy and paste technique of normative dispositions and precedents, both from the Mexican Supreme Court itself and other courts (as, for example, the Inter-American Court of Human Rights). Likewise, the presence of dissenting and concurring opinions (sometimes each of them longer than the majority one) contributes to this high number of pages. As already mentioned before, among the 40 leading cases, 33 have concurring or dissenting opinions, or in some cases, some of the judges share their intention to write a separate opinion. So, we can say that judges use this possibility quite often to manifest their personal reasoning.

F. Framing of Constitutional Issues

There are no typical ways of characterising constitutional issues; the framing depends on the nature of the dispute and the parties' choices. Also, framing is a problem of interpretation: it is sometimes difficult to distinguish between ordinary conventional statutory and proper constitutional adjudication (especially in human rights cases in which the constitutionality of a statute giving specific content and effect to a constitutional right is at stake). Moreover, the constitutional issue's formal characterisation is determined by the procedure through which the question reaches the Court (*acción de inconstitucionalidad, amparo* procedure, *controversia constitucional*, etc).

As far as the general topic of the 40 leading cases is concerned, 17 deal exclusively with 'Fundamental Rights', three with 'State Organisation' and one with 'Procedural Issues'. The three cases under the topic 'Other Issues' refer to the determination whether case law may have retroactive effects or be applied in cases that started before it was issued,[101] whether a rule establishing a fine was unconstitutional or not since it referred to another law which regulates an utterly different topic,[102] and whether the changes to the Constitution of the state of Aguascalientes on the composition of the state Congress violated the parameters established in the Federal Constitution on proportional representation and analyse the alleged irregularities of the legislative procedure.[103]

Four cases deal with both 'Fundamental Rights' and 'State Organisation' issues, and seven refer to both 'Fundamental Rights' and 'Procedural Issues'. In contrast, four touch fundamental rights and other issues.[104] Finally, there is only one case on both procedural and other issues: the *Acción de Inconstitucionalidad* 4/2004 on the determination whether the Federal District's regime of patrimonial state responsibility is congruent with the constitutional guidelines.

Thus, the great majority of the cases are on 'Fundamental Rights', mainly due to the fact that 30 out of 40 cases have been decided after the 2011 Human Rights constitutional reform, but also because even before 2011 the SCJN has shown a high sensitivity to Human Rights issues.

[101] See *Contradicción de Tesis 182/2014.*

[102] See *Acción de Inconstitucionalidad 4/2006.*

[103] See *Acción de Inconstitucionalidad 9/2005.*

[104] See *Acción de Inconstitucionalidad 1/1996, Contradicción de Tesis 293/2011, Recurso de Reclamación 9/2016-AI*, and *Amparo en Revisión 1359/2015.*

G. Key Concepts

i. The Most Cited Concept

The most popular concept invoked by the Mexican Supreme Court is 'equality' (present in 21 decisions), followed by 'human dignity' (19 decisions). It is not surprising that these two concepts are the most cited ones (often together, in 15 decisions), especially in the decisions on fundamental rights issued after the 2011 Constitutional Reform, which introduced the Human Rights Clause. It is also not a coincidence since the most relevant case law looks to transform a context of deep inequality based on equality and human dignity arguments.

Within this framework, it is possible to underline that the principle of equality has been invoked as far as gender issues are concerned. More specifically, it was invoked regarding gender discrimination,[105] abortion,[106] and the application of the gender perspective.[107] It is also frequently used in LGBTI+ cases[108] and in decisions on disabled persons,[109] cultural,[110] and indigenous[111] rights. Finally, some cases on due process also invoke 'equality' as a key concept such as the *Amparo Directo en Revisión 517/2011*, the 'Florence Cassez case',[112] determining whether the irregularities in the arrest violated the rights of the accused to consular assistance and presumption of innocence, and in cases on the determination of victims' compensation.[113]

In addition to the cases in which the principle of human dignity is invoked together with the 'equality' argument,[114] it is referred to freedom of speech,[115] to the relationship between international treaties and the constitution,[116] and the right to health.[117]

Furthermore, 'the rule of law' principle in its different forms is quite common, being present in 18 cases: the most popular one is the *seguridad jurídica* concept invoked alone in six cases[118] and together with the *estado de derecho* principle in one

[105] As in *Amparo en Revisión 208/2016*, with reference to parents' right to decide the order of their children's surnames.

[106] See *Acción de inconstitucionalidad 146/2007 y su acumulada 147/2007* on the constitutionality of the Mexico City Abortion Law.

[107] See *Amparo Directo en Revisión 2655/2013*, *Amparo Directo en Revisión 7134/2018* and *Amparo en Revisión 554/2013*, *Amparo Directo 9/2018 (relacionado con el Amparo directo 8/2018)* (with specific reference to social security) and *Amparo Directo en Revisión 1754/2015* (on compensatory alimony after divorce).

[108] See *Amparo directo civil 6/2008* and *Amparo en Revisión 581/2012.*

[109] See *Amparo en Revisión 159/2013* and *Amparo en Revisión 714/2017.*

[110] See *Amparo en Revisión 163/2018.*

[111] See *Acción de Inconstitucionalidad 151/2017.*

[112] See (nn 56 and 126).

[113] See *Amparo Directo 30/2013, Amparo Directo 35/2014 and Amparo Directo en Revisión 5490/2016.*

[114] See *Amparo Directo Civil 6/2008, Amparo en Revisión 581/2012, Amparo Directo en Revisión 517/2011, Amparo Directo en Revisión 517/2011, Amparo en Revisión 159/2013, Amparo Directo 30/2013, Amparo en Revisión 554/2013, Amparo Directo 35/2014, Acción de inconstitucionalidad 8/2014, Amparo Directo en Revisión 1754/2015, Amparo en Revisión 208/2016, Amparo Directo en Revisión 5490/2016, Amparo en Revisión 714/2017, Amparo en Revisión 714/2017, Amparo Directo 9/2018* and *Amparo Directo en Revisión 7134/2018.*

[115] See *Amparo Directo 28/2010.*

[116] See *Contradicción de Tesis 293/2011.*

[117] See *Amparo en Revisión 378/2014* and *Amparo en Revisión 237/2014.*

[118] See *Amparo en Revisión 159/2013, Recurso de Reclamación 9/2016-AI, Amparo en Revisión 208/2016, Acción de Inconstitucionalidad 15/2017, Contradicción de Tesis 182/2014* and *Acción de Inconstitucionalidad 151/2017.*

case[119] and with the *principio de legalidad* in one case[120] and two cases with both.[121] In four cases, only the *principio de legalidad* has been invoked,[122] and in three cases, only the *estado de derecho* principle has been invoked.[123] Usually, the reference made by the Mexican Supreme Court to the concept of rule of law is not rhetorical. Rather, the principle of *seguridad jurídica* has been considered as a general principle for constitutional interpretation (as in *Amparo en Revisión 159/2013*) or as rationale of a specific law (as in *Amparo en Revisión 208/2016*). When alone, the principle of rule of law is considered as corresponding to the *estado de regularidad constitucional* (as in *Amparo en Revisión 1359/2015*).

ii. Relatively Popular Concepts

'Democracy' is used by the Mexican Supreme Court in cases involving the form of government and the conflict of competencies between State powers,[124] the concept of 'democratic State', which may be affected by the functions performed by military forces,[125] but also to human rights, as their 'foundation',[126] and in cases regarding freedom of speech[127] and social and cultural rights.[128]

The form of government is also taken into consideration under the concept of 'government system by power structure' in cases on national security,[129] on vertical conflicts of competencies (both between states and the Federation and states and municipalities),[130] on the boundaries of the Court's competence,[131] on conflicts between laws[132] and authorities' omissions.[133]

The 'proportionality' principle, deeply inspired by Robert Alexy's proportionality and balancing theory,[134] is used about the proportionality of penalties,[135] same-sex

[119] See *Amparo en Revisión 57/2019.*

[120] See *Acción de Inconstitucionalidad 4/2006.*

[121] See *Amparo Directo en Revisión 517/2011* and *Acción de Inconstitucionalidad 6/2018.*

[122] See *Acción de Inconstitucionalidad 1/1996, Controversia Constitucional 14/2001, Acción de inconstitucionalidad 146/2007 y su acumulada 147* and *Amparo Directo en Revisión 6564/2015.*

[123] See *Amparo Directo 28/2010, Amparo en Revisión 1359/2015* and *Amparo Directo en Revisión 7134/2018.*

[124] See *Acción de Inconstitucionalidad 9/2005.*

[125] See *Acción de Inconstitucionalidad 6/2018 y acumuladas 8/2018, 9/2018, 10/2018 y 11/2018* on the invalidity of the Law of Interior Security.

[126] As in the *Acción de inconstitucionalidad 146/2007 y su acumulada 147/2007* on the constitutionality of the Mexico City Abortion Law. See also the Florence Cassez case (*Amparo Directo en Revisión 517/2011*).

[127] See *Amparo Directo 28/2010* and *Amparo en Revisión 1359/2015.*

[128] See *Amparo en Revisión 159/2013, Amparo en Revisión 378/2014* and *Amparo en Revisión 163/2018.*

[129] See *Acción de Inconstitucionalidad 1/1996.*

[130] See *Acción de Inconstitucionalidad 9/2005* and *Controversia Constitucional 14/2001.* See also *Acción de inconstitucionalidad 146/2007 y su acumulada, Acción de Incostitucionalidad 15/2017; Acción de Inconstitucionalidad 6/2018*, and *Amparo en Revisión 163/2018.*

[131] See *Controversia Constitucional 140/2006*, in which the Court stated that merely political questions are not subject to the Court's analysis.

[132] See *Acción de Inconstitucionalidad 119/2008* and *Amparo en Revisión 714/2017.*

[133] See *Controversia Constitucional 38/2015.*

[134] R Alexy, 'Constitutional Rights, Balancing and Rationality' (2003) 2 *Ratio Juris* 135–36.

[135] See *Acción de inconstitucionalidad 146/2007 y su acumulada 147/2007*, with reference to the penalties imposed in the case of abortion in the Mexico City Abortion Law.

couples rights,[136] and to determine whether or not a norm is contrary to the principle of equality.[137] The Court also refers to the concept of 'strict proportionality' with reference to the principle to be respected in the restriction of fundamental rights.[138]

The Court invokes the 'basic procedural rights' argument with reference to the Mariana Lima Buendía case, the first case of femicide to ever came to the Supreme Court, addressing the negligence and obstruction of justice by the local authorities,[139] and in six more decisions involving, among the others,[140] freedom of speech,[141] consular assistance and presumption of innocence,[142] and illegal detention and torture.[143]

In seven decisions, the Supreme Court invokes the 'rights to privacy' argument as one of the rights that can be violated in the use of the military force in national security tasks[144] but also in freedom of speech cases.[145] We considered the right to privacy as also including 'personal autonomy'[146] concerning sexual preference and gender orientation cases.[147]

The Mexican Supreme Court of Justice also makes quite extensive use of 'post-material values', including animal welfare,[148] gender identity,[149] gender perspective,[150] welfare State,[151] and the full inclusion of disabled persons,[152] among the others.[153] The 'justice' argument is referred to in nine decisions as the access to justice in conditions of equality (especially gender equality)[154] and also as social justice.[155] In comparison, 'custom' is invoked in seven decisions, referring to an ancient tradition of cultural type,[156] family,[157] gender discrimination and violence, prejudices and stereotypes,[158] and indigenous cultural rights.[159]

[136] See *Amparo en Revisión 581/2012*. See also *Acción de Inconstitucionalidad 8/2014* on same-sex couples adoption.

[137] See *Amparo Directo 9/2018* (relacionado con el *Amparo Directo 8/2018*).

[138] See *Acción de Inconstitucionalidad 6/2018 y acumuladas 8/2018, 9/2018, 10/2018 y 11/2018*, para 154. See also *Amparo en Revisión 208/2016*, para II.

[139] See *Amparo en Revisión 554/2013*. See also *Amparo Directo en Revisión 5490/2016*.

[140] See *Acción de Inconstitucionalidad 4/2006* and *Acción de Inconstitucionalidad 4/2004*.

[141] See *Amparo Directo 28/2010*.

[142] See *Amparo Directo en Revisión 517/2011*.

[143] See *Amparo Directo en Revisión 6564/2015*.

[144] See *Acción de Inconstitucionalidad 6/2018 y acumuladas 8/2018, 9/2018, 10/2018 y 11/2018*. See also *Amparo Directo en Revisión 6564/2015*.

[145] See *Amparo Directo 28/2010*.

[146] See *Amparo en Revisión 163/2018*. See also *Amparo en Revisión 208/2016* and *Amparo en Revisión 237/2014*.

[147] See *Amparo Directo Civil 6/2008*.

[148] See *Amparo en Revisión 163/2018*.

[149] See *Amparo Directo Civil 6/2008*.

[150] See *Amparo en Revisión 554/2013*, para 113 and *Amparo Directo en Revisión 2655/2013*.

[151] See *Amparo en Revisión 378/2014*, p 27.

[152] See *Amparo en Revisión 714/2017*.

[153] See also *Acción de Inconstitucionalidad 1/1996* and *Amparo Directo 28/2010*.

[154] See *Amparo Directo en Revisión 7134/2018*. See also *Amparo Directo en Revisión 2655/2013* and *Amparo Directo en Revisión 5490/2016* and *Acción de Inconstitucionalidad 151/2017*. The 'justice' argument is invoked also in *Amparo Directo 30/2013, Amparo Directo 35/2014* and *Amparo Directo en Revisión 1754/2015*.

[155] See *Amparo en Revisión 378/2014*.

[156] See *Amparo en Revisión 163/2018*.

[157] See *Amparo Directo en Revisión 7134/2018*. See also *Amparo en Revisión 208/2016*.

[158] See *Amparo Directo en Revisión 2655/*2013 and Amparo en Revisión 554/2013.

[159] See Acción de Inconstitucionalidad 151/2017. See also *Acción de Incostitucionalidad 15/2017*.

The 'family' argument is invoked on gender equality,[160] the right to health,[161] same-sex couples and LGBTI+ families.[162] At the same time, the Court refers to the concept of 'transition' in cases involving national security,[163] the conflict of competencies between state's organs,[164] due process rights,[165] and the hierarchical position within the constitutional system of human rights recognised in international treaties.[166] Finally, it is possible to find the 'economic, social, cultural and environmental rights; argument invoked in 10 decisions on the right to health,[167] gender discrimination and violence,[168] and cultural rights.[169]

iii. Very Rare Concepts

The concept of 'sovereignty' was invoked only in the *Acción de Inconstitucionalidad 146/2007 y su acumulada 147/2007* on the Mexico City Abortion Law's constitutionality, with specific reference to popular sovereignty. The Supreme Court referred to the 'state form' argument in two cases, with specific reference to the 'Democratic State' and 'Welfare State',[170] to the 'government system by procedural structure' argument in the *Acción de Inconstitucionalidad 1/1996* on presidential powers and to 'secularism' in a case on same-sex couples.[171]

The concept of 'nation' is invoked in the *Acción de Inconstitucionalidad 151/2017* on the right to prior consultation of indigenous people with a progressive interpretation of Article 2 of the Mexican Constitution. The only reference to the 'core of constitutional rights' can be found in the *Acción de Inconstitucionalidad 146/2007 y su acumulada 147/2007* with specific reference to the limits the legislator has with reference to criminal law.

Finally, only two decisions refer to the 'freedom of expression' argument,[172] to 'mechanism of political control', one of which referring to the limits the legislator has on penal issues,[173] and to 'judicial activism'.[174]

[160] See *Amparo Directo en Revisión 7134/2018*; *Amparo en Revisión 208/2016* and *Amparo Directo en Revisión 5490/2016*.

[161] See *Amparo en Revisión 57/2019*, a case involving a minor who needed marijuana for his medical treatments.

[162] See *Acción de Inconstitucionalidad 8/2014* and *Amparo en Revisión 581/2012*.

[163] See *Acción de Inconstitucionalidad 1/1996*.

[164] See *Acción de Inconstitucionalidad 9/2005, Controversia Constitucional 14/2001, Acción de Inconstitucionalidad 4/2004, Recurso de Reclamación 9/2016-AI* and *Amparo en Revisión 1359/2015*.

[165] See *Amparo Directo en Revisión 517/2011*.

[166] See *Contradicción de Tesis 293/2011*.

[167] See *Acción de inconstitucionalidad 146/2007 y su acumulada 147/2007, Amparo en Revisión 378/2014, Amparo en Revisión 714/2017* and *Amparo en Revisión 57/2019*.

[168] See *Amparo Directo en Revisión 1754/2015, Amparo Directo en Revisión 5490/2016, Amparo Directo 9/2018* and *Amparo Directo en Revisión 7134/2018*.

[169] See *Amparo en Revisión 163/2018*. The 'economic, social, cultural and environmental rights' argument was invoked also in *Amparo Directo 35/2014* and *Acción de Incostitucionalidad 15/2017*.

[170] See *Amparo en Revisión 378/2014*. See also *Acción de Inconstitucionalidad 9/2005*.

[171] See *Amparo en Revisión 581/2012*.

[172] See *Amparo Directo 28/2010*, on whether the expressions used by a publishing house to criticise the position of a newspaper are protected by freedom of speech, and *Amparo en Revisión 1359/2015* on whether the omission of the Legislative branch to issue a law regulating the hiring of state advertising is unconstitutional and affects the freedom of expression.

[173] See *Acción de inconstitucionalidad 146/2007 y su acumulada 147/2007*, on the constitutionality of the Mexico City Abortion Law. See also *Acción de Incostitucionalidad 15/2017*.

III. Comparative Perspective

A comparative analysis of Mexican contemporary constitutional law and especially the constitutional interpretation made by its constitutional court reveals that the Mexican Supreme Court of Justice shares a common trend with the other Latin American constitutional jurisdictions.

As it happens in other countries of the region, most of the Mexicana Supreme Court's interpretation is on legal materials rather than the constitutional text. This can be explained due to the procedural aspects of constitutional review of legislation since the Court concentrates both the concrete review of legislation (as in the US model) through the *juicio de amparo* (in its different modalities) which occupies the central part of the Court judicial agenda, and the abstract/concentrate review of legislation (as in the European model), thorough the *acción de inconstitucionalidad* against normative dispositions and the *controversia de constitucionalidad* as far as conflict of competences between states powers is at stake.

However, if we look at the specific relationship between legislative and executive power and the Court in terms of judicial deference or dialogue, we can see that the Mexican Supreme Court is more deferential to norms coming from the executive power and less to those produced by the legislature. Considering judicial deference from a quantitative point of view and taking into consideration the number of cases in which the Court has declared the unconstitutionality (in some cases at least partially) of the challenged law, act, or degree,[175] the Supreme Court of Mexico is more deferential to the federal legislator – as it happens in Uruguay – rather than state ones.[176]

Instead, it is possible to identify a more deferential attitude with respect to norms and acts coming from the executive power, as it happens in Venezuela, despite the very different political context.[177] If we go a little deeper and look at the judicial deference regarding the arguments used by the Court to declare the unconstitutionality of the challenged disposition, we can see that the great majority of them is based on formalistic arguments (as procedural or competence issues), as it happens in Colombia, Costa Rica and Ecuador. It is very sporadic for the Court to declare the unconstitutionality of the challenged norm, 'invading' the legislative discretion or invoking the core content of fundamental rights or competencies.

It is quite a common trend in many Latin America jurisdictions (as it happens in Colombia, Costa Rica and Ecuador), and it can be explained through two main reasons.[178] The first one refers to the presidential form of government highly predominant

[174] See *Amparo en Revisión 159/2013*, pp 74–75, in which the Court underlines its function as the ultimate guarantor of rights, highlighting how its judgments cannot be subjected to hypothetical scenarios of legislative action, which would imply ignoring its nature as a Constitutional Court. See also *Controversia Constitucional 38/2015*.

[175] Out of the 40 most relevant cases we selected for this paper, we have included 10 decisions of *acción de inconstitucionalidad* and four *controversias constitucionales*. In six *acciones de inconstitucionalidad* the Mexican Supreme Court declared the unconstitutionality (in some cases at least partially) of the challenged disposition, act or norm and in three *controversias constitucionales*.

[176] See *Acción de Inconstitucionalidad 8/2014*; *Acción de Inconstitucionalidad 4/2004* and *Acción de Inconstitucionalidad 4/2006*).

[177] See *Acción de Inconstitucionalidad 6/2018 y acumuladas 8/2018, 9/2018, 10/2018 y 11/2018*.

[178] We can identify a similar tendency in Bolivia, Chile, Colombia, Guatemala, Argentina and Paraguay among the others. See the corresponding national chapters in this book.

in Latin America. Despite the constitutional designs providing a scheme of checks and balances between a State's power, the reality shows executive powers predominating over legislative and judicial powers.

The second reason finds its root in the predominant style of constitutional interpretation. The Mexican Supreme Court, as well as other constitutional Latin American constitutional judges (as in Colombia, Costa Rica and Ecuador), is used to make a formalistic interpretation, usually not entering in the discussion of the constitutional text and not entering in the discussion, interpretation, and application of the core content of constitutional principles or rights, but instead prefers to make a more formalistic interpretation of the content of the challenged act. This interpretative attitude reflects the need for the text of the Constitution to be as complete as possible and comes along with the Mexican constitutional drafting style, which conceives, especially in comparison with the predominant European and US constitutional drafting style, hyper amended[179] and regulated texts, which leave little or no room at all for constitutional interpretation.[180]

This consideration is related to another significant trend in constitutional law in Latin America (as in Argentina or Uruguay). Even if the concept of the Constitution's supremacy was established since the very beginning of constitutionalism during the nineteenth century, it is also true that this supremacy was a political one.[181] The idea of a legal supremacy of the constitutional text arrived slightly later. This influences the configuration of constitutional justice and constitutional judges, sometimes resistant to interpretative tools that may directly affect the constitutional text. This attitude can also be explained with reference to the constitutional text features, which leave no room for constitutional interpretation and the dominant legal tradition that conceives judges as being under the positivistic-formalistic umbrella.

Finally, the Supreme Court of Justice of Mexico has also engaged in an essential dialogue with international law, mainly with the Inter-American System of Human Rights and the universal system. It is primarily related to conventionality control and represents a common trend in other countries as it is possible to identify this in Bolivia (contrary to countries like Paraguay, Guatemala, and Argentina).

IV. Evaluation, Pathology and Criticism

There are some pathologies that must change. Some of the rulings are very long by comparable standards. We commonly find rulings of more than 300 pages. Moreover, the language used in the rulings is sometimes baroque. The Court is struggling to leave behind a long legacy of a very formalistic judicial culture. In this sense, the lawyer jargon is still used to excess. In our opinion, this will change once the law clerks bear in mind

[179] MA Rivera León, 'Understanding Constitutional Amendments in México: Perpetuum Mobile Constitution' (2017) 9 *Mexican Law Review*, 3–27.

[180] See JR Cossío Díaz, *La teoría constitucional de la Suprema Corte de Justicia* (Fontamara, 2004) especially at 116–17.

[181] In this sense see E Ferrer Mac-Gregor and R Sánchez Gil, 'Mexico: Struggling For An Open View In Constitutional Adjudication' in T Groppi and MC Ponthoreau (eds), *The Use of Foreign Precedents by Constitutional Judges* (Hart Publishing, 2013) 301–20, at 303.

that their audience is not only the law community. Another serious pathology is the difficulty to find a single voice in the Court's rulings, especially in the Plenary rulings where the Court sessions are broadcast on TV. There is a high number of concurring and dissenting opinions in each ruling. Finally, an external constitutional pathology that affects the Court is the constitutional amendment mania[182] that makes it very difficult for the Court to develop solid doctrines with a long-term view.

[182] F Pou-Giménez, A Pozas-Loyo and C Saavedra-Herrera, *Interpreting the Ship Of Theseus: Constitutional Hyper-reformism and Judicial Review in Mexico (1917–2019)* (unpublished manuscript in file with the authors) 32, 40.

14

The Jurisprudence of the Supreme Court of Paraguay

MARÍA JOSÉ GARCÍA ASCOLANI AND JUAN PABLO IRRAZABAL

I. Introduction

This chapter identifies and addresses some of the main features of constitutional reasoning employed by the Paraguayan Supreme Court. In this sense, Paraguay is an interesting case study because its legal system has been strongly influenced by the North American and European systems with regard to substantive law and doctrine.[1] In addition, the beginning of the new democratic era following the dictatorship of Alfredo Stroessner was one of the essential motivations for the drafting and promulgation of the new Constitution of 1992.

Thus, in response to this long period of military coups, political instability and serious human rights violations,[2] the new Constitution was born, inspired by respect for human dignity in recognition of a supranational legal order that guarantees the full observance of human rights, peace, justice and international cooperation. It also expressly adopts democratic principles and values based on the social rule of law and constitutional supremacy.[3]

However, the stage of democratic transition has been accompanied by great challenges for Paraguayan society and the legal order, especially during those periods of crisis that have also impacted the Court and its work. Therefore, the central objective of this research is to analyse the Paraguayan judges' reasoning when issuing decisions on relevant constitutional issues. To this end, we have analysed 40 rulings related to constitutional review, which cover the time period between 1995 and 2018. The examination of the main features of the style, tools and strategies of judicial reasoning yields conclusive data not only on the legal culture in Paraguay – the main political, economic and

[1] D Moreno Rodríguez Alcalá, 'Veinticinco Años de Evolución de la Justicia Constitucional' in *Comentario a la Constitución*, vol V, Homenaje al Vigésimo Quinto Aniversario (Corte Suprema de Justicia: Instituto de Investigaciones Jurídicas, 2018) 284, www.pj.gov.py/ebook/coment-const-5.php.

[2] M Ramírez Candia, *Derecho Constitucional Paraguayo*, vol I (Litocolor, 2009) 217–21; E Camacho, *Lecciones de Derecho Constitucional*, vol I (Intercontinental, 2007) 78.

[3] See the preamble and, more explicitly, Arts 1 and 145 of the Constitution of 1992.

social challenges – but also on the judges' behaviour in situations of social and political instability.

One of the preliminary findings reveals that Paraguayan constitutional culture tends to be mostly classical and formalistic. As will be demonstrated, exegetical and teleological methods of interpretation prevail. In addition, not enough literature is employed, and dialogue with other regional courts and with the Inter-American Court of Human Rights (IACtHR) itself is still limited. Finally, the Court's rulings are considerably technical and are addressed to ordinary court judges and lawyers but not to the public. These are just some of the determining factors that have allowed us to see that our Court still has a long way to go before it can be labelled as activist.

To support this important finding, an overview of the prevailing legal culture in Paraguay is presented, followed by an identification and examination of the different types of arguments the Court employs.

II. Legal, Political, Institutional and Academic Context

A. Legal and Political Culture as Context for the Constitutional Reasoning

The current Constitution of 1992 is the fifth[4] since Paraguay fought for its independence in 1811. Paraguayan constitutional history is thus controversial to some extent, as it is characterised by continuous changes motivated by political, social and economic crises. This circumstance has undoubtedly influenced the constitutional system and, accordingly, judicial reasoning. However, the proper purpose of the various constitutions has not been to adapt the norms of human and social behaviour to new realities but rather to strengthen the prevailing political power, relying on the respective government programmes.[5]

One of the key effects of the Paraguayan process of constitutional reforms has been that it has not had a decisive impact either on citizens' quality of life or the strengthening of State institutions. Except for the new Constitution of 1992 (hereinafter, 'the Constitution'), the previous instruments lacked sufficient effectiveness with regard to citizen protection. This context favoured strong, charismatic and populist governments that did not encounter enough obstacles to their despotic impositions of decisions.[6]

As such, the new Constitution has become the centre of the Paraguayan legal system, influenced to a large extent by the neoconstitutionalist wave.[7] The Constitution

[4] See Ramírez Candia (n 2) 169–229; L Lezcano Claude, 'Historia Constitucional del Paraguay (Período 1870–2012)' (15 August 2012), see at luislezcanoclaude.wordpress.com/2012/08/15/169/.

[5] Camacho (n 2) 55–58.

[6] ibid 59–77.

[7] See R Guastini, *Estudios de la teoría constitucional* (Fontamara, 2001) 153–208.; L Ferrajoli, *Constitucionalismo más allá del Estado* (Editorial Trotta, 2018) 11–41; P Comanducci, *Formas de neoconstitucionalismo: un análisis metateórico* (2002) 16 *Isonomía* 89–112; N Bobbio, *Giusnaturalismo e positivismo giuridico* (Comunitá, 1988); G Bongiovanni, *Teorie 'constituzionalistiche' del diritto. Morale, diritto e interpretazione in R. Alexy and R. Dworkin* (Clueb, 2000); M Carbonell, *'Neoconstitucionalismo', Diccionario de*

strengthens its decisive presence in the development and interpretation of the legal order in accordance with its norms, principles and values. Therefore, judges play an important role within the constitutional system since their judgments must be the products of thorough argumentative reasoning. In short, mere reference to the use of one or another interpretative criterion and the method of subsuming the rule are no longer sufficient.

However, from different points of view, there is still a wide gap existing between the law and social reality – such as, for example, the deficient system of land distribution,[8] the disproportionate concentration of power in the hands of the legislative branch,[9] the questionable lack of judicial independence,[10] the repeated discussions regarding presidential re-election[11] and the permanent tenure of the Court's Ministers.[12] This, along with the high rate of social inequality, is hardly consistent with such essential constitutional principles as the respect for human dignity and the strengthening of the rule of law. For this reason, the historical, social, political and legal context of Paraguay merits great attention from academics since it reveals certain contradictions within the system itself and has direct effects on constitutional reasoning.

i. The Antecedents of the New Constitution of 1992 and its Conceptual Framework

The *coup d'état* of 2 and 3 February 1989, which overthrew the then-dictator, Alfredo Stroessner, constitutes the material source of the Constitution. Since this event, political and legal transformations have been facilitated relative to the process of the new constitutional system concluded on 20 June 1992.

Indeed, immediately after Alfredo Stroessner's fall, a period of political openness commenced, led by a transitional government under which strictly democratic reforms were carried out. Thus, the first law enacted in 1989 approved and ratified the American Convention on Human Rights[13] (Pact of San José, Costa Rica) (ACHR). Then, the electoral reform was implemented (1990),[14] which allowed – for the first time – the direct election of municipal mayors. These events reinforced the debate regarding the need

Derechos Humanos (Universidad de Alcalá, 2009) 1–6; R Gargarella, 'El periodo fundacional del constitucionalismo sudamericano (1810–1860)' (2003) 43 *Desarrollo Económico* 305–28; C Santiago Nino, *Introducción al Análisis del Derecho*, 2nd edn, 15th reprint (Astrea, 2010) 353–432; C Santiago Nino, *Fundamentos de Derecho Constitucional. Análisis filosófico, jurídico y politológico de la práctica constitucional*, 4th reprint (Astrea, 2013) 44–66.

[8] See Servicio de Paz y Justicia, *Compilación de Actuaciones del Sistema de Justicia en la Zona Norte del País* (SERPAJ, 2020).

[9] For example, in cases of the impeachment of Ministers of the Court, which is addressed below.

[10] *Case of Ríos Ávalos et al v Paraguay* (Merits, Reparations and Costs), Judgment Inter-American Court of Human Rights (19 August 2021) (English trans); World Justice Project, 'Rule of Law Index 2021', see at worldjusticeproject.org/sites/default/files/documents/WJP-INDEX_2021.pdf.

[11] See I González Bozzolasco, 'Paraguay: la reelección presidencial y los inicios de la carrera electoral 2018' (2017) 37 *Revista de Ciencia Política* 543–62. See at ojs.uc.cl/index.php/rcp/article/view/5286.

[12] Ac and Sent No 222/2000, 'permanent tenure of the Court's Ministers (I)'; Ac and Sent No 223/2000, 'permanent tenure of the Court's Ministers (II)'; Ac and Sent No 557/2007, 'permanent tenure of the Court's Ministers (III)'.

[13] See at www.bacn.gov.py/archivos/2619/20140924114553.pdf.

[14] J Silvero Salgueiro, 'La Constitución de la República del Paraguay del 20 de junio de 1992' (1998) 92 *Boletín Mexicano de Derecho Comparado* 503–35.

for constitutional reform to prompt the democratic transition with the rule of law as its central axis.

Thus, the abandonment of the authoritarian concentration of power in the hands of the Executive was promoted. A broad consensus was reached on the need for a fair balance between State powers, aspiring to the establishment of an independent judiciary and an autonomous parliament with sufficient powers to exercise control over the Executive.

In an environment of broad public freedoms, with the participation of all political sectors, the election of delegates to the Constituent Conventions (*Convencionales Constituyentes*) was held on 1 December 1991. Once the Convention's participants were installed, its internal regulations were approved, which, as a first step, provided for a period of 10 days for citizens to participate in the drafting of the constitutional text. As such, 128 projects from different organisations and civil society groups[15] were presented. Consequently, the new political and social openness towards democracy allowed the new Constitution to be enacted on 20 June 1992.

ii. Characteristics of the New Paraguayan Constitutionalism

The Paraguayan Conventions took great care to draft a rationalist, normative, liberal and systematic constitution. They gave it a focus that is central to the principle of the social rule of law while considering that the arbitrariness and irrationality in political decisions must be eliminated from the State. Therefore, power can only be exercised within the limits of the Constitution.

Another important feature is the entire legal system's express subordination to the Constitution (the principle of constitutional supremacy). The Constitution is specific, as it contains 291 articles and 20 final and transitional provisions. With regard to flexibility, we consider our Constitution to be rigid since it establishes two precise procedures for reformation (Art 289, Const.) or amendment (Art 290, Const.). In fact, the Constitution remains in force with only one amendment.[16]

The reform procedure can be initiated by 25 per cent of the legislators of either chamber, the President of the Republic or with the signatures of 30,000 electors. Once the reform has been initiated, the Superior Court of Electoral Justice (*Tribunal Superior de Justicia Electoral*) must call for elections of convention constituents for which a law will determine the conditions of eligibility and incompatibility. Its participants enjoy the same immunities as members of Congress. These convention constituents have broad powers to undertake the most profound and radical reform deemed necessary.

The amendment procedure is simpler and constitutes an important variation in our system. The initiative is set forth by a quarter of the legislators of either chamber, the President of the Republic or 30,000 electors. The legislature drafts the amendment, which must be approved in both houses by an absolute majority and, if rejected, cannot be reintroduced again for another year. Once approved, the Superior Court of Electoral Justice must put forth the proposed amendment in a referendum. Those provisions that

[15] Ramírez Candia (n 2) 219–21.

[16] Amendment referring to Art 120. Through it, Paraguayans living abroad are guaranteed the right to vote, see at www.bacn.gov.py/ENMIENDA_CONSTITUCIONAL_N_1.pdf.

affect the mode of election, composition, powers, duration of the mandates, any of the State powers and all those that refer to fundamental rights, freedoms and guarantees, cannot be modified through this procedure, only through reform.

Other institutions of contemporary constitutionalism have also been introduced. These are the Council of the Magistrature (*Consejo de la Magistratura*) and the Jury of Prosecution of Magistrates (*Jurado de Enjuiciamiento de Magistrados*),[17] while constitutional review rests exclusively in the hands of the Court. Additionally, in contrast with previous regimes, constitutional guarantees must remain in force even in times when internal security is threatened – that is, during a State of Emergency (*Estado de Excepción*).

Undoubtedly, the Constitution is the most progressive in Paraguayan history. The instrument attempts to overcome society's structural problems, highlighting human rights. The new Paraguayan constitutionalism emphasises the principles related to constitutional democracy, the universal value of constitutional norms and the rule of law. It also features social, economic and cultural rights, not just those of a political and civil nature. In this regard, the Constitution has created special legal and institutional means to vindicate and safeguard the rights of indigenous peoples, dedicating an entire chapter to them (Arts 62–67, Const.). In addition to recognising the existence of indigenous peoples, the Constitution defines them as extant groups that were present before the formation and organisation of the State. Further, it ensures the preservation and development of ethnic identity, the right to community ownership of land, and participation in national affairs and assistance.[18]

On the other hand, and although collective bodies are recognised as political actors (Art 123, Const.), the Constitution focuses mostly on representative democracy, the exception being popular referenda and social controls as a separate branch of power (Arts 121 and 122, Const.).[19]

Paraguay has thus succeeded in drafting a constitution responsive to its long authoritarian past, the weakness of republican institutions, the polarisation of civil society, the growing gap between rich and poor, the threat of corruption and the persistence of authoritarian sectors unamenable to democratic traditions.[20] From this emerges the importance of highlighting the Constitution as a cultural product of the new Paraguayan democratic era.

iii. The Formalistic Tendency in Constitutional Interpretation

The Constitution's new trend has marked the culmination of the struggle against the status quo, devising a new beginning as a demonstration of real change. On the contrary,

[17] See the critical position of R Campos Cervera, 'Teoría y Práctica de la Interpretación Constitucional – Intérpretes Naturales y Ocasionales de la Constitución' in *Comentario a la Constitución*, vol III (Corte Suprema de Justicia, División de Investigación, Legislación y Publicaciones, Centro Internacional de Estudios Judiciales, 2007) 113–44, at www.pj.gov.py/ebook/coment-const-3.php.

[18] Ac and Sent No 30/1997, 'rights of indigenous peoples (I)'; Ac and Sent No 365/1999, 'rights of indigenous peoples (II)'; Ac and Sent No 243/2008, 'rights of indigenous peoples (III)'.

[19] To date, a single popular referendum has been held (in 2011), regarding the possibility of Paraguayans living abroad having the right to vote in general elections. The results can be found at tsje.gov.py/referendum.html.

[20] Camacho (n 2) 93.

the Court – as an agent of change – has not taken sufficient care to recognise the gap existing between social reality and legal norms.

This circumstance could explain the public's disapproval of the judiciary and the numerous institutional dysfunctions that afflict it, which are not necessarily linked to the weak authority of the law.[21]

For its part, it is the Court's constitutional tradition to frequently resort to the textual interpretation of constitutional norms. This approach implies a rather formalistic view of the normativity of law, even more so when another characteristic feature is added: the strong link to the method of internal harmonisation. In other words, the Court interprets ordinary laws exclusively in light of the Constitution, a circumstance that in turn reinforces the top-down relationship between the Court itself and the ordinary courts.

The data collected for this chapter demonstrates that reasoning related to the Constitution's text has been sparsely substituted with references to international norms (eg, the Inter-American Human Rights System) (IAHRS) and foreign law. Likewise, we have not observed sufficient reference to legal concepts that the doctrine has analysed and developed. These practices allow us, therefore, to believe that the Court has a formalistic, classical tendency when interpreting the law.

B. The Court and Constitutional Litigation

i. Competences and Powers

Paraguay's constitutional review system is judicial and focused. It is characterised by its existence as a hybrid system, drawing on both the North American and European models of constitutional review.[22]

In this sense, the Constitution conceives, within the same Court, a specialised chamber (Arts 258 and 260, Const.) with the power and duty to review the constitutionality of judicial norms and judgments (Arts 132 and 259[5], Const.). The Constitutional Chamber is the only judicial body that has the final say on constitutional interpretation. Only in exceptional situations is there a possibility that the Court's plenary will rule on unconstitutionality.[23]

For its part, preventive review does not exist in our system because constitutional review is exercised solely and exclusively in a specific case or controversy. Thus, the Constitutional Chamber may declare the unconstitutionality of a law or a judgment only in the context of a judicial process and at the request of one of the parties. Such a requirement necessitates an individual to allege the violation of a constitutional right resulting from the application of a law or the derivation of a judgment that the party considers unconstitutional.

[21] See World Justice Project (n 10).

[22] Moreno Rodríguez Alcalá (n 1) 284; D Mendonca and JC Mendonca Bonnet, 'La Justicia Constitucional en Paraguay' (1997) *Anuario Iberoamericano de Justicia Constitucional* 293–302.

[23] Law 609/95, Art 16 'that organises the Supreme Court of Justice' provides for the enlargement of the Constitutional Chamber to the Court's plenary, especially for electoral or highly complex matters.

ii. The Process: Active Legitimisation, Avenues of Promotion and Declarative Effects

The process of reviewing constitutionality is regulated in the Code of Civil Procedure (CCP) (*Código de Procesal Civil*) (Arts 538–64). Any person whose fundamental rights and guarantees have been infringed by a rule or judgment that violates constitutional principles or norms may request in writing the declaration of unconstitutionality. While it is true that the scope of the expression 'every person' is nebulous, among our emblematic failures are actions promoted by the legislative and executive powers.[24]

Unconstitutionality can be processed by way of action or by way of exception. The first takes place when the plaintiff bases his or her claim directly on the Constitution, questioning the application of a law or the execution of a judgment.[25] The second occurs when the defendant opposes a claim, arguing that it is based on a rule that violates the Constitution.

To these are also added the Declaration of Office by the Court (*Declaración de Oficio por la Corte*), the Constitutional Consultation (*Consulta Constitucional*) and the Declaration of Constitutional Certainty (*Declaración de Certeza Constitucional*).

The Court is vested with the power to declare by its own motion the unconstitutionality of judicial and normative acts. In relation to the former, in processes submitted under the law (Art 563, CCP), the Court may declare unconstitutionality and the consequential nullity of other decisions of a judicial nature even if they have not been challenged. Regarding normative acts, ordinary judges, before sentencing and in case of doubt, may refer the trial – *ex officio* – to the Constitutional Chamber (Arts 18[a] and 582, CCP, modified by Law no. 609/95) so that it can carry out a constitutional review of the rules applicable to the case.[26]

In the Paraguayan constitutional design, there is no constitutional review outside a justiciable case, which contrasts with other countries where any organ or body charged with the review can lodge a consultation or request. However, by jurisprudential means, the Court has developed the Declaration of Constitutional Certainty, which, according to Moreno Rodríguez, 'was not provided for in the Constitution and in fact is unparalleled in any system of constitutional review in the region or in that of the most consolidated constitutional democracies whose models of constitutional justice usually serve as references at the level of comparative law'.[27] The Court defines this avenue as a species of the broader genre of merely declarative actions (Art 99, CCP) on the following grounds:

> Any doubt that arises as to the scope of a constitutional norm, concretised in a specific case that prompts judicial intervention, must be elucidated, as to its scope and effects, by the

[24] Ac and Sent No 706/1997, 'original jurisdiction of the Court in habeas corpus'; Ac and Sent No 415/1998, 'commutation of sentences – Lino Oviedo et al'; L Lezcano Claude, 'El Control de Constitucionalidad sobre Actos de los Poderes Legislativo y Ejecutivo en el Paraguay' (2000) *Anuario Iberoamericano de Justicia Constitucional* 221–41.

[25] See D Mendonca, *Sentencia arbitraria: análisis de la doctrina constitucional de la Corte Suprema de Justicia* (Intercontinental, 2006).

[26] Ac and Sent No 185/2014, 'constitutional consultation on the double renumeration of lawyers in public service'; Ac and Sent No 10/2018, 'constitutional consultation referred to an executive decree'; Ac and Sent No 119/2018, 'constitutional consultation referred to the right to health'.

[27] See Moreno Rodriguez Alcalá (n 1) 288–309.

> highest judicial instance of the Republic, in the exercise of its interpretative function. The Supreme Court of Justice is the only body that has jurisdiction to review the constitutionality of the legal norms that make up our positive order.[28]

As for the effects of a declaration of unconstitutionality of a norm, the declaration does not imply that the law should be repealed or deleted; it simply becomes inapplicable in the specific case. For its part, a judgment declared unconstitutional is null and void; therefore, the matter must be retried by another judge. This is the case regardless of the declaration's relevance in other areas, be they social, economic or political.

iii. Publication and Repercussions of the Decisions

The rulings handed down by the Constitutional Chamber are largely respected and obeyed not only by the ordinary courts but also by the other branches of government. Exceptionally, however, we note the well-known case involving the impeachment of Ministers of the Court, who were dismissed in 2003. They instigated actions of unconstitutionality against what was decided by Congress, which were finally admitted in December 2009. This situation created an ensuing schism between the legislature and the Court since the senators, through a resolution, intimidated the Court's Ministers to annul the resolved action, threatening to also initiate an impeachment trial. The Court ultimately decided to set aside its own decisions.[29]

On the other hand, in compliance with Law no. 6299/2019, establishing the electronic transmission of the Supreme Court of Justice's sessions, the Court's plenary meetings are transmitted as well as the Constitutional Chamber's live sessions (through the internet, social networks and the signal of TV Justice [*TV Justicia Paraguay*]). In addition, all the Court's decisions are posted on its website. Thus, in 2021, constitutional review was requested in 2,516 cases of which only 640 have been concluded.[30] This data reveals a slight increase over the number of cases resolved in previous years.[31]

iv. Judicial Activism

The role of the Court in relation to the other branches of government and its position vis-à-vis society is a topic still only minimally explored in Paraguayan doctrine.[32]

[28] Ac and Sent No 81/2017, 'Declarative Action of Constitutional Certainty' in Santiago Peña – Minister of Finance – Arts 217 and 202 inc. 10) of the National Constitution.

[29] See JP Irrazabal, *La Justicia y el Poder Político en Paraguay: ¿un ataque a la independencia judicial?*, Agenda Estado de Derecho (21 June 2021), see at agendaestadodederecho.com/la-justicia-y-el-poder-politico-en-paraguay-un-ataque-a-la-independencia-judicial/.

[30] Supreme Court of Justice, *Informe de Gestión 2021*, 59, 79, see at www.pj.gov.py/images/contenido/informes_gestion/informe2021.pdf.

[31] See Supreme Court of Justice, *Informes de Gestión*, see at www.pj.gov.py/contenido/505-informes-de-gestion-csj/505.

[32] See A Pérez-Liñán and A Castagnola, 'El Control Constitucional y la Defensa de los Derechos en Paraguay 1995–2015' in *Fragmentación política e independencia judicial. Un estudio de las acciones de inconstitucionalidad, 1995–2015* (Edición de Conferencia: Instituto Desarrollo, 2018) 15–29, see at www.conacyt.gov.py/sites/default/files/upload_editores/u294/Compendio-Judicial.pdf.
Both authors conclude that the Paraguayan Supreme Court is one of the most active in the world in view of the number of actions of unconstitutionality admitted against the legislative and executive powers. For this

However, we can provide a small sketch, taking into account some of the empirical results of our research.

As such, the actions of unconstitutionality were admitted in most of the cases analysed (21 rulings). However, this high rate does not necessarily imply that the Court has assumed a leading role in promoting public policies for society as a whole or for minority, vulnerable and excluded groups. It can be deduced, from the same technique used in the judgments, that the Court speaks to ordinary judges and the legal community, not to the rest of the population.

For example, there is Ac. and Sent. No. 191/1999,[33] 'double absence of leadership in the executive power', which was decided in a very specific political and social context. The Vice President of the Republic had died, and the President resigned from his position after a strong popular outcry. The question at hand was the following: 'Should general elections be called for the offices of President and Vice President while the leader of Congress holds the presidency on a temporary basis?'

Paradigmatically, the full Court answered this decisive question in favour of democracy – that is, the people could elect their Vice President but not their President. The arguments presented were primarily technical where the Court's Ministers analysed the limit and scope of dogmatic concepts such as the 'declaration of constitutional certainty' and 'constitutional doubt'.

Likewise, rulings with apparent justification are also not alien to the Paraguayan Court. For example, the case of Ac. and Sent. No. 30/1997, 'rights of indigenous peoples (I)', consists of three pages in which the facts are first presented extensively, then a 'precautionary measure' (a strictly procedural question) is analysed, and then finally the constitutional norm is set forth that protects indigenous peoples and guarantees their access to land. While it is true that the declaration of unconstitutionality favoured the petitioner indigenous community, the arguments presented were insufficient to protect groups historically excluded from the most basic rights, such as our native peoples.

Another fitting example is Ac. and Sent. No. 139/2007, 'diplomatic and consular service'. There, the Court's judges rhetorically noted the principle of equality for reasoning that, with or without a university degree, it is possible to access the diplomatic ladder under the same conditions and occupy representative positions in embassies and consulates.

From what we have unearthed, we can affirm that our Court carries out a '*sui generis* activism' even though most claims of unconstitutionality are admitted.[34] In other words, just because the Court is 'active' does not mean it is an activist tribunal.

result, they carried out a quantitative analysis of 5,000 decisions over a period of 20 years. At first glance, the results may be encouraging, but the decisive evidence would be the argumentative quality of these rulings and whether they have benefited society to some extent or whether they have only focused on blocking political decisions or goals.

[33] Most of the citations to the Paraguayan cases included in this chapter take the form of 'Ac. and Sent. No.', where 'Ac.' is the abbreviation for *Acuerdo* (Agreement), 'Sent.' is the abbreviation for *Sentencia* (Judgment) and 'No.' is the case number. Citations that take the form of 'A.I. No.' are citations to *Autos Interlocutorios* (Interlocutory Orders).

[34] D Moreno Rodríguez Alcalá, 'Sobre el "activismo" de la Corte Suprema y el rol de la justicia constitucional' (2020) *Anuario Paraguayo de Derecho Constitucional* 259–61.

Only in exceptional cases has the Court taken a different position involving the public. An important case in this regard is Ac. and Sent. No. 1306/2013, 'right of access to public information'. The antecedent of this ruling dealt with the Municipality of San Lorenzo's refusal to provide the number of public employees hired and appointed along with their personal data, positions and respective salaries.

Before resolving the case, the Constitutional Chamber asked[35] all social groups and those interested in the matter to submit their opinions under the proviso of 'Friends of the Court' ('*Amigos del Tribunal*'). This step was taken not only to collect various perspectives but also to provide a reasonable and reliable response to community interests.

C. The Judges

The Paraguayan judiciary is composed of ordinary courts and the Supreme Court of Justice, which consists of nine members and is divided into three chambers: Civil, Criminal and Constitutional. As far as its administration, the Court has budgetary independence (Art 249, Const.).[36]

The judges of the highest body for the administration of justice are called 'Ministers of the Supreme Court'. To be designated as such, they must meet certain requirements. Among these are Paraguayan nationality, an age of 35 or older, the academic degree of Doctor in Law and the exercise of the profession of attorney, judicial magistrature or university chair for at least 10 years (Art 258, Const.).

Thus, the exercise of the public function – in this instance, imparting justice – is compatible with the activity of teaching, this being the only additional work activity that judges can perform. Although almost all the Court's judges have the academic degrees of professor and Doctor in Law, not all of them teach. In addition, as will be seen in the descriptive part of our research, the analysed decisions do not incorporate sufficient academic content.

With regard to the form of selection and removal of judges, there are two bodies with extra powers provided for in the Constitution: The Council of the Magistrature (Arts 262–64, Const.) and the Jury of Prosecution of Magistrates (Art 253, Const.). The first is responsible for the selection process of judges for which it prepares and proposes the shortlists of candidates to populate the Court (Art 264[1], Const.). These lists are then submitted to the Senate for those members to decide but with the executive branch's subsequent approval.

Although it is true that the Council of the Magistrature is composed of representatives of the lawyers' guild and the academic establishment (Art 262, Const.), this does not imply that the rest of civil society actively participates in the process of selecting judges for the Court since no specific constitutional mechanism is foreseen for this purpose. In addition, authors like Campos Cervara have strongly criticised this body,

[35] See Acordada No 479 (9 October 2007), see at www.csj.gov.py/par97017/reglamentaciones/modulos/repdetallado.asp?codigo_acord=926.

[36] The judiciary has presented a budget expenditure in 2020 of 1,347,833,520,600 Gs (Guaranís), a sum that at the current exchange rate in U.S. dollars is USD $200,112,842.80.
See at www.pj.gov.py/images/contenido/presupuesto/2020/EPG_xls-Por-OG-Consolidado-Objeto-Gasto.

expressing scepticism about its legitimacy since some of its members are not disconnected from politics.[37]

With regard to the duration of the term of office, judges are irremovable and are appointed for periods of five years, starting from the day of their appointments (Art 262, Const.). The Constitution also dictates that the Court's Ministers may only be removed by impeachment and must cease to hold office at the age of 75 (Art 261, Const.).

These two constitutional norms have acquired an important role in academic discussion and have impacted judicial reasoning. Thus, some of the doctrine[38] maintains that it is a case of 'legal antinomy' since the impossibility of removal during the five-year period is only applicable to ordinary judges. On the contrary, the denomination of 'Ministers of the Court' elevates those judges to a superior hierarchical rank. Consequently, the Ministers can be removed solely and exclusively through impeachment. The argument of this line of thought is based on the fact that special law (Art 261, Const.) prevails over general (Art 262, Const.).

On the contrary, another branch of the doctrine[39] considers that the denominations of 'Magistrate' and 'Minister' should not be understood in a hierarchical sense, and the distinction is merely linguistic.

The Court has opted for the first of the aforementioned lines of thought and has interpreted that the two grounds for the cessation of a Minister of the highest court's functions are reaching the established age or removal after an impeachment trial.[40]

D. Legal Scholarship and Constitutional Reasoning

The study of constitutional law in Paraguay shares some characteristics with other countries in the region in terms of legal training and academia in general. The approach to legal theories and literature is primarily influenced by North American and European scholars. Likewise, Paraguayan academics focus largely on developments in Argentina. However, local voices with original ideas are still relatively scarce.

The Paraguayan academy focuses most of its critical attention on organic issues: for example, the question of the permanent tenure of the Court's Ministers, the declaration of unconstitutionality with *erga omnes* effects, the declaratory actions of constitutional certainty, and finally, the annulment of arbitrary sentences.

These positions are commonly published not only in manuals but also in legal journals. As for these materials' analyses, lawyers primarily use them although a minority of judges do as well, either arguing a claim or at the time of sentencing,[41] respectively.

[37] Campos Cervera (n 17) 113–44.

[38] JR Torres Kirmser, 'La Praxis del Control de Constitucionalidad en el Paraguay' (2010) *Revista de la Facultad de Derecho y Ciencias Sociales UNA* 100–02; Lezcano Claude (n 24) 236–40.

[39] J Seall-Sasiain, 'Cuestionable Inamovilidad Permanente de los Ministros de la Corte y Limitación al Consejo de la Magistratura, Crítica a los fallos No. 222 y No. 223 de 5/5/2000, y No. 1.033 de 29/12/2001 de la Corte Suprema de Justicia del Paraguay' (2003) *Anuario Iberoamericano de Justicia Constitucional* 606–07; Moreno Rodríguez Alcalá (n 1) 295–96.

[40] Ac and Sent No 222/2000, 'permanent tenure of the Court's Ministers (I)'; Ac and Sent No 223/2000, 'permanent tenure of the Court's Ministers (II)'; Ac and Sent No 557/2007, 'permanent tenure of the Court's Ministers (III)'.

[41] Above all, in decisions on democratic principles and human rights.

However, especially in recent years, a new type of academic community has emerged, which is influenced more by progressive theories that take a more critical position on the system. Many scholars are observers of constitutional transformations within the same region, gradually detaching themselves from traditional Western theories, seeking to adapt the Paraguayan legal system to the social reality and principles of equality and non-discrimination.[42]

III. Types of Arguments in Constitutional Reasoning

A. The Structure of Constitutional Arguments

Most of the analysed rulings follow a parallel-cumulative line of argument, which is observed in 22 out of 40 of the selected judgments. This could be due to the Constitutional Chamber's practice of deciding a case according to the majority vote. Indeed, the judges usually construct their arguments separately in the same judgment without necessarily implying any disagreement, the purpose being to transmit to their audience (ordinary judges and lawyers) a more complete and receptive opinion while relying on a certain legal interpretation. In addition, we should bear in mind that, in Paraguay, it is also very common to base an action on several different grounds or claims. For its part, the conclusive-argumentative structure was observed in 13 rulings, whereas the argument was dialogical in five.

The possible relevance of the decision in the legal, political, social or economic arena does not play a decisive role that allows us to explain the result.

B. Types of Arguments in Constitutional Reasoning

i. The Ordinary Meaning of Words

In our representative rulings, the use of the exegetical method predominates due to the Paraguayan judges' same formalistic tendency. Thus, in 17 of the 40 analysed decisions, the ordinary meaning of the words of the constitutional were directly and explicitly analysed.

However, the prevalence of this method does not imply that judges always agree on the grammatical interpretation of the rules. On the contrary, disagreements over terminology formed the bases of dissenting opinions in seven judgments.

For example, there is Ac. and Sent. No. 84/1998, 'Lino Oviedo – jurisdiction of the military court'. On the one hand, there has been discussion in Paraguay about the

[42] Currently, the Paraguayan Institute of Constitutional Law (*Instituto Paraguayo de Derecho Constitucional*) remains very active, promoting dialogue on current and pertinent issues of the new constitutional justice, see at ipdc.org.py. In addition, in the '2021 Report of the Human Rights Coordinator of Paraguay' ('*Informe 2021 de la Coordinadora de Derechos Humanos del Paraguay*'), there are numerous organisations mentioned that strive to promote discussion and the exchange of knowledge. See at codehupy.org.py/codehupy-presenta-informe-anual-sobre-derechos-humanos-2021/.

permanent existence of specialised courts to resolve military issues. On the other, the formation of extraordinary military tribunals is dependent on whether the nation is at peace or at war. To this end, the Court's judges have analysed the terms and scope of Organic Law no. 840/80, on the Military Courts (*Ley no. 840/80, Orgánica de los Tribunales Militares*) and its harmonisation with the Constitution.

On the contrary, and exceptionally, the systematic and harmonious method of constitutional norms has been used to argue rulings pertinent to the legal order and with the scope of *erga omnes*. Thus, there is Ac. and Sent. No. 222/2000, 'permanent tenure of the Court's Ministers (I)', and Ac. and Sent. No. 223/2000, 'permanent tenure of the Court's Ministers (II)'. In both decisions, the Court's nine judges declared the unconstitutionality of Article 19 of Law no. 609/95, which established the tacit renewal of the exercise of the Ministers' functions until they were confirmed, or their successors were appointed. The Ministers interpreted that the Constitution enshrines the principle of permanent tenure for the Court's Ministers (up to the age of 75) as opposed to the ordinary judges' temporary tenure (five years). In addition, the declaration had a general scope, based on the principle of constitutional supremacy (Art 137, Const.).

ii. Analogies

Paraguayan judges prefer to steer away from this method,[43] as they applied analogy rules in only two of the sample's 40 decisions.

Thus, in Ac. and Sent. No. 68/1996, 'conscientious objection to military service', the judges drew an analogy between individuals performing military service and those performing community service for the Red Cross, supporting the proposition that service was being performed for the Paraguayan nation in both situations.

iii. Domestic Harmonising Arguments

Due to the same formalistic tendency of Paraguayan judges and their adherence to the principle of normative hierarchy, we observed that in 25 of the 40 rulings the judges utilised arguments favouring internal harmonisation, using both constitutional norms as well as lower-ranking norms to preserve their consistency with the Constitution.

iv. International Harmonising Arguments

Nine of the selected 40 judgments referenced international regulations and instruments. In five of these, the Court cited the Inter-American Human Rights System (IAHRS), and two others invoked the Universal Declaration of Human Rights (UDHR). In the remaining decisions, the systems were combined. However, we note that the Court's inclination is to increasingly use this method.

[43] On the importance of analogy and the differences between it and precedents, see F Schauer, *Pensar como abogado. Una nueva introducción al razonamiento jurídico* (Marcial Pons, 2013) 99–114.

In this regard, we consider that A.I. no. 669/2009, 'recognition of IACtHR competence', is of the utmost importance. In that case, the Constitutional Chamber expressly affirmed the Paraguayan State's obligation to respect the binding nature of the IACtHR's decisions, excluding any appeal to national courts.

Likewise, in matters of fundamental rights and freedoms, such as those addressed in Ac. and Sent. No. 68/1996, 'conscientious objection to military service'; Ac. and Sent. No. 397/1997, 'pretrial detention'; and Ac. and Sent. No. 706/1997, 'original jurisdiction of the Court in habeas corpus', the judges argued that there must be harmonisation between domestic norms and the international norms of the IAHRS.

It is worth mentioning here that, in the Court's relevant jurisprudence, there is explicit reference to the review of the IAHRS's diffuse conventionality – specifically, in the Constitutional Chamber's decisions of Ac. and Sent. No. 2377/2012, Ac. and Sent. No. 805/2018, Ac. and Sent. No. 608/2018 and Ac. and Sent. No. 609/2018; in the Civil Chamber's opinion in Ac. and Sent. No. 83/2018; and in the Criminal Chamber's sentence of Ac. and Sent. No. 1283/2014.

v. Precedents

In 16 of the 40 decisions, the judges expressly referenced previous cases that the Court had already examined and resolved. This could be explained, on the one hand, by the relative significance of what was decided in these decisions, particularly regarding political power (eg, Ac. and Sent. No. 191/1999, 'double absence of leadership in the executive power', and A.I. No. 231/2017, 'constitutional certainty referring to the effect of the Executive's veto of the general expense budget'). On the other hand, judges are aware that, since a declaration of unconstitutionality only applies to a specific case, it must be applied consistently in future cases that address the same matter to preserve a certain level of jurisprudential uniformity. However, the term 'settled case law' is not expressly mentioned in the analysed judgments.

vi. Teleological Arguments Concerning the Purpose of the Text

In addition to the exegetical method, the teleological arguments of an objective nature cannot be ignored, as this type of argument was identified in 20 of the 40 opinions. This could be explained by the Constitution's very content, which, by accentuating a wide catalogue of rights, includes numerous references to the norms' protectionist purposes or objectives along with legal institutions that incorporate them. At the same time, the Constitution itself provides sufficient means to employ teleological arguments.

It should be noted that Paraguayan judges resort to this method to a large extent when they must protect procedural issues. For example, Ac. and Sent. No. 173/2000, 'admissibility requirements and origin of the action of unconstitutionality', delimits not only the parties' actions but also those of judicial analysis. Other examples of this practice are found in Ac. and Sent. No. 706/1997, 'original jurisdiction of the Court in habeas corpus'; Ac. and Sent. No. 84/1998, 'Lino Oviedo – jurisdiction of the military court'; and Ac. and Sent. No. 415/1998, 'commutation of sentences – Lino Oviedo et al.'

Judges also take advantage of the teleological method's potential when addressing human rights and collective rights matters. For example, in Ac. and Sent. No. 30/1997, 'rights of indigenous peoples (I)', the Court established – albeit briefly – that even the State cannot dispose of lands that legitimately belong to indigenous peoples. The Court based this on the Constitution, which considers indigenous peoples to be 'groups [present] prior to the formation and organisation of the Paraguayan State'.

Similarly, this has been argued in other important rulings for collective rights by granting those rights substantial rather than merely formal equality, such as in Ac. and Sent. No. 68/1996, 'conscientious objection to military service'; Ac. and Sent. No. 1306/2013, 'right of access to public information'; and Ac. and Sent. No. 540/1996, 'association of taxi drivers – municipal autonomy'.

vii. Teleological/Purposive Arguments

In 12 rulings, the judges analysed the legislator's intent (or what it might have been) behind a given norm. The correct use of this interpretative and argumentative method often makes it possible to determine the validity and scope of the invoked constitutional precept. To do this, the judges resort to the Journal of Sessions of the National Constituent Convention (*Diario de Sesiones de la Convención Nacional Constituyente*).[44]

viii. Non-Legal Arguments

The use of non-legal arguments was not very prevalent in the analysed decisions. There were sociological and moral arguments (or the combination thereof) in nine decisions. By contrast, economic arguments appeared only once.

However, Ac. and Sent. No. 1617/2004, 'custody of children and adolescents', must be considered because of the influence this type of judicial process has had on family law. In that case, the Court's judges emphasised the importance of the new environment to which a child must adapt after separation from the parents – 'without losing the vital emotional bond'. In addition, the Court warned 'the parents involved in the trial about the circumstances and the environment they [had] created for their minor children by taking them and subjecting them to a process of instability for more than four years'.

ix. Pro Homine/Pro Persona Principles

As pointed out at the beginning of the chapter, the Constitution indicates that the principle of respect for human dignity, which already appears in the preamble and in Article 1, serves as the very foundation of the Republic and the compulsory protection of human rights.

However, in one of the analysed rulings, the Court incorporated a standard of interpretation of the norm with a movement towards an amplification of rights. From this, the Ministers' application of the *pro persona* principle can be inferred, using the IACHR's doctrine in the scope of Article 13 of the ACHR as a reference. Here, we refer to Ac. and Sent. No. 1306/2013, 'right of access to public information'.

[44] See at www.bacn.gov.py/actas-de-sesiones-de-la-convencion-de-1992.

However, the reference to, and explicit incorporation of, the *pro persona* principle in Paraguayan jurisprudence is found in Ac. and Sent. No. 369/2016, and Ac. and Sent. No. 1007/2016, although neither is among the analysed judgments. However, these decisions merit attention because of their relevance not only for national jurists but also for foreign judges.

These decisions analyse the regulation of the judicial magistrates' teaching and scientific research activity. As such, the Court ruled forcefully on the *pro homine* principle with respect to the State's obligation to always consider the broadest norm in the context of human rights.

x. References to Scholarly Works and Foreign (National) Law

In 24 of the analysed judgments, the Court referenced academic works penned by both national and international authors. However, doctrinal references are addressed in separate paragraphs and are not always linked to what has been resolved. This practice is ripe for criticism because it breaks with the guiding discourse, undermines the very congruence of the sentence and causes difficulty determining or giving meaning to the terms used in the decision.

On the other hand, in 14 rulings that focus predominantly on procedural issues, the Ministers cited not only foreign legislation but also rulings issued by other courts, with those in Argentina being the most popular in this regard.

C. The Overall Weight of the Arguments

Based on the research analysis, we found that 33 judgments could be categorised as ratio decidendi and obiter dictum. Seven judgments used purely rhetorical arguments.

However, we could not verify in any of the analysed decisions that the judges attempted to craft a coherent doctrine on the justification and prioritisation of an interpretive method. Paraguayan judges first transcribe the facts of the case, then indicate the constitutional incompatibility of a norm or, where appropriate, the lower courts' or parties' errors, and then they finally analyse the meaning and grammatical scope of a norm, a word contained in the norm or a normative phrase. Ultimately, they primarily justify their decisions. The same goes for the analyses that derive from the teleological method and the low number of arguments from silence. However, this does not signify that there is a sufficient argumentative explanation for why a rule should be interpreted in one way or another.

For its part, the use of rhetorical arguments is unsurprising because it is a tool that all judges possess, not just those in Paraguay. If the number of these kinds of cases is increasing, and if the nature of this type of argument is decisive in specific cases, the academy would do well to analyse it more thoroughly.

As for the importance of what each judge states, there is no differentiation; there is simply an internal procedure that uses a lottery system to decide the order in which the judges will analyse the case's issue and present his or her arguments. The first examining judge is assigned the status of 'preopinion judge or [M]inister'. The order is irrelevant to the final outcome of the case.

D. Judicial Candour and Judicial Rhetoric

With regard to the style of opinions, technical-legal language predominates, utilising words that are not part of popular speech. This practice can be explained by the judges' custom of speaking preponderantly to the legal community in their opinions.

E. Length, Dissenting and Concurring Opinions

The arguments that each judge presents vary both in length and in terms of value judgments. We can explain these results from two perspectives. On the one hand, in decisions with significant political, social and media impact, the arguments are extensive. Each judge issues his or her own argument regardless of whether it is even concomitant with the previous one.

The length is thus determined from this premise: the greater the political or social involvement, the greater the argumentative length. For example, in those processes where the constitutional review involves the State's structure and political organisation, judicial independence or human rights, the arguments are varied and extensive.

On the other hand, in trials that individuals initiate, which attract no media interest, the arguments are short. This circumstance does not imply, however, that the issues discussed and decided are of little relevance. On the contrary, in some cases, the Constitutional Chamber could have spoken more broadly on constitutional issues relevant to the whole nation. For example, see A.I. No. 669/2009, 'recognition of the jurisdiction of the Inter-American Court'; Ac. and Sent. No. 30/1997, 'rights of indigenous peoples (I)'; Ac. and Sent. No. 365/1999, 'rights of indigenous peoples (II)'; and Ac. and Sent. No. 243/2008, 'rights of indigenous peoples (III)'.

The Court's decisions are based on the concurring opinions of the majority of the judges even if their reasons differ (Art 2, Law no. 609/95). Thus, each judge can issue his or her own opinion on the issue or 'adhere to the vote' (arguments) of their colleague(s). Judges can only vote against a decision if they present a dissenting opinion, which must be substantiated, as we observed in 10 rulings.

Dissenting opinions were found in four cases of disagreement regarding the interpretation of a norm or principle for the preservation – or restoration – of the democratic and political order, as well as for the safeguarding of the principle of the separation of powers.

There are, for example, cases involving considerable political instability, such as Ac. and Sent. No. 84/1998, 'Lino Oviedo – jurisdiction of the military court', and Ac. and Sent. No. 415/1998, 'commutation of sentences – Lino Oviedo et al.' Also relevant is Ac. and Sent. No. 1033/2001, 'selection and confirmation of judges', primarily because it addresses issues associated with the separation of powers and, above all, with judicial independence.

As for the dissenting views contained in the other judgments, these focused strictly on procedural issues (rules and principles).

F. Framing of Constitutional Issues

Most of the constitutional issues the Court decided concerned the absence of positive adaptation to the constitutional norm (21 rulings). Thus, the arguments presented there addressed the violation of recognised fundamental rights, the lack of the norm's reasonableness and even the overreach of functions in the legislative production process (laws, decrees, regulations, etc.). We also identified another important argument – the insufficient substantiation of a decision (cases of arbitrary sentences) – which led to declaring the sentence arbitrary or unconstitutional.

Another important topic among the selected cases was that of procedural rights (18 rulings), predominantly the guarantee of due process. In 12 decisions, the Court ruled on the organisation of the State and the relationship between the three government powers. These rulings were preceded by political and interinstitutional crises.

Finally, 18 judgments combined rights issues and structural disputes. We observed this combination not only in situations of national crisis but also in those cases that attempted to grant collective rights.

G. Key Concepts

In the judgments analysed, judicial independence, the rule of law, the principle of legality and the principle of equality were the key concepts of practice in judicial reasoning. The first appeared in 11 cases, the second in eight, and the third and fourth in seven cases each. In addition, basic procedural rights were also addressed in several decisions (five cases).

On the contrary, the concepts of legal certainty, justice, and economic, social and cultural rights appeared only once. Other concepts, such as secularism, sovereignty, the structure of the State and the government were practically invisible in the jurisprudence, except for controversies concerning democratic principles (two cases).

We emphasise that these key concepts were, on the one hand, mentioned in a combined way within the framework of political and social issues relevant to the country, as well as in those situations where judicial independence was at stake.

The principle of proportionality, freedom of expression, the right to privacy, human dignity and activism were mentioned exceptionally in two cases, which involved matters of general interest or collective rights.

IV. Comparative Perspective

The twentieth century constituted an important period of transformation aimed at the construction of constitutional democracies in Latin American States. Further, the inclusion of systems or models of constitutional justice developed to a greater or lesser extent during the same time period.[45]

[45] See G Bidart Campos, *Compendio de derecho constitucional* (Ediar, 2004); Santiago Nino (n 7); JE Roa Roa, *La justicia constitucional en América Latina* (Universidad Externado de Colombia, 2015) 1–31.

Thus, we observe in Latin America, an important diversity of systems referring to constitutional justice since, within it, the traditional European and North American models converge – alone, combined or even adapted to the experiences of constitutionalism in the region's countries.[46] In this sense, there are specialised court chambers and constitutional courts with the power to carry out constitutional review. There are also systems (of diffuse control) in which the judges of a lower hierarchy have subject matter jurisdiction to also hear such cases.[47]

In this sense, we note four aspects of judicial reasoning common to Paraguay and some of the other countries in the region. First, the declaration of unconstitutionality is always the exception. Therefore, a petition must be argued clearly and unequivocally. Second, most Latin American judges express their opinions in the form of parallel-cumulative arguments (Argentina, Uruguay, Mexico, Peru, Guatemala, Bolivia, Chile and Paraguay). Third, the language used in the judgments is technical, formalistic and closely linked to the normative text and, as such, is scarcely accessible to nonjurists. Fourth, the reference to key concepts, such as human dignity, the principle of equality, the rule of law, due process and democracy, without definitions or limitations of their own, is striking. Rather, judges use these concepts to reinforce their arguments. Of the latter, however, we exclude the Uruguayan judges, who address the principles of proportionality and equality in detail.

On the other hand, while Paraguayan judges are mostly limited to the method of literal interpretation, some of the region's magistrates have moved away from it (Peru), others have resorted to the use of different and varied methods (Argentina), and in other jurisdictions, judges are even normatively linked to fixed rules of interpretation (Bolivia and Ecuador). Thus, for example, precedents added to national and foreign doctrine play an important role in many countries in the region (Uruguay, Argentina, Bolivia, Mexico and Peru).

As for the length of the rulings, and contrary to Paraguayan opinions, in some Latin American countries, they reach more than 100 pages (Argentina, Bolivia, Mexico, Peru and Colombia). However, we consider that a greater length does not necessarily imply quality in the reasoning. However, this correlation is only possible to determine by evaluating each decision.

As for the intellectual and professional qualities of the judges that make up the different Latin American courts, we note that these are very diverse and do not allow for a compilation of common parameters beyond the fact that they are citizens and jurists. However, we can affirm that the more academics there are on a bench, the higher the quality of judicial reasoning.

We also observe that there is no correlation between a constitution's age and the possibility of amendment or reform in terms of procedural rigidity. However, we share the belief that an 'imbalance between the organic and dogmatic part' is a characteristic of

[46] P Navia and J Ríos-Figueroa, 'The constitutional adjudication mosaic of Latin America' (2005) 38 *Comparative Political Studies* 189–217.

[47] In this respect, see D García Belaúnde et al, *Los sistemas Constitucionales Iberoamericanos* (Dykinson, 1992); Navia and Ríos-Figueroa (n 46) 189–217; O Lara-Borges, A Castagnola and A Pérez-Liñán, 'Diseño Constitucional y Estabilidad Judicial en América Latina 1900–2009' (2012) 19 *Revista Política y Gobierno* 3–40.

the phenomenon called 'new Latin American constitutionalism'.[48] This is so because the regional constitutions contemplate various rights, while the organisation of constituted power does not contain innovations or limitations of great magnitude. Likewise, sufficient mechanisms for the participation of constituent power have not been activated.

Finally, Paraguay, Uruguay, Chile and Guatemala aspire to an enlargement of a more modern conception of human rights and fundamental guarantees in accordance with the various international instruments. This would contribute not only to a greater judicial dialogue but also to a delimitation of key concepts and sufficient substantiation when the *pro homine* principle must be applied.

V. Evaluation, Pathology and Criticism

The analysis of the judgments selected for this empirical research reveals four critical results regarding the Paraguayan constitutional mode of reasoning.

In the first place, the predominant use of the method of literal interpretation of the rule is problematic, although we will likely never agree on the most appropriate interpretative criteria.[49] On the contrary, we do concur that rational decisions do not necessarily emerge from literal interpretation, as the latter does not require a greater interpretative effort since the direct application of the rule is sufficient. Thus, the analytical capacity of judges has often been limited, even instrumentalised, and reduced to mere formalism. In addition, this trend is transmitted from the Court's judges to those of the lower courts. These assertions can be confirmed by the mere reading of any of the rulings because the Court's judges – and also those of ordinary courts – transcribe the applicable norm and then analyse its grammatical meaning and scope.[50] Therefore, a new approach to Paraguayan jurisprudence is necessary in which judgments are per se consistent and result from a high level and more systematic legal reasoning.

Second, the resource of the external interpreter must be promoted – that is, dialogue with other courts. Paraguayan judges don't sufficiently use the study of interpretative criteria, reasoning and solutions within the IASHR, together with doctrine and IACtHR jurisprudence and that of other regional courts. A paradigm shift, referring to a greater willingness of judges to use academic works and foreign judgments, could be of great help in improving constitutional reasoning, with a perspective of national and international harmonisation.

Third, the judgments' language reveals a rather formalistic judicial culture. In our opinion, this situation can be overcome once Paraguayan jurists realise that the public observer of judicial processes is not just the legal community. Thus, the interpretation

[48] R Gargarella, 'Sobre el nuevo constitucionalismo latinoamericano' (2018) 27 *Revista Uruguaya de Ciencia Política* 115–23.

[49] See NP Sagüés, 'Interpretación constitucional y alquimia constitucional. (El arsenal argumentativo de los Tribunales Supremos' (2004) 1 *Revista Iberoamericana de Derecho Procesal Constitucional* 151–70; R Gargarella, 'De la Alquimia Interpretativa al Maltrato Constitucional. La interpretación del derecho en manos de la Corte Suprema argentina' (2007) 2 *Jurisprudencia Argentina* (Lexis Nexis) 3–10; see also HLA Hart, *The Concept of Law*, 3rd edn (Oxford University Press, 2012); R Guastini, *Interpretar y argumentar* (Centro de Estudios Políticos y Constitucionales, 2014) 353 et seq.

[50] For example, Ac and Sent No 363/95, 'university autonomy'.

and application of the law does not imply that judges should make indiscriminate use of interpretative parameters, but rather that judges must contribute to public debate through words and analysis.

Fourthly, and finally, we address the question of judicial independence since the rule of law depends on it from three points of view: (i) the true independence of judges allows them to craft decisions without fear of external pressure; (ii) perceived independence gives citizens the confidence to bring their disputes before the national court; and (iii) compliance with the guarantees related to the judicial office's permanence and those linked to the appointment process support both real and perceived independence. In this sense, we have analysed rulings[51] where judicial independence has been flagrantly violated. On the one hand, the appointment processes were not disconnected from political (or sectoral) matters, and on the other, the permanent tenure in office of the Republic's highest-level judges was distorted. Thus, the question of judicial independence is one of the greatest challenges within our system. Its validity not only prevents the Executive and the legislature from imposing and controlling justice; it also prevents the issuance of judgments that may cause serious issues in the form of 'constitutional mutations'.[52] In this sense, it is undesirable that the practices and customs *contra constitutionem* expressly validated by the Court, end up consolidated and accepted without question or revoked and replaced several times depending on the Court's composition. Therefore, the great challenge for Paraguayan judges is to avoid what Sagüés[53] calls the 'deconstitutionalisation of the system'.

[51] Ac and Sent No 222/2000, 'permanent tenure of the Court's Ministers (I)'; Ac and Sent No 223/2000, 'permanent tenure of the Court's Ministers (II)'.

[52] For example, discussions around the *erga omnes* effect and the declaration of constitutional certainty. R Torres Kirmser, 'Panorama reciente de la acción declarativa de certeza constitucional en la jurisprudencia de la Corte Suprema de Justicia' (2017) *Revista Académica Facultad de Derecho y Ciencias Sociales de la Universidad Nacional de Asunción* 31–64.

[53] NP Sagüés, 'El concepto de desconstitucionalización' (2007) *Revista de Derecho de la Universidad Católica del Uruguay* 181, 195.

15

The Jurisprudence of the Constitutional Court of Peru

ABRAHAM SILES VALLEJOS,* ROSA NATALÍ LLIQUE RAMÍREZ AND MARÍA ALEJANDRA ESPINO LAYZA

I. Legal, Political, Institutional and Academic Context

A. Legal and Political Culture as Context for the Constitutional Reasoning

Although the Constitution entered into force at the end of 1993, the Constitutional Court was not operational until 24 June 1996.[1] From the onset, the Fujimori government maintained a hostile attitude towards constitutional jurisdiction to the extent that the Constitution's original drafts did not provide for a constitutional court.[2] Reluctantly accepting the Court's jurisdiction, however, the government set out to appoint magistrates who responded to the regime's dictates[3] and to enshrine in the Court's Organic Law a supermajority requirement for declaring the unconstitutionality of laws (six votes out of seven total). The latter action inextricably bound the Constitution's supreme interpreter to the nation's Fundamental Charter.[4]

Fujimori's second presidential re-election bid is especially relevant to this discussion, as it demonstrates the practical impossibility of the Court carrying out its

* I am grateful to Marilú Merzthal for her work organising the various judgments and also to my colleagues at GIDCYDEF for their comments on preliminary versions of this chapter.

[1] P Grández, 'Las "peculiaridades" del precedente constitucional en el Perú' in E Carpio and P Grández (eds), *Estudios al precedente constitucional* (Palestra Editores, 2010) 58.

[2] See the statement of Carlos Torres y Torres Lara at the Constituent Assembly, in Comisión de Constitución y de Reglamento del Congreso Constituyente Democrático, *Debate Constitucional - 1993*, vol III (Lima, Congreso de la República del Perú, 2001) 1967. See also S Abad, *Derecho Procesal Constitucional* (Gaceta Jurídica, 2004) 96–97; VJ Ortecho, *Jurisdicción y procesos constitucionales* (Editorial Rodhas, 2002) 76.

[3] Abad (n 2) 184; M Rubio, *Estudio de la Constitución Política de 1993*, vol VI (Pontificia Universidad Católica del Perú, 1999) 133.

[4] N Sagüés, 'Los poderes implícitos e inherentes del Tribunal Constitucional del Perú y el quórum para sus votaciones' in *La Constitución de 1993: análisis y comentarios III* (Comisión Andina de Juristas, 1996) 103–12; F Fernández Segado, 'El control normativo de la constitucionalidad en el Perú: Crónica de un fracaso anunciado' (1999) 19(56) *Revista Española de Derecho Constitucional* 11.

mandate at that time. This event led to the Parliament's gross interference, subject to the Executive, which the Inter-American Court of Human Rights (IACtHR) itself later recognised.[5]

In short, it was in this political and judicial terrain, with drastic cuts to its independence and democratic function, that the Constitutional Court would exercise its powers and perform its interpretive work. For this reason, this chapter will analyse the Court's decisions beginning in 2000, a milestone year in which the democratic transition began and, with it, the dismantling of intervening legislation and the reintegration of the Court. Since then, the Court has been able to deploy its interpretative and decision-making powers without political constraints or undue interference.

From the beginning, however, the Constitutional Court has performed its work in an environment imbued with a challenging political and legal culture. Here, a dividing line must be drawn that separates the two major periods of the Court's history. César Landa has referred to the first period as that of a 'captive' Court to underscore the political subjugation it experienced[6] between June 1996, the date of its opening, through November 2000, when the Fujimori regime collapsed and the Court's arbitrarily deposed judges were reinstated. For the following period, the beginning of which coincides with the democratic leadership transition led by President Valentín Paniagua, the same author speaks of a 'liberated' Court – that is, a Court released from the yoke of political subordination.[7]

It will be the 'liberated' Constitutional Court that will dedicate itself to the widest possible display of its potential as the Constitution's supreme interpreter and the defender of the community's fundamental order enshrined in the 1993 Charter, with particular emphasis placed on the protection of basic individual rights.The first instance of this display involved antiterrorist legislation, a topic of great political sensitivity in Peru and a very delicate one from a juridical-constitutional standpoint. The legislation was also the subject of separate IACtHR pronouncements.[8]

The Court has piloted the renewal of the approach to the Constitution, the role of constitutional jurisdiction and the function of constitutional interpretation and argumentation against a current of a rather conservative and restrictive tradition, well established in the country's legal and political arenas.[9] And with regard to Peruvian constitutional jurisdiction, it has historically been characterised as 'the preeminence of literal, legalistic interpretations and of limited argumentative development', such that 'it

[5] *Case of the Constitutional Court v Peru* (Merits, Reparations and Costs), Judgment Inter-American Court of Human Rights (31 January 2001) Series C No 71 paras 78–85 (English trans).

[6] C Landa, *Tribunal Constitucional y Estado Democrático*, 2nd edn (Palestra Editores, 2003) 260.

[7] ibid 285. See also Grández (n 1) 58–59. It should be noted that, whenever this chapter contains sentences or phrases in quotation marks ('…'), they are quotations from doctrine or jurisprudence of the Constitutional Court or the IACtHR, depending on which source the specific passage references.

[8] *Case of Loayza Tamayo v Peru* (Merits), Judgment Inter-American Court of Human Rights (17 September 1997) Series C No 33 (English trans); *Case of Castillo Petruzzi et al v Peru* (Merits, Reparations and Costs), Judgment Inter-American Court of Human Rights (30 May 1999) Series C No 52 (English trans); *Case of Durand and Ugarte v Peru* (Merits), Judgment Inter-American Court of Human Rights (16 August 2000) Series C No 68 (English trans).

[9] D García Belaunde, 'La jurisdicción constitucional en Perú' in D García Belaunde and F Fernández Segado (eds), *La jurisdicción constitucional en Iberoamérica* (Editorial Dykinson, 1997) 849–51; VJ Ortecho (n 2) 75.

has not contributed to the strengthening of democratic institutions', especially during the 1990s.[10]

Precisely, it has been the canon of constitutional review's deficiencies, democratic deficits, society's structural inequalities and the widespread noncompliance with fundamental rights, particularly those of a social and cultural nature, which have been at the root of the Court's display of a certain level of activism.[11]

In this way, the 'liberated' Court has attempted to maintain a midway position between the extremes that Pedro Grández has suggested – namely, that of the 'judge bound to the text of the Constitution' (ie, a textualist or originalist) and that of the 'sceptical judge', who approaches constitutional interpretation as a 'free creation' to garner a more average profile of a 'judge committed to values but limited by rational argumentation'.[12]

It should be recognised that the Constitutional Court's jurisprudential work has led to the general acceptance that constitutional interpretation is guided by specific principles and methods, which differ from those that are predominant in the classical interpretation of laws and are prevalent in other branches of Peru's domestic law.[13]

B. The Court and Constitutional Litigation

The Fundamental Charter defines the Peruvian Constitutional Court as the 'controlling body of the Constitution', characterised by its 'autonomy and independence' (Art 201, Const.). The Court's Organic Law (*Ley Orgánica del Tribunal Constitucional*) – Law 28,301 (*El Peruano*, July 23, 2004) – more precisely stipulates that the Court is the 'supreme body of interpretation, integration and constitutional review' (Art 1). As such, the Court has the final word on constitutional controversies in Peru, exercising the primordial functions of 'appraisal, pacification and arrangement'.[14]

In Peru, there are two types of constitutional proceedings. On the one hand, they can serve as the primary protector of fundamental rights – the 'constitutional jurisdiction of freedom' to use a celebrated expression.[15] On the other, they can function as the immediate means of protecting the Constitution's normative supremacy.[16] Included among the former are habeas corpus, amparo, habeas data and mandamus, while the latter encompasses the procedures involving unconstitutionality, popular action and jurisdictional conflicts (Arts 200 and 202.2, Const.).

Regarding constitutional review, Peruvian law enshrines a 'dual' or parallel double-mechanism model in which the Constitutional Court's focused and abstract review

[10] Abad (n 2) 189.
[11] Grández (n 1) 65, 69.
[12] ibid 111, 117, 124.
[13] Landa (n 6) 482–84; D García Belaunde, 'La interpretación constitucional como problema' (1994) 1(1) *Pensamiento Constitucional* 13, 14, 30–32.
[14] C Hakansson, *El proceso de inconstitucionalidad. Una aproximación teórica y jurisprudencial* (Palestra Editores, 2014) 28–29.
[15] M Cappelletti, *La jurisdicción constitucional de la libertad* (Palestra Editores–UNAM, 2010) 25.
[16] C Landa, *Derecho Procesal Constitucional* (Pontificia Universidad Católica del Perú, 2018) 109, 173.

coexists (without merging or intersecting) with the diffuse and concrete review powers conferred on all judges.[17]

For its part, the judiciary has the power to decide the unconstitutionality or illegality of regulatory norms (of lower rank than laws) within the framework of the popular action procedure (Art 200.5, Const.).

The integration of treaty review with constitutional review is especially noteworthy.[18] In Peru, faced with the constitutional text's failure to grant supremacy to international human rights treaties, the Constitutional Court, after a precarious beginning, has elected to recognise this supremacy in its jurisprudence.[19] In this sense, the Court has maintained that, even though the 1993 Constitution does not contain a clause recognising the 'constitutional hierarchy' of these treaties (as was the case with Art 105 of the 1979 Charter), 'the same conclusion can be reached from a systematic interpretation of some of its provisions'.[20]

Thus, a progressive interpretation of the Fourth of the Final and Transitory Provisions of the Constitution (*Cuarta de las Disposiciones Finales y Transitorias de la Constitución*), and Articles 3, 55, 57 and 205 of the Constitution, which Article V of the Preliminary Title of the 2004 Code of Constitutional Procedure (CCP) (*Código Procesal Constitucional*) later complemented, has allowed the Peruvian Constitutional Court to determine that the principle of constitutionality incorporates the norms of the Inter-American System of Human Rights (IASHR) and also the IACtHR's standards of interpretation and application.[21]

The CCP itself introduced a novelty into the Peruvian constitutional system. Specifically, the Court, as the supreme interpreter of the Fundamental Charter, can establish binding precedents and jurisprudential doctrine. In this way, a legal tradition like Peru's, which belongs to the Roman-Germanic family, incorporates institutions of Anglo-Saxon origin.[22]

The kinds of constitutional proceedings that come before the Constitutional Court most frequently are, by far, those of amparo (88,696 cases admitted and 83,243 resolved between 1996 and 2020), followed by those of habeas corpus, which are also quite numerous (17,505 admitted and 15,889 resolved during the same time period) but considerably less than the former. The number of procedures of concentrated and

[17] García Belaunde (n 9) 833–34; C Hakansson, *Curso de Derecho Constitucional* (Palestra Editores, 2009) 375–76.

[18] Landa (n 16) 51–53; N Torres, 'Control de convencionalidad y protección multinivel de los derechos humanos en el Sistema Interamericano de Derechos Humanos' (2013) 70 *Derecho PUCP* 347, 360–61.

[19] *Case of Lizana Puelles*, Constitutional Court of Peru, STC 5854-2005-PA (2005) subparas 22–23; *Case of Nina-Quispe Hernández*, Constitutional Court of Peru, STC 047-2004-AI (2006) subpara 61; *Case of Castillo Chirinos*, Constitutional Court of Peru, STC 2730-2006-PA (2006) subpara 9; *Case of PROFA 2*, Constitutional Court of Peru, STC 25-2005-AI and 26-2005-PI (2006) subpara 26.

[20] *Case of PROFA 2* (n 19) subpara 27.

[21] Landa (n 16) 53; Torres (n 18) 361; L Castillo, *Derechos fundamentales y procesos constitucionales. Vol 1: Teoría general de los derechos fundamentales*, 2nd edn (Zela, 2020) 774.

[22] R Rodríguez Santander, 'El precedente constitucional en el Perú: entre el poder de la historia y la razón de los derechos' in E Carpio and P Grández (eds), *Estudios al precedente constitucional* (Palestra Editores, 2007) 19; P Grández, 'Las "peculiaridades" del precedente constitucional en el Perú' in E Carpio and P Grández (eds), *Estudios al precedente constitucional* (Palestra Editores, 2007) 89–90; C Bernal Pulido, *El Derecho de los derechos* (Universidad Externado de Colombia, 2005) 149.

abstract reviews of the laws and equivalent norms is also considerable (570 unconstitutionality processes admitted and 507 resolved between the years 1996 and 2020).[23]

With regard to the modalities and efficacy of the Court's judgments, the adoption of the concept of the 'unconstitutional state of affairs' is worthy of mention. Originating in the Colombian constitutional jurisdiction, it seeks to remedy structural situations of systematic and massive infringements of fundamental individual rights, which must be addressed through public measures and policies involving various State institutions and eventually private actors.[24]

C. The Judges

The Constitutional Court has seven magistrates, each elected for five years without the possibility of immediate re-election, and they must meet the same requirements as those needed to be a member of the Supreme Court of Justice. The power of selection belongs exclusively to the Congress of the Republic, which can approve nominations with a positive vote of two-thirds of the legal number of its members (Art 201, Const.). In practice, the nomination system for the Court has been fraught with difficulties, and it merits future revision.

D. Legal Scholarship and Constitutional Reasoning

In general terms, the critical study of the Court's case law is executed with credibility and acuity, both by researchers and university professors, and by the authors of literature aimed at contributing to the legal profession's best practices. It cannot be said that there is academic deference to the Court or that analysts display hostile or unjustly critical attitudes towards the institution. The Court usually considers the works of national and foreign academics, citing those sources quite frequently.

II. Arguments in Constitutional Reasoning

The cases selected for this study of the Constitutional Court's reasoning cover the period from 2000 to 2019. Taking the establishment of precedent and the quality of constitutional reasoning as qualifying criteria, we can identify three stages within the sample. The first stage, the most productive and fruitful, spans from 2003 to 2007, which corresponds to the period when magistrates who were arbitrarily deposed in 1997 (Manuel Aguirre, Guillermo Rey and Delia Revoredo) were reinstated, and Javier Alva, Juan Bardelli, Víctor García and Magdiel Gonzáles replaced the magistrates who had

[23] See the website of the Constitutional Court of Peru, www.tc.gob.pe/institucional/estadisticas/.

[24] B Ramírez, *El 'estado de cosas inconstitucional' y sus posibilidades como herramienta para el litigio estratégico de Derecho Público. Una mirada a la jurisprudencia colombiana y peruana* (Pontificia Universidad Católica del Perú, 2013) 5–6.

maintained their positions under the Fujimori regime's oppression (Ricardo Nugent, Francisco Acosta, José García and Luis Díaz). During this period, the Court established its legal and social legitimacy and contributed to the affirmation of the constitutional, democratic and social rule of law by strengthening the protection of fundamental rights and limiting the exercise of power. The latter was accomplished through the development of innovative interpretations and turning to the introduction of new modalities of constitutional decisions (interpretive and manipulative).

The second stage corresponds to the 2008–2013 period when a turnover of the Court's membership led to a new majority comprising Magistrates Juan Vergara, Carlos Mesía, Ernesto Álvarez, Fernando Calle and Gerardo Eto, along with the important dissenting voices of Magistrates César Landa and Ricardo Beaumont. During this stage, the Court's jurisprudential orientation changed in certain cases of particular importance, becoming more conservative in its approach to the Constitution and fundamental rights, the constitutional judge's duties and the available interpretive techniques. The Court's regressive attitude and reasoning are illustrated in such cases as the *El Frontón* massacre, the distribution of the emergency oral contraceptive pill and the controversy involving the rules of due process in the Congress of the Republic's Commissions of Inquiry (*Comisiones de Investigación del Congreso de la República*).[25]

The third stage began in 2014, when six new magistrates joined the Court, and it continues through the present day. The Court's jurisprudence has regained force, and in addition to rectifying some of its previous transgressions, the Court has issued a series of judgments to strengthen the protection of basic individual rights and contribute to the preservation of the political regime model enshrined in the Supreme Charter. Warranting particular mention is the Court's use of the 'unconstitutional state of affairs' declaration with the widest and most careful attention. However, controversies with heavy political overtones within an institutional context of substantial tension between the Executive and Congress (ie, Government and opposition) have also polarised the Court. This, in turn, has resulted in ideological alignments, frequently divided rulings or even the impossibility of making substantive decisions due to a lack of consensus in causes of significant importance for the country's institutional life.[26]

It is worth mentioning that, in the study's sample, the Court found unconstitutionality in almost two-thirds of the cases – that is, in 26 decisions, representing 65 per cent of the total. The predominant general topic among the selected cases was fundamental rights (34 cases), followed by due process issues (19 cases), the organisation of the State (15 cases) and then 'other matters' (19 cases). There are numerous occasions in which judges issued concurring or dissenting opinions; this practice is observed in 23 cases, representing 57.5 per cent of the total.

Thus, the figures seem to reflect a high level of noncompliance and transgression with respect to constitutional mandates, but they concurrently show a constitutional court willing to confront violators and restore the reign of the Constitution, which overall represents a historic pivot in the Peruvian judiciary. The widespread historical disrespect

[25] *Case of Bernabé Montoya*, Constitutional Court of Peru, STC 03173-2008-HC (2008); *Case of ONG 'Anticorruption Action'*, Constitutional Court of Peru, STC 02005-2009-PA (2009); *Case of Tineo Cabrera* Constitutional Court of Peru, STC 00156-2012-PHC (2012).

[26] *Case of the dissolution of the Congress of the Republic*, Constitutional Court of Peru, STC 0006-2019-CC (2020). This decision falls outside the scope of this study's selected period of analysis.

for Peruvian citizens' fundamental rights has led to a predominance of processes aimed at the immediate protection of those rights, trusting their custodian with the restorative capacity of constitutional jurisdiction. However, the procedures related to conflicts between powers or institutional aspects of public life have been proliferating and gaining traction in recent years, accompanying an environment of extreme tension and crisis in democratic institutions – for example, during severe clashes between the Executive and the Congress of the Republic.

A. The Structure of Constitutional Arguments

In the vast majority of judgments, argumentation was configured as a cumulative-parallel structure in which two or more lines of reasoning converged to justify the decision, with each leading to the same solution. This is observed in 29 of the 40 sample cases. The Court abounds in constitutional reasoning, striving to base its rulings on solid argumentative grounds. The need to legitimise itself through its own jurisdictional activity has led the Court to explore and develop all lines of argumentation that can contribute to achieving the resolution of cases.

Thus, the discursive strategy, consisting of deploying a single conclusive line of argumentation (only seven cases), is relegated to the background. The dialogic structure, referring to the appearance of parallel arguments that are not conclusive separately but are so when considered as a whole, is only observed in four cases.

It is common for the Court to prepare expansive and lengthy complementary arguments (obiter dicta) or expound on theoretical frameworks and explain key concepts. This approach seems to fulfill a pedagogical purpose as well as a persuasive one when addressing institutional actors along with the general public. In this way, moreover, the Court seeks to strengthen the foundations of its own interpretative work.

B. Types of Arguments in Constitutional Reasoning

i. Establishment and Debate on the Text and Applicability of the Constitution

With respect to the procedures under analysis, there are no doubts as to whether certain norms are (or are not) part of the Constitution's text. Consequently, there is no discussion about whether or not particular normative statements qualify as constitutional mandates. On the other hand, the Court has only decided one case where the Constitution's applicability was expressly disputed – namely, in the *FONAVI* opinion. There, the Court examined the constitutionality of a law establishing the State's duty to refund money to workers who had contributed to the National Housing Fund (*Fondo Nacional de Vivienda*). Effectively, in that case, the Court analysed whether the Constitution could be applied as a parameter for reviewing a law approved by referendum.[27]

[27] *Case of FONAVI*, Constitutional Court of Peru, STC 00007-2012-PI (2012) subparas 9–21.

ii. Analogies

The Court only used or mentioned analogy in its argumentation in three of the decisions included in this study. One of these cases involved the Military Tribunal (*Fuero Militar*), where the Constitutional Court limited itself to confirming the constitutionality of prohibiting the analogous application of laws pertaining to on-duty soldiers' crimes to civilian criminal acts.[28] Likely of greater interest is the Court's recourse to analogy in a case involving the Applicant Training Program (*Programa de Formación de Aspirantes*) (PROFA) of the Judicial Academy (*Academia de la Magistratura*), where its argument was based on the constitutional clause on unnamed or implicit rights (Art 3, Const.). There, the Court recognised new fundamental rights 'of an analogous nature' to those declared by the Charter, such as those contained in international human rights law (IHRL) instruments.[29]

One judgment of particular importance in current Peruvian constitutionalism, where the Court justified its decision by employing analogical reasoning, is that related to the vote necessary to approve a parliamentary 'constitutional accusation' against high-ranking public officials who enjoy special constitutional protection. In that case, the Court held that 'constitutional silences' cannot be understood as an authorisation for the legislator to issue 'regulations unrelated to the Fundamental Norm' and, using the principle of reasonableness, established that the applicable rule should be similar to that existing for matters that suspend the immunity of members of Congress.[30]

iii. Ordinary Meaning of the Words

As indicated earlier, the Constitutional Court has consistently abandoned the classic method of literal interpretation, which was previously common in determining the meaning of laws and regulations and was also traditionally influential in Peruvian constitutionalism. As seen below, only five judgments in the selected sample alluded to the ordinary meaning of words but in no case was it a decisive remedy. Rather, these were usually acknowledgements that emphasised the insufficiency of textual interpretation and the superiority of integral interpretative techniques, which allowed for progression beyond mere linguistic statements. Or they usually invoked the constitutional clauses' textuality as an initial introduction to a normative understanding within the framework of a more complex argumentative strategy, which relied primarily on the uniqueness of principles recognised in the modern theory of constitutional interpretation.

Thus, in a case involving electoral protection (*amparo electoral*), the Court challenged 'literal and isolated interpretation' as a method contrary to the correct understanding of the constitutional order.[31] In another case, involving the approval of a judge, the Court maintained, as part of a more elaborate argumentation, that literal interpretation does not preclude the construction of creative and corrective argumentation since it must be

[28] *Case of the unconstitutionality of the Military Police Court*, Constitutional Court of Peru, STC 001-2009-AI (2009) subpara 26.

[29] *Case of PROFA 2* (n 19) subparas 29–30.

[30] *Case of the political trial and pretrial*, Constitutional Court of Peru, STC 00006-2003-AI (2003) subparas 9–12.

[31] *Case of Castillo Chirinos* (n 19) subpara 56.

understood that the omission of the constituent legislator empowers the ordinary legislator to create a gap-filling norm.[32] And in the case of the question of confidence, and the complete crisis of the ministerial Cabinet, the Court resorted to a textualist reading of Article 105 of the Constitution, emphasising that the Constitution grants 'express authorisation' to the Standing Rules of Congress (*Reglamento del Congreso*) to establish exceptions to the normal transmission of bills, allowing a waiver of the parliamentary committees' advisory opinions. The Court, however, then proceeded to refute the text during its final determination regarding the law in question.[33]

iv. Domestic Harmonising Arguments

Constitutional jurisprudence has already established that the interpretation of the Fundamental Charter must be made by reading its clauses together, such that the determination of meaning is a comprehensive process that considers the unity of the constitutional text and the systematic relationships among its provisions. In 32 proceedings out of 40, equivalent to 80 per cent of the sample, the Court used this technique, applying it to both resolve specific issues and to engage in an overall examination of the merits.

A seminal case of domestic harmonising interpretation is unquestionably the amparo petition brought by Pedro Lizana Puelles, who was removed from his position as district mayor and resorted to constitutional jurisdiction, alleging that the National Election Board (*Jurado Nacional de Elecciones*) had violated his right to due process. Although the Court dismissed the claim, it used the opportunity to affirm its power to review the constitutionality of the Board's decisions through an amparo procedure when there is a question involving a violation of fundamental rights. This affirmation was made even though two constitutional clauses expressly proclaim the irreversibility of the Board's decisions (Arts 142 and 181, Const.).

The Court, in order to justify its decision, set forth the essential content of the principles that must guide constitutional interpretation and indicated that it would use these to craft its argumentative strategy: constitutional unity, practical conformity, functional correction, integrative effectiveness and the Constitution's normative force.[34]

v. International/Harmonising Arguments

IHRL instruments are often referenced in the Constitutional Court's jurisprudence. A significant number of judgments – again 32 out of 40, that is, 80 per cent – considered international declarations or conventions to clarify the scope and content of the Fundamental Charter's provisions. The harmonisation with IHRL included the jurisprudence of international oversight bodies, whether of a jurisdictional nature (eg, the IACtHR) or of a promotional or quasi-jurisdictional nature (eg, the Inter-American

[32] *Case of Álvarez Guillén*, Constitutional Court of Peru, STC 03361-2004-AA (2005) subpara 40.

[33] *Case of the matter of confidence and total crisis of the Ministerial Cabinet*, Constitutional Court of Peru, STC 00006-2018-AI (2018) subparas 18, 21, 26.

[34] *Case of Lizana Puelles* (n 19) subpara 12.

Commission on Human Rights [IACHR]), as well as the decisions of the UN. Human Rights Committee, derived from the International Covenant on Civil and Political Rights (ICCPR). The Court also invoked soft law.

In some decisions, the invocation of IHRL served to legitimise the Constitutional Court's lines of argument. The norms of international conventions, the IASHR's jurisprudence or the universal system (ie, the international system for the protection of human rights) were invoked as sources of authority with interpretative or guiding value. This can be observed, for example, in the judgment on antiterrorism legislation. There, the Court affirmed that the death penalty provided for in Article 140 of the Constitution must be understood to be limited by the international human rights treaties to which the Peruvian State is a party, and even by the IACtHR's Advisory Opinion no. 14/94, but without referring to the normative or legal status of IHRL instruments.[35]

In the same vein, mention should be made of the *Castillo Chirinos* case, where the Court held that the Constitution requires public authorities to protect fundamental rights by interpreting them through the incorporation of 'the normative areas of human rights' provided for in the treaties.[36] In the Charter, the Court affirmed that there is 'an implicit recognition of the substantial nuclear identity shared by constitutionalism and the international system for the protection of human rights: the legal conviction of the value of the dignity of the human person, to whose protection and service the exercise of all power is ultimately and definitively redirected'.[37]

In other cases, however, the Court was more emphatic, explicitly resorting to IHRL as a normative instrument that is part of Peruvian domestic law and which integrates the canon of constitutional review – that is, it sits at the apex of the nation's legal hierarchy (although this is no longer expressly recognised in the Constitution). This situation can be noted in the *PROFA 2* case, where the Constitutional Court categorically declared that 'international treaties on human rights not only make up our system but they also have constitutional status', a conclusion which, in the face of the Charter's silence, was reached through a 'systematic interpretation' of various provisions.[38]

Despite the consistent and prevailing value that the Court attaches its reasoning to the interpretation that harmonises the Constitution's clauses with IHRL, it is essential to note that, exceptionally, it has also issued questionable decisions that represent setbacks in the use of international standards. Thus, for example, in a case involving the massacre at the *El Frontón* prison, the Court, in a split decision (four to three), favoured procedural reasons for disregarding the IACtHR's decisions in *Durand Ugarte* (2000) and *Neira Alegría* (1995).[39]

vi. Precedents

The Peruvian Constitutional Court has become a tribunal of precedents. Thus, in 38 of the 40 studied cases, the Court's argumentation included references to previous

[35] *Case of Tineo Silva*, Constitutional Court of Peru, STC 00010-2002-AI (2003) subpara 181.
[36] *Case of Castillo Chirinos* (n 19) subpara 9.
[37] ibid.
[38] *Case of PROFA 2* (n 19) subparas 26–27.
[39] *Case of Bernabé Montoya* (n 25) subpara 14.

decisions that had to serve as interpretive guides, or it set rules to be followed in future cases. In this way, the Constitution's supreme interpreter seeks to contribute to the guarantee of such principles as equality, legal certainty and predictability, thus providing uniformity and clarity to jurisdictional decisions in matters of constitutional relevance.

There are typical cases that set binding precedents as in the application of Article VII of the Preliminary Title of the CCP, which occurs in the areas of pensions, public employment or the Court's procedural rules aimed at limiting the number of incoming new cases and reducing the procedural burden.[40]

On other occasions, the Court has instead used the institution of the 'jurisprudential doctrine' – Article VI of the Preliminary Title of the CCP. Noteworthy in this regard is the decision in the *Romero Saldarriaga* case, which addressed a transsexual person's right to identity, and where the Court substantially modified the 'jurisprudential doctrine' established in a previous case (with a different bench composition). Indeed, in a four to three decision, the Court stressed the importance of subjecting judicial work to a 'constant evolution' and challenged any 'rigid and immutable interpretation' of fundamental rights with a view to endowing them with greater protection and guarantee. Thus, while reaching beyond its previous line of case law, the Court established new interpretative and argumentative guidelines.[41]

In certain procedures, the changes in the Constitutional Court's jurisprudence seem debatable and exhibit unsound argumentative bases. One example is the aforementioned *PROFA 2* case. There, the legal requirement to pass the Judicial Academy's training program (PROFA) before applying for the positions of judge and prosecutor through a public merit competition, was questioned for a second time. The requirement was again challenged under the basis of discrimination with respect to lawyers who had not taken such courses. This analytical shift can be observed in each case's protected legal principle: on the first occasion (the *PROFA 1* case), the Court held that the review parameter relied on the principle of equality (Art 2.2, Const.). And later (in the *PROFA 2* case), the Court noted that this parameter was in fact the right of access to a public service under conditions of equality (Art 25.c, ICCPR; Art 23.1.c, ACHR [American Convention on Human Rights]). Despite this pivot in constitutional analysis, which was merely rhetorical and weak in its substantive aspects, the Court held that this second case was valid, in contrast to its previous judgment even though the central issue was the same: equality and nondiscrimination.[42]

vii. *Doctrinal Analysis of Legal Concepts or Principles*

In an appreciable number of cases under study – 27, equivalent to 67.5 per cent of the total – the Court articulated principles or concepts that the constitutional text itself does not prescribe. This is part of the Court's intense interpretative work that seeks to develop

[40] *Case of Anicama Hernández*, Constitutional Court of Peru, STC 01417-2005-AA (2005); *Case of Huatuco Huatuco*, Constitutional Court of Peru, STC 05057-2013-PA (2015); *Case of Vásquez Romero*, Constitutional Court of Peru, STC 00987-2014-PA (2014).

[41] *Case of Romero Saldarriaga*, Constitutional Court of Peru, STC 06040-2015-PA (2016) subparas 2, 11, resolution point 2.

[42] *Case of PROFA 2* (n 19).

and specify the normative frameworks, which are frequently deficient and vague, and which the Fundamental Charter provides through its very nature.

Sometimes, these are principles that are component parts of others more general in scope that the Constitution contains. As such, the Court recognises the principle of judicial impartiality, which is not mentioned in any of the Charter's clauses but which the Constitutional Court considers to be incorporated in the principle/right of due process specified in Article 139.3.[43]

On other occasions, the Court has recognised implicit fundamental rights, relying on Article 3 of the Constitution, which acknowledges the existence of other rights 'of a similar nature' or derived from personal dignity, the basic principles of popular sovereignty, the democratic rule of law or the republican form of government. In this sense, the Constitutional Court has recognised the 'right to the truth' for cases of serious human rights violations, such as the forced disappearance of persons.[44]

Moreover, the recognition and development of concepts of enormous importance for the protection of fundamental rights, such as gender identity[45] or 'crimes against humanity', should also be highlighted.[46]

Finally, also noteworthy are the formulation and use of constitutional interpretative principles, such as those of constitutional unity, practical concordance, functional correction, integrative function and normative force,[47] as well as the declaration of the 'unconstitutional state of affairs' concept, which permits the adoption of structural decisions at the national level.[48]

viii. Arguments from Silence

The Constitutional Court applied this type of argument in only four of the selected cases. Undoubtedly, the most relevant decision in this category involved the constitutional omission pertaining to the vote necessary for the approval of a political trial and pretrial (as discussed above in section II(B)(ii)). In the other three cases, this kind of argument was only used with minor issues. For example, in a case that examined whether an exception to the ordinary legislative procedure was constitutional, the Court held that a normative gap incurred by the law does not justify a declaration of a constitutional defect which, without further argument, establishes that the challenged norm is harmonious with the 'constitutionality block'.[49]

ix. Teleological/Purposive Arguments Referring to the Purpose of the Text

In a significant number of cases in the sample, the Constitutional Court's argumentation incorporated references to the objective purposes of the constitutional clauses or

[43] *Case of Castillo Chirinos* (n 19) subpara 61.
[44] *Case of Villegas Namuche*, Constitutional Court of Peru, STC 02488-2002-HC (2004) subparas 8–20.
[45] *Case of Romero Saldarriaga*, Constitutional Court of Peru, STC 06040-2015-PA (2016) subparas 4, 14.
[46] *Case of Bernabé Montoya* (n 25), separate opinion of Judges Beaumont and Eto, subparas 20, 30–39; separate opinion of Judge Landa, subparas 30–34.
[47] *Case of Lizana Puelles* (n 19) subparas 12–21.
[48] *Case of Díaz Cáceres of Tinoco*, Constitutional Court of Peru, STC 00889-2017-PA (2018) subparas 46–53.
[49] *Case of tourist services in buildings that are part of the Nation's cultural heritage*, Constitutional Court of Peru, STC 0003-2008-PI (2010) subpara 21.

institutions. Indeed, in 23 cases (representing 57.5 per cent of the total), the Court proposed a certain purpose derived from the text under analysis – that is, without considering the historical Constituent Assembly's preparatory work or debates (when available).

Of course there is no such thing as an objective will of constitutional texts because it is always the interpreter who postulates what is to be understood as the intent of the provisions under review. In a case of fundamental rights, the Court adheres to an 'institutional interpretation' and defends a unitary and systematic understanding of the Supreme Charter's provisions, after which, quoting the Spanish academic Manuel García Pelayo, it dismisses the 'constituent's subjective will' and appeals to 'rationality and the objective will that emanates from the text'.[50]

Additionally, in a case alleging a violation of due process but with a backdrop of political rights – where the constitutionality of a mayor's dismissal was disputed – the Court aimed to establish an objective purpose by declaring that '[a]rticles 142 and 181 of the Constitution are intended to guarantee that no other power of the State appropriates the definitive administration of justice in electoral matters'.[51]

x. Teleological/Purposive Arguments Referring to the Intention of the Constitution-Maker

The research indicates that the constitutional judges only considered the drafters' historical intentions in eight decisions. On occasion, this is an argumentative strategy, indicating that the constituents did not debate the issue at hand, so the decision to select the preferred interpretative device is delegated to the democratic legislator (to the extent that it remains within the margins of constitutionality). This can be observed in the case on the waiver of parliamentary immunity in which the Court considered admissible both the broad protection traditionally accepted in Peruvian constitutionalism and the Congress of the Republic's recently introduced modification, which defines the prerogative of immunity in restrictive terms.[52]

Because of its significant conceptual value, it is useful to highlight Magistrate Ledesma's concurring vote in an amparo petition for a transsexual person's right to identity. Along with maintaining that the question was not foreseen, or therefore debated by the constituents in 1993, she rejected any 'originalist interpretation' that inquired about 'the will of the constituent power', and which led back to the 'historical moment in which the constitutional text was approved', instead proposing a 'constructivist interpretation', which implies 'broadly updating the content of the Constitution'.[53]

xi. Non-Legal (Moral, Sociological, Economic) Arguments

It is common for the Constitutional Court of Peru to employ non-legal arguments in its decisions. These appeared in 29 judgments of the sample, and they were of different

[50] *Case of ONG 'Anticorruption Action'* (n 25) subparas 26–27.
[51] *Case of Castillo Chirinos* (n 19) subpara 8.
[52] *Case of the lifting of parliamentary immunity*, Constitutional Court of Peru, STC 00026-2006-AI (2007) subparas 26–28.
[53] *Case of Romero Saldarriaga* (n 41) subparas 3–5, 9, concurring opinion of Magistrate Ledesma Narváez.

types: economic, sociological, moral or religious, and scientific or medical. This large number may be due to the Court's desire to adopt comprehensive approaches to the constitutional issues examined – that is, to those that transcend mere legalism and incorporate extra-legal explanations that contribute to the bases of decisions and their greater acceptance in society. The assumption is, of course, that law is a social practice and that its nature is not insular but is instead closely related to various disciplines.

However, it is common for such extra-legal reasons to accompany and reinforce deliberations of a legal nature without replacing them. In some cases, however, they may be exceptionally decisive. This is demonstrated in the case concerning emergency oral contraception in which scientific and medical criteria were crucial to such questions as the beginning of human life or the effects of the so-called 'morning-after pill'.[54]

Sociological arguments were the most numerous among those of an extra-legal nature; they were utilised in 12 judgments in the study sample. These arose in cases in which the general context of structural injustices was decisive, such as an amparo petition that established the right of Quechua speakers to be assisted by public entities in their own language; a case involving the right of transsexual individuals to self-identify as such; an action that recognised the fundamental right to potable water; another in which migrants' rights were defended; or a trial involving the protection of the right to education for poor girls in rural areas.[55]

Arguments of a moral or religious nature appeared in some procedures of the decisions selected for the research study. What was argued in the case of emergency oral contraception is noteworthy. There, the Court rejected 'moral perfectionism' and the 'paternalistic State' to immediately affirm, when facing the 'moral and ethical relativism of today's societies', the consensus of life's common moral criteria and basic values that represent fundamental human rights.[56] However, in other proceedings not included in the study, the Constitutional Court has recognised Catholicism's contribution to the nation's collective morality and cultural tradition.[57]

xii. References to Scholarly Works

The Constitutional Court's citations to national and foreign doctrine were abundant in the surveyed cases, without one type outnumbering the other. The practice is observed in 26 of 40 judgments (equivalent to 65 per cent of the total). For the Court, this is not just a question of utilising versation as a rhetorical device or making use of authoritative arguments; the Court moves beyond this, seeking to legitimise its decisions with arguments deeply rooted in the most solid contemporary legal-constitutional theories and doctrines. Further, as noted earlier, the Court's pedagogical objective and its

[54] *Case of ONG 'Anticorruption Action'* (n 25).

[55] *Case of Díaz Cáceres of Tinoco* (n 48); *Case of Romero Saldarriaga* (n 41); *Case of Távara Ceferino*, Constitutional Court of Peru, STC 06534-2006-PA/TC (2007); *Case of Mesquita Oliveira*, STC 02744-2015-PA (2016); *Case of Cieza Fernández*, Constitutional Court of Peru, STC 00853-2015-PA (2017).

[56] *Case of ONG 'Anticorruption Action'* (n 25) subpara 56.

[57] *Case of crucifixes in the Judiciary*, STC 06111-2009-AA (2011); *Case of the consecration of Señor de los Milagros as patron of Peru*, Constitutional Court of Peru, STC 03372-2011-AA (2013).

purpose to legitimise and distinguish its own work, presupposes that its discourse, beyond targeting a wide audience, often demands the approval of academics and legal experts.

The Peruvian Constitutional Court invokes doctrinal work with the intention of bolstering or clarifying its arguments, especially in those cases that generate the greatest controversy, such as the decision related to the contraceptive pill.[58]

xiii. References to Foreign (National) Law

On the other hand, and for reasons similar to those indicated in the previous section, foreign law was also often invoked: the laws of other countries were cited in 16 cases included in the study. Oddly, the number of citations to Latin American domestic legislation was the same as those made to countries outside the region (11 times in each instance).

Colombia is the Latin American country whose law was clearly referenced most often, with eight citations, followed by Argentina and Bolivia, with two references each, and then Chile, Costa Rica and Ecuador, each cited once. The predominance of Colombian law in the Peruvian Court's normative framework of comparative law is likely due to the Court's frequent consultation of Colombian constitutional jurisdiction, which requires a simultaneous review of Peruvian laws for an adequate understanding of the Court's own judgments.

Invocations of foreign law often serve to legitimise conceptual frameworks or normative schemes that have already gained acceptance in other countries as can be observed, for example, in a case decided by the Peruvian Court on parliamentary *transfuguismo* (change of parliamentary group). Indeed, in that case, the Court noted the existing rules in Colombia for the configuration of the so-called 'mixed parliamentary group', pointing out its residual character and the absence of an exact correspondence between political parties and parliamentary groups.[59]

xiv. Pro Homine/Pro Persona *Principles*

The Constitutional Court only expressly referred to the principles of *pro homine* or *pro persona* in five cases of the sample. The invocation of the principles in these cases failed to endorse a certain interpretation among several available for the provision under review, nor were they used to prioritise those rules that are more favourable to the effective protection of fundamental rights. Rather, these principles were cited to reinforce or guide a general orientation to the Court's argumentative construction in each case. Thus, for example, in a case that examined whether there was a violation of due process, but the substantive issue was the protection of privacy and honour against television media abuses, the Court indicated that it was 'empowered to respond to the

[58] *Case of ONG 'Anticorruption Action'* (n 25) subparas 22–23, 27–28, 36.

[59] *Case of the modification of article 37 of the Standing Rules of Congress on the regulation of parliamentary groups* [transfuguismo], Constitutional Court of Peru, STC 00001-2018-AI (2018) subpara 61.

concerns raised on the basis of a strict and *pro homine* analysis of the judicial decision in question'.[60]

xv. Other Methods/Arguments

There are many decisions included in the study that employed other types of methods or arguments – specifically, in 14 out of the 40 opinions, representing 35 per cent of the total. In some cases, the Constitutional Court proposed an 'institutional' interpretation, adding in another process with a 'social' interpretative dimension.[61] The Court also used the method that links law and social conditions – for example, when it considered the collective impact of illicit drug trafficking and the particular circumstances of the case, which included a judge's murder.[62] Likewise, in the political trial and pretrial case, the Court proposed the 'logical analysis' method, and in the *FONAVI* case, the Tribunal formulated an '*a contrario*' interpretation.[63]

C. The Overall Weight of the Arguments

Generally speaking, the judgments in the sample are not indicative that a theory exists for a priority or hierarchy of constitutional methods of interpretation. Clearly, the Court disqualifies the literal and isolated reading of the Constitution's clauses, instead signalling the need for a comprehensive and unitary understanding of the Fundamental Charter, as discussed above.

In addition to the special appraisal of systematic interpretation, the Court usually relies on its own precedent for relevant arguments, and it often resorts to IHRL harmonisation arguments, in particular giving weight to IACtHR decisions. Finally, references to academic works and foreign law play an important role in the Court's derivation of arguments (although less than that afforded to IASHR jurisprudence).

In almost all the cases studied – 36 out of 40, equivalent to 90 per cent of the total – the arguments contributed to substantiating the decision, both as ratio decidendi and as obiter dictum. A high proportion of rhetorical, ornamental or even misleading arguments are only observed in four cases. In this regard, it should be noted that, in a case where the constitutionality of criminal rights and guarantees was contested,[64] the arguments related to the fight against corruption gave the impression that they had no connection to the legal-constitutional question under consideration. This transpired because the judgment failed to explain the political and social context of the case, a phenomenon that originates in a congressionally approved law that intends to favour impunity for individuals involved in serious crimes of corruption.

[60] *Case of Medina Vela et al*, STC 06712-2005-PHC (2005) subpara 1.
[61] *Case of ONG 'Anticorruption Action'* (n 25) subparas 27–32; *Case of the political trial and pretrial* (n 30) subparas 5–6.
[62] *Case of Buitrón Rodríguez*, Constitutional Court of Peru, STC 07624-2005-HC (2006) subpara 34.
[63] *Case of the political trial and pretrial* (n 30) subpara 6; *Case of FONAVI* (n 27) subpara 32.
[64] *Case of the uniformity of house arrest*, Constitutional Court of Peru, STC 00019-2005-AI (2005).

D. Judicial Candour and Judicial Rhetoric

The examined judgments follow a specific format in which the case's facts and background are shared first, including the parties' approaches and the previous decisions on jurisdiction, if there were any (proceedings on the defence of fundamental rights). These are followed by the main section, which is clearly the most extensive, and which is dedicated to the decision's fundamentals. This section begins by addressing formal or procedural matters with a view to resolving them before the Court approaches the background issues. It is also common at the beginning of this section to present the conceptual framework or general theories that will allow a full understanding of the controversy and the decision.

The Court's language is technical and uses legal versation, containing multiple quotations from foreign doctrine and jurisprudence while simultaneously striving for simplicity to facilitate a lay reader's understanding. Therefore, it is noteworthy that the Court's discourse seemingly aims to reach all citizens, thereby seeking greater simplicity. Although in the event there are specialised legal pronouncements, the Court seeks the approval of academics and legal experts to a considerable extent to also legitimise itself in a legal, technical sense.

E. Length, Dissenting and Concurring Opinions

In general terms, it cannot be said that the Peruvian Constitutional Court's decisions are particularly extensive, which is likely because the Court's objective is to not overwhelm its eventual readers and because brevity can facilitate the coherence and understanding of its decisions. Of course, it is the quality of the Court's pronouncements that is important, not their number of pages. However, it should be emphasised that only 10 of the analysed judgments span 50 or more pages, including dissenting or concurring opinions, representing 25 per cent of the total cases under review. If the judges' individual opinions are not counted, then more than half of the judgments are 30 pages or less: 24 out of 40 decisions, equivalent to 60 per cent of the total. In addition, of these, six are quite brief, numbering 10 pages or less. On the other hand, the decisions in which there are dissenting or concurring votes number 15 – that is, 37.5 per cent of all the analysed cases.

F. Framing of Constitutional Issues

The Court's cases quite often involve more than one general issue – that is, they can be classified under more than one topical heading. However, the prevailing topic is fundamental rights, which our investigation assigned to 34 cases. This is followed, at a considerable distance away, by cases involving procedural or due process issues, which appear in 19 decisions. Next are those processes concerning the organic part of the Constitution – 12 in total – in which the dispute primarily involved the distribution of power among State organs. A likely explanation for these results can be found in the conclusion of the introductory part of section II in this chapter.

G. Key Concepts

It is common for the Constitutional Court to construct its argumentative strategies based on the establishment of broad theoretical frameworks, either with pedagogical intention or with the desire to propose conceptual anchors that the majority can accept. Thus, the constitutional model of principles and values that frames specific controversies is explained with legal-philosophical justifications in various decisions of the Court. These justifications, for example, have developed and supported personal dignity and fundamental rights,[65] the economic Constitution, the ecological Constitution, the democratic Constitution and the emergency Constitution.[66]

On the other hand, a pair of structural concepts/principles that the Court usually raises in different litigious contexts, both in relation to the Constitution's organic part and with respect to the catalog of rights, is also notable. We refer here to the concepts/principles of the rule of law and democracy. The first was invoked and had argumentative relevance in 26 of the 40 selected judgments; it appeared both in the context of the protection of basic rights[67] and in matters involving conflicts that concern the public authorities.[68] The second (democracy) was invoked in 13 of the Court's decisions (32.5 per cent of the sentences analysed), and it was employed in cases concerning the legitimacy of norms and institutions,[69] in the case of referendum as a mechanism of direct democracy[70] and in the realm of rights, fulfilling an interpretative role.[71]

III. Comparative Perspective

Certain characteristics of the Peruvian Constitutional Court's jurisprudence are also extant in comparable foreign courts' decisions. Among the most relevant similarities are the various courts' employment of teleological arguments and precedential case law, as seen, for example, in the former Ecuadorian Constitutional Court's decisions and in those of the current Plurinational Constitutional Court of Bolivia (in terms of the use of precedent, this is also observed in Argentina, Mexico and Uruguay). With these same constitutional jurisdictions, the Peruvian Court also shares the application of international law and the use of non-legal arguments. However, unlike in Ecuador during the Rafael Correa presidency, and in Bolivia, Peru's Constitutional Court has resorted to the latest interpretative methods, which have had a veritable impact on argumentation, not having served merely as rhetorical strategies or propositional adornments.

[65] *Case of Tineo Silva* (n 35).

[66] *Case of Nesta Brero*, Constitutional Court of Peru, STC 008-2003-AI (2003); *Case of Bustamante Johnson*, Constitutional Court of Peru, STC 03343-2007-PA (2009); *Case of constitutional reform*, Constitutional Court of Peru, STC 00014-2002-AI (2002); *Case of the unconstitutionality of states of emergency*, Constitutional Court of Peru, STC 0017-2003-AI (2004).

[67] *Case of ONG 'Anticorruption Action'* (n 25); *Case of Correa Condori*, Constitutional Court of Peru, STC 2016-2004-AA/TC (2004); *Case of Buitrón Rodríguez* (n 62).

[68] *Case of constitutional reform* (n 66); *Case of Castillo Chirinos* (n 19); *Case of the modification of article 37 of the Standing Rules of Congress on the regulation of parliamentary groups* [transfuguismo] (n 59).

[69] *Case of constitutional reform* (n 66); *Case of Tineo Silva* (n 35); *Case of the political trial and pretrial* (n 30).

[70] *Case of FONAVI* (n 27).

[71] *Case of Villegas Namuche* (n 44); *Case of Medina Vela et al* (n 60); *Case of Bustamante Johnson* (n 66).

The Court's use of IHRL sources, which is increasingly vigorous, is remarkable in the Peruvian case as well as in the current Ecuadorian Constitutional Court and in the comparable tribunals of Colombia, Mexico and Costa Rica. In all of these, there is characteristically low use, or even a complete disqualification, of literal interpretation alongside the desire to seek solid argumentative constructions in technical-legal terms, including theoretical and conceptual frameworks that are up-to-date with contemporary advances.

Finally, one of the most relevant regional commonalities of constitutional reasoning is the argumentative structure, which is usually that of conclusive-parallel arguments, as observed, for example, in the constitutional jurisdictions of Argentina, Bolivia, Chile, Guatemala, Mexico, Paraguay, Peru and Uruguay.

IV. Evaluation, Pathology and Criticism

The Constitutional Court has made an extremely important contribution to the affirmation of the constitutional rule of law in Peru. In its 25 years of existence, the Court has shown itself to be a key institution for defending fundamental individual rights and for serving as a controller of public authorities. This has occurred despite moments of political subjugation or sieges that politicians and groups possessing political power have orchestrated.

Despite having been 'captured' by the Fujimori autocracy during its early years, the Court was able to unfurl its potential in the service of Peru's institutions with the democratic transition in 2000. From the onset, it was the Court's interpretative force that established there were no areas exempt from constitutional review in the modern constitutional, democratic and social rule of law. The Court has indeed developed and clarified this model in its case law based on the 1993 Charter's text, which is often insufficient or limiting.

Some of the Court's innovative decisions addressing constitutional interpretation, and even traditional conceptions of the Constitution and constitutional jurisdiction, have introduced significant advances in terms of the availability of judgment types (interpretative and manipulative) and interpretative principles and techniques (constitutional unity, practical concordance, functional correction, etc). In this regard, the judgments on antiterrorist legislation, the legitimacy of the 1993 Constitution and the Court's review powers vis-à-vis the National Election Board are notable and represent a change of era. And later, the issuance of structural judgments and the use of the 'unconstitutional state of affairs' concept are of particular importance.

The current research confirms that the constitutional reasoning of the Peruvian Constitutional Court has established a solid foundation for the interpretation and application of the Fundamental Charter. It can be said that, as a historical trend, the Court has been consolidating itself as an independent court, generating lines of argumentation that are coherent and of juridical quality, especially in the most controversial cases, whether they refer to the catalogue of fundamental rights, or they address issues related to the organisation and exercise of public powers. It is worth highlighting the Court's desire to structure argumentation in the form of conclusive-parallel arguments to provide complementary reasons to better substantiate its decisions.

Mention should also be made of the Court's use of a series of argumentative remedies of primary importance, which depart from the conservative and formalist tradition of Peruvian jurisprudence, and which seemingly mark a clear path for the Court's forthcoming work. Among such innovative argumentative resources are the Court's rejection of mere literal and legalistic interpretations and its search for argumentative constructions in which the systematic reading of the Constitution, the harmonisation of its provisions with IHRL sources, the establishment of binding precedents and jurisprudential doctrine and the Court's frequent invocation of works of legal doctrine play a predominate role. All this, in addition, is occurring contemporaneously with a clear pedagogical purpose (aimed at a wide audience, without disdaining the academy), the construction of a legal-constitutional consensus based on constitutional reasoning founded on solid knowledge and the presentation of the justifying reasons for its decisions.

Among the main challenges that now threaten the Court, besides certain jurisprudential setbacks that have been exposed, is the will to submit, which is observed in certain political sectors and de facto powers (eg, economic, media, criminal). This phenomenon is already part of the Court's history, and this temptation to backtrack recurrently appears. In this regard, it is noteworthy that the nation's severe institutional crisis of 2019 occurred concurrently with the occasion of the Court's judicial election process. These events led to a second question of confidence, which the national representation denied, and the consequential total crisis of the ministerial Cabinet, triggering the President's dissolution of Congress through the application of Article 134 of the Constitution.

The hijacking of the Court and the placement of subjugated and uninformed judges must be avoided. Nor should the Court become a substitute forum for other political deliberation bodies. However, it is hoped that the Court will continue its institutional affirmation and its contribution to the constitutional, democratic and social rule of law. To achieve this, the Court must have independent and impartial judges who honour and carry out the 'duty of ingratitude' with the body that selects them, exercising a moderate level of activism, which consistently uses reasoning and argumentative and interpretative techniques with a solid foundation in constitutional law.

16

The Jurisprudence of the Supreme Court of Uruguay

MARIA PAULA GARAT DELGADO AND
ANNA LUISA WALTER DE SANTANA

This chapter will report the conclusions of the investigation carried out with respect to the State of Uruguay. To provide context, the political, institutional and academic perceptions of the Supreme Court and constitutional review will be presented alongside the system's essential characteristics: focused, restrictive legitimisation (ie, standing), a rather nonactivist Court and consequential impact on the concrete (ie, specific) case.

Next, the research's actual findings will be explored. It is observed that the study's conclusions point to a Court, which in general is quite restricted in its work for two essential reasons: the procedural requirements for constitutional review itself, and the starting points or standards the Supreme Court has developed when ruling on the constitutionality of laws.

Early on, the Supreme Court adopted a presumption of constitutionality, which has been applied consistently in the Court's jurisprudence, thus demonstrating a deference to the national legislator.[1] However, it is possible to identify a shift in this deference. In the selection of decisions for this study, it is observed that, since 1989 – the year of the first selected judgment – until 2009, the Court found norms under review to be unconstitutional on only two occasions (Judgments 49/2008 and 365/2009). Since 2010, the Court has found laws to be unconstitutional in 12 decisions out of 21.

Further, the Court's argumentation is characterised by: (i) being legally based, excluding political or other considerations; (ii) resorting to different types of arguments that can be categorised as ratio decidendi or as obiter dictum while generally disregarding other types (decorative, rhetorical, pseudo or inappropriate); (iii) invoking its previous jurisprudence and resorting to doctrinal analysis for interpretation; and (iv) having recently incorporated international parameters for the protection of fundamental rights. In 2016, especially, it is possible to observe a change – that is, an increase in the Court's recourse to international treaties and inter-American jurisprudence.

[1] Regarding this presumption and its different concepts, see M Risso Ferrand, *Algunas garantías básicas de los derechos humanos* (FCU, 2008) 158 et seq.

I. Legal, Political, Institutional and Academic Context

A. Legal and Political Culture as Context for the Constitutional Reasoning

The Constitution that currently governs Uruguay was approved in 1967, has subsequently been modified and has consistently been applied with the sole exception of the de facto period between 1973 and 1985.

The Constitution has political and legal importance, but it also garners an additional distinction of significance and respect.[2] Uruguay's constitutions, according to Gros Espiell,

> have also been normative instruments born of a historical reality, which have influenced that reality and which, without prejudice to the existence of other economic, social and cultural factors, have – within certain limits – shaped and modelled it. Its compliance, as well as its violations, its validity as well as the de facto periods born of its violation, have been and are unavoidable elements that are needed to understand the Uruguayan historical process and to capture the national reality.[3]

In this sense, the current Constitution reflects the State's commitment to Uruguayan society's democratic aspirations of, and respect for, human rights. In this context, it is also possible to highlight the overall respect for the Supreme Court of Justice – the highest organ of the judiciary – as an institution and, in particular, for its work monitoring the constitutionality of laws. As such, after the pronouncement of a Supreme Court opinion, the rest of the State powers, and in general the political ambit, respect and apply it.

Since 1934, the Supreme Court of Justice has been constitutionally assigned original and exclusive jurisdiction to declare the unconstitutionality of laws. The effects of a ruling are for the 'concrete case',[4] although some decisions of unconstitutionality have led the ruling party or certain political actors to promote initiatives to repeal or modify legislation to harmonise it with the Court's decision.[5]

During the de facto period (1973–85), through the government's various legal acts – called Institutional Acts (*Actos Institucionales*) – the process of appointing the members of the Supreme Court was modified, judicial independence was curtailed and the principle of the separation of powers was weakened.[6] Then, on 7 May 1985, the General Assembly – already re-established – declared that the Supreme Court's members had not been legitimately installed, and thus new members were appointed.[7]

[2] On this point, see M Risso Ferrand, *¿Qué es la Constitución?* (UCUDAL, 2011).

[3] H Gros Espiell, 'El derecho constitucional y la historiografía en Uruguay' (2006) 5 *Revista de Derecho de la Universidad de Montevideo* 29, 48.

[4] Art 259 of the Constitution of Uruguay.

[5] For example, in Judgment 17/2013, the Supreme Court of Justice declared Law 18,876 (creating a tax) to be unconstitutional. Then, the executive branch presented a bill to repeal this tax, an action that was finally embodied in Law 19,093.

[6] Institutional Act no 2 of 12 June 1976, and no 8 of 1 July 1977. On this point, see MP Garat Delgado, *Los derechos fundamentales ante el orden público* (Tirant lo Blanch, 2020) 240.

[7] H Gros Espiell, 'El estatuto jurídico del juez constitucional. Uruguay' in H Fix-Zamudio and CI Astudillo Reyes (eds), *Estatuto jurídico del juez constitucional en América Latina y Europa* (UNAM, 2012) 613–30.

With the end of the dictatorship, the Court resumed its institutional status relative to democracy, acting independently and impartially, and without experiencing constitutional deviations since the time of the restoration. However, although there is a formal respect for the Supreme Court's decisions, the academic and professional doctrine observes that, until the early years of the 2000s, the Court played a 'secondary role in national political history'[8] such that only in recent decades has it assumed a more important position.

B. The Court and Constitutional Litigation

Article 257 of the Constitution of Uruguay grants jurisdiction to the Supreme Court of Justice to determine the unconstitutionality of laws. Likewise, Article 260 adds that Decrees of the Departmental Governments (*Decretos de los Gobiernos Departamentales*) with the force of law in their jurisdictions can also be declared unconstitutional.

It is, then, a system concentrated in the Supreme Court of Justice, the highest organ of the judiciary and an institution that is generally highly esteemed in the country, as indicated above. Indeed, although there may be political issues at the time of the election and appointment of the Court's members, as will be discussed below, in general and in judgments, there are no political issues that interfere, as the judges make decisions independently.

The foregoing does not imply, however, that with certain assumptions there are no self-restraints. Indeed, the legal community's general perception is that the Uruguayan Supreme Court is not an activist court. Early on, the Court adopted as a premise, a presumption of the constitutionality of laws (eg, in Judgments 137/2010, 65/2014, 79/2016 and 271/2018), which prescribes a point of departure in favour of the legislator and contrary to the claimant's assertion of unconstitutionality. In addition, throughout its history, the Court has aggregated other starting points of a similar nature, some to be discussed later.[9]

To this is added the issue of required legitimacy, often used as the main argument to dismiss an action, and which can prevent the Court from reaching the underlying issue. In Uruguay, the process of unconstitutionality can be requested by means of a lawsuit, a plea of exception or an *ex officio* judicial action.[10] The legitimacy required is extraordinary since the claimant must have a 'direct, personal and legitimate interest'.[11] Therefore, it is the claimant who must be directly and personally affected by the provision.[12] This has led the Court to exclude some cases from analysis on the grounds that the claimant did not possess, or failed to prove, his or her standing. The most relevant case related to

[8] F Antía and D Vairo, 'Política y Justicia en Uruguay: el poder de la Suprema Corte de Justicia (1990–2018)' (2019) 28 *Revista Uruguaya de Ciencia Política* 61, 63; M Risso Ferrand, 'El "juez constitucional" en el Uruguay' (2014) 23 *Revista de Derecho Público* 61–86.

[9] For example, as will be noted later, the Court's starting point is that it 'does not judge the merit or legislative failure'. For all the Court's points of departure, consult Garat Delgado (n 6) 69, 345.

[10] Art 258, Constitution of Uruguay.

[11] ibid.

[12] We will not address the categorisation of the legitimate interest here, although in Uruguay, there are several works of doctrine that address it.

this issue involved the creation of the Single Vehicle Revenue System (*Sistema Único de Cobro de Ingresos Vehiculares*) (SUCIVE), Law 18,860, addressed in Judgment 568/2013. The doctrine had indicated that this law had various unconstitutional provisions, but the Court concluded that the claimant did not have standing to raise them, and consequently, it did not delve into a substantive analysis of the issue at hand.

Notwithstanding the above, it is possible to observe an evolution of sorts since the Court's interpretation of standing is currently slightly broader. For example, in the area of taxation, the Court's view that withholding agents did not have standing to claim the unconstitutionality of a tax for which they were responsible (only the taxpayer did) is a position that was recently modified (Judgment 301/2018).

On the other hand, the procedural rule requires the claimant to indicate 'with all precision and clarity, the precepts that are considered unconstitutional and the principle or constitutional norm that is violated or what the unconstitutionality consists of by reason of its form'.[13] In some cases, this burden is not met, and therefore the Court does not proceed to analyse some of the invoked rights. In other words, the party who invoked them did not indicate why they were doing so, and why the rights would be applicable in the case.

Within the framework of the unconstitutionality process, the Public Prosecutor intervenes in a necessary, albeit not binding, way. The Public Prosecutor or the parties' lawyers may make the claims of unconstitutionality *in voce*, which implies alleging them in a hearing before the Court, if they request it within three days of the notification of the order to convey the docket for the individual judges to study.[14] This option is sometimes used in practice.

The Court's judgments were originally unpublished although they formed part of a print register that could be consulted at the seat of the Court. Several years ago, the National Jurisprudence Database of the Judiciary (*Base de Jurisprudencia Nacional del Poder Judicial*) was created, which is a publicly accessible online database that contains all opinions from 1989 to the present.[15] Opinions decided prior to that year may be consulted in print at the Supreme Court of Justice's building, without prejudice to those cases appearing in contemporary print journals.

As explained above, a judgment affects the concrete case. Different views have been posited regarding the temporal effects of the decision. In general, the Court has favoured applying the judgment retrospectively from the date of filing. In a jurisprudential minority position appearing in some rulings and in dissents, and which has even greater doctrinal support, the 'concrete case' implies the application should be made from the time the interested party was impacted – therefore, even before the lawsuit was filed.

The unconstitutionality process has a current and approximate delay of one year from the initial filing. The executive and legislative branches of government exhibit a high level of compliance. As previously described, the Court is a respected institution, and many decisions – which legally only affect the specific case – have later prompted a

[13] Art 512, General Code of Procedure (*Código General del Proceso*).
[14] Arts 516 and 517, General Code of Procedure (*Código General del Proceso*).
[15] See Poder Judicial República Oriental del Uruguay, Base de Jurisprudencia Nacional Pública, bjn.poderjudicial.gub.uy/BJNPUBLICA/busquedaSimple.seam.

legislative change to the unconstitutional law, which has occurred in different governments and compositions of the Executive and legislature.

C. The Judges

The Court is composed of five members. The doctrine indicates that

> [t]he establishment of this number of Supreme Court members – undoubtedly the lowest in comparative constitutional law – has been the subject of criticism and amendment drafts. But these proposals have never moved forward, although it can be argued with some justification that with only five members the judges are inundated with work, which precludes more intense and rapid activity of the supreme judicial body.[16]

Since 2022, and for the first time in the Court's history, there are three female judges on the bench.[17] The requirements and procedure of appointment are provided for in Articles 235 and 236 of the Constitution.[18] Historically, judges with several years of experience in the judiciary have been appointed, although this is not required.

The above corresponds with the Court's argumentative characteristics since – as will be seen below – legal arguments are preferentially used, setting aside political or other types. In turn, the reasoning is similar throughout the Court's history, which is also a product of the judiciary being the source of its composition.

The appointment process requires a two-thirds favourable vote of the full membership of the General Assembly (legislative power). However, if in 90 days such a majority is not reached, the member of the Courts of Appeal with the longest service is automatically appointed. If there is equality of seniority in office, the appointment then goes to the individual who has served the longest in the judiciary or the Public Prosecutor's Office.

On several occasions, the full course of the 90 days has run. In others, the required majority has been reached, preceded by agreements reached between the different political parties with parliamentary representation and which collectively cover various vacancies in the Supreme Court of Justice and the Contentious-Administrative Tribunal (*Tribunal de lo Contencioso Administrativo*).

With regard to the Court's constitutional reasoning, and to the extent that the appointees come from the judiciary as judges, the existence (or nonexistence) of an earlier agreement has no significant impact. However, this could be the reason behind the characteristics of the type of reasoning found in this study.

For some authors, the established rule that distances the executive power from appointing the Court's members is proper since it places power in a pluralist and multiparty body that is popularly elected,[19]

[16] Gros Espiell (n 7) 613–30.

[17] The Court's composition at the date of this chapter's completion is as follows: Ministers John Pérez, Tabaré Sosa, Elena Martínez, Bernadette Minvielle and Doris Morales.

[18] Art 235, Constitution of Uruguay. To be a member of the Supreme Court of Justice, the requirements are: (1) Be forty years of age or older. (2) Native citizenship in practice, or legal citizenship with ten years exercise thereof and twenty-five years of residence in the country. (3) To have been a lawyer for ten years or, as such, to have been a judge in the Judiciary or a prosecutor in the Public Prosecutor's Office for eight years.

[19] Gros Espiell (n 7) 613–30.

> thus democratis[ing] the election of the Supreme Court's members and mak[ing] the constitutional judges in Uruguay appointed by the most politically and factually representative organ of national sovereignty. The appointment of members of the Supreme Court of Justice is a political act. Of the highest, noblest and greatest political significance. It is not a technical act or an internal contest. It constitutes a form of exercise of sovereignty, to embody a government power.[20]

Since the restoration of democracy after the last dictatorial period (1985), the Court has experienced no crises, has not been dissolved, and it has not experienced the effects of dictatorships or the like, given that the country has not endured a period with those characteristics.

D. Legal Doctrine and Constitutional Reasoning

The Court cited doctrine in virtually all the judgments selected for this study (39 out of 40 decisions). The doctrine could be critical of the Court, which was addressed numerous times, although gradually and in a progressive way. The doctrine has reflected on, and debated, the Supreme Court's transition, a slow but evolving pivot towards human rights and the rejection of more extreme concepts such as the presumption of constitutionality, which has impeded the review of some legislation.[21]

For example, the parameters for analysing cases involving limitations on fundamental rights or the principle of equality have varied over the years. The Court only recently invoked the principle of proportionality during the years 2015–16, although the doctrine had already started to develop in this area some time ago.

There is a mutual respect of the academy towards the Court, criticising with justifiable grounds and in pursuit of a positive progression,[22] and likewise from the Court to the academy. Indeed, it is common for the Court's members to consult and cite doctrine in their decisions and votes, relying on it for interpretation and analysis.

II. Arguments in Constitutional Reasoning

A. The Structure of Constitutional Arguments

For the purpose of the investigation, 40 significant Court decisions between 1989 and 2019[23] were selected, and in terms of argumentation, the structure was 'legs of a chair' –

[20] ibid.

[21] F Antía and D Vairo (n 8); M Risso Ferrand, 'Primeras reflexiones generales sobre las sentencias de inconstitucionalidad referidas a la ley de medios' (2016) 13 *Revista de Derecho* 141–87.

[22] An example of this is the evolution in the interpretation of the principle of equality following Professor Risso Ferrand's critique. See M Risso Ferrand, 'Algunas reflexiones sobre el principio de igualdad en la jurisprudencia de la Suprema Corte de Justicia del Uruguay' (2010) 5 *Revista de Derecho* 171–92.

[23] The selection of the 40 opinions was then checked with five outstanding professors of constitutional law representing various Uruguayan universities: Professors Eduardo Esteva, Diego Gamarra, Martín Risso Ferrand, María Elena Rocca and Jaime Sapolinski.

that is, cumulative-parallel arguments. This result is related, in our opinion, to the Court's makeup of judges rather than members with other types of backgrounds as seen in other jurisdictions.

Of the 40 judgments analysed, more than half (26) followed the structure of parallel and self-sufficient arguments, which allowed the Court to guide its decisions to the same conclusions. This is because the claimants' petitions for unconstitutionality proceedings were based on various principles or provisions where the Court had to analyse each one and then draw the conclusion that finally addressed all of them. Those arguments were therefore conclusive and cumulative.

The first selected opinion (Judgment 53/1989) is an example of the above. There, the Court structured its judgment in such a way as to respond to each of the grounds with parallel and cumulative arguments, which allowed it to sustain the conclusion it reached.

In general, the Court is quite moderate in the development of its arguments, limiting itself to addressing the issues raised in the case without invoking different arguments that would be inconclusive separately. This is even reflected in the number of pages of its decisions. Unlike comparable courts in other countries, such as Brazil or Colombia, the Court's opinions are relatively short (the maximum in the sample was 44 pages), and they seek to aggregate the necessary arguments that lead to the same conclusion.

The form of reasoning utilised is also reflected in the dissents, there being no difference on this point.

B. Types of Arguments in Constitutional Reasoning

i. Structure of Argument

The argumentation employed in the Supreme Court's judgments is characterised by being, in the first place, essentially legal, excluding political or other considerations. It is only possible in nine of the selected judgments to identify some type of non-legal argumentation. In the rare instances when the Court resorted to this type of argument, in most cases, it explicitly relied on an economic or sociological premise.

The second noteworthy point in the judgments' argumentation is the presumption of the constitutionality of the laws, which has been applied repeatedly in the Court's jurisprudence, demonstrating a deference to the national legislator. The Supreme Court adopted this position early on, which, in this study's analysis, was reflected in the applicability *ratione materiae* of the Constitution. According to the Court, the analysis of the constitutional question is based on at least two assumptions: (i) every law enjoys the presumption of constitutional regularity until proven otherwise; and (ii) the Court does not judge the merit or any legislative error, only whether the law is constitutionally valid (eg, Judgment 137/2010).

The presumption of constitutionality implies, in terms of the judgments analysed, that the unconstitutionality of laws is always exceptional and must be demonstrated clearly and unequivocally. In 18 of the 40 judgments, the Court expressly referenced this presumption of constitutionality, and, as a result, the Court's majority found that the norms at issue were constitutional.

In the analysed opinions, the argument of the presumption of constitutionality appeared expressly for the first time in Judgment 42/1993. However, in Judgment 234/1995, the Court referred to judgments from the 1960s, which had already referenced the constitutionality of laws as a principle and unconstitutionality as an exception.[24] In addition, the Court reaffirmed that its function was not to judge the merit or failure of the legislator but only whether the law was constitutionally valid: 'The legal norm, which within its institutional competence provides a wrong, erroneous, unwise solution with respect to the point it regulates, will be a bad Law, but it is not unconstitutional [for that reason]' (Judgment 234/95).

In this same sense, and in different rulings, the Court noted the understanding that it is alien to the process's purpose to venture into questions of legislative policy and to therefore remove it from the representative majority's decision – that is, from the competence of the legislative power. The interpreter is required to be cautious, and the person who invokes the constitutional violation much demonstrate unequivocally, reliably and indisputably the irreconcilability with, or opposition to, the Constitution's text or principles.

However, it is possible to identify a shift in this deference to the legislator. In the selection of judgments, it is observed that since 1989 – the year of the first judgment selected – until 2009, the Court found the reviewed norms to be unconstitutional on two occasions (Judgments 49/2008 and 365/2009). As of 2010, in 12 rulings out of 21, the Court declared the law at issue to be unconstitutional.

These same conclusions accord with other studies carried out on the Supreme Court of Justice's jurisprudence. Referring to the Supreme Court rulings through 2013, Risso Ferrand pointed to four characteristics of the Court's decisions: (i) the focus of the issue is on the act of authority under review and not on the human right or rights injured; (ii) only by exception is the act in question invalidated; (iii) self-restraint is considered (expressly or implicitly) as a virtue of the Court; and (iv) there is no particular tendency to delve into the human rights involved and the constitutional principles and values, but the invocation of these issues is made on the basis of long-standing doctrinal conceptions without resorting to or analysing modern developments.[25]

On the other hand, Antía and Vario's study[26] points to an expansion in recent years of the Supreme Court's power through a quantitative increase in declarations of unconstitutionality, which would imply a greater challenge to the elected powers and an eventual change in the legal vision that presumes the constitutionality of the laws.

ii. Types of Arguments in Constitutional Reasoning

The structure of the Supreme Court's arguments – characterised by self-limitation – is reflected in the small variety of interpretive methods used. Analogy, for example, appears in only four decisions, the argument from silence in one judgment, teleological interpretation in two decisions and historical interpretation (legislative history) in six opinions.

[24] In some cases, this resulted in the reversal of the burden of proof. Regarding this topic, see Garat Delgado (n 6) 346. On this presumption and its different concepts, see Risso Ferrand (n 1) 158 et seq.

[25] Risso Ferrand (n 8) 61–86.

[26] Antía and Vairo (n 8).

On the other hand, the Court usually invokes and applies its previous jurisprudence and resorts to doctrinal analysis for interpretation. In almost all the selected judgments, the Court referred to its precedents to support its final decision, and when there was a jurisprudential change, the Court highlighted it. Examples of this are found in Judgments 49/2008 and 80/2008. In Judgment 49/2008, the Court affirmed the unconstitutionality of Article 8 of Law 18,083, and in the same year – and after a change in the bench's composition – it dismissed the action of unconstitutionality. Similarly, in almost all the selected cases (39 out of 40), the Court relied on doctrine to support its interpretations.

Likewise, beginning in the first decade of the 2000s, the Supreme Court began to rely on principles or concepts not expressly found in the constitutional text. Among the 23 decisions where it is possible to identify the use of concepts or principles not contained in the Constitution, 15 of them appeared beginning in 2010.

The last highlight of the analysis is the recent incorporation of international parameters regarding the protection of fundamental rights. Starting in 2013, it is possible to observe the Court's openness to international law. The harmonisation of the Court's jurisprudence with international law was relatively insignificant at first. This is reflected in the Supreme Court's use of some very typical concepts of human rights-based argumentation that rarely appear in its decisions. The invocation of the *pro persona* principle was used in only one case and human dignity in five.

In the first set of judgments (covering 1989 to 2010), there were only three cases in which the Court referred to international legal sources: (i) a case on the law of the press (Judgment 54/2004), where the Court referred to inter-American standards; (ii) a case on the constitutionality of a tax (Judgment 49/2008), where a binding source of international law was broached; and (iii) a judgment on the law of revocation (amnesty), which applied a combination of regional and international law.

Beginning in 2013, out of 18 judgments, 12 sought harmonisation with international law, including the incorporation of soft law sources.

These changes coincided with the first conviction of the State of Uruguay (*Gelman v Uruguay*, 2011[27]) at the Inter-American Court of Human Rights (IACtHR) for acts committed during the military dictatorship (1973–85). This decision could justify a greater approximation of constitutional jurisprudence with the standards of regional and international law.[28]

Notwithstanding the foregoing, the Supreme Court does not utilise certain types of arguments to justify its decisions. Judicial independence and democracy were used as arguments in only five and six decisions, respectively – just at a time when it was possible to observe a lower level of deference to the legislator and a proclivity towards human rights.

Sovereignty appeared as an argument in two decisions, the State's administrative structure in three opinions and the form of government argument failed to appear in

[27] *Case of Gelman v Uruguay* (Merits and Reparations), Judgment Inter-American Court of Human Rights (24 February 2011) Series C No 221 (English trans); *Case of Gelman v Uruguay* (Monitoring Compliance with Judgment), Order of the Inter-American Court of Human Rights (20 March 2013) (English trans).

[28] On this point, see MP Garat Delgado, 'La Evolución en la Recepción de la Jurisprudencia de la Corte IDH en Uruguay. El impacto del "Caso Gelman" y su actual perspectiva' in M Tomé Gómez (ed), *El Derecho entre dos siglos. Estudios conmemorativos de los 25 años de la Facultad de Derecho de la Universidad Católica del Uruguay*, vol I (Montevideo, UCUDAL, 2015).

any. This is because, as previously mentioned, the legitimacy required to initiate an action of unconstitutionality is quite strict: the claimant must have a 'direct, personal and legitimate interest'. Therefore, cases related to the organisation of the State, in which this type of argument could be used, are scarce.

The concept of the rule of law, however, was utilised and can be found in several of the analysed decisions (16 out of 40). In most cases, the Supreme Court used the principle of legality to refer to the concept of the rule of law. In Judgment 576/2017, the Court relied on doctrine to conceptualise the rule of law as 'the idea of a government of Laws and not of men and characterised by the subjection of the State to the Law and the recognition of citizens' subjective rights'.

Proportionality was used as an argument in 13 of the 40 decisions. The concept was not often invoked in the first set of opinions and was mentioned without a detailed analysis. The principle of proportionality as derived from the German theory was expressly referenced and developed for the first time in 2015 (Judgment 104/2015).

The concept of equality was also one of the most-used arguments in the sample of Supreme Court decisions (23 out of 40 judgments). The number can be explained by the Court's need to promptly answer each argument presented; equality is an argument that is regularly invoked and about which the Court must rule.

C. The Overall Weight of the Arguments

The Court can be characterised, due to the structure of the argumentation used in all the analysed judgments, as resorting to different types of arguments that can be categorised as ratio decidendi or as obiter dictum while generally excluding those of other types (decorative, rhetorical, pseudo or inappropriate). These decisions ordinarily involved several independent and conclusive arguments that determined the final conclusion. Some judgments added secondary arguments that supported the same conclusion, which could be due to the composition of the Court, as already mentioned.

Although it cannot be said that the Supreme Court uses a specific method of argumentation, it is altogether evident that the Court's usual pattern is to focus on answering the plaintiff's arguments in an objective and technical way, using only the necessary legal arguments that determine or support the decision.

Although in some cases, the Court invoked concepts or principles that are not expressed in the constitutional text (23 cases of the 40 analysed), the interpretative method most often referenced in judgments was the literal method. Indeed, literal interpretation was used in 13 of the 40 decisions. As uncovered in the study, the Court rarely used other methods: analogy seldomly appeared (four judgments), the argument from silence only once, teleological interpretation twice and historical interpretation six times.

D. Judicial Candour and Judicial Rhetoric

The Court's arguments and language are technical. The judgment can be understood by any lawyer, without being a specialist in constitutional law. With some points, it can be difficult for a non-lawyer to understand the concepts being addressed.

In general, the Court focuses on the specific case, so it analyses the application of provisions, principles or rights involved in the controversy. However, with some topics, there is a typical pattern the Court follows based on its previous jurisprudence on point, which is possible to generalise. For example, the Court used its jurisprudence to cite the definition and requirements of rates (in tax matters);[29] also, and since 2016, to invoke the requirements to limit fundamental rights;[30] or to carry out differentiations in accordance with the principle of equality as required,[31] among others.

In the selection of analysed judgments, the Supreme Court did not employ rhetorical, emotional or political arguments.

E. Length, Dissenting and Concurring Opinions

It is possible for the judges to cast dissenting votes in the decisions, and it is typical for them to do so. The length varies in each case and for each magistrate with no limits or patterns to follow. In general, the dissents are not extensive, and they follow the mode of reasoning found in the rulings. Nor do dissents refer to certain issues and not to others. Unlike other comparable courts, there is no model that indicates when there will be dissenting votes. Despite this, the judges usually reiterate their positions in various dissenting votes scattered throughout different judgments.

In recent years, it has also been possible to find the judges' different or concordant positions in the opinions; indeed, some no longer mark their positions in a separate vote but in the text itself. This was the case, for example, in Judgment 667/2018, in which after presenting certain arguments, the following was added: 'Mrs. Minister Dr. Martínez, maintaining her previous jurisprudence on the subject of legal and constitutional interpretation, disagrees with the previous argumentative development and maintains what will be expressed below'.[32] Also, in Judgment 1148/2019, Ministers Turell, Martínez and Torres offered an additional argument, revealing themselves in the ruling's text.

F. Framing of Constitutional Issues

Historically, cases involving due process and the principle of equality have been more common than those involving other fundamental rights. This has been changing over time, and the Court's arguments used to resolve cases involving fundamental rights have

[29] For example, in Judgment 1980/2017, the Court maintained, 'The Court, in various pronouncements, has applied these concepts in cases in which the violation of article 297 of the Constitution was also alleged', then citing the ruling in 203/2013 and specifying that in the following decisions a similar conceptual orientation could be found: Judgments 45/2015, 386/2013, 379/2013 and 902/2012, among others.

[30] For example, in Judgment 576/2017, the Court referred to 'requirements for the restriction of the enjoyment of fundamental rights', specifying that 'such requirements have been studied and applied under the name of [the] "proportionality test"', carrying out a similar development to that already mentioned in an earlier case, Judgment 79/2016.

[31] For example, in Judgment 211/2016, and when referring to the principle of equality, the Court referenced and cited what had already been stated in Judgment 87/2015 regarding the judgment of reasonableness. It also cited what had already been expounded on this point in Judgment 255/2015.

[32] In that same decision, Judgment 667/2018, which was issued without a dissent or separate opinions, the judges expressed their opinions in the text itself regarding the conditions that enable the sentencing

also been changing. Since Judgment 79/2016 (on the unconstitutionality of the so-called 'Media Law'), the Court has utilised contemporary tools concordant with those that the rest of the comparable Latin American and European courts use in terms of rights limitations: the principle of proportionality and essential content, among others. At the same time, in matters of equality, the Court's jurisprudence has also evolved and introduced a new test for differentiation analysis.

We consider that there has been an evolution in the way in which constitutional cases are conceptualised throughout the law because of the State's constitutional rule of law, the constitutionalisation of the legal system, the interpretation from the Constitution and, more recently, the confluence with international human rights law and its development. This transformation has also been evident in the Supreme Court's jurisprudence on proportionality and essential content and in citations to IACtHR decisions, among others. The evolution is expected to continue to progress in the reception and development of these concepts and other standards in this area.

G. Key Concepts

From the data, it is possible to highlight some key concepts that are often invoked in the Court's decisions and that support the argumentation developed therein.

The structure of the judgments themselves and the fairly precise argumentation resorted to the concept of the rule of law in 16 of the 40 analysed judgments. It is possible to observe that the concept was substantially linked to the principle of legality and legal certainty (eg, Judgments 20/2013, 102/2016, 576/2017 and 680/2017).

The concept of proportionality was also invoked in some of the Court's judgments and appeared to a greater or lesser extent in 13 of the 40 analysed opinions. Initially, recourse to the idea of proportionality was not invoked in the form of a test or the German-based principle of proportionality as is common in the jurisprudence of other States with a substantial incorporation of the German doctrine, such as in Brazil. The first judgments (until 2015 and 2016) referred to the reasonableness of legislative activity, especially in the limitation of rights and based on the analysis of the reasons of general interest required for this limitation (Art. 7, Const.) but not with precise content or with the German theory's structure. With Judgment 104/2015, it is possible to observe an increase in the development of the concept of proportionality and a more specific discussion of the adequacy of the legislator's means of limiting the rights and purposes that the law pursues. Likewise, beginning with the aforementioned Judgment 79/2016, the Supreme Court finally adopted the German principle of proportionality and complemented it with a series of formal and substantive requirements for the restriction of fundamental rights based on Professor Jesús María Casal's doctrinal work.

On the other hand, and in the key concepts, it is useful to highlight the principle of equality, which was evident in 23 of the 40 studied judgments, always reaffirming the

of preventive detention in the new Code of Criminal Procedure (*Código de Proceso Penal*). Thus, Messrs. Ministers Hounie and Minvielle expressed one position, then Martínez stated another, then it was established that Chediak shared what Martínez maintained, and finally Turell's position was developed.

prohibition of privileges or inequalities for people who found themselves in a similar situation. This concept has also evolved in the Court's jurisprudence, which currently applies an equality test that allows the analysis of distinctions, their causes, purposes and their proportionality.[33]

The fourth and final concept that the Court frequently explored in its judgments' argumentation was procedural guarantees (13 out of 40 decisions), especially those related to due process.

III. Comparative Perspective

The comparative perspective of Uruguay's Supreme Court is complex to establish, because due to its composition, it does not have a political profile, and its arguments have a uniform style, typical of legal training.

Unlike comparable courts in the region, such as Colombia's, the Supreme Court of Justice is not activist but rather moderate, inextricably linked to the rules and their interpretation.

However, in comparison to the jurisprudence of similar courts in the region, it is possible to highlight the limited approach the Supreme Court of Justice of Uruguay has taken with some concepts, which are presented with greater assiduity and development in other courts. This is the case with the principle of *pro homine* or *pro persona*, which is addressed in only one case (Judgment 396/2016); with the concept of human dignity (mentioned in five of the 40 judgments); with democracy (invoked in six judgments); with judicial independence (four judgments) and justice (three decisions); and finally, with the concept of family, which was not evident in any of the rulings.

On the other hand, and considering the jurisprudence since 2009, there was only one opinion (Judgment 396/2016) that approached economic, social, cultural or environmental rights, which reflects the Supreme Court of Justice's limited jurisprudential development in this area, unlike what has occurred in comparable courts in the region, such as in Colombia's.

Likewise, and also within the comparative perspective, some positive aspects stand out in the Supreme Court of Justice's analysed jurisprudence, which, in our opinion, is connected to the respect that the institution and its rulings have garnered. In this sense, it is notable that the Court did not invoke custom in any of the analysed judgments, and there were no references to nonmaterial values such as '*buen vivir*' ('good living') and the '*pachamama*' ('Mother Earth'), which appear in the jurisprudence of corresponding courts in the region.

As already mentioned in this chapter, the Supreme Court's selected arguments were almost entirely legal in nature; in only nine of the 40 analysed judgments were other types of arguments presented, those being mostly economic (five of the nine) and sociological (four of the nine).

[33] The Court has been criticised in the doctrine with respect to its treatment of equality, being that the Court has referenced positions used in the jurisprudence of the United States, which were outdated and that compromised the analysis of the issue in Uruguay's national jurisprudence. Risso Ferrand (n 22) 171–92.

Finally, the argumentation of the ratio decidendi type was primarily evident in the judgments that ruled out other structures with inappropriate, political arguments or pseudo-arguments.

IV. Evaluation, Pathology and Criticism

In the study's selected and analysed jurisprudence, there are several aspects that can be assessed from a critical perspective:

(a) The adoption of points of departure and the presumption of constitutionality imply, in some cases, a deference to the legislator, which supports the Court's arguments of self-restraint.
(b) The analysis of legitimacy is another barrier to addressing the substance of a case, being that the Court has been strict in its interpretation of legitimisation, leading it to reject some cases for this reason, without delving into the substantive aspect of the case.
(c) In some areas, it is possible to note that parameters invoked in comparative jurisprudence are not used (eg, the principle of proportionality), or their use is even incipient. Notwithstanding the foregoing, in more recent times, it is possible to observe an evolution, as was mentioned in this chapter.
(d) Likewise, the following were key concepts in the analysed jurisprudence: (a) the rule of law, with a specific connection to the principle of legality; (b) the principle of proportionality, particularly since 2016; (c) the principle of equality, which has evolved in the Court's analysis; and (d) due process guarantees.
(e) Likewise, in a comparative perspective, some rarely used approaches have been pointed out (unlike in other comparable courts), but several positive aspects can also be highlighted from the Supreme Court of Justice's analysed jurisprudence.
(f) Finally, the Court's argumentation stands out for being structured, employing legal arguments (excluding political or other kinds of considerations), being mostly of the ratio decidendi type and for introducing more recent doctrines in accordance with the above.

17

The Jurisprudence of the Constitutional Chamber of the Venezuelan Supreme Court*

JUAN BERRÍOS ORTIGOZA AND RAÚL SÁNCHEZ URRIBARRÍ

I. Legal, Political, Institutional and Academic Context

A. Legal and Political Culture as Context for the Constitutional Reasoning

i. Historical Background: From a Dictatorial Past to Democracy

The Venezuelan constitutional system was shaped by a string of authoritarian governments since Venezuela became an independent nation state in 1830.[1] For over a century, these dictatorships were generally characterised by personalism, militarism, small and corrupt ruling cliques, limited state capacity, political violence, and instability. The Venezuelan economy was very small, and the government's ability to regulate and tax private activity was seriously limited.[2] In practice, the borders between the public and private domains were blurred, with local elites facing little legal constraints.

* Manuscript prepared for the Constitutional Reasoning in Latin America project (corelatam.com/), sponsored by the Konrad Adenauer Foundation and Universidad San Francisco de Quito (Ecuador). We thank Project Director Dr Johanna Fröhlich for her kind support and comments throughout the project. Special thanks to our colleagues Dr Carlos García Soto for reviewing the chapter, and to the colleagues who reviewed our case selection. We are also grateful for the valuable feedback received from the project's colleagues in the chapter's different iterations and presentations. We are also grateful to Silvina Sanchez Mera for excellent editing assistance.

[1] The country declared independence from Spain in 1810, and in 1811 a congress of representatives enacted the first Constitution of Hispanic America, the *Constitución Federal de los Estados de Venezuela* (21 December 1811), see AR Brewer-Carias, 'Historia Constitucional de Venezuela' in Francisco Manuel García García Costa and others (eds), *Historia constitucional de Iberoamérica* (Tirant lo Blanch 2019). For a comprehensive overview of Venezuela's constitutional and institutional history, see also AR Brewer-Carias, *Historia constitucional de Venezuela* (Alfa, 2008).

[2] F Coronil, *The Magical State: Nature, Money, and Modernity in Venezuela* (The University of Chicago Press, 1997).

The Constitution figured prominently in the legal and political system from the start, but overall, it was not a consequential text for political and social life. Rather, as was the case elsewhere in the region, the Constitution served mostly as a basic organisational text. Venezuela ranks amongst the countries in the world with the highest number of constitutions in its history.[3] Since 1830, the Venezuelan Constitution has been reformed over 25 times,[4] mostly under authoritarian rule.[5] Those constitutional texts were not entirely meaningless, and sometimes reflected significant historical changes. For example, the 1864 Constitution formally adopted federalism as a result of the *Guerra Federal*.[6] Yet, usually constitutions were replaced at the whim of a new government in power. As an old expression goes, '*la constitución sirve para todo*' (the constitution can be used for anything).[7]

This tradition changed with the development and expansion of the Venezuelan petrostate in the twentieth century. This period was characterised by military rule, increasing centralisation, an ever-complex socio-political life and the expansion of the legal system.[8] When the 1958 democratic revolution took place, the project's core civic and political ambitions were anchored in constitutional politics, including the creation of a new democratic constitution (1961). This constitution adopted liberal democratic features, with a commitment to constitutional supremacy, fundamental rights and the rule of law. It also created a new Supreme Court endowed with constitutional adjudication prerogatives. This period involved profound changes in Venezuela's socio-political culture. Democratic consolidation implied, on one hand, the elites' commitment to democratic rule, and on the other developing a political culture centred on citizen participation through elections, party politics and civil society.[9] It also fostered a culture of constitutional and legal supremacy, including holding the state accountable for transgressions of rights and empowering citizens to bring claims to court. This included creating legal proceedings to allow citizens to file claims against fundamental rights violations, most notably the creation of interim constitutional relief procedures (amparo) in the mid-1980s.[10] Moreover, the legal system's expansion came accompanied by an increase in the number of law schools and lawyers across the country.[11]

[3] On average, the Venezuelan constitutions have lasted about eight years (7.8 years since 1811, or 8.3 years since 1830). The constitution with the longest duration to date was the 1961 democratic Constitution (38 years, 1961–1999), over a decade longer than the 1830 Constitution (27 years).

[4] Brewer-Carias (n 1).

[5] The first democratic constitution in Venezuela was the 1947 Constitution, which lasted a year, until the coup against the democratically elected government of Rómulo Gallegos on 24 November 1948.

[6] C García Soto, 'De 1811 a 2017: Asambleas constituyentes y constituciones en la historia de Venezuela' *Prodavinci*, 2017, historico.prodavinci.com/blogs/de-1811-a-2017-asambleas-constituyentes-y-constituciones-en-la-historia-de-venezuela-por-carlos-garcia-soto/.

[7] Famous phrase attributed to President José Tadeo Monagas in 1848 to illustrate how the law was at the service of politics, and not the other way round. See JC Rey, 'La Constitución sirve para todo' (2017) REDIAJ 1559.

[8] R Pérez Perdomo, 'Estado y justicia en tiempos de Gómez (Venezuela 1909-1935).' (2007) 30 Politeia 121.

[9] M Kornblith, 'The Politics of Constitution-Making: Constitutions and Democracy in Venezuela' (1991) 23 *Journal of Latin American Studies* 61.

[10] CM Ayala Corao, *Del amparo constitucional al amparo interamericano como institutos para la protección de los derechos humanos* (Universidad Nacional Autónoma de México, Instituto de Investigaciones Jurídicas, 1998).

[11] Pérez Perdomo (n 8).

However, an embracement of a positivist approach to constitutional and legal interpretation remained, both at the courts and in law teaching and scholarship.[12]

These efforts fell short. Major problems in the Venezuelan state became increasingly evident. The same issues that afflicted the country plagued the judiciary and other legal institutions, including corruption, excessive bureaucratisation, inefficiency, dysfunctionality, social exclusion, politicisation, and resistance to change. It was common to find large backlogs across the judiciary, and reports abounded of the activity of groups of judges, legal officers, and lawyers in cartels manipulating legal proceedings.[13] These problems were the consequence of an incomplete process of state building, the lack of adequate implementation of the 1961 Constitution, and lack of attention to new needs in an ever-complex society. Whilst different attempts at reform were made in the face of the country's ongoing crisis (1980s–1990s), they were ineffective or rejected.[14] Following the *Caracazo* riots in February 1989, which took place in response to the first attempts at enacting a Neoliberal economic reform agenda, there were additional efforts to overhaul the state. This included frustrated attempts at constitutional redrafting, and important initiatives such as political and fiscal decentralisation. The unsuccessful military coups of February 1992 – headed by then Lt Col Hugo Chávez Frías – and November 1992 made it clear that the political crisis was more systemic than previously admitted. This propelled the impeachment of President Carlos Andrés Pérez in 1993 and, eventually, led to the collapse of the party system, with the two main political parties (AD and COPEI) losing influence against other political forces.

On the other hand, the 1990s experienced a notable increase of rights-based cases and, overall, the emergence of a human rights discourse similar to the rest of Latin America. Constitutional litigation became common and increasing attention to due process was given in Criminal Law, Administrative Law and Civil Procedural Law, among other areas. There was a notable effort to reform the judiciary via agreements with international financial institutions like the World Bank and the Inter-American Development Bank.[15] However, despite these and other related developments, challenges persisted across the legal system as a whole. By the end of the 1990s, the judiciary was still perceived as illegitimate as the regime.[16] Whilst it had become a more accessible institution – and a discourse centred on fundamental rights became more prominent – the judiciary was still seen as inextricably tied to the ruling elites.

The rise and earlier decline of constitutional democracy in Venezuela is critical to understand key elements of the country's constitutional life in the following years. Any analysis of the role of the Constitution in the past two decades needs to acknowledge

[12] RA Sánchez Urribarri, 'Courts between Democracy and Hybrid Authoritarianism: Evidence from the Venezuelan Supreme Court' (2011) 36 *Law & Social Inquiry* 854.

[13] M Gómez, 'Greasing the squeaky wheel of justice. Networks of Venezuelan lawyers from the pacted democracy to the Bolivarian Revolution' in Y Dezalay and B Garth (eds), *Lawyers and the Rule of Law in an Era of Globalization* (Routledge, 2011).

[14] C García Soto, MA Martínez Meucci and R Sánchez Urribarrí, 'Winds of Change: Comparing the Early Phases of Constitutional Redrafting in Chile and Venezuela' (2021) 13 *Hague Journal on the Rule of Law* 315.

[15] Similar to other judicial reform attempts across the region. *See* L Hammergren, *Envisioning Reform: Conceptual and Practical Obstacles to Improving Judicial Performance in Latin America* (The Pennsylvania State University Press, 2007).

[16] Sanchez Urribarri (n 12).

the previous existence and relevance of deficient – yet meaningful – liberal democracy and rule of law institutions.

ii. Hugo Chávez's Revolution and the 1999 Bolivarian Constitution

It was against this backdrop that Hugo Chávez was elected in 1998, ushering in a change of regime (the *Bolivarian Revolution*). The new institutions and logics proposed rested upon the country's authoritarian past and the successes and failures of the democratic project. They also relied on Chávez as a *caudillo* – a military populist leader who strongly criticised the previous regime and vouch to avenge Venezuelans against those who had betrayed them. Yet, he was elected in a free and fair voting process, and his project's legitimacy largely relied on his ability to count with the support of the majority via credible elections.[17] Thus, the country retained a nominal commitment to the liberal-democratic institutions developed under the 1961 Constitution – including free and fair elections, a commitment to the rule of law and separation of powers, judicial independence, and a federal system.

In this context, Chávez pushed for the creation of a new constitutional order. Despite not being established in the 1961 Constitution as a mechanism to replace the constitution, Chávez proposed a complete change via a constituent assembly. This idea counted with the reluctant, but definite support of the Venezuelan Supreme Court.[18] Based on a controversial interpretation of constituent power doctrine,[19] and dominated by Chávez's political coalition, the 1999 Constituent Assembly proceeded to make major modifications to Venezuela's architecture of power. This included expanded executive prerogatives, replacing the country's bicameral Congress with a new unicameral legislature, and allowing for a more expansive military role in politics. It also included creating new accountability institutions for the protection of rights and novel popular participation mechanisms, including an option of a recall referendum against elected leaders. Moreover, it envisioned a new Supreme Tribunal (*Tribunal Supremo de Justicia*, TSJ), that also included a division with all the powers of a constitutional tribunal, the *Sala Constitucional* (Constitutional Chamber).

The new *Bolivarian* constitutional order should be understood in connection to the development of *Chavismo* as a political regime, involving the progressive dismantlement of democracy and the eventual surge and consolidation of authoritarian rule.[20] This chapter chronicles this trajectory by assessing patterns of constitutional interpretation across the distinct regime phases: The first stage (1999–2006) involved a transition from failed democracy to a hybrid regime; the second phase (2007–2012) a hybrid regime undergoing a transition to an increasingly autocratic socialist system; and the third and

[17] Soto, Meucci and Sánchez Urribarrí (n 14).

[18] JI Colón-Ríos, 'Carl Schmitt and Constituent Power in Latin American Courts: The Cases of Venezuela and Colombia' (2011) 18 *Constellations* 365; J Braver, 'Hannah Arendt in Venezuela: The Supreme Court Battles Hugo Chávez over the Creation of the 1999 Constitution' (2016) 14 *International Journal of Constitutional Law* 555.

[19] AM Bejarano and R Segura, 'Reforma constitucional en tiempos de crisis: lecciones de Colombia y Venezuela' (2008) *Revista latinoamericana de política comparada* 151.

[20] AR Brewer-Carías, *Dismantling Democracy in Venezuela: The Chávez Authoritarian Experiment* (Cambridge University Press, 2010).

last phase (2013–current) encompasses the regime's transition to a hegemonic authoritarian regime.[21] The chapter focuses on the Constitutional Chamber as the storm centre of several political conflicts that took place along this trajectory. Against this backdrop, we look at 40 constitutional cases in detail, issued by different groups of justices over 20 years. The variation of court composition took place in relation with key milestones in the regime's evolution, helping to shape the Chamber's jurisprudence and political role.

Although the 1999 Constitution was tied to an authoritarian project, it is incorrect to assume that this text was (or is) irrelevant. Like other countries that have experienced democratic backsliding, constitutional life in Venezuela has gone through contradictions that are impossible to assess without considering social and political factors. In Venezuela there is a 'dual state' logic where regular appeals to the constitution and the law to justify state action coexist with widespread abuse.[22] Whilst the *Chavista* regime made a nominal commitment to democracy; expanded social, economic and political rights, and vowed to enhance political participation (inspiring similar developments in other countries such as Bolivia and Ecuador),[23] it also dedicated substantial efforts to politicising the judiciary and other accountability mechanisms,[24] and frustrating opposition expectations of seeking justice. Patterns and instances of constitutional interpretation in Venezuela and the performance of the court system are inextricably related to this process.[25]

B. The Court and its Litigation – The Constitutional Chamber of the Supreme Court

The Constitutional Chamber of the TSJ was a major innovation of the 1999 Bolivarian Constitution.[26] The Chamber was originally conceived as an institutionally powerful constitutional adjudication body, with wide constitutional prerogatives and generous rules of access. Despite the expansion of the prerogatives of the presidency (chief executive) in the 1999 Constitution, and the fact that this Constitution was promoted,

[21] RA Sánchez Urribarrí, 'Populism, Constitutional Democracy, and High Courts – Lessons from the Venezuelan Case' in A Czarnota, M Krygier and W Sadurski (eds), *Anti-Constitutional Populism* (Cambridge University Press, 2022).

[22] E Fraenkel and J Meierhenrich, *The Dual State: A Contribution to the Theory of Dictatorship* (Oxford University Press, 2017).

[23] See Fröhlich (ch 10); D Landau, 'Abusive Constitutionalism' (2013) 47 *UC Davis Law Review* 189; R Dixon and D Landau, *Abusive Constitutional Borrowing: Legal Globalization and the Subversion of Liberal Democracy* (Oxford University Press, 2021).

[24] L Castaldi 'Judicial independence threatened in Venezuela: the removal of Venezuelan judges and the complications of rule of law reform' 37 *Georgetown Journal of International Law* 477.

[25] JA Berríos Ortigoza, 'El concepto constitucional de Democracia y la judicialización de la política en Venezuela' (2013) 29 *Cuestiones Políticas* 13.

[26] Sánchez Urribarrí makes an explicit connection between the nature of the regime and the functions of the Constitutional Chamber, Sánchez Urribarri (n 12). For a discussion on the critical role played during the country's sharper turn towards authoritarianism after Chávez's death, see also RA Sánchez Urribarri, 'Between Power and Submissiveness: Constitutional Adjudication in Latin America' in R Dixon, T Ginsburg and L Spitz (eds), *Comparative Constitutional Law in Latin America* (Edward Elgar, 2017); J M Casal Hernández, 'The Constitutional Chamber and the Erosion of Democracy in Venezuela' (2021) *MPIL Research Paper Series* 913.

envisioned, and ultimately shaped by Chávez in the context of regime change, the Chamber constituted a formal expansion of judicial power in a legal and political sense.

There is abundant research – especially by Venezuelan constitutional scholars – that has reflected on the role of the TSJ throughout the *Chavista* regime, discussing key decisions proffered at different junctures. The Chamber never became a strong accountability mechanism against the government.[27] Despite an initial interest in expanding its jurisdiction, protecting fundamental rights and showing willingness to judicialise the country's political conflict, the Chamber became a reliable ally of the regime (as did the TSJ as a whole).[28] Today, it remains a vital tool in the regime's struggle to stabilise its rule in a country in crisis, providing judicial support in a variety of cases – from the legalisation of repression to the blockade of the opposition-leaning National Assembly.[29] Simultaneously, scholars have also analysed the rise of the Chamber's oversight role vis-à-vis the rest of the judiciary and the rest of the TSJ. This process is not only anchored on the Court's jurisdictional prerogatives, but also on the lack of tenure security of lower court judges and the need to avoid disciplinary action. Paradoxically, the same institution that is reluctant to challenge the Executive and other authorities, has asserted its role as maximum interpreter of the constitution within the judiciary. To these ends, it has relied on its case-law's binding character to define the content, scope and implementation of the values and principles of the constitutional project and its rules.[30]

A relatively unexplored dimension of this story is how the Constitutional Chamber interpreted the 1999 Constitution over time, ie, to what degree constitutional interpretation techniques shifted in tandem with the country's changes. The Chamber has concentrated an unusual amount of power yet, as we discuss below, it is 'hollow' judicial power, since it is not exercised in an autonomous and independent fashion. However, there are relatively few works that look systematically at how the justices interpret the law and craft their decisions. Whilst we know that the country's rule of law and the quality of judicial institutions have deteriorated dramatically,[31] we know little about how these changes have been reflected in constitutional reasoning and legal rhetoric. This is a critical indicator of the rule of law, including variation in terms of the consistency, quality, and effect as *ratio decidendi* of the court's rulings.[32]

[27] The politicisation of the Venezuelan Supreme Tribunal from the point of view of the populist features of the regime is discussed in Sánchez Urribarrí (n 21).

[28] A few years ago, a damning study by Canova et al described how the Supreme Tribunal simply refused to decide cases independently, and always ruled against the opposition. *See* Antonio Canova González, Luis A. Herrera Orellana, Rosa E. Rodríguez Ortega, and Giuseppe Graterol Stefanelli, *El TSJ al Servicio de la Revolución.* (Caracas: Editorial Galipán 2014). See also JA Berríos Ortigoza, 'El control jurisdiccional de la constitucionalidad y la política en Venezuela: estudio sobre la sala constitucional (2000–2010)' (Universidad Nacional de Educación a Distancia, España, Facultad de Derecho Departamento de Derecho Político, 2015).

[29] R Pérez Perdomo and AY Santacruz, 'La legitimidad de jueces y legisladores en el Estado constitucional de derecho: la Asamblea Nacional y el Tribunal Supremo venezolano en 2016' (2016) *Doxa. Cuadernos de Filosofía del Derecho* 405; V Capriles, A Santacruz and R Pérez-Perdomo, 'Represión, Justicia y Derecho En La Venezuela de Hoy (2013-2019) (Repression, Justice and Law in Today's Venezuela (2013–2019)' (2020) 10 *Oñati Socio-Legal Series* 789.

[30] Berríos Ortigoza (n 28) 391–411.

[31] See World Justice Project, *Rule of Law Index* (2021), worldjusticeproject.org/rule-of-law-index/country/Venezuela%2C%20RB. See also 'Informe Sobre El Cumplimiento de Los Requisitos Exigidos Por Parte Los Magistrados Del Tribunal Supremo de Justicia, Julio 2016' (Acceso a la Justicia, 2016) accesoalajusticia.org/wp-content/uploads/2016/07/Perfil-de-magistrados-del-TSJ-julio-2016.pdf.

[32] J Meierhenrich, *The Remnants of the Rechtsstaat: An Ethnography of Nazi Law* (Oxford University Press, 2018).

The Constitutional Chamber's main functions are listed in the 1999 Constitution.[33] However, from the start, the Chamber's preference has been to interpret these criteria expansively, on the basis that it is the final interpreter of the Constitution.[34] As autocratic logics became the norm, the Constitutional Chamber positioned itself as a major collaborator of the regime, interpreting its own jurisdiction and role as needed and doing away with its accountability role.[35] This offered a veil of legitimacy to actions that were at odds with the 1999 Constitution's tenets; expanding its own prerogatives when necessary, and even engaging in creative interpretive exercises to justify abuse. This had important effects on the structure, quality and content of the Chamber's decisions as well.[36] In this chapter we identify key traits of these techniques, including a selective (and often deceiving) engagement with the Inter-American Human Rights system's jurisprudence (despite its open opposition to it); a conscious and consistent appeal to its own case-law to justify its decisions, and the significant (yet apparently declining over time) interest in linking its interpretations to constitutional scholarship, among other trends.

[33] The 1999 *Constitution of the Bolivarian Republic of Venezuela* (Venezuelan Constitution), Article 336 states:

'The following are functions of the Constitutional Division of the Supreme Tribunal of Justice:

1. To declare the nullity, in whole or in part, of national laws and other acts of National Assembly with the force of law, which are in conflict with this Constitution.
2. To declare the nullity, in whole or in part, of state Constitutions and laws, municipal ordinances and other acts of the deliberating bodies of the States and Municipalities which are issued by way of direct and immediate implementation of the Constitution and are in conflict with the same.
3. To declare the nullity, in whole or in part, of acts of the National Executive with the force of law, which are in conflict with this Constitution.
4. To declare the nullity, in whole or in part, of acts issued by way of direct and immediate implementation of the Constitution by any other government organ exercising Public Power.
5. To verify, at the request of the President of the Republic or the National Assembly, the constitutionality of international treaties signed by the Republic, prior to ratification of the same.
6. To review in all cases, even ex officio, the constitutionality of decree of the President of the Republic decreeing states of exception.
7. To declare the unconstitutionality of omissions on the part of the municipal, state, national or legislatures, in failing to promulgate rules or measures essential to guaranteeing compliance with the Constitution, or promulgating it in an incomplete manner; and to establish the time limit and, where necessary, guidelines for correcting the deficiencies.
8. To resolve any conflicts existing between different provisions of law, and declare which of the same must prevail.
9. To resolve constitutional controversies arising between any of the organs of Public Power.
10. To review judgments embodying constitutional protective orders or control on the constitutionality of laws or juridical rules, handed down by the courts of the Republic, on the terms established by the pertinent organic law.
11. Any other functions established by this Constitution or by law'. *1999 Constitution of the Bolivarian Republic of Venezuela*, translation into English, www.constituteproject.org/constitution/Venezuela_2009?lang=en.

[34] As José Ignacio Hernández García points out, this was not immediately clear in the 1999 Constitution. However, both the subsequent *Exposición de Motivos* of the Constitution (an official document issued by the National Assembly to explain the rationale of the creation of the Constitution and some of its most important institutional innovations), and the interpretation of the Chamber itself at a volatile time led enabled the Chamber to establish itself as an effective court of last resort. JI Hernández García, '¿Se justifica preservar a la Sala Constitucional del Tribunal Supremo de Justicia?' (2017) *Revista de la Facultad de Derecho* 119.

[35] T Ginsburg and T Moustafa (eds), *Rule by Law: The Politics of Courts in Authoritarian Regimes* (Cambridge University Press, 2008).

[36] Sánchez Urribarrí (n 21).

C. The Judges – The Ever-Changing Composition of the Constitutional Chamber

In theory, justices of the Venezuelan Supreme Tribunal are supposed to be selected by the National Assembly (parliament) for a single (non-renewable) 12-year term;[37] following the conditions and procedures established in the Constitution. However, in practice that has not been the case. The nominations process has often been manipulated for political reasons.[38] Moreover, so far, no Constitutional Chamber justice has completed their 12-year term on the bench: they have all retired beforehand.[39] The changes in the composition of the Constitutional Chamber are directly linked to regime change and are the result of the government's needs to secure control. Hence, we can distinguish five eras in the Chamber's composition, depending on the total or partial changes made to the bench since the first interim appointments after the 1999 Constitution was approved (2000).[40]

i. The Year 2000

During this initial era of the Constitutional Chamber,[41] the justices were appointed in interim fashion, for only one year, and directly by the National Constituent Assembly. These appointments reflected the political composition of the Assembly, ie, they were linked to the actors and factions who had influence within the governing Chavista coalition (*Polo Patriótico*). The Chamber included Iván Rincón Urdaneta (who presided both the Chamber, and the TSJ as a whole); Jesús Eduardo Cabrera Romero (Vice-President of the Chamber), and José Manuel Delgado Ocando, Moisés Troconis Villarreal and Héctor Peña Torrelles.[42] A solid majority of four justices (Rincón, Cabrera, Delgado

[37] 1999 Venezuelan Constitution, Article 264: 'The justices of the Supreme Tribunal of Justice shall be elected for a single term of 12 years. The election procedure shall be determined by law. In all cases, candidates may be proposed to the Judicial Nominations Committee either on their own initiative or by organizations involved in the field of law. After hearing the opinion of the community, the Committee shall carry out a pre-selection to be submitted to the Citizen Power, which shall carry out a second pre-selection to be submitted to the National Assembly, which shall carry out the final selection. Citizens may file objections to any of the candidates, for cause, with the Judicial Nominations Committee or the National Assembly.'

[38] 'Informe Sobre El Cumplimiento de Los Requisitos Exigidos Por Parte Los Magistrados Del Tribunal Supremo de Justicia, Julio 2016' (n 31).

[39] The average length of a justice's term at the time of writing this chapter was about 7.4 years in the Constitutional Chamber. Two notable outliers are Arcadio Delgado Rosales and Carmen Zuleta de Merchán, who joined the Chamber as alternates and replaced retiring judges after 2005 and were eventually appointed *ex novo* in 2011. These two justices were in the Chamber for over 15 years until their recent replacement in 2022.

[40] According to the TSJ's official website (which cannot be regularly accessed since at least 2017, and it is blocked from overseas access now and then). See historico.tsj.gob.ve/eltribunal/magistradoshistorico.shtml.

[41] The justices began serving on 14 January 2000 and were appointed by the National Constituent Assembly (ANC). See Art 19.1, *Decreto sobre el Régimen de Transición del Poder Público* (decree governing the transition between the 1961 and 1999 constitutional orders), *Gaceta Oficial de la República*, number 36857, 27 December 1999, reprinted on *Gaceta Oficial de la República*, number 36859, 29 December 1999. We include the reprinted issue because it was in this second occasion that the appointments were finally made public.

[42] The alternate members of the TSJ were subsequently designated by the National Constituent Assembly's Legislative Commission ('Congresillo'), on 30 March 2000, and included justices Manuel Feo La Cruz, Pedro Bracho Grand, Carlos Enrique Peña, Humberto Briceño León and Emiro García Rosas. *Gaceta Oficial de la República*, number 36.927, 6 April 2000.

and Troconis) were responsible for some of the most consequential rulings of the Chamber. During this period, we see the origins of the expansive interpretation of jurisdiction rules and access that would characterise the Chamber's jurisprudence over its existence, and an interest in deciding political cases in the way that best reflected the interests and needs of the new *Chavista* regime. From the start, the Chamber began developing its case-law in a context of lack of procedural legislation for constitutional review cases. Existing legislation, such as the Civil Procedure Code or the Organic Law of Constitutional Amparo had not contemplated the existence of the Chamber and its prerogatives. Whilst this was a challenge for the Chamber, it also allowed it to use it as a pretence to 'fill the gap' through their own decisions. This was instrumental in defining the wide scope of its authority vis-à-vis the judiciary and other branches of power.

ii. Between 2001–2004

This second phase started in January 2001, after three of the Chamber's justices were ratified – Rincón (who remained President), Cabrera and Delgado – and two justices were added: Antonio García García and Pedro Rondón Haaz.[43] These justices were appointed by the National Assembly in a controversial designation process that co-opted part of the opposition (although these two justices had different links to the *Polo Patriótico* ruling coalition).[44] Initially supportive of the regime's interests, they eventually became pro-opposition after the fracture of Chávez's coalition in 2002. Several of the Chamber's most notable (and controversial) rulings happened in this phase. As the Chamber became an important venue for adjudicating political controversies and implementing the rights established in the 1999 Constitution, the pressure on the Chamber from government and opposition actors also increased. This was especially the case during the process that led to the August 2004 recall referendum against Chávez, including the appointment of the National Electoral Authority (which happened given the legislature's inability to achieve the required consensus).[45] Eventually, the National Assembly flunked different procedural rules to approve new legislation regulating the TSJ, leading to a court-packing round of designations in December 2004.

iii. Between 2005–2010

This third (and longest) era began in January 2005, with the expansion of the Supreme Tribunal to 32 justices, seven of whom served at the Constitutional Chamber. Four justices remained at the court (Rincón, Cabrera, García García and Rondón), and three justices were appointed: Luis Velásquez Alvaray, Luisa Estella Morales Lamuño and Francisco Carrasquero López.[46] All three justices had previous experience in the

[43] Pedro Bracho Grand, Carmen Zuleta de Merchán, Leoncio Abad Landáez Otazo, Argenis José Riera Encinoza and César Mata Marcano were appointed alternate justices.

[44] Appointed in an extraordinary session of the National Assembly on 20 December 2000, published in the *Gaceta Oficial de la República*, number 37105, 22 December 2000.

[45] AR Brewer Carías, RJ Chavero Gazdik and J Peña Solís, *La guerra de las Salas del TSJ frente al Referéndum Revocatorio* (Ed Aequitas, 2004).

[46] Appointed by the National Assembly on 13 December 2004, including seven alternate members. *Gaceta Oficial de la República*, number 30.086, 13 December 2004.

Chávez's government: Velásquez Alvaray had been a National Assembly member, Morales Lamuño spent time as a judge and allegedly had direct links to Chávez, and Carrasquero had just been President of the National Electoral Authority (CNE), which organised the referendum against Chávez. Over time, the composition of the Chamber changed following several justices' retirements: Rincón (February 2005), García García (May 2005), Cabrera (February 2008), and Rondón Haaz (March 2010). Rincón was replaced by Marcos Tulio Dugarte Padrón – appointed by the National Assembly in October 2005;[47] whilst the remaining justices were replaced by justices from the list of substitutes, until 2010.[48]

iv. Between 2011–2015

The fourth era began in January 2011, with the appointment of two new justices – former legislator Juan José Mendoza and ex-Solicitor General Gladys Gutiérrez Alvarado – and the appointments of alternate justices Carmen Zuleta de Merchán and Arcadio Delgado Rosales.[49] These designations reinforced the control of the ruling United Socialist Party (PSUV) over the Chamber. During this time, the Chamber continued to support the government in a variety of rulings and to exert control over the rest of the TSJ and the lower courts, whilst reducing its interest in protecting rights. The Chamber also issued several controversial rulings in connection to the regime's increasing autocratisation, including a string of decisions that helped the regime navigate the constitutional consequences of Chávez's absence from power due to illness (and his eventual death).[50]

v. From 2015 Until Now

Finally, the last era started with the incorporation of the justices appointed in unconstitutional fashion by the National Assembly in December 2015,[51] after the legislative elections in that same month resulted in a victory for the opposition. Justices Morales Lamuño, Carrasquero and Dugarte retired in October 2015,[52] and were replaced by Calixto Antonio Ortega Ríos, Luis Fernando Damiani Bustillos and Lourdes Benicia Suárez Anderson. These three justices had proven links with the PSUV.[53] Gutiérrez

[47] *Gaceta Oficial de la República*, number 38.287, 5 October 2005.

[48] The 2010 round took place in anticipation of the loss of a qualified majority in the National Assembly that the government coalition experienced in the legislative elections of that year. The appointment round included nine new principal justices and a complete slate of 32 alternate justices. The opposition protested the appointment round to no avail. 'La Mayoría Chavista Renueva a Jueces Del Supremo Entre Protestas Opositoras' *El Mundo* (12 August 2010) www.elmundo.es/america/2010/12/08/venezuela/1291834204.html.

[49] *Gaceta Oficial de la República*, número 39569, 8 December 2010.

[50] AR Brewer-Carías, 'Crónica constitucional del proceso venezolano de transición gubernamental, ocasionado por la enfermedad y muerte del presidente Hugo Chávez, y de la instauración por el juez constitucional de un gobierno sin legitimidad democrática (diciembre 2012/abril 2013)' (2013) 18 *Pensamiento Constitucional* 265.

[51] *Gaceta Oficial de la República*, number 40.816, 23 December 2015.

[52] As decided by the Plenary Chamber of the Venezuelan Supreme Tribunal, see www.tsj.gob.ve/-/sala-plena-del-tsj-acordo-aprobar-solicitud-de-jubilacion-de-13-magistrados-y-magistradas.

[53] See *Acceso a la Justicia* (Informe Anual 2019). accesoalajusticia.org/informe-anual-2019-persecucion-y-represion-la-consolidacion-de-un-estado-de-hecho-en-venezuela/.

retired after being appointed to the Electoral Council and was replaced by alternate justice René Degraves. This bench enacted at least 145 decisions against the opposition-leaning National Assembly, serving as a bulwark of authoritarian governance.[54]

D. Legal Scholarship and Constitutional Reasoning

Constitutional scholarship has traditionally played a critical role in shaping constitutional reasoning in Venezuela. However, the extent to which this is the case has changed over the last twenty years, as a result of the country's democratic backsliding process and, more recently, due to the country's complex humanitarian emergency. Although select academic journals and publishers remain operative, and several law schools continue to educate and graduate lawyers, it has been a difficult time for Venezuela's legal academics, many of whom have been forced to move overseas due to the country's dire circumstances. Interestingly, both Venezuelan and foreign scholarship are cited in the Chamber's rulings across different issue areas. This pattern has continued until today, since engaging with scholarship and justifying rulings based on legal doctrine help dispel claims that the Chamber does not engage seriously with the law and is a pro-regime institution.[55]

II. Arguments in Constitutional Reasoning

For this part of our work, we chose 40 decisions based on their relevance for socio-political life and the legal system. Inevitably, some of these rulings dealt with key regime change dilemmas. Additionally, we also selected cases that reflected the Chamber's efforts to establish its authority within the TSJ and vis-à-vis the rest of the judiciary and develop the 1999 constitutional order. This has included major rulings that have established new constitutional adjudication procedures; and defined the Chamber's jurisdiction to hear and decide over a wide range of cases.

A. The Structure of Constitutional Arguments

The structure of arguments in our sample showed a relatively balanced number of cases for each type of structure under analysis. We identified a one-line conclusive argumentation in about 13 out of 40 cases, a parallel-conclusive structure in 11 out of

[54] 'El TSJ vs. la AN | Acceso a la Justicia' (*Acceso a la Justicia*, 2021) accesoalajusticia.org/el-tsj-vs-la-an/; RA Sánchez Urribarri, 'I·CONnect – The Constitutional Chamber's Recent Decisions to Enable Legislative Elections in Autocratic Venezuela' www.iconnectblog.com/the-constitutional-chambers-recent-decisions-to-enable-legislative-elections-in-autocratic-venezuela/.

[55] For instance, in decision 9, where the Chamber cites constitutional scholar Brewer Carías, who holds critical views of the regime, as part of its reasoning to justify curtailing the opposition-controlled National Assembly's accountability prerogatives. Venezuelan Supreme Tribunal's Constitutional Chamber, Decision 9, 1 March 2016.

40 cases, and a slightly larger number of cases with parallel, individually inconclusive, but together conclusive arguments (also known as 'dialogic', 16 out of 40 cases). Whilst our sample is too small to make broader inferences about changes of type of interpretation over time, it is interesting that one-line argumentation seems to be relatively common during the years under examination (after 2010, nine out of 15 decisions employed this type of argumentation).

B. Types of Arguments in Constitutional Reasoning

i. Analogies

The use of analogy was observed in only seven cases out of 40.

ii. Ordinary Meaning of the Words of the Constitution

In the vast majority of the cases under analysis the Chamber's preferred constitutional reasoning approach was textual/literal interpretation. In 38 out of 40 cases, the Chamber resorted to textual interpretation in the ruling's main opinion, whilst in eight cases it was observed in dissenting/concurring opinions.[56] In only two cases the Chamber did not appeal to this type of interpretation.[57] The fact that the Chamber first and foremost appeals to the literal text of the constitution is a reflection of a positivist approach, which is at odds with region's emerging trends. It is also a notable feat in a growingly authoritarian context – the Chamber has continued to resort to literal interpretation, even if this implies making up controversial (or plainly misleading) readings of the text.

iii. Establishing/Debating the Text of the Constitution and Applicability of the Constitution

There is relatively little debate about the applicability of the Constitution in our sample, with only two cases out of 40. One of them was decision 1002 issued on 26 May 2004, in which the Chamber made an explicit distinction between protecting the right to healthcare established in the Constitution versus using its powers to control or effect healthcare policy (which it refused to do). The other case was issued on 22 July 2010, in which the Chamber ratified that it did not have jurisdiction to exercise judicial review over different acts related to constitutional amendment and reform processes, including the decision to convoke referendums on the constitutional amendment or reform in question.

[56] This approach is predominant in other areas of Law as well in Venezuela.

[57] These were the cases 1002, about the justiciability of the right to health (concluding that constitutional interim relief amparo proceedings were not suitable to control public policy in this field, but to protect the right to health in individual cases); and, more recently, see case 155 in which, together with decision 156, the Chamber interpreted the scope of parliamentary privilege/immunity and stripped the opposition-leaning legislature of its lawmaking powers. Venezuelan Supreme Tribunal's Constitutional Chamber, Decision 1002, 26 May 2004; Venezuelan Supreme Tribunal's Constitutional Chamber, Decision 155, 27 March 2017; RA Sánchez Urribarri and C García Soto, 'A Primer to Venezuela's Constitutional Crisis' (*IACL-IADC Blog*, 29 April 2019) blog-iacl-aidc.org/crisis-in-venezuela/2019/4/29/a-primer-to-venezuelas-constitutional-crisis.

iv. Harmonising Arguments

The Chamber seems to pay great attention to interpreting the Constitution as a whole, harmoniously (mentioning this in 35 out of 40 cases). This process was occasionally infused with interpretations driven by the judges' ideological preferences, with a strong nationalist orientation.[58] This also guides the Chamber's interpretation of the 1999 Constitution, which reflects a strong interest in appealing to domestic Venezuelan law as a matter of national interest vis-à-vis regional/international law, thus putting Venezuela at odds with the idea of a *Ius Constitutionale Commune* in the region. In the vast majority of cases (27), there was no mention whatsoever to the Inter-American Human Rights System, despite the Constitution's clear mandate to apply human rights treaties ratified by Venezuela over domestic law when it favours the claimant. Just four cases made explicit reference to the Inter-American Human Rights System, and only five cases mention other sources of international law (while five cases mention both). Moreover, as is well known and has already been documented in prior research, the Constitutional Chamber deliberately disengaged from the Inter-American System, first by conditioning the applicability of the findings, interpretations and decisions of the Inter-American system,[59] and later on by openly declaring that the Inter-American Court's decision in the dismissal of Judges Apitz Barbera, Ruggeri Cova and Rocha Contreras could not be executed, holding the decision at odds with the 1999 Constitution.[60] Moreover, in the latter decision, the Chamber went as far as requesting the Executive to withdraw from the Pact of San José (American Convention on Human Rights).[61]

v. Precedents

Interestingly, the sample also shows that the Chamber has a very strong interest in developing its case-law in a way that is coherent with previous rulings – even if it may veer from precedent for political reasons.[62] Only two of the decisions do not cite a previous interpretation or doctrine, which tends to be articulated as '*vinculante*' (formally binding).

vi. Doctrinal Analysis of Legal Concepts or Principles

The Chamber refrains from citing principles that are not specifically established in the Constitution. Only four decisions included non-constitutional principles, two of

[58] See Venezuelan Supreme Tribunal's Constitutional Chamber, Decision 1309, 19 July 2011, discussing the 1999 Constitution as a 'political-axiological project'.

[59] Venezuelan Supreme Tribunal's Constitutional Chamber, Decision 1942, 15 July 2003.

[60] Venezuelan Supreme Tribunal's Constitutional Chamber, Decision 1939, 18 December 2008.

[61] For an overall framework, see Alexandra Huneeus, rejecting the Inter-American Court, in A Huneeus, J Couso and R Sieder, 'Cultures of Legality: Judicialization and Political Activism in Contemporary Latin America' in A Huneeus, J Couso and R Sieder (eds), *Cultures of Legality: Judicialization and Political Activism in Latin America* (Cambridge University Press 2010). For a detailed explanation of the decision, see JA Berríos Ortigoza, 'Reseña "Sentencia de la Sala Constitucional sobre la inejecutabilidad de la decisión de 5 de agosto de 2008 de la Corte Interamericana de Derechos Humanos' (2009) III *Cuestiones Jurídicas* 85. See also E Meier García, 'Nacionalismo Constitucional y Derecho Internacional de Los Derechos Humanos' (2011) 9 *Estudios constitucionales* 329.

[62] A good example here is the decision 565, with the Chamber interpreting the Constitution federal structure and decentralisation in a way that gave the Federal/Central Government the power to rescind prerogatives

which dealt with the principle of constitutional continuity of presidential government to govern the temporary absence, and then the subsequent transition of power due to President Chávez's illness and death in 2012/2013.[63]

vii. Arguments from Silence

Arguments based on the 'silence of the legislator' or *non liquet* (absence of law) are rare – there was only one case of this type of interpretation in our sample.[64]

viii. Teleological/Purposive Arguments Referring to the Purpose of the Text

With respect to finding out the *telos* (purpose) of the constitution as a whole and/or its norms, also known as teleological argumentation, the Chamber employed teleological arguments with respect to specific norms in the 1999 Constitution in over half of our sample (22 decisions).

ix. Teleological/Purposive Arguments

The Chamber appealed to the overall intention of the *constituyente* (the constituent assembly's member) in 16 cases.

x. Non-Legal Arguments

The Constitutional Chamber frequently includes non-juridical criteria in its decisions, a finding that is directly linked to our previous discussion regarding the Chamber's sense of mission in the context of a new regime and its policy programme. At least 26 cases appeal to sociological reasons. Additionally, six decisions included economic or financial arguments, and one appealed to moral arguments.[65] Only 11 decisions did not entertain non-juridical arguments.

xi. References to Scholarly Works

The Constitutional Chamber frequently included references to constitutional scholarship, both Venezuelan and from other countries. This includes several decisions in

constitutionally allocated to Venezuelan states. As Justice Rondón Haaz highlighted in his dissenting vote, this differed significantly from the criteria in decision 2495/) – which was sidelined without compelling justification. Venezuelan Supreme Tribunal's Constitutional Chamber, Decision 565, 15 April 2008; Venezuelan Supreme Tribunal's Constitutional Chamber, Decision 2495, 19 December 2006.

[63] Venezuelan Supreme Tribunal's Constitutional Chamber, Decision 02, 9 January 2013; Venezuelan Supreme Tribunal's Constitutional Chamber, Decision 141, 8 March 2013.

[64] The only case in our sample was in the noteworthy decision 332, during the Chamber's jurisprudential 'first phase', when the Chamber asserted its jurisdiction to receive and decide writs of constitutional remedy for accessing information (*habeas data*) after noting there was no legislation regulating the matter. Venezuelan Supreme Tribunal's Constitutional Chamber, Decision 332, 14 March 2001.

[65] The latter is remarkable – the Chamber explicitly notes that 'following the most elementary moral imperatives', the composition of the Venezuelan Supreme Tribunal of Justice should not reflect changes in the relative proportion of seats held by different political forces in the legislature (National Assembly), since it would amount to a 'legal and ethical deviation'. Decision 9 (n 55).

which the justices cite their own scholarship (published or unpublished). At least 26 decisions include scholarly quotes, some of which are very long (ie, several paragraphs) and central to the decision's ratio decidendi.

xii. References to Foreign (National) Law

Additionally, general references to the law of other countries are also uncommon – only ten decisions engage with or mention other countries' legislation or preferred rights interpretation – with only two decisions citing law or legal/constitutional interpretations from other countries in the region, six cases citing law from outside of the region, and only two cases including references to both.

xiii. Pro Homine *or* Pro Persona *Principle*

Only two decisions out of 40 cases engage with the *pro persona* principle.

xiv. Other Methods/Arguments

A little over half of the cases (21 decisions) show a wide range of constitutional interpretation modalities different from the main interpretive canons discussed above. They include the 'dissociation argument', mentioned in eight decisions (including one together with *a contrario* argumentation, and another mentioning the thesis of the implicit powers/prerogatives of the State). Additionally, one of the decisions made findings based on facts communicated extensively via *hecho comunicacional* (media),[66] whilst in two other cases the Chamber based its conclusions on *lagunas axiológicas* (axiological lacunae). One ruling refers to implied rights, and another explicitly is premised upon historical argumentation. Furthermore, in another decision the Chamber created and established from scratch a special procedure to interpret constitutional norms in abstract, once again based on its authority as final interpreter of the Constitution.[67]

C. The Overall Weight of the Arguments

It is remarkable that the Chamber considers that arguments given outside of the ratio decidendi of the case, ie, obiter dictum, are also considered binding vis-à-vis other courts.[68]

D. The Impact and Quality of the Arguments

At least on paper, the arguments employed in the Chamber's decisions are relevant to the findings, whether they are part of the ratio decidendi or as obiter dictum.

[66] This type of argument has been employed by the Constitutional Chamber to claim that some situations are uncontroverted or 'truthful', because they have been broadcasted or published in the media. Venezuelan Supreme Tribunal's Constitutional Chamber, Decision 656, 30 June 2000).
[67] Venezuelan Supreme Tribunal's Constitutional Chamber, Decision 1077, 22 September 2000.
[68] For instance, Decision 1309 (n 58).

The Chamber is aware of the importance of constitutional interpretation, using the rulings' arguments as an excuse to increase its own jurisdiction, modify rules of access or alter other procedural rules in subsequent rulings.[69]

E. Judicial Candour and Judicial Rhetoric

On one hand, the rulings under analysis evidence the Chamber's ongoing use of constitutional/legal rhetoric over two decades. This, despite the substantive changes experienced in the institution and its pro-regime stance. During these years, the Chamber did not abandon the practice of crafting long, convoluted rulings, with frequent references to its own case-law and to national and international scholarship. Unfortunately, as has been the case in other authoritarian states, sophisticated constitutional and legal arguments can coexist with the erosion of judicial independence and the rule of law.

Although a separate empirical analysis project would be needed to properly explore this topic, the evolution of the Chamber's key institutional goals and objectives can be witnessed in the cases under analysis. At the start (2000–2004), the Chamber had an evident interest in developing its own constitutional interpretation principles,[70] or in defining key, controversial questions such as its own jurisdiction, scope and conception of constitutional review,[71] the meaning of a 'Democratic and Social State of Law and Justice',[72] or democracy broadly.[73] Conversely, most of the decisions after 2005 abandoned this approach, and focused instead on defending government interests without attempting to develop a constitutional doctrine as such. In this phase, the Chamber redefined the federal/subnational distribution of power,[74] ruled on different matters of governmental interest,[75] or issued key rulings interpreting constitutional rights[76] or regulatory measures[77] in a regressive, less principled way. Finally, the pro-government stance of the Chamber's decision-making became even more obvious throughout the

[69] A good example of the Chamber using its own precedent to assert jurisdiction in cases where there is a lack of explicit constitutional normative basis is in the decision 1547 /, referring to decision 1077, to justify its jurisdiction to review the constitutionality of the decisions of the Inter-American Court of Human Rights (since it was not established in the 2010 Organic Law on the Supreme Tribunal of Justice). Venezuelan Supreme Tribunal's Constitutional Chamber, Decision 1547, 17 October 2011; Decision 1077 (n 67).

[70] Decision 1077 (n 67); Decision 1309 (n 58).

[71] Venezuelan Supreme Tribunal's Constitutional Chamber, Decision 7, 1 February 2000; Decision 656 (n 66); Venezuelan Supreme Tribunal's Constitutional Chamber, Decision 93, 6 February 2001; Decision 332 (n 64); Venezuelan Supreme Tribunal's Constitutional Chamber, Decision 1571, 19 November 2001; Decision 1002 (n 57).

[72] Venezuelan Supreme Tribunal's Constitutional Chamber, Decision 85, 2002.

[73] Venezuelan Supreme Tribunal's Constitutional Chamber, Decision 1139, 21 June 2002; Venezuelan Supreme Tribunal's Constitutional Chamber, Decision and 23, 22 January 2003.

[74] Decision 565 (n 62).

[75] Venezuelan Supreme Tribunal's Constitutional Chamber, Decisions 49, 3 February 2009; Decision 02 (n 63); Decision 141 (n 63).

[76] Venezuelan Supreme Tribunal's Constitutional Chamber, Decision 190, 28 February 2008; Venezuelan Supreme Tribunal's Constitutional Chamber, Decision 1265, 5 August 2008; Venezuelan Supreme Tribunal's Constitutional Chamber, Decision, 796, 22 July 2010; Venezuelan Supreme Tribunal's Constitutional Chamber, Decision 993, 27 June 2013.

[77] Venezuelan Supreme Tribunal's Constitutional Chamber, Decision 1049, 23 July 2009.

2010s up until the present day, as we have seen in the controversial rulings that blocked the National Assembly's legislative function.[78]

F. Length, Dissenting and Concurring Opinions

The Chamber's decisions in key issue areas have varied length. They can be much longer than average, including lengthy dissents or concurring opinions, or be on the shorter side yet still solving important questions or setting precedent. All in all, in our sample the range in our sample was between ten and 88 pages, with 30 pages on average.[79]

It is possible for the TSJ's justices to submit both dissenting and concurring opinions. Although data on the number of dissents throughout the Chamber's history is not readily available, our sample shows a relatively large number of cases with either dissenting or concurring votes during the Chamber's first decade (16 cases), whilst there were only three cases with dissenting or concurring votes subsequently (ie, until 2017). During the first few years there were numerous dissents, as the Chamber decided varied matters of jurisdiction, review prerogatives, procedures, binding character of the rulings and power to issue specific mandates, among other matters.[80] However, over time, the most notable dissenter became Justice Rondón Haaz, who used to point out both formal and substantial matters and contradictions against prior precedent in his concurring/dissenting votes.[81]

In any case, the lack of dissents over time and, in fact, the eventual surge of *en banc* decisions after 2015 are associated with the turnover, changes of composition and overall regime politics described in the preceding sections. As Venezuela's democratic backsliding progressed, and the Court was subject to different court-packing attempts, the likelihood of dissenting opinions declined (with unanimous support for the government's preferred position in political cases).[82]

G. Framing of Constitutional Issues

The framing of constitutional issues is a very interesting aspect of the Venezuelan case. In our sample, 18 cases dealt with fundamental rights or were adjudicated on that premise, whilst a total of 12 cases were related to state organisation. Only four were related to matters of due process.[83] Based on our data, and corroborating our own prior

[78] Decision 9 (n 55); Venezuelan Supreme Tribunal's Constitutional Chamber, Decision 808, 2 September 2016; Decision 155 (n 57). See also Sánchez Urribarrí (n 21).

[79] The number of pages is based on printing out the decisions, as found on the TSJ database.

[80] There was one Justice in particular – Héctor Peña Torrelles – who became a 'chronic dissenter' during the first year because he didn't agree with the Chamber's jurisdiction to review constitutional interim relief requests (amparos) on appeal (which in turn became the lion's share of the Chamber's coursework and a key mechanism to position itself as the apex court vis-à-vis the rest of the court system).

[81] As pointed out above, Rondón Haaz became one of the few opposition-leaning justices during this era.

[82] Pérez Perdomo and Santacruz (n 29); Sánchez Urribarrí (n 21); Casal Hernández (n 26).

[83] In two cases the controversy was framed as involving both fundamental rights and state organisation; one as state organisation and due process combined, and another one as due process combined with another case. Decision 93 (n 71).

knowledge, we can perceive a decline over time in the Chamber's interest for adjudicating cases on fundamental rights or due process (including some cases that were critical to set up and reinforce the *Sala*'s ample jurisdiction and prerogatives), and an increase over time in deciding cases related to the organisation of the Venezuelan state – particularly after the regime's explicit transition to Socialism, as discussed above. This trend can also be linked to the country's broader de-democratisation process since both the Court became less interested in protecting citizens' rights overall – allowing the government to place more restrictions on individual liberties –; and Venezuelans who had been wronged also became less inclined to bring claims of this nature to the Chamber.

In fact, in our sample, after 2013, the key cases were related to the government's permanence in power (including the 2013 rulings related to Chávez's succession, and the effective veto and blocking of the National Assembly after the opposition took over following their victory in the 2015 Legislative elections). Although in our sample only 12 cases were triggered by a constitutional petition filed by a government actor, half of them correspond to the 2013–2017 period (a trend that would be more visible, and shocking, if we were to increase the sample and includes several cases brought by others non-official pro-government petitioners). In any case, as we pointed out before, it is virtually impossible for political opponents to secure a favourable decision in the Constitutional Chamber or in any of the TSJ's divisions.

H. Key Concepts

The Constitutional Chamber's jurisprudence – especially the cases included in this exercise – displays a remarkably wide range of concepts, theories and ideas included in their decisions. The salient cases under analysis demonstrate that the Chamber seems self-aware of its role within the regime as an 'activist' judicial adjudicator that fulfils a critical role in the implementation of the 1999 Constitution and, over time, in the regime's political project. Thus, in terms of defining its role vis-à-vis other branches, the Constitutional Chamber only mentioned judicial independence (or dealt with this concept) in three cases in the sample. This is remarkable, considering that the protection of judicial independence is established in the Constitution (and its erosion is precisely one of the strongest criticisms levelled against the Chamber). Quite telling, the activist role of the Chamber is not frowned upon by the judges – in fact, it is cherished, as it is present in at least 32 of the 40 decisions under study.[84]

There's also a strong willingness to engage with the democratic character of the regime (in at least 17 decisions) but with an interpretation that highlights national sovereignty as a premise (13 cases refer to the need to safeguard the country's sovereignty and three to nationalism alone, in line with the regime's overall populist-nationalist discourse).[85] There is also commonplace reference to the '*Estado de Derecho*' (Rule of Law) as an

[84] Pro-government judicial activism in authoritarian contexts is understudied. The Venezuelan case is a particularly interesting (and instructive) example of how the moniker 'judicial activism' can mean different things from different perspectives, even under autocratic conditions.

[85] On *Chavismo*'s populist discourse, see KA Hawkins, *Venezuela's Chavismo and Populism in Comparative Perspective* (Cambridge University Press, 2010).

important notion: 27 cases, sometimes defined as '*Estado Social de Derecho y de Justicia*' (which could be roughly translated as 'Social State of Law and Justice'). At least 12 decisions refer to justice as a key argumentative concept. These are all findings that relate to (and should be discussed in connection with) the trajectories of constitutional interpretation in the 'Andean Neo-Constitutionalism' country group (esp. Ecuador and Bolivia).

Conversely, the cases under analysis reflect lesser engagement and interest with the notion of fundamental rights from a liberal democratic perspective. Concepts like human dignity (four cases); freedom of expression (two cases), and privacy (one case) are relatively less used in our sample. Whilst due process is relatively noteworthy (in 13 cases), the actual protection of due process is less common, as discussed in the preceding section. In the sample, only five cases dealt with matters related to family or children's rights. It is interesting, however, that in at least ten cases the Chamber adjudicated, safeguarded, or engaged with a socioeconomic, cultural or environmental right, whilst equality/non-discrimination was referred to in ten cases. However, the Chamber's interest for these matters waned over time, as discussed above.

It is important to look into these examples in greater detail, since quite often mentioning a right or the need of protecting it does not necessarily mean the Chamber is making an actual effort to safeguard it, particularly in cases of political relevance. For example, although in eight cases the Chamber mentions the need for a proportional response by State actors, the rulings in question end up legitimising or favouring the state's use of coercive powers versus the individual.[86] On a similar note, the thesis of essential core State powers or constitutional rights is mentioned in seven cases, but usually to reinforce the state's regulatory powers.

A sample of only 40 cases does not allow us to discern the trajectories of constitutional interpretation or protection across all issue areas, but we can at least identify some areas of contention that are critical in order to understand the Chamber's role in a growingly illiberal context. For example, with respect to federalism, the Court issued rulings that sought to define the powers of subnational authorities, whilst respecting (and advancing) the regime's key interests. In 2006, the Chamber issued a ruling that interpreted the powers and prerogatives of subnational state governments.[87] Yet, in subsequent rulings, the decision in question was sidelined in order to prioritise the central government's coordinating powers over the prerogatives allocated to states (evidence of the regime's preference for centralising power).[88] However, other decisions illustrate that the protection of the government's interests from the bench can be more complex. For example, during the regime's first years, the Chamber's preference with respect to the subnational division of health policy responsibilities was to respect the existence of concurrent prerogatives across the central state and municipal levels.[89]

[86] See eg Decision 1049 justifying restrictions to property rights and the right to economic liberty. Decision 1049 (n 77); JA Berríos Ortigoza, 'El Concepto Constitucional de Estado Democrático y Social de Derecho y de Justicia, Como Parámetro Interpretativo Del Poder Coercitivo de La Administración Pública En Venezuela', in *La Justicia Constitucional y la Justicia Administrativa como garantes de los Derechos Humanos*, Homenaje a Gonzalo Pérez Luciani y en el marco del vigésimo aniversario de FUNEDA, III congreso de Derecho Procesal Constitucional, 1 (Caracas: Fundación Estudios de Derecho Administrativo, 2013).

[87] Decision 2495 (n 62).

[88] Decision 565 (n 62); Venezuelan Supreme Tribunal's Constitutional Chamber, Decision 256, 10 April 2008.

[89] Decision 1002 (n 57).

Later on, it issued rulings that respected the role of subnational levels of power in the control of public manifestations/demonstrations (although respecting the central government's authority and coordinating role);[90] and even constrained the accountability role fulfilled by the National Assembly vis-à-vis subnational entities (however, this happened when the Assembly was in the hands of opposition forces).[91]

Moreover, the Chamber also had an opportunity to support the Chief Executive (first Chávez and, later, Nicolás Maduro) by way of a generous interpretation of its prerogatives (at least seven decisions dealt with executive prerogative matters); the Executive's use and interpretation of emergency powers, and the ongoing control of the regime over the Executive branch in times of crisis, particularly during Chávez's illness and subsequently. Only nine cases made explicit reference to control government's actions (thus did not necessarily mean effective control). Finally, three cases referred to the transitional regime that operated between the 1961 and 1999 Constitutions.

Finally, secularism was not invoked as argument in any of these decisions. Post-material values were mentioned in 15 rulings as a decisive argument, whilst custom as a source of law was mentioned in at least ten decisions. A variety of expressions related to post-material values (in terms connected to both the constitutional project and the regime's dominant ideological project) pepper the Constitutional Chamber's decisions, including rulings appealing to 'quality of life', social harmony and 'spiritual values' in different ways. This is a very interesting finding in the regional context as well.[92]

III. Comparative Perspective

There are at least two types of comparisons that are relevant: One in connection to the *Ius Constitutionale Commune* – ie, to what degree the Chamber's case-law mirrors or reproduces traits discussed in this perspective – and another with respect to *Andean Neo-Constitutionalism*. A third form – less relevant in this analysis but important for future work – is to compare these findings with other countries experiencing increasingly authoritarian regimes or populist episodes. Additionally, it is important to highlight, once again, the need to study the Constitutional Chamber's case-law in longitudinal perspective, in a way that does justice to the different regime phases and shifts in its composition (as explained above).

IV. Evaluation, Pathology and Criticism

The Venezuelan case offers important lessons (or warnings) to those who place too much faith on the judiciary as a bulwark of democratic rule. Too much power allocated to judges can be detrimental to democracy if the judges lack a genuine commitment to

[90] Venezuelan Supreme Tribunal's Constitutional Chamber, Decision 276, 24 April 2014.
[91] Decision 9 (n 55).
[92] As early as 2000, the Chamber was already seeking to interpret social harmony and quality of life as key components of a Democratic and Social State of Law and Justice. See Decision 256 (n 88).

the rule of law, working in a highly politicised context, with much to lose from ruling against an elite uncommitted to respecting democratic rule. Judges need to be willing to operate with the level of ethics, integrity and professionalism required to better navigate an adverse structure of incentives.[93]

At face value, the Chamber might appear to be a strong court, endowed with the formal conditions to be an assertive judiciary vis-à-vis other branches of power. Moreover, the lion's share of its case-law shows that it is able to decide authoritatively vis-à-vis other state actors and was very successful at positioning itself at the top of the judicial hierarchy (even subjugating the other chambers of the Supreme Tribunal to its powers). However, as we have discussed in this chapter, this power is 'hollow': The Chamber has been able to do this because it has put its jurisdictional prerogatives at the service of the regime's interests of governance and political survival. This trend became clearer over time, as the country's process of democratic backsliding and authoritarian consolidation unfolded. In a context of low judicial independence, high polarisation and a very strong, populist leader at the helm, the Chamber abandoned its accountability duties and contributed greatly to the demise of the rule of law.

[93] D Kosař, *Perils of Judicial Self-Government in Transitional Societies* (Cambridge University Press 2016).

PART III

Principal Tendencies of Constitutional Reasoning in Latin America and the Caribbean

18

The Notion of the Rule of Law in the Constitutional Reasoning of Latin America and the Caribbean

MARIE-CHRISTINE FUCHS, JUAN CAMILO HERRERA AND MIGUEL ÁNGEL BARBOZA LOPEZ[1]

I. Introduction

Within the framework of this book's research project, we posed a specific question about the scope and use of the concept and elements of the 'Rule of Law' (RoL) in the 560 analysed judgments. This question and the project's empirical basis serve as the foundation for this composite chapter that provides an important approach to the scope and influence of one of the region's pillars of contemporary public law. Although there are a variety of elements that Latin American constitutional jurisprudence usually assimilates with the notion of the RoL – such as the principle of legality and legal certainty – there is no certainty about the RoL concept itself.

The current study delves into the RoL notion and provides insight into both the advantages and disadvantages of the concept's low usage and lack of uniformity. In addition, it proposes legal, historical and cultural reasons to support that, in Latin American constitutional reasoning, the concept of the RoL seems to resemble a rhetorical slogan more than a legally binding institution.

The first part of the chapter addresses the use of the notion of the RoL from historical, dogmatic and contemporary points of view (Sections II and III). Next, the RoL is analysed against the sample of the jurisprudence selected from the Inter-American Court of Human Rights (IACtHR) (Section IV) and the national constitutional courts and tribunals (Sections V and VI), which is followed by an assessment of the jurisprudential dialogue about the notion of the RoL (Section VII). Finally, we synthesise the theoretical and empirical parts in a section of conclusions (Section VIII).

[1] We are especially grateful to Sara Mejía Muñoz, who supported us in the study and classification of judgments on the RoL.

II. Notion, Definitions and Theories of the RoL

The term 'rule of law', '*estado de derecho*', '*Rechtsstaat*' or '*etát de droit*'[2] is widely addressed on global, regional and national scales. Throughout history,[3] the doctrine has differentiated and defined the elements of the RoL concept mostly through the formal 'thin' (Section II(A)) and substantive 'thick' (Section II(B)) theories. Although it is impossible to identify a single definition, there are certain categories, concepts or 'ingredients' that most definitions include when talking about the RoL.[4]

A. Formal Theories

'Thin' theories are characterised by the relevance granted to formality. (Purely) formal theories developed mostly in the nineteenth century with a high preponderance in the German-speaking region[5] and were taken up by Hans Kelsen[6] and, in its most extreme version, by US scholars Lon Fuller and Joseph Raz.[7] According to Fuller, the RoL is a moral value or concept, a 'must be', which is not associated with such concepts as 'the good' or 'the bad'.[8] Formal theories have in common the centrality or 'empire' of the law,[9] which has been characterised by a system of norms with the Constitution nowadays being the most preeminent among them.

According to 'thin' theories, the notion of the RoL includes at least the following three aspects:

(1) The proclamation of the total submission of every form of government to the law. In this way, only a political power that acts, governs and exercises its functions within the framework of the law is legitimate and authoritative.[10]

(2) The people's submission to the law.[11] The prerequisite of the normative system is prospective, clear, previously established and relatively stable norms articulated

[2] Regarding the differences between the terms 'rule of law' and '*Rechtsstaat*', see N MacCormick, 'Der Rechtsstaat und die rule of law' (1984) 39(2) *Juristenzeitung* 65–70.

[3] The first debates about the function of the law took place in ancient Greece and Rome. A Valcke, *The rule of law: Its origins and meanings* (ME Sharpe, 2012) 3.

[4] The Venice Commission summarises the different attempts to define the notion. See 'Report on the Rule of Law, Adopted by the Venice Commission at its 86th Plenary Session (Venice, 25–26 March 2011)', Study No 512/2009 (see section 2.3), www.venice.coe.int/webforms/documents/?pdf=CDL-AD(2011)003rev-e.

[5] FJ Stahl, *Die Philosophie des Rechts*, 2nd edn, vol 2 (Heidelberg University Publishing, 1846).

[6] H Kelsen, *Teoría pura del derecho*, RJ Vernengo, trans (Editorial UNAM, 1982).

[7] J Raz, *The authority of law: Essays on law and morality* (Oxford University Press, 1979).

[8] LL Fuller, *The morality of law* (Yale University Press, 1969) 39.

[9] E Díaz, *Estado de Derecho y sociedad democrática*, 9th edn (Taurus, 2011) 33–35; P Craig, 'Definition and conceptualization of the rule of law and the role of judicial independence therein' in P Craig, S Adam, N Díaz Abad and L Salazar, *Rule of law in Europe: Perspectives from practitioners and academics* (European Judicial Training Network, 2019) 1; Valcke (n 3) 2; P Badura, 'Über den Rechtsstaat' (1974) 4(1) *Recht und Gesellschaft* 13, 14.

[10] Craig (n 9) 2; J Jowell, 'El Estado de Derecho y sus valores fundamentales' in J Jowell, D Oliver and C O'Cinneide (eds), *La Constitución cambiante*, 8th edn (Oxford University Press, 2015) 10.

[11] BZ Tamanaha, 'The history and elements of the rule of law' (2012) *Singapore Journal of Legal Studies* 232–47.

in general terms in the abstract.[12] This presupposes that the process of enacting and administering the law is public and participatory. The requirements that the law imposes cannot be unrealisable.[13] In addition, without viewing the principle of equality as an ideal of justice, regulation must be the same for all without discrimination.[14]

(3) The existence of judicial mechanisms and institutions independent of the political power that are responsible for the enforcement of the legal system.[15] A high level of judicial independence is required to ensure that courts apply and (formally) interpret the law correctly and that the community respects judicial decisions.[16]

B. Substantive Theories

The 'thick' or substantive theories harken back mainly to the Enlightenment[17] and are characterised by interpreting the RoL as a juridical-political ideal that includes ethical considerations about 'what is fair' and what isn't. According to substantive theories with different nuances, a society's operating framework, which aims to guarantee common welfare and human dignity,[18] is based on three principal elements: democracy, human rights and the RoL. This triad is intrinsic, interdependent and indivisibly connected.[19] Among the main exponents of substantive theories is Dworkin, who stated that the RoL must include the ideals of justice and equity and that the RoL and the concept of law with its substantive principles must be interrelated.[20] These theories include most of the formal elements of 'thin' theories but specify that the RoL cannot exist in just any State or legal system; in this respect, only a system governed by legitimate (ie, democratic)[21] laws will qualify – that is, one that respects the principle of the separation of powers, equality before the law and human rights.[22]

The concept of human rights, according to these theories, encompasses democracy and the RoL. Human rights are a supposition for democracy,[23] and the RoL is a

[12] Venice Commission (n 4) 14.

[13] Tamanaha (n 11) 232–47.

[14] AV Dicey, *Introduction to the study of the law of the Constitution* (Liberty Fund, 1885); R Grote, 'Rule of Law, Rechtsstaat, y État de Droit' (2002) 8(8) *Pensamiento Constitucional* 128.

[15] Council of Europe, 'The Council of Europe and the Rule of Law – an overview', CM(2008)170, 21 November 2002, paras 39 and 43.

[16] S Adam, 'Judicial independence as a functional and constitutional instrument for upholding the rule of law in the European Union' in Craig et al (n 9) 15 et seq.

[17] J Fernández-Villaverde, 'Magna Carta, the rule of law, and the limits on government' (2016) 47 *International Review of Law and Economics* 22, 25.

[18] A Timmer, B Majtényi, K Häusler and O Salát, *EU human rights, democracy and rule of law: From concepts to practice* (European Commission, 2017) 6.

[19] S Carrera, E Guild and N Hernanz, *The triangular relationship between fundamental rights, democracy and the rule of law in the EU – Towards an EU Copenhagen mechanism* (Centro de Estudios de Política Europea, 2013) 35–36.

[20] 'I do not mean only what is often said, that we need justice as well as legality. I mean that legality makes no sense, even as an independent goal, unless the principles I have in mind are among its features'. RM Dworkin, 'What is the Rule of Law?' (1970) 30 *The Antioch Review* 151, 151.

[21] Díaz (n 9) 29; Carrera et al (n 19) 3.

[22] Timmer et al (n 18) 6.

[23] N Bobbio, *El futuro de la democracia* (Fondo de Cultura Económica, 2001).

'guarantor entity' of these rights[24] and a mechanism through which public power is organised to give concrete form to the legitimate organisation of power.[25] These are reasons why the involvement of any of the triad's elements would be a matter of moral and legal relevance within the framework of democratic political ethics.[26]

C. Contemporary Definitions and Conclusions

This last aspect constitutes the 'thin' theory exponents' main criticism of 'thick' theories in that there is no clear dividing line between the concepts of democracy, the RoL and human rights.[27] Later it will be observed that, in Latin America, this vagueness applies above all to the notions of democracy and the RoL. Some also defend the idea that the RoL (in the sense of legality) can exist without democracy and that an authoritarian system, even a dictatorship, can exist contemporaneously with the RoL.[28]

Regardless of academic controversies, most definitions found in contemporary doctrine, and which regional or international organisations and institutions promote, combine aspects of both theories. Beginning in the 1990s, various development banks, international organisations (eg, the United Nations)[29] and NGOs (eg, the World Justice Project) began to create benchmarks, indicators and indices of the RoL (often in combination with human rights indicators).[30]

In 2004, the UN Secretary-General defined the RoL as 'a principle of governance in which all persons, institutions and entities, public and private, including the State itself, are accountable to laws that are publicly promulgated, equally enforced and independently adjudicated, and which are consistent with international human rights norms and standards'.[31] In Europe, the RoL is a requirement for accession to, and continuation in, the European Union (EU).[32] If an EU Member State violates the RoL, it must face

[24] E Cruz Reyes, 'Derechos humanos, Estado de Derecho y Constitución' (2010) 2(2) *Criterio Jurídico Garantista* 62, 71.

[25] E-W Böckenförde, 'La democracia como principio constitucional' in E-W Böckenförde, *Estudios sobre el Estado de derecho y la democracia*, Rafael de Agapito Serrano, trans (Trotta, 2000) 118–31.

[26] J Zalaquett, *Transparencia, rendición de cuentas y lucha contra la corrupción en América* (Editorial Universidad de Chile, 2004).

[27] According to the Venice Commission's 'Report on the Rule of Law' (n 4) at 16, there is a high degree of overlap between both concepts. With respect to this discussion, see A von Bogdandy, P Bogdanowicz, I Canor, M Taborowski and M Schmidt, 'A potential constitutional moment for the European rule of law – The importance of red lines' (2018) 55 *Common Market Law Review* 983, 985.

[28] Cruz Reyes (n 24) 62, 72; Díaz (n 9) 35–55; With respect to this discussion, see von Bogdandy (n 27) 983, 985.

[29] *cf* United Nations, *The United Nations Rule of Law Indicators, Implementation Guide and Project Tools* (Geneva, United Nations, 2011).

[30] World Justice Project, 'Rule of Law Index 2020', worldjusticeproject.org/sites/default/files/documents/WJP-ROLI-2020-Online_0.pdf.

[31] U.N. Security Council, *Report of the Secretary-General: The rule of law and transitional justice in conflict and post-conflict societies* (23 August 2004) (S/2004/616).

[32] Art 49, Treaty on European Union; *cf* European Commission, *First Annual Report on the Rule of Law Situation across the European Union* (Brussels, European Commission) (30 September 2020); E Mak and S Taekema, 'The European Union's rule of law agenda: Identifying its core and contextualizing its application' (2016) 8 *Hague Journal on the Rule of Law* 25; Carrera, Guild and Hernanz (n 19) 1.

sanctions, such as the suspension of certain rights (Art 7, Treaty on European Union), the withholding of funds or – in an extreme case – expulsion from the EU.[33]

According to the Venice Commission, based on different attempts to define the RoL made by diverse legal and State systems, a consensus can be identified on the following necessary elements of the RoL:

(i) Legality, including a transparent, accountable and democratic process for the enactment of the law.
(ii) Legal certainty.
(iii) Prohibition of arbitrariness.
(iv) Access to justice before independent and impartial courts, including judicial review of administrative acts.
(v) Respect for human rights.
(vi) Nondiscrimination and equality before the law.[34]

As will be seen in Sections IV–VI below, many of these components of the RoL also arise in some way in the reviewed constitutional jurisprudence.

III. Notion of the RoL in Latin American Constitutionalism

The concept of the RoL arrived in Latin America with colonisation and later with the republican influence of the Constitution of Venezuela in 1811, that of Cádiz in 1812[35] and the many others that emerged from the newly independent nations in the region.[36]

The origins in Hispanic America of the RoL date back to the Hispanic Visigoth kingdom that blanketed the Iberian Peninsula between the fifth and eighth centuries. The apothegm of San Isidoro de Sevilla, '*rex eris si recte facias, si non facias non eris*' ('you will be king if you act properly, if not, you won't be')[37] was formed, words that demonstrated the primacy of the law over the State and the attempt to conform the monarch's power to the law. Proof of this is the formation of the *Audiencias* in 1528, a mechanism through which Native Americans or *mestizos* could formally defend themselves against the power of the Spanish Crown.[38] Subsequently, in the seventeenth century, other protective measures for indigenous peoples and *mestizos* appeared, particularly in South America – for example, the 'Multicultural Rule of Law' ('*Estado de Derecho Multicultural*') in which several prerogatives were contemplated favouring

[33] So far, the procedure to determine a clear risk of serious breach of the RoL (Art 7, para 1, Treaty on European Union) has been invoked with respect to Poland (2017 December) and Hungary (2018 September).

[34] Venice Commission (n 4) 13.

[35] MC Mirow, *Latin American Constitutions: The Constitution of Cádiz and its legacy in Spanish America* (Cambridge University Press, 2015).

[36] B Bravo Lira, 'El más antiguo Estado de derecho en Europa y en América (siglos XI al XXI). Parangón entre el *si recte facias* hispánico, el *rule of law inglés* y el *règne de la loi* ilustrado' (2010) *Anuario de Historia del Derecho Español-AHDE* 425.

[37] J Orlandis, 'En torno a la noción visigoda de tiranía' (1959) *Anuario de Historia del Derecho Español-ADHE* 5–44; P Ferreira da Cunha, 'Para uma história constitucional do direito portugués' (1995) *POLIS: Revista de Estudos Juridicos-Politicos* 291–95.

[38] Bravo Lira (n 36) 447.

the protection of certain elements of property[39] and the attainment of certain penal[40] or labour[41] guarantees, among others. At this time, the norms the Spaniards created were molded and adapted to the local realities of the colonial authorities.[42]

The struggle for the independence of some Latin American States was not only a reaction to Spanish domination but also to the concept of the judicial rule of law that had, from the outset, a vision favouring the interests of the nobility and landowners over those of Latin American peoples.[43] In this way, a path opened to a 'republican' period in which each independent nation, during the nineteenth and twentieth centuries, forged its own laws and regulations albeit with Spanish or, in the case of Brazil, Portuguese influence.[44]

The privileged classes, remnants of the colonial period, remained the same, and no local society existed that was guided by a constitutionally democratic and representative concept of the RoL since suffrage, for example, was limited and restricted.[45] This paved the way to a minority justice system – that is, one of patronage and private protection by status in which equality[46] continued to be a struggle. The republics of the nineteenth century were unable to create a citizen culture based on the protection of individual rights.[47] However, each new nation was tasked with determining what justice and equality meant from a constitutional standpoint and what their roles should be. At that time, a concept of the Latin American constitutional RoL began to form, which retained many aspects of the European/Spanish concept but still included genuine 'ingredients' based on local history and culture, especially plurinationality and slavery.

With the fall of military dictatorships and the end of armed conflicts, it has been possible to gradually return to, and reformulate, the regional conception of the constitutional

[39] F Silva Vargas, *Tierras y pueblos de indios en el Reino de Chile. Esquema histórico-jurídico* (Editorial Universidad Católica, 1962).

[40] A Ávila Martel, *Esquema del derecho penal indiano* (Editorial Universidad de Chile, 1941).

[41] M Salvat Monguillot, 'El derecho indiano del trabajo' in *Estudios de derecho del trabajo y de seguridad social ofrecidos a D. Francisco Walker Linares* (Editorial Jurídica de Chile, 1968) 277–95.

[42] M García Villegas, 'Law as hope: Constitution and social change in Latin America' (2004) 20 *Wisconsin International Law Journal* 353, 362.

[43] T Halperín Donghi, *Reforma y disolución de los imperios ibéricos, 1750–1850* (Alianza Editorial, 1985); F-X Guerra, *Modernidad e independencia* (Mapfre, 1992). In 1824, the Central American countries approved the Constitution of the Federal Republic of Central America, which was largely influenced by the Cádiz Constitution of 1812, but it incorporated new rights, such as the right to elect and be elected, the right to the non-confiscation of assets and the right to the abolition of slavery, among others. See F Meléndez, 'La Constitución Política de la Monarquía Española de 1812 y la Constitución de la República Federal de Centroamérica de 1824' in *Ayuntamiento de Cádiz. Las Cortes de Cádiz y su influencia en Centroamérica.* Presentaciones para el 'Diálogo sobre Integración Centroamericana', 5 and 6 October (SICA, Cádiz, Spain, 2012) 21–22.

[44] H Sábato, 'La reacción de América: la construcción de las repúblicas en el siglo XIX' in R Chartier and A Feros (comps), *Europa, América y el mundo: tiempos históricos* (Marcial Pons, 2006). The Imperial Constitution of Brazil of 1824, later replaced by the Republican Constitution of 1891, was directly influenced by the Portuguese Constitution of 1822; see H Gros Espiell, 'El constitucionalismo latinoamericano y la codificación en el siglo XIX' (2002) *Anuario Iberoamericano de justicia constitucional* 142, 145.

[45] Gros Espiell (n 44) 146.

[46] Proof of this is found in the agrarian revolutions in Latin America, which lasted until the beginning of the twentieth century. See R Alegrett, *Evolución y tendencias de las reformas agrarias en América Latina*, www.fao.org/3/j0415t/j0415t0b.htm.

[47] García Villegas (n 42) 362.

State.[48] This has been accomplished, in particular, by reinstalling such elements as the domination of law in the face of arbitrariness and despotism, regular political elections, peaceful government transitions, the understanding of the importance of the separation of powers, constitutional review of the legal system and the search for the effective protection of human rights.[49] The Latin American constitutions promulgated in recent decades have included additional elements belonging to the classic RoL category (see Table 1).

Table 1 The concept of RoL in Latin American constitutions

Country	Does the Constitution explicitly mention the RoL or a similar notion?
Brazil (1988)	Democratic Rule of Law State (Art. 1)
Peru (1993)	Democratic Rule of Law State (Art. 3)
Colombia (1991)	Social Rule of Law State (Art. 1)
Paraguay (1992)	Social Rule of Law State (Art. 1)
Venezuela (1999)	Democratic and Social Rule of Law State (Art. 2)
Dominican R. (2010)	Social and Democratic Rule of Law State (Art. 7)
Ecuador (2008)	Constitutional State of Rights and Justice (Art. 1)
Bolivia (2009)	Unitary Social State of Pluri-National Communitarian Law (Art. 1)
Honduras (1982)	Rule of Law State (Art. 1)
Guatemala (1985)	NO
El Salvador (1983)	NO
Costa Rica (1949)	NO
Nicaragua (1987)	NO
Argentina (1853)	NO
Uruguay (1967)	NO
Mexico (1917)	NO
Chile (1980)	NO

It is striking that Honduras is the only Latin American country that literally mentions the concept of the RoL in its constitution. Brazil and Peru coined the concept of the 'Democratic Rule of Law'. In the case of Brazil, the term is based on the 'general will' – that is, attending to society's common interest obtained through the consensus of the parties.[50] Peru shares

[48] L Hammergren, 'Latin American experience with rule of law reforms and applicability of nation building efforts' (2006) 38 *Case Western Reserve Journal of International Law* 63, 65; R Pérez-Perdomo, 'Rule of law and lawyers in Latin America' (2006) 603 *Annals of the American Academy of Political and Social Sciences* 179; SP Huntington, 'Patterns of violence in world politics' in SP Huntington (ed), *Changing patterns of military politics* (Columbia University Press, 1962); J Markof, *Olas de democracia: movimientos sociales y cambio político* (Tecnos, 1998).

[49] S Jost, 'El Estado de derecho hoy en América Latina' in SB Abad Yupanqui, *La importancia de la justicia constitucional en América Latina* (Instituto de Investigaciones Jurídicas, 2012) 57.

[50] Matheus Silveira, 'Estado Democrático de Direito: entenda o que é esse termo' *Politize!* (16 December 2019), www.politize.com.br/estado-democratico-de-direito.

the same position, and its Constitutional Tribunal (CT) has highlighted the importance of addressing the RoL issue from a constitutional rather than a legal perspective.[51] Colombia and Paraguay[52] incorporated the term 'Social Rule of Law' since both countries' constituent powers were strongly influenced by the reformulation of a State committed to social rights.[53] For their parts, the constitutions of Venezuela and the Dominican Republic, drawing from the elements addressed in the previous sections, speak of a 'Democratic and Social Rule of Law'.

The nation of Ecuador claims to base itself on a 'Constitutional State of Rights and Justice' and Bolivia on a 'Unitary Social State of Pluri-National Communitarian Law'. Apart from the particular emphasis on the social, these two political Charters highlight their respective concerns for a pluralism featuring their historical transversality, especially inclusive of indigenous peoples and peasant communities, an aspect of Latin American constitutionalism. Ecuador's Constitution recognises the 'rights of communities, peoples and nationalities' in a specific chapter, and Bolivia's contains a chapter on the 'rights of indigenous nations and indigenous peoples who are peasants'.

IV. Conception of the RoL in the OAS and the Jurisprudence of the IACtHR

Within the Organization of American States (OAS), neither its constituent document nor the American Convention on Human Rights (ACHR) explicitly mentions the concept of the RoL.[54] Only the Inter-American Democratic Charter (IADC) refers to it, among others, in Articles 2–4. Article 3 states that essential elements of representative democracy are 'inter alia, respect for human rights and fundamental freedoms, (…) in accordance with the rule of law'. In the event that an OAS Member State alters the constitutional regime, which produces an interruption of the democratic order, it could be subject to sanctions, including suspension (Arts 19–21). However, unlike the EU, although it is materially possible that the OAS could criminalise similar acts (such as a lack of judicial independence and the suspension of free elections, among other aspects), within the OAS, these sanctions are not the result of a violation of the RoL per se but occur in the event of 'an interruption of the democratic order'.

Of the 40 decisions selected from the jurisprudence of the IACtHR,[55] 17 mention elements of the RoL notion. Of these decisions, only 11 (judgments and advisory opinions) expressly mention the term RoL at least once, which you can see listed in Table 2.

[51] D Cabrera Leonardini, 'El Perú como Estado constitucional de derecho y su afectación por la corrupción' (2018) 11 *Revista Jurídica Científica SSIAS* 1–9, revistas.uss.edu.pe/index.php/SSIAS/article/view/932.

[52] G Delmás Aguiar, '¿El Estado paraguayo es un Estado de Derecho?' (2013) 1 *Revista Jurídica* 9–21.

[53] S Clavijo, 'Estado de derecho e instituciones' (March 2004), Banco de le República, Colombia, www.banrep.gov.co/sites/default/files/publicaciones/archivos/cortebr0304.pdf.

[54] Of the multiple regional organisations in Latin America, only two explicitly mention the RoL in their constituent documents: CELAC and the Pacific Alliance. In Central America, the 1994 Framework Treaty on Democratic Security in Central America contains a section on the RoL, which includes criteria for combating drug trafficking, impunity, corruption and more.

[55] Of the 40 IACtHR precedents, 33 are judgments, five are advisory opinions and two are provisional measures.

Table 2 Textual reference to the RoL in the selected jurisprudence of the IACtHR

Year	Contentious Case	Topic
1999	'Street Children' (Villagrán-Morales et al.) v Guatemala (rev. 28 June)	Children at risk – Torture and forced disappearance
2006	Ximenes Lopes v Brasil	Mental incapacity – Torture, cruel and inhumane treatment
2008	Castañeda Gutman v Mexico	Political rights
2011	Gelman v Uruguay	Forced disappearance – Extrajudicial executions – Amnesty
2012	Kichwa Indigenous People of Sarayaku v Ecuador	Indigenous peoples – Right to consultation – Communal property
	Furlan and family v Argentina	Incapacity – Children at risk – Reasonable time
2015	Granier et al. (Radio Caracas Television) v Venezuela	Freedom of information – Freedom of thought and expression
	López Lone et al. v Honduras	Freedom of expression, assembly and association – Political rights – Due process
2017	Advisory Opinion OC-24/17 of 24 November 2017	Gender identity – Rights of same-sex couples
2018	Advisory Opinion OC-25/18 of 30 May 2018	Asylum-Refugee
	Women Victims of Sexual Torture in Atenco v Mexico	Violence against women – Excessive use of police force

The RoL is not the central theme in any of these judgments nor is it the subject of in-depth considerations. In almost half of the 11 judgments, the Court mentions the RoL to reinforce elements of due process (Arts 1.1 and 25, ACHR), especially the effectiveness, simplicity and speed of judicial recourse[56] as well as effective judicial protection, which requires that the procedures for the execution of sentences be accessible, unobstructed and/or without undue delays.[57] These are all formal elements of the notion identified in section II of this chapter.[58] In OC-25/18, the Court clarified that each type of asylum procedure for politically persecuted individuals must 'be part of the justice systems that function under the rule of law'.[59]

[56] *Case of the 'Street Children' (Villagrán Morales et al) v Guatemala* (Merits), Judgment Inter-American Court of Human Rights (19 November 1999), para 234 (English trans); *Case of Ximenes Lopes v Brazil* (Merits, Reparations and Costs), Judgment Inter-American Court of Human Rights (4 July 2006), para 192 (English trans); *Case of Castañeda Gutman v Mexico* (Preliminary Objections, Merits, Reparations and Costs), Judgment Inter-American Court of Human Rights (6 August 2008), para 78 (English trans); *Case of Indigenous People of Sarayaku v Ecuador* (Merits and Reparations), Judgment Inter-American Court of Human Rights (27 June 2012), para 262 (English trans); *Case of Furlan and family v Argentina* (Preliminary Objections, Merits, Reparations and Costs), Judgment Inter-American Court of Human Rights (31 August 2012), para 210 (English trans).

[57] *Case of Furlan and family v Argentina* (n 56), paras 210 and 211.

[58] G Candia-Falcón, 'El Estado de Derecho y la Corte Interamericana de Derechos Humanos' (2015) 24 *Díkaion* 225–52.

[59] Advisory Opinion Inter-American Court of Human Rights, OC-25/18, para 78 (Spanish only).

The IACtHR has even argued – in a decision outside our sample – that the suspension of guarantees (art. 27, ACHR) does not imply 'a temporary suspension of the rule of law, nor does it authorise those in power to act in disregard of the principle of legality by which they are bound at all times'.[60] As for the principle of non-retroactivity, the Court has indicated in another judgment (also not included in Table 2), 'under the rule of law, the principles of legality and non-retroactivity govern the actions of all bodies of the State in their respective fields of competence',[61] so it has emphasised the importance of legal norms' prospectivity.[62]

In *Gelman v Uruguay*, the IACtHR affirmed that the full, timely and effective rule of justice[63] is a basic pillar of the RoL in the principle of legality sense. Therefore, 'amnesty laws are, in cases of serious violations of human rights, expressly incompatible with the letter and spirit of the Pact of San José'.[64] For the IACtHR, in *López Lone v Honduras*, the judicial function was intrinsically linked to the development and exercise of the RoL.[65]

On the other hand, in five of the 11 judgments, references to the RoL were associated, without pursuing a more in-depth development, with democracy and human rights.[66] In OC-24/17, the IACtHR established that the RoL, together with personal rights and freedoms and their guarantees within a democracy, formed a 'triad'.[67] In addition, the IACtHR has declared that the principle of the separation of powers is one of the RoL's essential elements.[68] Already in OC-8/87 (also not included in Table 2), the Court had understood that 'in a democratic society, the rights and freedoms inherent in the human person, the guarantees applicable to them and the rule of law form a triad. Each component thereof defines itself, complements and depends on the others for its meaning.'[69]

In the cases of *Castañeda Gutman v Mexico*,[70] *López Lone et al. v Honduras*[71] and *Granier et al. (Radio Caracas Television) v Venezuela*,[72] the IACtHR cited Articles 3 and 4 of the IADC, which lists the RoL as one of the elements of representative democracy (see above). The facts of the *López Lone* case related to the *coup d'état* on 28 June 2009,

[60] Advisory Opinion Inter-American Court of Human Rights, OC-8/87 'Habeas Corpus in Emergency Situations', para 24 (English trans).

[61] *Case of Baena Ricardo et al v Panama* (Merits, Reparations and Costs), Judgment Inter-American Court of Human Rights (2 February 2011), para 107 (English trans).

[62] Candia-Falcón (n 58) 225–52.

[63] *Case of Gelman v Uruguay* (Merits and Reparations), Judgment Inter-American Court of Human Rights (24 February 2011), para 226 (English trans).

[64] ibid.

[65] *Case of López Lone et al v Honduras* (Preliminary Objections, Merits, Reparations and Costs), Judgment Inter-American Court of Human Rights (5 October 2015) (English trans).

[66] *Case of the 'Street Children'* (n 56), para 234; *Case of Ximenes Lopes* (n 56), para 192; *Case of Castañeda Gutman* (n 56), para 142; *Case of Granier et al (Radio Caracas Television) v Venezuela* (Preliminary Objections, Merits, Reparations and Costs), Judgment Inter-American Court of Human Rights (22 June 2015), paras 54 and 140 (English trans); *Case of López Lone* (n 65), para 51.

[67] Advisory Opinion Inter-American Court of Human Rights, OC-24/17, 'Gender identity, and equality and non-discrimination with regard to same-sex couples' (24 November 2017), para 27 (English trans).

[68] *Case of López Lone* (n 65).

[69] Advisory Opinion (n 60), para 26.

[70] *Case of Castañeda Gutman* (n 56), para 142.

[71] *Case of López Lone* (n 65), paras 151–53.

[72] *Case of Granier et al (Radio Caracas Television)* (n 60), paras 54 and 140.

against former President Manuel Zelaya, through which the processes provided for in Article 20 of the IADC were initiated. In this context, the IACtHR decided that a protest demonstration by four judges 'against the *coup d'état* and in favour of the re-establishment of democracy and the rule of law' constituted a legitimate expression of their opinion.[73]

In conclusion, the IACtHR's jurisprudence, without establishing a fixed definition, has managed to unify elements of both the 'thin' and 'thick' theories, especially with the consistent reference to the 'triad'.[74] For the IACtHR, the RoL concept is not linked to a specific theme or to certain types of rights as contemplated in the ACHR. It appears as a transversal element, which has not required further development. In fact, as Candia-Falcón describes it, the IACtHR's jurisprudence on essential human rights (ie, life and personal integrity), which deals with a concept of material justice, can even create a tension with the (formal) elements of the RoL that the IACtHR itself recognises as fundamental.[75]

V. The Approach of the RoL in the Jurisprudence of the Countries of Latin America and the Caribbean

In this empirical part, we analyse the use of the notion of the RoL in the selected constitutional judgments. The graphs and data presented in this section have analytical and illustrative functions. They are presented collectively through the general averages of the region and also with data from each country.

Figure 1 Is the RoL invoked as an argument in court decisions? (Q26)

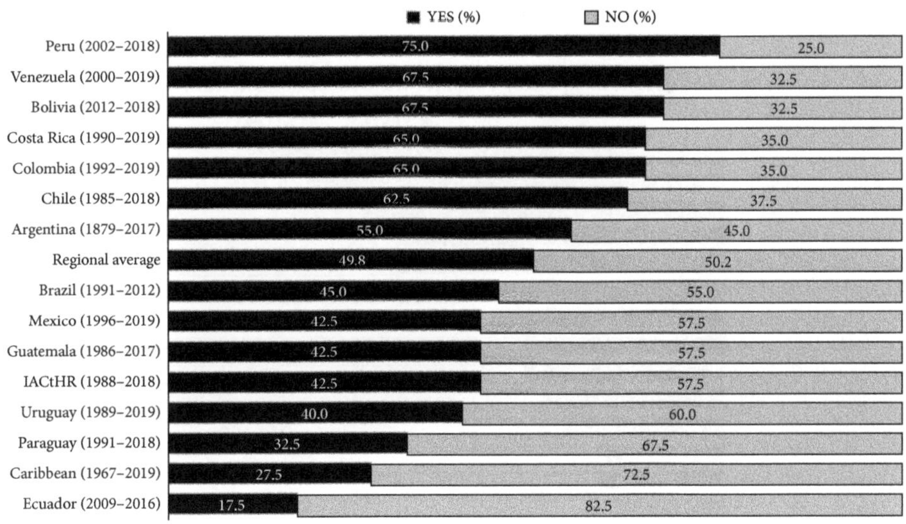

[73] *Case of López Lone* (n 65), para 153.
[74] Candia-Falcón (n 58) 225–52.
[75] ibid.

The data presented in Figure 1 corresponds to the 'backbone' of this part of the research – the presence of the RoL category in its many possible variations or definitions and its direct or indirect 'invocations' in the reviewed judgments.[76]

With regard to the overall results of the 15 countries, 49.8 per cent of the judgments invoked the RoL, while 50.2 per cent failed to reference it or develop any related ideas. What Figure 1 shows can be analysed both positively and negatively. It might be said that the idea of the RoL has lost momentum in the region. On the contrary, it is also possible to assume that the RoL has advanced and that it is following a steady path to consolidation.

These two interpretations are valid but for now are inaccurate. On the one hand, it is difficult to expect that 100 per cent of the judgments of a sample in a quantitative study of existing characteristics, which covers 50 indicators, will include such concepts as the RoL as a whole. On the other hand, being the first study of its kind, the research contributes to the measurement and illustration of, with a certain degree of certainty, the use and influence of one of the characteristic principles of contemporary public law. Precisely because of the indicated specificity and the heterogeneity of the notion of the RoL, we investigated several aspects of the RoL with the aim of testing its conceptual elements in greater depth.

A. Aspects of the Concept of the RoL in Latin America

In terms of the RoL's first sublevel, the concept's express characteristic was reviewed beyond its mere direct or indirect mention. The answers derived from this question reflect a decrease over time to the point that the overall average dropped from about 50 per cent to 32.1 per cent.

Figure 2 Does the court decision expressly consider the concept of the RoL? (Q26 1)

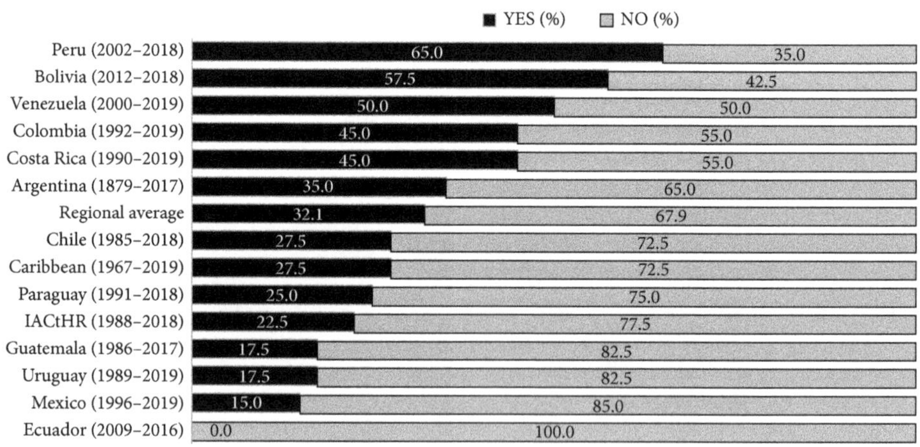

[76] Given the breadth and different meanings of the RoL, encoders were given a wide latitude of association with the concept at the time of coding.

It is remarkable that the sample of the 40 judgments from Ecuador, issued between 2009 and 2016, contains no RoL references and that jurisdictions such as Mexico, Uruguay and Guatemala reported around 16 per cent for 'yes' and 83 per cent for 'no'. The countries of the Andean region exhibit a repeated tendency to explicitly reference the RoL, with numbers higher than 51 per cent on average. From this distinctive feature, subregional-level proclivities regarding the elements and express uses of the RoL concept stand out. Are these similarities attributable to the influence of the Andean Community? To shared historical experiences in these countries?

In the selected judgments that mention the RoL, this concept moves closer to the idea of the principle of legality and legal certainty. The main reason for delving into these sublevels is that the selected judgments were reviewed with the aim of testing the following hypothesis: 'In Latin America, it seems that there is a slightly different conceptualisation of the rule of law. The "Rule of Law", or the "Social Rule of Law", is that which most closely resembles the "rule of law" and refers to a certain quality of the Rule. In addition, we can find that "the principle of legality" is more closely related to the "thin" version of the rule of law, while "judicial certainty" is limited to legal certainty'. The hypothesis investigates formal elements ('thin'; see section II(C)) and substantive elements ('thick'; see meaning in section II(C)) of the RoL concept in Latin American constitutional jurisprudence.

Figure 3 Does the court decision invoke the principle of legality? (Q 26 2)

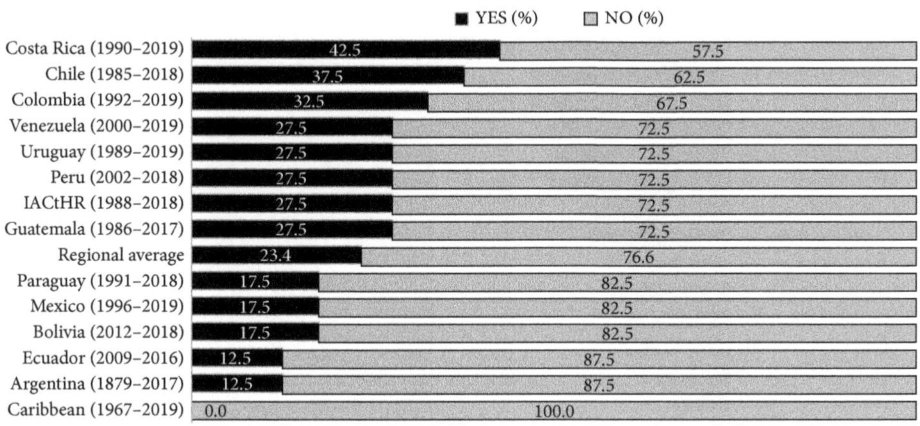

With regard to the assimilation of the principle of legality as an argument, Figure 3 indicates that Costa Rica and Chile are the countries that most often invoke legality as a key or associated element of the RoL notion. These results confirm the stability of two characteristic countries of the region that respect institutionalism and whose measurements coincide with those in the 2020 'Global Rule of Law Index'. The regional average is a 23.4 per cent invocation of the principle of legality in the context of the RoL.[77]

In most jurisdictions, the principle of legality was not invoked as a necessary feature for the development of the RoL concept (at least not directly) when trying to select the most characteristic judgments of each jurisdiction. This change may be due to the arrival

[77] World Justice Project (n 30).

of a wave of new constitutions and doctrines. Constitutional principles and values were removed from the programmatic spectrum in exchange for giving them real applicability on a day-to-day basis to the point that, today, it is perhaps more apt to think about 'constitutionality' than 'legality' in the strict sense. It is indeed possible to appreciate it in the relevance of the courts of last resort's pronouncements on the most pertinent aspects of contemporary societies. By removing the programmatic content from the constitutions, the legalisation of the law – while remaining important – has been displaced by the constitutionalisation of daily life.[78]

This change might be attributed to the simple idea of the RoL in Latin America; before the promulgations of the current constitutions, the jurisprudence and constitutional doctrine of the second half of the twentieth century were associated with the formal principle of legality and inflexible rigor. Closer to the idea of the '*dura lex, sed lex*' ('it is harsh, but it is the law') as the ultimate source of the legal system, the labour, civil or criminal code occupied the highest normative position to gradually assist with constitutionalisation and, therefore, the preeminence of 'the constitutional' both in its formal and substantive spectrum as a complement to legality (constitutional review).[79] It is also possible that the principle of legality is so clearly one of RoL's foundations that, at the time of substantiating it, law clerks and judges take the principle for granted and find it unnecessary to explain it or delve into it more deeply.[80]

Figure 4 Does the court decision expressly refer to legal certainty? (Q26 3)

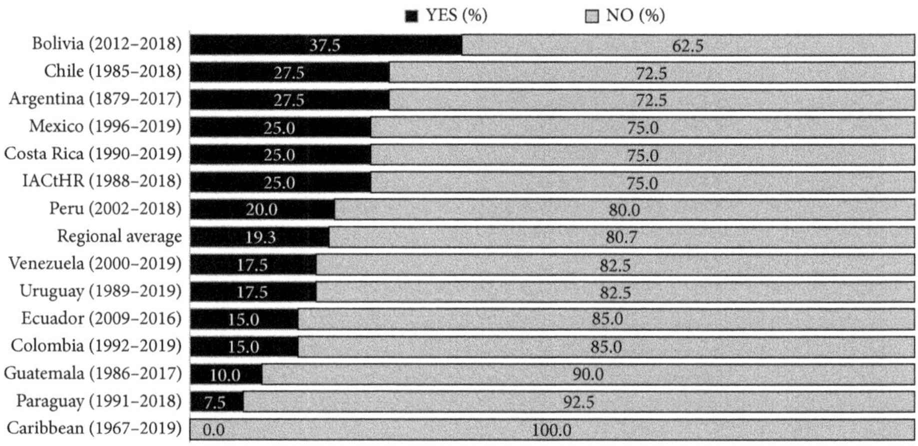

Similarly, in terms of utilising legal certainty to reinforce the argumentation or association with the RoL, Figure 4 shows that the highest result was Bolivia with 37.5 per cent, and the lowest was the Caribbean with zero. From this, it can be concluded that legal certainty is a residual element of the selected case law when defining the RoL. One explanation for why Caribbean countries do not refer to legal certainty is their

[78] L Eslava, 'Constitutionalization of rights in Colombia: Establishing a ground for meaningful comparisons' (2009)(22) *Revista Derecho del Estado* 183–230.

[79] C Rodríguez, M García Villegas and R Uprimny, 'Justice and society in Colombia: A sociolegal analysis of Colombian courts' in L Friedman and R Pérez-Perdomo (eds), *Legal culture in the age of globalization: Latin America and Latin Europe* (Stanford University Press, 2003).

[80] P Salazar, 'Una aproximación al concepto de legalidad y su vigencia en México' (1998) 9 *Isomonía* 193.

membership in the common law legal family, which assimilates the RoL notion to the mere principle of legality and not to the broad idea of constitutionality.[81] The concept of the 'rule of law' is not so much focused on legality or legal certainty and is instead equated more with the idea of the uniform application of ordinary law to any individual subject in the jurisdiction of ordinary courts.[82]

B. Deepening the Measurement of the RoL Concept

To collect more evidence to understand the use of the RoL concept, we added the following aspects[83] to the study: (i) references to decisions that offer an express or literal explanation of the content of the RoL concept; and (ii) a connection with other concepts, such as human rights or democracy.

Figure 5 shows the trend of in-depth treatment of the RoL concept. In 73.6 per cent of the sample, the question about the concept's in-depth treatment was not included since it was not addressed in that part of the selected decisions. As for 14.3 per cent being the regional average, 3.6 per cent of the case law sample crafted a more specific notion or concept and, in 8.6 per cent, there was no specific definition. The 3.6 per cent with the greatest depth represents 20 judgments out of the total of 560, the majority of which (ie, 14) addressed issues related to fundamental rights; five dealt with the organisation of the State; five others tackled procedural issues; and four addressed matters other than the aforementioned. These disparate results stem from the fact that, in a judgment, the deciding court addressed more than one issue.

Figure 5 Apart from mentioning 'the RoL', does the judgment include in-depth treatment or clarify the concept?

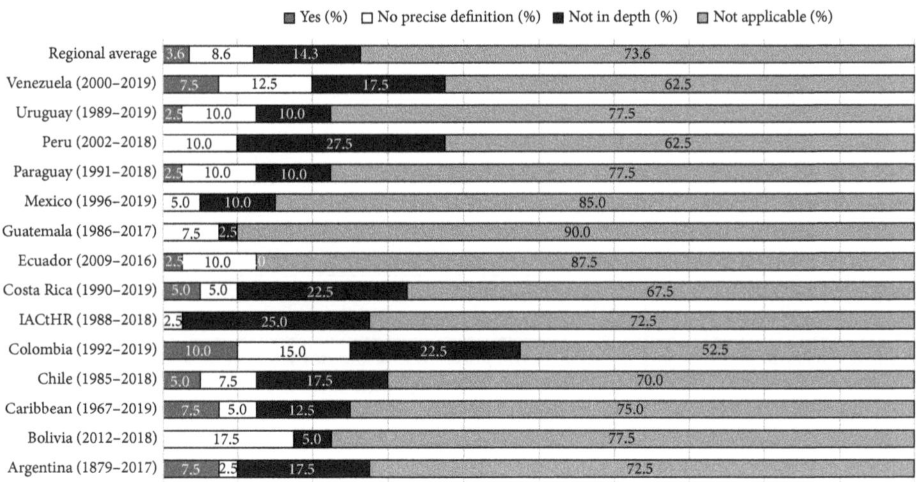

[81] SF Joireman, 'Colonization and the rule of law: Comparing the effectiveness of common law and civil law countries' (2004) 15 *Constitutional Political Economy* 315–38; Fernández-Villaverde (n 17) 22–23; Valcke (n 3) 10.

[82] Grote (n 14) 128.

[83] The database with the described aspects that we used to craft this part of the research is available at core-latam.com.

The 3.6 per cent result correlates with the jurisprudence that proceeded to develop its own characteristics of a jurisprudential understanding of the precise concept of the RoL. From this percentage, we extracted representative and literal examples of how each court in the sample attempted to define the RoL concept (see Table 3).

Table 3 Conceptual definitions of the RoL

Tribunal or Court	**Reference in the judgment (S.)**
SCJ of Argentina	— '*the empire of law*'. S. Kot, Samuel S.R.L., S/Writ of Habeas Corpus (1958).
SCJ of Argentina	— '*primacy of objective law over the rulers' will*'. S. Sejean, Juan Bautista with Ana Maria Saks de Sejean, 308:2268 (1986).
CC of Colombia	— '*rationalize the exercise of political power*' S. C-027 (1993).
CT of Chile	— '*State bodies must submit their action to the Constitution and the rules issued in accordance with it*'. S. Morning-after pill, 740-2007 (2007).
Constitutional Chamber of the SCJ of Costa Rica	— '*compromise formula that unites fundamental rights within a constitution that enshrines the division of powers and the principle of legitimacy and legality*'. S. 02771-2003 (2003).
SCJ of Venezuela	— '*exercise of power solely through legal norms with judicial review of legality from the Constitution*'. S. 1326, AA50-T-2009-0266 (2009).
CC of Ecuador	— '*Constitutional State as an evolution of the Rule of Law, which involves submission to the Constitution*'. S. 002-09-SAN-CC (2009).
CC of Colombia	— '*widespread compliance with legal norms together with the principle of legality, separation of powers and democracy*'. S. C-252 (2010).
SCJ of Paraguay	— '*Social Rule of Law as an evolution, which intervenes in the economic sphere and abandons legal abstentionism*'. S. AyS 10 of (2018).
CT of Chile	— '*Constitutional state as an evolution of the rule of law, which gives authentic legal power*'. S. Free Higher Education, Budget Law 2935 (2015).
SCJ of Belize	— '*right to the protection of the law. Obligation of the State to honor its international commitments*'. Maya Leaders Alliance v Attorney General Belize [2015] CCJ 15 (AJ).
SCJ of Uruguay	— '*government of laws and not of men with recognition of subjective rights*'. S. 576/2017.
SCJ of Guyana	— '*right to the protection of the law from abuses and arbitrary exercise of power*'. S. McEwan et al. v Attorney General Guyana [2018] CCJ 30 (AJ).
CC of Colombia	— '*principle of legality, guarantee of the rights of individuals, legal certainty, separation of powers and judicial resolution of conflicts*'. S. C-252 (2019).

It is not possible to derive a general rule of understanding of the RoL concept from the transcriptions of the cited judgments. But the sample in Table 3 serves to provide an idea of what is behind the 3.6 per cent overall regional average.

Regarding the connection with the doctrinal section (see Section II above), we observe that many of the subtopics addressed in the RoL notion are found in the examined Latin American constitutional judgments. Likewise, the interaction with European and US theories is noteworthy in terms of the key points of connection that have historically characterised the RoL notion and its contemporary understanding. On the other hand, the analysis of 3.6 per cent of the judgments confirms that, in Latin America over the last 20 years, the notion of the RoL has evolved towards the prevalence of the constitutional State (of law) in contrast to that of mere legality.

Since only three of the investigated judgments predate the 2000s, the referenced RoL notions correspond to a longitudinal view of the last 20 years. For those pre-2000 decisions, the references to the empire or primacy of the law are potent enough to allow the observance of a gradual submission to the Constitution in contemporary RoL notions. As for a question that traverses all notions, it is interesting to highlight the importance or emphasis of definitions on the need to control or rationalise power through not only its division but also through the need to protect the governed from a leader's abuses. It could be concluded that the RoL's aspect of constraining those that govern is something typical in Latin America, a region where hyper-presidentialism prevails. Finally, it is interesting to note the notion's expanded use to accentuate such aspects as the role of a passive State becoming that of an active State, which intervenes in the economy, honors international commitments and infuses real legal power into the idea of the RoL.

Figure 6 illustrates the RoL notion's proximity to, and interrelationship with, the other two elements of the triad (ie, the association with democracy or human rights) (see Section II). Regarding the methodology of measuring the associations among the triad elements, when interpreting the references to the RoL, we verified whether the concepts of democracy or human rights were also mentioned or developed in the sentences or paragraphs that referenced the RoL.

Figure 6 Is the concept of the RoL associated with democracy or human rights?

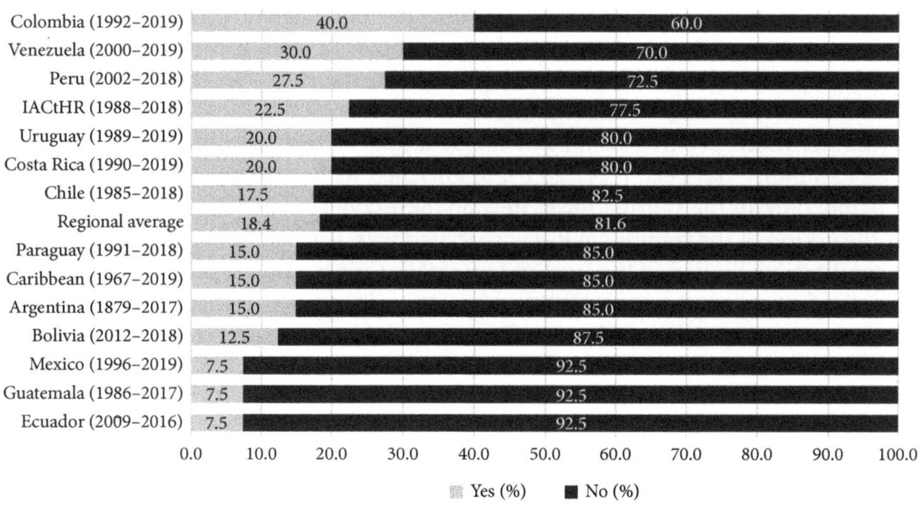

Figure 6 shows that, in most cases, the RoL was presented as an autonomous concept that would support 'thin' theories. Colombia is the country that is associated most with the triad (40 per cent), followed by Venezuela, Peru and the Inter-American Court (on the IACtHR, see Section IV). The overall percentage was 18.4 per cent. While in many international and regional treaties the triad is recurrent, in national constitutional jurisprudence, the RoL notion (still) has a more formal reading, as Nagle has confirmed.[84] Formality could explain the notion's sometimes negative connotation. However, in the previous Section, we found that among the few judgments that delved into the notion of the RoL, most did so in a human rights context. Therefore, the interpretation that CTs associate the RoL with situations involving the protection of fundamental rights, without the need to directly invoke the triad, is valid.

C. Analytical Summary of Data Analysis

Summarising the data, the simplest and perhaps negative reading that only 32.1 per cent of the analysed judgments expressly considered the concept of the RoL, and only 3.6 per cent explored it more deeply, is that the RoL notion in Latin America has not managed to reach the level of precision in its definition and the powerful role that it has in Europe. Its function is somewhat more rhetorical or decorative in Latin America. This can be attributed to various factors – for example, the crisis of indirect representation and, above all, the weak normative force. García Villegas spoke of a constitutionalism of expectations, whose risk is that the Constitution may lead to a devaluation of the RoL. The law is characterised by its enormous flexibility and is nothing more than a changing expression of the ruler's political will.[85]

As explained in Section III, it is a relic of the nineteenth and twentieth centuries that the Constitution's application is less focused on the materialisation of rights and serves more as a political instrument of the upper class. Esquirol speaks of 'failed law' and explains there is a negative image of the law not only because of citizens' distrust of the ruling class but also because of the 'importation' of neoliberal legal models from the global North, especially from the United States where the main goal has been to protect private property.[86] In Latin America's legal culture, the RoL – in the formal sense of legality – has historically lacked legitimacy.

Another more 'positive' reading of the data may be that the RoL concept, without losing its validity, has been replaced by, or enriched with, such elements as the 'social', the 'democratic' or the 'plurinational'. Beyond these conceptual additions, we have noted that the notion of the traditional RoL, associated with legality, has been regenerated by the constitutionalisation of the legal system rather than by mere legality.

In the first years after the adoption of a new political charter/major amendment, a CT needs to conceptualise different components of the new charter/amendment (which

[84] LE Nagle, *The Rule of Law in Latin America* (Routledge, 2010) 88 et seq.

[85] Garcia Villegas (n 42) 353–70.

[86] JE Esquivel, 'The turn to legal interpretation in Latin America' (2011) 26 *American University International Law Review* 1032, 1049.

possibly created it). This was part of the need to provide conceptualisations of a new understanding of the RoL notion. For example, given the replacement of an entire constitutional scheme in the jurisprudence of the Constitutional Court of Colombia (CCC) during the 1992–2000 period, judgments with high dogmatic or conceptual content covering multiple articles and postulates of the Constitution stand out. On what is the 'Social Rule of Law' in the 1991 Constitution, as opposed to the RoL of the 1886 Charter, the CCC clarified: 'The first thing that must be noted is that the term "social", now added to the classic formula of the Rule of Law, should not be understood as a simple rhetorical slogan that provides an elegant touch of philanthropy to the traditional idea of the Rule of Law'.[87]

In the spirit of the current constitutional framework, in which constitutionality has reinforced 'legality', all of a constitution's content is completely relevant. Hence, some CTs have a transformative intention to awaken the many provisions or dormant clauses from their 'constitutional slumber', which were historically considered to be 'programmatic', 'aspirational' or rhetorical crutches.[88] The fact that many constitutional judgments do not explicitly mention the RoL can be explained by the so-called jurisprudential reiteration that some courts practice.[89] This contradicts the widespread thesis that in Latin America the mention of the RoL is merely rhetorical and that the concept is irrelevant.

VI. Dialogue and Cooperation in the Construction of the Concept of the RoL

A. National Constitutional 'Dialogue'

Looking at aspects related to judicial dialogue to broaden the scope of the RoL concept, we reviewed the references of Latin American CTs against national jurisprudential precedents of their own jurisdictions (horizontal and vertical) and against precedents from other countries in the region. Regarding fidelity to national precedent, in only 10.8 per cent of the cases do the CTs reference a domestic precedent. The country that most often referenced such a decision was Colombia (30 per cent), followed by Venezuela (22.5 per cent) and then Costa Rica, Chile and Argentina (about 15 per cent each). In general, the reference to the RoL in Latin American constitutional jurisprudence is autonomous from the judgment and is not justified in a previous decision.

[87] CCC, Judgment T-406 (1992).

[88] R Gargarella and C Courtis, *The New Latin American Constitutionalism: Promises and Questions* (ECLAC, 2009).

[89] For example, in the jurisprudence of the CCC between 2010 and 2020, the concept was reviewed only when a case was relevant or when the Plenary Chamber wanted to unify/change the jurisprudence. Otherwise, concepts such as 'multiculturality' or the 'Social Rule of Law' are simply affirmed with or without conceptual reinforcement. MJ Cepeda Espinosa and DE Landau, *Colombian constitutional law: Leading cases* (Oxford University Press, 2017).

Along the same lines, a significant self-referential element was observed during the review of precedents. In the few cases that practiced this, horizontal self-reference to the so-called 'closing' or 'supreme' courts was the general rule. In no instance was the argumentation of the RoL's scope based in courts that were not seated in the capital city or were not courts of last resort. In other words, the elaboration of the RoL concept from the point of view of a constructive judicial dialogue between center and periphery, as with many other matters, hardly exists.[90] Among judges, the belief seemingly persists that jurisprudence considered lesser known or inferior is not cited.[91]

Regarding horizontal constitutional dialogue, in only seven cases of the 560 analysed judgments did the CTs proceed to cite other such courts in the Latin American region to broaden the concept of the RoL. Of these seven references, five were from the Caribbean Court of Justice pertaining to national cases in the Caribbean,[92] one was from the CT of Chile regarding a judgment of the CCC[93] and another was from the Supreme Court of Justice (SCJ) of Paraguay, which cited another judgment of the CCC.[94] By all accounts, the results were poor in terms of collective construction, at least insofar as the most direct expression in the form of direct reference was concerned.

B. Influence of Inter-American and European Jurisprudence

In addition, we identified those judgments of each country that expressly mentioned the RoL notion or developed the concept and concurrently referred to the Inter-American Human Rights System (IAHRS) and/or the IACtHR with the aim of measuring their/its (direct) impact on the RoL in Latin American constitutional jurisprudence.

Only 13 judgments of those analysed referred to the IAHRS, of which nine corresponded to IACtHR decisions.[95] The SCJ of Uruguay issued the remaining three: one[96] referred to OC-9/87 to reinforce the idea of due process, and in the other two, the same court extensively cited *Kimel v Argentina* and *Fermín Ramírez v Guatemala*, pointing out that the principles of legality and non-retroactivity are principles of the RoL.[97] The Plurinational Constitutional Court (PCC) of Bolivia cited to the same IACtHR affirmation,[98] although referring instead to the cases of *De La Cruz Flores v Peru* and *Vélez Loor v Panama*.

[90] P Acosta Alvarado, *Diálogo judicial y constitucionalismo multinivel, el caso interamericano* (Universidad Externado de Colombia, 2015) 32 et seq.

[91] G de Vergottini, 'El diálogo entre tribunales' in E Ferrer Mac-Gregor and A Herrera García (eds), *Diálogo jurisprudencial en derechos humanos entre Tribunales Constitucionales y Cortes Internacionales* (Inter-American Court of Human Rights, 2013). See at 498 against the practice of direct citations of the Hungarian to the German FCC but not vice versa.

[92] See *Nervais and Severin v The Queen* [2018] CCJ 19 (AJ); *Attorney General of Belize v Zuniga* [2014] CCJ 2 (AJ); *McEwan et al v Attorney General Guyana* [2018] CCJ 30 (AJ); *Christopher Ram v Attorney General, the Leader of the Opposition, Joseph Harmon and Guyana Elections Commission* [2019] CCJ 10 (AJ); *Toussaint v Attorney General of St. Vincent and the Grenadines* [2007].

[93] CT of Chile, *Case of Cascadas* 3236-2016 (2018).

[94] Case: AyS.191.

[95] The others refer to the American Declaration of the Rights and Duties of Man, the ACHR or the IADC.

[96] Judgment 1148/2019, SCJ of Uruguay, 8–9.

[97] SCJ of Uruguay, Judgments 102/2016, 19, 20, and 104/105, S.10.

[98] PCC of Bolivia, Judgment SCP 770/2012, 20.

On the other hand, the SCJ of the Argentine Nation cited twice (in two separate cases)[99] to the IACtHR[100] in relation to the effective judicial remedy serving as a basic pillar of the RoL. The CT of Peru, in two judgments,[101] cited the IACtHR case *García Asto and Ramírez Rojas v Peru*, which recognised the principles of separation of powers and legality as key elements of the RoL. Finally, the CCC referred to OC-8/87 in one of its decisions,[102] highlighting the inextricability of the RoL, the principle of legality and democratic institutions.

Regarding the SCJ of Uruguay's cases that cited the IACtHR more frequently and broadly, it is conceivable that this is related to the presence of Ricardo Pérez Manrique, who was a Minister of the Court from 2012 to 2020. In 2020, he was appointed as an IACtHR judge. Manrique had an affinity with the jurisprudence of the IACtHR; the SCJ of Uruguay's three rulings citing the IACtHR were issued when he served on its bench.

The same trend can be observed regarding explicit references to European constitutional decisions. Only one of the 11 IACtHR judgments that mentioned the RoL (see Table 2), *Furlan and family v Argentina*,[103] referred to a decision of the European Court of Human Rights in order to focus on the RoL – more specifically to explain the standards for the execution of sentences. With regard to the judgments of the national CTs, a Peruvian CT decision[104] and one from the SCJ of Uruguay[105] were identified that referred to the German Federal Constitutional Court (FCC) in RoL matters.

Uruguay is a particularly interesting case because it cites the FCC to explain why the principles of formal legal certainty in a sense of non-retroactivity and material justice can sometimes conflict. This 'train wreck' that can be created at times between 'thin' and 'thick' theories (see section 2), and which Latin American jurisprudence has yet to resolve, leaves the concept of the RoL somewhat diffuse. Finally, a ruling of the Chilean CT[106] was noted that cited a Spanish CT opinion, which reiterated that constitutional review is part of the RoL principle.

[99] Appeal of fact deduced by the State and the Government of Chile in the case of *Arancibia Clavel, Enrique Lautaro s/ qualified homicide and illicit association and others*, Case No 259, SCJ of the Nation, p 107; *Simón, Julio Héctor et al s/ unlawful deprivation of liberty, etc.*, Case No 17,768, SCJ of the Nation, 110.

[100] *Case of Castillo Páez v Peru* (Merits), Judgment Inter-American Court of Human Rights (3 November 1997) Series C No 34, paras 82 and 83 (English trans); *Case of Suárez Rosero v Ecuador* (Merits), Judgment Inter-American Court of Human Rights (12 November 1997) Series C No 35, para 65 (English trans); *Case of Paniagua Morales et al v Guatemala* (Merits), Judgment Inter-American Court of Human Rights (8 March 1998) Series C No 37, para 164 (English trans); *Case of Loayza Tamayo v Peru* (Reparations and Costs), Judgment Inter-American Court of Human Rights (27 November 1998) Series C No 42, para 169 (English trans).

[101] Judgment STC No 5854-2005-PA/TC, CT of Peru, p 14; Judgment STC No 00156-2012-PHC/TC, CT of Peru, p 6.

[102] CCC, Judgment C-252/10, 68.

[103] *Case of Furlan and family* (n 56), paras 210 and 211.

[104] CT of Peru, STC No 025-2005-AI / 00026-2005-AI, 2006, p 21, with reference to p 21: Judgment BVerfGE 92, 140 (p 151), *Case of 'Special Dismissal' (Sonderkündigung)*, Judgment (21 February 1995).

[105] SCJ of Uruguay, Judgment 680/2017, p 22: 'And the German FCC goes on to say: the postulate of legal certainty, inherent in the rule of law, requires that the citizen be able to foresee the possible interventions of the State against him and that he be able to behave accordingly. (…) To the RoL, however, belongs not only legal certainty, but also material justice (…). If legal certainty is opposed to justice, then it will be up to the legislator to decide in favor of one or the other'.

[106] CT of Chile (n 93) paras 56–57.

C. Analysis of Influences

Although a growing legal-cultural dialogue can be identified in the current globalised world[107] (including the inter-American sphere),[108] this trend cannot be affirmed in the analysed judgments. The percentages of explicit citation to foreign judgments are low. However, this does not necessarily indicate that CTs do not consult this jurisprudence or that European concepts do not have persuasive influence in Latin America.[109]

One explanation for the small percentages may be that foreign-judgment citation is practiced more in common law systems, whereas Latin American countries adhere more to the civil law tradition in which explicit citations are used less frequently. As Groppi has observed, the constitutional argumentation in civil law countries more often follows the logic of 'doing it but not admitting'[110] in which 'implicit references prevail, which are difficult to identify, with rare exceptions'.[111] The study's results suggest that this logic is sound.[112] Another explanation may be that those who are charged with the substantiation of judgments find it irrelevant to develop the notion of the RoL conceptually, leaving the dogmatic elaboration to the doctrine.

VII. Conclusions

About half of the 560 analysed judgments directly or indirectly pertained to the RoL (see Figure 1). The statistics also show that variations in the RoL notion as they relate to the concept's traditional content are high – for example, in terms of assimilation with the principle of legality or legal certainty (see Figures 2–5). This analysis aligns with the results of the conceptual part of this study (see Section II(C)), which also shows that there is no single definition of the RoL. Also, the review of the different conceptual 'layers' that the jurisprudence used when addressing the RoL demonstrates the notion's heterogeneity (see Figure 5 and Table 3).

If we compare the results of the empirical chapter with the theories of the RoL notion, the impacts of the elements of both 'thin' and 'thick' theories are evident in Latin America. For example, when the IACtHR has referred to the RoL category, it has done so mainly to reinforce central ideas related to the principle of legality, non-retroactivity and due process (elements of formal theories), and it has also referenced the triad repeatedly (tradition of substantive theories).

[107] T Groppi, '¿Bottom up globalization? El uso de precedentes extranjeros por parte de las cortes constitucionales' (2010) *Rivista di Diritti Comparati*, www.diritticomparati.it/bottom-up-globalization/; P Häberle, *Rechtsvergleichung im Kraftfeld des Verfassungsstaates* (Berlin, Duncker & Humboldt GmbH, 1992); B Ackerman, 'The Rise of World Constitutionalism' (1997) 83 *Virginia Law Review* 771–97.

[108] L García Jaramillo, 'Variaciones en torno a la interamericanización del derecho. A propósito del Ius Constitucionale Commune' (2016) 18 *Araucaria. Revista Iberoamericana de Filosofía, Política y Humanidades* 511, 512.

[109] Groppi (n 107).

[110] B Markesinis and J Fedtke, 'The judge as comparatist' (2005) 80 *Tulane Law Review* 11; B Markesinis and J Fedtke (coords), *Giudici e diritto straniero* (Il Mulino, 2009).

[111] Groppi (n 107). Groppi cites decisions of Italy's Court of Cassation and Germany's FCC, which are exceptions in this sense.

[112] C Dupré, *Importing law in post-communist transitions* (Hart Publishing, 2003).

In Europe, at both the national and EU levels, the violation of the RoL can have severe and concrete legal consequences, such as nonacceptance to, or expulsion from, the EU, which presupposes a clear definition of the notion (see Section II(C)). In Latin America, however, the use of the RoL serves more as an argumentative reinforcement whose absence does not affect the argument's substance and which has no practical effects beyond the symbolic. In Latin America's supranational organisations, as demonstrated by the Inter-American Commission, the predominant notion is (representative) democracy for which the RoL is nothing more than a prerequisite, one of several requirements or an expression of good intentions without a binding character (see Section IV).

At present, only the Honduran Constitution literally uses the expression 'rule of law'. The rest of the constitutions in force in Latin America have added new elements, such as 'social', 'democratic' or 'constitutional', or they simply do not mention the RoL at all (see Section III). As evidenced by the analysis of the few judgments in the sample that delve into the notion of the RoL (Table 3), the idea that the RoL acts in favour of the separation of powers to diminish hyper-presidential powers with abusive or *caudillismo* tendencies also seems to be something purely Latin American.

Additionally, it has been proven that, in most of the precedents included in the study, the 'activating' element of human rights led the courts to conceptualise the RoL. Above all, the IACtHR has tended to invoke the RoL in contexts of serious human rights violations committed during dictatorships or armed conflicts or in the ensuing stages of democratic restoration.

Finally, this study serves as a point of departure from which to explore the scope and influence of one of the pillars of contemporary public law in the region. It is plausible that Latin American constitutional case law began a broad dialogue with the academy and the supranational system's different actors to further clarify the understanding of the RoL notion and to be more explicit about the scope of Latin American 'contributions' – not only to the notion itself but also to the materialisation of the presumptions of the classic and contemporary RoL, with binding and not merely symbolic effects.

19

The Constitutional Dialogue between the Inter-American and the European Courts of Human Rights: Toward an Increasing Influence of the Inter-American Jurisprudence?

ANNA MARIA LECIS AND TANIA GROPPI

I. Introduction

A. The Judicial Dialogue between the IACtHR and the ECtHR

The interpretative methods and judicial reasoning of the regional courts of human rights have drawn the attention of doctrine for a long time. In the last ten years, authors have especially put their attention on the transjudicial communication among these courts,[1] and especially between the Interamerican Court of Human Rights (hereinafter also IACtHR) and the European Court of Human Rights (hereinafter also ECtHR) because of their seniority and their greater effectiveness. Several authors have thus recently highlighted the emergence of a certain tendency of the two Courts to look at each other and in some cases even to quote each other.[2] These studies often come to different conclusions on the existence of a real 'dialogue' between the two Courts.

This chapter will provide the results of an empirical research in order to verify some scholarly conclusions and to develop further reflections on the interactions between

[1] B Dickson and L Burgorgue-Larsen, *Les Trois Cours Régionales Des Droits de l'Homme in Context: La Justice Qui n'allait Pas de Soi* (Éditions A. Pedone, 2020); (2021) 21(2) *Human Rights Law Review* 499–502. T Groppi, 'El uso de Precedentes Extrasistémicos por el Tribunal Europeo de Derechos Humanos y por la Corte Africana de Derechos Humanos y de los Pueblos', communication présentée au *VIII Congrès international de droit processuel. El Precedente Judicial y el Ejercicio des Derecho ante las Altas Cortes* (Cartagena, Colombia, 29 August 2015).

[2] Within the enormous number of studies, the collective work dedicated to dialogue and convergences between the European and American systems stands out in particular: J García Roca, PA Fernández, P Santolaya and R Canosa (eds), *El Diálogo entre los Sistemas Europeo y Americano de Derechos Humanos* (Civitas, 2012).

these two regional courts. Therefore, its aim partially differs from the general aim of national chapters. Whilst, following the general criteria, the national reports consider references to foreign law (or 'extra-systemic' law) as one of the judicial arguments taken into account for the purpose of the study, here we will take this argument as a key indicator to select the relevant case law (as we will explain in the following paragraph) and to analyse the Inter-American Court judicial reasoning and its role as a receiver and as a contributor in a cross-fertilisation perspective, especially compared to its European homologue.

The methodology, fitting with the general criteria applied to the project, will combine quantitative and qualitative analysis of the case law of the two Courts containing reciprocal references.[3]

B. Methodological Premises

The empirical analysis is based on the decisions of each one of the two regional courts, selected on the basis of the presence of at least one citation of decisions issued from the other Court.[4] The present chapter used the criteria of the reference to foreign law, and a particular category of foreign law, as an indicator to select the decisions taken into account in the analysis.

Once the judgments containing references to the case law of the other regional Court had been identified, they were analysed from a quantitative and qualitative perspective, following some of the criteria considered in the National Reports of the project.

Through the quantitative analysis, the judgments containing at least one citation of the jurisprudence of the other Court have been considered, evidencing the relationship between the number of decisions that present at least one citation and the total number of judgments issued. The references will also be analysed in a diachronic perspective.

From a qualitative point of view, first we tried to evaluate the 'overall weight of the citation' on all the decisions selected by means of formal indicators, such as the 'place' of the decision in which it is situated (considerations of fact or right; majority vote or individual vote), the length of the citation and the inclusion of other extra-systemic references. Then, we will try to 'weight' the influence of the other regional Court, according to the criteria we point out in this paragraph.

[3] For further indications about the methodology, see below.

[4] The research was made on all the judgments issued by the two Courts in the exercise of their contentious function since 1987 (the year in which the Inter-American Court delivered its first judgment) until 31 December 2020. The research was carried out, as regards the jurisprudence of the ECtHR, on the databases in English and in French, using the keywords 'interamerican', 'inter-american' (due to the double spelling used to the term in question), 'interaméricaine', 'interam' and 'inter-am' (the latter, in consideration of the fact that citations in the notes are frequently abbreviated); with reference to the jurisprudence of the Inter-American Court, the investigation was carried out on each decision in English and Spanish, with the keywords 'European', 'European', 'Europea' and 'Eur'. A certain margin of error must be considered. We updated for the purpose and methodology of this project a previous research, based on the judgments issued until August 2017: see T Groppi and AM Lecis, 'El uso de precedentes extra sistémicos en el diálogo entre la Corte Interamericana y el Tribunal europeo de Derechos Humanos: una investigación empírica' (2018) 21 *IurisDictio* 29.

As a matter of fact, the citation of foreign case law can fulfil several functions, depending in particular on whether it is carried out in the 'cognitive' or in the 'decision-making' phase.[5] In the cognitive phase, extra-systemic jurisprudence can be cited to show knowledge of other systems, by illustrating the range of interpretative solutions adopted elsewhere, with a technique defined as the 'window-dressing approach'.[6] The citation of other extra-systemic references would thus be a useful indicator to evaluate that.

Within the decision-making phase, then, extra-systemic case law can be used to a different extent and with different purposes. First, it can form the basis of the decision[7] as a 'ratio decidendi argument'. This hypothesis rarely finds application, as it can expose courts to strong criticism. Outside this rare scenario, it can be used as a contribution to the interpretation and judicial reasoning, for example with the following purposes: to harmonise the interpretation of a concept with that given by other jurisdictions and thus avoid conflicts, to show the framework of the possible interpretative solutions who can be applied, to justify the interpretative solution adopted, especially when it is an evolving interpretation which departs from the text and the 'original intent' of its authors, or to strengthen the legitimacy of own precedents by citing case law that refers to them. Sometimes, though, the extra-systemic argument is cited only with a rhetorical or even deceptive purpose,[8] without being really taken into account in the reasoning.

In order to identify the purpose of the citation, we thus used also substantial indicators, such as the general topic and the specific topic, the harmonisation with international law requirements, the invocation of its own precedents, the invocation of a concept not present in the text of the Convention, the invocation of the *pro homine* principle and a general appreciation of the weight of the citation from a substantial perspective, evaluating the way the Court refers to the argument in its assessment and how it uses it in its judicial reasoning.

Before presenting the results of the analysis, the institutional, historical and social context in which the two Courts operate must be introduced.

II. Juridical and Cultural Context: Similarities and Differences between the Two Courts

A certain inclination to look at the jurisprudence of other legal systems is inherent in the nature of Human Rights regional courts, which are called upon to relate to the different

[5] See especially T Groppi and MC Ponthoreau, 'Introduction: The Methodology of the Research: How to Assess the Reality of Transjudicial Communication?' in T Groppi and M-C Ponthoreau (eds), *The Use of Foreign Precedents by Constitutional Judges*, 1st edn (Hart Publishing, 2013) 1–10; O Pfersmann, 'Le sophisme onomastique: changer au lieu de connaître. L'interprétation de la constitution', in F Mélin-Soucramanien, (eds), *L'interprétation constitutionnelle* (Dalloz, Paris, 2005) 146; HH Koh, 'International Law as Part of Our Law' (2004) 98 *Am. J. Int'l Law* 43.

[6] L Garlicki, 'Conferencia introductoria: Universalism v. Regionalism? The Role of The Supranational Judicial Dialog' in J García Roca, PA Fernández, P Santolaya and R Canosa (eds), *El Diálogo entre los Sistemas Europeo y Americano de derechos Humanos* (Civitas, 2012) 27.

[7] This is what G de Vergottini calls the 'comparative judgment', opposed to the 'comparative argument' which only fulfil a rhetoric purpose: G de Vergottini, *Oltre il dialogo tra Corti*, (Il Mulino, 2010).

[8] M Bencze and G Yein Ng, *How to Measure the Quality of Judicial Reasoning* (Springer, 2018).

systems of the Member States and must deal with varied legal and cultural contexts. Therefore, to some extent, they are by nature comparatist.[9] Furthermore, the composition of these courts, made up of jurists from different countries and with different legal cultures, can have a significant impact on the citation of extra-systemic decisions.

However, despite these common features, the two Courts present significant differences which may have influenced their interpretative techniques, eventually leading them to different approaches towards extra-systemic citations.

First, the two systems diverge significantly as regards the procedural rules and the workload of the respective Courts. In the evolution of the ECHR system, Protocol no. 11 marked a real turning point, as it imposed the jurisdiction of the Court on all States parties and eliminated the filter by the Commission introducing the possibility of an individual complaint to the Court. This reform, together with the geographical enlargement to new States parties, has led to a multiplication of appeals and, thus, to the resulting overload of work for the Court. In the American system, instead, the filter by the Commission still exists: individual complaints cannot be addressed directly to the Court but they must pass through the scrutiny of the Commission, which eventually refers to the Court. Consequently, the workload of the two courts is very different. As regards the subject of this study, the lower workload to which the IACtHR is burdened implies that it may be able to devote greater attention to each individual case, thus being able to develop extensive and in-depth comparative studies and arguments.[10]

Regarding the composition of the Courts, then, some differences must be underlined. The European Court is made up of 47 judges sitting on a permanent basis. They are made up of one from each Member State, who therefore come from very different legal and cultural backgrounds. Conversely, the Inter-American Court is not a permanently seated jurisdiction but sits in ordinary and extraordinary sessions several weeks per year. It is composed of only seven judges from OAS Member States (who have ratified the Convention but not necessarily who have accepted the jurisdiction of the Court), who, with the exception of a few Anglo-Saxon jurists, usually come from Latin American legal and cultural contexts. Moreover, regarding the background of the judges of the Interamerican jurisdiction, the majority is nowadays represented by scholars and constitutional judges.[11] This circumstance has consequences for the subject of this study, if we consider the propensity of many Latin American jurisdictions to cite extra-systemic sources, including foreign precedents, as the national reports show.[12]

The nature of the recipients to whom they are addressed must also be taken into account. Since the motivation of judicial decisions has as its main objective making

[9] de Vergottini (n 7) 11; G de Vergottini, 'Tribunales constitucionales y comparación en la extensión de las declaraciones de derechos', in *La ciencia del derecho procesal constitucional. Estudio en homenaje a Héctor Fix-Zamudio*, Volume II (UNAM, 2008) 637, 641.

[10] See also González Domínguez and Ortega (ch 12) in this volume.

[11] ibid.

[12] See MJ Garcia-Mansilla, 'La Corte Suprema de los Estados Unidos y su debil influencia en Iberoamerica' in P Manili (ed), *Tratado de derecho procesal constitucional*, III (La Ley, 2010) 109; VA da Silva, 'Integração e Diálogo Constitucional na América do Sul' in A von Bogdandy, F Piovesan and M Morales Antoniazzi (eds), *Estudos Avançados de Direitos Humanos – Democracia e Integração Jurídica: Emergência de um novo Direito Público* (Campus Elsevier, 2013) 530; M Neves, 'Breves Considerações com Especial Referência à Experiênica Latino-Americana' in F Alves Correia, JEM Machado and JC Loureiro (eds), *Estudos em Homenagem ao Prof. Doutor José Joaquim Gomes Canotilho*, vol 3 (Coimbra Editora, 2012) 615–52.

them persuasive and accepted in the eyes of their recipients, the selection of arguments made by the courts is strongly influenced by the perception they have of the sensitivity and preferences of their target audience, in terms of legal culture and geopolitical preferences.[13]

Unlike the European regional human rights system, the Inter-American regional system was born in a markedly authoritarian environment characterised by violations of core rights by the Member States. Unlike the European system, which emerges in parallel with the European integration process and has served as a relevant instrument to strengthen this integration process, in the Inter-American case there was only an embryonic movement for regional integration.[14]

All these factors have an influence on the interpretative techniques and the judicial reasoning of the two Courts and will thus be considered in the qualitative analysis.

III. The Quantitative Analysis

The data on the number of reciprocal citations, in relation to the number of decisions issued in the contentious venue, show an impressive difference between the two Courts.

Between 1987 and 2020 (until 31 December), the Inter-American Court issued 416 judgments,[15] 56 per cent of which (233) contain at least one citation of the jurisprudence of the ECtHR or its Commission. In 15 of those cases, references to the European jurisprudence are made only in a separate opinion. The ECtHR, in the same period, issued 23.286 decisions: just 85 of them (which is equivalent to 0.36 per cent of the total) refer to the Inter-American Court or Commission case law. In addition, in 22 of those cases, the references to the Inter-American jurisprudence can be found only in a separate opinion.

The diachronic perspective clearly shows that for many years the relationship between the two Courts has been articulated around the influence exerted by the ECtHR on its Inter-American counterpart. In fact, the Inter-American Court started from the beginning of its activity to cite European jurisprudence, first in its advisory opinions[16] and then also in its judgments. Such a trend does not seem to decrease over time, as shown either in the number of decisions that contain at least one reference, or even in the

[13] See T Groppi and MC Ponthoreau, 'The Use of Foreign Precedents by Constitutional Judges: A Limited Practice, An Uncertain Future' in T Groppi and MC Ponthoreau (eds), *The Use of Foreign Precedents by Constitutional Judge* (Hart Publishing, 2013) 413.

[14] F Piovesan, 'Ius constitutionale commune latino-americano em Direitos Humanos e o Sistema Interamericano: perspectivas e desafios' (2017) 8 *Revista Direito e Práxis* 1356.

[15] We are counting here the totality of judgments made by the Court, but some of these judgments are 'clarifications' of the judgment on the merits, reparations, and costs, based on Art 67 of the American Convention, where the Court does not develop a legal analysis in a strict sense. If we consider only the decisions on merits, reparations and costs, the percentage of citations is even higher.

[16] Empirical research on advisory opinions carried out in 2008 has shown that this practice was maintained over time and that, of the 19 advisory opinions issued up to the date of the study in question, 8 contained citations of the jurisprudence of the ECtHR. In an opinion on the rights of the child, issued in 2002, it was possible to identify up to 25 judgments of the ECHR. See A Garro, 'La influencia de Tribunal Europeo de Derechos Humanos en el ejercicio de la función consultiva de la Corte Interamericana de Derechos Humanos' (2009) *Cuestiones constitucionales* 191.

percentage, read diachronically. This suggests that the attention of the Inter-American Court towards European jurisprudence does not represent a contingent phenomenon, destined to be reversed once the referring Court itself obtains a greater degree of acceptance and influence,[17] but rather a structural element, also confirmed by the analysis of the 40 landmark cases in the chapter dedicated to the IACtHR in this book.[18]

Conversely, the analysis of the jurisprudence of the ECtHR shows that the number of citations of the Inter-American Court's case law is very small and, compared to the percentage of the total number of decisions, almost irrelevant. In addition, most of the references happen on the facts of the decisions, in which the Court quotes parties' opinions or reviews the international and comparative law considered relevant to the case. Nonetheless, during the last 20 years, the European Court also begins to make sporadic references to the jurisprudence of the IACtHR in the decision-making part of its own motivations.[19]

A first explanation of the phenomenon is based on the entry into force of Protocol no. 11 and the consequent increase in the total amount of decisions, which implies a greater probability of recourse to jurisprudential citations. Indeed, in accordance with this hypothesis, the percentage shows that while the absolute number of decisions containing citations increases, the percentage decreases.

Nonetheless, as we will see, the qualitative analysis of the decisions brings another explanation, showing the increasing interest of the European Court in the Inter-American Court's case law. As a matter of fact, during those years, the ECtHR had to hear issues concerning gross violations of rights much more frequently, as a consequence of the Balkan wars in the 1990s and of the increasing degradation of human rights protection in countries such as Turkey and Russia. On those matters, the Inter-American jurisprudence was already richer and more advanced. Therefore, the ECtHR had new reasons to be interested in the activity of the newest IACtHR.[20]

[17] Such a trend has been observed among national Courts, with the newest Court citing the case law of more ancient and influential Courts as long as they do not have a substantial burden of their own precedents, and then decreasing the number of citations thereafter: See Groppi and Ponthoreau (n 5); MC Ponthoreau, 'Le recours à l'argument de droit comparé par le juge constitutionnel. Quelques problèmes théoriques et techniques' in F Mélin-Soucramanien (ed), *L'interprétation constitutionnelle* (Dalloz, 2005) 168.

[18] See González Domínguez and Ortega (ch 12) in this volume.

[19] The decisions of the ECtHR are normally divided into three parts, to which can be added the separate opinions of each judge. Different parts and sections are numbered and have a title. Also, each one of the paragraphs is numbered. In the first part ('The facts') the Court reports on the development of the facts, including the trial before national judges, the relevant national law and practice, and the interventions of the parties and third parties (amici curiae). In this part, the Court often includes a section presenting the relevant international, European, and comparative law, including normative references, jurisprudence and soft law. The second part ('The Law') contains the judicial reasoning with the actual 'ratio decidendi' for the decision: in this part, the Court examines the reasons for appeal. Usually, the Court lists each specific ground of appeal, summarising the positions of the appellant, the national government and the third parties, followed by the considerations of the Court. The latter regularly begin with a reconstruction of its relevant previous jurisprudence, in order to later apply it to the case. Finally, the third part contains the device of the sentence, with an indication of the measures that the State must eventually take, in case of violation of the Convention.

[20] M Philip-Gay, 'La poursuite des auteurs de graves violations de droits de l'homme: une influence de la jurisprudence interaméricaine sur le système européen ?' in E Lambert Abdelgawad and K Martin-Chenut (eds), *Réparer les violations graves et massives des droits de l'homme: la Cour interaméricaine, pionnière et modèle?* (Société de Législation Comparée, 2010) 263 ff.

Furthermore, most recently, some references appeared beyond gross violations matters, suggesting an increasing influence of the IACtHR in other fields. Some observations based on the qualitative analysis results will allow us to better understand these conclusions.

IV. The Qualitative Analysis

A. Interpretative Methods Allowing the Reference to Extra-Systemic Case Law

Analysing the interpretative methods of the two Courts may help to explain the big difference in the number of citations revealed through the quantitative analysis.

As a starting point, we should consider that there are some common features. Invested in the function of interpreting and applying human rights treaties, the two Courts gave priority to the purpose of protecting individuals over their nature as an interstate agreement. This resulted in the adoption and development of specific interpretative methods which, despite the differences between the two Courts that we will outline, present a common denominator: the interpretation most favourable to the human person.

Human rights treaties, in fact, are not ordinary multilateral treaties, sources of reciprocal obligations between States, but are conventions which confer rights and guarantees on individuals vis-à-vis States Parties. The affirmation of the international subjectivity of the human person has thus 'humanised' the interpretation of treaty provisions,[21] until then largely submitted to the principle of the will of the State. In application of the teleological criterion, the two Courts have thus developed the principle of the *pro homine* interpretation. The analysis of the 40 landmarks cases of the Interamerican Court of Human Rights also confirms this attitude, showing that the Court has given 'secondary interpretative status to the intention of the Parties to the treaty or to textual and historical methods in favour of a teleological interpretation supported by the values that the Inter-American System seeks to support' and that 'ordinary meaning of words' and 'historical context', even when invoked, are usually not decisive.[22] If this interpretative principle is somehow rooted in the Vienna Convention on the Law of the Treaties,[23] concerning the American system, it also finds its basis in the American Convention itself. Article 29 of the American Convention sets out some 'standards of interpretation' clearly inspired by the principle of *pro homine*. The Inter-American Court drew from

[21] On the 'humanisation' of International law, the essential reference is the work of Cançado-Trindade. Within its academic work, see AA Cançado Trindade, *International Law for Humankind: Towards a New Jus Gentium* (Martinus Nijhoff Publishers, 2010). Within its jurisdictional work, see especially his separate opinion in the IACtHR, OC-18/03, n° A 18, para 88.

[22] See González Domínguez and Ortega (ch 12) in this volume.

[23] Based on the teleological criterion, set out in Art 31 of the Vienna Convention, prescribing in its first paragraph that a treaty must be interpreted 'in the light of its object and purpose': see L Calfish and AA Cançado Trindade, 'Les Conventions Américaine et Européenne des Droits de l'Homme et le Droit International Général' (2004) 108 *Revue Générale de Droit International Public* 5.

this a general rule according to which 'when interpreting the Convention, it is always necessary to choose the alternative that is most favourable to the protection of the rights enshrined in said treaty, based on the principle of the rule most favourable to the human being'.[24]

Despite the fact that a provision of the same content is not included in the European Convention, the ECtHR stated very early on that 'the object and purpose of the Convention as an instrument for the protection of individual human beings require that its provisions be interpreted and applied so as to make its safeguards practical and effective'.[25] Therefore, in the European jurisprudence, the criterion of 'useful effect' ('*effet utile*') is applied so as to guarantee the effectiveness of the provisions of the treaty in the name of the guarantee of human rights.

The guiding principle of the effectiveness of the protection has thus made it possible to both Courts to broaden the content and the scope of the rights entrenched in their Conventions, according to an interpretation that has increasingly become detached from the text.

By following this principle, the two Courts have made evolutionary interpretation an essential method in the application of the respective conventions. This method constitutes in fact the technique which characterises the two Courts examined in the panorama of the international courts,[26] by bringing them closer to the national judges who are supposed to interpret the catalogues of the rights included in the national constitutions.

The ECtHR constantly recalls, since *Tyrer v United Kingdom*, that 'the Convention is a living instrument which [...] must be interpreted in the light of present-day conditions'.[27] And it is precisely by referring to this judgment of its European counterpart that the IACtHR, in its opinion on the right to information on consular assistance, applies the same method.[28]

We should also consider that taking into account 'the context' in the interpretative reasoning, as stated in Article 31 of the Vienna Convention, implies a 'normative openness',[29] by which the courts may have recourse to a multitude of sources, binding or not, international or national, infra-systemic or extra- systemic.[30] In addition, the two regional Courts broadened the scope of this provision: to determine the useful context for interpreting the terms of the Convention, they also use texts and case law not directly

[24] IACtHR, *Mapiripán Massacre v Colombia*, 2005, para 106. See also OC-5/85, para 46.

[25] ECtHR, *Soering v UK*, 7 July 1989, para 87. See J Gerards, 'The European Court of Human Rights' in A Jakab, A Dyevre and G Itzcovich, *Comparative Constitutional Reasoning* (Cambridge University Press, 2017) 237 ff., spec. 256.

[26] See J Ferrero, *L'interprétation évolutive des conventions internationales de protection des droits de l'homme : contribution à l'étude de la fonction interprétative du juge international* (Pedone, 2019).

[27] ECtHR, *Tyrer v Roayume-Uni*, n° 5856/72, 25-4-1978, para 31. See also *Christine Goodwin v UK*, GC, para 75; C Prebensen, 'Evolutive Interpretation of the European Convention on Human Rights', in P Mahoney et al (eds), *Protecting Human Rights: The European Perspective. Studies in Memory of Rolv Ryssdal* (Carl Heymanns Verlag KG, 2000) 1123.

[28] IACtHR, OC-16/99, 1er/10/1999, Série A n° 16, para 114.

[29] L Burgorgue-Larsen, 'Les méthodes d'interprétation de la Cour interaméricaine des droits de l'homme' (2014) 25 *Revue Trimestrielle des Droits de l'homme* 46.

[30] See D French, 'Treaty interpretation and the incorporation of extraneous legal rules' (2006) 55 *International and Comparative Law Quarterly* 281.

applicable to State parties. This approach can lead to an interpretation which differs from the original intent of the States. The 'context' is reconstructed by the two Courts by taking into account other non-binding references for the parties, which would show the evolution 'in the light of the general principles of international law, the law of treaties and international case law',[31] which represents the 'international *corpus juris*' according to the terminology used by the Inter-American Court.[32]

Ultimately, whether it is for applying the principle of *pro homine* or the *utile effect* or an evolutive interpretation, the flexibility of the criteria of interpretation used by the two Courts allows them to refer to several sources other than their respective conventions in their judicial reasoning.

Notwithstanding those common features, the two Courts differ in many aspects, beginning from the different approaches to the 'useful effect' doctrine. Actually, the ECtHR usually refrains from directly providing for abstract, wide and deeply morally reasoned interpretations and strongly prefers case-based reasoning, elaborating general criteria from its own precedents, according to an 'incremental approach'.[33]

However, the most important difference, for the scope of this study, is that, as far as the evolutive interpretation is concerned, the ECtHR uses a special interpretative technique, which does not exist in the Interamerican case law: the 'common ground' or 'consensus' interpretation. This method implies that the Court only accepts a novel interpretation of the Convention if there is a sufficiently clear European consensus supporting such an interpretation.[34] This approach, as we will point out later, implies that the ECtHR is much more interested in the case law of the Courts which are part of the system, whereas the IACtHR is much more open to extra-systemic sources, including the case law. In the end, we cannot ignore the impact of the factual context on the interpretative techniques, as the democratic fragility of the Latin America and Caribbean region makes the intra-systemic references useless, as far as democracy and human rights protection are concerned.

B. Functions of the Citations in the Judicial Reasoning of the Two Courts

Studies on the circulation of case law in international law suggest that, within the international courts, the main function fulfilled by the recourse to the decisions of other

[31] *Mamaktulov and Others v Turkey*, paras 121–23.

[32] On the notion of 'international *corpus juris*', see OC-16/99, para 115. Moreover, the greater inclination of the Inter-American Court to cite the extra-systemic references derived also from the breadth of its consultative competence. According to the large interpretation that it retains of this competence, indeed, the Court has jurisdiction to interpret any treaty to which the States of the Organization of American States are parties: see Art 64 ACHR and Art 71 of the Procedural rules of the IACtHR. On the citation of extra-systemic sources in the consultative competence, which is not covered by this study, see L Hennebel, 'Les références croisées entre les juridictions internationales des droits de l'homme' in J Allard, B Frydman and L Hennebel (eds), *Le dialogue des juges: Colloque Les Cahiers de l'Institut d'études sur la justice* (Bruylant, 2007) 31.

[33] Gerards (n 25) 258.

[34] On the evolutive interpretation of the ECtHR, pointing out the role played by the 'consensus', see Gerards (n 25) 255–56.

international bodies is the harmonisation in the interpretation of a concept to avoid conflicts among courts and the fragmentation of the international law.[35]

The case law of the two Courts does not completely escape this observation: as we showed in a previous study,[36] the harmonising function seems to have effectively guided the interpretation, in light of the international case law of other judicial bodies, regarding the qualification of acts of torture,[37] slavery,[38] enforced disappearances,[39] as well as on several procedural guarantees such as the right to a fair trial[40] or the independence of the judiciary.[41] However, the harmonising aim does not seem to be the main function of these citations.

In the jurisprudence of the two regional Courts, citations turn out to be used prevalently at the initial moment of the interpretive activity, that is, in the 'cognitive phase' of the interpretation, to guide it (in this case, it begins with a sort of list of decisions from other jurisdictions, member and non-member countries, to show the various possible interpretative options), or they are used based on a 'comforting comparison' or 'evidence', by means of which it is intended to show how a decision that the Court is preparing to adopt on the basis of the Convention has also been taken up by other international or national courts.[42]

First, both Courts have used citations from the other court's jurisprudence to confirm the interpretation adopted by autonomous interpretative methods. This is what happened, first of all, in the development of the interpretive techniques themselves. It may be recalled, as an example, the doctrine of useful effect, taken up in the *Ivcher-Bronstein v Peru*, 24 September 1999; or that of the evolutionary interpretation of the Convention, cited in *Mapiripán Massacre v Colombia*, 15 September 2005. On

[35] PM Dupuy, 'The Danger of Fragmentation or Unification of the international Legal System and the International Court of Justice' (1999) 31 *New York University Journal of International Law and Politics* 791; French (n 30) 281.

[36] AM Lecis, 'Les référents jurisprudentiels extra-systémiques dans la jurisprudence de la Cour EDH et de la Cour IDH: le recours aux 'précédents' d'autres organes internationaux au service d'un corpus juris des droits de l'homme ?' (2018) 2 *Revue du droit public et de la science politique en France et à l'étranger* 499.

[37] IACtHR, *Caesar v Trinidad and Tobago*, 11-03-2005, n° C 123; IACtHR, *González and Others ('Cotton Field') v Mexico*, 16-11-2009, n° C 205.

[38] ECtHR, *Rantsev v Cyprus and Russia*, paras 273–74; IACtHR, *Trabajadores de La Hacienda Brasil Verde v Brazil*, 20-10-2016, n° C 318.

[39] IACtHR, *Anzualdo-Castro v Peru*, 22-09-2009, n° C 202; *Chitay Nech and Others v Guatemala*, 25-05-2010, n° C 212; *Ibsen Cárdenas and Ibsen-Peña v Bolivia*, 1-09-2010, n° C 217; in *Gudiel Álvarez and Others ('Diario Militar') v Guatemala*, 20-11-2012, n° C 253, the IACtHR finally underlined that this qualification became *jus cogens*.

[40] IACtHR *Suárez-Rosero v Ecuador*, 12-11-1997; *Villagrán-Morales and Others v Guatemala* 19-11-1999, n° C 63; *Constitutional Court v Peru*, 31-01-2001; *Lori Berenson Mejía v Peru*, 25-11-2004, n° C 119; *Fermín Ramírez v. Guatemala*, 20-06-2005, n° C 126; *Palamara Iribarne v. Chili*, 22-11-2005, n° C 135; *Pueblo Bello Massacre v Colombia*, 31-01-2006, n° C 140; *López Mendoza v Venezuela*, 1-09-2011, n° C 233; *Norín Catrimán and autres v Chile*, 29-05-2014, n° C 279.

[41] ECtHR, G.C., *Baka v Hungary*, 23-06-2016, n° 20261/12; ECtHR, *Allanazarova v Russia*, 14-02-2017, n° 46721/15.

[42] This 'confrontational' use of the citation of the precedents of the other Court can be defined as a form of judicial communication based on 'empathy', where resorting to the extra-systemic precedent does not represent a mere example of comparative law, but an interpretive reference endowed with great persuasive effectiveness thanks to the conviction that there is a common ground between the system in which the decision has been made and the system in which it is cited.

the contrary, the Inter-American Court has not adopted the doctrine of the margin of appreciation (which it has rejected, lately, in *Atala Riffo and daughters v Chile*, 24 February 2012, paras 34–35 and in *Artavia Murillo et al. v Costa Rica*, 28 November 2012, para 316), although it admits a certain level of state discretion with regard to the discipline of the active and passive electorate, 'in light of the evolution of the country concerned'.[43]

Second, some of these functions have characterised the case law of one of the Courts more than the other Court, in accordance with the tradition of judicial reasoning of each one.

Through the citations of the other Court's case law, the Inter-American Court seeks in particular the most protective interpretations of human rights, or even the most daring, according to a 'cherry picking' method inspired by the principle of *pro homine* interpretation.[44] This attitude seems to be a common feature of Latin American jurisdictions, as national reports show. The style of the citations is very varied. Citations are sometimes long and accurate, with the reproduction of entire paragraphs: they are thus used by the Court as real legal arguments to build the interpretation of a concept or even to solve the case. Sometimes, however, they are short, limited to the indication of the case law reference, in the text or at the bottom of the page, without the illustration of the legal question dealt with: they are then used to confirm the chosen solution and show the existing consensus around it.

References to the European Court case law are also often used by the Inter-American Court to reinforce the legitimacy of its own precedents. For instance, concerning the qualification of enforced disappearances, when the qualification that the Court had previously given was adopted by other international jurisdictions, it cited this case law to show that this qualification was subjected to international consensus.[45] Similarly, concerning amnesty laws, when the prohibition of laws that would prevent victims and families of victims from having justice was developed in the case law of the European Court as well as of several international bodies, the Interamerican Court cited these case laws alongside its own precedents to show that 'the universal trend has consolidated'.[46] Whilst the IACtHR mostly refers to international and extra-systemic sources rather than to the case law of domestic jurisdictions to interpret human rights according to a universalist interpretative approach,[47] the European Court, instead, rarely refers to the

[43] *Castañeda Gutman v Mexico*, 6 August 2008, para 165. See AA Cançado-Trindade, 'Le développement du Droit international des droits de l'homme à travers l'activité et la jurisprudence des Cours européenne et interaméricaine des droits de l'homme' (2004) 16 *Revue universelle des droits de l'homme* 177; see also MA Benavides Casals, 'El consenso y el margine de apreciación en la protecciòn de los derechos humanos' (2009) 15 *Ius et Praxis* 295.

[44] See Hennebel (n 32) 31. This technique has also been qualified 'opportunistic nomadism': see S Turgis, *Les interactions entre les normes internationales relatives aux droits de la personne* (Pedone, 2012) 443.

[45] *Anzualdo Castro v Peru*, 22-09-2009, n° C 202; *Chitay Nech et al v Guatemala*, 25-05-2010, n° C 212; *Ibsen Cárdenas and Ibsen-Peña v Bolivia*, 1-09-2010, n° C 217; *Contreras et al v El Salvador*, 31-08-2011, n° C 232; *González Medina and Family v Dominican Republic*, 27-02-2012, n° C 240; *Gudiel Álvarez et al ('Diario Militar') v Guatemala*, 20-11-2012, n° C 253; *García and Family v Guatemala*, 29-11-2012, n° C 258; *Gudiel Álvarez et al ('Diario Militar') v Guatemala*, 19-08-2013, n° C 262; *Osorio Rivera and Family v Peru*, 26-11-2013, n° C 274.

[46] IACtHR, *Gelman v Uruguay*, 24-02-2011, n° C 221.

[47] See also the IACtHR Report, 14 ff, showing that international sources are cited in 38 out of 40 decisions. However, the report also seems to show an increasing number of citations of domestic courts since 2008. On the lack of a 'looking down approach', see the remarks of G Ferrari, cit, 24 ff.

case law of courts outside Europe in the core of its reasoning. Most of the time, to determine the context and guide the interpretation of a provision, the Court of Strasbourg prefers to draw inspiration from the laws and jurisprudences of the States parties, using an 'infra-systemic comparison' more in line with its regionalist approach,[48] also as a consequence of the important role played by the 'consensus' interpretation, which is based on Member States legal orders. Professor and former judge of the ECtHR Lech Garlicki thus observed that, in the case law of the ECtHR, the 'looking down' perspective – towards the national legal traditions of the States Parties – prevails over the 'looking up' perspective – oriented towards the international dimension of rights protection.[49]

Unlike what has been observed in the case law of the Inter-American Court, we do not find the tendency to use extra-systemic references to reinforce the legitimacy of its own case law. The ECtHR, in fact, has built this legitimacy on the respect of its own precedents[50] to which it systematically refers and whose acceptance is based on the respect for the legal traditions of the States Parties.[51]

Nonetheless, the qualitative analysis showed that, even if the ECtHR refers to the IACtHR case law very rarely, when it does it, it ascribes value to these citations. Citations of the Interamerican Court case law are always long and detailed, often with the transcription of entire paragraphs of the cited decision and with an accurate contextualisation. In not less than 25 judgments, those citations are used in the decision-making phase, in different fields and with different functions, as the qualitative diachronic analysis will show.

V. An Evolving Transjudicial Communication

A. The First Phase: A One-Direction Influence

In the first phase, lasting until the late 1990s, we assisted in a one-direction citation of the European jurisprudence in the Inter-American Court case law. At the beginning of its activity, the Inter-American Court cited almost systematically the case law of the ECtHR which, as the prototype of regional courts of human rights, constituted a model for its American younger sister. It is interesting to notice that, during the same period, the Inter-American Court also cited the jurisprudence of the ICJ with almost the same frequency. From the quantitative and qualitative analysis of the citations during the first

[48] Professor Paolo G Carozza uses the expression 'interstate comparison', noting that this is not a real recourse to legal comparison: PG Carozza, 'Uses and Misuses of Comparative Law in International Human Rights: Some Reflections on the Jurisprudence of the European Court of Human Rights' (1998) 73 *Notre Dame Review* 1217, 1218.

[49] Garlicki (n 6) 36.

[50] Even if their respect is not mandatory, because the Court is not bound by a stare decisis rule: see D Szymczak, 'La manipulation par la Cour européenne des droits de l'homme de ses propres précédents' in F Houcquerbie and MC Ponthoreau (eds), *La motivation des décisions des cours suprêmes et des cours constitutionnelles* (Bruylant, 2012) 61; G Guillaume, 'The Use of Precedents by International Judges and Arbitrators' (2011) 2 *Journal of International Dispute Settlement* 5.

[51] Y Lupu and E Voeten, 'The Role of Precedent at the European Court of Human Rights: A Network Analysis of Case Citations' (2010), Paper 12. opensiuc.lib.siu.edu/pnconfs_2010/12.

years, we can infer that it cited the case law of the ICJ and the ECtHR in order to assert its legitimacy as an international court and as a human rights court, before building its own heritage of precedents.

As we outlined above, though, the citation of the ECtHR jurisprudence did not decrease in a diachronic perspective. Conversely, the citation of the ICJ did, as other studies showed.[52] We can thus infer that, from the moment when it could count on a considerable number of its own precedents, the Inter-American Court didn't feel the need to turn to extra-systemic case law to reaffirm classic principles of international law as often. The citations of the case law of the ICJ then decreased drastically. On the other hand, as it developed its interpretative methods dedicated to broadening the scope of the guarantees provided by the ACHR, the IACtHR had every interest in seeking extra-systemic references which would have been useful in its approach. It finds them in the judgments and opinions of bodies engaged in the monitoring of concrete human rights violations. It then continues to cite the case law of the ECtHR and, alongside it, the decisions and observations of the Human Rights Committee as well as other judicial and quasi-judicial bodies guaranteeing treaties signed within the framework of the United Nations.[53]

B. The second Phase: The Beginning of Mutual References in Gross Violations Matters

From the late 1990s and the early 2000s, then, a certain reciprocity of citations could be observed in matters such as due process, and the definition of inhuman and degrading treatment, especially with references to cases on forced disappearances and amnesty laws.

Concerning due process, the Inter-American Court cited at first the European jurisprudence.[54] However, the Inter-American Court did not remain on the threshold established by its European counterpart but continued to develop a broader interpretation of procedural guarantees.[55] Therefore, the European Court has then cited this

[52] Lecis (n 36).

[53] Even if the citations of the decisions of these bodies were not the subject of our empirical research, it is useful to observe that during this period the citations of the case law of other judicial and quasi-judicial bodies guaranteeing treaties signed within the framework of the United Nations also became very frequent: several dozens of decisions also cite the jurisprudence and quasi-jurisprudence of the Committee on Economic, Social and Cultural Rights, the Committee for the Elimination of Racial Discrimination, the Committee for the Elimination of Discrimination against Women, Committee against Torture, Committee on the Rights of the Child, Committee on the Rights of Persons with Disabilities: See Lecis (n 36).

[54] See especially *Suárez-Rosero v Ecuador*, 12/11/1997; *Villagrán-Morales and Others v Guatemala* ('Niños de la Calle'), 19/11/1999; *Corte Constitucional v Perú*, 31 January, 2001; *Lori Berenson-Mejía v Perú*, 25 November, 2004; *Fermín Ramírez v Guatemala*, 20/6/2005; *Cabrera García and Montiel Flores v México*, 26 November, 2010; *Palamara-Iribarne v Chile*, 22/11/2005; *Masacre de Pueblo Bello v Colombia*, 31/12006; *La Cantuta v Peru*, 29/11/2006; *Acevedo Buendía and Others v Peru* (case 'Cesantes y jubilados de la Contraloría'), 1/7/2009; *Barbani Duarte and Others v Uruguay*, 1/10/2011.

[55] In the decision *Hilaire, Constantine y Benjamín and Others v Trinidad y Tobago* the Inter-American Court observed that: 'Taking into account the exceptionally serious and irreparable nature of the death penalty, the observance of due process, with its bundle of rights and guarantees, becomes all the more important when human life is at stake ' (*Hilaire, Constantine y Benjamín and Others v Trinidad y Tobago*, 21/6/2002, para 148).

jurisprudence, especially regarding the absolute non-derogability of the rules of due process when the death penalty is foreseen,[56] or regarding the impartiality of the military courts[57] and the removal from office of the judges.[58]

Another matter that has been revealed to be of reciprocal influence is the definition of 'inhuman and degrading treatment'. At first, the European Court began to influence the Inter-American jurisprudence,[59] but later, from the 1990s onwards, it happened more and more frequently that the European Court, invested with appeals concerning systematic violations such as arbitrary detentions, illegal executions and forced disappearances, looked at the Inter-American case law. However, from a numerical point of view, the influence of Inter-American jurisprudence on the European Court case law in this area seems less relevant than might have been expected. Despite the absence of a conspicuous number of reciprocal references, though, during these years the two Courts have shown a growing convergence in the approach they have with respect to such violations, even if the ECtHR did not expressly refer to the decisions of the Inter-American Court.[60]

Another field of convergence worth mentioning concerns amnesty laws and war crimes. In the judgment in *Marguš v Croatia*,[61] the ECtHR makes extensive references to the jurisprudence of the Inter-American Court, which is not only cited page by page in the part 'on the facts' but is also used in the Court's considerations to interpret Article 6.5 of Additional Protocol II of the Geneva Conventions. Following the interpretation of the Inter-American Court of Human Rights, the ECtHR considers that this provision does not apply to perpetrators of war crimes and crimes against humanity.[62]

C. The Third Phase: Toward an Increasing Influence of the Inter-American Court Jurisprudence?

During the last 20 years, the relationship between the two Courts has changed. They have started to look at each other more frequently, within and outside their judicial activity.

On the one hand, common studies and seminars have been increasing, not only at an academic level[63] but also directly involving the two Courts.[64] On the other hand, this

[56] *Ocalan v Turkey*, (GC), 12/3/2003, para 203.

[57] *Ergin v Turkey*, (4th Ch.) 4/5/2006, paras 25 and 54.

[58] *Baka v Hungary*, n° 20261/12, 23/06/2016.

[59] *Loayza-Tamayo v Peru*, 17/9/1997, para 57, citing *Ireland v United Kingdom*, 18/1/1978 and *Ribitsch v Austria*, 4/12/1995. See also *Cantoral-Benavides v Peru*, 18/8/2000, para 89.

[60] E Fernàndez, 'Nuevos retos para el Tribunal europeo de derechos humanos: la jurisprudencia sobre desapariciones forzadas' (2009) 61 *Persona y derecho*, 195.

[61] *Marguš v Croatia*, (G.Ch.), 27/5/2014.

[62] *Marguš v Croatia*, (G.Ch.), 27/5/2014, para 131.

[63] To mention only one initiative, the ICCAL project of the Max-Planck Institute in Heidelberg facilitates the circulation of InterAmerican case law in Europe. See A von Bogdandy, E Ferrer Mac-Gregor, M Morales Antoniazzi and F Piovesan (eds), *Transformative Constitutionalism in Latin America: The Emergence of a New Ius Commune* (Oxford University Press, 2017).

[64] When we realised our first empirical research on this topic in 2012 (later published in T Groppi and AM Lecis, 'Las referencias recíprocas entre la Corte Europea y la Corte Interamericana de Derechos Humanos: ¿de la influencia al diálogo?' (2014) 80 *Revista de Derecho Público*, 85), the two Courts had never drawn up internal studies on it, while they have been doing it since: see www.echr.coe.int/Documents/

reciprocal attention was eventually reflected in the jurisprudence, with citations of the Inter-American case law from its European counterpart on matters other than gross violations.

In the 'facts part' of its judgments, the European Court now cites almost systematically the Inter-American case law, in the section reserved for the 'relevant international law materials'. Even if most of the time it does not explicitly refer to those citations in the Court's considerations, some convergences can be found in the solution eventually adopted.

For instance, in a case concerning in vitro fertilisation, *Parrillo v Italy*, the ECtHR cited, in the section concerning relevant international law, the judgment *Artavia Murillo et al. v Costa Rica* concluding that 'the human embryo prior to implantation could not be understood to be a person for the purposes of Article 4 § 1 of the American Convention'. Even if it does not refer to this citation in the core part of the judgment, the Court finally reached a similar decision, establishing that, according to its previous jurisprudence, there is no assessment on the recognition of rights of the human embryo (para 167).

On occasion the ECtHR refers to the IACtHR case law in the decision-making part of the judgment. This happened in another recent case concerning the right to private and family rights, this time with reference to the best interests of the child in a case concerning administrative detention of minors in the context of immigration controls. In *G.B. and others v Turkey*, the European Court relies, inter alia, on the Advisory Opinion of the Inter-American Court on the Rights and Guarantees of Children in the Context of Migration and/or in Need of International Protection in order to affirm that 'when the child's best interests require keeping the family together, the imperative requirement not to deprive the child of liberty extends to the child's parents and requires the authorities to choose non-custodial solutions for the entire family' (para 168).

A certain interaction between the two Courts has even been observed – which could lead to a surprise in the field of freedom of expression. The Inter-American Court has made extensive use of European jurisprudence in the interpretation of admissible restrictions on freedom of expression in a democratic society, between 1985 and 1986 in advisory opinions, and since 2001, also in jurisdictional cases.[65] More recently, the European Court has been citing the Inter-American jurisprudence on freedom of expression.[66] The reciprocal attention shown by the two Courts with regard to the limitations on freedom of expression could signal the beginning of a true dialogue

Research_report_inter_american_court_ENG.pdf. Furthermore, Joint seminars, reports and summits are often organised: see the 'Joint public seminar of the European Court of Human Rights and Inter-American Court of Human Rights: Optimization of a methodology in adjudicating large-scale human rights violations' Strasbourg, 9 November 2018, www.echr.coe.int/Documents/Seminar_Inter_American_Court_20181109_ENG.pdf; the 'Joint Law Report 2019 by AfCHPR, ECHR and IACHR' www.corteidh.or.cr/sitios/libros/todos/docs/Libro_tres_cortes.pdf and, more recently, the 'Dialogue between the Three Human Rights Courts of the World: The impact of COVID-19 on Human Rights' www.youtube.com/watch?v=FMWOFS4WjB0&t=2102s.

[65] *Olmedo-Bustos and Others v Chile* (case 'La última tentación de Cristo'), 5/2/2001; *Ivcher-Bronstein v Perú*, 6/2/2001; *Herrera-Ulloa v Costa Rica*, 2/7/2004; *Ricardo Canese v Paraguay*, 31/8/2004; *Kimel v Argentina*, 2/5/2008; *Fontevecchia and D'amico v Argentina*, 29/11/2011; *Usón Ramírez v Venezuela*, 20/11/2009; *Granier and Others (Radio Caracas Televisión) v Venezuela*, 22/6/2015.

[66] *Stoll v Switzerland*, (G.Ch.), 10/12/2007, citing *Claude Reyes and Others v Chile*, 19/9/2006.

to determine international standards on this issue, but such a conclusion still seems premature and will require analysis of future developments.[67]

This third phase, characterised by a greater interaction, could eventually bring a bigger convergence both in the interpretative methods and the interpretative solutions.

The context in which the Inter-American Court operates is undergoing a rapid transformation: since gross violations no longer constitute the general rule in the Latin American continent, the Court, as with the European Court, is more often invested with questions concerning the definition and standard of protection of rights other than the 'core rights'. Such a mutation gave rise to a debate on the need to introduce into the Inter-American system an instrument analogous to the margin of appreciation, which had always been refused by the IACtHR until now, to avoid subordinating the human rights standard to the regional consensus.[68] References to the national systems of Member States are used by the Inter-American Court only when it is affirmed around the most favourable interpretation for the human person.

Otherwise, the Inter-American Court does not hesitate to compare regional approaches and trends with international consensus, to ensure the second prevails over the first when it is more favourable to human rights. The reasons that led the Inter-American Court to reject the margin of appreciation and the comparison between the legal systems of the Member States for the determination of standards are therefore essentially due to two kinds of reasons: on the one hand, the lack of a common standard of democracy between the States Parties and the fact that the Court has been regularly invested with complaints concerning violations of core rights; and on the other hand, the universalist approach in human rights protection, according to which the Court has never constructed a concept corresponding to that of 'European public order'.

However, this second order of reasons is the consequence of the first and therefore we can wonder whether it is not destined to succumb to the changes in the political context, leaving room for the development of a regional public order as the Court finds itself dealing with issues that have arisen in the context of more stable democracies and which therefore do not have gross violations as their object.

From a transjudicial communication perspective, this mutation of paradigm makes the Inter-American case law more interesting for the European Court in a field other than gross violations. The Inter-American Court has reached a recognised legitimation, which allows it to try to spread its jurisprudence in some fields where it has developed higher standards. The environmental rights constitute a clear example. Even if the European Court has never cited the Inter-American case law on this matter, the IACtHR paved the way for possible future convergences, outlining the higher standards of the Inter-American jurisprudence on environmental protection. In the Advisory opinion on Environment and Human Rights (OC-23/17), the Inter-American Court cites the European jurisprudence, implicitly highlighting its most advanced position

[67] E Bertoni, 'The Inter-American Court of Human Rights and the European Court of Human Rights: A Dialogue on Freedom of Expression Standards' (2009) 3 *European Human Rights Law Review* 332; FG Eguiguren Praeli, R Bustos Gisbert and I Torres Muro, 'Las libertades de pensamiento, información y expresión, y los derechos de reunión y asociación: pautas para un diálogo' in García Roca (n 2) 185.

[68] S Bertelsen, 'A margin for the margin of appreciation: Deference in the Inter-American Court of Human Rights' (2021) 19 *International Journal of Constitutional Law* 887–913.

on the matter, based on the recognition of an autonomous right to the protection of the environment, which is not dependent, as is the case in the European system, on the protection of people's rights.

Another field of possible future convergences is the definition of 'femicide'. While the Inter-American Court introduced this notion in its famous *Cotton field* decision,[69] the European Court only recently referred to this notion, considering the persistency of 'socio-cultural attitudes of tolerance of domestic violence' as a form of discrimination based on sex.[70] However, the decision did not mention the Inter-American case law, preferring to rely instead on documents and rapports of international bodies concerning the defendant State[71] rather than looking outside the European region.

VI. Conclusions: The IACtHR, from Greater Receiver to Greater Contributor?

The greater openness of the IACtHR to European jurisprudence finds its roots in its historical and cultural development. Even though extra-systemic references have been fulfilling several functions in its case law, the main purpose of those comparative arguments seems to be the application of the *pro homine* principle in the interpretation of the ACHR and the elevation of the standard independently from the regional standard of protection, at the cost of exposing itself to the criticism of cherry-picking.[72] Through this approach to extra-systemic case law, the IACtHR affirms its conception of human rights: a universal conception, which questions state voluntarism and national particularisms in the name of the highest protection of the person, and which has been advocated within the Court by the engagement of illustrious jurists who sat there.[73] The Court clearly assumes this conception in its case law, when it positions itself explicitly in a universalist perspective, in opposition to other regional systems and especially to the European system.

Unlike its European counterpart, the IACtHR has thus been an extra-systemic receiver more than a contributor. However, its growing affirmation and the development of advanced jurisprudence in certain areas may lead it to become an important contributor to a cross-judicial fertilisation perspective.

If this has been true, up to now, in areas such as forced disappearances and other gross violations, other areas of its specialisation, such as the case law on environmental protection or violence against women, could soon become a field of judicial export.

[69] IACtHR, *González et al ('Cotton Field') v Mexico*, Series C 205 (16 November 2009).

[70] ECtHR *Talpis v Italy*, Court (First Section), n° 41237/14, 02/03/2017, para 145.

[71] The decision cites the concluding comments on Italy of the Committee on the Elimination of Discrimination against Women ('the CEDAW Committee') and the conclusions of the United Nations Special Rapporteur on violence against women, its causes and consequences, drawn up following his official visit to Italy.

[72] For a synthesis of those critiques, see L Hennebel, 'La Cour interaméricaine des droits de l'homme: entre universalisme et particularisme' in L Hennebel and H Tigroudja (eds), *Le particularisme interaméricain des droits de l'homme* (Pedone, 2009) 75 ff., especially 117.

[73] The first reference goes to AA Cançado-Trindade, but also to other judges such as Diego Garcia Sayán, Cecilia Medina Quiroga and E Ferrer Mac-Gregor Poisot. On the influence of the formations and convictions of the judges who composed it on the doctrine of the Court, see also Burgorgue-Larsen (n 29) 39–46.

On the other hand, the context in which the Inter-American Court operates is rapidly changing: gross violations are no longer the rule in the Latin American continent, so the Court is increasingly called upon to rule on issues concerning the definition and standards of protection of rights other than core rights. This change has revived the debate on the need to introduce in the Inter-American system an instrument similar to the margin of appreciation, which requires that regional consensus be taken into consideration in determining standards.

In the dialectic between universalism and particularism of human rights, the regional courts find themselves in a privileged position, right on the dividing line between the universality of rights and the enhancement of the specificities of the reference area.

The two Courts examined have so far taken a different approach with respect to these positions as a result of the different contexts in which they have found themselves operating: the one more devoted to universalism, the other more careful to safeguard a certain amount of diversity and pluralism among the Member States. But the more the political and social context in which the two Courts are located changes, the more they will be called to an evolution, which can be more fruitful if they manage to dialogue more, not only through reciprocal citations but also through further promotion of relationships and encounters between people. As 'intermediaries' between the international and national legal systems, they have the chance to find the best balance that prevents harmonisation from degenerating into homogenisation.

20

The Argumentative Turn in Constitutional Reasoning in Latin America and the Caribbean

JOHANNA FRÖHLICH*

There is an argumentative turn sweeping through constitutional courts in the region, which suggests that the formalist era of constitutional reasoning in Latin America and the Caribbean is over. As others have pointed out not so long ago,[1] the once 'sleepy and sovereigntist' landscape of constitutional review has been drastically transformed at the highest levels of constitutional adjudication. It is not just that constitutional review has become the dominant[2] way of resolving human rights violations in this part of the world. The argumentative turn I mention is neither a simple by-product of the wave of new constitutions that began in the 1980s nor a mere consequence of the extensive legal reforms that several Latin American countries have implemented.[3] With our database, and throughout this volume's chapters on the analysed courts' jurisprudence, we can observe a transformation that reaches the level of the constitutional courts' general reason-giving practices, up to the way those courts contemplate their obligation to justify their reasoning in concrete cases.

This transformation is neither unidirectional nor without contradictions or paradoxes. This argumentative turn is a multifaceted phenomenon that has at least three elements that continually interact with one another. These elements are the following: (i) a mostly unpremeditated, dysfunctional, but continually weakening textual component; (ii) a transformative-creative element emerging to dominance; and finally, (iii) the game-

* Thanks to András Jakab, Katalin Kelemen, Pier Paolo Pigozzi, Julio Ríos-Figueroa, Sergio Verdugo and Cristián Villalonga Torrijo for their valuable comments and suggestions and a special thanks to Sebastián Umpierrez de Reguero for his help with the data and graphs that were used in this chapter.

[1] A Hunees, 'Introduction to the Symposium on the Constitutionalization of International law in Latin America' (2015) *University of Wisconsin Law School Legal Studies Research Paper Series*, no 1428. 89.

[2] P Navia and J Ríos-Figueroa, 'The Constitutional Adjudication Mosaic of Latin America' (2005) 38 *Comparative Political Studies* 189–217; see also the first wave of judicial review in M Cappelletti, *Judicial Review in the Contemporary World* (1971); D Lustig and JHH Weiler, 'Judicial Review in the Contemporary World – Retrospective and Prospective' (2018) 16 *International Journal of Constitutional Law*.

[3] S Huntington, *The third wave: Democratization in the late twentieth century* (University of Oklahoma Press, 1993); H Frühling, 'Judicial reform and democratization in Latin America' in F Agüero and J Stark (eds), *Fault lines of democracy in post-transition Latin America* (Lynne Rienner, 1998) 237–62.

changer rhetorical element. I argue that the overall empirical results can be best understood by engaging with the complexity of this dynamic, which is behind the reason-giving practices of the selected judgments.

The unique efforts of this volume and others to unearth the twists and turns of the Latin American argumentative puzzle have limitations and must necessarily be incomplete. These constraints must be particularly acknowledged when we encounter the extremely colourful and rich constitutional heritage that Latin America and the Caribbean possess. Facing this tremendous abundance of historical events, opinions and theories, as well as a constitutional reality that is so mysteriously tangled, an outside observer cannot but choose the humblest standpoint and apply as much self-reflection as possible – especially if the observer is not native to this culture. Any exaggeration or understatement, misunderstanding or confusion, is a product of the enthusiasm for making sense of this complexity, which of course is not any less detrimental than any other mistake one can make. It is in this spirit, as a non-native, that I offer my insights.

I. Contours of a Paradigm Change?

Our data on constitutional reasoning in the region has the potential to point to various features. As explained in the book's Introduction, our database contains temporally unbalanced samples since most of the selected landmark judgments were pronounced during the past two decades. Having said that, the empirical results gathered from the 15 jurisdictions, together with the in-depth doctrinal analysis that focuses on the last two or three decades, allow us to point to regional features and emerging tendencies. Our data and its analysis suggest that competing visions of the textual and creative elements in constitutional reasoning comprise the explanatory framework that has the greatest potential to effectively explain constitutional adjudication practices. Although results vary across jurisdictions, this distinction can trigger divisive judicial behaviour, shape judicial attitudes and redefine interpretive concepts throughout the region. While the textual approach[4] prefers to maintain an immediate link with the authoritative text, the creative approach chooses to use sources from outside the constitutional text to shape the tenor of the constitution. The age-old dynamic of these two opposing views has created a unique and complex system of reasoning culture in constitutional law cases in Latin America and the Caribbean, which is outlined in the following sections.

A. Unpremeditated, Dysfunctional and Weakening Textual Component

There are three elements that interact with one another, shaping the argumentative practices of courts in Latin America and the Caribbean. The first element is a latent

[4] See especially JF Manning, 'Textualism as a Nondelegation Doctrine' (1997) 97 *Columbia Law Review* 673–739. For a detailed analysis and categorisation of constitutional interpretive methods see A Jakab,' Judicial Reasoning in Constitutional Courts: A European Perspective' (2013) 14 *German Law Journal* 1215–75. For more specific information on the textual method, see 1231–33.

textual component that seemingly functions as the customary basis to which judges in the region usually appeal. For purposes of this research, the textual element is primarily defined as the use of the ordinary (or plain, literal or textual) meaning and the constitution-maker's intent.

In the cultural context of Latin America, textual methods are viewed with suspicion. By the twentieth century, judicial decision-making and legal reasoning developed 'the most primitive sort of formalist legal positivism'[5] according to that theory's critics. In light of the usual criticism of formalism, this was meant to remove any creative component from the act of interpretation and contributed to an almost complete deference to the legislative body. Furthermore, Latin American judges exhibited a strong preference for procedural rules over substantive components of the normative text,[6] which was said not only to be unnecessary but also inconsistent with arguments related to natural law that were usually familiar to those judges.[7]

The word 'formalism' in the Latin American context thus does not simply refer to a value-neutral way of judicial meaning-making in the sense that it disregards the good and wellbeing of the person and their communities during interpretation and application.[8] Instead, in Latin America, it refers to a timid, short-sighted or even abusive and deficient mode of reasoning that has been used to deny justice to the masses throughout Latin American history.[9] However, this concept of formalism, shaped by the traumatic experience in Latin America, should be distinguished from the classical, textual and interpretive methods that rely on the (ordinary) meaning of the normative text's words and phrases. This textual element serves legitimate goals,[10] such as recognising and channelling the value of representative democratic bodies' decisions by maintaining the authoritative text as the starting point of the interpretive journey for judicial sentences, along with fomenting legal security,[11] foreseeability and coherence through its consistent application. The value of textual interpretation has rarely been demonstrated[12] through authentic examples in Latin America, but that does not eradicate its value or render its correct application impossible. On the contrary, looking at our data on how this method was in fact used in the region could contribute to resolving the mystery around formalism and its present-day potential for application.

Our overall data confirms at least two characteristics of the use of the textual element in this area of the globe. First, academic criticism of formalism reached regional constitutional and supreme courts, and consequently, its use began to notably decrease. Second, the textual component remains part of a 'persistent cultural

[5] J Couso, 'The transformation of constitutional discourse and the judicialization of politics in Latin America' in Couso et al (eds), *Cultures of Legality* (Cambridge University Press, 2010) 151.

[6] ibid.

[7] ibid.

[8] J Finnis, 'Priority of Persons' in J Finnis, *Intention and Identity. Collected Essays: Volume II* (Oxford University Press, 2011) 27.

[9] DE López Medina, *Teoría Impura del Derecho. La transformación de la cultura jurídica latinoamericana* (Legis, 2004) 417–34.

[10] Jakab (n 4) 1229; C Casey, 'Constitutional Design and the Point of Constitutional Law' (2022) 67 *The American Journal of Jurisprudence* 173–97.

[11] SJ Brison and W Sinnott-Armstrong, 'A Philosophical Introduction to Constitutional Interpretation' in SJ Brison and W Sinnott-Armstrong (eds), *Contemporary Perspectives on Constitutional Interpretation* (Routledge, 1993) 1, 5.

[12] As an example, see the Colombian Constitutional Court's Decision C-590/05 about permitting the admissibility of *tutelas* based on the literal interpretation of Art 86 of the Colombian Constitution.

attitude'[13] but mostly in an unpremeditated and dysfunctional way. The Chilean Constitutional Court, for instance, continued to steadily apply the textual method even after the reform of its constitutional review system in 2005. Similarly, in Argentina, the Supreme Court used the textual method frequently (in about 60 per cent of the selected cases, 25 out of 40), even though Argentine legal scholarship is well-known for having inspired a transformative progressive turn in the region's constitutional culture.[14]

At first glance, Graph 1 paints a contradictory picture of references to the textual component. We see that, until 2000, the number of references to the literal meaning and the constitution-maker's intent (either one or both) was below 20 per cent in all jurisdictions, whereas in the last two decades, these numbers were close to or above 40 per cent. This might be explained by the fact that there were very few selected cases from the first three decades of the project's temporal coverage,[15] as most of the courts we analysed began operating in the late 1990s. The growth we see starting in the 2000s is not truly an increase since that was the first decade with a considerable number of selected cases. The contrast between the last two decades, however, is meaningful, and it points to a decreasing use of the textual element.

Graph 1 The use of the textual element in all jurisdictions over time

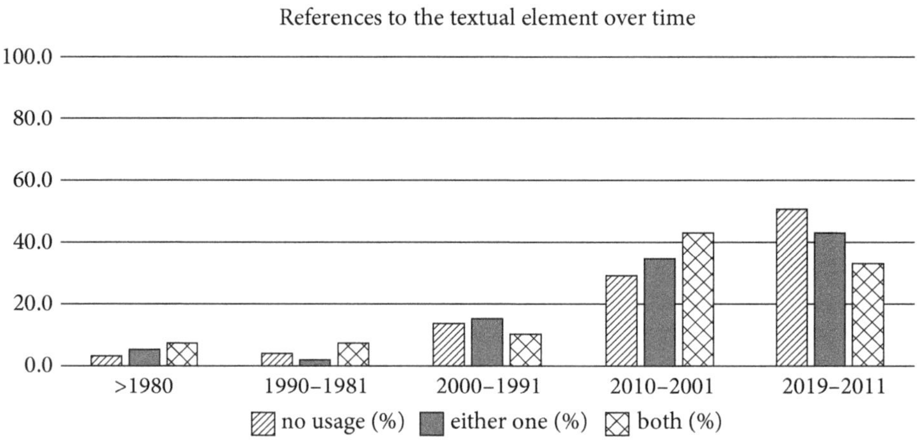

Graph 2 adds the national bits and pieces to the big picture. References to the textual element either stagnated or decreased in the last two decades except for Argentina and Brazil. While the case of Brazil is related to the hyperbolic nature of constitutional reasoning in general, the selected Argentine jurisprudence seems to maintain a dominant textual component as a customary basis of the court's argumentative practice. One could argue that stagnation is also an important feature that cannot be interpreted as a decrease but rather a sign of a solid and long-lasting tendency of the court's reasoning. As we will see below in the section on the rhetorical element, textual methods

[13] Couso (n 5) 3.
[14] Couso (n 5) 152.
[15] See the graph on the temporal division of the selected landmark judgments in the Introduction (Fröhlich, Umpierrez de Reguero and Meléndez (ch 1)).

are usually not used in a functional, straightforward way. The main trend is instead a clear drop in the use of the textual component, which can be observed in the following sections and graphs.

Graph 2 The use of the textual method in each jurisdiction throughout the entire period of the research

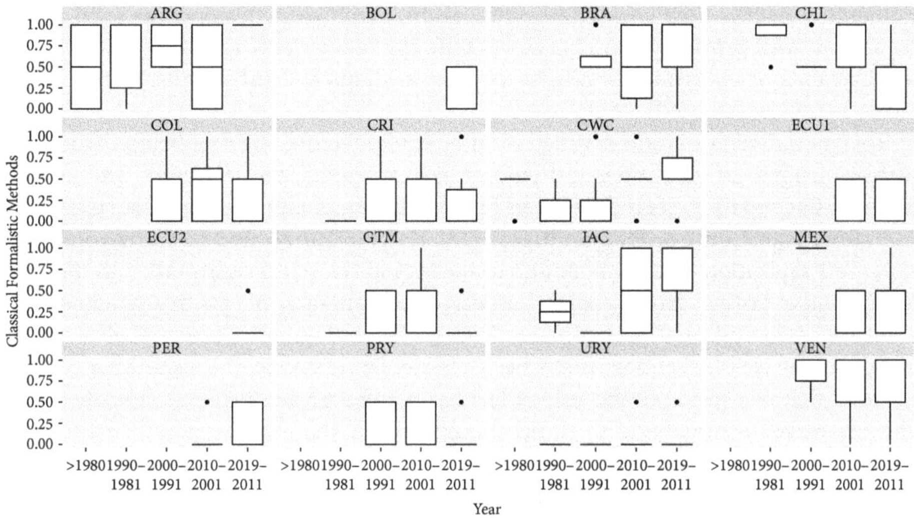

B. Transformative, Creative Component Emerging to Dominance

The above-depicted image would be both incomplete and incomprehensible without identifying other recent features of constitutional reasoning that emerged with the theories of neo-constitutionalism and transformative constitutionalism in Latin America and the Caribbean.[16] In response to criticism of an overly formalist and positivist legal culture, where methodological rigidity meets a social and political reality that is fundamentally disengaged from the normative text's aspirations, the primary expectation of new constitutional theories has been to transform the courts' jurisprudence and make it more responsive and judicially enforceable.

The first seeds of this change can be identified in a tendency described and conceptualised for instance, in the law and courts literature. The expansion of the courts' role[17] in fighting inequality and injustice through legal discourse and individual rights is a global phenomenon.[18] There are, however, at least three characteristics of this trend in Latin America that make it a rather remarkable case.[19] First, an ever-wider sphere of social and political issues has been translated into legal problems and voiced

[16] See Pigozzi (ch 2) regarding the constitutional culture in Latin America and the Caribbean.

[17] R Hirschl, *Towards Juristocracy. The Origins and Consequences of New Constitutionalism* (Harvard University Press, 2007); J Finnis, 'Judicial Power: Past, Present and Future' in R Ekins (ed), *Judicial Power and the Balance of Our Constitution* (Policy Exchange, 2018) 31.

[18] Lustig and Weiler (n 2).

[19] A Huneeus, J Couso and R Siedel (eds), *Cultures of Legality* (Cambridge University Press, 2010) 9–10.

through legal institutions and legal terms. For example, the attempt to promote social justice triggered the emergence of economic, social and cultural rights as enforceable rights.[20] This process of the 'formalisation' of social and political deficiencies has brought the other two features to the fore: a wide range of new legal instruments and the transformation of legal language as a strategy to effectively use law and courts for fighting inequality and injustice.[21] While the formalisation of socioeconomic problems concerns how social and political problems are redesigned as legal issues, the second and third aspects pertain to how this alters legal language by inventing new concepts or instruments to fight for human rights and substantive justice claims and by using them expeditiously.

This metamorphosis was sparked by at least two factors, the first being the region's historic struggle to guarantee and enforce human rights, the standards and content of which have mainly been developed by constitutional and supreme courts and the Inter-American Court of Human Rights (IACtHR).[22] The second factor encompasses those new aspirations that were added to the region's classical rights talk[23] in the form of substantive justice claims, social justice and indigenous concepts that reached Latin American constitutional and supreme courts. On a dogmatic, theoretical level, the change in key classical concepts has been visible. For instance, it is clear on a conceptual level that the notion of the rule of law has undergone a sea change. Those scholars who are rather sympathetic to these changes admit that 'in the new constitutional orthodoxy the value of legal certainty has been substituted by that of substantive justice, developments that would have shocked any legal theorist in the region just two or three decades ago'.[24] This shift, however, was not limited to certain key concepts or methods, although it re-established the basic approach to constitutional reasoning since it went 'from a strict adherence to a formalist legal positivism hostile to judge-created law and routine interference with the elected branches of government' to a new vision 'based on the pre-eminence of human rights and constitutional principles over legislated law, as well as an activist conception of the role of courts in a democracy'.[25] Beyond the transformation on a theoretical level, one of the questions this chapter puts forth is whether and how these shifting theories have impacted the jurisprudence of the region's constitutional courts.

Our data shows both the overall picture and the bits and pieces of this argumentative shift. Regarding the objectives of this research, these types of arguments were designated as creative methods that used an extra-textual source as a reference point

[20] J Fröhlich, 'The Paradox of Social Justice Constitutionalism' *International Journal of Constitutional Law Blog* (4 October 2022) at www.iconnectblog.com/i-connect-symposium-on-the-chilean-constitutional-referendum-the-contradiction-of-social-justice-constitutionalism/.

[21] Couso (n 5) 152. Referring to a 'conceptual revolution' that started in the 1980s.

[22] See generally, P Carozza and D Shelton, *Regional Protection of Human Rights* (Oxford University Press, 2013) on how Latin American countries contributed to the idea of human rights, see PG Carozza,' From Conquest to Constitutions: Retrieving a Latin American Tradition of the Idea of Human Rights' (2003) 25 *Human Rights Quarterly* 281–313.

[23] MA Glendon, *Rights Talk. The Impoverishment of Political Discourse* (Free Press, 1993).

[24] Couso (n 5) 166. Contrary to this trend, see eg T Győrfy, *Against the New Constitutionalism* (Edward Elgar, 2016). For the critique of a 'moral-political primacy of rights', see J Finnis, 'Human Rights and Their Enforcement' in J Finnis, *Human Rights and Common Good. Collected Essays Volume III.* (Oxford University Press, 2011) 29.

[25] Couso (n 5) 166. Contrary this trend, see G Webber, P Yowell, R Ekins, M Köpcke, BW Miller and F Urbina, *Legislated Rights. Securing Human Rights Through Legislation* (Cambridge University Press, 2018).

to define the constitution's meaning. Thus, the creative element referenced later in this chapter consists of: (i) the method of harmonisation with international law; (ii) reference to concepts and principles that cannot be found in the constitution's text; (iii) non-legal methods; (iv) reference to scholarly work; (v) reference to foreign law; and (vi) the *pro personae* principle. We will see in the forthcoming sections that some of these methods are relatively new, such as the *pro personae* principle, which in a different context could be considered an established, classical method like the interpretation applying international law. While applying international law was considered a creative interpretive method because it has developed into a flexible, extra-textual tool for questioning the validity of domestic law, the objective teleological (or purposive) method was not deemed as such because Latin American constitutions have strong aspirational features containing numerous open-ended purposive phrases that can be interpreted in distinct ways. For purposes of this research, the methods considered creative were chosen as such to identify those arguments that Latin American courts have used to replace the textual component.

Graph 3 The use of creative methods in all jurisdictions throughout the entire period of the research

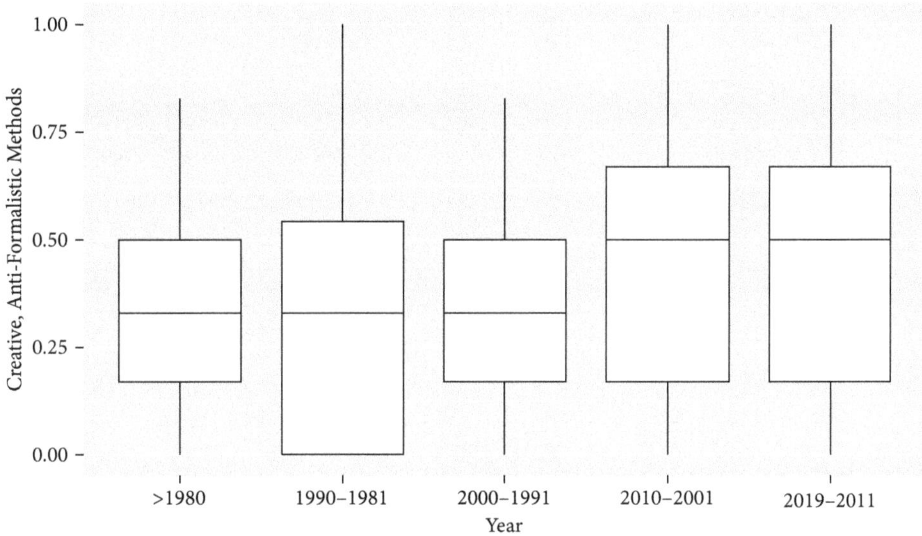

Graph 3 depicts a more clear-cut picture of the use of the aforementioned creative methods. The results and the range of observations are contained and concentrated in each period and delineate a clear tendency to increase, displaying a statistically significant correlation of the use of creative methods over time (Fligner-Killeen:med chi-squared = 11.378, df = 4, p-value = 0.02263). If we look at the data for each jurisdiction as shown in Graph 4, we can see that in most of the cases there was an augmentation in the use of creative methods when comparing the last two decades (2000–2010 to 2010–2019). Graph 4 confirms the region's commitment to furthering the mission of transformative constitutionalism in the case of some courts that are well-known for their proclivity for these theories, such as the Costa Rican, Brazilian and Colombian and the IACtHR courts, while some other jurisdictions' results call for more explanation.

Interestingly, there were courts included in the study that were not necessarily expected to be creative. For instance, the Chilean Constitutional Court has been steadily advancing its use of creative argumentative skills despite its rather unfavourable reputation at both the national and regional levels.[26] Meanwhile, the common-law area of the Caribbean is known as a moderate jurisdiction in terms of argumentative and conceptual diversity, but the methods these courts use have become increasingly more creative in the last decade. On the other hand, we find courts that seemingly refute their renown as advocates of the transformative agenda. One example is Ecuador, whose court is currently among the fiercest proponents of the transformative agenda, although its number of references to creative methods do not seem to confirm this. One explanation is that while the first Ecuadorean court (Ecuador 1) was well-known for its deference to former President Rafael Correa, the second Ecuadorean court (Ecuador 2) was under more pressure to demonstrate the legitimacy of its decisions and thus maintained a more moderate style. Argentina is the only country where the use of creative methods among the selected decisions decreased over the last decade and is therefore a clear outlier of this almost homogenous regional trend.

Graph 4 The use of creative methods in each jurisdiction throughout the entire time period of the research

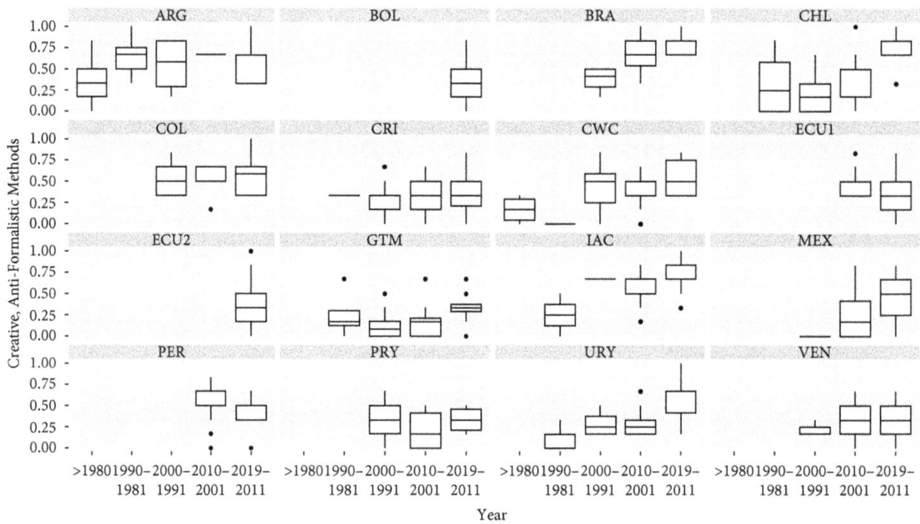

C. The Game-Changer Rhetorical Component

The textual and creative components represent two contrasting or even competing visions of law and constitutional reasoning. However, although they offer interpretive tools for two ideologically opposed judicial self-understandings, they are not mutually exclusive. Further, although interpretive methods – like those that pertain to either the textual or the creative component in this research – are legitimate elements in the

[26] L Hilbink, *Judges beyond Politics in Democracy and Dictatorship: Lessons from Chile* (Cambridge University Press, 2007).

argumentative toolkit of courts, it is possible to invoke them rhetorically. In other words, the rhetorical use of arguments, whether applied to textual or creative methods, is a characteristic that does not necessarily follow ideological currents but could emerge in distinct situations and in courts that favour different ideological views. The rhetorical component can appear in the jurisprudence of various Latin American and Caribbean courts at many distinct points in their histories, precisely because it can be employed in distinct, even opposing directions. As shown below, a rhetorical twist could exploit interpretive methods and turn constitutional provisions into empty shells or cause their escalation to the point where their meaning is obscured, blurred or even lost.

Thus, any method could be the victim of a rhetorical tangle. Depending on the objective, a rhetorical move can be utilised to minimise, downplay or escalate different arguments. However, rhetorical arguments are, by definition, dishonest in the sense that they allow judges to say things they don't mean, or conversely, they allow them to do things they don't want to say. Notwithstanding the aforementioned, I don't consider rhetorical arguments as altogether inappropriate or illegitimate. As part of a court's political communication[27] or pedagogical mission, it can be acceptable to incorporate arguments that have no bearing on a decision. Rhetorical arguments are not desirable in the sense that they are not the richest or truest accounts of the practice of judicial reason-giving but rather a practice that only resembles the true instantiation of constitutional reasoning by constitutional court judges. Given this, a rhetorical argument can still be an argument, although it is not the *central case* of this practice.[28]

Moving forward, the chapter will distinguish two specific types of rhetoric use, without relinquishing the possibility that there might be other objectives behind this strategy.[29] First, rhetorical downplaying is quite a common practice, following which courts invoke an argument based on the constitution's normative text, although they do not expound its meaning since it is usually left as an empty shell with no real significance. It is a fine line that distinguishes this practice from another common routine, when courts simply cite to the constitution's text without using it to develop an argument. In this latter instance, it is impossible to even find the necessary logical link between a proposition (the constitution's text) and the conclusion (its meaning); therefore, in the strict sense, it cannot be treated as an argument.[30]

In the case of rhetorical downplaying, the logical link can be tracked down, but the argument appears to be unpremeditated and irrelevant because it is unclear what the text's meaning is and how the court reached it. For instance, the first Ecuadorean Constitutional Court (Ecuador 1) seemingly applied the textual method in almost half of the selected landmark cases but failed to provide a clear meaning for the constitutional provision. As a consequence of turning textual arguments so peripherally, other interpretive methods, such as referencing scholarly arguments or to comparative sources, were used instead of the textual method. Similarly, the Venezuelan Constitutional Chamber invoked textual arguments in almost all the selected cases but without

[27] A Jakab and A Dyevre, Foreword: Understanding Constitutional Reasoning. Special Issue on Constitutional Reasoning' (2013) 14 *German Law Journal* 983–1015.

[28] J Finnis, *Natural Law and Natural Rights* (Oxford University Press, 2011) 14.

[29] Further differentiations could and should be made in light of advanced research on this topic, such as the possible impact and consequence of rhetorical reasoning on the public opinion, on the reasoning of lower courts and on the academic and public discourse.

[30] See M Bencze and GY Ng (eds), *How to Measure the Quality of Judicial Reasoning* (Springer, 2019) 91–96, 97.

seriously engaging with their meaning. While in the Ecuadorean case, rhetorical downplaying of textual arguments appears to be part of a persistent ambivalence towards the normative text, in Venezuela, the textual component is practically empty, even if it serves as the dominant narrative in which the Chamber safeguards the legal system's harmony with the letter of the constitution.[31] Furthermore, the principle of the rule of law is a potential victim of rhetorical downplaying at a regional level, which is seen in the IACtHR's jurisprudence.[32]

Rhetorical use cannot only eliminate or weaken an argument but also boost and excessively strengthen it. Rhetorical escalation is, therefore, another way that arguments can be tangled rhetorically. In this instance, arguments are invoked in an overly detailed and abundant way with various citations and examples, making the arguments excessive and overstated. This hyperbolic practice causes ambiguity and uncertainty from another aspect, as it blurs the result of the interpretation and the main lines of argument. The extreme example is clearly the Brazilian Supreme Federal Tribunal (SFT), a court discussed in chapter five, which frequently employs 'an endless line of reasoning'[33] using various methods and concepts to the point where the judges' opinions and the *ratio decidendi* of the decisions become practically unidentifiable. This becomes even clearer by looking at the textual component results from Brazil, according to which the textual method was invoked as many as 18 times out of the 40 selected cases, which is the least (!) frequently used method in its jurisprudence. Instead, the domestic harmonising, purposive and non-legal methods were among the most often recurring interpretive methods, which were utilised 39, 35, and 30 times, respectively, in the Brazilian court's jurisprudence. Unsurprisingly, this approach affected the length of the decisions as well, which was an average of 260 pages in the Brazilian case. During its cosmopolitan period, the Guatemalan Constitutional Court used multiple lines of argument adorned with several principles and abstract concepts borrowed from foreign law that did not contribute directly to the decision's outcome.

Because of the nature of rhetorical arguments, it is challenging to identify them, and even more so to measure them. As rhetorical use depends mostly on the objective one has in mind, it is very difficult if not impossible to capture this intention empirically. Despite the challenges and risks, we decided to experiment and create a new indicator to measure the overall weight of the arguments, which together with the doctrinal analysis serves as a basis for the following observations.

In some cases, the rhetoric use of arguments works differently when applied to textual versus creative methods. In case there is rhetoric use at all, rhetorical downplaying is typically applied to textual methods, and rhetorical escalation occurs more frequently with creative methods as shown in Table 1. It can be hard-pressed to find a court that applies rhetorical downplaying with creative methods, as it seems to go against the very nature of textual methods to rhetorically escalate them. Furthermore, it could easily happen that a court with creative jurisprudence adopts a decision by applying the rhetorical downplaying of textual methods. For instance, the Guatemalan Court, during its creative cosmopolitan period, used the rhetorical downplaying of textual

[31] For instance, in Decision 23, Expediente 03-0017, 22 January 2003, the Chamber refers to itself as the 'maximum guarantor of the Fundamental Text'.

[32] See Fuchs, Camilo Herrera and Barboza (ch 18).

[33] See Werneck Arguelhes, Bellem de Lima and Hartmann (ch 5).

methods to uphold a decision to bar the daughter of Ríos Mont, a former *coup d'état* president, from running for the presidency.[34] Similarly, Ecuador 1, which was packed by former President Rafael Correa, reviewed the constitutionality of a constitutional amendment allowing the indefinite re-election of the president, which it had approved in 2015 during Correa's regime.[35] This happened at a politically sensitive moment, just a few weeks before Ecuador 1's operations ceased, when it referred extensively to the constitution's text without including conceptual content or relying on dogmatic construction.[36]

The rhetorical downplaying of textual methods and the rhetorical escalation of creative arguments seem to occur at moments of political turmoil, when courts are pressured to invoke reasons against their better judgement, or they choose to use arguments that reflect their own institutional and personal interests without expending sufficient effort to justify them. Indeed, an unpremeditated automatic escape route with textual methods (rhetorical downplaying) and the hyperbolic stockpiling of creative methods (rhetorical escalation) have something in common – the corrosion of the weight of the arguments that could lead to the discredit of law. Consequently, both the rhetorical downplaying of textual methods and the rhetorical escalation of creative methods seem to favour outcomes preferred by transformative and neo-constitutional theories and social justice constitutionalism.[37]

Table 1 On the rhetorical use of textual and creative methods

	Textual methods	Creative methods
Rhetorical downplaying	Ecuador 1 and 2, Peru, Paraguay, Bolivia, Guatemala in its formalist period, Venezuela	Ecuador 1 (with references to international law)
Rhetorical escalation		Brazil, Costa Rica, Colombia, Guatemala cosmopolitan period
Outcome	Social justice constitutionalism	

Some courts seem to lack rhetorical use following the results on the overall weight of the arguments, such as in the Commonwealth Caribbean, Uruguay, Chile and Mexico. As the Chilean case shows, courts taking an apolitical approach can also mask rhetorical practices,[38] and therefore our numbers should be carefully read within the concrete political and social contexts. While the results for the Caribbean Commonwealth and Uruguay are less surprising, the present experiment to single out and measure rhetorical arguments has left several questions open, and perhaps even added new ones to the list, further proving that the topic needs more academic attention.

[34] *Zury Rios case*, Expediente 1584-2019, Apelación de Sentencia de Amparo, 13 May 2019.

[35] Judgment No 018-18-SIN-CC, ECC.

[36] See more J Fröhlich and PP Pigozzi, 'Ecuador' in R Albert et al (eds), *2018 Global Review of Constitutional Law* (I•CONnect – Clough Center, 2019) 88.

[37] The 'all-things-considered moral reasoning' frequently applied in human rights cases in the region (and elsewhere) requires rhetorical reasoning in the sense of 'make believe' where judges are merely applying the law and not engaging in legislative activity. Casey (n 10) 190.

[38] See Hilbink (n 26).

D. An Integral Look at the Classical vs Creative Division

In political science, those who study the judicialisation of politics or law and courts have seemingly already prepared the basic terminology to capture the division that looms among constitutional courts in Latin America and the Caribbean:

> The transformation of Latin American constitutional doctrine signalled the abandonment of the strong legal formalism that had dominated throughout the previous century and a half. The traditional insistence on the superiority of codified and statutory law and the prescription of a modest role for the judiciary (to apply the law without scrutinizing its fairness) was suddenly replaced by a constitutional discourse emphasizing the relevance of human rights, constitutional principles, and value-oriented judges.[39]

I argue that changes went beyond a simple intensification of creative methods. The creative versus formalist battlefield in constitutional interpretation is not novel in itself; it is an age-old tension that has had and will continue to have novel manifestations. The current Latin American and Caribbean tendency is novel in at least two aspects.

First, we have seen in Latin America and the Caribbean that the debate over the ideal interpretive approach is conducted with different methods and concepts than elsewhere. However, because we know so little about the judicial practices of most of the world outside the countries that this and the CONREASON project covered (eg, African countries and the Far East), this comparison could and should be further explored. Second, renouncing the 'formalist and anti-judicial review' position and accepting the new orthodoxy that is 'pro-judicial review'[40] deconstructed, indicates an attempt to redesign the basic concept of constitutional interpretation and its methods in light of transformative constitutional theories. Consequently, interpretation in the framework of this attempt is not considered an action involving 'guided 'moral' principles and rules' that 'are a matter of objective reasonableness, not of whim, convention or mere 'decision''[41] but rather a tool of judicial empowerment freely adjustable to the perceived injustices that judges seek to resolve with their decisions.

The rise of judicial review and the dominance of international law in constitutional adjudication happened somewhat hand in hand in Latin America, as the inclusion of international human rights law in constitutions was simultaneously a sign of the state's commitment to the constitution.[42] As the IACtHR has led an activist interpretation of rights[43] and its own competences, states have begun to consider different exit options[44] (see the cases of Trinidad and Tobago, Peru, the Dominican Republic, Argentina and

[39] Couso (n 5) 149; see also, 148.

[40] ibid 157.

[41] Finnis (n 28) 141.

[42] MC Mirow, *Latin American Law: A History of Private Law and Institutions in Spanish America* (University of Texas, 2004) 237.

[43] J Contesse, 'Resisting the Inter-American Human Rights System' (2019) 44 *Yale Journal of International Law* 179, 218.

[44] The exit scenario could be part of the third wave of judicial review and be identified as a complex set of reactions to the tensions that existed between the first two waves, which were triggered by 'the sensitivity to the rule of law and democratic deficits which exist in international and transnational governance' and the increasing counterforces against a diminishing national identity. See Weiler and Lustig (n 2) 345.

Venezuela).[45] The Latin American experience[46] invites deeper analysis of the quality of judicial argumentation and judicial independence vis-à-vis the region-specific manifestation of backlash and voice.

Because of judges' self-perceptions and their impact on judicial behaviour, earlier studies have already theorised the abovementioned division. According to these studies, the difference between the traditional-positivists and the new constitutionalist worldviews is that while the former interpreted constitutions like ordinary statutes, with the new constitutionalist approach, judges read the constitutions more broadly.[47]

Graph 5 The use of creative versus classical methods based on the selected cases from all analysed jurisdictions

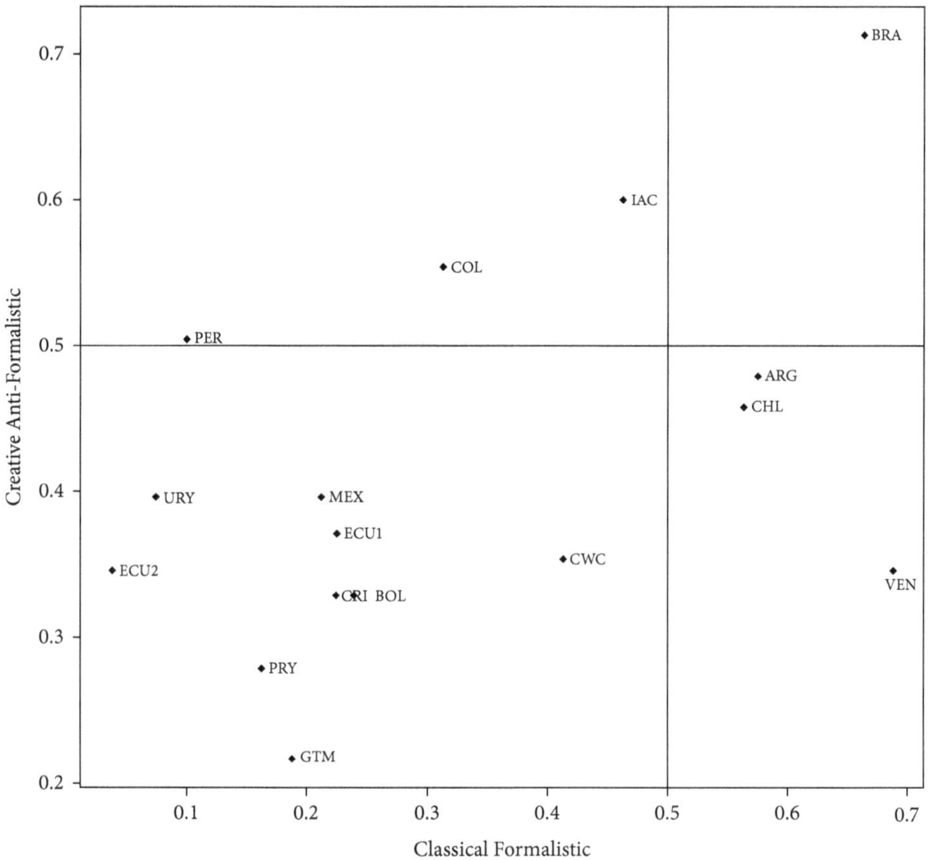

[45] X Soley, 'Parting Ways or Lashing Back? Withdrawals, Backlash and the Inter-American Court of Human Rights' (2018-01) *Max Planck Institute for Comparative Public Law and International Law Research Paper*.

[46] J Ríos-Figueroa, 'Judicial review and democratic resilience: Afterword to the Foreword by Doreen Lustig and J. H. H. Weiler' (2019) 17 *International Journal of Constitutional Law* 17–23.

[47] D Landau, 'The Two Discourses in Colombian Constitutional Jurisprudence: A New Approach to Modeling Judicial Behavior in Latin America' (2005) 37 *The George Washington International Law Review* 709. According to Landau, the basic reason why a judge would accept one or another worldview is his or her pre-constitutional court experience and exposure to different ideas.

Graph 5 provides a picture of references to classical and creative methods among the selected cases in Latin America and the Caribbean. Divided by the half point (or 50 per cent) of each approach, there are four categories of courts. In the upper-right corner, we find Brazil, a truly hyperbolic court that relies on an excessive number of references to both creative and classical methods. The section to its left contains courts such as the IACtHR, the Colombian and Peruvian, which have a rather creative jurisprudence, with fewer references to formalist methods. In contrast, the lower-right corner shows courts that are more classical and formalist (the Argentine and Chilean tribunals), which had quite high scores on creative methods as well but comparatively used more classical arguments. In this same cluster, Venezuela had double the number of references to formalist methods compared to creative ones. Finally, when considering the total number of observations, most courts pertained to the group with around 30 to 40 per cent of references to both types of arguments. In this same category, we had relatively varied results, as we find Ecuador 2 and Uruguay's tribunal, which both excluded almost all classical methods from their reasoning, and on the other hand, Guatemala's, with few references to the creative component.

Graph 5 is like a photograph of a busy street with many people. We capture a moment when they all appear close to one other for a second, but we know that they are all moving in different directions. Our data shows that, just a decade ago, many if not all the countries would have been in the bottom-left cluster with a more formalist type of reasoning. In the last decade or so, this practice changed dramatically, and as a result, various courts now employ a verifiably more cosmopolitan and creative reason-giving practice, such as in the cases of Colombia, the IACtHR and Brazil. We also observe that some countries, such as Chile, Guatemala, Ecuador, Argentina and Mexico, are on this same path but in an earlier stage of the process. In absolute terms, the true outliers of this regional tendency seem to be the Venezuelan formalist court because of the authoritarian context, and the Commonwealth Caribbean because of the differences its legal culture implies. Indeed, it will be the task of future researchers to determine whether these trends proceed in the same direction or change in light of novel emerging circumstances.

II. Constitutional Reasoning in Latin America and the Caribbean

A. 'Rights Talk' in Latin America and the Caribbean

In Latin America, the global doctrine according to which human rights law is the central category[48] of constitutionalism is especially strong, and the present research's results attest to this. It is well-known that before the end of the 1980s, constitutional courts did not undertake human rights cases on a massive scale. Even law courses at that time focused mostly on the so-called 'organic part' of the constitution, and the

[48] Couso (n 5) 163.

'dogmatic' section dedicated to fundamental rights was reduced to a mere enumeration of the rights mentioned in the constitutions.[49]

Most of the selected landmark cases, about 70 per cent, focused on fundamental rights in the region, which could cast doubt on any claim about the end[50] of 'the age of rights'[51] in Latin America and the Caribbean. Unsurprisingly, the IACtHR fielded most of these types of cases (about 95 per cent, 38 out of 40), followed by Peru (34), Mexico and Chile (32), Costa Rica, Guatemala and Colombia (31), and finally the Commonwealth Caribbean and Argentina (30). It is interesting to note that courts from the Andean region with an extensive rights catalogue were below the regional average. In Bolivia and Venezuela, this number was around 50 per cent, and in the case of the current Ecuadorian court, it was below 40 per cent.

The second most common topic among the selected cases was not interbranch or structural problems but procedural issues. The regional average of this type of case was 36 per cent, which means that almost every third case included this theme. This subcategory was created precisely because a common feature of several Latin American and Caribbean courts is lengthy and detailed reasoning on procedural aspects, sometimes avoiding a response on the merits.[52]

Finally, around 23 per cent of the selected cases dealt with interbranch issues – that is, the relationships among and the competences of different state organs. Ecuador 1 of the Correa era and the Uruguayan tribunal did not field any such cases, whereas the courts of Bolivia (almost 50 per cent), Venezuela, Peru and Brazil (37.5 per cent) and Guatemala (35 per cent) that had the most interbranch issues among their selected judgments.

B. The Structure of the Arguments and the Length of the Decisions – An Argumentative Labyrinth?

While most courts analysed in the CONREASON project applied a chain structure of arguments[53] with only a few exceptions (eg, the Brazilian and South African cases), in our samples from Latin America and the Caribbean, the parallel argument structure was the most common. Only the Chilean, Ecuadorian (Ecuador 1) and Commonwealth Caribbean courts employed the classical linear argumentative structure in more than half of their selected decisions, while Mexico and Argentina were still above the regional average (34 per cent) with 40 per cent each. The first three courts with above-average scores are known as courts that take a more formalist approach to reasoning – Chile and the Caribbean for cultural reasons, and Ecuador 2 for reasons more related to the high pressure to quickly process an accumulated caseload and a desire to separate itself from its predecessor's rhetorical practices.

[49] ibid 152.

[50] MW Mutua, 'Is the Age of Human Rights Over?' in SA McClennen and A Schultheis Moore (eds), *Routledge Companion to Literature and Human Rights* (Routledge, 2016) 450–58.

[51] L Henkin, *The Age of Rights* (Columbia University Press, 1990).

[52] Couso (n 5) 151.

[53] A Jakab et al (eds), *Comparative Constitutional Reasoning* (Cambridge University Press, 2017) 788–89. However, as the data in this volume shows, while the one-line conclusive structure is declining, parallel and dialogical structures are on the rise.

Contrary to the global tendency, the most frequent structure of arguments was the parallel conclusive type used in an average of 47 per cent of the selected cases from all jurisdictions. While those countries that scored the highest on the linear structure were now the last ones on the list, such as Chile, Ecuador 1 and the Commonwealth Caribbean, courts that scored the lowest before, now had the highest values. These are the courts that employed two or more simultaneous lines of argument that together led to the decision's conclusion. For instance, the IACtHR used the parallel conclusive structure in 87.5 per cent of its selected cases, followed by Peru, Ecuador 2, Uruguay, Brazil and Paraguay, which all used the parallel structure in more than half of their selected sentences.

The least used reasoning structure was the 'individually inconclusive, but together conclusive arguments' (dialogic structure), referring to a court's practice of employing several different lines of argumentation without establishing a clear relation among them or to the conclusion. The generally volatile character of the IACtHR's jurisprudence is less of a surprise, although it is still a startling detail that 95 per cent of its selected decisions followed the dialogic structure. The IACtHR was followed by the courts from Colombia (50 per cent), Bolivia (45 per cent), Venezuela (40 per cent), Costa Rica and Guatemala (35 per cent). On the other end of the spectrum, we find results of courts with fewer than 10 per cent of cases with dialogic reasoning, such as the Caribbean Commonwealth, Chile, Ecuador 1, Peru and Mexico, which were the only jurisdictions without even one decision with a dialogic structure.

All in all, the great majority of the selected decisions went beyond a simple linear structure of argumentation and opted for a more complex, often-hyperbolic style of reasoning. The accumulation of various arguments implies that there are evident consequences to the average length of the decisions. Our data, in fact, supports the unsurprising correlation between the more complex (parallel or dialogic) reasoning structure and the length of the judicial decision, meaning the more complex the structure applied, the longer the sentence will be. The most extensive decisions were from Brazil (with an average of 260 pages), Colombia (164), Mexico (147) and the IACtHR (112). All these courts had high scores on either the parallel or dialogic structures of arguments, and they occupied a leading position among the region's transformative courts. Courts with the shortest decisions were those in Paraguay (an average of 10.5 pages), Uruguay (12), Ecuador (Ecuador 2, 16.5) and Costa Rica (22.5). The explanation might be slightly more complex for these cases, as Uruguay, Paraguay and Ecuador 2 all had high scores for parallel arguments, although this seemingly did not impact the length of their decisions. The cases of Uruguay and Costa Rica prove that a dominant creative element in the reasoning can coexist with a more moderate structure, and vice versa, the cases of Chile (an average of 88 pages) and Mexico (147) prove that a moderate reasoning style can also lead to relatively long decisions. The regional average of the length of the selected decisions was 68.5 pages.

C. Constitutional Interpretive Methods in Latin America and the Caribbean

Human rights cases were the rule among the selected landmark judgments in Latin America and the Caribbean, and most of the region's courts preferred to use two or more simultaneous lines of reasoning to justify the outcome in those types of decisions. In this section, we examine the most and least frequent methods that courts invoked, by creating three categories of methods according to the rates of their occurrence in the 40 selected cases in each jurisdiction. First, conventional instruments of constitutional reasoning were those that had a median close to or more than 20, meaning that they were invoked in around half of the selected sentences. Second were the methods that have been trending in the region since the 2000s, and third were those methods that started to lose their relevance or were used rarely throughout the analysed period.

Graph 6 below shows the interpretive methods invoked in the selected decisions from all analysed jurisdictions. Between the two ends of the long, thin lines (whiskers or error bars), we see the country with the least and most uses of that certain method, while all other cases (except for the two outliers mentioned earlier) are visualised in the rectangles (or two-coloured boxes). The line that divides these boxes indicates the median value. The median value shows the middle or halfway point of the data, meaning that there are an equal number of observations (in our case, case numbers) towards the bottom (lower quartile) and the top (upper quartile). Whisker plots allow us to observe more details about the results than a simple average.

Graph 6 Reference to interpretive methods in all jurisdictions among the selected case law

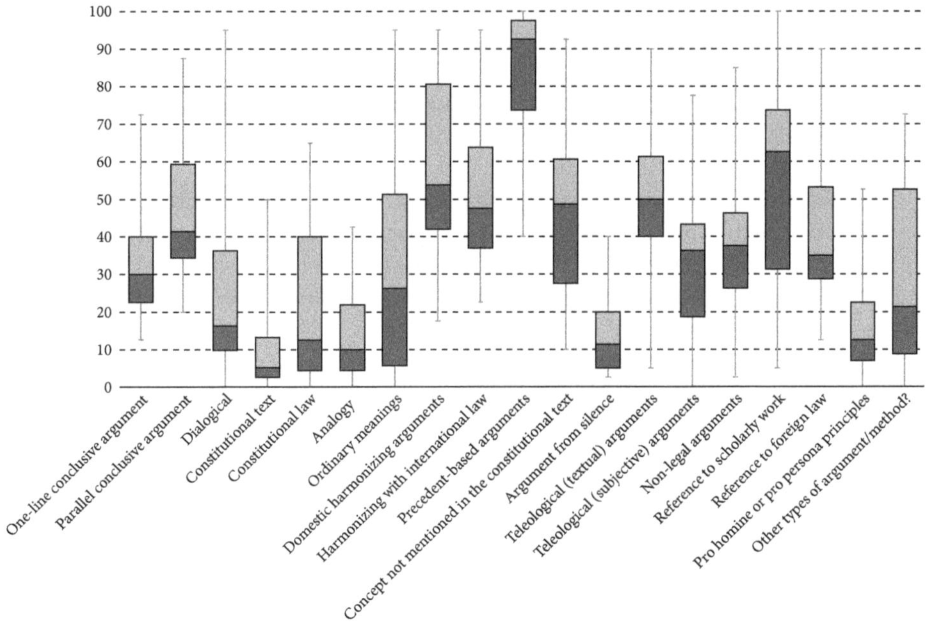

i. The Conventional Methods of Interpretation

Certain methods seem to function as part of a conventional set of interpretive tools for Latin American and Caribbean courts. These methods have evidently not been identified with or expropriated by any political ideology as the only desirable methods to resolve constitutional law issues. Conventional methods are the precedential method, the domestic harmonising method and the objective teleological method. There are two more methods that have a median close to 0.5 – reference to scholarly work, and international law and concepts and principles – but these methods have become popular only recently so their use is better explained in the second category.

Reference to precedents was the most frequent method of interpretation among all selected decisions in the region. As depicted in Graph 6, the median was 37 out of 40 points (using the number of selected landmark judgments as the scale of measurement), and the regional average was 92.5 per cent, while even in Paraguay and Guatemala, the negative outliers referred to precedents in 40 to 42 per cent of the selected cases. Brazil, where the Constitutional Court used this method in each selected case, is not really an outstanding example, as most courts in the study referred to their own earlier caselaw between 75 and 95 per cent of the time, which is a high enough number to support the idea that Latin America and the Caribbean share the global trend of the 'commonlawisation' of civil law.[54] It is noteworthy that the only common-law jurisdiction among the countries included in the research used this method 'only' in 37 cases out of the selected 40 (92.5 per cent).

Domestic harmonising was the second most invoked interpretive method in the selected cases among all jurisdictions, with a median of 21.5 points out of 40, and a regional average of 56.5 per cent, although there was equally great variation. Indeed, the method that seeks the inner coherency of the constitutional text seems to be less politicised and more neutral and perhaps more suited to courts that are seeking to provide a more established justification for their decisions. The great variation shows, however, that there is no complete agreement on this, as Brazil and Colombia, with the highest values (both with 38 points), and the courts from Uruguay, Ecuador (Ecuador 2) and Guatemala are those that seem to refute this hypothesis (7, 8, and 9 decisions out of 40, respectively).

The objective teleological, or purposive method, has been mainly understood to be a creative method because of its unique capacity to combine the normative text's legitimacy and the proactivity of the embedded norm's aim. This method could be an indicator for more advanced constitutional reasoning practices in other contexts, thanks to the creative, self-empowering approach it implies.[55] Our data, however, reflects a different picture in Latin America and the Caribbean. Most constitutions in the region have a strong aspirational and aversive character,[56] with abundant references to different aims, characterising at the same time the nature of authority.[57] The constitutional text does not fully function as an action-guiding normative framework but rather as a normatively deficient collective wish. Therefore, instead of self-empowerment, this method allows a certain level of deference in the decision-making process.[58] Our data seems to confirm this, showing that the Bolivian court and Ecuador 1 under Rafael Correa employed this tool most frequently (in 36 and 33 cases out of 40, respectively), together with Brazil (in 35 cases out of 40). On the other end, we find Uruguay with

[54] Jakab et al (n 53) 768.

[55] Jakab (n 4) 1241–43.

[56] KL Scheppele, 'Aspirational and Aversive Constitutionalism: The Case for Studying Cross-Constitutional Influence through Negative Models' (2003) 1 *International Journal of Constitutional Law* 296.

[57] M García-Villegas, 'Law as Hope: Constitutions, Courts, and Social Change in Latin America' (2004) 16 *Florida Journal of International Law* 133.

[58] As pointed out by M Hailbronner, 'A View From Western Europe' in C Hübner Mendes, R Gargarella and S Gaudi (eds), *The Oxford Handbook of Constitutional Law in Latin America* (Oxford University Press, 2022).

only two cases using a purposive method. With a regional average of more than 50 per cent, most countries in the region applied this method in several landmark cases but without a clear correlation to a transformative agenda that seemed to favour other interpretive tools.

ii. Recently Ascending Methods of Interpretation

The use of international law, foreign law, extra-constitutional concepts, scholarly work and non-legal arguments, collectively identified earlier as the creative component, are among the rising interpretive methods in Latin America and the Caribbean. Graph 6 shows that all these methods were close to a 50 per cent average use among the jurisdictions except for the principle of *pro personae*, which was present in less than 10 cases throughout the analysed jurisdictions but is nonetheless ascending as a new principle of public law in the region.

It might be somewhat surprising that the interpretive method that references scholarly works was the second most frequent method of interpretation in Latin American and Caribbean courts, with a 25-point median and a regional average of 56 per cent. Most courts examined in the research study referred to this method between 50 and 75 per cent of the time in their selected cases; however, there is great variation in the results, with outliers at the two extreme ends of the spectrum. The Brazilian court used this argument in all its selected cases, and the Uruguayan court in 38, followed by Argentina (31), Chile (31) and Colombia (29), while the regional human rights court, the IACtHR, was a clear exception, using this method in only two cases, followed by Guatemala, Costa Rica and the Commonwealth Caribbean with 11 cases each.

Especially beginning in the 1990s, courts needed robust doctrinal support to live up to the expectations of the new constitutional orthodoxy and create a conceptual framework in which the legal community could legitimately express and accept creative argumentations. The argumentative repertoire was mostly guaranteed by doctrinal transplants, which is why Latin American authors were not among the most cited scholars in the selected decisions. Although in some countries, like Chile before 2005, Brazilian, Spanish, Portuguese, Argentine and Chilean authors had a stronger impact, but after the 2000s, Italian, North American and German authors had a greater influence. The 'sudden popularity within Latin America's constitutional academic community of three important global exponents of higher-law constitutionalism: Ronald Dworkin (from the Anglo-American academic world); and Robert Alexy and Luigi Ferrajoli (from the Continental European one)'[59] was a widespread phenomenon that deeply shaped Latin American constitutional culture.[60] Furthermore, others point to the enormous explanatory power of Hans Kelsen's Pure Theory of Law, which has been used to support myriads of different legal positions and used rather incoherently,[61] or even erroneously.[62]

[59] Couso (n 5) 166.
[60] López (n 9).
[61] J Esquirol, 'Continuing Fictions of Latin American Law' (2003) 55 *Florida Law Review* 59–60.
[62] See M Gassner,' Der Kreis um Hans Kelsen in Lateinamerika. Wie die Reine Rechtslehre Lateinamerika eroberte' (2014) 1 *Beiträge zur Rechtsgeschichte Österreichs* 64–83, about Kelsen's presence in Latin America and the incorrect ('ecological') interpretation of his Pure Theory of Law by an Argentine professor, Carlos Cossio.

Even the outlier IACtHR has maintained a close and active relationship with academia, contributing to a relationship based on mutual influence without citations. Academia greatly influenced the court's jurisprudence on economic, social and cultural rights, and at the same time, the court contributed to the emerging relevance of this topic in academic circles. However, not all courts have the same motivation for referring to scholarly opinions. Examples of rhetorical escalation are found in the practice of the Brazilian court, which has been criticised for referring to scholarship in a decontextualised and superficial way, without engaging with the substance of the cited academic works. The Venezuelan court, on the other hand, uses this method to banish arguments about the court's ideological or institutional captivity and demonstrate its serious engagement with the law. Graph 7 confirms this. Beginning in the 2000s, there was an exponential growth in the judicial practice of citing to scholarly opinions, which by 2019, was present in every four selected decisions in the region.

Graph 7 The temporal division of the use of scholarly opinion among the selected cases across all jurisdictions

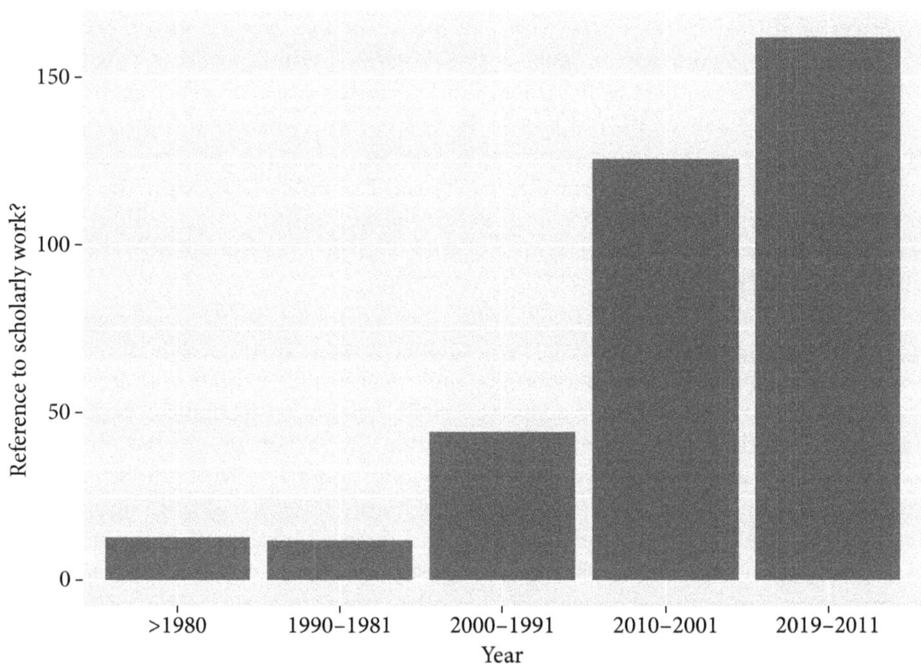

The use of concepts and principles is another interpretive tool that has been turned into a powerful transformative instrument. We note ample variation among the jurisdictions, with the lowest regional value from Venezuela with four cases, and the highest from the IACtHR with 38 cases out of 40. Brazil, with 30 cases, was second, while Colombia came in third with 25 mentions. In the case of Venezuela, there was seemingly a general refrain from referring to extratextual sources. Among the four cases where this happened, we find decisions that ensure the continuity of presidential power in instances of temporal absence or transition. While the IACtHR's frequent dogmatic construction might be explained by its intent to develop the standards and content of human rights, in other cases, such as Brazil's, criticism points to the oftentimes abusive, distorted or rhetorical references to concepts and principles.

Harmonising with international law or foreign law are methods that have had an enigmatic role in the region over the last two decades. Reference to international law in Latin America and the Caribbean can be understood better as a creative method than a classical one. In the region, international law is not primarily understood to be a complement to national law when appeals are lodged in instances of constitutional malfunction, but it has come to be a customary reference point for opposing the national constitution.[63] Contrasting deficient and incomplete national constitutions with the robust body of international law and its redemptive capacity has created quite successful arguments, especially during the last two decades. While it is unsurprising to find cosmopolitan practices in the IACtHR (using this method in 38 out of 40 sentences), Colombia (28) or Brazil (27), it is somewhat unexpected in Peru (33). Because of the doctrine of conventionality control (*control de convencionalidad*),[64] which the IACtHR developed, constitutional judges have a duty to ensure that their interpretation and enforcement of domestic law – including the constitution – are conducted in accordance with international law. The Peruvian court for instance used it to argue that the death penalty provided for in Article 140 of the constitution must be understood to be limited by the international human rights treaties to which Peru is a party. On the other end of the spectrum, we find Paraguay, Chile and Venezuela with 9, 12 and 13 cases, respectively, using international law arguments out of the 40 selected decisions. While the case of Chile might be explained by the fact that the Chilean court started to employ these kinds of arguments only after a 2005 constitutional amendment, the lower numbers from Venezuela would perfectly fit the third wave of constitutional review[65] that made some countries reject the excessive power of international courts.[66] It is also clear from our sample that the sources of the Inter-American System of Human Rights were referenced most frequently in the IACtHR's jurisprudence (95 per cent), Peru's (72 per cent), Brazil's (55 per cent) and Colombia's (50 per cent) and reach a regional average of 40 per cent, while the use of binding international law from outside the region was less frequent (32.5 per cent as a regional average). Finally, the IACtHR invoked international soft law in 95 per cent of the selected caselaw, followed by Mexico with a 47.5 per cent average.

Reference to foreign law is another ascending element of the creative argumentative turn. Looking at the total number of cases from the last two decades, we see somewhat fewer cases with foreign references, but there was a clear upsurge of foreign borrowing starting in the 2000s, which continued between 2010 and 2019. There was great divergence between the two extremes, where Brazil stood out with 36 cases out of 40, while Guatemala, with 5 out of 40 cases, was the least open to foreign legal experiences. While these numbers alone might optimistically suggest that there is an increasing

[63] See more about the use of international law to strike down national legislation in Huneeus (n 1) 89.

[64] See *Almonacid Arellano and others v Chile* (Judgment of 26 September 2006) 124.

[65] See Lustig Weiler (n 2).

[66] So far, Argentina, Chile and Venezuela have rejected the jurisprudence of the Inter-American Court. See A Huneuss, 'Rejecting the Inter-American Court: Judicialization, National Court and Regional Human Rights' in Couso et al (eds), *Cultures of Legality* (Cambridge University Press, 2010) 113.

amount of international or regional judicial dialogue, the chapters that address this issue caution against drawing such a conclusion too quickly. One reason is that comparative sources (such as foreign constitutions, foreign laws or foreign court decisions) are taken out of context and selected and applied in an arbitrary manner,[67] while another is the relatively few references made to regional sources. A good example of the latter is an Ecuador 1 case regarding the indefinite re-election of the country's president. There, the court referred to a Colombian case on the passive right to vote, attempting to justify the constitutionality of the constitutional amendment that then-President Rafael Correa proposed. At the same time, the court failed to mention the Colombian case that prohibited the second re-election of President Álvaro Uribe, using arguments on the rule of law. Regarding the issue of judicial dialogue, Brazil, as a regional leader in the use of foreign references, shows that Latin American foreign law is almost always invoked together with non-Latin American sources (in the Brazilian case, there was only one exception). Graph 8 depicts the overall augmentation of references to international law and foreign law in Latin America and the Caribbean throughout the analysed period.

Graph 8 The use of international law and foreign law over time in all the selected cases

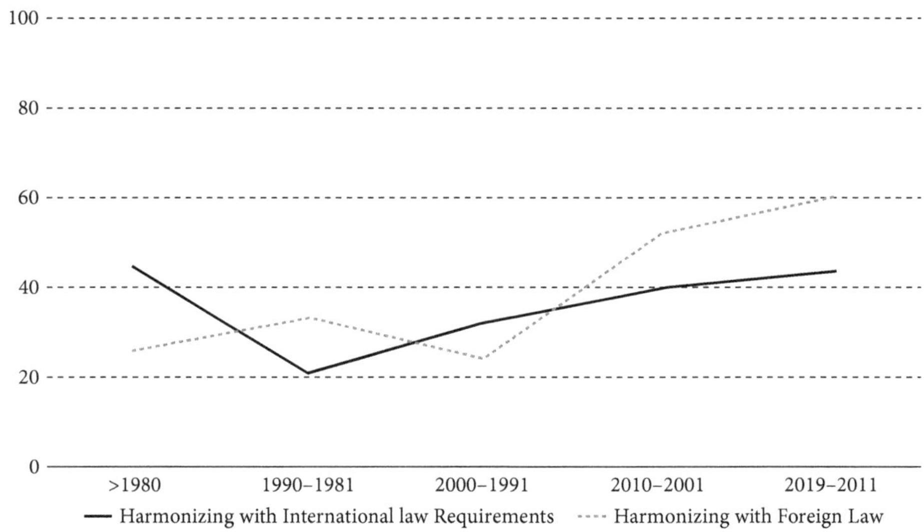

The *pro personae* principle is another type of argument that has become an important element of the judicial self-empowerment in Latin America and the Caribbean. The IACtHR's first specific reference to this principle was in Consultative Opinion 8/85, a Costa Rican freedom-of-expression case.[68] To maximise the content of rights and minimise the possibly applicable restrictions, the *pro personae* principle became a

[67] See R Dixon and D Landau, *Abusive Constitutional Borrowing: Legal Globalization and the Subversion of Liberal Democracy* (Oxford University Press, 2021).

[68] X Medellin, 'Principio Pro Personae: Una Revisión Crítica Desde el Derecho Internacional de los Derechos Humanos' (2019) *Estudios Constitucionales* 420–21.

guiding element not only in the IACtHR's jurisprudence but also in many other courts in the region. Thus, it is somewhat surprising that the Commonwealth Caribbean's courts invoked this principle the most in their selected decisions, namely in half of the cases, followed by the IACtHR with 17 cases out of 40. On the other hand, countries that had the lowest numbers of references to this principle have courts that are otherwise quite creative and produce an argumentatively diverse jurisprudence, such as those in Colombia, Costa Rica and Ecuador (Ecuador 2). One possible explanation could be that the *pro personae* principle mainly works as a meta-legal principle, functioning as a blueprint for the court's reasoning. Additionally, in some courts' jurisprudence, or in some cases, this principle was limited to a specific use, such as in the case of Ecuador 2, which applied it in criminal proceedings to protect the defendant.[69] The 18 per cent regional average could be deemed low as an absolute value, but this principle was among the arguments recognised and massively invoked just two decades ago.

Regarding non-legal arguments, we differentiated among economic, social, moral and scientific arguments and found that courts in the region invoked all these types at an average rate of 40 per cent among the chosen cases, with a 15-point median. As non-legal arguments openly introduce extra-legal content to the decision-making process, the practice could signal a court's deviation from the normative text and shed light on the process of the deformalisation of legal norms and institutions in view of social, economic or moral considerations. In this context, the 40 per cent average might confirm that in many of the selected landmark cases legal issues were being delegalised through the frequent use of non-legal arguments. Our data also shows that social arguments were by far the most powerful, with a 30 per cent regional average, followed by economic (14 per cent), scientific (10 per cent) and moral (7.5 per cent regional average) arguments. We also observe that Brazil, Colombia and the IACtHR occupied the top three places in all categories, which seems to confirm the trend of viewing the constitution as a conduit for social transformation.

iii. Weakening and Sporadic Methods of Interpretation

While creative interpretive methods are ascending in prominence, those that maintain a solid link to the normative text are declining in most courts' landmark cases in Latin America and the Caribbean. Regionally, on average, courts invoked the ordinary meaning of the constitutional text in 33 per cent of the selected cases. There are at least three factors that might help explain this value.

First, literal meaning is precisely the method that is usually rhetorically downplayed in real practice. The long-standing misuses and abuses of the textual argument have prompted a rather superficial and empty reference to the constitutional text, which is almost analogous to a mere citation to its words, with no explanation of its meaning or how it supports a certain outcome. This downplaying type of rhetorical use explains in part why textual meaning was present in at least every third selected case in the region. Second, courts with results above this average, such as the Venezuelan, Chilean, Brazilian, Argentine, Commonwealth Caribbean and the IACtHR, have

[69] Decision of the Ecuadorean Constitutional Court No 7-16-CN/19 and No 10-16-CN/19.

specific explanations for exceeding this value. The Venezuelan court's use of the textual method, with a 95 per cent average, presents an image at odds with the current regional trend. Instead of an explicit commitment to a textual philosophy of interpretation, the Venezuelan court maintains a close link with the text to demonstrate its decisions' legitimacy to the Venezuelan public. The cases of Chile, (57.5 per cent average), Argentina (50 per cent) and Brazil (50 per cent), showcase a persistent reasoning culture, where referring to the constitution's text is still a classical must-do even if it is unpremeditated and ultimately defeated by other arguments. Results from the Commonwealth Caribbean (42.5 per cent average) resemble the common English practice of statutory interpretation. The IACtHR produced the same value as the Caribbean courts, but this might be because the American Convention includes references to the use of ordinary meaning as a means of interpretation. In practice, however, these IACtHR arguments are rarely conclusive and usually overruled by other arguments, such as concepts and principles not expressed in the normative text, precedents or comparative sources. Third, the temporal distribution of references to ordinary meaning can be equally instructive. The overall decline over the last decade is even more pronounced if we look at Graph 9, which shows how steadily courts began to put this interpretive approach aside, especially after 2010. Like previous indicators, most selected judgments were from the last two decades, which increased the absolute number of cases with references to ordinary meaning. However, while during the first two decades there were either more or an equal number of landmarks with textual arguments, the first substantive drop occurred between 1991 and 2000, and the second between 2011 and 2019, when there were only 71 out of 291 selected cases that contained references to ordinary meaning.

Graph 9 The use of the ordinary meaning method in all jurisdictions over time

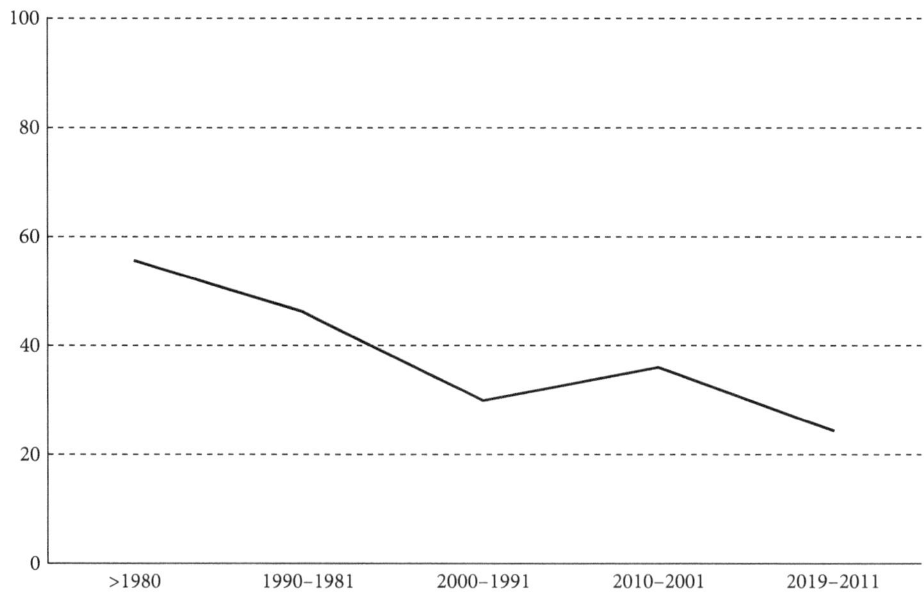

As foreseeable, references to the constitution-maker's intent (or the subjective teleological method) were not among the arguments that define the current tendencies. With a regional average of 30 per cent (a median of 16 points), it is an interpretive method that is present among the possible arguments known to courts in the region, although it is not used creatively and is therefore not among the current popular methods. The Brazilian court had this indicator's highest value, with 65 per cent, followed by the courts of Argentina and Venezuela (42.5 per cent) and those of Colombia and the Commonwealth Caribbean (40 per cent).

D. Key Concepts in Constitutional Reasoning in Latin America and the Caribbean

Most of the analysed concepts, 17 out of 24, were rarely invoked, with a median less than 10 points out of 40. In this group, we find judicial independence, sovereignty, state form, government systems, secularism, nation, core of constitutional rights, human dignity, freedom of expression, privacy, post-material values, justice, custom, family, transition, mechanisms of political control and judicial activism. As human rights cases comprised the clear majority of the selected cases, these results are mostly unsurprising. Concepts that are more useful for adjudicating human rights matters has a higher median, even among those that were rather scarce, such as the core of constitutional rights and dignity.

Graph 10 Reference to different concepts in all jurisdictions among the selected case law

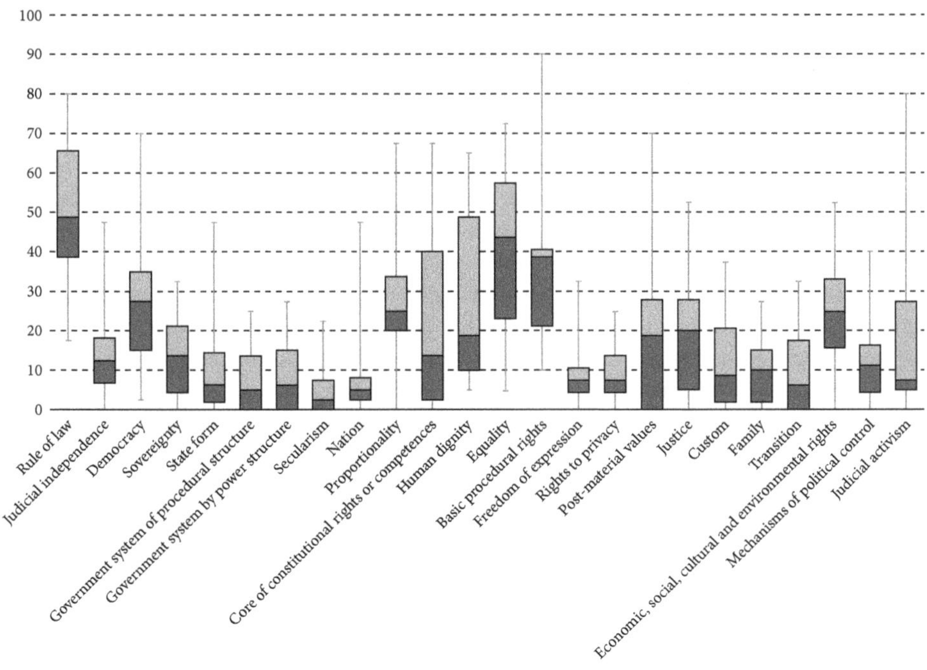

Democracy, proportionality and economic, social, cultural and environmental rights had a 10- or 11-point median out of 40, which means that they appeared in every fourth selected case, although all indicators showed great variation. In all three instances, Brazil was the upper outlier with 28, 27 or 21 cases, respectively, while Guatemala represents the lower end of the extreme with 1 case on democracy and no cases invoking proportionality. Similar to Guatemala, Ecuador 1 and Paraguay had very low values (2 and 3, respectively) on proportionality, which might be because these countries had the fewest human rights cases among their selected sentences. Paraguay continued to be one of the outliers when it came to invoking economic, social, cultural and environmental rights. With 1 case, however, the Paraguayan court was second to last, just one position above the Commonwealth Caribbean, which had no cases among its selected jurisprudence that referred to these rights. However, the Commonwealth Caribbean courts were above the regional average in terms of human rights cases, but many of them involved the death penalty, which was not addressed through the concept of human dignity but primarily through the right to a fair procedure and the rule of law. In the Commonwealth Caribbean, the imposition of the death penalty is mandatory for murder, and the argument for the defendant is usually that his or her basic procedural rights were denied when a judge had no opportunity to mitigate circumstances when imposing the sentence for murder.

The rule of law, equality and basic procedural rights were evidently the most powerful concepts among the selected cases from all jurisdictions. We dedicated a separate chapter to the rule of law in this volume, in which the authors looked closely at the references to the rule of law, and found that in most cases there was no substantial reasoning behind this principle.[70] The practice of rhetorical downplaying and rhetorical escalation is essential for understanding the dynamics behind the results from Brazil (32), Peru (30), Bolivia and Venezuela (27), and Colombia and Costa Rica (26) – the courts that had the most references. Those that had the lowest value for the rule of law seemingly reflect a more authentic and functional use, such as in Ecuador 2 (7) or the Commonwealth Caribbean courts (11). However, these numbers are close to each other, and whereas the latter employed the rule of law argument in the framework of the Westminster model of government, using it to strike down provisions of the Gun Court Act and fight the death penalty, the former diverged from its original concept and referred to it as an essentially transformed concept (ie, the rule of rights and justice).

The relatively high number of cases using the concept of equality is perhaps best interpreted in the unique Latin American social context characterised by a long-standing and deeply rooted structural inequality. As courts' profiles have been redesigned to make them more responsive to social justice issues, the high number of references to equality could be seen as a logical consequence of their reasoning practices. Equality was invoked most often by Colombia (29), Bolivia (28) and Brazil (24). The Bolivian court's most cited concept besides equality was post-material values. In various countries in the Andean region, equality across peoples is connected to harmony with the natural world and the establishment of the plurinational state, and in Bolivia, it is also linked to the recognition of human rights. Bolivia was an absolute outlier with 28 references to post-material values, invoking indigenous concepts such as the wellbeing or good-living

[70] See Fuchs, Camilo Herrera and Barboza (ch 18).

principle (*buenvivir*) and the harmony between man and nature (*Pachamama*). Other indigenous concepts, such as *Ama Qhilla* ('do not be lazy'), were invoked to determine their applicability to cases regarding judicial delay. On the other hand, references to equality were lowest in the Commonwealth Caribbean (2) and Paraguay (7).

With 36 mentions, the IACtHR occupied the first position regarding references to basic procedural rights, while Costa Rica with four mentions was a regional outlier from this trend. With respect to the IACtHR, the explanation could easily be attributed to the fact that the court usually analyses whether there was a violation of the right to access a judicial remedy, as all remedies must first be exhausted at the national level. It is no wonder that basic procedural rights form an essential part of the region's key concepts since several countries' constitutions, as well as the Inter-American Convention on Human Rights, expressly mention and protect the principle of due process and its distinct aspects.

Graph 11 References to proportionality, equality, post-material values and economic, social, cultural and environmental rights over time

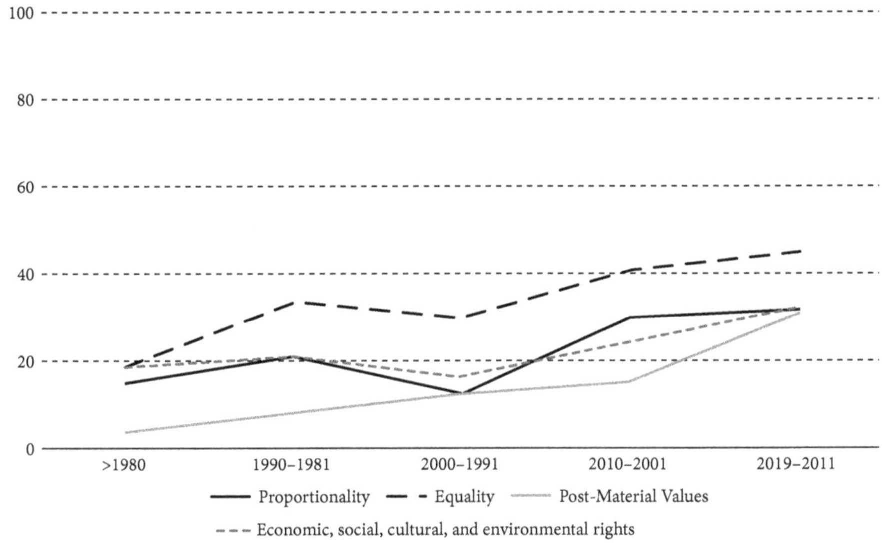

Graph 11 provides a summary of how some of the key concepts in the region are becoming increasingly powerful, based on the number of references. The appearance of these concepts is on the rise, approaching 40 to 50 per cent among the selected cases, while concepts that concern structural issues, such as the state's interbranch dimensions or competences, were rather sporadic and weak, which signals that Latin American courts in general place more emphasis on developing the necessary reasoning tools to settle human rights cases than to combat power abuse.

E. Overall Weight of the Arguments and Separate Opinions

Arguments with no logical connection to the final decision is a structural feature of court decisions in Latin America and the Caribbean. An extreme case can occur when a court uses long and detailed lines of argument that favour a certain outcome, then at the end of the opinion, it claims the case or the historical moment is an exception and raises new, often contrary arguments to conclude the case. Taking a harsh turn in judicial reasoning is not completely unprecedented in courts outside the region, but in Latin America, this practice has become standard in many courts. The indicator of the overall weight of the arguments was designed to make this practice visible and measurable.

The challenges posed by this measurement are explained in the volume's Introduction.[71] It is only fair to admit that we engaged in an experiment by asking our team to contrast the arguments invoked with the arguments that had a textually provable link to the conclusion, using the following descriptive three-level scale: (1) decisions with a majority of reasons that had a direct, logical connection to the conclusion were designated as conclusive or ratio decidendi arguments; (2) decisions with an equal number of reasons with and without such logical connections were designated as persuasive or obiter dicta arguments; and (3) decisions with more reasons invoked without such logical connections were called rhetorical (decorative or deceptive) arguments.

The overall hypothesis was that there were a significant number of cases that displayed the ample rhetorical element in constitutional reasoning, which I claim is a central feature in the region. Our results are neither conclusive nor irrelevant.

Graph 12 Decisions with conclusive, persuasive or rhetorical arguments in all selected cases

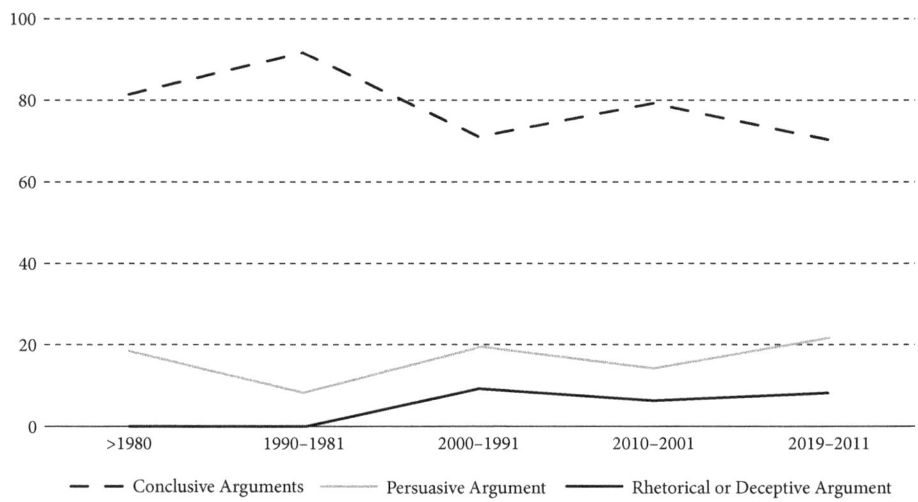

We can see that most courts maintained the relationships between the arguments and invoked concepts as well as the conclusions they reached, which is demonstrated by the high number of selected judgments that qualified as containing conclusive reasoning. The regional average of this type of reasoning was roughly 75 per cent. The Bolivian, Guatemalan, Costa Rican, Brazilian and Argentine courts, as well as the IACtHR, fell below this average. Ecuador 1 could possibly be in this group if we had the same type of

[71] See Fröhlich, Umpierrez de Reguero and Meléndez (ch 1).

data available, as 10 times out of 35, the court simply recalled the facts of the case, noted the lower court's mistakes or stated that the rules were violated. The Bolivian court's aim to advance the decolonisation project and apply the neo-constitutionalist approach has resulted in heavily decorated judgments with oftentimes ambiguous reasoning. In the case of Guatemala, the court, in its last cosmopolitan era, began to embrace a multiple-line structure of arguments where several reasons were rather auxiliary. While the Bolivian court has used precedents rhetorically, the Guatemalan court has frequently referred to foreign sources to distract from the actual line of reasoning. Similarly, the Brazilian court has been criticised for invoking reasons unconnected to the case and issue at hand, either to appear knowledgeable or exhibit sensitivity regarding certain issues. Indeed, the Brazilian chapter emphasises that the concept of human dignity has primarily been the victim of empty generalisations.

However, not all courts that fell below the regional average of reasoning coherency employed deceptive practices. For example, to comply with a pedagogical mission, the Costa Rican court provided reasons without establishing a clear link to the conclusion. Using a case on fair procedure in criminal proceedings to tackle general principles of due process, or even citing to Victor Hugo, the French writer, could be interpreted as an example of such motivation. The IACtHR reportedly had the same motivation behind its use of rhetorical arguments in various cases.

On the other end, courts that led a coherent jurisprudence in terms of maintaining a clear, logical connection between what they said and how they decided were those in the Commonwealth Caribbean, Uruguay, Mexico, Chile, Ecuador 2 and Venezuela. The Venezuelan court was perhaps the most curious of all, revealing that a court operating in a hegemonic authoritarian regime can also build coherent reasoning if the practice is in its own best interest.[72]

Despite the evident methodological difficulties, analysing the coherency of decisions and tackling rhetorical elements in the act of reasoning could contribute to a better understanding of judicial decision-making and foster judicial responsibility, which is why future research of both these aspects is needed.

Dissenting opinions[73] are not indispensable for a well-functioning constitutional review system; however, if permitted, they could attest to the quality and honesty of constitutional discourse inside and outside a court. Discouraging the submission of dissenting opinions in constitutional courts is a common feature of traditional civil law systems, where law is supposed to have a clearer and more stable meaning and where judicial decision-making is viewed as more distanced from politics.[74] In such an environment, a constitutional court can follow the strategy of the consensual decision-making approach, where decisions are made 'by unanimity and negotiated to achieve

[72] The court often uses constitutional interpretation to assert jurisdiction in cases where there is a lack of an explicit constitutional normative basis or to modify rules of access and other procedural rules. See Sánchez Urribarri and Berríos (ch 17).

[73] For a historical and empirical approach to understanding dissenting opinions in the civil law tradition of Europe, see K Kelemen, *Judicial Dissent in European Constitutional Courts. A Comparative and Legal Perspective* (Routledge, 2018).

[74] N Garoupa and T Ginsburg, *Judicial Reputation: A Comparative Theory* (University of Chicago Press, 2015) 252.

a consensus of all judges',[75] and the court can promote a public perception of an independent, law-abiding and neutral court. Alternatively, if a constitutional court chooses the strategy of fragmentation, concurring and dissenting opinions can unveil the different opinions expressed during the decision-making process. This strategy can foster a court's prestige and the constitution's supremacy, whereas in authoritarian regimes or those with weak public institutions, unanimous decisions might be interpreted as signs of unconditional deference to the executive branch or a lack of autonomous and independent decision-making.[76]

In Latin America and the Caribbean, the regional average of separate opinions in the selected cases was 53 per cent, meaning every second case in our database had either a dissenting or concurring opinion. There are various reasons why courts might fall below this average, but in general, there is a weak culture of academic discourse that often impedes the expression and mutual cultivation of disagreement. The negative outlier, Ecuador 1, which only had a dissenting or concurring opinion in 4 out of the 40 selected decisions, was harshly criticised for being not only deferential but also generally subservient to the executive and personally servile to then-President Rafael Correa. Ecuador 2, despite representing a different ideology and level of academic quality, occupied the second to last place, which might be due to the pressure imposed on that court to transmit an image of a strong and unanimous tribunal in politically sensitive cases.[77] While in Guatemala, dissenting opinions are only present in highly politicised cases, in Bolivia, judges have short tenures (six years), which seems to encourage the practice of hiding their preferences to ensure better opportunities after their tenures end. Finally, the Caribbean, with 17 decisions out of 40, represents an interesting case. As the CCJ is only the final appellate court in Barbados, Belize, Dominica and Guyana, the JCPC remains the court of last resort for the majority of Commonwealth Caribbean countries. In common-law courts, however, separate opinions should not be taken for granted because of the 'unity in judgement' principle, which was in force until 1966. As the Caribbean chapter explains, 17 decisions is still considered a high number. Usually, courts have 70 per cent or more decisions that include separate opinions, such as the Brazilian court with 90 per cent,[78] the Chilean with 85 per cent and the Mexican with 82.5 per cent.[79]

[75] ibid 147.

[76] ibid 148, 251–52.

[77] S Basabe-Serrano, 'Determinants of Judicial Dissent in Contexts of Extreme Institutional Instability: The Case of Ecuador's Constitutional Court' (2014) 6 *Journal of Politics in Latin America* 83.

[78] D Werneck Arguelhes and L Molhano Ribeiro, '"The Court, It Is I"? Individual Judicial Powers in the Brazilian Supreme Court and Their Implications for Constitutional Theory' (2018) 7 *Global Constitutionalism* 236; VA da Silva, 'Deciding without Deliberating' (2013) 11 *International Journal of Constitutional Law* 557–84.

[79] See generally R Davis and D Taras (eds), *Justices and Journalists: The Global Perspective* (Cambridge University Press, 2017). VA da Silva argues that the public broadcasting of plenary sessions produces more separate opinions in Brazil and Mexico, and identifies 'deliberative losses'. VA da Silva, 'Big Brother is Watching the Courts: Effects of TV Broadcasting on Judicial Deliberation' (2018) 51 *Verfassung und Recht in Übersee* 437; F Pou Giménez,' Constitutionalism and Rights Protection in Mexico and Brazil: comparative remarks' Dossier – The 30th Anniversary of the 1988 Brazilian Constitution (2018) 5 *Journal of Constitutional Research* at doi.org/10.5380/rinc.v5i3.60972.

F. Comparison of Global Trends in Constitutional Reasoning

As we have access to the dataset of the CONREASON project, which measured and compared 18 courts from various countries of the world, we have the possibility of making a novel comparison.[80] These courts, although not connected geographically, shared a relatively advanced standard of Western constitutionalism that makes it possible to have a common understanding of different interpretive methods and concepts. Although Latin America and the Caribbean is a region with specific characteristics that can affect the criteria of interpretive methods and concepts, a comparison of the results of the two projects still seems worthwhile. On the one hand, following the path of the CONREASON methodology was done precisely to make comparability possible, while on the other, the comparison offered an additional opportunity to test our hypothesis and the conceptualisation of our results.

Graph 13 below displays the most contested interpretive methods mentioned earlier. We see that Latin American and Caribbean courts indeed used the ordinary meaning method less frequently than jurisdictions analysed in the CONREASON project, which in reality must be even less if we consider the region's rhetorical downplaying of the textual method. With regard to the methods categorised earlier as the creative component, the only value higher in the CONREASON project was the number of the studied courts' references to concepts and principles. A possible explanation might be that, while the use of concepts in the traditional Western democracies is related more to judicial empowerment, in Latin America and the Caribbean, this impact is associated more with references to international law. This seems to be supported by the fact that the greatest difference between the analysed methods is observed in the harmonisation with international law, where we observe a 16 per cent variance between the results.

Graph 13 The comparison of some of the most contested interpretive methods with the results of the CONREASON project

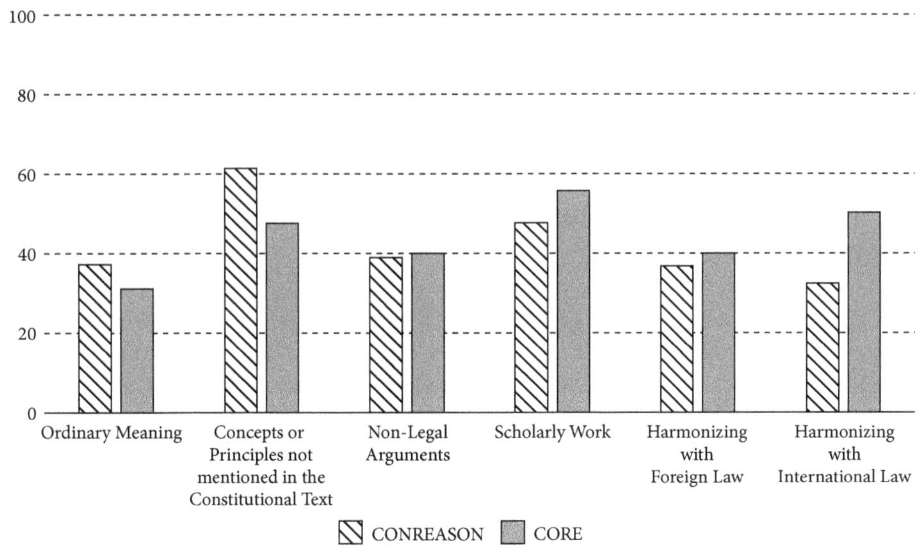

[80] See Jakab et al (n 53).

Another worthwhile experiment is comparing the results of the studies of the regional international courts included in these projects. Graph 14 paints an image of the IACtHR, which is excessively and abundantly equipped with concepts and interpretive methods. The IACtHR's use of concepts and principles without a textual basis, non-legal arguments and references to international law reaches extraordinary levels that are incomparable to its European peers. Indeed, the IACtHR produces an exceptionally creative jurisprudence, considering the results of those methods that use extratextual sources to define the meaning of the American Convention. The only instances when the IACtHR occupied the second position in the results were in the use of comparative sources and the mention of the constitution's text.

Graph 14 The comparison of some of the most contested interpretive methods invoked by international courts with the results of the CONREASON project

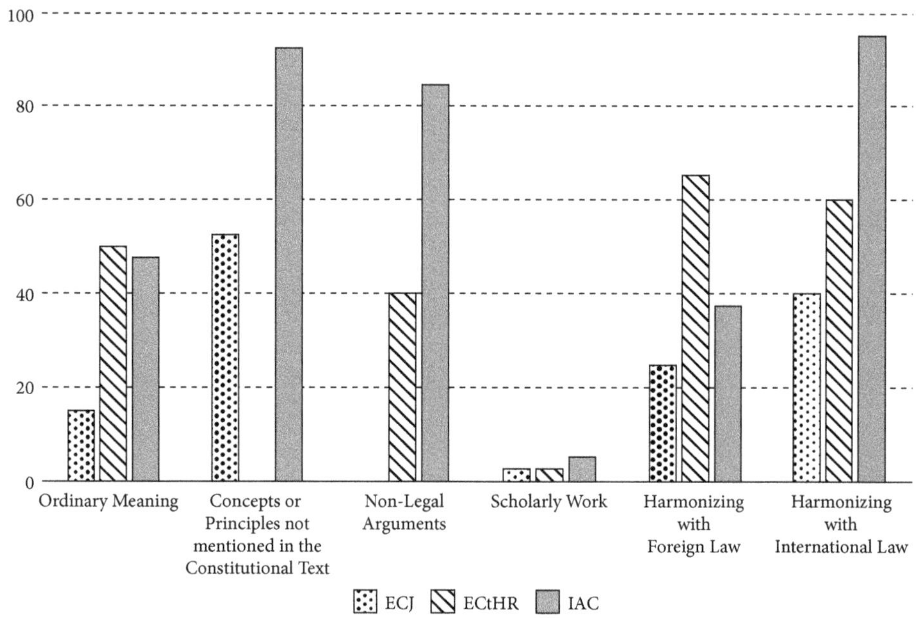

G. The Diminishing Value of the Rule of Law and a Weakening Normative Culture

Latin American constitutional and supreme courts do not generally follow the classical interpretive methods. However, if they do, they do so with a distinct meaning designed to fulfil social justice aspirations defined by the neo-constitutionalist and transformative constitutional theories. The current features of constitutional reasoning thus pertain to an interpretive empowerment of constitutional and supreme courts, which satisfy substantive justice claims by using creative methods and ignoring and contravening the normative text.

When it comes to the direct application of fundamental rights principles, judicial activism or references to substantive justice, it is common to refer to a higher law constitutionalism as the leading paradigm in Latin America and the Caribbean.[81] The 'higher' nature of constitutionalism, however, must embrace a robust formal element that credits the constitution's language by acknowledging its supreme character through entrenched constitutional clauses properly emphasised and executed in a constitutional court's reasoning. Posited law can promote human flourishing in multiple ways.[82] Preserving a direct link to the authoritative text has the additional functions of maintaining a standard for measuring judicial activity, keeping a court's power under control and ensuring judges' independence.[83] This formal aspect, when called into question, results in a sharpening contradiction between the classical and creative divisions as we have seen throughout the pages of this chapter.

There is an ambivalence that exists in the region about the authority of law and the constitution and those instruments' overall capacity to efficiently direct the actions of those who are obligated to follow their rules in concrete matters.[84] There is a deeper reality of historical and social rupture[85] that produced and has been producing conflicting attitudes about authority in general and legal authority in particular – a reality in which the individual is either subjugated by coercion or defies and revolts against it. Submission and deference to authority has undoubtedly been a frequent historical experience in the region, and according to our data, the opposite extreme has recently started to prevail in the form of defiance and confrontation. This false dichotomy in the approach to law's authority (ie, between submission and revolt) seems to reflect the sharp contrast existing between the oftentimes rhetorical downplaying of the authoritative text and the rhetorical escalation of creative interpretive methods. The third option (ie, making a reasoned and personally reflected choice about committing to the law and 'having an obligation'[86]) is rather an exceptional relationship to authority in the region.

Today, in Latin America and the Caribbean, constitutional authority is a diminishing façade in which is being replaced by international legal norms and society's substantive justice claims. International law, nevertheless, is itself existing in an epoch of challenges and relative normativity.[87] Additionally, by nature, the language of international law is even more abstract and general, which raises further difficulties for its ability to substitute the authority of national constitutions. This tendency has its roots, among others, in the fact that the basic principles of the rule of law, such as legal certainty, foreseeability and the principle of constitutional supremacy, have been

[81] Couso (n 5) 157.

[82] See Finnis (n 28) chs IX and X.

[83] Jakab (n 4) 1228–29.

[84] My understanding of this ambivalence was informed by an interview conducted with the Chilean sociologist, Pedro Morandé on 17 December 2023. He drew attention to the fact that Spanish language, especially the one used in the Spanish colonies, was initially spoken and not written, resulting in the absence of a strong unifying character concerning what was correct or clear; indeed, the language's grammar rules were not officially laid down until 1492.

[85] Pedro Morandé, *Cultura y Modernización en América Latina* (Instituto de Estudios de la Sociedad, 2017) 225–32; O Paz, *El laberinto de la soledad*, 9th edn (Fondo de Cultura Económica, 1981) 59–80.

[86] HLA Hart, *The Concept of Law* (Oxford University Press, 1961) chs II and V.

[87] M Goldmann, 'Relative Normativity' in J d'Aspremont and S Singh (eds), *Concepts for International Law: Contributions to Disciplinary Thought* (Edward Elgar, 2019); J Klabbers and G Palombella (eds), *The Challenge of Inter-Legality* (Cambridge University Press, 2019).

discredited for being artificial, dishonest and imposed by those in positions of power.[88] The void of authority has not been filled with any coherent theory or concept, and the inherent contradictions embedded in the constitution's text have been cloaked in darkness and open to arbitrariness and the advance of ideologically motivated agendas.

When law itself is deprived of its capacity to be valuable, and it becomes useful only relative to the objectives of those in power, the legal character of norms can disappear and be absorbed by politics, sociology or psychology. Indeed, abandoning the formal characteristics of law evokes the condemnation of classical methods of constitutional interpretation, such as the textual method, and it foments the reinforcement of interpretive methods with no connection to the normative text.[89] This approach seems to attach an imminent blindness to the consequences of law's weak authority and to the robust conceptual overreach in terms of rights that contrast with the context and practice in which they should be applied and exercised.

When the concrete demands of social justice change in light of the needs of distinct situations, the notion of constitutional interpretive methods are pressed to change as well. This requirement has transformed the essential quality of constitutional adjudication and constitutional interpretation too, as it abolished the rule-like character of interpretive methods,[90] turning them into a tool for transformative agendas. As courts thwart attempts to link the global and regional legal systems to the national and local dimensions of authority through judicial reasoning, the crisis of authority on the national level seems to be hardly avoidable.

We do not have the data to confirm if this rupture had existed in such a sharp form before the 1980s and the 1990s. We also lack the future data to say that this trend will continue the same way as it looks like now. It is therefore important to keep observing and critically analysing the judicial reasoning practice in the region, which is essential for maintaining a constant demand for well-founded, coherent and responsive judicial decisions.

[88] For a criticism of legal formalism as an artificial neutrality imposed by the wealthy, see R Pérez Perdomo, *El formalismo jurídico y sus funciones sociales en el siglo XIX venezolano* (Monte Ávila, 1978).

[89] For instance, a previous judge who served on the Ecuador 2 court argued that the source of human rights and constitutional guarantees is not only the constitution and the laws, but also the people themselves. R Ávila Santamaría, *Retos de una nueva institucionalidad estatal para la protección de los derechos humanos. Neoconstitucionalismo y sociedad* (Ministerio de Justicia y Derechos Humanos, 2008) 39.

[90] J Wróblewski, 'Legal Reasoning in Legal Interpretation' (1969) 12 *Logique at Analyse* 3, 7, in Jakab (n 4) 1227.

APPENDIX A: THE SELECTED LANDMARK CASES BY JURISDICTION

Argentina

1. Siri, Angel S. - 239:459
2. Sojo, Eduardo - causa CVIII - 32:120
3. F.A.L - 259 XLVI - 335:197
4. Acordada sobre reconocimiento del Gobierno Provisional de la Nación
5. Sejean, Juan Bautista con Ana María Saks de Sejean - 308:2268
6. Fallo Díaz Vélez Contra Provincia de Buenos Aires
7. Fallo Ercolano contra Lanteri de Renshaw
8. Fallo Avico contra de la Pesa, por consignación de intereses
9. Fallo Amador Spagnol, María Elena Alvarez de Schuster y otros
10. Fallo de la Municipalidad de la Capital contra Isabel A. de Elortondo
11. Fallo Ponzetti de Balbín v. Editorial Atlantida S.A.
12. Fallo Ana María Perez de Smith
13. Simón, Julio Héctor y otros s/ privación ilegítima de la libertad, etc. Causa N° 17.768
14. Kot, Samuel S.R.L. s/recurso de Habeas Corpus
15. Ekmekdjián, Miguel Angel c/ Sofovich, Gerardo y otros
16. Celestino M. Rey c/ Alfredo y Eduardo Rocha, por falsificación de mercaderías y de marca de fábrica
17. Rizzo, Jorge Gabriel (apoderado lista 3 Gente de Derecho) s/ acción de amparo c/ Poder Ejecutivo Nacional, ley 26,855, medida cautelar (Expte. N° 3034/13)
18. Juana Ana Soria de c/ Bodegas y Viñedos Pulenta Hnos. S.A.
19. Timerman, Jacobo s/ recurso de Habeas Corpus
20. Comunidad Homosexual Argentina c/ Resolución Inspección General de Justicia s/ personas jurídicas
21. Sociedad Anónima Compañía Azucarera Tucumana c/Provincia de Tucumán s/ cobro de pesos
22. Halabi, Ernesto c/P.E.N. - ley 25.873 - dto. 1563/04 s/ amparo ley 16.986
23. Recurso de hecho deducido por el centro de Estudios Legales y Sociales en la causa Verbitsky, Horacio s/ habeas corpus
24. Alem, Leandro N. y Candioti, Mariano N. (causa CCCLIII)
25. Dromi, José Roberto (Ministro de Obras y Servicios Públicos de la Nación) S/avocación en autos: Fontela, Moisés Eduardo c/ Estado Nacional

26. Recurso de hecho deducido por el Estado y el gobierno de Chile en la causa Arancibia Clavel, Enrique Lautaro s/ homicidio calificado y asociación ilícita y otros -causa n° 259
27. Schiffrin, Leopoldo Héctor c/ Poder Ejecutivo Nacional s/ acción meramente declarativa
28. Giroldi, Horacio David y otro s/ recurso de casacion- causa N 32/93
29. Enrique Arlandini
30. Peralta, Luis Arcenio y otro c/ Estado Nacional (Mrio. de Economía – BCRA.) s/ amparo
31. Angel Mattei
32. Arriola, Sebastián y otros s/ causa n 9080
33. Criminal c. López Jordán
34. Provincia de Chaco c/ Estado Nacional
35. Saguir y Dib, Claudia Graciela
36. S.A. Merck Quimica Argentina v. Nacion Argentina
37. Bazterrica, Gustavo Mario s/ tenencia de estupefacientes
38. Callao (Cine) s/ interpone recurso jerárquico c/ resolución dictada por la Direc. Nac. Serv. Empleo
39. Portillo, Alfredo s/ infr. art 44 ley 17.531
40. Ramon Juan Alberto Camps y Otros. "Causa incoada en virtud del decreto 280/84 del Poder Ejecutivo Nacional"

Bolivia

1. SCP 211/2018-S3
2. SCP 37/2018-S4
3. SCP 93/2017
4. SCP 84/2017
5. SCP 1086/2017-S1
6. SCP 691/2017-S3
7. SCP 60/2016
8. SCP 617/2016-S2
9. SCP 575/2016-S3
10. SCP 96/2016-S3
11. DCP 194/2015
12. SCP 783/2015-S1
13. SCP 832/2015-S3
14. SCP 426/2015-3
15. SCP 1954/2014
16. SCP 874/2014
17. SCP 778/2014
18. SCP 572/2014
19. SCP 551/2014
20. SCP 487/2014

21. DCP 8/2014
22. SCP 206/2014
23. SCP 1864/2013
24. SCP 1787/2013
25. DCP 6/2013
26. DCP 3/2013
27. DCP 2/2013
28. DCP 1/2013
29. SCP 2143/2012
30. SCP 2056/2012
31. SCP 2055/2012
32. SCP 1250/2012
33. SCP 846/2012
34. SCP 790/2012
35. SCP 770/2012
36. SCP 693/2012
37. SCP 300/2012
38. SCP 258/212
39. SCP 140/2012
40. SCP 15/2012

Brazil

1. RE 511961
2. ADPF 187
3. ADI 4815
4. ADPF 130
5. RE 389808
6. ADI 19694
7. RE 2018198
8. ADPF 186
9. ADPF 572
10. ADI 4439
11. ADPF 132
12. ADI 4650
13. ADC 43
14. ADPF 378
15. ADO 26
16. ADC 42
17. ADI 1351-3
18. MS 26603
19. ADPF 378
20. MS 21689-1
21. ADC 29

22. ADI 3367
23. ADI 6431
24. ADI-MC 939-7
25. ADI 4983
26. HC 82424
27. HC 82959
28. MI 670
29. ADI 3510
30. ADPF 54
31. STA 175 AgR
32. RE 888815
33. RE 670422
34. ADC 9 – MC
35. AG REG RE 410.715-5
36. ADPF 153
37. ADI 3105
38. RE 466443
39. ADI 3239
40. ADI MC 1480

Chile

1. Tribunal Calificador de Elecciones 33-1985
2. Requerimiento contra Clodomiro Almeyda 46-1987
3. Partidos Políticos 43-1987
4. Votaciones populares 53-1988
5. Municipalidades II 141-1992
6. Publicidad caminera 146-1992
7. Gobierno y Administración Regional 155-1992
8. Juzgados de policía local 171-1993
9. Tarifas de peajes 183-1994
10. Transplantes de órganos 220-1995
11. Sistema previsional FF.AA. 237-1996
12. Ley de presupuesto 254-1997
13. Código de Aguas 260-1997
14. Convenio pueblos indígenas 309-2000
15. Vehículos Catalíticos 325-2001
16. Liceo Manuel de Salas 352-2002
17. Corte Penal Internacional 346-2002
18. Jornada escolar completa II 423-2004
19. Sanción Empresas Eléctircas 480-2006
20. Panguipulli 505-2006
21. Presupuesto 2007 1005-2007
22. Abogado de Turno art.523 COT. 755-2007
23. Píldora del día después 740-2007

24. Transantiago II 1153-2008
25. Art.169 Código Sanitario 1518-2009
26. Recursos y tipicidad penal 1432-09
27. Art.38.ter Ley de Isapres 1710-2010
28. Intereses tributarios 1951-2011
29. Inhabilidad para contratar con el Estado prácticas antisindicales 1968-2011
30. Propaganda electoral 2487-13
31. Administrador Provisional Educación Superior 2731-2014
32. Curtidos Bas 2684-2014
33. Elimina Financiamiento Compartido y Prohibe Lucro 2787-2015
34. Reforma sistema electoral y cuotas 2777-2015
35. Gratuidad Educación Superior. Ley de Presupuesto 2935–2015
36. Sobre modernización de las relaciones laborales (Libertad sindical) 3016-2016
37. Ley Emilia 2983-2016
38. Despenalización del Aborto en Tres Causales 3729-2017
39. Sernac 4012-2017
40. Cascadas 3236-2016

Colombia

1. T-406/1992
2. T-494/1992
3. C-027/1993
4. C-221/1994
5. C-318/1995
6. C-239/1997
7. SU- 047/1999
8. SU-166/1999
9. SU-337/1999
10. C-371/2000
11. C-1052/2001
12. C-578/2002
13. T-881/2002
14. SU 383/2003
15. T-025/2004
16. C-590/2005
17. C-591/2005
18. T-1090/2005
19. C-355/2006
20. T-391/2007
21. C-070/2009
22. C-141/2010
23. C-252/2010
24. T-418/2010
25. T-617/ 2010

26. T-629/2010
27. C-644/2012
28. C-123/2014
29. T-057/2015
30. C-182/2016
31. SU-214/2016
32. C-699/2016
33. T-236/2017
34. C-332/2017
35. T-543/2017
36. C-674/2017
37. C-590/2017
38. C-117/2018
39. C-111/2019
40. C-252/2019

Commonwealth Caribbean

1. Barbados: Attorney General v Boyce and Joseph [2006] CCJ 3
2. Guyana: Attorney General Guyana v Cedric Richardson [2018] CCJ 17 (AJ)
3. Trinidad and Tobago: Attorney General Trinidad and Tobago v McLead [1984] 1 WLR 522
4. Trinidad and Tobago: Privy Council Appeal No.60 of 1998, Darrin Roger Thomas and Another v Cipriani Baptiste and Others [2002] AC
5. Barbados: Privy Council Appeal No.99 of 2002, Boyce and Another v The Queen [2005] 1 AC 400
6. Jamaica: Natalie Campbell-Rodrigues, Valrene Bennett, Andrew Wheatley, Anton Young, Keith Vlake v Attorney General of Jamaica [2007] UKPC 65
7. Trinidad and Tobago: Learie Collymore and Another v AG Trinidad and Tobago Privy Council Appeal No.26 of 1967
8. Trinidad and Tobago: Privy Council Appeal No.20 of 1974, De Freitas v Benny [1976] AC 239
9. Antigua and Barbuda: Elloy de Freitas v Permanent Secretary of Ministry of Agriculture, Fisheries, Lands and Housing [1999] 1 AC
10. Jamaica: Director of Public Prosecution of Jamaica v Mollison [2003] 2 AC 411 (Privy Council Appeal No.88 of 2001)
11. The Bahamas: Privy Council Appeal of 1999 Higgs v Minister National Security [2000] 2 AC 228
12. Jamaica: Privy Council Appeal No.s 4 and 5 of 1975 Hinds v The Queen and Another [1977] AC 195
13. The Bahamas: Privy Council Appeal No.45 of 2004 Austin Knowles and Others v Superintendent Culmer (Superintendent of HM Prison Fox Hill) and Others 2005 WL 699570

14. Jamaica: Privy Council Appeals Nos. 60 of 1999, 65 of 1999, 69 of 1999 and 10 of 2000. Neville Lewis v Attorney General of Jamaica and Another, Patrick Taylor and Another v Attorney General of Jamaica and Another, Christopher Brown v Attorney General of Jamaica and Another, and Desmond Taylor and Another v Attorney General of Jamaica and Another [2001] 2 AC 50.
15. Trinidad and Tobago: Matthew v State of Trinidad and Tobago [2005] 1 AC 433
16. Belize: Maya Leaders Alliance v Attorney General Belize [2015] CCJ 15 (AJ)
17. Guyana: McEwan et al v Attorney General Guyana [2018] CCJ 30 (AJ)
18. Belize: Privy Council Appeal No.9 of 2003. George Meerabux v Attorney General of Belize [2005] 2 AC 513
19. Bermuda: Privy Council Appeal No.4 of 1978 Minister of Home Affairs (Bermuda) v Fisher [1980] AC 319
20. Guyana: Zulfikar Mustapha v Attorney General of Guyana and Chairman of the Guyana Elections Commission [2019] CCJ 9 (AJ)
21. Barbados: Nervais and Severin v The Queen [2018] CCJ 19 (AJ)
22. Trinidad and Tobago: Panday v Gordon [2006] 1 AC 427
23. Belize: Prime Minister of Belize v Vellos [2010] UKPC
24. Jamaica: Privy Council Appeal N0.10 of 1993, Earl Pratt and Another v Attorney General for Jamaica and Another [1994] 2 AC 1
25. Guyana: Christopher Ram v Attorney General, the Leader of the Opposition, Joseph Harmon and Guyana Elections Commission [2019] CCJ 10 (AJ)
26. The Bahamas: Thomas Reckley v Minister of Public Safety and Immigration and Others [1995] 2 AC 491
27. Jamaica: Riley and Others v Attorney General Jamaica. Privy Council Appeal No.41 of 1981
28. Trinidad and Tobago: Privy Council Appeal No.18 of 2003, Roodal v State of Trinidad and Tobago [2005] 1 AC 328
29. St. Lucia: R v Hughes [2002] AC 259
30. Trinidad and Tobago: Privy Council appeal No. 73 of 2006, Sharma and Others v Attorney General of Trinidad and Tobago [2007] 1 WLR 2223
31. Trinidad and Tobago: Privy Council Appeal No.84 of 2006, Suratt and Others v Attorney General of Trinidad and Tobago [2008] 1 AC 655
32. Trinidad and Tobago: Thornhill v Attorney General Trinidad and Tobago [1981] AC 61
33. St. Vincent and the Grenadines: Toussaint v Attorney General of St Vincent and the Grenadines
34. Jamaica: Privy Council Appeal No. 36 of 2003, Watson v The Queen [2005] 1 AC 472
35. Belize: Attorney General of Belize v Zuniga [2014] CCJ 2 (AJ)
36. Grenada: Petition for Special Leave to Appeal form the Court of Appeal of Grenada July 1985, Andy Mitchell and Others v Director of Public Prosecutions and Another [1986] AC 73
37. Jamaica: Director of Public Prosecution v Nasralla Privy Council Appeal No.36 of 1965

38. The Bahamas: The Bahamas District of the Methodist Church in the Caribbean and the Americas and Others v The Hon. Vernon J. Symonette MP Speaker of the House of Assembly and 7 Others: Ormond Hilton Poitier and 14 Others v The Methodist Church of the Bahamas, Reverend Dr. Colin Archer, The Attorney General of the Bahamas [2000] 7 WLUK 758
39. Belize: Reyes v The Queen Privy Council Appeal No.64 of 2001
40. Jamaica: Privy Council Appeal No. 41 of 2004. Independent Jamaica Council for Human Rights (1998) Ltd and Others v Marshall-Burnett and Another [2005] 2 AC 356

Costa Rica

1. 00300-1990
2. 00980-1991
3. 01739-1992
4. 03003-1992
5. 03435-1992
6. 01313-1993
7. 03705-1993
8. 02313-1995
9. 05934-1997
10. 05347-1998
11. 02306-2000
12. 03220-2000
13. 07818-2000
14. 01486-2002
15. 02771-2003
16. 03656-2003
17. 06322-2003
18. 09992-2004
19. 14293-2005
20. 09469-2007
21. 09345-2008
22. 17620-2008
23. 02023-2010
24. 06922-2010
25. 13313-2010
26. 14821-2010
27. 06247-2013
28. 09122-2013
29. 10540-2013
30. 04037-2014
31. 18643-2014
32. 18836-2014
33. 13885-2015

34. 01692-2016
35. 15711-2016
36. 11212-2017
37. 11723-2018
38. 12782-2018
39. 19511-2018
40. 05560-2019

Ecuador

Constitutional Court 2009–2016

1. 0001-09-SIC-CC
2. 0004-09-SIC-CC
3. 0006-09-SIC-CC
4. 002-09-SAN–CC
5. 003-09-SIN-CC
6. 008-09-SEP-CC
7. 021-09-SEP-CC
8. 001-10-PJO-CC
9. 001-10-SIN-CC
10. 007-11-SEP-CC
11. 011-11-SCN-CC
12. 011-11-SEP-CC
13. 031-11-SEP-CC
14. 055-11-SEP-CC
15. 085-12-SEP-CC
16. 129-12-SEP-CC
17. 147-12-SEP-CC
18. 148-12-SEP-CC
19. 169-12-SEP-CC
20. 182-12-SEP-CC
21. 184-12-SEP-CC
22. 001-13-SCN-CC
23. 030-13-SCN-CC
24. 034-13-SCN-CC
25. 048-13-SCN-CC
26. 080-13-SEP-CC
27. 086-13-SEP-CC
28. 001-14-PJO-CC
29. 110-14-SEP-CC
30. 112-14-SEP-CC
31. 113-14-SEP-CC
32. 141-14-SEP-CC

33. 022-15-SEP-CC
34. 090-15-SEP-CC
35. 302-15-SEP-CC
36. 001-16-PJO-CC
37. 011-16-SIS-CC
38. 016-16-SEP-CC
39. 021-16-SIS-CC
40. 309-16-SEP-CC

Constitutional Court 2019

1. 10-18-CN/19
2. 11-18-CN/19
3. 282-13-JP/19
4. 1-19-CP/19
5. 20-19-TI/19
6. 2-19-IC/19
7. 4-19-RC/19
8. 71-14-CN/19
9. 7-17-CN/19
10. 5-13-IN/19
11. 154-12-EP/19
12. 88-11-IS/19
13. 14-15-CN/19
14. 1-18-RC/19
15. 66-15-JC/19
16. 002-19-DOP-CC
17. 5-19-RC/19
18. 18-17-IS/19
19. 2-19-TI/19
20. 2-19-CP/19
21. 13-18-TI/19
22. 7-16-CN/19
23. 9-19-CP/19
24. 5-18-CN/19
25. 10-16-CN/19
26. 5-19-EE/19
27. 323-13-EP/19
28. 61-12-IS/19
29. 7-11-IA/19
30. 7-19-RC/19
31. 209-15-JH/19
32. 4-18-RC/19
33. 176-14-EP/19
34. 9-17-CN/19

35. 12-19-CN/19
36. 280-13-EP/19
37. 1944-12-EP/19
38. 6-19-CP/19
39. 904-12-JP/19
40. 23-18-IN/19

Guatemala

1. Expediente 12-86, Inconstitucionalidad de Leyes, Reglamentos y Disposiciones de Carácter General, 17 September 1986
2. Expediente 96-86, Dictamen, 25 November 1986
3. Expediente 25-88, Inconstitucionalidad de Ley, 26 May 1988 (Interpretative Judgments)
4. Expediente 93-89, Amparo en Unica Instancia, 28 July 1989
5. Expediente 364-90, Apelacion de Sentencia de Amparo, 26 June 1991
6. Expediente 290-01 y 292-91, Inconstitucionalidad General, 3 November 1992
7. Expediente 225-93, Inconstitucionalidad General, 25 May 1993
8. Expediente 167-95, Inconstitucionalidad Parcial, 28 September 1995
9. Expediente 199-95, Opinion Consultiva, 18 May 1995
10. Expediente 300-95. Inconstitutcionalidad, 12 March 1996
11. Expediente 305-95, Inconstitucionalidad General, 26 September 1996
12. Expediente 313-95, Amparo en Unica Instancia, 29 August 1995
13. Expediente 639-95, Inconstitucionalidad General, 11 December 1996
14. Expediente 916-97, Apelacion de Sentencia de Amparo, 27 May 1998
15. Expediente 266-99, Apelacion de Sentencia de Amparo, 20 May 1999
16. Expediente 30-2000, Amparo en Unica Instancia, 31 October 2000
17. Expediente 890-2001, Inconstitucionalidad Parcial, 9 December 2002
18. Expediente 171-2002, Opinion Consultiva, 25 March 2002
19. Expediente 855-2003, Apelacion de Sentencia de Amparo, 27 October 2003
20. Expediente 1250-2004, Opinion Consultiva, 5 August 2004
21. Expedientes Acumulados 1555-2002 y 1808-2002, Inconstitucionalidad General Total, 13 August 2003
22. Expediente 1089-2003, Apelacion de Sentencia de Amparo, 14 July 2003
23. Expediente 2395-2006, Solicitud de Anulacion, 10 October 2006
24. Expediente 794-2007, Inconstitucionalidad General Parcial, 6 November 2007
25. Expedientes Acumulados 1202-2006, 1288-2006 y 1451-2007, Inconstitucionalidad General, 8 January 2008
26. Expediente 3300-2009, Apelacion de Sentencia de Amparo, 21 October 2010
27. Expediente 548-2010, Amparo en Unica Instancia, 25 August 2010
28. Expediente 3729-2009, Amparo en Unica Instancia, 30 September 2010
29. Expediente 1566-2011, Apelacion de Sentencia de Amparo, 26 de Agosto de 2011
30. Expediente 1822-2011, Inconstitucionalidad General Parcial por Omision, 17 July 2012

31. Expediente 2151-2011, Apelacion de Sentencia de Amparo, 23 August 2011
32. Expediente 2729-2011. Inconstitucionalidad General Parcial, 14 August 2012
33. Expediente 3005-2011, Apelacion de Sentencia de Amparo, 7 December 2011
34. Expediente 4371-2001, Inconstitucionalidad General Parcial, 9 de octubre de 2012
35. Expediente 56-2012, Inconstitucionalidad General Parcial, 3 de mayo de 2012
36. Expediente 2846-2012, Apelacion de Sentencia de Amparo, 18 September 2012
37. Expediente 5986-2016. Inconstitucionalidad General, 24 Octiber 2017
38. Expediente 4783-2013, 48-2013 y 4813-2013, Apelacion de Sentencia de Amparo, 5 july 2016
39. Expedientes Acumulados 4639-2014, 4645-2014 y 4647-2014, Amparo en Unica Instancia, 19 November 2014
40. Expedientes Acumulado 90-2017.91-2017 y 92-2017, Apelacion de Sentencia de Amparo, 26 May 2017

Inter-American Court of Human Rights

1. Velásquez Rodríguez Vs. Honduras
2. Caso de los niños de la calle Vs. Guatemala (Rev.28.06)
3. "La Última Tentación de Cristo" (Olmedo Bustos y otros) Vs. Chile
4. Comunidad Mayagna (Sumo) Awas Tingni Vs. Nicaragua
5. Barrios Altos Vs. Perú
6. Baena Ricardo y otros (270 Trabajadores) Vs. Panamá Supervisión de Cumplimiento de Sentencia 6/6/2003
7. Myrna Mack Chang Vs. Guatemala
8. Herrera Ulloa Vs. Costa Rica
9. Fermín Ramírez Vs. Guatemala
10. Yatama vs. Nicaragua
11. Comunidad indígena Yakye Axa Vs. Paraguay
12. Ximenes Lopes Vs. Brasil
13. Almonacid Arellano y otros Vs. Chile
14. Penal Miguel Castro Castro Vs. Perú
15. Kimel Vs. Argentina
16. Castañeda Gutman Vs. México
17. Gelman Vs. Uruguay
18. Campo Algodonero Vs. México
19. Radilla Pacheco Vs. México
20. Fernández Ortega y otros Vs. México
21. Resolución de medidas provisionales respecto de Honduras. Asunto Gladys Lanza Ochoa
22. Atala Riffo y niñas Vs. Chile
23. Pueblo Indígena Kichwa de Sarayaku Vs. Ecuador.
24. Furlan y familiares Vs. Argentina
25. Masacres de El Mozote y lugares aledaños Vs. El Salvador
26. Artavia Murillo y otros ("Fecundación In Vitro") Vs. Costa Rica

27. Masacre de Santo Domingo Vs. Colombia
28. Rodríguez Vera y otros (Desaparecidos del Palacio de Justicia) Vs. Colombia
29. Personas Dominicanas y Haitianas Expulsadas Vs. República Dominicana
30. Granier y otros (Radio Caracas Televisión) Vs. Venezuela
31. Gonzales Lluy y otros Vs. Ecuador
32. López Lone y otros Vs. Honduras
33. Trabajadores de la Hacienda Brasil Verde Vs. Brasil
34. Cuscul Pivaral y otros Vs. Guatemala
35. Mujeres Víctimas de Tortura Sexual en Atenco Vs. México
36. Opinión Consultiva 11/90. Excepciones al agotamiento de los recursos internos
37. Opinión Consultiva 17/02. Condición Jurídica y Derechos Humanos del Niño
38. Opinión Consultiva 23/17. Medio ambiente y Derechos Humanos
39. Opinión Consultiva OC-24/17 de 24 de noviembre de 2017
40. Opinión Consultiva OC-25/18 de 30 de mayo de 2018

Mexico

1. Acción de Inconstitucionalidad 1/1996
2. Acción de Inconstitucionalidad 9/2005
3. Controversia Constitucional 14/2001
4. Acción de Inconstitucionalidad 4/2006
5. Controversia Constitucional 140/2006
6. Acción de Inconstitucionalidad 4/2004
7. Acción de inconstitucionalidad 146/2007 y su acumulada
8. Amparo directo civil 6/2008
9. Acción de Inconstitucionalidad 119/2008
10. Amparo Directo 28/2010
11. Amparo en Revisión 581/2012
12. Amparo Directo en Revisión 517/2011
13. Contradicción de Tesis 293/2011
14. Amparo en Revisión 159/2013
15. Amparo Directo en Revisión 2655/2013
16. Amparo Directo 30/2013
17. Controversia Constitucional 32/2012
18. Amparo en Revisión 378/2014
19. Amparo en revisión 554/2013
20. Amparo directo en revisión 1250/2012
21. Amparo Directo 35/2014
22. Acción de inconstitucionalidad 8/2014
23. Amparo Directo en Revisión 1754/2015
24. Amparo en Revisión 237/2014
25. Recurso de Reclamación 9/2016-AI
26. Amparo Directo en Revisión 6564/2015
27. Amparo en Revisión 208/2016

28. Controversia Constitucional 38/2015
29. Acción de Incostitucionalidad 15/2017
30. Contradicción de Tesis 182/2014
31. Amparo en Revisión 1359/2015
32. Amparo Directo en Revisión 5490/2016
33. Amparo en revisión 1170/2017
34. Acción de Inconstitucionalidad 151/2017
35. Amparo en revisión 714/2017
36. Acción de Inconstitucionalidad 6/2018
37. Amparo en Revisión 163/2018
38. Amparo Directo 9/2018
39. Amparo directo en revisión 7134/2018
40. Amparo en revisión 57/2019

Paraguay

1. AyS.208
2. AyS.260.
3. AyS.395
4. AyS.363
5. AyS.399
6. AyS.586
7. AyS.551
8. AyS.68
9. AyS.540
10. AyS.30
11. AyS.397
12. AyS.706
13. AyS.84
14. AyS.415
15. AyS.365
16. AyS.191
17. AyS.173
18. AyS.222
19. AyS.223
20. AyS. 1033
21. AyS.673
22. AyS.1617
23. AyS.1905
24. AyS.364
25. AyS.642
26. AyS.139
27. AyS.557
28. AyS.268

29. AyS.243
30. AyS. N° 952
31. A.I. Nº 669
32. AyS.947
33. AyS.385
34. AyS.474
35. AyS.1306
36. AyS.185
37. AyS.1113
38. A.I. N° 231
39. AyS.10
40. AyS.119

Peru

1. STC N° 2005-2009-PA/TC
2. STC N° 7624-2005-HC/TC
3. STC N° 00889-2017-PA/TC
4. STC N° 5057-2013-PA/TC
5. STC N° 1204-2017-PA/TC
6. STC N° 2016-2004-AA/TC
7. STC N° 6040-2015-PA/TC
8. STC N° 06534-2006- PA/TC
9. STC N° 02744-2015-PA
10. STC N° 01575-2007-PHC/TC
11. STC N° 014-2002-AI
12. STC N°010-2002-AI
13. ATC N° 03173-2008-PHC/TC
14. STC N° 01151-2010-AA/TC
15. STC N° 2730-2006-PA
16. STC N° 0006-2003-AI/TC
17. STC N° 0008-2003-AI/TC
18. STC N° 00987-2014-PA/TC
19. STC N° 02488-2002-HC
20. STC Nº 0001-2018-PI/TC
21. STC Nº 003-2008-PI/TC
22. STC Nº 0019-2005-PI/TC
23. STC Nº 1417-2005-AA/TC
24. STC Nº 6712-2005-HC/TC
25. STC Nº 00853-2015-PA/TC
26. STC Nº 0026-2006-PI/TC
27. STC N° 03343-2007- PA/TC
28. STC N° 01126-2011- HC/TC
29. STC N° 2663-2003-HC/TC

30. STC N° 5854-2005-PA/TC
31. STC N° 0017-2003-AI/TC
32. STC N° 006-2018-AI/TC
33. STC N° 3361-2004-AA/TC
34. STC N° 0006-2017-PI/TC
35. STC N° 0007-2012-PI/TC
36. STC N° 0001-2009-PI/TC
37. STC N° 00048-2004-PI/TC
38. STC N° 00156-2012-PHC/TC
39. STC N° 004-2004-CC
40. STC N° 025-2005-AI / 00026-2005-AI

Uruguay

1. 53/1989
2. 54/1990
3. 96/1990
4. 12./1991
5. 55/1991
6. 42/1993
7. 234/1995
8. 54/2004
9. 61/2005
10. 39/2008
11. 49/2008
12. 55/2008
13. 80/2008
14. 58/2009
15. 79/2009
16. 156/2009
17. 365/2009
18. 259/2009
19. 271/2009
20. 60/2010
21. 137/2010
22. 17/2013
23. 20/2013
24. 568/2013
25. 65/2014
26. 734/2014
27. 738/2014
28. 104/2015
29. 311/2015
30. 79/2016
31. 87/2016

32. 102/2016
33. 211/2016
34. 396/2016
35. 576/2017
36. 680/2017
37. 1980/2017
38. 271/2018
39. 667/2018
40. 1148/2019

Venezuela

1. Sentencia 7, expediente 00-0010, 1 de febrero de 2000
2. Sentencia 656, expediente 00-1728, 30 de junio de 2000
3. Sentencia 1077, expediente 00-1289, 22 de septiembre de 2000
4. Sentencia 93, expediente 00-1529, 6 de febrero de 2001
5. Sentencia 332, expediente 00-1797, 14 de marzo de 2001
6. Sentencia 1309, expediente 01-1362, 19 de julio de 2001
7. Sentencia 1571, expediente 01-1274, 22 de agosto de 2001
8. Sentencia 85, expediente 01-1274, 24 de enero de 2002
9. Sentencia 1139, expediente 02-0429, 5 de junio de 2002
10. Sentencia 23, expediente 03-0017, 22 de enero de 2003
11. Sentencia 1942, expediente 01-0415, 15 de Julio de 2003
12. Sentencia 2073, expedientes 03-1254 y 03-1308, 4 de agosto de 2003
13. Sentencia 1002, expediente 02-2167, 26 de mayo de 2004
14. Sentencia 233, expediente AA50-T-2004-003227, 11 de marzo de 2005
15. Sentencia 2495, expediente 02-0265, 19 de diciembre de 2006
16. Sentencia 2087, expediente 07-1282, 06 de noviembre de 2007
17. Sentencia 190, expediente 03-2630, 28 de febrero de 2008
18. Sentencia 565, expediente 07-1108, 15 de abril de 2008
19. Sentencia 1265, expediente 05-1853, 5 de agosto de 2008
20. Sentencia 1431, expediente 07-1121, 14 de agosto de 2008
21. Sentencia 1684, expediente 08-1016, 4 de noviembre de 2008
22. Sentencia 1939, expediente 08-1572, 18 de diciembre de 2008
23. Sentencia 49, expediente 08-1617, 03 de febrero de 2009
24. Sentencia 1049, expediente 04-2233, 23 de julio de 2009
25. Sentencia 1326, expediente AA50-T-2009-0266, 19 de octubre de 2009
26. Sentencia 365, expediente 09-0458, 10 de mayo de 2010
27. Sentencia 796, 09-0555, 22 de julio de 2010
28. Sentencia 2, expediente 12-1358, 9 de enero de 2013
29. Sentencia 141, expediente AA50-T-2013-0196, 8 de marzo de 2013
30. Sentencia 993, expediente 13-0230, 16 de julio de 2013
31. Sentencia 245, expediente 14-0205, 9 de abril de 2014
32. Sentencia 256, expediente AA50-T-2010-0459, 10 de abril de 2014
33. Sentencia 276, expediente 14-0277, 24 de abril de 2014

34. Sentencia 446, expediente 14-0094, 15 de mayo de 2014
35. Sentencia 1865, expediente 14-1343, 26 de diciembre
36. Sentencia 9, expediente 16-0153, 1 de marzo de 2016
37. Sentencia 327, expediente 16-0363, 28 de abril de 2016
38. Sentencia 808, expediente 16-0831, 2 de septiembre de 2016
39. Sentencia 1187, expediente 16-0357, 15 de diciembre de 2016
40. Sentencia 155, expediente 17-0323, 27 de marzo de 2017

APPENDIX B: CORE CODEBOOK[1]

This document is a manual to conduct the empirical pillar of the research on each of the 15 jurisdictions, resulting in 16 excel sheets (as from Ecuador we have two samples). Each Excel sheet contain 40 landmark cases selected by the Authors of each Country Chapter following the indications in the CORE Project Guide. We will work with 640 observations in total.

The authors should be able to complete every cell of the Excel Table. If a given argument or concept was explicitly considered or invoked by the judicial opinion, it shall be counted as 'YES'. If the argument or concept was not invoked in a verifiable way, please indicate 'NO'. If the expert cannot fill the cell based on the required information, either because she does not have the information or the requirement does not apply to the realm of her country/case study, she should mark 'NA' or '0' to identify her response as 'missing'.

Almost all the responses are categorical (mostly, they are coded in 'YES' or 'NO'). However, in the case of certain indicators we included different categories of 'YES' by differentiating among options referred to as (1), (2), (3) etc. For the effect of these indicators, if an answer was 'YES', there were consecutively numbered options to choose from. Depending on the nature of the issue, different options could be marked at the same time.

Questions for Overall Identification (Q1–Q8)

Coding	Question or variable label	Conceptualisation	Indicator(s)/ Measurement
Q1 **Reference**	Reference of the decision?	Please write in English, Spanish or Portuguese the official reference of the decision. If the reference of the decision is in a native language other than the above-mentioned, please write it in English.	Please name of the reference of the decision.
Q2A **Year**	Year of the decision	Year when the decision was rendered.	Please specify the exact year of the decision.

[1] Updated and edited version of the Questionnaire for the purposes of the present publication. The present structure was borrowed from A Jakab et al, *Comparative Constitutional Reasoning* (Cambridge University Press, 2017). See more about the methodology here, A Jakab, A Dyevre and G Itzkovich, CONREASON – The Comparative Constitutional Reasoning Project. Methodological Dilemmas and Project Design. *MTA Law Working Papers* 2015/9.

Coding	Question or variable label	Conceptualisation	Indicator(s)/ Measurement
Q2B **Range**	Range of decision's year		2019–2011 = 1 2010–2001 = 2 2000–1991 = 3 1990–1981 = 4 >1980 = 5
Q3 **Opinion**	Dissenting or concurring opinion in the case?	If the case was adopted unanimously or there is no traceable sign of disagreement, the judgment shall be considered as not containing any minority decisions. Whereas if there is an official record that one or more judges disagreed on the reasoning, but agreed on the decision (to reject or to accept the complaint), it is a 'concurring opinion', and if one or more judge disagreed both on the reasoning and on the decision, it is a 'dissenting opinion'.	Please, indicate if the decision includes minority opinions. Please specify (YES) if you have found either dissenting or concurring opinions, or both, and 'NO' if there's no minority decision. If separate decisions are not allowed, please leave it blank.
Q4 **Disposition**	Case disposition?	The case disposition refers to whether the decision of the Court was favourable for the complainant, or it was rejected. Solely if the judgment prescribes a binding interpretation (of the constitution's statutes), then the question should be left blank. If the Court states an 'unconstitutional omission' or grants a 'preventive control', then the cell should be 'YES'. Acceptability decisions can also be categorised as 'YES', if the acceptability was granted, or as 'NO' if the acceptability was denied. An interim relief is also a 'YES'.	Please indicate 'YES' if the Court found (at least partially) against the challenged law, act, decree or ordinary court decision or 'NO' if the unconstitutionality was rejected.

Coding	Question or variable label	Conceptualisation	Indicator(s)/ Measurement
Q5 **Topic**	General topic?	The general topic refers to whether the case could be considered as a human rights/fundamental rights case, a case of constitutional structure or a case that has procedural aspects at its heart. It is important, that this element (too) shall be evaluated on the substance and not the form only – meaning, however, if the complaint is about the right to housing, but the Court avoids dealing with the substantial aspects of this right and rather deviates from it towards the procedural/due process aspects, this should be considered as the option (3).	Please indicate (1) Fundamental Rights; (2) State Organisation; (3) Procedural, due process; (4) Other. Note: This column also serves to specify if the response is a combination of the above- indicated alternatives.
Q5A		ONLY: 'Fundamental Rights'.	0 = No 1 = Yes
Q5B		ONLY: 'State organisation'.	0 = No 1 = Yes
Q5C		ONLY: 'Procedural, due process'.	0 = No 1 = Yes
Q5D		ONLY: 'Other'	0 = No 1 = Yes
Q6 **Issue**	Concrete issue?	The concrete issue refers to the substantial topic of the case at hand, characterised by the expert's own words.	Please, characterise briefly the issue at hand, using your own words.
Q7 **State**	Top- down/ bottom- up involvement?	Top-down involvement refers to whether any organs or bodies of the government (branches, authorities, offices, ministries, state-owned companies etc.) or the president initiated the constitutional review procedure in the concrete case. Some countries	Please indicate 'YES' if the government or any of its bodies initiated the case at hand. Please indicate 'NO' if a civil society organisation or a (group of) citizen(s) initiated or proposed the case at hand.

Coding	Question or variable label	Conceptualisation	Indicator(s)/ Measurement
		granted fundamental rights protection to the government organs. This means that these bodies could start constitutional review cases before the Courts and they could win them against citizens or private companies. Bottom- up involvement refers to constitutional review cases initiated by citizens or civil society organisation.	
Q8A **Length of the judgment?**	How long is the judgment?	This includes the complete length of the sentence from the very beginning until the end of the concurring and dissenting opinions. Please to count the pages, use the official format of the decision (in the *Gaceta Oficial* or the redaction you find on the official webpage of the Court).	Please indicate the number of pages of the judgment.
Q8B **(Range) Length of the judgment?**	How long is the judgment in range?		1 = 0–49 pages 2 = 50–99 pages 3 = 100–199 pages 4 = ≥ 200 pages

Questions Related to the Interpretive Methods (Q9 – Q26)

Coding	Question or variable label	Conceptualisation	Indicator(s)
Q9	Structure of argument?	By one-line conclusive arguments, we refer to a standalone structure, in which every premise represents a necessary component of the argument. By parallel conclusive arguments, we refer to a cumulative parallel structure, in which two or more divergent and self-sufficient considerations lead to the same conclusion.	Please select (1), if you identify a one-line conclusive argument; (2) if you identify a parallel conclusive argument; and (3) if you find a parallel, individually inconclusive, but together conclusive arguments.

Coding	Question or variable label	Conceptualisation	Indicator(s)
		By individually inconclusive, but together conclusive arguments, we refer to several different arguments that would not be conclusive separately, but together they are sufficient to reach the conclusion.	
Q9A		ONLY: 'one-line conclusive argument'	0 = No 1 = Yes
Q9B		ONLY: 'parallel conclusive argument'	0 = No 1 = Yes
Q9C		ONLY: 'parallel, individually inconclusive, but together conclusive argument'	0 = No 1 = Yes
Q10	Identifying or explicitly discussing the Constitution's text?	Arguments that define the scope of the constitution means to discuss explicitly what counts as part of the constitutional text. These arguments usually emerge when it is not clear whether a norm is part of the supreme law of the land, ie if it's recognised as a constitutional text or not.	Please check 'YES' if the judicial opinion openly discusses what counts as constitutional text; otherwise indicate 'NO'.
Q11	Is the applicability of constitutional law discussed?	This question relies on the applicability *ratione materiae* of the constitution, its binding force, and the constitutional enforceability and justiciability. Statements to illustrate this are eg 'the case at hand has no constitutional relevance; the case falls within the discretion of the legislator [or other non-judicial institution]' Using the doctrine of conventionality control or the concepts like the margin of appreciation would fall under this category as well.	Please check 'YES' if the judicial opinion openly considers whether constitutional law can be applied by the Court or not. Otherwise, check 'NO'.
Q12	Analogy?	Analogy is an argument to fill in gaps and to resolve the case at hand that is not regulated in the constitution by using similar institutions or principles from other fields of jurisprudence.	Please check 'YES' if the judicial opinion explicitly discusses analogy. Otherwise, indicate 'NO'.

Coding	Question or variable label	Conceptualisation	Indicator(s)
Q13	Ordinary meaning of words?	By ordinary meaning of words, we refer to the grammatical-literal interpretation of the words/phrases/ articles of the constitution, following its everyday or professional meaning.	Please check (1) if the judicial opinion openly refers to the ordinary meaning of the text of the constitution in the majority decision. Please, check (2) if the ordinary meaning method is openly referred in dissenting or concurrent opinions. Otherwise, indicate 'NO'.
Q13A		ONLY: 'ordinary meaning of the text of the constitution in the majority decision'	0 = No 1 = Yes
Q13B		ONLY: 'dissenting or concurrent opinions'	0 = No 1 = Yes
Q13C		BINARY AGGREGATION: '(Q13A+Q13B)'	0 = No 1 = Yes
Q14	Domestic harmonising arguments?	This method refers to those types of arguments that interpret different articles, sections or provisions of the same constitution in harmony with each other. It can also be called 'integrative' method. This only applies at the domestic level, meaning with respect to the national constitution.	Please check 'YES' if the judicial opinion expressively refers to domestic harmonising arguments. Otherwise, indicate 'NO'.
Q15	Harmonising with international law requirements?	This question assumes that international law and domestic law can concur each other. This method refers to the use of international legal instruments in order to interpret the constitution. While deciding about this component, the universally accepted sources of international law shall serve as guidance.	Please check (1) if the judicial opinion openly refers to international legal instruments from the Inter-American system. Please, check (2) if the judicial opinion openly refers to any other binding sources of international law; (3) if the judicial opinion openly refers to sources of international soft law. Otherwise, please check 'NO'.

Coding	Question or variable label	Conceptualisation	Indicator(s)
Q15A		ONLY: 'international legal instruments from the Inter-American system'	0 = No 1 = Yes
Q15B		ONLY: 'other binding sources of international law'	0 = No 1 = Yes
Q15C		ONLY: 'sources of international soft law'	0 = No 1 = Yes
Q15D		BINARY AGGREGATION: (Q15A+Q15B+Q15C)	0 = No 1 = Yes
Q16	Precedent-based arguments?	A precedent-based argument means the use of previous judgments or preliminary rulings of the same court, already resolved, in order to interpret the text of the constitution.	Please check 'YES' whether the judicial opinion explicitly precedent-based arguments. Otherwise indicate 'NO'.
Q17	Invokes a concept or a principle not mentioned in the constitutional text?	This method means the application of those principles and concepts that are not mentioned or defined explicitly in the text of the constitution, but courts can employ them to interpret the constitution.	Please check 'YES' if the judicial opinion invokes a concept or a principle not specified expressively in the constitutional text. Otherwise indicate 'NO'.
Q18	Argument from silence?	An argument from silence (*argumentum ex silentio)* is based on the omission or lack of expressive reference to something to interpret the constitution.	Please indicate 'YES' if the judicial opinion considers argument from silence. Otherwise indicate 'NO'.
Q19	Teleological (textual) arguments?	This type of teleological argument refers to the purpose or aim of the provision in question that has expressive textual basis in the constitution (therefore, it is 'objective').	Please indicate 'YES' if the judicial opinion explicitly invokes the supposed purpose of the constitutional provision (or part thereof). Otherwise indicate 'NO'.
Q20	Teleological (historical-intentional) arguments?	This kind of teleological argument (often denominated as subjective teleological argument) considers the constitution-maker's purpose or intention to interpret the constitution. It might take the form of a reference to a work-in- progress or *travaux préparatoires.*	Please check (1) if the judicial opinion openly refers to the intention of the constitution-maker in the majority decision. Please, check (2) if it is used in dissenting or concurrent opinions. Otherwise indicate 'NO'.

Coding	Question or variable label	Conceptualisation	Indicator(s)
Q20A		ONLY: 'intention of the constitution-maker in the majority decision'.	0 = No 1 = Yes
Q20B		ONLY: 'dissenting or concurrent opinions.'	0 = No 1 = Yes
Q20C		BINARY AGGREGATION: (Q20A+Q20B)	0 = No 1 = Yes
Q21	Non-legal arguments?	Non-legal arguments are explicitly moral/religious, economic, scientific/medical or sociological arguments (ie arguments that are clearly grounded on externalities to the legal process or the law) during constitutional interpretation.	Please indicate if the judicial opinion invokes or considers: (1) Economic, (2) Sociological, (3) Moral/Religious; (4) Scientific/Medical. Otherwise indicate 'NO'.
Q21A		ONLY: 'Economic'	0 = No 1 = Yes
Q21B		ONLY: 'Sociological'	0 = No 1 = Yes
Q21C		ONLY: 'Moral/Religious'	0 = No 1 = Yes
Q21D		ONLY 'Scientific/Medical'	0 = No 1 = Yes
Q21E		BINARY AGGREGATION: (Q21A+Q21B+Q21C+Q21D)	0 = No 1 = Yes
Q22	Reference to scholarly work?	Both concrete or generic references such as 'dominant doctrine' or 'authoritative doctrine' should be considered as scholarly contributions. The use of concepts and theories associate with academic origins should not count as scholarly contributions if no explicit references to legal-constitutional scholarship is emitted. Foreign or national scholarly sources are equally treated as scholarly work.	Please check 'YES' if the judicial opinion explicitly invokes scholarly contributions. Otherwise indicate 'NO'.

Coding	Question or variable label	Conceptualisation	Indicator(s)
Q23	Reference to foreign law?	By referring to foreign law, we allude to arguments that explicitly invoke or consider foreign legal sources (foreign countries' legal norms, foreign courts' sentences or 'the results of comparative law', meaning the experience of foreign legal institutions). Neither words nor expressions in other languages count as a positive response.	Please mark (1) if the judicial opinion invokes or consider foreign laws from Latin American countries. Please check (2), if the judicial opinion invokes or considers foreign laws of other regions. Otherwise indicate 'NO'.
Q23A		ONLY: 'foreign laws from Latin American countries'	0 = No 1 = Yes
Q23B		ONLY 'foreign laws of other regions'	0 = No 1 = Yes
Q23C		BINARY AGGREGATION: (Q23A+Q23B)	0 = No 1 = Yes
Q24	Pro homine or Pro persona principles	This is an interpretive principle that aims at maximising the protection of human rights and at the same time, minimalise restrictions pertaining to them. It has an interpretive aspect and an aspect of application of the law. The first means an extensive interpretation or a restrictive interpretation depending on which one is more in favour of the effective protection of rights, while the other aspect means the preference of norms that are more favourable to the effective protection of human rights.	Please check 'YES' if the judicial opinion explicitly uses *pro homine* or *pro persona* principles of interpretation. Otherwise indicate 'NO'.
Q25	Other types of argument or method?	Including references to all the other types of arguments that cannot be fitted to any of the previous categories.	Please check 'YES' if the judicial opinion invokes other type of arguments that could not be specified as any of the previous ones. Otherwise indicate 'NO'.

Questions Related to Key Concepts Used in the Argumentation (Q26 – Q49)

Coding	Question or variable label	Conceptualisation	Indicator(s)
Q26	The rule of law invoked as an argument?	We can differentiate between the 'thin' and the 'thick' version of rule of law. The former refers to the basic formal requirements of law (ie general, universally applicable laws, publicity, equality under the law, clear, understandable, coherent laws, prohibition of retroactive laws, judicial review, separation of powers). The 'thick' version basically refers to the proper implementation and well-functioning of these rules, such as foreseeability, legal security, accountability, stability, judicial accountability, judicial independence, fair trial. (Voigt 2009. Also see, World Justice Project, 2019, 9.). In Latin America there seems to exist a slightly different conceptualisation of rule of law. 'Estado de derecho', or 'Estado social de derecho' is the one that is the most similar to 'rule of law' and refers to a certain quality of the state. Besides this, we can find 'el principio de legalidad' more related to the thin version of rule law, while 'seguridad jurídica' is limited to legal certainty.	Please check (1) if the judicial opinion expressively invokes or considers the concept of 'estado de derecho' or rule of law. Please check (2) if the judicial opinion invokes 'el principio de legalidad' or 'legalidad' or legality. Please check (3) if you find an expressive reference to 'seguridad jurídica' or legal security. Otherwise indicate 'NO'.
Q26A		ONLY: 'concept of '*estado de derecho*' or rule of law'	0 = No 1 = Yes
Q26B		ONLY: 'concept '*el principio de legalidad*' or '*legalidad*' or legality.	0 = No 1 = Yes
Q26C		ONLY: 'concept 'seguridad jurídica' or legal security'	0 = No 1 = Yes
Q26D		BINARY AGGREGATION: (Q26A+Q26B+Q26C)	0 = No 1 = Yes

Coding	Question or variable label	Conceptualisation	Indicator(s)
Q27	Judicial independence invoked as an argument?	The concept of judicial independence means that no other state function can interfere with the judicial branch, as it shall enjoy independence from the interventions of other branches. The judges while interpreting and applying the laws shall only be subjected to the constitution and the laws. Judicial independence has a structural aspect, according to which the judicial branch shall have an independent organisation, and a financial one which refers to the budgetary independence that this branch shall enjoy.	Please check 'YES' if the judicial opinion expressively invokes the concept of judicial independence. Otherwise indicate 'NO'.
Q28	Democracy invoked as an argument?	Following the conceptualisation offered by Dahl (1971), a substantive perspective of democracy categorises political regimes in relation to the outcomes that they generate. A minimalist, or procedural, perspective of democracy refers to political regimes in relation to their institutions and procedures. In this regard, democracy can be conceptualised and measured into two dimensions: (1) contestation or the extent to which the demos are free to create political organisations in order to channel the social demands into decision-making process; and (2) inclusion or the degree of participation in the democratic process.	Please check 'YES' if the judicial opinion invokes or considers the concept of democracy. Otherwise indicate 'NO'.
Q29	Sovereignty invoked as an argument?	According to the Westphalia Pax, sovereignty means state authority (Krasner, 2001). Following Thomas Hobbes, sovereignty relapses on the ultimate decision unit. Sovereignty within a state comprises a permanent population, a geographically defined territory, and a government with the capacity to establish (cooperative) relations with other sovereign states.	Please check 'YES' if the judicial opinion invokes or considers the concept of sovereignty. Otherwise indicate 'NO'.

Coding	Question or variable label	Conceptualisation	Indicator(s)
Q30	State form invoked as an argument?	The form of the state can be basically (constitutional) monarchy or republic.	Please check 'YES' if the judicial opinion expressively invokes the concept of the state form. Otherwise, please, mark 'NO'.
Q31	Government system by procedural structure invoked as an argument?	Government system by procedural structure could be classified in three different clusters: parliamentarian system (whether in a monarchy or in a republic); presidential systems (whether with a prime- minister or with a president as the head of state); and semi- presidential system (whether as premier- presidential system or presidential- parliamentary system). Yet, as of Latin America largely has presidential systems, we suggest indicating the nuances of different sub-types of presidentialism.	Please check (1) if the judicial opinion invokes the concept of hyper-presidential system. Mark (2) if the judicial opinion considers presidential emergency power. Indicate (3) if the judicial opinion refers to presidential term/ decision. Please indicate (4) if the judicial opinion invokes other forms of government systems such as parliamentarism or semi/presidentialism. Otherwise indicate 'NO'.
Q31A		ONLY: 'concept of hyper-presidential system'	0 = No 1 = Yes
Q31B		ONLY: 'concept of presidential emergency power'	0 = No 1 = Yes
Q31C		ONLY: 'concept of presidential term/ decision'.	0 = No 1 = Yes
Q31D		ONLY: 'other forms of government systems such as parliamentarism or semi/presidentialism'	0 = No 1 = Yes
Q31E		BINARY AGGREGATION: (Q31A+Q31B+Q31C+Q31D)	0 = No 1 = Yes
Q32	Government system by power structure invoked as an argument?	Government system by power structure could be understood as unitary or federal systems. The concept includes references to 'regionalism', 'autonomous regions', or 'autonomy of local governments'.	Please check 'YES' if the judicial opinion invokes or considers the concept of federalism. Otherwise indicate 'NO'.

Coding	Question or variable label	Conceptualisation	Indicator(s)
Q33	Secularism invoked as an argument?	Following Max Weber (1905), secularism could be defined as the way in which government remain objective or neutral regarding any religious affair, and neither enforce, nor forbid the freedom of cult, religion, or the religious choice to the citizenry. We count references to the concept of laic state as well. This includes references to 'secularism', 'the separation of church and state', 'the state neutrality in religious affairs' or to 'laic state'.	Please check 'YES' if the judicial opinion invokes or considers arguments regarding the state-religion separation. Otherwise indicate 'NO'.
Q34	Nation invoked as an argument?	By the term of nation we refer to the concept of nation- state, which is a sovereign territory whereby the vast majority of inhabitant shares a similar culture and identity. We also mean to include the competing notions of nation, such as 'plurinationality'.	Please check 'YES' if the judicial opinion invokes or considers the different concepts of nation. Otherwise indicate 'NO'.
Q35	Proportionality invoked as argument?	Proportionality is a legal construct used to adjudicate human rights disputes, ie to resolve collisions between colliding values and rights. There are different versions of the test, but usually the model includes the following steps: legitimate aim, suitability of the aim, suitability of the restriction, proportionality of the restriction. We mean to include all versions of the test, such as plain 'balancing' and 'scrutiny', as well as the different versions of the proportionality test.	Please check 'YES' if the judicial opinion invokes or considers the concept of proportionality or similar means-end test. Otherwise indicate 'NO'.
Q36	Core of constitutional rights or competences?	The legal construct of 'core content of rights' *(Wesensgehalt)* that refers to the unchangeable or inviolable essential origin of all fundamental and human rights.	Please check 'YES' if the judicial opinion invokes or considers doctrines of the core content of either fundamental rights or of competences. Otherwise indicate 'NO'.

Coding	Question or variable label	Conceptualisation	Indicator(s)
Q37	Human dignity invoked as an argument?	According to Steinmann (2016), 'human dignity' is a contested concept. At the ontological level, the author defined 'human dignity' as a value or a right, directly associated with the unique qualities of every individual and the recognition of the second-generation social and economic human rights.	Please check 'YES' if the judicial opinion invokes or considers the concept of human dignity. Otherwise indicate 'NO'.
Q38	Equality invoked as an argument?	By the concept of equality, we mean both general legal and political equality, in which all citizens in a given state are of equal standing before the law, and the equal treatment in terms of (human) rights (prohibition of unjustified discrimination).	Please check 'YES' if the judicial opinion invokes or considers the concept of equality. This includes references to non- discrimination too. Otherwise indicate 'NO'.
Q39	Basic procedural rights invoked as an argument?	The concept of 'basic procedural rights' includes references to procedural due process, right to effective judicial review, adversarial principle, rights of the defence, right to be heard, *ne bis in idem*, principle of the legality of criminal offences and penalties, presumption of innocence. However, it excludes references to the constitutional requirements of the legislative and constitution-making procedures.	Please check 'YES' if the judicial opinion invokes or considers the concept of basic procedural rights. Otherwise indicate 'NO'.
Q40	Freedom of expression as an argument?	The freedom of expression is the right of every individual to manifest her/ his opinion through any means of the public discourse.	Please check 'YES' if the judicial opinion invokes or considers the concept of freedom of expression. Otherwise indicate 'NO'.
Q41	Rights to privacy as an argument?	Privacy refers to protection of the private sphere, family, home or correspondence, as well as the person's honour and reputation. This concept also includes references to data protection and copyrights.	Please check 'YES' if the judicial opinion invokes or considers the concept of privacy rights. Otherwise indicate 'NO'.

Coding	Question or variable label	Conceptualisation	Indicator(s)
Q42	Post-material values as an argument?	Post-material values highlight self-expression and quality of life over economic and physical security (Inglehart, 1977). According to Inglehart and Welzel (2005), post-material values trigger individuals' demand for freedom and provide a new type of civic culture, which shifts political institutions making them more efficient and responsive. These values include happiness, trust, pro-social norms and principles, ecology, social capital, social ties, civil culture, and civil engagement. Mentions to '*buen vivir*', '*Pacha Mama*' or similar indigenous concepts that refer to the harmony with nature shall be considered here as well.	Please check 'YES' if the judicial opinion invokes expressively post-material values. Otherwise indicate 'NO'.
Q43	Justice as an argument?	We consider here the material concept of justice (both in the corrective and distributive sense). Justice has three basic elements: it is interpersonal, meaning that it can only exist in relation to another person(s), it involves a duty, meaning there is something that is owed to another person, and it implies equality, meaning an equilibrium or balance in relation to what is owed.	Please check 'YES' if the judicial opinion invokes or considers the concept of justice. Otherwise indicate 'NO'.
Q44	Custom as an argument?	Custom refers to the legal tradition on a national level, either with or without an explicit mention of a concrete source from the domestic legal history. On a high level of generality, references to the 'constitutional tradition', 'customs of law' or the like should be included in this category. It applies only if one cannot qualify it as subjective teleological argument.	Please check 'YES' if the judicial opinion invokes or considers the concept of custom. Otherwise indicate 'NO'.
Q45	Family as an argument?	References to family in general, or specifically to the social, legal and cultural aspects, conditions or values of family shall be considered here.	Please check 'YES' if the judicial opinion invokes or considers the concept of family. Otherwise indicate 'NO'.

Coding	Question or variable label	Conceptualisation	Indicator(s)
Q46	Transition as an argument	References to transition, as a legal, cultural and institutional phenomena that involves change on a structural level. In the original, strict sense, transition is understood as a process of transformation from an authoritarian regime to democracy. However, recently it has been used to refer to transition from a democracy to an authoritarian regime too, as well as to allude to the process of remodelling of social and cultural institutions.	Please check 'YES' if the judicial opinion invokes or considers the concept of transition. Otherwise indicate 'NO'.
Q47	Economic, social, cultural and environmental rights as an argument?	Economic, social, cultural and environmental rights incorporate the rights to adequate food, housing, education, health, social security, as well as to take part in cultural life, to adequate water and sanitation, and to work. Lately, the jurisprudence of the IACHR has included environmental rights under this category as well.	Please check 'YES' if the judicial opinion invokes or considers social, economic and cultural rights. Otherwise indicate 'NO'.
Q48	Mechanisms of political control as an argument?	By mechanism of political control, we refer to constitutional mechanisms to make politicians accountable to citizens as Adserá, Boix & Payne (2003) suggested. Mainly these types of mechanisms occur in relation to corruption cases or issues of good government and efficiency.	Please check 'YES' if the judicial opinion invokes or considers control mechanism. Otherwise indicate 'NO'.
Q49	Judicial activism as an argument?	By the concept judicial activism, we refer to following features of the judicial decision: (1) extend or amplify the scope of the court's competences of constitutional review compared to what is expressively given by law; (2) derive completely new powers that are/were not written explicitly in the Constitution; (3) amplify or create a new remedy not included in law; (4) create new constitutional norms or interpret them in a evolutive/extensive way. For our present purposes, the expressive use of the concept of (judicial) activism would count here.	Please check 'YES' if the judicial opinion invokes or considers the concept of (judicial) activism. Otherwise indicate 'NO'.

Question Related to Overall Weight of the Arguments (Q50)

Q50	Overall weight of the arguments	The overall weight of the arguments refers to the ratio between those arguments that were mentioned but not taken into consideration, and those that in fact contributed to conclusion of the issue at hand (on 'conclusion' we mean the Case Disposition in Q4). Arguments could be categorised based on their weight as follows: conclusive (*ratio decidendi)* arguments are the ones that determine the conclusion. Supportive arguments (*obiter dictum)* are those that are not conclusive, but they support the conclusion. Finally, *decorative or rhetorical arguments* are those that do not have any persuasive effect from a conceptual/legal point of view, but only from a political-communication point of view. Also, you might find *pseudo arguments or inappropriate arguments* that are not even arguments, because the Court does not express the logical connection between its assertions and the conclusion. First you need to identify the arguments mentioned by the Court (this is what you have been doing already by filling out the previous rubrics of the Excel) and then experiment by imagining deleting them one by one. If by deleting an argument, the conclusion would be different, you have found the conclusive argument. If by deleting an argument, the final decision would still be the same, but less persuasive, you have found the supportive argument. If the deleted argument does not affect at all the conclusion, you might have found a decorative or rhetorical argument.	Please check (1) if most of the arguments mentioned in the judicial opinion were conclusive or supportive arguments. Please check (2) if the proportion between the conclusive and supportive arguments on the one hand, and the decorative, rhetorical, or deceptive arguments were equal. Please, check (3) if the majority the judicial opinion used rhetorical, or deceptive arguments.
Q50A		ONLY: 'ratio decidendi or obiter dictum arguments'	0 = No 1 = Yes

Q50B		ONLY: 'if the proportion between the ratio decidendi and obiter dictum arguments on the one hand, and the decorative, rhetorical or deceptive use of arguments were practically equal'	0 = No 1 = Yes
Q50C		ONLY: 'rhetorical, or deceptive arguments'.	0 = No 1 = Yes
Q51	Classical Formalistic Methods	BINARY AGGREGATION: (Q13C+Q20C)	Scale 0-1
Q52	Creative, Anti-Formalistic Methods	BINARY AGGREGATION: (Q15D+Q17+Q21E+Q22+Q23C+Q24)	Scale 0-1
Region			Southern Cone (ie, Argentina, Brazil, Chile, Paraguay and Uruguay) = '1'; Andean Region (ie, Bolivia, Colombia, Ecuador, Peru, and Venezuela) = '2'; Central America (Costa Rica, Guatemala and Mexico) = '3' Other (ie, Commonwealth Caribbean and Inter-American Court) = '4'.

APPENDIX C: QUESTIONNAIRE FOR COUNTRY REPORTS[1]

Each chapter that analyses a certain jurisdiction is meant to provide a description of the argumentative practices of the Court under consideration on the basis of an in-depth analysis of the Court's 40 selected landmark judgments and the relevant legal, political and academic context. Authors can refer to cases outside of the 40 landmark judgments, if this seems necessary in order to explain the wider context or to show contrasts. The present guidelines are there to ensure comparability and transparency across the Country Reports. Hence it is crucial for the comparative analysis and the validity of the research results that the authors read these guidelines carefully and follow them strictly while writing their chapters.

The answers should form a full-text, self-contained essay. Care should be taken to avoid repetitions and to present the answers in order that appears most relevant and appropriate. Besides the Questionnaire, each author should complete a separate Excel table in light of the analysis of the 40 selected judgments. As far as possible, the questions should be answered in the order given below. Authors may change the structure of the questionnaire and alter the order of sections and paragraphs, but only to the extent that is necessary to improve the readability and logical coherence of the Country Reports.

I. Legal, Political, Institutional and Academic Context

The exposition of the institutional context should not be overly detailed and should be limited to those general aspects or characteristic features that allow for a meaningful comparison with other experiences.

A. Legal and Political Culture as Context for the Constitutional Reasoning

The prevailing legal and political culture, including traditional conceptions of the nature of law, the constitution and the proper role of courts; attitudes and reactions of the other

[1] Updated and edited version of the Questionnaire for the purposes of the present publication. The present structure was borrowed from A Jakab et al, *Comparative Constitutional Reasoning* (Cambridge University Press, 2017). See more about the methodology here, A Jakab, A Dyevre, G Itzkovich, CONREASON – The Comparative Constitutional Reasoning Project. Methodological Dilemmas and Project Design. MTA Law Working Papers. 2015/9.

branches of government towards perceived judicial 'activism'; and the extent to which judges have felt compelled to 'stretch' their constitutional authority in order to deal with problems such as corruption, oppression, injustice and abuse of power. What are the typical implied political philosophical presuppositions (the existence of a pre-legal state or human rights as natural rights) in general and related to the legitimacy of law? What are the usual spoken or unspoken premises about the purpose of the political community and of its constitution?

Are methods of legal reasoning different in ordinary courts? How far do the literature of your system and the judgments themselves consider the extent to which constitutions differ from statutes, and require different methods of interpretation? If there are such differences in practice and/or they are analysed in the literature, how are these differences explained? By the intended longevity of constitutions, their inclusion of broad, abstract terms, or the difficulty of amending them? Are ordinary courts following the judgments of the constitutional court?

B. The Court and Constitutional Litigation

What are the relevant competences (eg abstract review, individual complaint etc) of the court? Who has standing (MPs, ombudsman, ordinary courts, individuals …) to bring a case and under what circumstances can the court choose among the cases brought? Does the court have any discretionary power to refuse to review a case or to select a case for review? How responsive is the Court, how much is it responding to the arguments contained in the petition?

Do other courts have the competence to annul statutes?

Are cases (always, frequently, never) orally argued? Who are the parties to the procedure? Can the State (government organs, authorities, ministries, or the President) or state-owned companies bring a case to the Court? Under what conditions?

Are there any specific (constitutional/statutory) rules about the admissibility of proof/argument in the court? How often are they used? Please provide examples.

What is the workload of the Court (number of cases decided per year, incl. *a limine* rejections for formal reasons or for being obviously unfounded)? How has it varied throughout the years? Are all the decided cases published (what is the percentage of published vs. unpublished cases)?

What kind of judgments does the Court adopt as to their legal nature? Is there a commonly accepted typology of constitutional judgments? (eg, judgments on admissibility/on the merits, 'interpretative judgments', 'warning decisions', etc). What kind of remedies could the Court order as consequence for the unconstitutionality? Are they based on the constitution or on the laws or has the Court derived new means of remedies in its jurisdiction?

How could you characterise the efficiency of the Court's decisions in general terms? Are the decisions of the Court usually respected by other state branches? Have the decisions of the Court been overruled by the legislative or executive? How often has that happened? What is the perception of the academic and professional community on the level of compliance of the decisions of the Court?

C. The Judges

How many members does the Court have? How are the judges selected? Are they elected/ appointed for life or for a shorter period? Is there any mechanism pertaining to the removal of individual judges? Has the Court throughout its history with constitutional review been dissolved, or has it gone through dictatorships? If yes, how was the Court affected by this, especially from the point of view of its competences, case load and efficiency?

Are the judges, academics, politicians, judges or other practitioners? Has the ratio of these four groups changed significantly over time?

D. Legal Scholarship and Constitutional Reasoning

Is legal scholarship critical/deferential towards the court? Are the works of law professors (who are not sitting on the Court) perceived to have an impact on the way the Court argues or on the court's jurisprudence? How do you see the prestige of a constitutional court judge compared to that of a constitutional law professor or a litigating lawyer in your system? Can you compare the salaries?

Are there any generally (or at least widely) accepted theories about constitutional reasoning, constitutional interpretation, or legal interpretation (including the ranking of interpretive methods) in general in the country under consideration? If yes, please outline them (two pages max.). Are these theories explicitly mentioned in the judgments? What do you think are the main divisions among the existing theories?

II. Arguments in Constitutional Reasoning

For this part of the Country Report the authors are required to base their analysis on the 40 selected landmark judgments of the Court. Each author should strive to identify the 40 judgments that are perceived, in the legal community broadly defined (ie encompassing judges, law professors and practitioners), as being the Court's most influential ever (both in the scholarly discourse and the legal practice). Authors should also include the separate (dissenting or concurring) opinions of the judgments in the analysis. Note that the Excel table as Appendix is attached as a separate file.

A. The Structure of Constitutional Arguments

What is the usual structure of arguments? What is your assessment of the frequency of use of the following argumentative structures in judicial opinions on constitutional matters:[2]

- One-line conclusive structure: deploying one conclusive argument (or chain of arguments following from one another)?

[2] Abbreviations of these indicators are based on the original terms of the options ('chain structure' as C, 'legs of a chair' as L, and 'dialogic' as D) that were later changed for more clarity.

- Parallel conclusive structure (legs of a chair): cumulative-parallel arguments, i.e. the arguments support a certain legal interpretation independently; every argument would suffice on its own; the reasoning thus resembles the legs of a chair?
- Parallel, individually inconclusive structure: the opinion presents a range of relevant considerations, none of which is really conclusive, yet taken together they indicate a certain way of solution (discursive or dialogic style)?

B. Types of Arguments in Constitutional Reasoning

Which of the following arguments are used (or explicitly rejected) in the 40 opinions? Please do not consider those arguments which are used to interpret statutes or regulations (ie infra-constitutional norms). Please fill in the summary table of the 40 judgments in the attached Excel table on the use of the following arguments:[3]

- Identifying or explicitly discussing the text of the Constitution.
- Applicability of constitutional law (eg, political question doctrine, conventionality control, state-centred arguments in a state of emergency).
- Analogies.
- Ordinary meaning of the words of the Constitution or reference to the 'wording of the Constitution' in general.
- Harmonising arguments (separate domestic harmonising and international/EU harmonising arguments).
- Precedents (former own cases).
- Doctrinal analysis of legal concepts or principles.
- Arguments from silence.
- Teleological/purposive arguments referring to the purpose of the text.
- Teleological/purposive arguments referring to the intention of the Constitution-maker (incl. travaux préparatoires).
- Non-legal (moral, sociological, economic) arguments.
- References to scholarly works.
- References to foreign (national) law.
- Pro homine/pro persona principles.
- Other methods/arguments (explain in the text especially these arguments).

Please also mark those judgments with 'YES' where a certain argument was considered but eventually rejected (eg if the opinion distinguishes the case at hand from former precedents, it does count as an 'argument from precedent'). However, do NOT mark 'YES' if the argument was rejected altogether or marked as irrelevant or inappropriate

[3] The present terminology and list of interpretive methods were borrowed from Jakab et al (n 1), which is based on the conceptual-doctrinal framework elaborated in A Jakab, 'Constitutional Reasoning. A European Perspective on Judicial Reasoning in Constitutional Courts' (2013) 8 *German Law Journal* 1215–78.

(eg the argument 'we do not consider here moral arguments because it is a court of law' does not count as a non-legal argument).

What are the typical situations in which these arguments are resorted to? Is there any self-reference in the Constitution about how to interpret its provisions?

C. The Overall Weight of the Arguments

What is the result of the analysis on the weight of the arguments? Does the Court usually consider the arguments that it mentions, by connecting them to the final conclusion of the case? Are there any specific doctrine in your country or in the jurisprudence of the Court on how to weight arguments (methods)? If yes, please give illustrations.

Can you identify any pattern regarding the conclusive argument? Which type of argument is usually the ratio decidendi? Is it possible to categorise arguments as auxiliary/secondary (offering only a backup or additional argument for the result which has already been derived from another argument) as opposed to main or primary arguments? Does the weight of a specific argument (eg, literal, purposive argument, or reference to precedents) differ depending on the specific area of constitutional law (human rights vs. power allocation)?

D. Judicial Candour and Judicial Rhetoric

Judges make value judgments while adjudicating cases, but to what extent are these value judgments acknowledged in their opinions? Do you see a correlation between opinion length and the judges' degree of candour?

Do the opinions deal with possible counterarguments (and/or the arguments of the parties, if there are parties to the procedure; and/or from legal scholars, even if not referring to them explicitly)?

How technical is the language used by the opinion writers? Is it understandable for non-lawyers and/or for lawyers not specialised in constitutional law?

Who are the target audience of the reasoning of the judgment? Courts? Parties in the proceedings? Lawyers? Politicians? General public? Law students? Academic constitutional lawyers? Judges of the same court? Foreign or international courts (aiming at judicial dialogue)? Please weigh the relevance of the audiences.

What is the degree of generalisation? Do judgments concentrate on the very specific issue to be decided or are they trying to develop a general conceptual frame and/or principle for future cases?

What is the degree of rhetoric? Do you find (legally irrelevant) political and/or emotional language in the text of judgments?

E. Length, Dissenting and Concurring Opinions

Does the length of the opinions show any correlation with the topic? Has it been growing by time or not? Are there any other factors influencing it (eg changes in political power, changes in constitutional text, changes in the personnel of the court)?

Is it possible to submit dissenting or concurring opinions? If yes, then how often does it happen? On what does it depend, whether there are dissenting and concurring opinions to a judgment? Are there any factors (the nature of the topic, changes in political power, changes in constitutional text, changes in the personnel of the court) that make it more it likely?

F. Framing of Constitutional Issues

Can you see any typical ways of characterising constitutional issues (eg as procedural/due process issue rather than as fundamental rights issue)?

Have there been changes over time in the way constitutional cases are conceptualised?

G. Key Concepts

Taking a broader look at the Court's jurisprudence and argumentative practices, how frequently, if ever, does it make use of the following concepts (please give a definition only where a constitutional lawyer with a general basic knowledge of comparative law might be surprised: the purpose is not to analyse any concept, but only to avoid misunderstandings when comparing with other countries):

- Rule of law (incl. 'separation of powers', 'primacy of the constitution', 'legality', 'legal certainty').
- Judicial independence.
- Democracy (incl. sovereignty of the people).
- Sovereignty ('international independence', 'state' or 'statehood').
- State form ('monarchy', 'republic').
- Government system by procedural structure (focusing on the different aspects of presidentialism, but containing the parliamentary system as well).
- Government system by power structure ('regionalism', 'autonomous regions', 'devolution', 'autonomy of local governments', 'subsidiarity).
- Secularism (or the separation of state and church).
- Nation (civic, ethnic or a mixture, plurinationalism).
- Proportionality.
- Core of constitutional rights (Wesensgehalt, of competences or of fundamental rights).
- Human dignity.
- Equality (or non-discrimination).
- Basic procedural rights (incl. 'due process' and 'presumption of innocence', but excl. procedure of law making).
- Freedom of expression.
- Rights to privacy (right to privacy, data protection).

- Post-material values (quality of life over material and physical aspects, like happiness, trust, ecology, civic culture).
- Justice (both corrective and distributive).
- Custom (as constitutional culture, customs of law).
- Family (legal, cultural, economic or social aspects of family).
- Transition (democratic transition or structural transition of legal or cultural institutions).
- Economic, social, cultural and environmental rights (women, indigenous people, ethnic minorities, refugees, rights of nature).
- Mechanisms of political control (corruption, good government, efficiency).
- Judicial activism.

Are there any further key concepts widely used by the Court? If yes, which ones and how are they defined? Are there are other peculiarities in constitutional terminology which could be surprising to foreign constitutional lawyers (max. one page)?

Are the key constitutional concepts spelled out in the constitutional text(s) (respectively in the text of the founding treaty)? Are the key concepts somehow derived from higher ranked constitutional provisions (Infinity clauses or alike)?

Are they used in an operative manner in the sense of triggering specific legal consequences, or are they essentially deployed as rhetorical device? Has the frequency of use of any of these concepts changed throughout the years? If yes, what would be the most plausible explanation?

III. Comparative Perspective

(*Authors should write this part after having read the first drafts of the other country reports, thus after our workshop on 11–12 June 2020.*)

Can you see any major differences in the applied key concepts, typical arguments etc as compared to the other countries as seen in the country reports? How can this be explained?

Please also consider: (1) the possible correlation between procedural aspects of constitutional review and the style of reasoning, (2) differences in political theory in the countries (relative roles of courts and legislature), (3) differences in legal culture, including legal theory, and (4) differences in personnel (including training and background) for explaining the differences in constitutional reasoning.

Hypotheses to be tested: (1) 'Without a full posterior constitutional review and a great amount of cases, the conceptual sophistication in constitutional law remains underdeveloped', (2) 'The older the Constitution is and the more difficult it is to amend it, the more likely the judges are to use purposive arguments instead of literal arguments', (3) 'The more academics are sitting in a court, the longer and more detailed the judgments/the more abstract the judgments/the more references to academic literature', (4) 'The closer the case in time to the dictatorial past, the more likely for it to use creative means of interpretation and extend its powers', (6) 'The closer to the contemporary times, the more likely that Courts would use foreign legal sources from Latin America'.

As a conclusion, list a handful of important general unwritten premises (implied presuppositions) that you think a foreign lawyer needs to know to understand a judgment of your constitutional court, for instance, 'the Constitution says something about every single legal case', 'constitutional law should only be considered, if it is an important political issue'.

IV. Evaluation, Pathology and Criticism

What features of the argumentative practices of the Court in your country do you consider to be pathological? Highly subject to criticism? For example, do judges manipulate constitutional language? Do they make bad arguments of a given type? What else? Or the opposite: do you see any exemplary elements which other countries should consider borrowing? How common are these? How would you summarise and explain the results of the indicators on the impact and quality of the Court's reasoning?

The authors are invited to conclude their chapters with some overall critical observations, on issues such as whether the courts have been either too legalistic or too creative, and the contribution they have made to their societies.

INDEX

Graphs, figures, and tables are located by page number followed by *G, F, T* respectively.

www.ingramcontent.com/pod-product-compliance
Ingram Content Group UK Ltd.
Pitfield, Milton Keynes, MK11 3LW, UK
UKHW020225290926
15470UKWH00001B/382

9 781509 960170